Introduction to the Sociology of
"Developing Societies"

Antonio García
#2F WAH
X853 5716

Sociology of "Developing Societies"

General Editor: Teodor Shanin

THEMATIC VOLUMES

INTRODUCTION TO THE SOCIOLOGY OF "DEVELOPING
SOCIETIES"
Hamza Alavi and Teodor Shanin

SOCIALIST "DEVELOPING SOCIETIES"?
(in preparation)

THEORIES OF SOCIAL TRANSFORMATION
(in preparation)

REGIONAL VOLUMES

SUB-SAHARAN AFRICA
Chris Allen and Gavin Williams

THE MIDDLE EAST
Talal Asad and Roger Owen

LATIN AMERICA

SOUTH-EAST ASIA
John Taylor and Andrew Turton (forthcoming)

CENTRAL AMERICA AND THE CARIBBEAN
(in preparation)

SOUTH ASIA
Hamza Alavi and Kathleen Gough (in preparation)

Introduction to the Sociology of "Developing Societies"

edited by Hamza Alavi and Teodor Shanin

Monthly Review Press
New York

Library of Congress Cataloging in Publication Data
Main entry under title:

Introduction to the sociology of "developing
    societies"

    (The Sociology of "developing societies"; 1
    Bibliography: p.
    1. Underdeveloped areas—Social conditions—
Addresses, essays, lectureš. I. Alavi, Hamza,
1921-   II. Shanin, Teodor. III. Series.

HN980.I59   909'.09724   81-16892
ISBN 0-85345-595-3   AACR2
ISBN 0-85345-596-1 (pbk.)

Monthly Review Press
122 West 27th Street
New York, N.Y. 10001

Manufactured in the United States of America
10 9 8 7 6 5 4

Contents

Preface   xi

Introduction   1

I. The Making of the Third World

1. Imperialism: A Historical Survey   *Harry Magdoff*   11

2. The Rise and Future Demise of the World Capitalist
   System: Concepts for Comparative Analysis
   Immanuel Wallerstein   29

3. The Origins of Capitalist Development: A Critique of
   Neo-Smithian Marxism   *Robert Brenner*   54

4. Colonialism in the Words of Its Contemporaries:
   Cecil Rhodes, Jules Harmand, Albert Beveridge,
   Joseph Conrad, James Connolly   72

5. The Losers   *Eric Hobsbawm*   78

6. Colonialism's Last Days:
   The "Emergency" in Malaya   *Han Suyin*   81

7. Colonialism's Last Days:
   An Orderly Decolonization in Malawi
   The Times (London)   85

8. White-Settler Colonialism and the Myth of
   Investment Imperialism   *Arghiri Emmanuel*   88

II. The Global Context

9. Pathways of Social Development: A Brief Against
   Suprahistorical Theory   *Karl Marx*   109

10. Dependency and Development in Latin America
    Fernando Henrique Cardoso   112

11. The Multinational Corporation and the Law
    of Uneven Development   *Stephen Hymer*   128

12. Developing Societies as Part of an International
    Political Economy   *Michael Barratt Brown*   153

13. The Structure of Peripheral Capitalism
    Hamza Alavi   172

III. Political Economy

14. A Morphology of Backwardness   *Paul A. Baran*   195

15. The Disarticulation of Economy Within
    "Developing Societies"   *Samir Amin*   205

16. Center, Periphery, and the Crisis of the System
    Paul M. Sweezy   210

17. Industrialization, Development, and Dependence
    Henry Bernstein   218

18. Poverty in the Third World: Ugly Facts
    and Fancy Models
    Keith Griffin and Azizur Rahman Khan   236

19. The Political Ideology of Population Control
    Lars Bondestam   252

20. The Dimension of Environment
    Malcolm Caldwell   260

21. Class Formation as an "Articulation" Process:
    East African Cases   *Lionel Cliffe*   262

22. Workers in Developing Societies   *Robin Cohen*   279

IV. State and Revolution

23. State and Class Under Peripheral Capitalism
    Hamza Alavi   289

24. Class, State, and Revolution: Substitutes and
    Realities   *Teodor Shanin*   308

25. Samuel Huntington and the End of Classical
    Modernization Theory   *Colin Leys*   332

26. The Death of Salvador Allende
    Gabriel García Márquez   350

V. Community, Culture, and Ideology

27. The New Metropolis   *Raymond Williams*   363

28. Cities in Developing Societies   *Bryan Roberts*   366

29. Family Structure and the Division of Labor:
    Female Roles in Urban Ghana   *Frances Pine*   387

30. Culture of Dependency: Arts and Political Ethos
    Octavio Paz   406

31. Learning to Be...What? Shaping Education in
    "Developing Societies"   *Roger Dale*   408

32. Reflections and Refractions on the Flow of
    Information   *Anthony Smith*   422

33. Nationalism and "Development"   *Tom Nairn*   430

34. Ideology and Identity: An Approach from History
    Basil Davidson   435

VI. Appendix

Further Reading on the Sociology of "Developing
Societies"   *Chris Allen*   459

Preface

The question of the so-called developing societies lies at the very heart of the political, economic, and moral crises of contemporary global society. It is central to relations of power, diplomacy, and war in the world we live in. It is decisive when the material well being of humanity is concerned, that is, the ways some people make a living and some people hunger. It presents a fundamental dimension of social inequality and of struggles for social justice. During the last generation it has also become a main challenge to scholarship, a field where the perplexity is deeper, the argument sharper, and the potential for new illuminations more profound. This challenge reflects the outstanding social relevance of the problems. It reflects too an essential ethnocentrism that weighs heavily on contemporary social science. The very terminology that designates "developing" or "underdeveloping" or "emerging" societies is impregnated with a teleology that identifies parts of Europe and the United States as "developed." Images of the world at large as rising unilinearly from barbarity to modernity (or vice versa, as a descent to hell) have often substituted for the analysis of actuality, as simplistic metaphors often are. To come to grips with a social reality that is systematically different from one's own, and to explain its specific logic and momentum, are most difficult conceptual and pedagogic tasks. It is the more so because the fundamental questions about "developing societies" are not of difference only but of relationships past and present with the countries of advanced capitalism and industrialization. It is in this light that we encounter, as analysts and teachers, not only a challenge to the "sociology of development," but a major challenge to radical scholarship itself.

The "Sociology of 'Developing Societies'" series aims to offer a systematically linked set of texts to be used as a major teaching aid at the university level. It is being produced by a group of teachers and scholars related by common interest, general outlook, and commitment sufficient to provide an overall coherence but by no means a single monolithic view. The object is, on the one hand, to bring relevant questions into focus and, on the other hand, to teach through debate. We think that at the current stage a "textbook" would necessarily gloss over the very diversity, contradictions, and inadequacies of our thought which must be focused on. On the other hand, collections of articles are often accidental in content. The format of a conceptually structured set of readers was chosen as one sufficiently open to accommodate a variety of views within a coherent system of presentation. These readers bring together works by sociologists, social anthropologists, historians, political scientists, economists, literary critics, and novelists in an intended disregard of the formal disciplinary divisions of the academic enterprise.

Three major alternatives of presentation stand out: first, a comparative discussion of the social structures within the "developing societies," focusing on the generic within them; second, the exploration of the distinct character of the main regions of the "developing societies"; third, consideration of context and content of theories of social transformation and change. Accordingly, the *Introduction* volume deals with the general issues of comparative study. Other volumes cover different regions, while the final volume is devoted to an examination of basic paradigms of the theories of social transformation. The volumes taken together thus represent the three main dimensions of the problem area, leaving it to teachers and students to choose from them and to compose their own courses.

The topic is ideologically charged, relating directly to the outlook and the ideals of everyone. The editors and many of the contributors share a broad sense of common commitment, although there is among them a considerable diversity of political viewpoint and theoretical approach. The common ground may be best indicated in terms of three fundamental negations. First, there is an implacable opposition to every social system of oppression of humans by other humans. That entails also the rejection of scholastic apologia of every such system, be it imperialism, class oppression, elitism, sexism, or whatever. Second, there is the rejection of "preaching down" easy solutions from the comfort of air-conditioned offices and campuses, whether in the "West" or in the "developing societies" themselves, and of the tacit assumption of our privileged wisdom that has little to learn from the common people in the "developing societies." Third, there is the rejection of the notion of scholastic detachment from social commitment as a pedagogy and as a way of life. True scholarship is not a propaganda exercise, even of the most sacred values. Nor is it without social consequence, however conceived. There are students and teachers alike who think that indifference improves vision. We believe the opposite to be true.

Manchester, England, 1982   *Teodor Shanin*

Acknowledgments

The editors and publishers wish to thank the following, who have kindly given permission for the use of copyright material: Academic Press, Inc. (London) for extracts from *Poverty and Population Control* by Lars Bondestam; Carmen Balcells Agencia Literaria on behalf of Gabriel García Márquez for the article "The Death of Salvador Allende," translated by Gregory Rabassa, © 1974 by Gabriel García Márquez; Booker McConnell Limited for the advertisement placed in *The Times Supplement on Malawi* (6 July 1964); Cambridge University Press for an abridged version of an essay that appeared in *The Capitalist World-Economy* by Immanuel Wallerstein; Jonathan Cape Limited for an extract from *. . . and the Rain My Drink* by Han Suyin, reproduced by permission of the author; Frank Cass & Co. Limited for "Class Formation as an 'Articulation' Process," abridged by Lionel Cliffe from his article "Rural Class Formation in East Africa" published in *Journal of Peasant Studies* 4, no. 2 (January 1977); Chatto & Windus Limited and Oxford University Press, Inc. for extracts from *The Country and the City* by Raymond Williams (1973); Grove Press Inc. for extracts from *The Other Mexico: Critique of the Pyramid* by Octavio Paz, translated by Lysander Kemp, copyright © 1972 by the publisher: *Journal of Contemporary Asia* (Stockholm) for the article "Class and Revolution: The Empirical Peasantry, the Hypothetical Proletariat, and the Evasive Intelligentsia" by Teodor Shanin, published in vol. 1, no. 1 (1969) and expanded by the author into "Class, State, and Revolution: Substitutes and Realities"; Macmillan Publishing Co., Inc. for the article "The Multinational Corporation and the Law of Uneven Development" by Stephen Hymer, from *Economics and World Order from the 1970s to the 1990s*, edited by Jagdish N. Bhagwati, copyright © 1972 by the publisher; Monthly Review Press for "A Morphology of Backwardness" from *The Political Economy of Growth* by Paul A. Baran; "The Disarticulation of Economy Within 'Developing Societies' " from *Accumulation on a World Scale: A Critique of the Theory of Underdevelopment*, vol. 1 by Samir Amin; "Imperialism: A Historical Survey" by Harry Magdoff, which is an expanded version of a chapter in *Imperialism: From the Colonial Age to the Present*; and "Center, Periphery, and the Crisis of the System" abridged by Paul M. Sweezy from his *Four Lectures on Marxism*; *New Left Review* and the authors for the abridged versions "The Origins of Capitalist Development: A Critique of Neo-Smithian Marxism" by Robert Brenner, vol. 104 (1977), "White-Settler Colonialism and the Myth of Investment Imperialism" by Arghiri Emmanuel, vol. 73 (1972), "Nationalism and 'Development' " by Tom Nairn from his article "Marxism and the Modern Janus," vol. 94 (1975), and "Latin American Capitalism" by Fernando Henrique Cardoso, originally published as "Dependency and Development in Latin America," vol. 74 (1972); Pergamon Press Limited for an extract from *World Development* 6, no. 3 (1978) by Keith Griffin and Azizur Rahman Khan; The Times Newspapers Limited for extracts from *The Times*, "Towards Self-Sufficiency—an Editorial Comment" (6 July 1964), "A Message from the Prime Minister—Dr Hastings Banda" (6 July 1964), "Colonialism's Last Days: An Orderly De-Colonisation in Malawi" (7 July 1964), and "Reflections and Refractions on the Flow of Information," published in *The Times Higher Education Supplement* (28 March 1980); Weidenfeld (Publishers) Limited for an extract from *The Age of Capital 1848-1875* by E. J. Hobsbawm; Zed Press Limited for an extract from *The Wealth of Some Nations* by Malcolm Caldwell.

*This book is dedicated to the
memories of Orlando Letelier (1932-1976)
and Malcolm Caldwell (1931-1978)*

Introduction to the Sociology of "Developing Societies"

Introduction

The world has moved into the 1980s with prospects and problems radically different from those of earlier decades. These changes in the world situation are not merely conjunctural; underlying the day-to-day signs of the global crisis that surrounds us are far-reaching structural changes. To study them is to look at the continuities and to identify fresh issues and new debates that will, in turn, inform our perspectives on the future. The aim of this volume is to identify and elucidate issues at the center of contemporary debate about the nature and characteristics of so-called developing societies while locating them in historical and global contexts.

The "sociology of development" as an academic enterprise came into its own in the 1950s and 1960s as a product of the new world situation that emerged after World War II. Projects of active intervention for the purpose of "development" in poor and backward countries that had undergone the experience of direct or indirect colonial domination were now being widely discussed. The postwar decade was characterized by a radical realignment of the balance of economic and political power, with the ascendancy of the United States as the dominant power of the capitalist world and the concomitant consolidation of the power of the Soviet Union and the victory of the Chinese Communist Party. In that period the powerful resurgence of national liberation movements and the dismantling of the colonial system became central. Those changes took one of two directions. There were countries where national liberation was associated with a radical break with the framework of world capitalism and effective social revolution with varying characteristics and internal dynamics. Elsewhere, nationalistic movements, while usually also employing the rhetoric of socialism, did not try, or were unable, to break with the institutions and the international framework of the capitalist world or to radically overturn their own class structure. That did not mean, however, simple repetition of the road along which the major capitalist societies of today had already trodden, for the conditions, context, and content differed considerably. It is this category of countries and types of social transformation that this volume is primarily addressed to.

1

A master program of promoting a few specific kinds of "development," through state intervention and international assistance, mostly from the advanced capitalist countries, was adopted in these areas by the powers that be, and also appropriated by academics and conceptualized and systematized as "modernization theory." Its essence lies in its teleology and in its claim to scientific objectivity. It assumed that all countries had to "develop" along a single upward slope—to become roughly like the United States, the idealized model and ultimate goal of "development." To do so, they had to identify and remove social and ideological obstacles to such development. The image of such transformation was in its essence that of the transfer of Western technology and rationality in order to increase production without changing class structure. The ensuing strategy can be designated as "developmentalism," a conception that came to be adopted by the United Nations, by scholars, and by the mass media in the phrase "developing societies."

A wide variety of terms has been used to designate such societies. We have decided not to embroil ourselves in a long semantic debate and have opted for a term that is easily recognizable and formally used by international institutions to delimit a group of countries within the global framework. Whatever the wording, we accept the category of societies delimited thereby as real, relevant, and illuminating. We have placed the term "developing societies" in the title of this volume within quotation marks to underline its ideological underpinnings and the questions it begs. Something must be said about the way that the terminology developed. An earlier label, "backward societies," informed a colonial vision. With decolonization, the term "emergent nations" came into use, expressing a "Western" ethnocentric outlook, as if those newly independent nations had no history and no past. The term soon gave way to the expression "underdeveloped societies," naturally interpreted within the "modernization" paradigm as meaning those countries that were "still underdeveloped," but on their way, in time, to join those already "developed," once the right medicine was applied. As the postcolonial societies began to take their place in international forums, and as "developmentalist" projects got under way, those ideas found expression in the more flattering and optimistic alternative term, "developing societies." This word-producing industry is not yet at a standstill. More recently, the term "less developed societies" or "LDCs" has been gaining ground in the vocabulary of developmentalism.

The alternative expression "Third World" had its origin in the confrontation of the two hostile camps led by the United States and the USSR respectively in the Cold War of the 1950s and in the populist beliefs or rhetoric of those leaders of the Afro-Asian countries who professed "nonalignment" as a "third way." It represented an early and partial attempt to break out of the language of the "modernization" paradigm, which assumed it to be necessary for every society to proceed along a road already taken by the industrial capitalist societies. The dramatic failure of "developmentalist" strategies, expressed in the growing economic gap between the advanced capitalist countries and the "developing societies," by that time universally acknowledged, led in the 1960s and 1970s to major shifts in theoretical orientation and terminology. Attention moved from the dichotomy between "traditional" and "modern" societies, and especially the values and attitudes that were thought to impede modernization or favor it, to greater concern with structural considerations. "Developmental" experts, disillusioned by their own "grand theory," which did not seem to be delivering the goods, increasingly left the field of theory to focus upon specific problems of particular societies, without making much effort to view them any longer within any broader analytical context. The theoretical void thus created was increasingly filled by "dependency theory," which emphasized, above all, the subordinate location of Third World societies within the capitalist world-system and the determination of their fate by external forces. Simultaneously and interdependently, a revival and renewal of Marxist theories placed a new emphasis upon political economy, class structure, and the dynamics of capital accumulation within a global matrix and, in particular, the nature of the transformation of precapitalist societies by colonial and neocolonial capitalism. The political experience that found its climax and its symbols in the year 1968 in Saigon, Paris, Prague, Washington, and Peking brought all this into focus. In the changed intellectual climate, a conceptual shift took place from the duality "tradition" versus "modernity" to a new pair of major concepts, "core" and "periphery." This brought two sets of countries within the capitalist world-system (and the subregions within each of these) into a single framework of unequal relationships. Used rather loosely, the paired concept of core/periphery has become the most pervasive image of the 1970s, both in the literature of developmentalism on the right and in radical critiques of developmentalism by the left. The analytical edge of these concepts became increasingly blunted, for their connotations ranged from sophisticated conceptions of global structures of exploitation to simple descriptions dividing countries into "rich" and "poor."

While important in developing a devastating critique of earlier modernization theories, the new paradigm was often expressed in strongly deterministic terms, a bias sustained by a lack of conceptual clarity. The "development of underdevelopment" in the periphery was assumed to be a necessary and inexorable process inherent within the core/periphery interdependence. It was the basic dynamic of the "core" economies only, and/or the logic of the world capitalist system, that determined the outcome of contemporary world history. Social and economic processes in the periphery had little significance and were treated as secondary, the mere result of external determination. The effects of indigenous social forces within the developing societies themselves, the variety of strategies introduced by governments in those countries that were not necessarily dictated from the outside; industrialization in some of the "developing societies"; the influence of class struggles within some of the developing societies on the ways in which those countries actually developed; the experience of a multiplicity of roads and diversity of outcomes—all these demonstrated the inadequacies of oversimplified "underdevelopment" and "dependency" theories, and brought into focus fresh questions for the 1980s.

Sociology of developing societies must begin not with stereotypes of "traditional" and "modern" societies but with a historical analysis of the making of the contemporary Third World—the world we live in. A closer examination shows a complex and reciprocal relationship between the rise of industrial capitalism in Europe and colonial policies, whether accompanied by direct colonial rule or not. Also, and contrary to much of Western ethnocentric scholarship and popular myth, we must question the paternalistic assumptions of colonial history that viewed the colonized as barbaric or simple people who had to await the arrival of colonialism to be "civilized." European expansion spread barbarism as much as civilization. In many territories, the indigenous population was exterminated; elsewhere it was subjugated. A trail of devastation, physical as well as cultural, followed where sophisticated civilizations had existed. A more balanced view of the past is essential for a more perceptive view of the present and sounder judgments about the future.

Direct colonial rule did not prove to be an essential condition for capitalism. Typically, the burgeoning industrial capitalism of Britain in the first half of the nineteenth century did not necessarily undertake further territorial conquest. On the contrary, given its unrivalled economic power at the time, its slogans were "open door" and "free trade." The nineteenth-century scramble for direct colonial possessions and the division of the world among powerful advanced capitalist countries was very much a pre-emptive strategy, a response to their mutual rivalry. But direct colonial rule by established powers was an obstacle for those who were late-comers as capitalist powers, in particular the United States, which after

1945 acquired a hegemonic position in the capitalist world. Their interest therefore lay in prying open the grip of the old colonial powers and opting for the "open door." The rapid decolonization that followed World War II, with a prostrate Europe, a dominant United States, and an increasingly powerful USSR, must be considered in the light of the rise of the new superpowers, and not only as a consequence of the growing pressures of nationalist movements struggling for independence. The alignment of forces within the international capitalist system and within the world at large was altered radically by the end of World War II, which inaugurated the era of decolonization.

The character of the global scene has changed considerably in the last generation. The international context has been altered with the emergence of a large number of independent states in Africa and Asia, a greater degree of effective independence in some of the states in peripheral capitalist countries, and the rise of a new framework of interstate relationships and international organizations. On the other hand, a number of factors have contributed toward a relative consolidation of the bloc of advanced capitalist countries, forcing them to collaborate without wholly eliminating rivalry between them. Among these factors, there is firstly the economic and military power of the United States, although in more recent times U.S. predominance in the capitalist world has been qualified by the rise of European and Japanese economic power. For the governments of the advanced capitalist countries the compulsion to collaborate has been reinforced by the need to coordinate policies in a variety of spheres, including international monetary management and the military, political, economic, and ideological confrontations with a variety of "others": the USSR, the oil suppliers, the "developing societies," etc.

Since the late 1950s, with the growing awareness of revolutionary pressures and the emergence of the Soviet bloc as a provider of aid to Third World countries, the "aid policies" of the advanced capitalist nations were placed on a new footing and coordinated through the World Bank, and later the International Monetary Fund. Through these bodies, the advanced capitalist countries collectively confronted individual developing societies in a process of granting "aid" and credits, which involved detailed consideration and stringent conditions concerning their internal economic policies, including those concerning foreign investment. The rise of multinational corporations, whose interests and power transcend the boundaries of nation states, and which require, for their effective operation, international "order and stability," has also contributed to the mitigation of interimperialist rivalry. The coordination of policies imposed collectively by the advanced capitalist countries through agencies such as the World Bank differs considerably from the unmitigated interimperialist rivalry that was at the center of Hobson's and Lenin's analysis of early imperialism. These agencies have an overriding common interest in maintaining the structures of peripheral capitalism and the corresponding political order. When regimes (or political movements) emerge that do not meet those political or economic goals, policies of "destabilization" and of direct intervention follow—Chile has been but the most dramatic case in point.

This volume will focus, in Parts I and II respectively, on the historical background and global context of the developing societies. The subsequent chapters are devoted to the social structures of these countries. Such divisions are necessarily relative: each section therefore signifies a focus of attention within an interlocking set of problems and not a separated compartment or topic. The division of the book suggests shifts in perspective rather than wholly different contents.

Parts III, IV, and V center on political economy, state power, and the issues of consciousness and community, all treated within the specific context of the "developing societies." Central to the problems of political economy are issues of the "morphology of backwardness"—the specific economic characteristics of developing societies—and their class structures and alternative economic strategies. At the center of the political problems in those countries stand the issues of power and of the state, of dissent and of revolution. The last chapter is focused on the changing nature of the communities within which life is lived in the "developing societies"— the town, the village, and the family—and on issues of consciousness produced by, and in turn shaping, the nature of those societies.

In every part a range of views is introduced in order to foster debate, without pretending to purvey the absolute truth. Works of particular significance to the field have been used, but about half the text was specifically commissioned for this publication. The editors themselves do not necessarily agree on every issue. Likewise, they are not necessarily in agreement with the content of every contribution. The preface indicates the principles and criteria that have guided their selection.

The preparation of this volume was carried out by a team that consisted of Hamza Alavi, Rod Aya, and Teodor Shanin. The editors regret that Rod Aya could not join us in the book's finalization, and on its cover; his impact and considerable help are here acknowledged. The volume would have been less rich without his suggestions and challenge.

It is the nature of social transformation, political strategies, contradictions and, often, their unexpected results that constitute the center of attention in this volume. It was designed to stand on its own in content, design, and internal coherence. It is obvious that a single book cannot exhaust or even fully present the riches of theory and empiria, problems and alternatives relevant to our topic. An extension of the volume is offered in two ways. First, a further reading list is appended, its content and design aimed to encourage wider exploration of relevant problems. Second, the volume is part of a series. A number of further volumes extend and specify the issues presented in the *Introduction to the Sociology of "Developing Societies,"* relating them to different regions of the globe. The final volume of the series will extend it further and systematically relate the major questions presented in the introductory volume to the different schools of thought, and the controversies among them. Once again, the division of items between the different volumes is relative. Most of them will be relevant to several volumes.

The three decades of "developmentalism" have indeed seen massive social changes in "developing societies." Towns and villages have been transformed, as has the balance between industry and agriculture, and the technologies employed. Political organizations have changed, and wars have been fought both within and between countries. Many of these changes were unpredicted, often the "unintended result" of plans and strategies. Those changes challenged and undermined neat analytical systems. To the mass of people in developing societies, these transformations have often produced conditions of life that are even harsher and more difficult to bear than before. This has generated mass unrest and demand for change in the social order, for reforms as well as for social revolution. It has also generated vicious regimes of repression and terror. The political tension within developing societies breaks surface every day.

In the vocabulary of developmentalism, this syndrome has been recognized, but not as a movement of forces that might lead to a reconstitution of a more just social order that would generate well being and extend the liberties of the majority of people. Rather, it has been portrayed as a dysfunctional "hypermobilization" of the people, and a "revolution of rising expectations" that the political system must be geared to moderate, institutionalize, and control. The brutality of political struggle and the monstrosity of some of the regimes in developing societies are explained in terms of "political underdevelopment" or the innate inferiority of some peoples, rather than in relation to the cruelty of the choices and the acuteness of the conflict imposed by poverty, privilege, and inequality, both national and international. Solutions to challenges from below were sought in repression and ideological reinforcement of the established order, and also in attempts to moderate the course of popular discontent— at not too high a price for established interests and "social peace." The newest in the long line of these responses is epitomized by the so-called basic needs approach, a less optimistic version of developmentalism for the 1980s, an aspiration to mitigate only the worst of the effects of the social devastation within developing societies. When even these moderate hopes run aground, repression, institutionalized terror, and torture follow.

This volume is committed to the idea that while people do not make history as they please, they do make history; they can take history in their hands and untie the shackles that bind them. Things said about the cruelty of choices within "developing societies" shape also the nature of the alternative regimes and not only of the defenders of the status quo. The struggle against oppression is not only a battle against the past but also against new forms of oppression and new privileges, under different ideological banners. That being so, the struggle for radical social reconstruction and for participation by the broadest masses of the population in political life is still the only way for the mass of the people in "developing societies" to arrive at conditions of freedom, equality, and well-being, truly to emerge into a world worth living in. We believe that knowledge serves that cause. That is why this book came into being.

Part I

The Making of the Third World

Part I is devoted to the origins of "developing societies." It begins with a paper by Harry Magdoff in which he discusses the rise and development of imperialism as a historical sequence, relating it to our own times. This conception constitutes the central thread that runs through the issues which are debated in the articles brought together here. The chapters by Immanuel Wallerstein and Robert Brenner represent two positions in a major contemporary debate about the development of capitalism as a world system, its structure, and the genesis of developing societies in the course of their social transformation and incorporation into the capitalist world economy.

The order in which the contributions are presented does not imply any view on the part of the editors that the articles that follow have disposed of the arguments of those that precede them—or vice versa. The major issues are both important and wide open, and the controversy over them will continue. A number of short statements present images of colonialism in the words of its contemporaries. Eric Hobsbawm's concise statement identifies and broadens the list of the "losers" in confrontations that have marked the age of the blossoming of global capital, both in colonized and "noncolonial" societies. Two more short items present a picture of colonialism in its last days, one of independence struggles and the other of independence "granted" by the colonial powers. The chapter by Arghiri Emmanuel concludes this part with a critique of some earlier theories of imperialism and lays particular stress on the different interests of colonial settlers and international capital, an issue of major significance to the context of decolonization and the development of neocolonialism.

A major missing component, in the light of the initial design of this section, is a full discussion of the noncolonial road leading to transformations of societies into developing societies, for example, the cases of Turkey or China. The issue is raised, however, by Hobsbawm and Wallerstein. The items in Part II are closely related to those in Part I, as are contributions from Paul Baran, Paul Sweezy, and Basil Davidson elsewhere in this volume.

[1]
Imperialism: A Historical Survey

Harry Magdoff

History is full of examples of the annexation of foreign territory and the domination of weaker by stronger powers. Nevertheless, there is a vital difference between the empire-building of precapitalist times, such as the Iberian conquest of Latin America, and that of capitalist times. Apart from outright pillage, the precapitalist colonizers benefited from their domination by exacting a continuous flow of tribute. On the whole, though, they did not interfere with the economic basis of the conquered territories: the tribute skimmed off the economic surplus that was produced traditionally in the subjugated areas.

On the other hand, the roughly five centuries of conquest and domination that began at the end of the fifteenth century was distinguished by the extent to which the conquerors imposed social and economic changes on their victims and the degree to which the latter became appendages of the economies at the core of empire. This did not happen all at once. At first, the new colonial powers of Western Europe used their military prowess to pursue the well-trodden paths of plunder, piracy, and annexation of foreign territory. But at that time Europe was on the threshold of major upheavals: the feudal system was in crisis, trade and commodity production were becoming increasingly important, and the seeds of the capitalist mode of production were sprouting. The exploitation of the business opportunities found overseas stimulated a vast growth in worldwide trade. The commercial revolution of the sixteenth and seventeenth centuries, which unfolded along with the geographical discoveries and overseas conquests, helped break down the feudal barriers to production and accelerated the rise of capitalism.

It was not only at the birth of capitalism in Western Europe, however, that territorial expansion and domination over foreign lands played a crucial role. As this dynamic system evolved, the interest of the leading capitalist nations in manipulating and utilizing the rest of the world's resources grew and became more varied. The budding capitalists concentrated at first on acquiring gold, silver, sugar, spices—and slaves to work the colonial plantations. Then, with the spread of industrialization, came a rising demand

11

for raw materials to be processed and food for the burgeoning cities. But the industrializing nations did not remain merely buyers of colonial products. They soon became sellers too, as they urgently searched for new markets in which to unload the growing volume of machine-produced goods. Still later, as capitalist industry and finance matured, manufacturers and bankers looked to the colonial world for new and profitable fields in which to invest capital.

The traditional social systems and culture of the foreign possessions, however, stood in the way: they were not suited to the creation of a sufficient volume of the desired agricultural and mineral exports or to the furnishing of good markets for manufactured imports. Therefore colonial policy and practice was from time to time adapted in different ways to overcome these constraints. This was done by forcefully altering the subjugated societies in order that they might become more profitable adjuncts of the centers of capitalism. Thus, private property in land was introduced where it did not previously exist. Land was expropriated for the use of white settlers and for plantation agriculture. Where foreign entrepreneurs could not find a sufficient labor supply (to extract minerals, grow commercial crops, and build ports, roads, and railways) either slaves were imported or the indigenous population was forced, by direct and indirect means, to work for wages. The use of money and commodity exchange was stimulated by imposing money payments for taxes and land rent and by inducing a decline of home production. Where precolonial society already had a developed industry, production and exports by native manufacturers were curtailed. (India, for example, was converted from an exporter to an importer of cotton goods.)

On the top of all this came social and political innovations designed to support and perpetuate such radical economic transformations. Local elite strata that would benefit from cooperation with the foreign rulers were activated. Effective administrative techniques were introduced. New or amended legal codes were installed to facilitate the operation of a money, business, and private property economy. Above all, police and armed forces were developed to assure social stability and to sustain environments conducive to the new social order. The imposition of the language and the permeation of the culture and ideology of the dominating power tied all of this together—leading to a social psychology based on the presumed superiority of the colonizers and the inferiority of the colonized.

As a result of these societal changes ushered in during the centuries-long wave of capitalist expansion, the rest of the world was brought into the orbit of the leading capitalist nations. Although initially created by force and chicanery, the new institutions and class alignments of the periphery served to maintain and reproduce a hierarchy of nations—a hierarchy that was distinguished by great inequalities in standards of living, levels of technology, and freedom for self-development. In fact, the changes resulting from decades and centuries of colonialism became so deep-seated that they served to perpetuate the essential economic dependency of the peripheral nations on the leading capitalist centers even after the widespread post-World War II decolonization.

What has thus far been discussed telescopes a long and varied history. The specific aspects of this history differed from territory to territory and from time to time, influenced by the special conditions in each area, by the process of conquest, by the circumstances at the time when economic exploitation of the possessions became desirable and feasible, and by the competitive struggles among rival colonial powers. Yet distinct patterns do emerge in the midst of the extensive diversity. And these can best be recognized against the background of stages in the development of the capitalist system. The focus of this essay is to suggest in outline form distinct stages in the evolution of imperialism. The purpose is not merely to clarify past history but to better understand the present, since, in our opinion, many of today's constraints to the development of the underdeveloped areas are rooted in the imperialist experience.

1. European Commerce Enters the World Stage: From the End of the Fifteenth Century to the Mid-Seventeenth Century

The outward thrust of European commerce at the end of the fifteenth century had to overcome two obstacles: the blockade (and counterpressure) of the Ottoman Empire, and the fact that trade with and between countries outside Europe was controlled by Asians and Africans. The blockade stimulated the ocean voyages that opened up the Americas, where the inferiority of Indian weapons and the susceptibility of the population to European diseases facilitated European conquest. However, in striving for trade opportunities in other parts of the world, the Europeans came up against well-entrenched commercial systems, as for example in the Indian Ocean:

> After journeying through the inhospitable seas of Southern Africa the Portuguese ships had come into regions where there was a complex of shipping, trade and authority as highly developed as the European: forms of political capitalism at least as large in dimensions as those of Southern Europe, and probably larger; shipping in bottoms many of

them carrying more than those used in European merchant shipping; a trade in every conceivable valuable high quality product carried on by a great multitude of traders; merchant gentlemen and harbor princes wielding as great financial power as did the merchants and princes of Europe.[1]

Here the Europeans had nothing to offer in superiority of goods, finance, or trading ability which would enable them to break into the traditional trade. They did have one decisive advantage, however: the great superiority of European ships of war. Sailing ships strong enough to mount cannon provided sufficient destructive power to force the issue: to cripple the ships of other nations, transfer the trade into European hands, and establish forts for control of the seas.

The main features of this period of expansion—conquest of South America, exploitation of the gold and silver resources found there, and the diversion of established trade—reflect the state of the arts of the period. The relatively undeveloped means of production and the consequently small currently produced economic surplus left direct robbery, whenever practical, as one of the most effective means of accumulating wealth. Hence looting, plunder, and piracy were primary agents of redistribution and new concentrations of wealth. This redistribution took two forms: (1) skimming off by the Europeans of as much as possible of the accumulated surplus of the rest of the world, and (2) conflict among leading European nations—Spain, Portugal, Holland, France, and England—for access to the wealth of other continents, including what they could pirate from each other on the high seas. As one economic historian described the foreign commerce those days: "The prize in distant commerce went not to the best producers and merchants, but to the group of the best fighters; not size and resources, but ability to organize and willingness to risk resources in conflict, determined the question of success."[2]

In the long run, the flood of new products from the East, the huge flow of precious metals from America, the opening of new markets, and the demand generated by the several states in the pursuit and establishment of colonies enormously stimulated the expansion of Western manufactures and the ascendancy of the European bourgeoisies—in short, paved the way for the global triumph of capitalism. But there was a limit to the profitability of this first wave of overseas expansion: the wealth obtained by plunder of hoards amassed over years can only be taken once.

There were, moreover, further contradictions contributing to the drying up of the benefits from the first wave of overseas expansion: (1) The handsome profits derived from taking over the trade routes of others do not grow unless the trade itself keeps on expanding, and this did not occur as long as the old modes of production remained intact. (2) Profits from the spice trade dropped, squeezed by restricted supplies on the one side and increasing costs of defending monopolistic control against rival nations on the other. The flow of precious metals from South America declined as the richest mines became exhausted, given the backward techniques then in use, and as the labor force of the superexploited Indians dried up. These were among the reasons why, as Eric Hobsbawm put it, "The old colonial system passed through a profound crisis. . . . Old colonialism did not grow over into new colonialism; it collapsed and was replaced by it."[3]

2. Commercial Capital Dominant: Mid-Seventeenth Century to the Late Eighteenth Century

The political and military conditions that set off and distinguish this period are: (1) the waning of Spain's pre-eminence; (2) the shift in Portugal's dependence on France to dependence on England; (3) the end of a virtual Dutch monopoly of shipping; (4) the growth of colonial rivalry between France and England, and the emergence of Britain's pre-eminence on the sea and in international commerce. Central to these changes was the triumph of commercial interests in the class struggles that ripened in the English revolution of the seventeenth century. This development puts its stamp on the whole era, conditioning the rise of Britain's leading role in empire, finance, and trade.[4]

In contrast with the vacillation of Britain in earlier decades, the political triumph of commercial capital is reflected in the adoption of clear-cut policies to assure Britain's commercial supremacy. Under Cromwell, Britain set out to build for the first time a national and professional navy. But while a strong navy was needed to back up ocean commerce,[5] the shipping trade itself needed special promotion, in part to compete for commerce, and in part to train a reserve of competent seamen for the growing navy. These considerations, aimed at overcoming Dutch ocean-trade dominance, were behind the Navigation Acts of 1650-1651. These acts not only created a monopoly for Britain's ships in its trade with Asia, Africa, and America, but also created the basis for a whole set of restrictions on its colonies which gave an important boost to the demand for British manufacturers. The aim of colonial policy became crystal clear: to create a self-sufficient empire, producing as much as possible of the raw materials and food needs of the mother country and providing exclusive markets for its manufactures.

This goal fitted in with the state of productive resources of those times. We are dealing here with the period of rapid growth of manufactures that preceded the Industrial Revolution. Given the fact that domestic markets were weak and that prices could not be drastically slashed, it followed that the demand for manufactures could be most successfully stimulated in a controlled environment. This meant exclusivity both at home and in the colonies, and also a drive for more colonies, involving wars to take away the proven colonies of other powers.

The search for foreign markets had to overcome many hurdles prior to the Industrial Revolution and to the time when Europe had the military and technical resources to penetrate into the interior of foreign continents, thereby creating markets through the breaking up and restructuring of noncapitalist societies. The populated, relatively advanced countries of the East, such as India and China, had little interest in acquiring European manufactures. And in a large part of the Asian world Europe bought more than it sold, until the nineteenth century.[6] Under these conditions, the growth of plantation colonies (with a new emphasis on expanded production to meet growing European demand) and of white-settler colonies was a major contribution to that burst of demand for manufactures to meet the needs of the settlers in both types of colonies that helped stimulate the Industrial Revolution.

At the heart of this wave of expansion was the slave trade. The prosperity of the extremely profitable sugar plantations was based on the import of African slaves. More than that, the slave trade itself was a most lucrative business, as well as an important prop to British exports via the well-known triangular trade. In sum, the Industrial Revolution germinated in this period—in the boom of export markets and the trade in merchandise and slaves, under monopoly conditions secured through war, control of the seas, and political domination.

On the other hand, this source of European prosperity had its own limitations and began to dry up in the latter half of the eighteenth century. This process was pointedly summarized by Hobsbawm:

> The new colonial economies were not capable of permanent expansion... their use of land and labor was essentially extensive and inefficient. Moreover, the supply of slaves (who rarely reproduced themselves on a sufficient scale) could not be increased fast enough, as is suggested by the rapidly rising trend of slave prices. Hence, exhaustion of the soil, inefficiencies of management, and labor difficulties led to

something like a "crisis of the colonial economy" from the 1750s.[7] This found various forms of expression—for instance, anti-slavery sentiment, and the Home Rule movements of local white settler oligarchies which grew up rapidly in the last third of the eighteenth century in Latin America, in the West Indies, North America and Ireland, and contributed to the revolution in western Europe.[8]

3. Rise of Industrial Capital: Late Eighteenth Century to the 1870s

The declining profitability of the old colonies on the eve of the Industrial Revolution led to an intensification of the search for new colonies and to renewal of warfare between rival empires for redistribution of existing colonies. In the 1760s, England launched a campaign of exploration for new markets in Asia and Africa (on both of which continents Portugal and Holland had taken the lead) and in South America (via establishment of bases for smuggling through the barriers imposed by Spain around her colonies). At the same time, the intense Seven Years War (1756-1763) led to France's losing nearly the whole of its colonial empire, and to Britain's doubling its possessions in North America and opening a clear road to the takeover of India and the domination of the Indian Ocean.

In the previous stage, the major struggles among colonial powers resulted in the triumph of Britain over Holland and Spain (from which the victor obtained, as one of the rewards, control over the slave trade to the Spanish colonies). In the period now being discussed, the primary struggle was between England and France, finally decided in the Napoleonic Wars. It is these wars which set the stage for Britain's hegemony for most of the nineteenth century. Competition among the industrializing capitalist nations continued, but an era of relative peace prevailed in the years between Waterloo and the rise of the new imperialism. The wars of these years were wars of conquest as the imperial powers proceeded further into continental interiors, rather than wars among the imperial powers themselves. And one of the major reasons for this was Britain's undisputed mastery of the seas. As put by one student of imperial history: "In the nineteenth century, as a consequence of one nation's overwhelming naval supremacy, such phrases as 'the struggle for command of the sea' had lost all meaning."[9]

Another effect of the Napoleonic Wars, which helped stamp the future of imperialism, was the opportunity given to Britain to grab the overseas markets of rival powers—to build up its trade and banking network in South America, Africa, West and South Asia, and the Far East. As seen most clearly in its support of the independence of the Spanish and Portuguese colonies in South America and in its subsequent commercial and financial pre-eminence on that continent, the benefits made possible by the Industrial Revolution (in contrast with the situation prevailing in the previous stage of dominant merchant capital) could be acquired through informal as well as formal empire.

The basic strategy of economic relations between the advanced capitalist nations and the rest of the world necessarily changed with the growth of mass production and the ascendancy of industrial capital. Instead of colonial products (such as sugar and spices) and slaves, the needs of the industrializing nations broadened out to include an ever mounting hunger for raw materials to be processed (cotton, oilseeds, dyestuffs, jute, metals) and for food for rapidly expanding urban populations. More important, the previous closed markets of the plantation and settlement colonies were small beer in the light of the flood of products pouring out of the new factories. The pressures of the capital accumulation process and of constantly advancing technology propelled an effort to transform the noncapitalist areas into customers, a process entailing the breakup of the noncapitalist societies. This "breakup" was needed both to create markets and to obtain supplies via commercial agriculture and mining. And while the tactics used to reach these goals varied from one colonial power to another, the basic strategy was universal, involving to a lesser or greater extent the disruption of traditional self-sufficient and self-perpetuating communities; introduction of private property in land; extending the use of money and exchange; imposition of forced labor and recruitment of a labor force depending on wages; destroying competitive native industry; creating a new class structure, including fostering of new elite groups as political and economic junior partners of the imperial powers; imposition of the culture of the metropolitan centers, along with racism and other sociopsychological characteristics of minority foreign rule.

Accompanying the changing character of colonial strategy was the enabling technology, civilian (notably railroads) as well as military. For, in contrast with the previous two stages during which the colonies, except for South America, were largely located along coasts or on small islands, the colonial expansion of this period was characterized by the conquest of continental interiors—including the conquest by the United States of its transcontinental empire, and the tsarist absorption of Central Asia.[10]

During the transition from the colonial system based on merchant capital to that based on industrial capital, some of the ideological and political leaders of triumphant capitalism began to question the utility of colonies, but it would be wrong, I believe, to make too much of this tendency. These anti-imperialists were thinking primarily of the white-settler colonies. As a rule they had no objections to, and for the most part supported, among other things, the wars in India, the Opium Wars, and the retention of Ireland as a colony.[11] What is especially striking about this "anti-imperialism" is its negative aspect: it was directed against special-privilege hangovers in the colonies from the days of merchant capitalism. And its positive aspect was that it provided ideological support and justification for the informal empire of trade and finance which rested on Britain's position as master of the seas, center of international finance, leading exporter of capital, and overwhelmingly foremost manufacturer.

Whether by means of informal or formal empire, the epitome of this stage of imperialism, in contrast with all previous history, is the imposition of the conqueror's mode of production on the society of the conquered. This was achieved in two ways: (1) the use of force or threat of force to transform existing societies to meet the raw material, trade, and investment needs of the conqueror, thereby instituting the division of labor most beneficial to the metropolitan centers, along with the mechanisms for reproducing this division of labor; and (2) killing off the indigenous population and/or moving them into reservations in order to create room for the transplantation of the capitalist system by migration of people and capital from the advanced imperialist centers. In this fashion, the European nations spread their control (in Europe itself as well as in the colonies and ex-colonies) from 35 percent of the globe's land surface in 1800 to 67 percent in 1878, when a new major wave of expansion started.[12]

4. Monopoly Capital and the New Imperialism: 1880s to World War I

Two features distinguish the expansionism of this period: (1) a marked acceleration of the seizure and annexation of foreign territory, and (2) an increase in the number of countries seeking colonies. The rate at which foreign lands were seized in the period from 1878 to 1914 was *three times greater* than it had been during the preceding seventy-five years.[13] This startling increase in the tempo of expansion was most noteworthy in the scramble for Africa. Thus, before 1880 colonial possessions in Africa were relatively few and limited to some coastal areas; twenty years later, almost the entire African continent was split into separate territories owned by European nations.[14] As a result of the conquest of the people of Africa and military adventures elsewhere, the empire-building powers had by 1914 divided among themselves about 85 percent of the globe. Rivalry between expanding nations interfered with outright annexation or absorption of some areas (e.g., China, Persia, and Turkey). In such cases, limited military intervention, the ever-present threat of invasion, and indirect measures were employed by the imperial powers to exercise control and influence. In effect, by the time World War I broke out almost the entire world, including the islands of the seven seas, were under direct or indirect rule of a handful of nations. Once this partitioning had been more or less completed, further expansion by any one power could only be achieved at the expense of another power.

The intensification of the drive for the division of the world was accompanied by an increase in the number of countries that had the means and the urge to get slices of the colonial pie: Germany, the United States, Belgium, Italy, and Japan joined the club of expansionists. This very multiplication of colonial powers, occurring in a relatively short period, accelerated the tempo of colonial growth. Unoccupied space that could potentially be occupied was limited. Therefore, the more nations there were seeking additional colonies at about the same time, the greater was the premium on speed. Hence, the rivalry among the colonizing nations reached new heights, which in turn strengthened the motivation for preclusive occupation of territory and for attempts to control areas useful for the military defense of existing empires against rivals.

The mad rush for foreign land, the mounting conflicts arising from the rivalry for possession of as yet unconquered territory and for the redivision of established empires, the accompanying armaments race, the resurgence of wars among the empire-builders, and finally the outbreak of World War I—all of these clearly indicated the emergence of a new era. In order to clearly underscore the unique features of this stage of capitalist history, as distinguished from earlier phases of colonialism and expansionism, many Marxists follow Lenin's practice (proposed in his seminal work, *Imperialism: The Highest Stage of Capitalism*) of restricting the use of the term "imperialism" to describe the period since the end of the nineteenth century. This historical differentiation is especially important because the new phenomena just described were not accidental events but were clearly correlated with (1) major structural changes in the economies of the advanced capitalist countries, and (2) the rise of competing industrial and financial powers who were increasingly challenging Great Britain's hegemony in world affairs—a hegemony that had been a determining aspect of the preceding period.

The most important structural change in the leading capitalist nations during this period was the transformation from competitive to monopoly capitalism. In the former stage, a large number of firms participated in each industry, turnover of enterprises was high, and the market power of any one firm was quite limited. But as investment in each industry grew alongside intense competition, the weaker firms lost out and capital became increasingly concentrated in fewer hands. Eventually this drift toward monopoly (or oligopoly) led to the emergence of giant firms able to exercise considerable power over their markets and suppliers. The increased strength of these large corporations, supported and at times stimulated by the accompanying growth and concentration of financial capital markets, generated an enhanced ability for, and spurred the thrust to, greater involvement in the world economy. The export of capital became an increasingly important instrument not only for political domination but also as a means to boost exports, control foreign markets, and assure a supply of needed raw materials.

It was also during the blossoming of the monopolistic phase that a number of industrializing nations reached the point at which, besides getting involved in the race for colonies, they were able and willing to challenge Great Britain's lead in industry, finance, and foreign trade. In the mid-nineteenth century Britain's economy far outdistanced its potential rivals. But, by the last quarter of that century, Britain was confronted by restless competitors seeking a greater share of world trade and finance; the industrial revolution had gained a strong foothold in these nations, aided by the spread of railroads and the attainment of integrated national markets.

In addition, the major technological innovations of the late nineteenth and early twentieth centuries improved the competitive ability of the newer industrial nations. Great Britain's advantage as the progenitor of the first industrial revolution diminished as the newer products and sources of energy of what some call a second industrial revolution began to take hold. The late starters, having digested the first industrial revolution, now had a more equal footing with Great Britain: they were all starting out from more or less the same base to exploit the second industrial revolution.[15] This new industrialism, notably featuring mass-produced steel, electric power, and oil as sources of energy, industrial chemistry, and the internal-combustion engine, spread over Western Europe, the United States, and Japan.

The large-scale industries based on the new technology accelerated the trend toward monopoly. They needed heavy capital investment and a firm base for research and design. Thus, the new industries, as well as the giants in the older industries, grew in tandem with capital markets that became large and flexible enough to finance them. The more substantial capital markets and industrial enterprises, in turn, helped push forward the geographic scale of operations of the industrialized nations: more capital could now be mobilized for foreign loans and investment, and the bigger businesses had the resources for the worldwide search for, and development of, the raw materials essential to the success and security of their investments. Not only did the new industrialism generate a voracious appetite for raw materials, food for the swelling urban populations in Europe was now also sought in the far corners of the world. Advance in ship construction made feasible the inexpensive movement of bulk raw materials and food over long ocean distances. Under the pressures and opportunities of the later decades of the nineteenth century, more and more of the world was drawn upon as producers of primary agricultural and mineral products for the industrialized nations. Self-contained economic regions dissolved into a world economy— one that was characterized by an international division of labor in which the leading industrial nations made and sold manufactured goods and the rest of the world supplied them with raw materials and food.

5. The Imperialist World Begins to Shrink: Between the Two World Wars

Colonies were reshuffled after World War I. The victors—with the exception of the United States, which had adopted a separate strategy for strengthening its influence in the international community—carved up the colonies owned by the defeated nations. But the war and its aftermath also brought about countertrends to imperialism. A Communist Revolution in Russia created in one-sixth of the globe a nation that was boldly anti-imperialist: privileges in foreign lands that had been obtained by tsarist governments were renounced and the secret machinations of the imperial powers were exposed by public airing of tsarist archives. For the people of the colonies, the Russian Revolution sounded the knell of a new day: it showed that the masses could successfully rebel and set a country on a totally new path. Less dramatic but still instructive to the colonial world was the attainment of independence in Southern Ireland and the creation of the Irish Free State in 1923.

The interwar period as a whole was characterized by a major surge of nationalism in the colonies. In several areas, this gave rise to active rebellion, in others to various forms of militant political and trade-union struggles. The common thread of these movements was the determination to win freedom from foreign rule. But it took another wave of expansion, a second world war, and numerous wars of national liberation before the colonies attained independence.

In addition to the redivision of the colonies of the defeated nations, World War I induced changes in the relative positions of the victors. Especially noteworthy was the ascendance of the United States over Great Britain. With the growth of both U.S. and Japanese naval power, Great Britain rapidly lost its pre-eminent position on the seas. This played a role in the increase of U.S. influence in Canada and Australia. The wartime weakening of the British economy along with the strengthening of the U.S. financial position as a major supplier of the Allies allowed the United States soon to become the leading capital market, to expand its international banking and overseas investments, and to compete with Great Britain for the world's oil reserves. Long before the war, the United States had begun to spread its influence in Latin America, most markedly in Central America, where, by military intervention and occupation, Cuba, the Dominican Republic, Panama, Nicaragua, and Haiti had in effect become U.S. protectorates. Because of the opportunities arising from the war-induced disruptions of trade and investment, U.S. economic penetration of Latin America increased considerably. During the interwar years Latin America came more and more into the U.S., instead of the British, economic and political orbit.

Apart from the spread of U.S. influence on the world scene, a new expansionary thrust emerged during the Great Depression of the 1930s from the nations that subsequently formed the Axis in World War II. Japan invaded Manchuria in 1931, and, after swallowing that area, began in 1937 a war of conquest for the rest of China. Italy enlarged its empire in northeast Africa by conquering and then in 1936 annexing Ethiopia. Demand for repossession of Germany's former colonies cropped up from time to time in the Weimar Republic, but it did not become a key item of government policy until the Nazis came to power. Although the Nazis featured this goal, the initial strategy of conquest, which initiated World War II, concentrated on building an empire in Central and Eastern Europe.

6. Decolonization and the Rise of the Multinational Corporation: Since World War II

The forces set in motion or accelerated by World War II led to a sharp reversal of the expansionism of the preceding centuries. The imperialist system contracted as a result of the increase in the number of socialist countries, and it was further weakened as more and more colonies attained political independence. Behind the tidal wave of decolonization in the aftermath of the war were three factors: (1) the realignment of world power, with the United States and the Soviet Union emerging as the leading giants; (2) the declining ability of the old colonial powers to hold on to their far-flung empires; and (3) the evolution of independence movements and wars of national liberation powerful enough to remove foreign rule.

The postwar colonial system in Asia was shaken by the growth of resistance movements that originated and gained experience in struggles against Japanese occupation. Elsewhere in Asia, where the Japanese had not penetrated, and on other continents one colony after another was on the verge of revolt by war's end. The weakening of the hold over the colonies by the home countries engaged in a life-and-death struggle with the Axis powers had raised the will of the colonial people to resist. Moreover, depleted financial and military resources on top of postwar reconstruction problems severely limited the ability of the European powers to exercise as much control over the colonies as they had in the past.

The United States was the only power at the end of the war and in subsequent decades that had sufficient strength to try maintaining the old colonial system. But it was confronted with diverse motives, interested at one and the same time in (1) rebuilding the Western European nations as allies in the struggle against the Soviet Union; (2) countering social revolutions that would close the door to United States trade and investment; (3) enlarging its own sphere of influence in the very areas where its allies had prior claims; and (4) minimizing the influence the Soviet Union might obtain through support of anticolonial liberation movements. Such a complex of aims at times served to intensify U.S. support of imperial wars against national liberation struggles, while in other cases it facilitated the transition to political independence. In general, the transition to independence came sooner and with less bloodshed wherever the home country and/or the United States was confident that power was being turned over to governments that would remain in the economic and political orbit of the imperialist nations. The most intense and longest lasting warfare occurred where the independence movements were not only nationalist but also revolutionary—where independence was likely to result in confiscation of foreign investments, severance of economic ties with the former home country, and a shift to the orbit of a socialist country.

The spread of political independence throughout the colonial world created new challenges for the centers of imperialism, since the underlying imperialist nature of the leading capitalist nations and the expansionist imperatives of monopoly capital did not change. The central problem was to keep as much of the colonial world as possible in informal empires, whereby the peripheral nations would be kept open for the exploitation of their natural resources and trade and investment opportunities. This task became more urgent as the nationalist impulses generated by decolonization brought the issue of local industrialization and self-development to the fore. It soon became clear that if the metropolitan centers were to retain the benefits of informal empire they would have to influence the course of economic development in the neocolonies. This was facilitated by the method of decolonization itself: in most cases the key economic and financial components of dependency on the metropolitan centers were retained intact. Control and influence over the periphery was also sustained by the way economic aid was granted and administered, and by the conditions imposed when loans were granted by the newly created international institutions, such as the World Bank and the International Monetary Fund. All of this was backed up by direct and indirect interference by the United States and other powers in the politics and class conflicts of the ex-colonies, aimed at strengthening the most reliable sections of the ruling class, and providing them with needed military assistance and military alliances. Further, the United States, using a chain of military bases around the globe, built up a highly mobile air force and navy as instruments to restrain defection from the imperialist network.

In fact, the economic penetration by the advanced capitalist nations in the areas that remained in the imperialist periphery increased substantially since the end of World War II. The major agents of this form of expansion were the multinational corporations and the multinational banks. Foreign investment had slowed down during the interwar period, because of several factors: the effect of the Great Depression; the rise of cartels that parceled out world markets among competitors and prevented poaching on each other's territory; and the tendency of colonial powers to keep their possessions as exclusive investment preserves for themselves. One after another of these restraints faded away during and after World

War II. Many cartels evaporated during the war. Decolonization created new opportunities for trade and investment competition from metropolitan centers that formerly were excluded. The pervasive U.S. military presence around the globe inspired confidence in foreign investors about the security of their foreign assets. Finally, government war contracts had fattened U.S. industrial giants and thus gave a push to further concentration of economic power, ending up in the creation of supergiants that could exercise control over a large and geographically widespread number of affiliates.

The upshot was an explosion of U.S. foreign investment in other metropolitan centers and in the periphery. In contrast with earlier foreign investment, when a typical international enterprise had two to four foreign branches, the postwar multinational corporation spread out to twenty or more countries. The rapid growth and the extent of the U.S. multinationals aroused a competitive reaction in other metropoles, speeding up further concentration of industry there and the rise of West European and Japanese multinationals. These corporations became the major sources of capital and technology for the newly independent as well as the older periphery. That, together with the fact that the multinationals only invest in ways that suit their own profit aims, worked to reinforce the economic ties of the ex-colonies to the metropoles. These ties were still further entrenched by the multiplying network of multinational banks, whose branches help finance foreign investment and trade as well as participate actively in the financial markets of the periphery.

In all of these changes, the United States played the most decisive role. Indeed, during the first two postwar decades the United States was the undisputed hegemonic power in the imperialist system. The heart of the international financial system was located in New York City, which became the capitalist world's banker and money market. The international money system was tied to the dollar, and, similar to Britain in the previous century, the United States was the largest manufacturer and foreign trader.

By the late 1960s, however, significant changes at the top of the capitalist hierarchy began to appear. On the one hand, the costs of maintaining a globe-straddling military establishment, extending economic and military aid, supplying funds for multinational investment, and financing the war in Vietnam resulted in an unending U.S. balance-of-payments deficit and a vast overload of dollars abroad. This forced two devaluations of the dollar in rapid succession in the early 1970s and subsequent further weakening of the international value of the dollar. (The dollar was no longer "as good as gold": the linchpin of earlier U.S. economic and political dominance.) On the other hand, the revitalized and rapidly growing economies of Western Europe and Japan significantly cut into the U.S. lead in trade and manufacturing: as the decades rolled by, the competition among the leading imperialist nations intensified. Although these developments did not remove the United States from the top of the heap, they increasingly created new challenges to U.S. hegemony and added constraints to U.S. policies and programs. During the 1970s tendencies emerged which pointed to the possibility, especially under the stress of economic crisis, of the emergence of competing trade and currency blocs to replace the earlier more harmonious arrangements (under U.S. leadership) among the imperialist powers.

Notes

1. A. Toussaint, *Archives of the Indian Ocean*; as quoted in G.S. Graham, *The Politics of Naval Supremacy* (Cambridge: Cambridge University Press, 1965), p. 37.
2. Clive Day, *A History of Commerce* (New York: Longman, 1938), p. 166.
3. E.J. Hobsbawm, "The Crisis of the Seventeenth Century," in Trevor Aston, ed., *Crisis in Europe 1560-1660* (New York: Doubleday Anchor, 1967), p. 24. The entire paragraph is based on Hobsbawm's path-breaking articles (originally appearing in *Past and Present*) in which, among other things, he clearly spells out the historical significance of, and the differences between, the earlier colonies of plunder and the subsequent plantation and settlement colonies.
4. The resolution of the class struggle in England necessarily influenced the direction of movement in other leading powers, even those where the commercial classes were as yet in a subordinate position. The increasing strength of England entailed the weakening of their rivals' commercial position. The impact of such competition obliged the others to play England's game or fall by the wayside. And in the process the status of merchants, shippers, and manufacturers waxed in those competing nations which succeeded in staying in the game. In similar fashion, the subsequent Industrial Revolution in England made it imperative for other nations to industrialize.
5. Some interesting data on the correlation between the ups and downs of British trade and its power at sea are given in J. Holland Rose, "Sea Power and Expansion 1660-1763," *The Cambridge History of the British Empire*, vol. 2 (New York: Macmillan, 1929), p. 537.
6. The diversion of trade discussed in the preceding section applied, as far as Asia was concerned, to the displacement of shipping by Asians rather than to any basic changes in the character of Asian trade, which came much later.
7. The "crisis" of the new colonialism does not contradict the previous point about the decisive benefit obtained for the Industrial Revolu-

tion from these colonies. Thus, for a long time prior to 1770 the colonies (including Ireland) bought at least 90 percent of Britain's cotton piece-goods exports.

8. Hobsbawm, "The Crisis of the Seventeenth Century," pp. 55-56.

9. Graham, *The Politics of Naval Supremacy*, p. 105.

10. The new space conquered by imperial powers provided land and jobs for the unemployed and the dislocated produced by rampant capitalism, and no doubt contributed somewhat to the abatement of the social-revolutionary potential of the European working classes.

11. On this, see the useful study by Bernard Semmel, *The Rise of Free Trade Imperialism* (Cambridge: Cambridge University Press, 1970).

12. Grover Clark, *The Balance Sheets of Imperialism* (New York: Columbia University Press, 1936), pp. 5-6.

13. An annual average of about 240,000 square miles of foreign possessions were acquired by the colonial powers in the period from 1878 to the outbreak of World War I. The comparable figure for the first three quarters of the nineteenth century was 83,000. These averages were calculated from data in Clark, *Balance Sheets of Imperialism*, pp. 5-6.

14. The only exceptions were Liberia, generally regarded as being under the special protection of the United States; Morocco, conquered by France a few years later; Libya, later taken over by Italy; and Ethiopia.

15. The same phenomenon is seen with respect to Britain's naval supremacy. Britain lost its advantage (the largest navy) when armor-clad ships were perfected. Since Britain, in effect, had to start anew to build a modern fleet, other nations with sufficient industrial capacity had the opportunity to build up competitive strength that could challenge Britain's hegemony.

[2]
The Rise and Future Demise
of the World Capitalist System:
Concepts for Comparative Analysis

Immanuel Wallerstein

The growth within the capitalist world-economy of the industrial sector of production, the so-called industrial revolution, was accompanied by a very strong current of thought which defined this change as both a process of organic development and of progress. There were those who considered these economic developments and the concomitant changes in social organization to be some penultimate stage of world development whose final working out was but a matter of time. These included such diverse thinkers as Saint-Simon, Comte, Hegel, Weber, Durkheim. And then there were the critics, most notably Marx, who argued, if you will, that the nineteenth-century present was only an antepenultimate stage of development, that the capitalist world was to know a cataclysmic political revolution which would then lead in the fullness of time to a final societal form, in this case the classless society.

One of the great strengths of Marxism was that, being an oppositional and hence critical doctrine, it called attention not merely to the contradictions of the system but also to those of its ideologists, by appealing to the empirical evidence of historical reality which unmasked the irrelevancy of the models proposed for the explanation of the social world. The Marxist critics saw in abstracted models concrete rationalization, and they argued their case fundamentally by pointing to the failure of their opponents to analyze the social whole. As Lukacs put it, "It is not the primacy of economic motives in historical explanation that constitutes the decisive difference between Marxism and bourgeois thought, but the point of view of totality."[1][. . .].

Does Marxism give us a better account of social reality? In principle yes. In practice there are many different, often contradictory, versions extant of "Marxism." But what is more fundamental is the fact that in many countries Marxism is now the official state doctrine. Marxism is no longer exclusively an oppositional doctrine as it was in the nineteenth century. The social fate of official doctrines is that they suffer a constant social pressure toward dogmatism and apologia, difficult although by no means impossible to counteract, and that they thereby often fall into the same intellectual dead end of ahistorical model building. [. . .].

29

Nothing illustrates the distortions of ahistorical models of social change better than the dilemmas to which the concept of stages gives rise. If we are to deal with social transformations over long historical time..., and if we are to give an explanation of both continuity and transformation, then we must logically divide the long term into segments in order to observe the structural changes from time A to time B. These segments are however not discrete but continuous in reality; ergo they are "stages" in the "development" of a social structure, a development which we determine however not a priori but a posteriori. That is, we cannot predict the future concretely, but we can predict the past.

The crucial issue when comparing "stages" is to determine the units of which the "stages" are synchronic portraits (or "ideal types," if you will). And the fundamental error of ahistorical social science (including ahistorical versions of Marxism) is to reify parts of the totality into such units and then to compare these reified structures.

For example, we may take modes of disposition of agricultural production, and term them subsistence cropping and cash cropping. We may then see these as entities which are "stages" of a development. We may talk about decisions of groups of peasants to shift from one to the other. We may describe other partial entities, such as states, as having within them two separate "economies," each based on a different mode of disposition of agricultural production. If we take each of these successive steps, all of which are false steps, we will end up with the misleading concept of the "dual economy," as have many liberal economists dealing with the so-called underdeveloped countries of the world.

Marxist scholars have often fallen into exactly the same trap. If we take modes of payment of agricultural labor and contrast a "feudal" mode wherein the laborer is permitted to retain for subsistence a part of his agricultural production with a "capitalist" mode wherein the same laborer turns over the totality of his production to the landowner, receiving part of it back in the form of wages, we may then see these two modes as "stages" of a development. We may talk of the interests of "feudal" landowners in preventing the conversion of their mode of payment to a system of wages. We may then explain the fact that in the twentieth century a partial entity, say a state in Latin America, has not yet industrialized as the consequence of its being dominated by such landlords. If we take each of these successive steps, all of which are false steps, we will end up with the misleading concept of a "state dominated by feudal elements," as though such a thing could possibly exist in a capitalist world-economy. [...].

Not only does the misidentification of the entities to be compared lead us into false concepts, but it creates a nonproblem: can stages be skipped? This question is only logically meaningful if we have "stages" that "coexist" within a single empirical framework. If within a capitalist world-economy, we can define one state as feudal, a second as capitalist, and a third as socialist, then and only then can we pose the question: can a country "skip" from the feudal stage to the socialist stage of national development without "passing through capitalism"? But if there is no such thing as "national development" (if by that we mean a natural history), and if the proper entity of comparison is the world-system, then the problem of stage skipping is nonsense. [. . .].

If we are to talk of stages, then—and we should talk of stages—it must be stages of social systems, that is, of totalities. And the only totalities that exist or have historically existed are minisystems and world-systems, and in the nineteenth and twentieth centuries there has been only one world-system in existence, the capitalist world-economy.

We take the defining characteristic of a social system to be the existence within it of a division of labor, such that the various sectors or areas within are dependent upon economic exchange with others for the smooth and continuous provisioning of the needs of the area. Such economic exchange can clearly exist without a common political structure and even more obviously without sharing the same culture.

A minisystem is an entity that has within it a complete division of labor, and a single cultural framework. Such systems were found only in very simple agricultural or hunting and gathering societies. Such minisystems no longer exist in the world. Furthermore, there were fewer in the past than is often asserted, since any such system that became tied to an empire by the payment of tribute as "protection costs" ceased by that fact to be a "system," no longer having a self-contained division of labor. For such an area, the payment of tribute marked a shift, in Polanyi's language, from being a reciprocal economy to participating in a larger redistributive economy.[2]

Leaving aside the now defunct minisystems, the only kind of social system is a world-system, which we define quite simply as a unit with a single division of labor and multiple cultural systems. It follows logically that there can, however, be two varieties of such world-systems, one with a common political system and one without. We shall designate these respectively as world-empires and world-economies.

It turns out empirically that world-economies have historically been unstable structures leading either toward disintegration or conquest by one group and hence transformation into a world-empire. Examples of such world-empires emerging from world-economies are all the so-called great civilizations of premodern times, such as China, Egypt, Rome (each at appropriate periods of its history). On the other hand, the so-called nineteenth-century empires, such as Great Britain or France, were not world-empires at all, but nation-states with colonial appendages operating within the framework of a world-economy.

World-empires were basically redistributive in economic form. No doubt they bred clusters of merchants who engaged in economic exchange (primarily long-distance trade), but such clusters, however large, were a minor part of the total economy and not fundamentally determinative of its fate. Such long-distance trade tended to be, as Polanyi argues, "administered trade" and not market trade, utilizing "ports of trade."

It was only with the emergence of the modern world-economy in sixteenth-century Europe that we saw the full development and economic predominance of market trade. This was the system called capitalism. Capitalism and a world-economy (that is, a single division of labor but multiple polities and cultures) are obverse sides of the same coin. One does not cause the other. We are merely defining the same indivisible phenomenon by different characteristics.[. . .].

On the "feudalism" debate, we take as a starting point Frank's concept of "the development of underdevelopment," that is, the view that the economic structure of contemporary underdeveloped countries is not the form which a "traditional" society takes upon contact with "developed" societies, nor an earlier stage in the "transition" to industrialization. It is rather the result of being involved in the world-economy as a peripheral, raw material producing area, or as Frank puts it for Chile, "underdevelopment . . . is the necessary product of four centuries of capitalism itself."[3]

This formulation runs counter to a large body of writing concerning the underdeveloped countries that was produced in the period 1950-1970, a literature which sought the factors that explained "development" within nonsystems such as "states" or "cultures" and, once having presumably discovered these factors, urged their reproduction in underdeveloped areas as the road to salvation.[4] Frank's theory also runs counter, as we have already noted, to the received orthodox version of Marxism that had long dominated Marxist parties and intellectual circles, for example in Latin America. This older "Marxist" view of Latin America as a set of feudal societies in a more or less prebourgeois stage of development has fallen before the critiques of Frank and many others as well as before the political reality symbolized by the Cuban revolution and all its many consequences. Recent analysis in Latin America has centered instead around the concept of "dependence."[5]

However, recently, Ernesto Laclau has made an attack on Frank which, while accepting the critique of dualist doctrines, refuses to accept the categorization of Latin American states as capitalist. Instead Laclau asserts that "the world capitalist system. . .includes, *at the level of its definition*, various modes of production." He accuses Frank of confusing the two concepts of the "capitalist mode of production" and "participation in a world capitalist economic system."[6] Of course, if it's a matter of definition, then there can be no argument. But then the polemic is scarcely useful since it is reduced to a question of semantics. Furthermore, Laclau insists that the definition is not his but that of Marx, which is more debatable. [. . .].

There is [. . .] a substantive issue in this debate. It is in fact the same substantive issue that underlay the debate between Maurice Dobb and Paul Sweezy in the early 1950s about the "transition from feudalism to capitalism" that occurred in early modern Europe.[7] The substantive issue, in my view, concerns the appropriate unit of analysis for the purpose of comparison. Basically, although neither Sweezy nor Frank is quite explicit on this point, and though Dobb and Laclau can both point to texts of Marx that seem clearly to indicate that they more faithfully follow Marx's argument, I believe both Sweezy and Frank better follow the spirit of Marx if not his letter and that, leaving Marx quite out of the picture, they bring us nearer to an understanding of what actually happened and is happening than do their opponents.

What is the picture, both analytical and historical, that Laclau constructs? The heart of the problem revolves around the existence of free labor as the defining characteristic of a capitalist mode of production: "The fundamental economic relationship of capitalism is constituted by the *free* [italics mine] labourer's sale of his labourpower, whose necessary precondition is the loss by the direct producer of ownership of the means of production."[8] [. . .]. There in a nutshell it is. Western Europe, at least England from the late seventeenth century on, had primarily landless, wage-earning laborers. In Latin America, then and to some extent still now, laborers were not proletarians, but slaves or "serfs." If proletariat, then capitalism. Of course. To be sure. But is England, or Mexico, or the West Indies a unit of analysis? Does each have a separate "mode of production"? Or is the unit (for the sixteenth to the eighteenth centuries) the European world-economy, including England *and*

Mexico, in which case what was the "mode of production" of this world-economy?

Before we argue our response to this question let us turn to quite another debate, one between Mao Zedong and Liu Shaoqi in the 1960s concerning whether or not the Chinese People's Republic was a "socialist state." This is a debate that has a long background in the evolving thought of Marxist parties.

Marx, as has been often noted, said virtually nothing about the postrevolutionary political process. Engels spoke quite late in his writings of the "dictatorship of the proletariat." It was left to Lenin to elaborate a theory about such a "dictatorship," in his pamphlet *State and Revolution*, published in the last stages before the Bolshevik takeover of Russia, that is, in August 1917. The coming to power of the Bolsheviks led to a considerable debate as to the nature of the regime that had been established. Eventually a theoretical distinction emerged in Soviet thought between "socialism" and "communism" as two stages in historical development, one realizable in the present and one only in the future. In 1936 Stalin proclaimed that the USSR had become a socialist (but not yet a communist) state. Thus we now had firmly established *three* stages after bourgeois rule: a postrevolutionary government, a socialist state, and eventually communism. When, after World War II, various regimes dominated by the Communist Party were established in various East European states, these regimes were proclaimed to be "peoples' democracies," a new name then given to the postrevolutionary stage one. At later points, some of these countries, for example Czechoslovakia, asserted that they had passed into stage two, that of becoming a socialist republic.

In 1961, the Twenty-Second Congress of the Communist Party of the Soviet Union (CPSU) invented a fourth stage, in between the former second and third stages: that of a socialist state which had become a "state of the whole people," a stage it was contended the USSR had at that point reached. The program of the Congress asserted that "the state as an organization of the entire people will survive until the complete victory of communism." One of its commentators defines the "intrinsic substance (and) chief distinctive feature" of this stage: "The state of the whole people is the first state in the world with no class struggle to contend with and, hence, with no class domination and no suppression."[9]

One of the earliest signs of a major disagreement in the 1950s between the Communist Party of the Soviet Union and the Chinese Communist Party (CCP) was a theoretical debate that revolved around the question of the "gradual transition to communism." Basically, the CPSU argued that different socialist states would proceed separately in effectuating such a transition whereas the CCP argued that all socialist states would proceed simultaneously.

As we can see, this last form of the debate about "stages" implicitly raised the issue of the unit of analysis, for in effect the CCP was arguing that "communism" was a characteristic not of nation-states but of the world-economy as a whole. This debate was transposed onto the internal Chinese scene by the ideological debate, now known to have deep and long-standing roots, that gave rise eventually to the Cultural Revolution.

One of the corollaries of these debates about "stages" was whether or not the class struggle continued in postrevolutionary states prior to the achievement of communism. The Twenty-Second Congress of the CPSU in 1961 had argued that the USSR had become a state without an internal class struggle; there were no longer existing antagonistic classes within it. Without speaking of the USSR, Mao Zedong in 1957 had asserted in China:

> The class struggle is by no means over.... It will continue to be long and tortuous, and at times will even become very acute.... Marxists are still a minority among the entire population as well as among the intellectuals. Therefore, Marxism must still develop through struggle. ...Such struggles will never end. This is the law of development of truth and, naturally, of Marxism as well.[10]

If such struggles never end, then many of the facile generalizations about "stages" which "socialist" states are presumed to go through are thrown into question.

During the Cultural Revolution, it was asserted that Mao's report *On the Correct Handling of Contradictions Among the People* cited above, as well as one other, "entirely repudiated the 'theory of the dying out of the class struggle' advocated by Liu Shao-Chi...."[11] Specifically, Mao argued that "the elimination of the system of ownership by the exploiting classes through socialist transformation is not equal to the disappearance of struggle in the political and ideological spheres."[12]

Indeed, this is the logic of a *cultural* revolution. Mao is asserting that even if there is the achievement of political power (dictatorship of the proletariat) and *economic* transformation (abolition of private ownership of the means of production), the revolution is still far from complete. Revolution is not an event but a process. This process Mao calls "socialist society"—in my view a somewhat confusing choice of words, but no matter—and "socialist society covers a fairly long historical period."[13] Furthermore, "there are classes and class struggle throughout the period of socialist society." The Tenth Plenum of the Eighth Central Committee of the CCP,[14] meeting from

September 24-27, 1962, in endorsing Mao's views, omitted the phrase "socialist society" and talked instead of "the historical period of proletarian revolution and proletarian dictatorship,...the historical period of transition from capitalism to communism," which it said "will last scores of years or even longer" and during which "there is a class struggle between the proletariat and the bourgeoisie and struggle between the socialist road and the capitalist road."[15]

We do not have directly Liu's counter arguments. We might however take as an expression of the alternative position a recent analysis published in the USSR on the relationship of the socialist system and world development. There it is asserted that at some unspecified point after World War II, "socialism outgrew the bounds of one country and became a world system...." It is further argued that: "Capitalism, emerging in the 16th century, became a world economic system only in the 19th century. It took the bourgeois revolutions 300 years to put an end to the power of the feudal elite. It took socialism 30 or 40 years to generate the forces for a new world system." Finally, this book speaks of "capitalism's international division of labor" and "international socialist cooperation of labor" as two separate phenomena, drawing from this counterposition the policy conclusion: "Socialist unity has suffered a serious setback from the divisive course being pursued by the incumbent leadership of the Chinese People's Republic," and attributes that to "the great-power chauvinism of Mao Zedong and his group."[16]

Note well the contrast between these two positions. Mao Zedong is arguing for viewing "socialist society" as process rather than structure. Like Frank and Sweezy, and once again implicitly rather than explicitly, he is taking the world-system rather than the nation-state as the unit of analysis. The analysis by USSR scholars by contrast specifically argues the existence of two world-systems with two divisions of labor existing side by side, although the socialist system is acknowledged to be "divided." If divided politically, is it united economically? Hardly, one would think; in which case what is the substructural base to argue the existence of the system? Is it merely a moral imperative? And are then the Soviet scholars defending their concepts on the basis of Kantian metaphysics?

Let us see now if we can reinterpret the issues developed in these two debates within the framework of a general set of concepts that could be used to analyze the functioning of world-systems, and particularly of the historically specific capitalist world-economy that has existed for about four or five centuries now.

We must start with how one demonstrates the existence of a single division of labor. We can regard a division of labor as a grid which is substantially interdependent. Economic actors operate on some assumption (obviously seldom clear to any individual actor) that the totality of their essential needs—of sustenance, protection, and pleasure—will be met over a reasonable time span by a combination of their own productive activities and exchange in some form. The smallest grid that would substantially meet the expectations of the overwhelming majority of actors within those boundaries constitutes a single division of labor.

The reason why a small farming community whose only significant link to outsiders is the payment of annual tribute does not constitute such a single division of labor is that the assumptions of persons living in it concerning the provision of protection involve an "exchange" with other parts of the world-empire.

This concept of grid of exchange relationships assumes, however, a distinction between *essential* exchanges and what might be called "luxury" exchanges. This is to be sure a distinction rooted in the social perceptions of the actors and hence in both their social organization and their culture. These perceptions can change. But this distinction is crucial if we are not to fall into the trap of identifying every exchange activity as evidence of the existence of a system. Members of a system (a minisystem or a world-system) can be linked in limited exchanges with elements located outside the system, in the "external arena" of the system.[. . .].

We are, as you see, coming to the essential feature of a capitalist world-economy, which is production for sale in a market in which the object is to realize the maximum profit. In such a system production is constantly expanded as long as further production is profitable, and men constantly innovate new ways of producing things that will expand the profit margin. The classical economists tried to argue that such production for the market was somehow the "natural" state of man. But the combined writings of the anthropologists and the Marxists left few in doubt that such a mode of production (these days called "capitalism") was only one of the several possible modes.

Since, however, the intellectual debate between the liberals and the Marxists took place in the era of the Industrial Revolution, there has tended to be a de facto confusion between industrialism and capitalism. This left the liberals after 1945 in the dilemma of explaining how a presumably noncapitalist society, the USSR, had industrialized. The most sophisticated response has been to conceive of "liberal capitalism" and "socialism" as two variants of an "industrial society," two variants destined to "converge." This argument has been trenchantly expounded by Raymond Aron.[17] But the same confusion left the Marxists, including Marx, with the problem of explaining what was the mode of production that predominated in Europe from the sixteenth to the eighteenth centuries, that is, before the Industrial Revolution. Essentially, most Marxists have talked of a "transitional" stage, which is in fact a blurry nonconcept with no operational indicators. This dilemma is heightened if the unit of analysis used is the state, in which case one has to explain why the transition has occurred at different rates and times in different countries.[18]

Marx himself handled this by drawing a distinction between "merchant capitalism" and "industrial capitalism." This I believe is unfortunate terminology, since it leads to such conclusions as that of Maurice Dobb who says of this "transitional" period:

> But why speak of this as a stage of capitalism at all? The workers were generally not proletarianized: that is, they were not separated from the instruments of production, nor even in many cases from occupation of a plot of land. Production was scattered and decentralized and not concentrated. *The capitalist was still predominantly a merchant* who did not control production directly and did not impose his own discipline upon the work of artisan-craftsmen, who both laboured as individual (or family) units and retained a considerable measure of independence (if a dwindling one).[19]

One might well say: why indeed? Especially if one remembers how much emphasis Dobb places a few pages earlier on capitalism as a mode of *production*—how then can the capitalist be primarily a merchant—on the concentration of such ownership in the hands of a few, and on the fact that capitalism is not synonymous with private ownership, capitalism being different from a system in which the owners are "small peasant producers or artisan-producers." Dobb argues that a defining feature of private ownership under capitalism is that some are "obliged to [work for those that own] since [they own] nothing and [have] no access to means of production [and hence] have no other means of livelihood."[20] Given this contradiction, the answer Dobb gives to his own question is in my view very weak: "While it is true that at this date the situation was transitional, and capital-to-wage-labour relations were still immaturely developed, the latter were already beginning to assume their characteristic features."[21]

If capitalism is a mode of production, production for profit in a market, then we ought, I should have thought, to look to whether or not such production was or was not occurring. It turns out in fact that it was, and in a very substantial form. Most of this production, however, was not industrial production. What was happening in Europe from the sixteenth to the eighteenth centuries is that over a large geographical area going from Poland in the northeast westward and southward throughout Europe and including large parts of the Western Hemisphere as well, there grew up a world-economy with a single division of labor within which there was a world market, for which men produced largely agricultural products for sale and profit. I would think the simplest thing to do would be to call this agricultural capitalism.

This then resolves the problems incurred by using the pervasiveness of wage labor as a defining characteristic of capitalism. An individual is no less a capitalist exploiting labor because the state assists him to pay his laborers low wages (including wages in kind) and denies these laborers the right to change employment. Slavery and so-called second serfdom are not to be regarded as anomalies in a capitalist system. Rather the so-called serf in Poland or the Indian on a Spanish *encomienda* in New Spain in this sixteenth-century world-economy were working for landlords who "paid" them (however euphemistic this term) for cash-crop production. This is a relationship in which labor power is a commodity (how could it ever be more so than under slavery?), quite different from the relationship of a feudal serf to his lord in eleventh-century Burgundy, where the economy was not oriented to a world market, and where labor power was (therefore?)in no sense bought or sold.

Capitalism thus means labor as a commodity to be sure. But in the era of agricultural capitalism, wage labor is only one of the modes in which labor is recruited and recompensed in the labor market. Slavery, coerced cash-crop production (my name for the so-called second feudalism), sharecropping, and tenancy are all alternative modes. It would take too long to develop here the conditions under which differing regions of the world-economy tend to specialize in different agricultural products. I have done this elsewhere.[22]

What we must notice now is that the specialization occurs in specific and differing geographic regions of the world-economy. This regional specialization comes about by the attempts of actors in the market to avoid the normal operation of the market whenever it does not maximize their profit. The attempts of these actors to use nonmarket devices to ensure short-run profits makes them turn to the political entities which have in fact power to affect the market—the nation-states.[. . .].

In any case, the local capitalist classes—cash-crop landowners, (often, even usually, nobility) and merchants—turned to the state, not only to liberate them from nonmarket constraints (as traditionally emphasized by liberal historiography) but to create new constraints on the new market, the market of the European world-economy.

By a series of accidents—historical, ecological, geographic— northwest Europe was better situated in the sixteenth century to diversify its agricultural specialization and add to it certain industries (such as textiles, shipbuilding, and metal wares) than were other parts of Europe. Northwest Europe emerged as the core area of this world-economy, specializing in agricultural production of higher skill levels, which favored (again for reasons too complex to develop) tenancy and wage labor as the modes of labor control. Eastern Europe and the Western Hemisphere became peripheral areas specializing in export of grains, bullion, wood, cotton, sugar— all of which favored the use of a slavery and coerced cash-crop labor as the modes of labor control. Mediterranean Europe emerged as the semiperipheral area of this world-economy specializing in high-cost industrial products (for example, silks) and credit and specie transactions, which had as a consequence in the agricultural arena sharecropping as the mode of labor control and little export to other areas.

The three structural positions in a world-economy—core, periphery, and semiperiphery—had become stabilized by about 1640. How certain areas became one and not the other is a long story.[23] The key fact is that given slightly different starting points, the interests of various local groups converged in northwest Europe, leading to the development of strong state mechanisms, and diverged sharply in the peripheral areas, leading to very weak ones. Once we get a difference in the strength of the state machineries, we get the operation of "unequal exchange,"[24] which is enforced by strong states on weak ones, by core states on peripheral areas. Thus capitalism involves not only appropriation of the surplus value by an owner from a laborer, but an appropriation of surplus of the whole world-economy by core areas. And this was as true in the stage of agricultural capitalism as it is in the stage of industrial capitalism.[. . . .].

Capitalism was from the beginning an affair of the world-economy and not of nation-states. It is a misreading of the situation to claim that it is only in the twentieth century that capitalism has become "worldwide," although this claim is frequently made in various writings, particularly by Marxists[. . . .]. Capital has never allowed its aspirations to be determined by national boundaries in a capitalist world-economy, and that the creation of "national" barriers— generically, mercantilism—has historically been a defensive mechanism of capitalists located in states which are one level below the high point of strength in the system.[. . . .]. In the process a large number of countries create national economic barriers whose consequences often last beyond their initial objectives. At this later point in the process the very same capitalists who pressed their national governments to impose the restrictions now find these restrictions constraining. This is not an "internationalization" of "national" capital. This is simply a new political demand by certain sectors of the capitalist classes who have at all points in time sought to maximize their profits within the real economic market, that of the world-economy.

If this is so, then what meaning does it have to talk of structural positions within this economy and identify states as being in one of these positions? And why talk of three positions, inserting that of "semiperiphery" in between the widely used concepts of core and periphery? The state machineries of the core states were strengthened to meet the needs of capitalist landowners and their merchant allies.[. . .].

The strengthening of the state machineries in core areas has as its direct counterpart the decline of the state machineries in peripheral areas.[. . .]. In peripheral countries, the interests of the capitalist landowners lie in an opposite direction from those of the local commercial bourgeoisie. Their interests lie in maintaining an open economy to maximize their profit from world-market trade (no restrictions in exports and access to lower-cost industrial products from core countries) and in elimination of the commercial bourgeoisie in favor of outside merchants (who pose no local political threat). Thus, in terms of the state, the coalition which strengthened it in core countries was precisely absent.

The second reason, which has become ever more operative over the history of the modern world-system, is that the strength of the state machinery in core states is a function of the weakness of other state machineries. Hence intervention of outsiders via war, subversion, and diplomacy is the lot of peripheral states.

All this seems very obvious. I repeat it only in order to make clear two points. One cannot reasonably explain the strength of various state machineries at specific moments of the history of the modern world-system primarily in terms of a genetic-cultural line of argumentation, but rather in terms of the structural role a country plays in the world-economy at that moment in time.[. . .].

The second point we wish to make about the structural differences of core and periphery is that they are not comprehensible unless we realize that there is a third structural position: that of the semiperiphery. This is not the result merely of establishing arbitrary cutting-points on a continuum of characteristics.[. . .]. The semiperiphery is needed to make a capitalist world-economy run smoothly. Both kinds of world-system, the world-empire with a redistributive economy and the world-economy with a capitalist market economy, involve markedly unequal distribution of rewards. Thus, logically, there is immediately posed the question of how it is possible politically for such a system to persist. Why do not the majority who are exploited simply overwhelm the minority who draw disproportionate benefits?[. . .].

There have been three major mechanisms that have enabled world-systems to retain relative political stability (not in terms of the particular groups who will play the leading roles in the system, but in terms of systemic survival itself). One obviously is the concentration of military strength in the hands of the dominant forces. The modalities of this obviously vary with the technology, and there are, to be sure, political prerequisities for such a concentration, but nonetheless sheer force is no doubt a central consideration.

A second mechanism is the pervasiveness of an ideological commitment to the system as a whole. I do not mean what has often been termed the "legitimation" of a system, because that term has been used to imply that the lower strata of a system feel some affinity with or loyalty toward the rulers, and I doubt that this has ever been a significant factor in the survival of world-systems. I mean rather the degree to which the staff or cadres of the system (and I leave this term deliberately vague) feel that their own well-being is wrapped up in the survival of the system as such and the competence of its leaders. It is this staff which not only propagates the myths; it is they who believe them.

But neither force nor the ideological commitment of the staff would suffice were it not for the division of the majority into a larger lower stratum and a smaller middle stratum. Both the revolutionary call for polarization as a strategy of change and the liberal encomium to consensus as the basis of the liberal polity reflect this proposition. The import is far wider than its use in the analysis of contemporary political problems suggests. It is the normal condition of either kind of world-system to have a three-layered structure. When and if this ceases to be the case, the world-system disintegrates.

In a world-empire, the middle stratum is in fact accorded the role of maintaining the marginally desirable long-distance luxury trade, while the upper stratum concentrates its resources on controlling the military machinery which can collect the tribute, the crucial mode of redistributing surplus. By providing, however, for an access to a limited portion of the surplus to urbanized elements who alone, in premodern societies, could contribute political cohesiveness to isolated clusters of primary producers, the upper stratum effectively buys off the potential leadership of coordinated revolt. And by denying access to political rights for this commercial-urban middle stratum, it makes them constantly vulnerable to confiscatory measures whenever their economic profits become sufficiently swollen so that they might begin to create for themselves military strength.

In a world-economy, such "cultural" stratification is not so simple, because the absence of a single political system means the concentration of economic roles vertically rather than horizontally throughout the system. The solution then is to have three *kinds* of states, with pressures for cultural homogenization within each of them—thus, besides the upper stratum of core states and the lower stratum of peripheral states, there is a middle stratum of semiperipheral ones.

This semiperiphery is then assigned as it were a specific economic role, but the reason is less economic than political. That is to say, one might make a good case that the world-economy as an economy would function every bit as well without a semiperiphery. But it would be far less *politically* stable, for it would mean a polarized world-system. The existence of the third category means precisely that the upper stratum is not faced with the *unified* opposition of all the others because the *middle* stratum is both exploited and exploiter. It follows that the specific economic role is not all that important and has thus changed through the various historical stages of the modern world-system.[. . .].

Where then does class analysis fit in all of this? And what in such a formulation are nations, nationalities, peoples, ethnic groups? First of all, without arguing the point now,[25] I would contend that all these latter terms denote variants of a single phenomenon which I will term "ethno-nations."

Both classes and ethnic groups, or status groups, or ethno-nations are phenomena of world-economies and much of the enormous confusion that has surrounded the concrete analysis of their functioning can be attributed quite simply to the fact that they have been analyzed as though they existed within the nation-states of this world-economy, instead of within the world-economy as a whole. This has been a Procrustean bed indeed.

The range of economic activities being far wider in the core than in the periphery, the range of syndical interest groups is far wider there.[26] Thus, it has been widely observed that there does not exist in many parts of the world today a proletariat of the kind which exists in, say, Europe or North America. But this is a confusing way to state the observation. Industrial activity being disproportionately concentrated in certain parts of the world-economy, industrial wage workers are to be found principally in certain geographic regions. Their interests as a syndical group are determined by their collective relationship to the world-economy.[. . .]. The same might be said about industrial capitalists. Class analysis is perfectly capable of accounting for the political position of, let us say, French skilled workers if we look at their structural position and interests in the world-economy. Similarly with the ethno-nations. The meaning of ethnic consciousness in a core area is considerably different from that of ethnic consciousness in a peripheral area precisely because of the different class position such ethnic groups have in the world-economy.[27]

Political struggles of ethnonations or segments of classes within national boundaries of course are the daily bread and butter of local politics. But their significance or consequences can only be fruitfully analyzed if one spells out the implications of their organizational activity or political demands for the functioning of the world-economy. [. . .].

The functioning then of a capitalist world-economy requires that groups pursue their economic interests within a single world market while seeking to distort this market for their benefit by organizing to exert influence on states, some of which are far more powerful than others but none of which controls the world market in its entirety. Of course, we shall find on closer inspection that there are periods where one state is relatively quite powerful and other periods where power is more diffuse and contested, permitting weaker states broader ranges of action. We can talk then of the relative tightness or looseness of the world-system as an important variable and seek to analyze why this dimension tends to be cyclical in nature, as it seems to have been for several hundred years.

We are now in a position to look at the historical evolution of this capitalist world-economy itself and analyze the degree to which it is fruitful to talk of distinct stages in its evolution as a system. The emergence of the European world-economy in the "long" sixteenth century (1450-1640) was made possible by an historical conjuncture: on those long-term trends which were the culmination of what has been sometimes described as the "crisis of feudalism" was superimposed a more immediate cyclical crisis plus climatic changes, all of which created a dilemma that could only be resolved by a geographic expansion of the division of labor. Furthermore, the balance of intersystem forces was such as to make this realizable. Thus a geographic expansion did take place in conjunction with a demographic expansion and an upward price rise. [. . .].

Each of the states or potential states within the European world-economy was quickly in the race to bureaucratize, to raise a standing army, to homogenize its culture, to diversify its economic activities. By 1640, those in northwest Europe had succeeded in establishing themselves as the core states; Spain and the northern Italian city-states declined into being semiperipheral; northeastern Europe and Iberian America had become the periphery. At this point, those in semiperipheral status had reached it by virtue of decline from a former more pre-eminent status.

It was the system-wide recession of 1650-1730 that consolidated the European world-economy and opened stage two of the modern world-economy. For the recession forced retrenchment, and the decline in relative surplus allowed room for only one core state to survive. The mode of struggle was mercantilism. [...]. In this struggle England first ousted the Netherlands from its commerical primacy and then resisted successfully France's attempt to catch up. As England began to speed up the process of industrialization after 1760, there was one last attempt of those capitalist forces located in France to break the imminent British hegemony. This attempt was expressed first in the French Revolution's replacement of the cadres of the regime and then in Napoleon's continental blockade. But it failed.

Stage three of the capitalist world-economy begins, then, a stage of industrial rather than of agricultural capitalism. Henceforth, industrial production is no longer a minor aspect of the world market but comprises an ever larger percentage of world gross production—and even more important, of world gross surplus. This involves a whole series of consequences for the world-system.

First of all, it led to the further geographic expansion of the European world-economy to include now the whole of the globe. This was in part the result of its technological feasibility both in terms of improved military firepower and improved shipping facilities which made regular trade sufficiently inexpensive to be viable. But, in addition, industrial production *required* access to raw materials of a nature and in a quantity such that the needs could not be supplied within the former boundaries. At first, however, the search for new markets was not a primary consideration in the geographic expansion since the new markets were more readily available within the old boundaries, as we shall see.

The geographic expansion of the European world-economy meant the elimination of other world-systems as well as the absorption of the remaining minisystems. The most important world-system up to then outside of the European world-economy, Russia, entered in semiperipheral status, the consequence of the strength of its state machinery (including its army) and the degree of industrialization already achieved in the eighteenth century. The independences in the Latin American countries did nothing to change their peripheral status. They merely eliminated the last vestiges of Spain's semiperipheral role and ended pockets of noninvolvement in the world-economy in the interior of Latin America. Asia and Africa were absorbed into the periphery in the nineteenth century, although Japan, because of the combination of the strength of its state machinery, the poverty of its resource base (which led to a certain disinterest on the part of world capitalist forces), and its geographic remoteness from the core areas, was able quickly to graduate into semiperipheral status. [. . .].

The creation of vast new areas as the periphery of the expanded world-economy made possible a shift in the role of some other areas. Specifically, both the United States and Germany (as it came into being) combined formerly peripheral and semiperipheral regions. The manufacturing sector in each was able to gain political ascendancy, as the peripheral subregions became less economically crucial to the world-economy. Mercantilism now became the major tool of semiperipheral countries seeking to become core countries, thus still performing a function analogous to that of the mercantilist drives of the late seventeeth and eighteenth centuries in England and France. To be sure, the struggle of semiperipheral countries to "industrialize" varied in the degree to which it succeeded in the period before World War I: all the way in the United States, only partially in Germany, not at all in Russia.

The internal structure of core states also changed fundamentally under industrial capitalism. For a core area, industrialism involved divesting itself of substantially all agricultural activities (except that in the twentieth century further mechanization was to create a new form of working the land that was so highly mechanized as to warrant the appellation industrial). Thus whereas, in the period 1700-1740, England not only was Europe's leading industrial exporter but was also Europe's leading agricultural exporter—this was at a high point in the economy-wide recession—by 1900, less than 10 percent of England's population was engaged in agricultural pursuits.

At first under industrial capitalism, the core exchanged manufactured products against the periphery's agricultural products—hence, Britain from 1815 to 1873 was the "workshop of the world." Even to those semiperipheral countries that had some manufacture (France, Germany, Belgium, the United States, Britain) in this period supplied about half their needs in manufactured goods. As, however, the mercantilist practices of this latter group both cut Britain off from outlets and even created competition for Britain in sales to peripheral areas, a competition which led to the late nineteenth-century "scramble for Africa," the world division of labor was reallocated to ensure a new special role for the core: less the provision of the manufactures, more the provision of the machines to make the manufactures as well as the provision of infrastructure (especially, in this period, railroads).

The rise of manufacturing created for the first time under capitalism a large-scale urban proletariat. And in consequence for the first time there arose what Michels has called the "anticapitalist mass spirit,"[28] which was translated into concrete organizational forms (trade unions, socialist parties). This development intruded a new factor as threatening to the stability of the states and of the capitalist forces now so securely in control of them as the earlier centrifugal thrusts of regional anticapitalist landed elements had been in the seventeenth century.

At the same time that the bourgeoisies of the core countries were faced by this threat to the internal stability of their state structures, they were simultaneously faced with the economic crisis of the latter third of the nineteenth century resulting from the more rapid increase of agricultural production (and indeed of light manufactures) than the expansion of a potential market for these goods. Some of the surplus would have to be redistributed to someone to allow these goods to be bought and the economic machinery to return to smooth operation. By expanding the purchasing power of the industrial proletariat of the core countries, the world-economy was unburdened simultaneously of two problems: the bottleneck of demand, and the unsettling "class conflict" of the core states—hence, the social liberalism or welfare-state ideology that arose just at that point in time.

World War I was, as men of the time observed, the end of an era; and the Russian Revolution of October 1917 the beginning of a new one—our stage four. This stage was, to be sure, a stage of revolutionary turmoil but it also was, in a seeming paradox, the stage of the *consolidation* of the industrial capitalist world-economy. The Russian Revolution was essentially that of a semiperipheral country whose internal balance of forces had been such that as of the late nineteenth century it began on a decline toward a peripheral status. [. . .]. The Revolution brought to power a group of state managers who reversed each one of these trends by using the classic technique of mercantilist semiwithdrawal from the world-economy. In the process of doing this, the now USSR mobilized considerable popular support, especially in the urban sector. At the end of World War II, Russia was reinstated as a very strong member of the semiperiphery and could begin to seek full core status. [. . .].

It was World War II that enabled the United States for a brief period (1945-1965) to attain the same level of primacy as Britain had in the first part of the nineteenth century. United States growth in this period was spectacular and created a great need for expanded market outlets. The cold war closure denied not only the USSR but Eastern Europe to U.S. exports. And the Chinese Revolution meant that this region, which had been destined for much exploitative activity, was also cut off. Three alternative areas were available and each was pursued with assiduity. First, Western Europe had to be rapidly "reconstructed," and it was the Marshall Plan which thus allowed this area to play a primary role in the expansion of world productivity. Secondly, Latin America became the reserve of U.S. investment from which now Britain and Germany were completely cut off. Thirdly, Southern Asia, the Middle East, and Africa had to be decolonized. On the one hand, this was necessary in order to reduce the share of the surplus taken by the Western European intermediaries, as Canning covertly supported the Latin American revolutionaries against Spain in the 1820s.[29] But also, these countries had to be decolonized in order to mobilize productive potential in a way that had never been achieved in the colonial era. Colonial rule after all had been an *inferior* mode of relationship of core and periphery, one occasioned by the strenuous late-nineteenth-century conflict among industrial states but one no longer desirable from the point of view of the new hegemonic power.[30]

But a world capitalist economy does not permit true imperium. Charles V could not succeed in his dream of world-empire. The Pax Britannica stimulated its own demise. So too did the Pax Americana. [. . .].

Such a decline in U.S. state hegemony has actually *increased* the freedom of action of capitalist enterprises, the larger of which have now taken the form of multinational corporations which are able to maneuver against state bureaucracies whenever the national politicians become too responsive to internal worker pressures. Whether some effective links can be established between multinational corporations, presently limited to operating in certain areas, and the USSR remains to be seen, but it is by no means impossible.

This brings us back to one of the questions with which we opened this paper, the seemingly esoteric debate between Liu Shaoqi and Mao Zedong as to whether China was, as Liu argued, a socialist state, or whether, as Mao argued, socialism was a *process* involving continued and continual class struggle. No doubt to those to whom the terminology is foreign the discussion seems abstrusely theological. The issue, however, as we said, is real. If the Russian Revolution emerged as a reaction to the threatened further decline of Russia's structural position in the world-economy, and if fifty years later one can talk of the USSR as entering the status of a core power in a *capitalist* world-economy, what then is the meaning of the various so-called socialist revolutions that have occurred on a third of the world's surface? First let us notice that it has been neither Thailand nor Liberia nor Paraguay that has had a "socialist revolution" but Russia, China, and Cuba. That is to say, these revolutions have occurred in countries that, in terms of their internal economic structures in the prerevolutionary period, had a certain minimum strength in terms of skilled personnel, some manufacturing, and other factors which made it plausible that, within the framework of a capitalist world-economy, such a country could alter its role in the world division of labor within a reasonable period (say thirty to fifty years) by the use of the technique of mercantilist semiwithdrawal. (This may not be all that plausible for Cuba, but we shall see.) Of course, other countries in the geographic regions and military orbit of these revolutionary forces had changes of regime without in any way having these characteristics (for example, Mongolia or Albania). It is also to be noted that many of the countries where similar forces are strong or where considerable counterforce is required to keep them from emerging also share this status of minimum strength. I think of Chile or Brazil or Egypt—or indeed Italy.

Are we not seeing the emergence of a political structure for *semiperipheral* nations adapted to stage four of the capitalist world-system? The fact that all enterprises are nationalized in these countries does not make the participation of these enterprises in the world-economy one that does not conform to the mode of operation of a capitalist market system: seeking increased efficiency of production in order to realize a maximum price on sales, thus achieving a more favorable allocation of the surplus of the world-economy. If tomorrow U.S. Steel became a worker's collective in which all employees without exception received an identical share of the profits and all stockholders are expropriated without compensation, would U.S. Steel thereby cease to be a capitalist enterprise operating in a capitalist world-economy?

What then have been the consequences for the world-system of the emergence of many states in which there is no private ownership of the basic means of production? To some extent, this has meant an internal reallocation of consumption. It has certainly undermined the ideological justification in world capitalism, both by showing the political vulnerability of capitalist entrepreneurs and by demonstrating that private ownership is irrelevant to the rapid expansion of industrial productivity. But to the extent that it has raised the ability of the new semiperipheral areas to enjoy a larger share of the world surplus, it has once again depolarized the world, recreating the triad of strata that has been a fundamental element in the survival of the world-system.

Finally, in the peripheral areas of the world-economy, both the continued economic expansion of the core (even though the core is seeing some reallocation of surplus internal to it) and the new strength of the semiperiphery has led to a weakening of the political and hence economic position of the peripheral areas. The pundits note that "the gap is getting wider," but thus far no one has succeeded in doing much about it, and it is not clear that there are very many in whose interests it would be to do so. Far from a strengthening of state authority, in many parts of the world we are witnessing the same kind of deterioration Poland knew in the sixteenth century, a deterioration of which the frequency of military coups is only one of many signposts. And all of this leads us to conclude that stage four has been the stage of the *consolidation* of the capitalist world-economy.

Consolidation, however, does not mean the absence of contradictions and does not mean the likelihood of long-term survival.[. . . .].

There are two fundamental contradictions, it seems to me, involved in the workings of the capitalist world-system. In the first place, there is the contradiction to which the nineteenth-century Marxian corpus pointed, which I would phrase as follows: whereas in the short run the maximization of profit requires maximizing the withdrawal of surplus from immediate consumption of the majority, in the long run the continued production of surplus requires a mass demand which can only be created by redistributing the surplus withdrawn. Since these two considerations move in opposite directions (a "contradiction"), the system has constant crises which in the long run both weaken it and make the game for those with privilege less worth playing.

The second fundamental contradiction, to which Mao's concept of socialism as process points, is the following: whenever the tenants of privilege seek to coopt an oppositional movement by including them in a minor share of the privilege, they may no doubt eliminate opponents in the short run; but they also up the ante for the next oppositional movement created in the next crisis of the world-economy. Thus the cost of "co-optation" rises ever higher and the advantages of co-option seem ever less worthwhile.

There are today no socialist systems in the world-economy any more than there are feudal systems because there is only *one* world-system. It is a world-economy and it is by definition capitalist in form. Socialism involves the creation of a new kind of *world*-system, neither a redistributive world-empire nor a capitalist world-economy but a socialist world-government. I don't see this projection as being in the least utopian but I also don't feel its institution is imminent. It will be the outcome of a long struggle in forms that may be familiar and perhaps in very few forms, that will take place in *all* the areas of the world-economy (Mao's continual "class struggle"). Governments may be in the hands of persons, groups, or movements sympathetic to this transformation but *states* as such are neither progressive nor reactionary. It is movements and forces that deserve such evaluative judgments. [. . .].

Notes

1. George Lukacs, "The Marxism of Rosa Luxemburg," *History and Class Consciousness* (London: Merlin Press, 1968), p. 27.
2. See Karl Polanyi, "The Economy as Instituted Process," in Karl Polanyi, Conrad M. Arsenberg, and Harry W. Pearson, eds., *Trade and Market in Early Empire* (Glencoe: Free Press, 1957), pp. 243-70.
3. Andre Gunder Frank, "The Myth of Feudalism," in *Capitalism and Underdevelopment in Latin America* (New York: Monthly Review Press, 1967), p. 3.
4. Frank's critique, now classic, of these theories is entitled "Sociology of Development and Underdevelopment of Sociology," and is reprinted in *Latin America: Underdevelopment or Revolution* (New York: Monthly Review Press, 1969), pp. 21-94.
5. See Theotonio Dos Santos, *La Nueva Dependencia* (Buenos Aires: s/ediciones, 1968).
6. Ernesto Laclau, "Feudalism and Capitalism in Latin America," *New Left Review* 67 (May-June 1971):37-38.
7. The debate begins with Maurice Dobb, *Studies in the Development of Capitalism* (London: Routledge & Kegan Paul, 1946). Paul Sweezy criticized Dobb in "The Transition from Feudalism to Capitalism," *Science and Society* 14, no. 2 (Spring 1950): 134-57, with a "Reply" by Dobb in the same issue. From that point on many others got into the debate in various parts of the world. I have reviewed and discussed this debate in extenso in chap. 1 of *The Modern World-System: Capitalist Agriculture and the Origins of the European World-Economy in the Sixteenth Century* (New York: Academic Press, 1974).
8. Laclau, "Feudalism and Capitalism," pp. 25, 30.
9. Cited in F. Burlatsky, *The State and Communism* (Moscow: Progress Publishers, n.d. [1961]), pp. 95-97.
10. Mao Zedong, *On the Correct Handling of Contradictions Among the People*, 7th ed., revised trans. (Peking: Foreign Languages Press, 1966), pp. 37-38.
11. *Long Live the Invincible Thought of Mao Tse-Tung!*, undated pamphlet, issued between 1967 and 1969, translated in *Current Background* 884 (18 July 1969): 14.
12. This is the position taken by Mao Zedong in his speech to the Work Conference of the Central Committee at Peitaiho in August 1962, as reported in the pamphlet, *Long Live . . .*, p. 20. Mao's position was subsequently endorsed at the Tenth Plenum of the Eighth CCP Central Committee in September 1962, a session this same pamphlet describes

52   *Immanuel Wallerstein*

as "a great turning point in the violent struggle between the proletarian headquarters and the bourgeois headquarters in China." Ibid., p. 21.

13. Ibid., p. 20.
14. Mao Zedong, "Talk on the Question of Democratic Centralism," 30 January 1962, in *Current Background* 891 (8 October 1969): 39.
15. "Communiqué of the 10th Plenary Session of the 8th Central Committee of the Chinese Communist Party," *Current Background* 691 (5 October 1962): 3.
16. Yuri Sdobnikov, ed., *Socialism and Capitalism: Score and Prospects* (Moscow: Progress Publications, 1971), pp. 20-26.
17. See Raymond Aron, *Dix-huit leçons de la société industrielle* (Paris: Gallimard, 1962).
18. This is the dilemma, I feel, of E. J. Hobsbawm in explaining his so-called crisis of the seventeenth century. See his *Past and Present* article reprinted (with various critiques) in Trevor Aston, ed., *The Crisis of the Seventeenth Century* (London: Routledge & Kegan Paul, 1965).
19. Maurice Dobb, *Capitalism Yesterday and Today* (London: Lawrence and Wishart, 1958), p. 21. My emphasis.
20. Ibid., pp. 6-7.
21. Ibid., p. 21.
22. See my *The Modern World-System*, chap. 2.
23. I give a brief account of this in "Three Paths of National Development in the Sixteenth Century," *Studies in Comparative International Development*, 7:2 (Summer 1972): 95-101.
24. See Arghiri Emmanuel, *Unequal Exchange* (New York: Monthly Review Press, 1972).
25. See my fuller analysis in "Social Conflict in Post-Independence Black Africa: The Concepts of Race and Status-Group Reconsidered," in Ernest Q. Campbell, ed., *Racial Tensions and National Identity* (Nashville: Vanderbilt University Press, 1972), pp. 207-26.
26. "Range" in this sentence means the number of different occupations in which a significant proportion of the population is engaged. Thus peripheral society typically is overwhelmingly agricultural. A core society typically has its occupations well distributed over all of Colin Clark's three sectors. If one shifted the connotation of range to talk of style of life, consumption patterns, even income distribution, quite possibly one might reverse the correlation. In a typical peripheral society, the differences between a subsistence farmer and an urban professional are probably far greater than those which could be found in a typical core state.
27. See my "The Two Modes of Ethnic Consciousness: Soviet Central Asia in Transition?" in Edward Allworth, ed., *The Nationality Question in Soviet Central Asia* (New York: Praeger, 1973), pp. 168-75.
28. Robert Michels, "The Origins of the Anti-Capitalist Mass Spirit," *Man in Contemporary Society* (New York: Columbia University Press, 1955), vol. 1, pp. 740-65.

29. See William W. Kaufman, *British Policy and the Independence of Latin America, 1804-28* (New Haven: Yale University Press, 1951).
30. Cf. Catherine Coquery-Vidrovitch, "De l'impérialisme britannique à l'impérialisme contemporaine—l'avatar colonial," *L'Homme et la société* 18 (October-December 1970): 61-90.

[3]
The Origins of Capitalist Development: A Critique of Neo-Smithian Marxism

Robert Brenner

The appearance of systematic barriers to economic advance in the course of capitalist expansion—the "development of underdevelopment"—has posed difficult problems for Marxist theory. There has arisen, in response, a strong tendency sharply to revise Marx's conceptions regarding economic development. In part, this has been a healthy reaction to the Marx of the *Manifesto*, who envisioned a more or less direct and inevitable process of capitalist expansion: undermining old modes of production, replacing them with capitalist social productive relations and, on this basis, setting off a process of capital accumulation and economic development more or less following the pattern of the original homelands of capitalism. [. . .].

Many writers have quite properly pointed out that historical developments since the mid-nineteenth century have tended to belie this "optimistic," "progressist" prognosis, in that the capitalist penetration of the "Third World" through trade and capital investment not only has failed to carry with it capitalist economic development, but has erected positive barriers to such development. [. . .]. It was clearly on the premise that capitalist expansion would lead to the establishment of capitalist social relations of production on the ruins of the old modes that Marx could predict worldwide economic development in a capitalist image. But, suppose capitalist expansion through trade and investment failed to break the old modes of production (a possibility which he later envisaged); or actually tended to strengthen the old modes, or to erect other noncapitalist systems of social relations of production in place of the old modes? In this case, Marx's prediction would fall to the ground. For whatever Marx thought about the origins of capitalist social-productive relations, he was quite clear that their establishment was indispensable for the development of the productive forces, i.e., for capitalist economic development. If expansion through trade and investment did not bring with it the transition to capitalist social-productive relations—manifested in the full emergence of labor power as a commodity— there could be no capital accumulation on an extended scale. [. . .].

Faced with this problem the *method* of an entire line of writers in the Marxist tradition has led them to displace class relations from the center of their analyses of economic development and under-development. It has been their intention to negate the optimistic model of economic advance derived from Adam Smith, whereby the development of trade and the division of labor unfailingly bring about economic development. Because they have failed, however, to discard the underlying individualistic-mechanist presuppositions of this model, they have ended up by erecting an alternative theory of capitalist development which is, in its central aspects, the mirror image of the "progressist" thesis they wish to surpass.[...]. They fail to take into account either the way in which class structures, once established, will in fact determine the course of economic development or underdevelopment over an entire epoch, or the way in which these class structures themselves emerge: as the out-come of class struggles whose results are incomprehensible in terms merely of market forces.[...].

It has thus been maintained that the very same mechanisms which set off underdevelopment in the "periphery" are prerequisite to capital accumulation in the "core." Capitalist development cannot take place in the core unless underdevelopment is developed in the periphery, because the very mechanisms which determine under-development are required for capitalist accumulation [...]. As a case in point, Andre Gunder Frank's primary focus has in fact been on the roots of underdevelopment, so it has not been essential for him to go into great detail concerning the origins and structure of capitalist development itself. Yet, to clarify his approach, it was necessary to lay out the mainsprings of capitalist development, as well as underdevelopment; accordingly, Frank did not neglect to do this, at least in broad outline. The roots of capitalist evolution, he said, were to be found in the rise of a world "commercial net-work," developing into a "mercantile capitalist system." Thus "a commercial network spread out [...] until the entire face of the globe had been incorporated into a *single organic* mercantilist or mercantile capitalist, and later also industrial and financial, system, whose metropolitan center developed in Western Europe and then in North America and whose peripheral satellites underdeveloped on all the remaining continents."[1] With the rise of this system, there was "created a whole series of metropolis-satellite relationships, interlinked as in the surplus appropriation chain noted above." As the "core" end of the chain developed, the "peripheral" end simul-taneously underdeveloped.

Frank did not go much further than this in filling out his view of capitalism as a whole, its origins and development. But he was unambiguous in locating the dynamic of capitalist expansion in the rise of a world commercial network, while specifying the roots of both growth and backwardness in the "surplus appropriation chain" which emerged in the expansionary process: surplus appropriation by the core from the periphery, and the organization of the satellite's internal mode of production to serve the needs of the metropolis. In this way, Frank set the stage for ceasing to locate the dynamic of capitalist development in a self-expanding process of capital accumulation by way of innovation in the core itself. [...].

It has been left for Immanuel Wallerstein to carry to its logical conclusion the system outlined by Frank. [...]. Indeed, in his magisterial work, *The Origins of the Modern World-System*,[2] Wallerstein attempts nothing less than to establish the origins of capitalist development and underdevelopment and to locate the mainsprings of their subsequent evolutions.[...]. His focus is on what he terms the "world-economy," defined negatively by contrast with the preceding universal "world-empires." So the world-empires, which ended up by dominating all economies prior to the modern one, prevented economic development through the effects of their overarching bureaucracies, which absorbed masses of economic surplus and prevented its accumulation in the form of productive investments. [...]. The essential condition for modern economic development was the collapse of world-empire, and the prevention of the emergence of any new one from the sixteenth century until the present. Wallerstein can argue in this way because of what he sees to be the immanent developmental dynamic of unfettered world trade. Left to develop on its own, that is, without the suffocating impact of the world-empires, developing commerce will bring with it an ever more efficient organization of production through ever increasing regional specialization—in particular, through allowing for a more effective distribution by region of what Wallerstein terms systems of "labor control" in relation to the world's regional distribution of natural resources and population. The trade-induced world division of labor will, in turn, give rise to an international structure of unequally powerful nation states: a structure which, through maintaining and consolidating the world division of labor, determines an accelerated process of accumulation in certain regions (the core), while enforcing a cycle of backwardness in others (the periphery).[3]

[...] Wallerstein's [...] master conceptions of world-economy and world-empire were developed to distinguish the modern economy, which can and does experience systematic economic development, from the precapitalist economies (called world-empires), which were capable only of redistributing a relatively inflexible product, because they could expand production only within definite limits. Such a distinction is both correct and necessary. For capitalism differs from all precapitalist modes of production in its *systematic* tendency to unprecedented, though neither continuous nor unlimited, economic development—in particular through the expansion of what might be called (after Marx's terminology) relative as opposed to absolute surplus labor. That is, under capitalism, surplus is systematically achieved for the first time through increases of labor productivity, leading to the cheapening of goods and a greater total output from a given labor force (with a given working day, intensity of labor, and real wage). This makes it possible for the capitalist class to increase its surplus, without necessarily having to resort to methods of increasing absolute surplus labor which dominated precapitalist modes—i.e., the extension of the working day, the intensification of work, and the decrease in the standard of living of the labor force.

To be specific, a society can achieve increases in labor productivity leading to increases in *relative surplus* product/labor when it can produce a greater mass of use values with the same amount of labor as previously. Put another way, a given labor force achieves an increase in labor productivity when it can produce the means of production and means of subsistence which make possible its own reproduction (continued existence) in less time than previously (working at the same intensity); or when, given the same amount of time worked as before, it produces a larger surplus above the means of production and means of subsistence necessary to reproduce itself than previously. This cannot take place without qualitative changes, innovations in the forces of production, which have historically required the accumulation of surplus, i.e., "plough back of surplus," into production. The basis, in turn, for the operation of this mechanism as a more or less regular means to bring about economic development was a system of production organized on the basis of capitalist social-productive or class relations. As Marx put it: "[. . .] The production of absolute surplus-value turns exclusively on the length of the working day, whereas the production of relative surplus-value *completely revolutionizes the technical processes of labor* and the groupings into which society is divided. It therefore requires a specifically capitalist mode of production, a mode of production which, along with its methods, means and conditions, arises and *develops spontaneously on the basis of the formal subsumption of labour under capital.* This formal subsumption is then replaced by a real subsumption."[4]

It is the fundamental difficulty in Wallerstein's argument that he can neither confront nor explain the fact of a systematic development of relative surplus labor based on growth of the productivity of labor as a regular and dominant feature of capitalism. In essence, his view of economic development is *quantitative*, revolving around: (1) the growth in size of the system itself through expansion; (2) the rearrangement of the factors of production through regional specialization to achieve greater efficiency; (3) the transfer of surplus. Thus, according to Wallerstein, the collapse of world-empire made possible a worldwide system of trade and division of labor. This, in turn, determined that what for Wallerstein were the three fundamental conditions for the development of the world economy would be fulfilled: "An expansion of the geographical size of the world in question [incorporation], the development of variegated methods of labor control for different products and different zones of the world-economy [specialization] and the creation of relatively strong state machinery in what would become the core states of this capitalist world-economy [to assure transfer of surplus to the core]" (MWS, p. 38). However, as we shall show, neither the expansion of trade leading to the *incorporation* of greater human and natural material resources, nor the *transfer of surplus* leading to the build-up of wealth in the core, nor the *specialization* of labor control systems leading to more effective ruling-class surplus extraction can determine a process of economic development. This is because these cannot determine the rise of a system which "develops itself spontaneously," which can and must continually "revolutionize out and out the technical processes of labor and composition of society."

Wallerstein does not, in the last analysis, take into account the development of the forces of production through a process of accumulation by means of innovation ("accumulation of capital on an extended scale"), in part because to do so would undermine his notion of the essential role of the underdevelopment of the periphery in contributing to the development of the core, through surplus transfer to underwrite accumulation there. More directly, Wallerstein cannot—and in fact does not—account for the systematic production of relative surplus product, because he mislocates the mechanism behind accumulation via innovation in "production for profit on the market." [. . .].

Now, there is no doubt that capitalism is a system in which production for a profit via exchange predominates. But does the opposite hold true? Does the appearance of widespread production "for profit in the market" signal the existence of capitalism, and more particularly a system in which, as a characteristic feature, "production is constantly expanded and men constantly innovate new ways of producing." Certainly not, because production for exchange is perfectly compatible with a system in which it is either unnecessary or impossible, or both, to reinvest in expanded, improved production in order to "profit." Indeed, we shall argue that this is the norm in precapitalist societies. For in such societies the social relations of production in large part confine the realization of surplus labor to the methods of extending absolute labor. The increase of relative surplus labor cannot become a *systematic feature* of such modes of production.

To state the case schematically: "production for profit via exchange" will have the systematic effect of accumulation and the development of the productive forces only when it expresses certain specific social relations of production, namely a system of free wage labor, where labor power is a commodity. Only where labor has been separated from possession of the means of production, and where laborers have been emancipated from any direct relation of domination (such as slavery or serfdom), are both capital and labor power "free" to make *possible* their combination at the highest possible level of technology. Only where they are free will such combination appear *feasible* and *desirable*. Only where they are free will such combination be *necessitated*. Only under conditions of free wage labor will the individual producing units (combining labor power and the means of production) be forced to sell in order to buy, to buy in order to survive and reproduce, and ultimately to expand and innovate in order to maintain this position in relationship to other competing productive units. Only under such a system, where both capital and labor power are thus commodities—and which was therefore called by Marx "generalized commodity production"—is there the necessity of producing at the "socially necessary" labor time in order to survive, and to surpass this level of productivity to ensure continued survival.

What therefore accounts for capitalist economic development is that the class (property/surplus extraction) structure of the *economy as a whole* determines that the reproduction carried out by its component "units" is dependent upon their ability to increase their production (accumulate) and thereby develop their forces of production, in order to increase the productivity of labor and so cheapen their commodities. In contrast, precapitalist economies, even those in which trade is widespread, can develop only within definite limits, because the class structure of the economy as a whole determines that their component units—specifically those producing the means of subsistence and means of production, i.e., means of survival and reproduction, rather than luxuries—neither can nor must systematically increase the forces of production, the productivity of labor, in order to reproduce themselves.

If, then, the class-structured system of reproduction in which labor power is a commodity lies behind capitalist economic development, while "production for profit in the market" cannot in itself determine the development of the productive forces, it follows that the historical problem of the origins of capitalist economic development in relation to precapitalist modes of production becomes that of the origin of the property/surplus extraction system (class system) of free wage labor—the historical process by which labor power and the means of production become commodities. Wallerstein, like Gunder Frank, is explicit in his renunciation of this position. Consistently he argues that since "production on the market for profit" determines capitalist economic development, the problem of the origins of capitalism comes down to the origins of the expanding world market, unfettered by world-empire. He is at pains to distinguish the emergence of the capitalist world-economy in the sixteenth century—the rise of the world division of labor which emerged with the great discoveries and expansion of trade routes—from the emergence of a system of free wage labor, and contends that the latter is derivative from the former.

The issues raised here were, of course, at the center of the controversy in the 1950s over the transition from feudalism to capitalism,[5] as well as of subsequent controversy over the rise of capitalist underdevelopment. Indeed, it is necessary to understand Wallerstein's position as a direct outgrowth of the arguments put forward then by Paul Sweezy, as well as of the theses advanced more recently by Frank. To grasp this line of thought, what is essential is to see that the basic theoretical underpinnings for the positions set out by all three of these writers is the model put forward by Adam Smith in *The Wealth of Nations*. The elements of Smith's model are very familiar. The development of a society's wealth—quite sensibly equated with the development of the productivity of labor—is a function of the degree of the division of labor. By this, Smith simply means the specialization of productive tasks—classically achieved through the separation of agriculture and manufacturing, and their assignment to country and town respectively. In turn, for Smith the degree of specialization is bound up with the degree of development of trade: the degree to which a potentially interdependent, specialized labor force can be—and is—linked up via commercial nexus. Thus, we get Smith's famous principle that the division of labor is limited by the extent of the market—literally, the size of the area and population linked up via trade relations.[...].

The parallels between the positions of both Sweezy and Wallerstein and that of Adam Smith are striking, and the defects of their arguments are the result of their adopting his assumptions. Like Smith, both Sweezy and Wallerstein, implicitly or explicitly, equate capitalism with a trade-based division of labor. They thus understand its special dynamic of accumulation through innovation as a function of the imperatives of exchange on the market and the productive effects of specialization. As a result, their accounts of the transition from feudalism to capitalism end up by assuming away the fundamental problem of the transformation of class relations—the class struggles this entailed—so that the rise of distinctively capitalist class relations of production are no longer seen as the *basis* for capitalist development, but as its *result*.

Of course, Wallerstein and Sweezy appear to differ from Smith precisely in their apparent concern for "class." But, in fact, their conception of the "capitalist effects" of the growth of exchange and the division of labor—the tendency to increasing output and productivity advance built into "production for profit on the market" —lead them to *assimilate* the emergence of new class relations of production to commercial development. Explicitly or implicitly, they regard the transformation of class relations as a necessary effect of continuing commercialization. [...]. Smith's model of development is thereby "extended" to subsume the transformation of class relations within the broader process of the development of a trade-based division of labor. [...].

Sweezy and Wallerstein, like Smith, implicitly regard "surplus maximization" and "competition on the market" as essentially transhistorical forces, requiring only the original impetus of commerce, the rise of the market, to start working their progressive effects within the extant individual productive units. To them, therefore, as to Smith, historical problem of the origins of capitalism becomes that of the origins of trade-based division of labor. [...].

In Wallerstein's *The Modern World-System*, the Smithian theory embedded in Sweezy's analysis of the transition from feudalism to capitalism is made entirely explicit, and carried to its logical conclusion. [...]. Thus Wallerstein straightforwardly defines capitalism as a trade-based division of labor, and it is here that he locates the dynamic of capitalist economic development.[...].The mainspring of the developing division of labor is simply the "profit motive," which is induced by trade and the market and which, in turn, induces accumulation (plough-back of surplus) and innovation. Capitalism, says Wallerstein, is "*a mode of production, production for profit in a market*" (emphasis added) (RFD, p.399). Wallerstein draws the logical consequences of this position[...]: trade in itself will lead to accumulation and innovation via the profit-motivated development of the division of labor; therefore, it logically follows that *any* region which is part of the apparently interdependent system of exchange which constitutes the world division of labor is capitalist, whatever its methods of "labor control" and of "rewarding labor power." Once embedded within the world-economy/world-market, the productive regions based on serfdom (what Wallerstein calls "coerced cash-crop labor"), in particular the grain-exporting regions of the Eastern European "periphery," cease to be one bit less capitalist than the regions whose production for the market is based on free wage labor.

Once, says Wallerstein, "[the] so-called reciprocal nexus we identify with feudalism, the exchange of protection for labor services...is contained *within* a capitalist world-economy, its autonomous reality disappears. It becomes rather one of the many *forms of bourgeois employment of proletarian labor* to be found in a capitalist mode of production, a form that is maintained, *expanded or diminished in relation to its profitability on the market"* (emphasis added) (FFC, pp. 278-79). So that, for Wallerstein, "Capitalism thus means labor as a commodity to be sure. But in the era of agricultural capitalism, wage labor is only one of the modes in which labor is recruited and recompensed on the labor market. Slavery, coerced cash cropping (...the so-called second feudalism), sharecropping and tenancy are all alternative modes" (RFD, p. 400). Indeed, it is precisely the specialization of "capitalist" systems of labor control/reward to labor by region, made possible by trade, which constitute the basis of the capitalist world-economy, and account for its ability to develop. Specifically, "The emergence of an industrial sector [in the core] was important [in the rise of the world capitalist division of labor], but what made this possible was the transformation of agricultural activity from feudal to capitalist forms. Not all these capitalist "forms" were based on "free" labor—only those in the core of the economy. But the motivations of landlord and laborer in the non-"free" sector [in the periphery] were as capitalist as those in the core" (MWS, p. 126).

For Wallerstein, then, the growth of the world division of labor *is* the development of capitalism. Not surprisingly, therefore, he can forthrightly state that the rise of free labor is merely an *aspect* of the development of the world division of labor, determined by the technical requirements of the development of the productive forces in given types of production and specific regions. Sweezy could not have come explicitly to this conclusion, for he seems to accept Marx's massive emphasis, in both *Capital* (especially Part 8 on "So-called Primitive Accumulation of Capital") and the *Grundrisse* (especially the passages on precapitalist economic formations), on the rise of free wage labor/*labor power as a commodity*, presented as the fundamental basis for the capitalist mode of production—for the accumulation of capital. [. . .].

[I]t was no doubt Sweezy's position that a system of free wage labor is a precondition for a built-in tendency to capital accumulation and the development of the productive forces. However, in arguing that the pressures of market production would lead to an evolution away from serfdom toward capitalism due to market-induced needs of the ruling class to increase production and thus to adopt new productive forces inoperable under the old mode, he ended up contradicting this viewpoint. For the latter argument implicitly entails the idea that serfdom itself will develop a tendency to sociotechnical innovation under market pressure (bringing with it ultimately a change to free labor), so that free labor becomes a consequence rather than a condition of capitalist development.

Wallerstein attempts to cut through this contradiction by banishing it. If one contends that labor power as a commodity is *the* essential condition for economic development via accumulation and innovation, it is illogical to argue that trade will induce processes of development via accumulation and innovation within the old mode of production which will bring about the transformation of the old mode itself—toward free wage labor. In that case, the dynamic of development clearly resides in trade, not in the class relations of labor power as a commodity. Thus Wallerstein simply denies from the start that free wage labor is a condition for accumulation via innovation, so that he can consistently argue that a trade-based division of labor is not only responsible for the origins of capitalism, but also the source of its dynamic of development. Thus various forms of "labor control/reward to labor"—free wage labor included—emerge merely to facilitate the market-induced processes of economic development (and underdevelopment). Yet, as we have already seen with regard to Adam Smith, the general consequence of such a position is an ahistorical, nonclass conception of the division of labor, which fails to notice that the very development of the trade-based division of labor can only be a product, not the source, of the development of the productive forces (the productivity of labor), which in turn are dependent upon and limited by the class relations in which they evolve. [. . .].

Wallerstein seems to have two modes of explaining the putative transfer of surplus from core to the periphery: one directly "economic," the other "political." Thus, he states: "The division of the world-economy involves a hierarchy of occupational tasks, in which tasks requiring higher levels of skill and greater capitalization are reserved for higher ranking areas. Since a capitalist world-economy essentially rewards accumulated capital, including human capital, at a higher rate than 'raw' labor power, the geographical maldistribution of these occupational skills involves a strong trend toward self-maintenance. The forces of the marketplace reinforce them rather than undermine them" (MWS, p. 350). At the same time, Wallerstein argues that the system of labor control/rewards to labor gives rise to strong states in the core and weak ones in the periphery. As a consequence, the strong states are able to assure, ultimately by force it appears, an unequal economic relationship between the core economies and those of the periphery. "In [the core] states, the creation of a strong state machinery...serves...as a mechanism to protect disparities that have arisen within the world-system" (MWS, p. 349). "Once we get a difference in the strength of the state-machineries, we get the operation of unequal exchange which is enforced by strong states on weak ones, by core states on peripheral areas. Thus [agricultural] capitalism [of the early modern period] involves not only appropriation of the surplus-value by an owner from a laborer, but an appropriation of surplus of the whole world-economy by core areas" (RFD, p. 401).

[. . .] As to the economic argument, the first question which must be asked is what determines Wallerstein's "hierarchy of tasks," such that some productive tasks are carried on with more capital and skilled labor than others. Wallerstein goes far in the direction of arguing that it is actually the *tasks themselves* which determine the amount of capital and skill which is used to carry them out. Thus, he states: "Given the great expansion of the geographic and demographic scope to world commerce and industry, some areas of Europe could amass the profits of this expansion all the more if they could specialize in the activities essential to reaping the profit. They thus had to spend less of their time, manpower, land, and other natural resources on sustaining themselves in basic necessities. Either Eastern Europe would become the 'breadbasket' of Western Europe or vice versa" (MWS, pp. 98-99). According to this account, food production apparently necessitated less capital and skill, hence less of a share in the total surplus, than manufacturing. Wallerstein can thus conclude that the "development of underdevelopment" is the "result of being involved in the world-economy as a peripheral raw-material-producing area" (RFD, p. 392). [. . .].

Clearly, such a logic cannot work. It is not necessary to resort to such modern comparisons as that of American export agriculture with Third World export manufacturing, the former often using far greater amounts of capital and skill than the latter. For during the early modern era itself, by Wallerstein's own testimony, it was not just core manufacturing which was more capital and skill-intensive than peripheral agriculture; *all* core productive activities had those qualities. And this includes, as Wallerstein fails to emphasize, *basic*

food production, where for the same products English agricultural-
ists applied far more capital and skill (to much greater effect) than
did their Polish counterparts.

Clearly, the product itself could not determine the skill and capital used to produce it. Yet, on the other hand, if Wallerstein is
contending that it is the fact of *presence in the core* which itself determines superior equipment by capital and skill in *all* productive
lines, he must explain *why* this should be so, especially in order to
avoid the tautologous conclusion that what determines a region's
place (core or periphery) is the capital and skill applied to the
productive tasks there. As we have seen already, the world market
cannot determine the type of production carried out in any area,
especially the level and character of the productive forces applied,
except insofar as its impact is, in turn, determined by the region's
class structure. On the other hand, it would contradict Wallerstein's
whole line of reasoning to contend that indeed it was not a region's
position in the world market that determined the level of its productive forces; but that it was the level of development of its productive forces—labor productivity—which determined its place in
the world market. This must, in turn, be referred back to the class
structure in which those forces of production do or do.not, could
or could not, be developed. [. . .].

What then of Wallerstein's notion that surplus transfer was assured politically, by the strong states of the core against the weak
ones of the periphery? Again, it is necessary to back up one step to a
prior question: that of the distribution of strong and weak states
themselves. Wallerstein says: "In the sixteenth century, some monarchs achieved great strength. . . . Others failed. This is closely
related . . . to the role of the area in the division of labor within the
world-economy. *The different roles led to different class structures* which
led to different politics" (MWS, p. 157). Yet again, Wallerstein sets
up a strictly economically determined structure, which breaks down
over his contradictory conception of systems of labor control/rewards
to labor. On the one hand, Wallerstein wishes to see class structures
(systems of labor control/reward to labor) as determined by the
world-economy, by the organization of work in a particular line of
production, in the last analysis by a region's role in the division of
labor—i.e., as a product of market-determined technical-economic
exigencies. On the other hand, it is also class structure, now considered as a relationship of ruling-class exploiters to laboring exploited, which, for Wallerstein, in turn determines the character of the
state: "The modes of labor control greatly affect the political system
(in particular the strength of the state apparatus), and the possibilities for an indigenous bourgeoisie to thrive" (MWS, p. 87).

As I have argued, however, to view the labor control system as a class structure of exploitation precludes its being conceptualized in essentially technical-functional terms. Since, from this viewpoint, the region's class structure conditions the very development of its productive forces, and thus by extension its role in the world economy, the region's class structure, in determining the structure of the state, cannot be viewed as merely "transmitting" the pressures of the world market and division of labor. Wallerstein cannot have it both ways: a labor control system as a class structure of exploitation which determines the character of the state, and a labor control system as reflecting the most suitable "productive" technique for a given region in the world economy. His attempting to do so leads him to explicitly contradict his central contention that the state structure of a region is determined by that region's place in the world division of labor. Thus at one point Wallerstein explains Japan's and Russia's unusual economic success, their ability to enter the world economy in semiperipheral rather than peripheral status, as a result of their strong state structures. Yet if so, does not the state determine the region's economic role, rather than vice versa? On the other hand, France was by any reckoning an unusually strong state in the seventeenth century, yet it did not reside in the core. [. . .].

In fact neither development in the core nor underdevelopment in the periphery was determined by surplus transfer. Economic development was a qualitative process, which did not merely involve an accumulation of wealth in general, but was centrally focused on the development of the productivity of labor of the direct producers of the means of production and means of subsistence. This development of labor productivity, most significantly in agriculture, which occurred in parts of Western Europe in the early modern period, was dependent in turn upon the emergence of a social system which tended not only to equip the direct producers with capital and skill at the highest level of existing technique, but possessed the capacity to continue to do so on an increasing scale. In short, the uniquely successful development of capitalism in Western Europe was determined by a class system, a property system, a system of surplus extraction, in which the methods the extractors were obliged to use to increase their surplus corresponded to an unprecedented, *though enormously imperfect*, degree to the needs of development of the productive forces. Capitalism was therefore distinguished from precapitalist modes of production in requiring those who controlled production to continue to increase their "profits" (surplus) largely by increasing what we have termed relative, not merely absolute, surplus labor. To account for capitalist economic development is, therefore, at least to explain the basis for this conjunction between the requirements for surplus extraction and the needs of the developing productive forces: on the one hand, its structure, or the reasons it held true; on the other hand, its origins, or how it came into being. It is a fundamental weakness of Wallerstein's analysis that it never forces these questions to be directly posed.[. . .].

The onset of a capitalist dynamic of development was in its first appearance made possible as an unintended consequence of class conflicts—conflicts in which the peasantry freed themselves from the extra-economic controls of the ruling class, while the latter secured ownership of the land. The resulting overall class structure of production and reproduction made possible an unprecedented degree of correspondence between the needs of surplus extraction and the *continuing development* of the productive forces through accumulation and innovation, especially in agriculture, by way of the application of fixed capital on the basis of increasingly cooperative labor. The original emergence of capitalist development is, therefore, incomprehensible as a phenomenon of "money," "trade," "the production of commodities," or of "merchant capital." The very significance of these forms depends on the class structure of production with which they are associated. They perform indispensable functions in production and reproduction under capitalist social-productive relations. On the other hand, by themselves, by their "self-development" (the widening of commodity production alone) they cannot bring about the emergence of capitalist social-productive relations and a pattern of economic development in response to the demands of profitability on the market.

To see the action of money or trade or of merchant capitalists as being behind the original emergence of capitalism is, therefore, circular: for it is to account for the origins of capitalism by the action of capitalists functioning in a capitalist manner. It is for analogous reasons that it is necessary to reject the idea that the mere extension of the world market via the action of merchants to stimulate increasing commodity production in new areas determines a pattern of underdevelopment, as in Eastern Europe. For this is merely to turn the Smithian argument on its head: to contend that the demands of production for profit on the market determine the rise of class relations and productive forces which enforce, not the development of capitalist production (as with Paul Sweezy), but the rise of economic backwardness (as with Andre Gunder Frank and Immanuel Wallerstein). [. . .].

From this perspective, it is impossible to accept Frank's view, adopted by Wallerstein, that the capitalist "development of underdevelopment" in the regions colonized by Europeans from the six-teenth century—especially the Caribbean, South America, and Africa, as well as the southern part of North America—is comprehensible as a direct result of the incorporation of these regions within the world market, their "subordination" to the system of capital accu-mulation on a world scale. Frank originally explained this rise of underdevelopment largely in terms of the transfer of surplus from periphery to core, and the export-dependent role assigned to the periphery in the world division of labor. These mechanisms clearly capture important aspects of the functioning reality of underde-velopment. But they explain little, for, as the more searching critics of Frank's earlier formulations pointed out, they themselves need to be explained. In particular, it was stated, they needed to be rooted in the class and productive structures of the periphery.[. . .].

This is not to deny that there was a long-term transfer of surplus away from the periphery. It is to root this in a different dynamic. [. . .]. Frank's comment that "*because of commerce and foreign capital, the economic and political interests of the mining, agricultural and commercial bourgeoisie were never directed toward internal eco-nomic development*"[6] could be misleading. It was not the specific national character of the capital or the commercial connection with the metropolis which determined a flow of potential investment funds "out of the system." It was the class-structured character of the profit opportunities which determined that: (1) there would be relatively little investment even in the home industry (the mines and plantation); (2) what industrial production there was for the home market would be carried on largely in the metropolis because it could be more profitably organized there, leading to a flow of investment funds from periphery to core; (3) there would be con-siderable expenditure on luxury production which would not in-crease the productive capacity of the system.

In other words, the development of underdevelopment was rooted in the class structure of production based on the extension of abso-lute surplus labor, which determined a sharp *disjuncture* between the requirements for the development of the productive forces (productivity of labor) and the structure of profitability of the econ-omy as a whole. On the one hand, this class structure determined a general antagonism between the demands of profit-making and the development of the productive forces in the fields subject to world market demand, by discouraging the advance of fixed capi-tal and undermining the development of skill, since production was based on forced labor (while low payments to labor power encouraged the adoption of labor-using techniques). On the other hand, it determined a generalized lack of profitability for the remainder of the economy, precisely because this was generally compelled to support export production through "contributing" cheap or free labor power and means of subsistence (by way of forced levies), without receiving any investment to raise labor productivity. Thus the "subsidizing" of the "export sector" was generally accomplished on the basis of the intensification of various forms of peasant production; and this, in turn, posed powerful barriers to development throughout the economy, through making difficult the application of fixed capital and the rise of cooperative labor, as well as, more generally, the full emergence of labor power as a commodity.

In the second place, it cannot be deduced from Frank's revised account of the class structure of underdevelopment that what determined the colonies' backwardness was their role in the world system, their production of raw materials for export. During the early modern period, grain for example was produced for export in many different areas of Europe under different class structures of production, with very different resulting patterns of economic development or underdevelopment. So Frank's comment that "ultra-underdevelopment...was characteristic of an export economy"[7] must be carefully qualified. It was not the fact of production for export which determined export dependence; it was the class structure through which export production was carried out (based on ultraexploitation/methods of absolute surplus labor) which determined that increasing export production would lead to underdevelopment rather than development. Otherwise it would not be possible, for example, to account for the impressive development of the grain-exporting economy of the Middle Atlantic colonies in the colonial period. [. . .].

Frank's original formulations aimed to destroy the suffocating orthodoxies of Marxist evolutionary stage theory upon which the Communist parties' political strategies of "popular front" and "bourgeois democratic revolution" had been predicated.[8] Frank rightly stressed that the expansion of capitalism through trade and investment did not automatically bring with it the capitalist economic development that the Marx of the *Manifesto* had predicted. In the course of the growth of the world market, Chinese walls to the advance of the productive forces might be erected as well as battered down. When such "development of underdevelopment" occurred, Frank pointed out, the "national bourgeoisie" acquired an interest not in revolution for development, but in supporting precisely the class system of production and surplus extraction which fettered economic advance. In particular, the merchants of the periphery backed the established order, for they depended for their profits on the mining and plantation enterprises controlled by the "reactionaries," as well as the industrial production of the imperialists in the metropolis. But even the industrial capitalists of the periphery offered no challenge to the established structure—partly as a consequence of their involvement in luxury production serving the upper classes—while they merged with the "neofeudalists" through family connections and state office. As Frank asserted, to expect under these circumstances that capitalist penetration would develop the country was, by and large, wishful thinking. To count on the bourgeoisie for a significant role in an antifeudal, antiimperialist revolution was to encourage a dangerous utopia.

Yet, the failure of Frank [. . .] and Wallerstein [. . .] to transcend the economic determinist framework of their adversaries, rather than merely turn it upside down, opens the way in turn for the adoption of similarly ill-founded political perspectives. Where the old orthodoxy claimed that the bourgeoisie must oppose the neofeudalists, Frank said the neofeudalists were capitalists. Where the old orthodoxy saw development as depending on bourgeois penetration, Frank argued that capitalist development in the core depended upon the development of underdevelopment in the periphery. At every point, therefore, Frank—and his cothinkers such as Wallerstein—followed their adversaries in locating the sources of both development and underdevelopment in an abstract process of capitalist expansion; and like them, failed to specify the particular, historically developed class structures through which these processes actually worked themselves out and through which their fundamental character was actually determined [. . .]. Hence, they did not see the degree to which patterns of development or underdevelopment for an entire epoch might hinge upon the outcome of specific processes of class formation, of class struggle. The consequence is that Frank's analysis can be used to support political conclusions he would certainly himself oppose, for so long as incorporation into the world market/world division of labor is seen automatically to breed underdevelopment, the logical antidote to capitalist underdevelopment is not socialism, but autarky. [. . .].

Notes

1. Andre Gunder Frank, *Capitalism and Underdevelopment in Latin America* (New York: Monthly Review Press, 1969), pp. 14-15.
2. New York: Academic Press, 1974; hereafter MWS. In the following discussion, I treat this book together with a series of closely related articles

by Wallerstein which further clarify and amplify his themes. These include: "The Rise and Future Demise of the World Capitalist System: Concepts for Comparative Analysis," *Comparative Studies in Society and History* 16 (January 1974): 387-415 (RFD) and abridged in this volume; "From Feudalism to Capitalism: Transition or Transitions?" *Social Forces* (December 1976): 273-81 (FFC); "Three Paths of National Development in Sixteenth-Century Europe," *Studies in Comparative International Development* 7 (Summer 1972): 95-101 (TPN); "Dependence in an Interdependent World: The Limited Possibilities of Transformation Within the Capitalist World Economy," *African Studies Review* 17 (April 1974): 1-27 (DIW). Henceforth, when quoting from Wallerstein's works, I will indicate the source through using the indicated abbreviations, with page numbers, placed in parentheses in the text.

3. MWS, pp. 16-20. See also "Rise and Future Demise," pp. 390-92.
4. *Capital*, vol. I (Harmondsworth: Penguin, 1976), p. 645 (emphasis added).
5. *The Transition from Feudalism to Capitalism* (expanded edition; London: New Left Books, 1976). The critique of Sweezy in this exchange by Maurice Dobb, as well as (implicitly) in Dobb's *Studies in the Development of Capitalism* (Cambridge: Cambridge University Press, 1963) is, of course, of fundamental importance—as is Ernesto Laclau's critique of Frank in "Feudalism and Capitalism in Latin America," *New Left Review* 67 (republished in his *Politics and Ideology in Marxist Theory* [London: New Left Books, 1977]). I hope my great debt to both these writers will be apparent throughout this essay.
6. Andre Gunder Frank, *Lumpenbourgeoisie, Lumpendevelopment* (New York: Monthly Review Press, 1972), p. 23 (emphasis added).
7. Ibid., p. 22.
8. See Andre Gunder Frank, "Not Feudalism—Capitalism," *Monthly Review* (December 1963): 468-78 and passim.

[4]
Colonialism in the Words of Its Contemporaries

Cecil Rhodes, Jules Harmand, Albert Beveridge, Joseph Conrad, James Connolly

The Colonial Rule in Plain Speech

Cecil Rhodes, the man after whom the colony of Rhodesia was named—at a reception after coming back from England

[...] And, sir, my people have changed. I speak of the English people, with their marvellous common sense, coupled with their powers of imagination—all thoughts of a little England are over. They are tumbling over each other, Liberals and Conservatives, to show which side are the greatest and most enthusiastic Imperialists. The people have changed, and so do all the parties, just like the Punch and Judy show at a country fair. The people have found out that England is small, and her trade is large, and they have also found out that other people are taking their share of the world, and enforcing hostile tariffs. The people of England are finding out that "trade follows the flag," and they have all become Imperialists. They are not going to part with any territory. And the bygone ideas of nebulous republics are over. The English people intend to retain every inch of land they have got, and perhaps, sir, they intend to secure a few more inches. And so the thought of my country has changed. When I began this business of annexation, both sides were most timid. They would ask one to stop at Kimberley, then they asked one to stop at Khama's country [...]. Now, sir, they won't stop anywhere; they have found out that the world is not quite big enough for British trade and the British flag; and that the operation of even conquering the planets is only something which has yet to be known.

—in the white-only parliament of a South African province

[...] I will lay down my own policy on this Native question. Either you have to receive them on an equal footing as citizens, or to call them a subject race. Well, I have made up my mind that there must be class legislation, that there must be Pass Laws, and Peace Preservation acts, and that we have got to treat natives, where they are in a state of barbarism, in a different way to ourselves. We are to be lords over them. These are my politics on native affairs, and these are the politics of South Africa. Treat the natives as a subject people as long as they continue in a state of barbarism and communal tenure; be the lords over them, and let them be a subject race [. . .]. The native is to be treated as a child and denied the franchise; he is to be denied liquor also; and upon the principles of the honourable member for Stellenbosch himself, I call on him to go with me on this [. . .].

—and again, in the parliament

[. . .] There is, I think, a general feeling that the natives are a distinct source of trouble and loss to this country. Now, I take a different view. When I see the labour troubles that are occurring in the United States, and when I see the troubles that are going to occur with the English people in their own country on the social question and the labour question, I feel rather glad that the labour question here is connected with the native question, for I see that at any rate we do not have here what has lately occurred in Chicago, where, on account of some question as to the management of the Pullman Car Company, the whole of these labour quarrels have broken out, and the city has been practically wrecked. This is what is going on in the older countries on account of the masses, as against the classes, getting what they term their rights, or, to put it into plain English, those who have not, trying to take from those who have. If they cannot get it by what might be termed Irish legislation, they mean to get it by physical force. That is another aspect of government by the people. The proposition that I would wish to put to the House is this, that I do not feel that the fact of our having to live with the natives in this country is a reason for serious anxiety. In fact, I think the natives should be a source of great assistance to most of us. At any rate, if the whites maintain their position as the supreme race, the day may come when we shall all be thankful that we have the natives with us in their proper position. We shall be thankful that we have escaped those difficulties which are going on amongst all the old nations of the world.

—in an 1898 report to shareholders

[. . .] I have very little more to add. I think this—I may repeat it—that the English people have themselves done very well. They have a new territory and a clause that will give them the trade of it for ever. And even I myself have not come out badly[. . .]. You have again elected me your director, but the picture would not be complete and the imaginative thought would fail if I did not remember now that I am again responsible for your affairs—that on the lines I have sketched out to you as to the future of the country, it will fall to me with my co-directors to make you—and I think long in saying that—a full and ample return for the money you have spent and for the support which you have given us; and I have not the slightest doubt about it.

(Vindex, *Cecil Rhodes, His Political Life and Speeches 1891-1900*
[London, 1900])

Jules Harmand, *the commissaire-general in Tonkin (Indochina)*

[...] To transpose democratic institutions into such a setting is aberrant nonsense. The subject people are not and cannot become citizens in the democratic sense of the term.

France has tried to resolve the contradiction by assimilation, based on a previous faith in the equality of all men and their rapid perfectibility. [...] The time has come to substitute other conceptions for these utopias, perhaps less generous but assuredly more useful and more fruitful, for they alone are in conformity with the nature of things.

[...] It is necessary, then, to accept as a principle and point of departure the fact that there is a hierarchy of races and civilizations, and that we belong to the superior race and civilization, still recognizing that, while superiority confers rights, it imposes strict obligations in return. The basic legitimation of conquest over native peoples is the conviction of our superiority, not merely our mechanical, economic, and military superiority, but our moral superiority. Our dignity rests on that quality, and it underlies our right to direct the rest of humanity. Material power is nothing but a means to that end.

Peoples who lack this belief and this frankness about themselves should not try to conquer.

(Jules Harmand, *Domination et colonisation* [Paris, 1910])

U.S. Senator **Albert Beveridge**

God has not been preparing the English speaking and Teutonic peoples for a thousand years for nothing but vain and idle self-contemplation and self-admiration. No! He has made us the master organizers of the world to establish system where chaos reigns. He has made us adept in government that we may administer government among savage and servile peoples.

(Albert Beveridge, *The Russian Advance* [New York, 1903])

A Look from the Outside

Joseph Conrad *in a major biographical novel about the Congo*

[...] When near the buildings I met a white man, in such an unexpected elegance of get-up that in the first moment I took him for a sort of vision. I saw a high starched collar, white cuffs, a light alpaca jacket, snowy trousers, a clear necktie, and varnished boots. No hat. Hair parted, brushed, oiled, under a green-lined parasol held in a big white hand. He was amazing, and had a penholder behind his ear.

I shook hands with this miracle, and I learned he was the Company's chief accountant, and that all the book-keeping was done at this station.

[...] One day he remarked, without lifting his head, "In the interior you will no doubt meet Mr Kurtz." On my asking who Mr. Kurtz was, he said he was a first-class agent; and seeing my disappointment at this information, he added slowly, laying down his pen, "He is a very remarkable person." Further questions elicited from him that Mr. Kurtz was at present in charge of a trading post, a very important one, in the true ivory-country, at "the very bottom of there. Sends in as much ivory as all the others put together...." [...] "When you see Mr. Kurtz," he went on "tell him from me that everything here"—he glanced at the desk—"is very satisfactory. I don't like to write to him—with those messengers of ours you never know who may get hold of your letter—at that Central Station." He stared at me for a moment with his mild, bulging eyes. "Oh, he will go far, very far," he began again. "He will be a somebody in the Administration before long. They, above—the Council in Europe, you know—mean him to be."

[And after meeting Mr. Kurtz.]"...I am not trying to excuse or even explain—I am trying to account to myself for—for—Mr. Kurtz—for the shade of Mr. Kurtz. This initiated wraith from the back of Nowhere honoured me with its amazing confidence before it vanished altogether. This was because it could speak English to me. The original Kurtz had been educated partly in England, and—as he was good enough to say himself—his sympathies were in the right place. His mother was half-English, his father was half-French. All Europe contributed to the making of Kurtz; and by-and-by I learned that, most appropriately, the International Society for the Suppression of Savage Customs had intrusted him with the making of a report, for its future guidance. And he had written it, too. I've seen it. I've read it. It was eloquent, vibrating with eloquence, but

too high-strung, I think. Seventeen pages of close writing he had
found time for! But this must have been before his—let us say—
nerves, went wrong, and caused him to preside at certain midnight
dances ending with unspeakable rites, which—as far as I reluctantly
gathered from what I heard at various times—were offered up to
him—do you understand? —to Mr. Kurtz himself. But it was a
beautiful piece of writing. The opening paragraph, however, in the
light of later information, strikes me now as ominous. He began
with the argument that we whites, from the point of development
we had arrived at, 'must necessarily appear to them [savages] in the
nature of supernatural beings—we approach them with the might
as of a deity,' and so on, and so on. 'By the simple exercise of our
will we can exert a power for good practically unbounded,' etc. etc.
From that point he soared and took me with him. The peroration
was magnificent, though difficult to remember, you know. It gave
me the notion of an exotic Immensity ruled by an august Benevo-
lence. It made me tingle with enthusiasm. This was the unbounded
power of eloquence—of words—of burning noble words. There
were no practical hints to interrupt the magic current of phrases,
unless a kind of note at the foot of the last page, scrawled evidently
much later, in an unsteady hand, may be regarded as the exposition of a method. It was very simple, and at the end of that moving
appeal to every altruistic sentiment it blazed at you, luminous and
terrifying, like a flash of lightning in a serene sky: 'Exterminate all
the brutes!'"

(Joseph Conrad, *Heart of Darkness* [London, 1902])

A Look from the Inside:
A Socialist Response

James Connolly, *leader of the Irish Socialists, executed for high treason
in 1916 by the British authorities*

[. . .] The section of the Socialist army to which I belong, the Irish
Socialist Republican Party, never seeks to hide its hostility to those
purely bourgeois parties which at present direct Irish politics.

But, in inscribing on our banners an ideal to which they also give
lip-homage, we have no intention of joining in a movement which
could debase the banner of revolutionary Socialism. The Socialist
parties of France oppose the mere Republicans without ceasing to
love the Republic. In the same way the Irish Socialist Republican
Party seeks the independence of the nation, whilst refusing to con-

form to the methods or to employ the arguments of the chauvinist Nationalist.

As Socialists we are not imbued with national or racial hatred by the remembrance that the political and social order under which we live was imposed on our fathers at the point of the sword; that during 700 years Ireland has resisted this unjust foreign domination; that famine, pestilence and bad government have made of this western isle almost a desert and scattered our exiled fellow-countrymen over the whole face of the globe.

The enunciation of facts such as I have just stated is not able today to inspire or to direct the political energies of the militant working-class of Ireland; such is not the foundation of our resolve to free Ireland from the yoke of the British Empire. We recognise rather that during all these centuries the great mass of the British people had no political existence whatever; that England was, politically and socially, terrorised by a numerically small governing class; that the atrocities which have been perpetrated against Ireland are only imputable to the unscrupulous ambition of this class, greedy to enrich itself at the expense of defenseless men; that up to the present generation the great majority of the English people were denied a deliberate voice in the government of their own country; that it is, therefore, manifestly unjust to charge the English people with the past crimes of their Government; and that at the worst we can but charge them with a criminal apathy in submitting to slavery and allowing themselves to be made an instrument of coercion for the enslavement of others. An accusation as applicable to the present as to the past.

But whilst refusing to base our political action on hereditary national antipathy, and wishing rather comradeship with the English workers than to regard them with hatred, we desire with our precursors the United Irishmen of 1798 that our animosities be buried with the bones of our ancestors—there is not a party in Ireland which accentuates more as a vital principle of its political faith the need of separating Ireland from England and of making it absolutely independent.

(James Connolly, *Socialism and Nationalism* [Paris, 1897])

[5]
The Losers

Eric Hobsbawm

An imitation of European customs, including the
perilous art of borrowing, has been lately affected:
but, in the hands of Eastern rulers, the civilisation of
the West is unfruitful; and, instead of restoring a tot-
tering state, appears to threaten it with speedier ruin.
Sir T. Erskine May (1877)[1]

The Word of God gives no authority to the modern
tenderness for human life. . . . It is necessary in all Eastern lands to establish a fear and awe of the Government. Then, and only then, are its benefits appreciated.
J. W. Kaye (1870)[2]

In that "struggle for existence" which provided the basic metaphor of the economic, political, social, and biological thought of the
bourgeois world, only the "fittest" would survive, their fitness certi-
fied not only by their survival but by their domination. The greater
part of the world's population therefore became the victims of
those whose superiority, economic, technological, and therefore
military, was unquestioned and seemed unchallengeable: the economies and states of northwestern and central Europe and the
countries settled by its emigrants abroad, notably the United States.
With the three major exceptions of India, Indonesia, and parts of
North Africa few of them became or were formal colonies in the
third quarter of the nineteenth century. (We may leave aside the
areas of Anglo-Saxon settlement like Australia, New Zealand, and
Canada which, though not yet formally independent, were clearly
not treated like the areas inhabited by "natives," a term in itself
neutral, but which acquired a strong connotation of inferiority.)
Admittedly these exceptions were not negligible: India alone accounted for 14 percent of the world's population in 1871. Still, the
political independence of the rest counted for little. Economically
they were at the mercy of capitalism, insofar as they came within
its reach. From a military point of view their inferiority was blatant.
The gunboat and the expeditionary force appeared to be all powerful.
   In fact, they were not quite as decisive as they looked, when
Europeans blackmailed feeble or traditional governments. There

were plenty of what British administrators liked to call, not without admiration, "martial races," which were quite capable of defeating European forces in pitched battles on land, though never at sea. The Turks enjoyed a well-merited reputation as soldiers, and indeed their ability not only to defeat and massacre the rebel subjects of the Sultan but to stand up to their most dangerous adversary, the Russian army, preserved the Ottoman Empire as effectively as the rivalries between the European powers, or at least slowed down its disintegration. British soldiers treated the Sikhs and Pathans in India and the Zulus in Africa, French ones the North African Berbers, with considerable respect. Again experience showed that expeditionary forces were severely troubled by consistent irregular or guerrilla warfare, especially in rather remote mountainous areas where the foreigners lacked local support. The Russians struggled for decades against such resistance in the Caucasus, and the British gave up the attempt to control Afghanistan directly, and contented themselves with little more than supervising the northwestern frontier of India. Lastly, the permanent occupation of vast countries by small minorities of foreign conquerors was extremely difficult and expensive, and, given the ability of the developed countries to impose their will and interests on them without it, the attempt hardly seemed worth making. Still, hardly anybody doubted that it could be done if necessary.

The greater part of the world was therefore in no position to determine its own fate. It could at best react to the outside forces which pressed upon it with increasing weight. By and large this world of the victims consisted of four major sectors. First, there were the surviving non-European empires or independent large kingdoms, of the Islamic world and Asia: the Ottoman Empire, Persia, China, Japan, and a few lesser ones such as Morocco, Burma, Siam, and Vietnam. The greater ones of these survived, though— with the exception of Japan—[. . .] increasingly undermined by the new forces of nineteenth-century capitalism; the smaller ones were eventually occupied after the end of our period, with the exception of Siam which survived as a buffer state between British and French zones of influence. Second, there were the former colonies of Spain and Portugal in the Americas, now nominally independent states. Third, there was sub-Saharan Africa, about which little need be said since it attracted no major attention in this period. Finally, there were the already formally colonized or occupied victims, mainly Asian.

All of them faced the fundamental problem of what their attitude should be to the formal or informal conquest by the West. That the whites were too strong to be merely rejected was, alas, evident [. . .].

Notes

1. T. Erskine May, *Democracy in Europe* (London, 1877), vol. I, p. lxxi.
2. J. W. Kaye, *A History of the Sepoy War in India* (1870), vol. II, pp. 402-3.

[6]
Colonialism's Last Days:
The "Emergency" in Malaya

From Han Suyin's novel, ... and the Rain My Drink

[...] One afternoon Evangeline was dropped. Evangeline was twelve and had been a bandit for two years in the jungle. Captured by the Gurkhas in a raid on the terrorist camp where she lived, wounded by bullets in the assault, she was treated at the hospital for seven weeks and became rather spoilt. Everyone in the hospital, from the friendly and vigorous English matron to the sleepy, coconut oil-smelling Malay sweepers, brought her toys and sweets and petted her and sat on her bed, admiring her.

Evangeline came up our stairs dressed in a gingham cotton gown with red, green and yellow checks, made by a Scots nursing sister at night and fitted on Evangeline with the whole of the nursing staff brimful of advice standing round. Her two hands clutched the first toy she had been given, a duck fluffy with white downy feather, on wheels, and with a yellow papier-mâché beak. Evangeline's hair was cut crew style, parted and brilliantined like a boy's, and to cultivate a wave she wore a large curler on a spring. But her hair was too thick and alive and the curler snapped off and fell to the ground when she moved. Then she clipped it on again, firmly.

Gravely she bowed. Her eyes lingered upon the polished wooden floor and remained scanning it, measuring its extent, noting its surface.

"Go ahead," I said, "try it." Immediately she produced a large key from her pocket, wound up the spring and put down her duck. It went round and round in wide ecstatic circles, rolling its wheels with tremendous whirrs and whooshes, beating its wings in time together, veering upon the slight bumps on the floor and saying quack, quack, quack.

The duck having adopted our floor, Evangeline signified she would stay, and remained eleven weeks.[...].

Days later two detectives and an official from the Ministry of Information came to see Evangeline. The Information official was an amiable and gay ex-officer of the Chinese Nationalist Army, Jimmy Lo. "What a pretty little girl, and so intelligent," he said, "how I wish she were my daughter." [...]

81

Jimmy Lo returned with a camera man, a wire recorder, two aides and a box of chocolates slightly mouldy with heat. His pretty wife was with him. She sat in a corner, gazing at Evangeline. The Information Department had decided to broadcast Evangeline's story as good propaganda. There were quite a few child bandits about, but not many as intelligent as this little girl.

They sat on the large pink and white Malay mat on the floor and placed the wire recorder on a stool in front of Evangeline and Jimmy held the microphone and began.

"Now how long were you in the jungle, little girl?"

Already trained by police interrogation, having answered this question many times, Evangeline replied: "Two years and four months."

"Now tell us," said Jimmy, "how you came to the jungle."

"I went with my mother," said Evangeline.

"What happened to your father?" asked Jimmy's sympathetic voice.

And his silent lips framed the answer for lip-reading Evangeline.

"My father died," said Evangeline, "so my mother and I went to the jungle."

"Who killed your father?" asked Jimmy.

"Bad people," replied Evangeline, rolling her eyes at the machine squatting attentive in its maroon shagreen skin, its slow wheels turning, "very bad people."

"Aha," said Jimmy happily, "communist bandits, wasn't it, little girl? Say yes," he mouthed to Evangeline.

"Yes," said Evangeline.

Jimmy looked pleased. "We're getting on, she's really quite wonderful," he whispered aside, and produced a memorandum sheet out of his pocket, upon which he had jotted the main points of the interview. He now ticked off point 1, "Parents," and continued:

"Now when you were in the jungle camp with the wicked bandits, did they beat you?"

"No," said Evangeline.

"Not even once?"

"No...but once or twice my mother beat me. And the men they shouted at me." Warming up she added, "Especially when the food was not ready they cursed me, and tried to leave me behind when they moved."

"Point 2. Ill treatment," checked Jimmy and continued:

"Now what did you do in the jungle, little girl?"

"I cooked, I washed clothes, I sang songs, and we walked and walked and sometimes we ran. And I helped to chop wood. And I threw stones to kill birds and lizards. And one day," her voice rose vibrant out of its artificial submission, "I saw a tiger. A real one."

"Weren't you afraid?" asked Jimmy, forgetting the recorder.

"Oh no," said Evangeline. "But we were afraid of the Gurkhas, because they are terrible people. They chop heads and hands. They are Kling devils," she said.

"Cut," said Jimmy. "I think we'll have to prepare her a bit more, to give some shape to the broadcast. Now," he resumed, "what happened to your mother?"

"She was killed," said Evangeline. "She was killed when I was taken."

But no tears fell, she said it stolidly and wriggled her red sandals on the floor, and looked at her duck and patted it.

"Now we'll take a photograph," said Jimmy. We walked downstairs and stood in the garden in front of the bungalow, Evangeline with her duck, and the camera man snapped her alone; then with Ah Mei; then with all of us round her, a gay company smiling strenuously and blinking our eyes in the harsh sun.

Three more times did Jimmy come to the house, until Evangeline was ready and then they recorded her. Each time Mrs. Lo came with him, to watch Evangeline with a rapt tenderness, with love to stroke her hair, and to offer her little drives in the car, and to bring her handkerchiefs and oranges and a bright red plastic belt to match her sandals.

One day Jimmy asked Evangeline what songs she sang in the jungle, and she started:

> Arise, ye who do not want to be slaves,
> ——With flesh and blood
> ——We shall build our new Great Wall.

"Ha," said Jimmy, "that's a communist song, little girl."

But I remembered the song, many times heard during the war against Japan; in Chungking hummed by servants as they swept the courtyards.

"Surely, Mr. Lo, you remember this, our war song, yours too. It was not only a communist song."

"Yes, I know," replied Jimmy. "But many things which were not communist have become communist now...in fact it is so difficult sometimes...but not for you," he added, his brow clearing. "Not for you or me...we are positively not communists." He meant to make me feel secure, above suspicion, in these suspicious days when all liberalism is suspect which is not tainted with servile acquiescence, but instead I felt suddenly a traitor, and nothing else.

"I know another song," said Evangeline. "Our teacher in the jungle sang it, after lessons, playing it on the flute. He said it was old, from the ancestors' country. But we could not march to it. He sang it alone, after food was eaten, and I listened."

She sang in a harsh, unmelodic voice pitched higher than normal, off-key and haunted with the old longing and grievance, old as the world of man:

> I will go to the forest for justice,
> For justice and righteousness,
> And become a green-clad man.
> The rulers pursue me with soldiers,
> With riders, chariots, and spears.
>
> I will go to the forest for justice,
> The people will flock to me.
> I will right their wrongs from the green shade,
> And kill the rulers with arrows.
> Their horsemen will stumble with fear.
>
> I will go to the forest for justice.
> The wind for my garment I wear.
> Together with my many companions,
> The wind for my garment and the rain my drink,
> We build a new heaven on earth.

"Ah, how typical, isn't it?" mused Jimmy. "Justice...the justice of the forest. It's old and steeped in tradition...A corrupt, incompetent government, and the just and good men going to the green forest and becoming bandits, but right is on their side...." Suddenly he became nostalgic, uneasy, and fretful. "Of course we call them bandits, I don't think the English understand their idea...."

"Of course they do, they've got Robin Hood, you know," I said.

[7]
Colonialism's Last Days:
An Orderly Decolonization in Malawi

The Times (London)

After 73 years of colonial rule, the Union Jack was lowered and the new state of Malawi came into being at midnight last night. Watched by the Duke of Edinburgh, representing the Queen, and by representatives of more than 80 countries, the raising of the Malawi flag was the climax of four days of celebrations to mark the country's independence.

Today, at an open-air ceremony in bright sunshine, the instruments of government were handed over to Dr. Hastings Kamuzu Banda, the Malawi Prime Minister. The Duke of Edinburgh read a message from the Queen. Tomorrow the Duke will read the Speech from the Throne at the state opening of Parliament in Zomba.

Malawi's independence is the crowning achievement for Dr. Banda. After the new flag had been raised last night a portrait of the Prime Minister was illuminated in fireworks amid cheers, and the ceremony concluded with a rousing song of praise, "Everything belongs to Kamuzu Banda," led by Mr. Kanyama Chiume, the Minister in charge of the celebrations.

In his speeches during the celebrations Dr. Banda has reiterated his appeal for peace and calm and his pledge to build a state "in which race, colour or creed will be no barrier to anybody's progress."

He was confident that tolerance, stability, and good government would bring Malawi the investments so vital to its economic progress and prosperity. This aspect, however, was "insignificant" when compared with the achievement of independence.

"Poverty is preferable to tyranny. National independence under rule of law is a vital condition of peace and happiness"[. . .].

(*The Times Supplement on Malawi*, July 6, 1964)

Toward self-sufficiency—an editorial comment

Malawi's emergence does not mean that it can become a spearhead of anti-European pressure against southern Africa. The country's entire trade links run through European-governed countries—notably Mozambique. Its development will depend largely on Western aid. The many thousands of emigrant Nyasas, whose remittances are so important to Malawi's balance of payments, work largely in Southern Rhodesia and South Africa, though some work in the Northern Rhodesia copperbelt. There are hard facts which will dictate Malawi's relations with her neighbours. It is already clear that Dr. Banda perfectly understands the limitations of Malawi independence, at least for the time being. Ardent nationalist though he is, and a professed admirer of Dr. Nkrumah, he does not intend to destroy his country on unwise crusades. He has come to an understanding with the Portuguese, and has invited the Prime Minister of Southern Rhodesia, Mr. Ian Smith, to the Malawi independence celebrations.

(Ibid.)

A message from the Prime Minister—Dr. Hastings Banda

Malawi has today become an independent sovereign State. Our people celebrate their independence with heartful joy and they look forward to playing their part in the affairs of the world in general and in the Commonwealth in particular. They are grateful to the British Government and its people for all the assistance they have given them in the past.

(*The Times*, July 7, 1964)

A Booker Group advertisement

[Extract from the Annual Statement of the Chairman, Sir Jock Campbell, in 1960.] "As I write, in April, Dr. Banda has, I am happy to say, just been released from prison (but not yet some of his lieutenants and many of his followers). The Monckton Commission are at work in Central Africa, and Mr. Macleod's visit has apparently done much to set the scene for restoring African confidence and progress. We in Bookers, with our business in Northern Rhodesia and Nyasaland, have a direct as well as a moral stake in what happens. I have previously expressed the view that no form of federation or association in Central Africa can command African acceptance and support if its effect, however veiled, is to inhibit African constitutional progress in Northern Rhodesia and to sustain European domination. The choice in Africa does not lie between continuing white supremacy and early effective African constitutional advancement. The catastrophic events in South Africa have finally shown that the doctrine of white supremacy is as dangerous and unworkable as it is wrong and inhuman. African constitutional advancement there must be. The choice lies between its achievement by constructive and imaginative statesmanship or in violence and bitterness."

[. . .]The Booker Group in Malawi operate the following divisions:

Kandodo—a chain of forty retail shops

McConnell & Company and Pelletier Ltd.—manufacturers' agents, with six depots

London & Blantyre Wholesale Company—wholesalers of general merchandise, with ten depots

Shire Clothing—manufacturers of clothing

Bookers Shipping and Travel (Malawi)—travel bureau, and clearing and forwarding, in Blantyre and Zomba

Sugar Services—importers and distributors of sugar

Chombe Tea Estate—growers of tea.

(The Times Supplement, July 6, 1964)

[8]
White-Settler Colonialism and the Myth of Investment Imperialism

Arghiri Emmanuel

"Financial" imperialism is a fashionable term. It is supposed to be different in nature from the "mercantile" imperialism of the seventeenth and eighteenth centuries, to have matured during the last quarter of the century and to have led to the "informal" and then the "formal" takeover of the world, culminating in the sharing out of the last unoccupied territories—Africa, the Ottoman Middle East, and Indochina. This theory has been put to severe trial recently. The huge colonial empires, which had taken centuries to build, broke up in a few years without proportionate violence and without any marked impoverishment of the great imperial parent states or any reduction in their capacity to exploit the rest of the world.

The concepts of neocolonialism and neoimperialism are unsatisfactory. They were devised for argument's sake, in the face of an unexpected situation, and they fail to save the traditional theory. For it is becoming increasingly obvious that political domination, far from having been the condition or even the crowning of economic domination (or what I would call exploitation), really ran counter to it.[. . .].

Unfortunately a certain piety toward Lenin's writings still prevents Marxists from disengaging themselves intellectually from the influence of work as marginal as *Imperialism: The Highest Stage . . .*, which never had any scientific pretensions, and which was written rapidly, in the difficult conditions of exile, with no other documentation to hand but the Bern library. The author himself described it as a simple "popular outline," and far from being a general theory of imperialism, it was only an empirical analysis conditioned by a particular historical situation.

I believe this quasi-religious attitude explains the repeated misunderstandings and deficiencies of revolutionary Marxism in the face of all the major events that have accompanied decolonization. [. . .]. Marxists seem to circle round and round these problems without knowing from which angle to tackle them. Innumerable "minitheories" are produced that contradict one another; words are refuted by other words; and no current doctrine of imperialism is accepted by more than a small group, even within the great "left-wing" parties themselves on those occasions when reflection is encouraged, allowed, or simply tolerated. This confusion becomes unbearable when the inadequacy of the old concepts is recognized and people try to save them with a multitude of deductive developments instead of firmly replacing them by new ones.

The main aim of this article is to show up a particular deficiency of the traditional schemas. This is their failure to recognize a third factor that intervenes between imperialist capitalism and the peoples of the exploited countries, viz., the colonialists themselves. Not only does this deficiency seem to us to be the most topical one and the one most immediately linked to certain present-day problems of the utmost urgency, but its examination will enable us to consider in logical order a whole series of other contradictions between accepted notions and reality.

The Second Wave of Colonialism

It is useless to go into the various constraints and inducements that suddenly launched the policy of colonial conquest and expansion at the end of the nineteenth century. As J. Galagher and R. Robinson put it, "Why, after centuries of neglect, the British and other European governments should have scrambled to appropriate nine-tenths of the African continent within sixteen years, is an old problem, still awaiting an answer."[1] One thing seems certain, however, and is beginning to be widely accepted. Whatever the motivating forces behind this adventure, the advanced capitalist world did not receive any *supplementary* benefit from the direct administration of these new territories.

Without going into details [. . .] one can say that the imperialists' easy renunciation of their colonies and the fact that it caused them no loss or reduction of earnings provides a strong argument, at any rate a posteriori, in favor of the theory according to which direct administration of the underdeveloped countries ceased, at a certain moment, to be profitable, and from then on added nothing to the automatic machinery of exploitation and "blocking" constituted by the free play of world economic forces and relations of production.

This does not necessarily mean that colonialism was a technical error. As Paul Sweezy has said so well, speaking of British colonialism: "Though English capitalists may have little to gain through annexation...they may have much to lose through annexation by [others]....The result may appear to be a net loss...[but] what is important is not the loss or gain compared to the pre-existing situation, but rather the loss or gain compared to the situation which would have prevailed had a rival succeeded in stepping in ahead." [...] Impelled by competition and by their internal contradictions, capitalists are often obliged, within each country, to act in a way that is prejudicial to their class and their system. The same is true in the international sphere. Imperialism as a whole would perhaps have gladly avoided the expense of administering the backward countries directly, but each imperialist taken separately had no choice. It was, in fact, on these antagonisms and this competition that Lenin based his refutation of Kautsky's theory of ultraimperialism, according to which the trend toward concentration would culminate in some kind of monopolistic planning on a planetary scale, which would in turn lead to universal peace and the rational organization of the world economy.

This explanation is plausible. It is confirmed by some of the most pertinent historical analyses. Fear of foreign interference on the route to India seems to have determined England's takeover in South Africa and its intervention in Egypt. Then, during a second period, and indirectly, the link-up between these two areas seems to have conditioned the English predilection for East Africa, which in turn incited the French to seize the western side, and so on. National prestige, military ambition, "retaliation," pure power politics, the various "civilizing missions," often provided sufficient immediate motivations for this or that costly and irrational colonialist operation. But all this belongs in turn to an ideological superstructure that would not have existed if international imperialism itself had not been there already, with its need for economic expansion and exploitation.

An Independent Factor: The Colonials

This explanation is, however, neither complete nor sufficient. If the colonial problem, as an "avatar of the imperialist process," was only due to the internal political contradictions (and complications) of international imperialism, it would be difficult to account for the determination of small countries like Belgium, Holland, and Portugal to establish and above all to preserve empires showing a deficit, whose political appropriation ran counter to the properly understood interests of the capitalists. Leaving Portugal aside, it is difficult to see what particular advantages the colonies brought to the great Belgian and Dutch financiers by contrast with those of countries like Denmark, Switzerland, Sweden, etc.[2][...].

Things change and everything becomes clear, however, if one admits that beyond the causes that are so to speak "inherent" in capitalism, there exists another independent motive force that generates the colonial phenomenon, a social factor proper to it that embodies the contradiction referred to earlier. This motive force proper to colonialism is none other than the colonials themselves—and in this category I include not only the settlers but a whole import-export world, including the local staff of the great home-based companies and the colonial civil servants (at any rate the lower grades), not forgetting the agents and backers of these interest-groups in the parent country.

For these people, the colonial adventure was neither a "hindrance," a "contradiction," nor a "distortion," but the mainspring of their existence and their supreme justification. They benefited from colonialism and therefore promoted it, without reserve or contradiction— and for this very reason they were basically anti-imperialistic, however paradoxical this may seem. From the very beginning they were in conflict with their respective parent countries and therefore with imperialism itself—objectively so at all times, subjectively so at times of crisis, going so far as to take up arms against it (Algeria, Belgian Congo, Biafra, etc.).

This highly retrograde and reactionary element led the struggle on two fronts—unyieldingly and wholeheartedly against the natives of the occupied territories, relatively and occasionally, but often very violently against the great capitalists "back home." However, precisely on account of its antagonistic relation with big capital, this element was for long viewed favorably, even supported, by the left-wing parties in the respective metropolitan countries. The result was a mechanical transposition into the colonies of slogans from the antimonopoly struggle as waged within the metropolises. Everything was now back to front. For, in the specific conditions of certain colonies and notably those in Black Africa, where neither national bourgeoisies nor genuine indigenous proletariats existed, and where there were strong tribal residues and no infrastructure or socioeconomic development to speak of—in such conditions the great capitalist enterprise constituted, paradoxical as this may appear, if not the most progressive factor at least the most positive in historical terms.

Few in number, very often integrated both vertically and horizontally, controlling all resources and outlets, enjoying a technocratic interpenetration with an administration whose political and economic tasks merged at every level, these enterprises were naturally impelled toward a planned optimization of the whole. From the point of view of production, they represented the most rational forms of organization; from that of distribution, they were relatively the most tolerable. At the political level, these big capitalist enterprises were able to come to terms with the essential aspirations of the local elite: with Africanization of cadres very willingly; with national independence with greater or lesser reservations depending on the circumstances.

By contrast, the settler community could not come to terms with anything: neither with the trusts, nor with the metropolitan country—far less with Africanization or independence. It could be saved only by secession from the metropolis and by setting up an independent "white" state. The settlers did not fail to appreciate that this was the case, and soon gave it the concrete form of an explicit demand.

On the economic plane, the settler community constituted a dead weight—if not a parasitic and harmful element. A competitive and anarchic sector, existing at the margins of the dirigism and planning of the trusts, controlling only a small portion of the economy and consequently little aware of the imperatives of the whole, greedy for immediate profit, a great waster of labor-power and resources, the settler community also spent and invested a large part of its income abroad; it thus caused an outflow of funds in place of the external finance, however minimal, ensured by the big companies and so badly needed by these countries.

On the political plane, the relative weight of the settlers and their ability to act independently differed widely according to whether they were in a settlers' or a mainly administrative colony; but their position and their attitude were essentially the same, while their aggressiveness and efficacy depended on the relation of forces at a particular time. There were few of them in the Belgian Congo and they were beaten, but only after obliging the imperialists to use all the means at their disposal. They were scarcely more numerous in Rhodesia, but they succeeded with disconcerting ease. In Algeria, however, although they were far more numerous both in absolute and in relative terms, they nevertheless succumbed—though not until they had endangered the parent country itself and obliged a French prime minister to scurry to the radio in the middle of the night to stir up the populaton against a hypothetical descent of parachutists over the capital.

The Antagonism Between the White Settlers and Imperialism

There was nothing new in all this, however. The most difficult struggles of the imperialist countries since the eighteenth century had not been with the natives in their colonies but with their own settlers. And it should not be forgotten that if England is a second-class power today, this is due to its defeat in a conflict of this type and the subsequent founding of the United States. Without this, North America would now be an ex-colony of American Indians recently promoted to independence and therefore still exploited by England.

Marx and Engels did not fail to make references here and there to "white settlers," "poor whites," etc., although during the period in which they lived the problem was not acute. But Lenin came out strongly in favor of the Boers in 1900, just as Mao Zedong's China gave unexpected support to Biafra and its mercenaries. Finally, the exaggerated schematization in which Marxism was confined after Lenin's death meant that no place could be made for this uncomfortable "third element" in the noble formulas of the "people's struggle against financial imperialism." [. . .].

The Imperatives of Decolonization

People have been struck by the ease with which decolonization in Africa was carried out and they have concluded that imperialism was eager to eliminate noneconomic liabilities. It is true that the colonies were not or were no longer profitable for the parent countries and that direct political domination had become a burden. But this negative factor is not enough. Elimination of the cost of direct administration would explain a certain passive attitude, but it cannot account for the *extraordinary haste* with which independence was granted in many cases, particularly in the Congo. This can only be explained by a positive motive, i.e., the home countries' need at a certain moment *to steal a march on their own settlers who were threatening nearly everywhere to secede and form white states.* This is obvious in the Belgian Congo, where it was suddenly and cold-bloodedly decided to grant immediate independence, although nobody expected it for two or three years. But in varying degrees the same factor weighed in the balance more or less everywhere.[3]

This was not the first time in history that imperialist countries had been obliged to reckon with their own settlers. Selborne showed remarkable foresight when he wrote to Chamberlain in 1896 that so far as South Africa was concerned, he was much more apprehensive of the setting up of republics by the English white settlers than of Boer domination in the Transvaal. What were to be avoided at all costs, he added, were new Canadas or United States. This does not mean, of course, that England's opposition to the Boers was a secondary one. Galagher and Robinson are right when they say that since Great Britain annexed the Cape their administration was much more often pro-Bantu than pro-Boer.[4] As Demangeon states, "The Boer's hatred of British domination was largely caused by English protection of the natives. It was because they considered the abolition of slavery to be intolerable that thousands of Boers emigrated from the Cape Colony in 1835, starting the great treks that resulted in the founding of the Natal, Orange and Transvaal colonies."[5]

Although he is arguing from an ethical point of view, Bennett uses striking terms when, referring to Hobson, he describes the group that has always been the most implacable enemy of backward peoples: "If organized Governments of civilized Powers refused the task, they would let loose a horde of private adventurers, slavers, piratical traders, treasure hunters, concession mongers, who, animated by greed of gold or power, would set about the work of exploitation under no public control and with no regard to the future.... The contact with white races cannot be avoided, and it is more perilous and more injurious in proportion as it lacks governmental sanction and control."[6] The same point of view is adopted by L. S. Woolf: "Economic imperialism has itself created conditions in which that control must inevitably continue.... The European State, if it remains in Africa, is necessarily an instrument of that exploitation of Africans by Europeans; if it withdraws, it merely hands over the native to the more cruel exploitation of irresponsible white men."[7]

The whole history of imperialism and colonization demonstrates plainly that the opposition between backward peoples and the small white settler is the worst of all; and our refusal to allow for it in our classical descriptions of the class struggle will not eliminate this "stubborn fact," which finds ample confirmation today in the bloody conflict between Catholics and Protestants in Ireland and the merciless war in the Middle East.

As Demangeon reminds us again, Ireland was Britain's first real colony. In the sixteenth century, "thousands of Englishmen... settled on the land of the depossessed Irish clans and Anglo-Saxon property and exploitation were substituted for Celtic communal ways of life. English colonization of Ireland dates from this time, when the first wave of British immigrants came over," driven from the English countryside by the enclosures and the substitution of grazing for tilling. This is a striking example of the irrevocable nature of the antagonism we are discussing. After four centuries of coexistence, the two communities have not been able to take the least step toward integration. In relation to the Catholics, the Belfast Protestants are neither capitalists nor imperialists; they are still settlers. If they do not demand secession, it is for easily understood historical and geographical reasons. They still demand a large measure of autonomy, however, which allows them to deal with the oppressed people in their own way.

As for Israel, it is all too often forgotten that if this country represents a spearhead of imperialism in the particular present international context of antagonism between the two great blocs, this is only a result of special circumstances. Its true nature is to be a mass of small "white" settlers spreading out more and more to colonize an underdeveloped territory. It is this that makes their conflict with the peoples of the region so ruthless, even where the latter live under pro-Western regimes which are themselves the satellites of imperialism. In spite of its circumstantial and unnatural alliance with American imperialism (which is not all that reliable) [...], Israel is a secessionist colonial state. Its foundation was the object of a long and bloody struggle with England, who played the role of the imperialist parent country.

The case of Algeria should not be forgotten either. After the Front de Libération Nationale (FLN) was neutralized, following the "battle of Algiers" and the immobilization of its regular army beyond the barrage along the Algero-Tunisian frontier, the struggle mainly took place between France and the French settlers and assimilated groups, who—as mentioned earlier—went so far as to threaten the French state itself.

Financial Imperialism or Imperialism of Trade

If this analysis is accepted, a crucial question arises: why was imperialism so bitterly opposed to the white settlers' secession? If decolonization was to come, what did it matter whether it was to the advantange of the native population or the settlers?

According to fashionable theory, imperialism's essential feature is the investments of multinational corporations. If this were true, what little difference there might be between the two ways of decolonization would favor the white-settler states. Multinational corporations invest a great deal more in Canada, Australia, South Africa, and even Rhodesia, than they do in Tanzania or Uganda. But I do not believe that direct or portfolio investments and capital movements in general constitute the essence of imperialism, and this is what I shall try to demonstrate further on. The essential element is trade. On this level, it makes an enormous difference to the parent country whether power is taken over by the white settlers or by the natives. A "native" state is far more exploitable, commercially speaking, than a white state, whatever the volume of the trade flows involved. Britain can sell and buy much more in Canada than in Tanzania, but it exploits Tanzania, whereas it is exploited by Canada.[8] Both countries were British colonies in the past. In one, the English settlers took power; in the other, the natives. The result is that today Canada is much less English than Tanzania is.[9]

De Gaulle, who was a leading representative of French capitalism, saw all that clearly where Algeria was concerned. If the partisans of "French Algeria" had won, Algeria would have been much less French than it still is today, in spite of the profound breaches made by the revolution and the war. It was so that Algeria might remain as French as possible that he fought the Organisation Armée Secrète (OAS), exactly as Salan or Soustelle would have done if they had been responsible for government in France.[10]

The Export of Capital

The question therefore arises as to whether the export of capital is as essential to imperialism as most Marxists have considered it to be up to now. The core of this argument is to be found in J. A. Hobson's theory, which was approved by Lenin, at any rate in its main elements, and remodeled later by Strachey and a number of other economists. It can be summarized as follows:

At a certain stage in its development, capitalism is faced with the problem of reinvesting the profits it has saved. On the one hand, the concentration of industry in trust companies, combines, etc., results in economies of capital at the very moment when the elimination or reduction of competition has increased profits and therefore increased the sum of fresh capital formed during each production or sales cycle. On the other hand, income distribution in the capitalist system is such that the consumption of the masses remains relatively stagnant. This limits the expansion capacity of the concentrated industries and therefore their capacity to absorb new capital. Capitalists can no longer find opportunities for investing their spare profits in their own cartelized industries. So they are faced with a dilemma. They must either redistribute the national income through increased wages (which would lead to higher internal investments but lower profits) or else maintain the low rate of wages and the high rate of profits but find some other use for their spare capital. So the only way of avoiding a "blockage" of the system is through external investment. And this entails imperialist protection, which leads to the partition of the world. (Lenin added that the unequal development of capitalism among the great imperial powers results in a contradiction between the flexibility of the economic potential and the rigidity of the political framework. Because of this, there must be a periodical redistribution by war.)

With a view to verifying the historical truth of this theory, Lenin identified the foreign *assets* of England, France, and Germany during the period 1870-1914 with the *export* of capital. This identification is unacceptable. A foreign investment can be increased by the ploughing back of profits without there being any need for further export of capital. It can even increase simultaneously with the net *import* of capital toward the holding country. This is what happened during the period in question, as we shall show.

Lenin did not invent this identification, of course. Many bourgeois economists used it before him, and they still use it now for the purposes of national accounts. It is then convenient, and frequently done, to include all the interest and dividends earned abroad in the national income, whether it is reimported or not, and to balance the accounts by showing the interest and dividends that are reinvested on the spot as a net *export* of capital. This is just a question of terminology and accountancy procedures, and everybody knows what it means.

The Accumulation of International Investments

But when it is a question of verifying a theory of imperialism based on the *internal* accumulation of capital, as in the present case, things change radically. Because, between a situation where capital formed internally is invested abroad and one where on the contrary part of the profits made abroad are reimported and consumed internally, the remainder being reinvested on the spot, *there is all the difference between producing more than one can consume and consuming more than one actually produces.* And it then becomes quite inadmissible to explain imperialist expansion by the first situation when the figures one quotes show that the true situation is exactly the opposite.

If we limit ourselves to the two countries that best represent so-called investment imperialism during that period—England and France—we shall see that, roughly speaking, the former's investments

Foreign investments of the main capitalist countries in millions of pounds sterling:[11]

Year	United Kingdom	France	Germany	United States
1870	1006	513	negligible	negligible
1885	1602	678	390	negligible
1900	2485	1068	986	103
1914	4004	1766	1376	513

increased in forty four years from £1 to £4 billion and the latter's from a half to £1.75 billion. In other words, England's multiplied by four and France's by three-and-a-half. But if one takes into account the fact that after 1871 France had to liquidate part of its foreign assets to pay Germany the famous war indemnity of 5 billion francs, i.e., £200 million, one can say that the rate of increase of these countries' foreign investments between 1870 and 1914 was extraordinarily similar, i.e., 400 percent in forty-four years.

Now it is obvious that to obtain this result there is no need for fresh capital at all. Not only would reinvestment of returns suffice, but it should normally exceed the required sum by a wide margin. At 5 percent, a capital grows in forty-four years by over 850 percent and at 4 percent by over 560 percent. Four or 5 percent (more often 5—or even a higher figure—than 4) are the percentages generally adopted by those who have studied the question, such as Giffen, Hobson, Lenin, Frankel, Feis, Seyd, Beaulieu, Léon Say, R.L. Nash, Nogaro, et al. They either specifically mention these percentages or imply them indirectly by giving the amount of the financial earnings and the amount of investments for a given year. So if one adopts even the lowest figure—4 percent—one finds that if England had left the billion pounds it had invested in 1870, without adding any exported funds or deducting any reimported funds, these foreign investments would, by 1914, have totaled some £5.6 billion. As they only reached £4 billion, one is forced to conclude that not only did England not "export" capital during this period, but that England "imported" it.

But there is no need to use a more or less hypothetical percentage. We now have the genuine figures of Great Britain's annual accounts for the period under review, as well as partial but significant figures for France. For Britain, they are those of C. K. Hobson (not to be confused with J. A. Hobson, author of *Imperialism*), but above all the much more precise and reliable figures of Cairncross.[12] Hobson's figures stop at 1912. Adding them up, one finds that from 1870 to 1912 England's trade balance, which was constantly negative, showed for goods—including gold and silver—an overall surplus of imports over exports of £5517.1 million. If we extrapolate the average figures for the last five years, we have, for 1914, an overall surplus of imports, in round figures, of £5.8 billion. From this we must, of course, deduct the service-sector balance, which is positive. The surplus of this balance was, in 1912, £4071.2 million. Proceeding in the same way as for the trade-balance deficit, we have, for 1914, a total of £4.3 billion.

A final deficit of £1.5 billion therefore remains, which England could only make good by using an equivalent part of its external income, leaving the other part to accumulate on the spot. This means that from 1870 to 1914, England not only did not export new funds, but that it drew on external funds to cover its overall goods-and-services balance deficit. According to Hobson's figures, these withdrawals amounted to £1.5 billion, which is not far from the £1.6 billion suggested above, that was calculated on the basis of a hypothetical yield of 4 percent.

Yet Hobson's figures are rather unfavorable to my theory, for two reasons:

(1) He does not take into account any money spent by Englishmen traveling abroad that was not covered by ordinary bank remittances. This expenditure would have increased the trade-balance deficit.

(2) He counts among English service exports the "expenditure of the Indian government in this country," i.e., the salaries of members of the Indian Civil Service paid by drafts on London banks. But even if one accepts the (somewhat humorous) idea that England supplied the "services of good government" to India, it is doubtful whether these "services" can be included in England's (visible and invisible) *domestic* product. And, as we have already had occasion to repeat, this is what is in question here: i.e., whether the *domestic* product really tended, during the period under review, to exceed consumption and hence bring about an export of capital.

Cairncross meticulously revised all Hobson's figures one by one, and the overall results he obtained only differed by a few negligible fractions.[. . .].

Although French statistics for the same period are not so abundant, everything—similar rate of accumulation of assets, persistent trade balance deficit—goes to show that we are in the presence of the same phenomenon, i.e., a net import of funds.[13] What differences there may be are not sufficient to reverse the direction of the flows. Far from exporting their excess capital, the two main imperialist countries—and Germany too, at any rate from 1900—drained part of the capital from the rest of the world, merely by reimporting the income from their earlier investments, and without counting commerical exploitation and terms of trade. Far from being hampered by their limited consumption, they consumed part of the product of others.

So much for the famous second period of imperialism, from 1870 to 1913. But what about the earlier period? Before 1870, things are more uncertain. Statistics are rare and less reliable, and estimates more divergent. Keynes went so far as categorically to deny any net export of capital since...1580, when Queen Elizabeth invested Drake's treasure in the Levant Company and later used the profits to found the East India Company.[14] But one thing seems sure: if there was any export of capital, however small, it was before 1870. The most plausible version seems to be that there was a small export of capital between 1800 and 1850 or 1855, and that the situation changed radically between then and 1870. In any case, Britain's trade balance was positive until 1824; and one can say with certainty that there was at that time an export of capital, whatever the amount involved. After 1824, the trade balance became negative, but this does not justify the conclusion that there was a reversal of flows, since the invisibles may well have more than compensated for a few years and produced a positive balance of payments.[15] It is therefore very difficult to situate the "break" exactly; but it came somewhere about the middle of the century.

The Failings of the Traditional Theory

It could be argued that the dominant element of financial imperialism is not net capital exports, but the level of external investments, whatever their source, whether internal or external. But in this case, all our accepted ideas about imperialism have to be revised.

(1) Imperialism would then have nothing to do with an internal "overripeness" of capitalism that induced the export of capital. The basis of imperialist expansion would be neither the overaccumulation of capital nor the overproduction of goods.

(2) If external investments were an essential, if not unique, dimension of imperialism, we should then have to admit that English and French imperialism has been curiously attenuated since 1914, because after this date the level of their external investments fell progressively until they became an insignificant quantity compared with the 1914 figures.

(3) To say that North American imperialism has taken over the investment role would not save the theory, since *the present amount*

of U.S. investments and even the total amount of those of all the advanced capitalist countries added together is an insignificant quantity compared with the investments of England alone in 1914, and an absolutely negligible quantity compared with the investments of the four advanced capitalist countries in 1914.

To take the highest estimate, the present foreign investments of the United States total $70 billion. This seems an enormous sum. But England's 4 billion gold-backed pounds of 1914 are worth, according to the most conservative estimate, £40 billion of today's paper pounds. This is the equivalent of 96 billion present-day dollars, i.e., already a considerably higher sum, *in absolute terms*, than the current investments of the United States.[16] But a comparison in absolute terms between an England with 45 million inhabitants, at the 1914 economic level, and a United States of over 200 million inhabitants, at the 1970 level, has little meaning. These investments must be examined in the light of the national income of the investing and perhaps even the recipient countries. We then find that England's accumulated investments in 1914 represented something like twice its annual national income, whereas the present accumulated investments of the United States only represent the eleventh or twelfth part of its annual national income. If the national income of the recipient countries were taken into account, the results would be of the same order.

Finally, if one compares the total investments of all the imperialist countries in 1970 and in 1914, those of 1970 would come out even worse, since in 1914 England's £4 billion must be added to the £3.6 billion of the other three investing countries—France, Germany, and the United States—whereas today there is nothing much to be added to the $70 billion of the United States. What is the point, then, of laying such stress today on external investments in order to explain imperialism (and even a certain "superimperialism" of America), since over half a century ago England did *twenty times* better and all the advanced capitalist countries together, about *thirty-five times* better?

(4) In any case—whether the main symptom of imperialism is the actual export of capital or only the level of external investments—there is no possible link between the accumulation of these investments from 1870 to 1914 and the territorial expansion of the imperialists during the same period. This expansion took the forms of the partition of Africa, the dismantling of the Ottoman Empire, and the completion of the conquest of Indochina. But during the period under review, and even after it, these new territories were completely neglected by investors. And apart from the mining areas of South Africa, Rhodesia, and Katanga, where the reason for in-

vesting was not the placing of surplus capital but the need for certain essential products, investment in the territories acquired during the imperialist "scramble" was practically nil.[17] [...].

(5) At the same time as he advanced the theory of surplus capital seeking external outlets, J. A. Hobson put forward the theory of "overripeness" that produces a parasitical capitalism and a "Rentier State." Lenin used this theory in his *Imperialism*. But the two images are self-contradictory. According to the first one, capitalism is incapable of using its own surplus and invests part of it abroad. According to the second, capitalism ekes out its living with the help of a surplus that comes in from the rest of the world. It cannot even be said that the first situation necessarily precedes the second, nor that the latter is the corollary of an overripeness which Lenin called the "last stage" and Bukharin the "putrefaction" of capitalism.[18]

After another half century of further "ripening," both the idle rentiers *and* the "coupon clippers" have disappeared, in England as well as in France, and it is the active, direct-investing capitalists who have taken their place on the Promenade des Anglais.... If, under certain historical conditions, the producer-state does become the rentier-state, in others (particularly when there are no more coupons to clip) the rentier-state turns back into the producer-state. Without giving any warning, capitalism regains its youth and vigor after its "rotting," and one after another the elements that Marxism has periodically considered to be structural prove in time to have been only historical.

Conclusions

(1) Does this mean that the dilemma, redistribution of income or overproduction, has never existed? No, it is always latent in capitalism and it does become manifest under certain conditions. In England, in fact, it was relatively as severe before 1870 as afterward. After 1870, the trade union struggle and the rise in wages helped advanced capitalism out of this dilemma, at any rate to a certain extent. This does not mean that a relapse could not take place again in the future.

(2) When this dilemma does appear, it does not lead to the search for outlets for capital but for outlets for goods. Marx explained this very well when he said the overproduction of capital ultimately meant nothing more than overproduction of goods. But if the new capital is already formed, the product has already been sold, in which case there is neither overproduction nor lack of investment opportunities. Nobody has ever had difficulty in placing his capital.

However, it can happen that the need to sell products incites capitalism to export goods over and beyond its capacity to import other goods, the exporting country being ready if necessary to transform the equivalent of the surplus into foreign assets. It is then that the export of capital takes place, as a derivative form of the surplus export of goods, even if the credits precede the sales and induce them. This is why the post-Marxian idea of an export of capital taking precedence over the export of commodities does not make sense at all.[19] It is quite another thing to say that at certain periods the export of capital goods takes precedence over the export of consumer goods. This is correct, but it is still a question of export of goods.

(3) It is not the export of capital that prevented the development of backward countries, and Marx was right in theory when he forecast that India would become a capitalist country like England.[20] It is on the contrary the interruption of these exports and the reversal of the flows that is detrimental to the underdeveloped countries. This reversal happens when the servicing of earlier debts exceeds the influx of new capital, and when in addition the little surplus that has been produced on the spot is sent abroad by local capitalists and invested in the developed countries. The essential factor in this situation was the considerable rise in the standard of living of the masses within the great capitalist countries, following a particularly successful reformist struggle of the working classes that Marx could not have foreseen.

This does not mean that the allocation of this foreign capital is the best one for the national economy of the underdeveloped countries, from the point of view of specialization and the international division of labor. But if the underdeveloped countries cannot make the most desirable use of these investments, this is not because of the nationality of the capital involved, but because of the particular structures of the recipient countries, and notably the narrow limits of their local market—due to low wages—compared with markets and wages in the developed countries.[21] Whether it is national or international, capital is in search of profit, and it behaves in the same way.

Those who stress the obnoxiousness of foreign investments and multinational companies are therefore completely out of touch with the reality of the underdeveloped countries, since all capitalist under- or semideveloped countries, without exception, and even some "socialist" countries of Eastern Europe, are doing their utmost to institute investment codes and multiplying the exemptions and privileges to be granted to attract foreign capital.

(4) International antagonisms cannot always be automatically reduced to the terms of the class struggle. We must pass from factory

antagonisms to national antagonisms. On this level, there is no common measure between on the one hand the contradictions of great international capital and the underdeveloped peoples, and on the other hand the total enslavement and even physical extermination with which some of these peoples are threatened by true colonialism, which is that of the white settlers and their states, where these exist.

Notes

1. P. Galagher and R. Robinson, *Africa and the Victorians* (London: 1963), p. 17.
2. Neither these territories, nor generally speaking any of those that were acquired during this second period of imperialism (that has been called "investment imperialism"), were choice areas for financial capitalism. Moreover, England, which was at the spearhead of the colonial scramble, could scarcely be said to be the country of cartels and other forms of capitalist concentration, particularly at that time. On the contrary, says Werner Sombart, these phenomena are to be observed in certain countries like Switzerland, which show no tendency toward imperialist expansion, with or without political domination (*L'Apogée du capitalisme* [Paris: 1932], vol. I, p. 90).
3. J. de Staercke, general secretary of the Belgian Catholic Employers' Federation, knew what he was talking about when he wrote already in 1959: "What has to be done is to lead the Congo towards independence in good order and good understanding with Belgium. If, to maintain this order and understanding, it is necessary to grant independence a little earlier than is technically desirable, we should not hesitate to do so." The "order" of which J. de Staercke speaks was threatened by the settlers' plotting. At other times, on the contrary, this same fear of the settlers impelled the parent countries to cling to their colonies and postpone the granting of independence. For example, the French communists saw this danger of secession when they took part in the first postwar government and held responsible posts in the colonial administration. Suret-Canale, among others, has given a pertinent answer to those who blamed the French Communist Party for not having launched the idea of independence at the time, pointing out that in the absence of any political structure in the native population, independence meant secession and the founding of white states on South African or Rhodesian lines.
4. Galagher and Robinson, *Africa and the Victorians*, p. 53.
5. Albert Demangeon, *L'Empire Britannique* (Paris: 1923), p. 217. It was certainly not for humanitarian reasons that imperialist England opposed the local settlers so violently. The Protestant missionaries' campaign for "protection of the Bantu peoples" was certainly a deceptive

pretext justifying English imperialism's policy of using force against the Boers, which was itself determined by economic reasons. But this does not justify Lenin for having so ardently espoused the cause of the Boers against England in 1900 and the same goes for Mao Zedong backing the Biafra secession in 1969.

6. George Bennett, *The Concept of Empire* (London: 1962), p. 376.

7. L. S. Woolf, *Empire and Commerce in Africa* (London: 1920), pp. 334-35, 356-58.

8. I hope this has been sufficiently demonstrated in my book *Unequal Exchange* (New York: Monthly Review Press, 1972). It is not possible to discuss this theory here.

9. I have chosen Tanzania as the most unfavorable example for my theory, since this country has adopted a neutralist attitude that keeps it relatively separate from the Western world. If I had chosen Kenya or Uganda, the comparison would be much more striking. These two countries remain as English as one could wish. They buy English, transport English, insure English, and operate through English banks. This is not the case for Australia and New Zealand, although they had been colonized by the purest English stock, and it is even less true of Canada, which today is more American than anything.[...].

10. [...]. On March 24, 1971, General Salan declared during an interview on Radio Luxemborg that the type of French presence in Algeria he had in mind at the time was "like Rhodesia, but without apartheid." Which is extraordinarily naive! For if his Algeria was not to be more French than Rhodesia is English, how can he be surprised that France refused it?

11. S. H. Frankel, *Capital Investment in Africa* (Oxford: 1938), p. 6. [...].

12. C. K. Hobson, *The Export of Capital* (London: 1914), pp. 170-204; A. K. Cairncross, *Home and Foreign Investment 1870-1913* (Cambridge: 1953), pp. 176-80.

13. France's cumulative trade-balance deficit from 1875 to 1913 was 25,187 million francs, i.e., about £1 billion.

14. J.M. Keynes, *Essays in Persuasion* (London: 1930).

15. This is the opinion of François Crouzet, *L'Economie du commonwealth* (Paris: 1950).

16. The exchange rate used is that current in early 1971, before the last devaluation of the dollar.

17. Frankel, *Capital Investment in Africa*, p. 158.

18. Curious "putrefaction" that sets in before death, as Lucien Laurat remarked!

19. If certain Marxists did not have an unfortunate tendency to "by-pass" political economy instead of "going beyond it," they would not have forgotten this elementary proposition, i.e., that the export of capital is nothing but the export of *unpaid* goods. No other material means for transferring capital between countries exists.

20. Lenin was of the same opinion when he wrote: "The export of capital affects and greatly accelerates the development of capitalism in those countries to which it is exported. While, therefore, the export of capi-

tal may tend to a certain extent to arrest development in the capital-exporting countries, it can only do so by expanding and deepening the further development of capitalism thoughout the world" (*Selected Works* [Moscow: 1967], I, pp. 725-26).

21. This question has been considered in detail in *Unequal Exchange*, and cannot be further discussed here.

Part II

The Global Context

The contributions in Part II place the nature and dynamics of "developing societies" in their international context. It opens with the retort by Marx against those who used his writings to justify unilinear theories of development—that all societies would necessarily proceed along the same road. This point is well taken not only with reference to variants of Marxist analysis but, not least, to the teleological visions of modernization theory. That is followed by a paper by Cardoso, both a co-author and a strong critic of "dependency theory," in which he examines new forms of economic dependency that give rise to novel political and social adaptations in "developing societies." Hymer's paper is a classic contribution to the discussion of the role of multinational corporations in peripheral capitalism. Barratt Brown takes that discussion forward, relating it to the new global division of labor that is taking shape, and introduces current discussions of the "New International Economic Order." Alavi's paper argues that the internal structure of "developing societies" can be understood only by locating them in their global context, but offers a different theoretical conception to that of Wallerstein.

The issues exposed in Part II follow closely from those in Part I and likewise provide the background against which those brought up in Part III are discussed. Contributions of Harry Magdoff, Immanuel Wallerstein, Arghiri Emmanuel, and Basil Davidson are particularly relevant to these issues.

[9]
Pathways of Social Development:
A Brief Against Suprahistorical Theory[1]

Karl Marx

The chapter on primitive accumulation[2] does not claim to do more than trace the path by which, in Western Europe, the capitalist economic order emerged from the womb of the feudal economic order. It therefore presents the historical movement that, by divorcing the producers from their means of production, converted the former into wage workers (proletarians in the modern sense of the word) and the possessors of the latter into capitalists. In this history "all revolutions[3] are epoch-making that serve as levers to the emergent capitalist class, above all those that, by stripping great masses of people of their means of production and traditional existence,[4] suddenly hurl them onto the labor market. But the basis of this whole development is the expropriation of the agricultural producers. It has been accomplished in a radical manner thus far only in England...but all countries of Western Europe are going through the same movement," etc.[5] At the end of the chapter, the historical tendency of production is summed up thus: that it "begets its own negation with the inexorability that governs the metamorphoses of nature"; that it has itself created the elements of a new economic order by giving the greatest impetus at once to the productive forces of social labor and to the complete development of every individual producer; that capitalist property, already resting de facto on a collective mode of production,[6] cannot but be transformed into social property. I furnish no proof at this point for the good reason that this statement itself is nothing but the brief summary of long expositions given previously in the chapters on capitalist production.

Now, what application to Russia could my critic make of this historical sketch? Only this: if Russia is tending to become a capitalist nation like the nations of Western Europe—and during the last few years it has been at great pains to achieve this—it will not succeed without first having transformed a large part of its peasants into proletarians; and, after that, once brought into the fold of the capitalist regime, it will endure its pitiless laws like other profane peoples. That is all. But it is too little for my critic. He absolutely insists on transforming my historical sketch of the genesis of capitalism in Western Europe into a historico-philosophical theory[7] of the general course fatally imposed on all peoples, whatever the historical circumstances in which they find themselves placed, in order to arrive ultimately at this economic formation that ensures, together with the greatest expansion of the productive powers of social labor, the most complete development of man. But I beg his pardon. (It does me both too much honor and too much discredit.) Let us take an example.

At various points in *Capital* I allude to the fate that befell the plebeians of ancient Rome. They were originally free peasants tilling their own plots, each on his own account. In the course of Roman history they were expropriated. The same movement that divorced them from their means of production and subsistence involved not only the formation of large landed property, but of big money capitals as well. Thus, one fine morning, there were on the one side free men, stripped of everything but their labor-power, and, on the other, to exploit this labor, the possessors of all acquired wealth. What happened? The Roman proletarians became, not wage workers, but an idle mob[8] more abject than those who were called "poor whites" in the southern United States; and alongside them there developed, not a capitalist, but a slave mode of production. Thus events that are strikingly analogous, but taking place in different historical milieu, lead to totally disparate results. By studying each of these developments separately, and then comparing them, one can easily discover the key to this phenomenon, but one will never arrive there with the master key of a historico-philosophical theory whose supreme virtue consists in being suprahistorical.

Notes

1. This is the concluding section of a letter Karl Marx wrote (but never sent) to the editors of *Otechestvennye Zapiski* (Fatherland Notes), a journal published in St. Petersburg. Marx composed the letter to explain his views on how Russia might develop, and to correct the interpretation of *Capital* given—prophetically, it turned out—by N. K. Mikhailovskii (1842-1904), a positivist philosopher and prominent theoretician of later-day populism. It has usually been assumed that the letter was written in November 1877 but recent research would assign it to 1878, i.e., after the collapse of hopes that Russian defeat in the war with Turkey would be followed by revolution (H. Wada, "Karl Marx and Revolutionary Russia," in T. Shanin, *Late Marx and the Russian Road* [to be published in 1983]). The letter is Marx's clearest statement of the scope and limits of

the historical analysis in chap. 24 of *Capital*, as well as his sternest warning against overgeneralizing that sketch of how capitalism emerged in Western Europe. Engels found the letter among Marx's papers. It was first published in Russian in 1884 in *Vestnik Narodnoi Voli* (Messenger of the People's Will) in Geneva. For the history of its publication, see Wada's article. Having decided to reprint this excerpt because of its clear significance for contemporary debate, we soon discovered a number of different and conflicting English translations—which, it became clear, had been made from two different texts: Marx's French original and Engels' German translation (which departs from Marx's wording on at least one substantive point). Subsequent translators, stylizing the text, have shifted its meaning still further.

Under these circumstances, it seemed best to make a fresh translation from the French. This was initiated and carried out by Rod Aya with the help of Annie Hlasny, Rosemary Mellor, Elfie Nunn, and Ton Zwaan. The few places where Engels' translation departs from Marx's original are footnoted below. For the original French text, published for the first time in 1902, see Karl Marx and Friedrich Engels, *Ausgewählte Briefe* (Berlin: Dietz, 1953), pp. 365-68.

2. The French reads "accumulation primitive" for "ursprüngliche Akkumulation," the title of chap. 24 of *Capital*, vol. 1 (1867). "Primary accumulation" seems more appropriate to the modern ear.

3. Engels rendered "revolution" as "Umwälzung" (upheaval), after Marx's wording of the original passage in *Capital*.

4. Engels gives "traditionellen Produktions—und Existenzmitteln" for "moyens de production et d'existence traditionnels."

5. Marx here cites *Capital*, French edition, p. 315. The wording of the German original is somewhat different, especially the last sentence: "Its history assumes different coloring in different countries and runs through the different phases in different sequences and in different historical epochs. Only in England, which we therefore take as an example, has it the classic form." *Das Kapital, Marx-Engels Werke* (Berlin: Dietz, 1962), chap. 23, p. 744. For the conceptual significance of the changes Marx introduces in the French edition of *Capital* see Wada, "Karl Marx and Revolutionary Russia."

6. Engels gives "Art kollektiver Produktion" (kind of collective production) for "mode de production collectif."

7. This is a literal rendering of the French adjective form of "philosophy of history." The German equivalent is "geschichtsphilosophisch."

8. In English in the original.

[10]
Dependency and Development in Latin America

Fernando Henrique Cardoso

The theory of imperialist capitalism, as is well known, has so far attained its most significant treatment in Lenin's works. This is not only because Lenin attempts to explain transformations of the capitalist economies that occurred during the last decade of the nineteenth century and the first decade of the twentieth, but is mainly because of the political and historical implications contained in his interpretations. In fact, the descriptive arguments of Lenin's theory of imperialism were borrowed from Hobson's analysis. Other writers had already presented evidence of the international expansion of the capitalist economies and nations. Nevertheless, Lenin, inspired by Marx's views, was able to bring together evidence to the effect that economic expansion is meaningless if we do not take into consideration the *political* and *historical* aspects with which economic factors are intimately related. From Lenin's perspective, imperialism is a new form of the capitalist mode of production. This new form cannot be considered a *different* mode of economic organization, insofar as capital accumulation based on private ownership of the means of production and exploitation of the labor force remain the basic features of the system. But its significance is that of a new *stage* of capitalism. The historical "momentum" was a new one, with all the political consequences of that type of transformation: within the dominant capitalist classes, new sectors tried to impose their interests and ideologies; the state, the army, and all basic social and political institutions were redefined in order to assure expansion abroad. At the same time new types of liberation and social struggles came onto the historical scene—the colonial liberation movements and the fight against "trade unionism," the latter a struggle against an initial form of working-class compromise with the bourgeoisie made possible by the exploitation of the colonial world.

From that broad picture of a new historical stage of capitalist development Lenin inferred new political tasks, tactics, and strategies for socialist revolution.

Lenin's Characterization of Imperialism

The main points of Lenin's characterization of imperialism that are essential to the present discussion can be summarized as follows:

(1) The capitalist economy in its "advanced stages" involves a concentration of capital and production (points that were well established by Marx in *Capital*) in such a way that the competitive market is replaced in its basic branches by a monopolistic one.

(2) This trend was historically accomplished through internal differentiation of capitalist functions, leading not only to the formation of a financial stratum among entrepreneurs but to the marked prominence of the banking system in the capitalist mode of production. Furthermore, the fusion of industrial capital with financial capital under the control of the latter turned out to be the decisive feature of the political and economic relations within capitalist classes, with all the practical consequences that such a system of relations has in terms of state organization, politics, and ideology.

(3) Capitalism thus reached its "ultimate stage of development" both internally and externally. Internally, control of the productive system by financiers turned the productive forces and the capital accumulation process toward the search for new possibilities for investment. The problem of "capital realization" became in this way an imperative necessity to permit the continuing of capitalist expansion. In addition there were internal limits that impeded the continuous reinvestment of new capital (impoverishment of the masses, a faster rate of capital growth than that of the internal market, and so on). *External outlets* had to be found to ensure the continuity of capitalist advance and accumulation.

(4) The increased and increasing speed of the development of productive forces under monopolistic control also pushed the advanced capitalist countries toward the political control of foreign lands. The search for control over *raw materials* is yet another reason why capitalism in its monopolistic stage becomes expansionist.

In short, Lenin's explanations of why advanced capitalist economies were impelled toward the control of backward lands was based on two main factors. One stressed movements of capital, the other outlined the productive process. Both were not only linked to each other but also related to the global transformation of the capitalist system that had led to the control of the productive system by financiers. It is not difficult to see that such modifications deeply affected state organizations and functions as well as the relationships among nations, since a main thrust of capitalist development in the stage of imperialism was toward the territorial division of the world among the leading capitalist countries. This process guaranteed capital flows from the overcapitalized economies to backward countries and assured provision of raw materials in return.

Imperialism and Dependent Economies

From that perspective, the consequence of imperialism with respect to dependent economies and nations (or colonies) was the integration of the latter into the international market. Inequality among nations and economies resulted from imperialism's development to the extent that import of raw materials and export of manufactured goods were the bases of the imperialist-colonial relationship. The reproduction and amplification of inequality between advanced economies and dependent economies developed as a by-product of the very process of capitalist growth.

Certainly, Lenin was aware of particular types of interconnections, as in Argentina and other economies dependent on Great Britain, where local bourgeoisies controlled sectors of the productive system creating more complex patterns of exploitation. The same was true with respect to the political aspects of dependence in those countries where the state tried to defend the national bourgeoisie against imperialist pressures.

Nevertheless, from the theoretical point of view, as a mode of exploitation, imperialism should tend to restrict the economic growth of backward countries to mineral and agricultural sectors in order to assure raw materials for the advanced capitalist nations in their drive for further industrialization. For the same reasons the indigenous labor force could be kept at low wage and salary levels. By that means the dominant central economies were assured of cheap raw material prices. Consequently, in colonized or dependent nations, internal markets did not have any special strategic significance.

Of course, in terms of "capital realization," selling products abroad had importance. But even so, the main imperialistic tie in terms of direct capital investment was oriented toward the concession of loans to the dependent state or to private local entrepreneurs. In both cases, however, political and financial guarantees were assured by the state or the administration of the receiver country.

In short, imperialist profit was based on unequal trade and financial exploitation. The latter could be measured by the increasing indebtedness of exploited economies to the central economies. The former was evidenced through the different types of products exchanged, i.e., raw materials for manufactured goods. This process of exploitation of the indigenous labor force thus insured an unevenness in both types of economies. Moreover, technological advances in the industrial sectors of central economies provided a high level of exploitation, increasing the relative surplus value extracted through a continuously advancing technology of production (leading in turn to unevenness of the rate of organic composition of capital), while in the dominated economies the direct over-exploitation of labor prevailed in the productive system.

Politically, this type of economic expansion thus reinforced colonial links, through wars, repression, and subjugation of peoples that previously were not only marginal to the international market, but were culturally independent and structurally did not have links with the Western world. Such were the African and Asian regions where nations, in spite of previous commercial-capitalist expansion, remained largely untouched in terms of their productive systems.

Latin America from the beginning was somewhat different in its links to the imperialist process. It is true that this process of colonialistic penetration obtained with respect to some countries (mainly the Caribbean nations). Yet throughout most of Latin America, the imperialistic upsurge occurred by way of a more complex process, through which Latin American countries kept their political independence, but slowly shifted from subordination to an earlier British influence to American predominance.

Ownership of the productive system was the site of the main differences. Some Latin American economies, even after imperialist predominance, were able to cope with the new situation by maintaining proprietorship of the local export economy in the hands of native bourgeoisies. Thus in some countries (such as Argentina, Brazil, Uruguay, Colombia, Chile), the export sector remained at least to some extent controlled by the local bourgeoisie and the links of dependence were based more on trade and financial relations than directly on the productive sectors. In some countries the internal financial system was itself mainly dominated by internal bankers, and financial dependence was based on international loans contracted, as noted above, by the state or under state guarantees.[1]

In spite of numerous political and economic variations, Lenin's basic picture remained valid; the internal market of Latin American countries grew in a limited way during the period of the first imperialist expansion; the industrial sector was not significantly expanded; external financial dependence grew enormously; raw materials including foodstuffs constituted the basis of export economies.

At the same time not only were the majority of Latin American countries unable to keep control of the export sector, but some of the countries that had previously retained dominance of raw materials or food production now lost that capacity (as in the Chilean mineral economy).

New Patterns of Capital Accumulation

In spite of the accuracy of Lenin's insights as measured against historical events during the first half of the century in many parts of the world, some important recent changes have deeply affected the pattern of relationship between imperialist and dependent nations. These changes demand a reappraisal of emergent structures and their main tendencies. Even if these modifications are not so deep as the shift that enabled Lenin to characterize a new stage of capitalism during the period of imperialist expansion, they are marked enough to warrant a major modification of the established analyses of capitalism and imperialism. Nevertheless, contemporary international capitalist expansion and control of dependent economics undoubtedly prove that this new pattern of economic relationships among nations remains imperialist. However, the main points of Lenin's characterization of imperialism and capitalism are no longer fully adequate to describe and explain the present forms of capital accumulation and external expansion.

With respect to changes that have occurred within the more advanced capitalist economies (chiefly the rise of monopoly capital and corporate enterprise) there are some consistent analyses. Baran and Sweezy's works, as well as those of Magdoff, Mandel, and O'Connor, come to mind. These offer a comprehensive body of descriptive and explanatory material showing the differences between capitalism now and during Lenin's life.

In spite of some recent criticism, Baran and Sweezy argued convincingly (and Sweezy's article, "The Resurgence of Financial Control: Fact or Fancy?"[2] helps to affirm that conviction) that corporations operate as quasi-self-sufficient units of decision and action vis-à-vis capital accumulation. Hence previous notions of banking control over industry need to be rethought. Similarly, the conglomerate form of present big corporations and the multinational scope of production and marketing adds considerable novelty to the capitalist form of production.[3]

These transformations (and we are only suggesting some of the principal ones which affect all processes of capitalist transformation) have led to important consequences that have been already analyzed by the authors noted, as well as others. These writers stress, for instance, the increasing secular growth of profit rates under administered prices in a monopoly system. Of course, this is a central point in Marxian theory and in Lenin's analysis. Yet now important modifications, such as those mentioned, alter the type of political response that the capitalist system is able to produce in order to cope with the challenging situations created by its expansion.

It is equally necessary to approach the problem of surplus realization with a fresh perspective. In this connection some authors have considered the strengthened ties between militarist expansion and the reinforcement of military control over society, through a war economy, as the basic means of capital realization. As a second argument, but a still important factor, state expenditures in welfare are emphasized as alternative outlets for capital accumulation.

Though the adequacy of this analysis may be questioned, Marxist authors have carried out a fairly comprehensive *economic* reinterpretation of the mode of functioning of monopoly capitalism. The same is not true, however, when one considers the *political* aspects of the problem and especially the *politicoeconomic* consequences of monopoly capitalism in dependent economies. Let us start with the last aspect of the question.

New Forms of Economic Dependency

Recent figures demonstrate (see Tables 1 and 2) that foreign investment in the new nations and in Latin America is moving rapidly away from oil, raw materials, and agriculture and in the direction of the industrial sectors. Even where the bulk of assets continues to remain in the traditional sectors of imperialist investment, the rate of expansion of the industrial sector is rapid. This is true not only for Latin America but also for Africa and Asia.

The point is not only that multinational corporations are investing in the industrial sectors of dominated economies, instead of in the traditional agricultural and mineral sectors. Beyond that, even the "traditional" sectors of dependent economies, they are operating in technically and organizationally advanced modes, sometimes accepting local participation in their enterprises. Of course, these transformations do not mean that previous types of imperialistic investment, i.e., in oil or metals, are disappearing, even in the case of the most industrialized dependent economies, i.e., Argentina, Brazil, and Mexico in Latin America. However, the dominant traits of imperialism in those countries, as the process of industrialization continues, cannot be adequately described and interpreted on the

Table 1
Growth of U.S. Direct Investment—1929 to 1968

	Investment (Billion $)				Rate of growth (percent)		Percent distribution		
	1929	1950	1960	1968	1950-60	1960-68	1950	1960	1968
All regions	7.5	11.8	31.9	64.8	10.4	9.3	100	100	100
Canada	2.0	3.6	11.2	19.5	12.0	7.2	31	36	30
Latin America	3.5	4.6	8.4	13.0	6.2	5.6	39	26	20
Europe	1.4	1.7	6.7	19.4	14.7	12.4	14	21	30
Other areas	0.6	1.9	5.6	12.9	11.4	11.0	16	17	20
Sectors							100	100	100
Manufacturing	1.8	3.8	11.1	26.4	11.3	11.5	32	35	41
Oil	1.1	3.4	10.8	18.8	12.3	7.2	29	34	29
Mining	1.2	1.1	3.0	5.4	10.6	7.6	9	9	8
Others	3.4	3.5	7.0	14.2	7.2	9.3	30	22	22

Source: *Survey of Current Business*, and in F. Fajnzylber, *Estrategia Industrial y Empresas Internacionales* (Rio: United Nations, ECLA, November 1971).

basis of frames of reference that posit the exchange of raw material for industrialized goods as the main feature of trade, and suppose virtually complete external ownership of the dependent economies' means of production.

Even the mineral sector (such as manganese in Brazil, copper in Chile during Frei's government, or petrochemicals in various countries) is now being submitted to new patterns of economic ownership. The distinguishing feature of these new forms is the joint venture enterprise, comprising local state capital, private national capital, and monopoly international investment (under foreign control in the last analysis).

As a consequence, in some dependent economies—among these, the so-called developing countries of Latin America—foreign investment no longer remains a simple zero-sum game of exploitation as was the pattern in classical imperialism. Strictly speaking—if we consider the purely economic indicators—it is not difficult to show that *development* and *monopoly penetration* in the industrial sectors of dependent economies are not incompatible. The idea that there occurs a kind of development of underdevelopment, apart from the play on words, is not helpful. In fact, *dependency, monopoly capitalism*, and *development* are not contradictory terms: there occurs a kind of *dependent capitalist development* in the sectors of the Third World integrated into the new forms of monopolistic expansion.

As a result, in countries like Argentina, Brazil, Mexico, South Africa, India, and some others, there is an internal structural frag-

Table 2
U.S. Direct Investment in Manufacturing as a Percent of Total

Years	Total for Latin America	Argentina	Brazil	Mexico	Other countries
1929	7	25	24	1	4
1940	8	20	29	3	3
1946	13	39	39	21	6
1950	18	45	44	32	7
1952	21	50	51	43	1
1955	22	51	51	45	7
1956	22	51	50	46	8
1959	17	43	53	47	7
1960	19	45	54	49	8
1961	20	43	54	50	7
1962	22	51	56	51	8
1963	24	55	59	55	8
1964	26	57	67	59	9
1965	29	62	67	64	11
1966	31	63	68	64	12
1967	32	63	67	66	13
1968	34	64	69	68	14

Source: *Survey of Current Business*, several issues; *U.S. Investments in Latin America* in F. Fajnzylber, *Estrategia Industrial*, p. 204.

mentation, connecting the most "advanced" parts of their economies to the international capitalist system. Separate although subordinated to these advanced sectors, the backward economic and social sectors of the dependent countries then play the role of "internal colonies." The gap between both will probably increase, creating a new type of dualism, quite different from the imaginary one sustained by some non-Marxist authors. The new structural "duality" corresponds to a kind of internal differentiation of the same unity. It results directly, of course, from capitalist expansion and is functional to that expansion, insofar as it helps to keep wages at a low level and diminishes political pressures inside the "modern" sector, since the social and economic position of those who belong to the latter is always better in comparative terms.

If this is true, to what extent is it possible to sustain the idea of *development* in tandem with dependence? The answer cannot be immediate. First of all I am suggesting that the present trend of imperialist investment allows some degree of local participation in the process of economic production. Let us indicate a crucial feature in which present and past forms of capitalism differ. During the previous type of imperialism, the market for goods produced in dependent economies by foreign enterprise was mostly, if not fully, the market of the advanced economies: oil, copper, coffee, iron bauxite, manganese, etc., were produced to be sold and consumed in the advanced capitalist countries. This explains why the internal market of dependent economies was irrelevant for the imperialist economies, excepting the modest portion of import goods consumed by the upper class in the dominated society.

Today for General Motors or Volkswagen, or General Electric, or Sears Roebuck, the Latin American market, if not the particular market in each country where those corporations are producing in Latin America, is the immediate goal in terms of profit. So, at least to some extent, a certain type of foreign investment needs some kind of internal prosperity. There are and there will be some parts of dependent societies tied to the corporate system, internally and abroad, through shared interests.

On the other hand, and in spite of internal economic development, countries tied to international capitalism by that type of linkage remain economically dependent, insofar as the production of the means of production (technology) are concentrated in advanced capitalist economies (mainly in the United States).

In terms of the Marxist scheme of capital reproduction, this means that sector I (the production of means of production)—the strategic part of the reproductive scheme—is virtually nonexistent in dependent economies. Thus, from a broad perspective, the realization of capital accumulation *demands* a productive complementarity which does not exist within the country. In Lenin's interpretation the imperialist economies needed external expansion for the realization of capital accumulation. Conversely, within the dependent economies capital returns to the metropole in order to complete the cycle of capitalist reproduction. That is the reason why "technology" is so important. Its "material" aspect is less impressive than its significance as a form of maintenance of control and as a necessary step in the process of capital accumulation. Through technological advantage, corporations make secure their key roles in the global system of capital accumulation. Some degree of local prosperity is possible insofar as consumption goods locally produced by foreign investments can induce some dynamic effects in the dependent economies. But at the same time, the global process of capitalist development determines an interconnection between the sector of production of consumption goods and the capital goods sector, reproducing in this way the links of dependency.

One of the main factors which explained imperialist expansion in Lenin's theory was the search for capitalist investment. Now since foreign capital goes to the industrial sector of dependent economies in search of external markets, some considerable changes have occurred. First, in comparison with expanding assets of foreign corporations, the net amount of foreign capital actually invested in the dependent economies is decreasing: local savings and the reinvestment of profits realized in local markets provide resources for the growth of foreign assets with limited external flow of new capital. This is intimately related to the previously discussed process of expansion of the local market and it is also related to the mounting of "joint ventures" linking local capitalists and foreign enterprise (see Table 3).

Secondly, but no less important, statistics demonstrate that dependent economies during the period of monopolistic imperialist expansion are *exporting* capital to the dominant economies.

As a reaction against that process, some dependent countries have tried to limit exportable profits. Nevertheless, international corporations had the foresight to sense that the principal way to send returns abroad is through the payment of licenses, patents, royalties, and related items. These institutional devices, together with the increasing indebtedness of the exploited nations vis-à-vis international agencies and banks (in fact controlled by the big imperialist countries), have altered the main forms of exploitation.

It is not the purpose of this presentation to discuss all the consequences of this for a monopoly capitalist economy. However, some repercussions of the new pattern of imperialism on the United States and other central economies are obvious. If a real problem of capital realization exists under monopoly capitalism, the new form of dependency will increase the necessity to find new fields of application for the capital accumulated in the metropolitan economies. Witness the push toward more "technical obsolescence" administered by corporations. Military expenditures are another means of finding new outlets for capital.

Nevertheless, I am not considering the whole picture. In fact, some of these conclusions might change if the capital flows and trade interrelations among advanced capitalist economies were taken into consideration. Thus the preceding remarks are presented with the single aim of stressing that the present trend of capital export from the underdeveloped countries to the imperialist ones leads to a redefinition of the function of foreign expansion for capital realization.

The idea that the growth of capitalism depends on Third World exploitation requires some further elaboration. In fact, the main trends of the last decade show that Latin American participation in both the expansion of international trade and investment is decreasing. If we accept the distinction between two sectors of inter-

Table 3
Sources of Investment
(in percents)

Areas and sectors	1957/1959 Source of investment			1960/1962 Source of investment			1963/1965 Source of investment			1957/1965 Source of investment		
	IF	LF	USF	IF	LF	USF	IF	LF	USF	IF	LF	USF
All areas												
Total	0.52	0.22	0.26	0.57	0.24	0.19	0.48	0.32	0.20	0.52	0.27	0.21
Mining	0.46	0.13	0.41	0.63	0.20	0.17	0.68	0.26	0.06	0.06	0.20	0.20
Oil	0.48	0.23	0.29	0.61	0.15	0.24	0.43	0.29	0.28	0.50	0.23	0.27
Manufg.	0.57	0.24	0.19	0.53	0.30	0.17	0.49	0.35	0.16	0.51	0.32	0.17
Canada												
Total	0.57	1.13	0.30	0.70	0.12	0.18	0.64	0.22	0.14	0.64	0.17	0.19
Mining	0.40	0.20	0.40	0.52	0.14	0.34	0.75	0.23	0.02	0.58	0.19	0.23
Oil	0.42	0.24	0.34	0.66	0.11	0.23	0.58	0.18	0.24	0.55	0.18	0.27
Manufg.	0.77	0.01	0.22	0.81	0.11	0.08	0.63	0.24	0.13	0.71	0.15	0.14
Latin America												
Total	0.50	0.17	0.33	0.71	0.23	0.06	0.60	0.31	0.09	0.59	0.24	0.17
Mining	0.46	0.01	0.43	1.08	0.26	−0.34	1.04	0.13	−0.17	0.78	0.14	0.08
Oil	0.57	0.09	0.34	1.06	0.01	0.07	0.96	0.14	−0.10	0.79	0.08	0.13
Manufg.	0.36	0.40	0.24	0.38	0.40	0.22	0.38	0.40	0.22	0.38	0.40	0.22

Europe

Total	0.44	0.30	0.19	0.42	0.30	0.28	0.40	0.38	0.22	0.41	0.35	0.24
Mining	—	−0.50	0.50	1.25	−0.50	0.25	0.32	0.23	0.45	0.44	0.04	0.52
Oil	0.30	0.44	0.26	0.33	0.18	0.49	0.22	0.40	0.38	0.27	0.35	0.38
Manufg.	0.52	0.33	0.15	0.46	0.35	0.19	0.47	0.37	0.16	0.48	0.36	0.16

Other Areas

Total	0.58	0.23	0.19	0.51	0.29	0.20	0.38	0.35	0.27	0.46	0.23	0.23
Mining	0.82	−0.18	0.36	0.48	0.30	0.22	0.29	0.41	0.30	0.40	0.31	0.29
Oil	0.57	0.23	0.20	0.55	0.24	0.21	0.36	0.28	0.36	0.47	0.26	0.27
Manufg.	0.56	0.29	0.15	0.43	0.39	0.18	0.42	0.42	0.16	0.44	0.39	0.17

IF = Internal Funds (reinvestment of profits and depreciation funds)
LF = Local Funds., or funds coming from third countries
USF = Funds coming from the United States

Source: Survey of Current Business, several issues; ECLA analysis , in F. Fajnzylber, Estrategia Industrial, p. 65

national trade—the center and the periphery—one finds that the trade rate of growth was 7.9 percent per year in the central economies and 4.8 percent in the peripheral ones. As a consequence, exports of the peripheral economies which reached a peak in 1948 (32 percent of the international trade) decreased to 26 percent in 1958 and to 21 percent in 1968 (below the 28 percent of the prewar period). In the Latin American case this participation decreased from 12 percent in 1948 to 6 percent in 1968.[4] The same is happening with respect to the importance that the periphery has for U.S. investments. The periphery absorbed 55 percent of the total U.S. investment in 1950 and only 40 percent in 1968. Latin American participation in this process fell in the same period from 39 percent to 20 percent.

Of course, these data do not show the increase of "loans and aid" which—as was stressed before—has been of increasing importance in economic imperialism. However, the fact that the interrelations among the most advanced economies are growing cannot be utilized as an argument to infer the "end of imperialism." On the contrary, the more appropriate inference is that the relations between advanced capitalist countries and dependent nations lead rather to a "marginalization" of the latter within the global system of economic development (as Anibal Pinto has outlined).[5]

Some Political Consequences

The new forms of dependency will undoubtedly give rise to novel political and social adaptations and reactions inside the dependent countries. If my analysis is correct, the above-mentioned process of fragmentation of interests will probably lead to an internal differentiation that in very schematic terms can be suggested as follows. Part of the "national bourgeoisie," (the principal one in terms of economic power—agrarian, commercial, industrial, or financial) is the direct beneficiary, as a junior partner, of the foreign interest. I refer not only to the direct associates, but also to economic groups that benefit from the eventual atmosphere of prosperity derived from dependent development (as is easily demonstrated in Brazil or Mexico). The process goes further and not only part of the "middle class" (intellectuals, state bureaucracies, armies, etc.) is involved in the new system, but even part of the working class. Those employed by the "internationalized" sector structurally belong to it.

Of course, structural dependence does not mean immediate political co-optation. Effective political integration of groups and persons depends on the political processes, movements, goals, and alternatives that they face.

Nevertheless, as the process of internationalization of dependent nations progresses, it becomes difficult to perceive the political process in terms of a struggle between the nation and the antination, the latter conceived as the foreign power of imperialism. The antination will be inside the "nation"—so to speak, among the local people in different social strata. Furthermore, to perceive that, in these terms, the nation is an occupied one is not an easy process: there are very few "others" in cultural and national terms physically representing the presence of "the enemy."

I do not wish to give the impression that I conceive the political process in a mechanistic way. Consequently, my intention is not to "derive" some political consequences from a structural economic analysis. Rather, the point is that most socialist interpretations of the Latin American political situation not only run in that direction but also assume the wrong structural point of departure.

Some more general remarks can be summarized thus:

(1) Analysis which is based on the naive assumption that imperialism unifies the interests and reactions of dominated nations is a clear oversimplification of what is really occurring. It does not take into consideration the internal fragmentation of these countries and the attraction that development exerts in different social strata, and not only on the upper classes.

(2) The term "development of underdevelopment" (in Andre Gunder Frank) summarizes another mistake. In fact, the assumption of a structural "lack of dynamism" in dependent economies because of imperialism misinterprets the actual forms of economic imperialism and presents an imprecise political understanding of the situation. It is necessary to understand that in specific situations it is possible to expect *development* and *dependency*.

It would be wrong to generalize these processes to the entire Third World. They only occur when corporations reorganize the international division of labor and include parts of dependent economies in their plans of productive investment.

Thus the majority of the Third World is not necessarily involved in this specific structural situation. To assume the contrary will lead to political mistakes equivalent to those derived from, for instance, Debray's analysis of Latin America. Debray once accepted the view that imperialism homogenized all Latin American countries (with one or two exceptions) and assumed a frame of reference which stressed the old-fashioned type of imperialist exploitation with its attendant reinforcement of oligarchic and landlord-based types of dominance.

Now, I am assuming that there are different forms of dependency in Latin America and that in some of them, development produces a shift in internal power, displacing the old oligarchical power groups and reinforcing more "modern" types of political control. In that sense, the present dictatorships in Latin America, even when militarily based, do not express, by virtue of pure structural constraints, a traditional and "antidevelopmentalist" (I mean antimodern capitalism) form of domination.

It is hardly necessary to repeat that from the left's point of view there are strong arguments to maintain its denunciation of both new forms of imperialism or dependency and political authoritarianism. But clearly, new political analyses are needed to explain the bureaucratic-technocratic form of authoritarian state which serves the interests of the internationalized bourgeoisie and their allies.

In this context, and in order to avoid a mechanistic approach, a correct orientation of the struggles against capitalist imperialism demands special attention to cultural problems and the different forms of alienation.

If the capitalist pattern of development in industrialized dependent countries pushes toward internal fragmentation and inequalities, values related to national integrity and social participation might be transformed into instruments of political struggle. To permit the state and bourgeois groups to command the banner of nationalism—conceived not only in terms of sovereignty but also of internal cohesion and progressive social integration—would be a mistake with deep consequences. I am not supporting the idea that the strategic (or revolutionary) side of dependent industrialized societies is the "marginalized sector." But denunciation of marginalization as a consequence of capitalist growth, and the organization of unstructured masses, are indispensable tasks of analysis and practical politics.

For this reason it is not very realistic to expect the national bourgeoisie to lead resistance against external penetration. Consequently, denunciation of the dependency perspective cannot rest on values associated with bourgeois nationalism. National integrity as cited above means primarily popular integration in the nation and the need to struggle against the particular form of development promoted by the large corporations.

In the same way that trade unionism may become a danger for workers in advanced capitalist societies, development is a real ideological pole of attraction for middle class *and workers'* sectors in Latin American countries. The answer to that attractive effect cannot be a purely ideological denial of economic progress, when it occurs. A reply must be based on values and political objectives that enlarge the awareness of the masses with respect to social inequalities and national dependency.

Notes

1. See F. H. Cardoso and E. Faletto, *Dependencia y Desarrollo en America Latina* (Mexico: 1972).
2. See P. Sweezy, "The Resurgence of Financial Control: Fact or Fancy?" *Socialist Revolution* 2, no. 8 (March-April 1972): 157-92.
3. See H. Magdoff and P. Sweezy, "Notes on the Multinational Corporation," K. H. Fann and D. C. Hodges, eds. *Readings in U.S. Imperialism* (Boston: 1972), pp. 93-116.
4. These data and analyses can be found in Anibal Pinto and Jan Knakel's interesting paper "El sistema centro-periferia 20 años después," ECLA, 3rd version, November 11, 1971, pp. 14 and following.
5. A comprehensive and pioneer analysis on new forms of imperialism can be found in J. O'Connor, "The Meaning of Economic Imperialism," Radical Education Project, Detroit. See also H. Alavi, "Imperialism, Old and New," *Socialist Register 1964* (London: Merlin Press, 1964).

[11]
The Multinational Corporation and the Law of Uneven Development

Stephen Hymer

We have been asked to look into the future toward the year 2000. This essay attempts to do so in terms of two laws of economic development: the Law of Increasing Firm Size and the Law of Uneven Development.[1]

Since the beginning of the Industrial Revolution there has been a tendency for the representative firm to increase in size from the *workshop* to the *factory* to the *national corporation* to the *multidivisional corporation* and now to the *multinational corporation*. This growth has been qualitative as well as quantitative. With each step, the business enterprise acquired a more complex administrative structure to coordinate its activities and a larger brain to plan for its survival and growth. The first part of this essay traces the evolution of the corporation stressing the development of a hierarchical system of authority and control.

The remainder of the essay is concerned with extrapolating the trends in business enterprise (the microcosm) and relating them to the evolution of the international economy (the macrocosm). Until recently, most multinational corporations have come from the United States, where private business enterprise has reached its largest size and most highly developed forms. Now European corporations, as a by-product of increased size, and as a reaction to the American invasion of Europe, are also shifting attention from national to global production and beginning to "see the world as their oyster."[2] *If* present trends continue, multinationalization is likely to increase greatly in the next decade as giants from both sides of the Atlantic (though still mainly from the United States) strive to penetrate each other's markets and to establish bases in underdeveloped countries, where there are few indigenous concentrations of capital sufficiently large to operate on a world scale. This rivalry may be intense at first but will probably abate through time and turn into collusion as firms approach some kind of oligopolistic equilibrium. A new structure of international industrial organization and a new international division of labor will have been born.[3]

What will be the effect of this latest stage in the evolution of business enterprise on the Law of Uneven Development, i.e., the tendency of the system to produce poverty as well as wealth, underdevelopment as well as development? The second part of this essay suggests that a regime of North Atlantic multinational corporations would tend to produce a hierarchical division of labor between geographical regions corresponding to the vertical division of labor within the firm. It would tend to centralize high-level decision-making occupations in a few key cities in the advanced countries, surrounded by a number of regional subcapitals, and confine the rest of the world to lower levels of activity and income, i.e., to the status of towns and villages in a new imperial system. Income, status, authority, and consumption patterns would radiate out from the centers along a declining curve, and the existing pattern of inequality and dependency would be perpetuated. The pattern would be complex, just as the structure of the corporation is complex, but the basic relationship between different countries would be one of superior and subordinate, head office and branch plant.

How far will this tendency of corporations to create a world in their own image proceed?[. . .]. Right now, we seem to be in the midst of a major revolution in international relationships as modern science establishes the technological basis for a major advance in the conquest of the material world and the beginnings of truly cosmopolitan production.[4] Multinational corporations are in the vanguard of this revolution because of their great financial and administrative strength and their close contact with the new technology. Governments (outside the military) are far behind, because of their narrower horizons and perspectives, as are labor organizations and most nonbusiness institutions and associations. (As John Powers, president of Charles Pfizer Corporation, has put it, "Practice is ahead of theory and policy.") Therefore, in the first round, multinational corporations are likely to have a certain degree of success in organizing markets, decision making, and the spread of information in their own interest. However, their very success will create tensions and conflicts which will lead to further development. The last part of this essay discusses some of the contradictions that are likely to emerge as the multinational corporate system overextends itself. These contradictions provide certain openings for action. Whether or not they can or will be used in the next round to move toward superior forms of international organization requires an analysis of a wide range of political factors outside the scope of this essay.

The Evolution of the Multinational Corporation

The Marshallian Firm and the Market Economy

What is the nature of the "beast"? It is called many names: Direct Investment, International Business, the International Firm, the International Corporate Group, the Multinational Firm, the Multinational Enterprise, the Multinational Corporation,[...] or, as the French Foreign Minister called them, "The U.S. corporate monsters" (Michel Debré quoted in *Fortune* [August 1965], p. 126).

Giant organizations are nothing new in international trade. They were a characteristic form of the mercantilist period when large joint-stock companies, e.g., The Hudson's Bay Company, The Royal African Company, The East India Company, to name the major English merchant firms, organized long-distance trade with America, Africa, and Asia. But neither these firms, nor the large mining and plantation enterprises in the production sector, were the forerunners of the multinational corporation. They were like dinosaurs, large in bulk, but small in brain, feeding on the lush vegetation of the new worlds.

The activities of these international merchants, planters, and miners laid the groundwork for the Industrial Revolution by concentrating capital in the metropolitan center, but the driving force came from the small-scale capitalist enterprises in manufacturing, operating at first in the interstices of the feudalist economic structure, but gradually emerging into the open and finally gaining predominance. It is in the small workshops, organized by the newly emerging capitalist class, that the forerunners of the modern corporation are to be found.

The strength of this new form of business enterprise lay in its power and ability to reap the benefits of cooperation and division of labor. Without the capitalist, economic activity was individualistic, small-scale, scattered, and unproductive. But a man with capital, i.e., with sufficient funds to buy raw materials and advance wages, could gather a number of people into a single shop and obtain as his reward the increased productivity that resulted from social production. The reinvestment of these profits led to a steady increase in the size of capital, making further division of labor possible and creating an opportunity for using machinery in production. A phenomenal increase in productivity and production resulted from this process, and entirely new dimensions of human existence were opened. The growth of capital revolutionized the entire world and, figuratively speaking, even battered down the Great Wall of China.

The hallmarks of the new system were *the market* and *the factory*, representing the two different methods of coordinating the division of labor. In the factory, entrepreneurs consciously plan and organize cooperation, and the relationships are hierarchical and authoritarian; in the market, coordination is achieved through a decentralized, unconscious, competitive process.[5]

To understand the significance of this distinction, the new system should be compared to the structure it replaced. In the precapitalist system of production, the division of labor was hierarchically structured at the *macro* level, i.e., for society as a whole, but unconsciously structured at the *micro* level, i.e., the actual process of production. Society as a whole was partitioned into various castes, classes, and guilds, on a rigid and authoritarian basis so that political and social stability could be maintained and adequate numbers assured for each industry and occupation. Within each sphere of production, however, individuals by and large were independent and their activities only loosely coordinated, if at all. In essence, a guild was composed of a large number of similar individuals, each performing the same task in roughly the same way with little cooperation or division of labor. This type of organization could produce high standards of quality and workmanship but was limited quantitatively to low levels of output per head.

The capitalist system of production turned this structure on its head. The macro system became unconsciously structured, while the micro system became hierarchically structured. The market emerged as a self-regulating coordinator of business units as restrictions on capital markets and labor mobility were removed. (Of course the state remained above the market as a conscious coordinator to maintain the system and ensure the growth of capital.) At the micro level, that is, the level of production, labor was gathered under the authority of the entrepreneur capitalist.

Marshall, like Marx, stressed that the internal division of labor within the factory, between those who planned and those who worked (between "undertakers" and laborers), was the "chief fact in the form of modern civilization, the 'kernel' of the modern economic problem." Marx, however, stressed the authoritarian and unequal nature of this relationship based on the coercive power of property and its antisocial characteristics. He focused on the irony that concentration of wealth in the hands of a few and its ruthless use were necessary historically to demonstrate the value of cooperation and the social nature of production.

Marshall, in trying to answer Marx, argued for the voluntary cooperative nature of the relationship between capital and labor. In his view, the market reconciled individual freedom and collective production. He argued that those on top achieved their position because of their superior organizational ability, and that their relation to the workers below them was essentially harmonious and not exploitative. "Undertakers" were not captains of industry because they had capital; they could obtain capital because they had the ability to be captains of industry. They retained their authority by merit, not by coercion; for according to Marshall, natural selection, operating through the market, constantly destroyed inferior organizers and gave everyone who had the ability—including workers—a chance to rise to managerial positions. Capitalists earned more than workers because they contributed more, while the system as a whole provided all its members, and especially the workers, with improved standards of living and an ever expanding field of choice of consumption.[6]

The Corporate Economy

The evolution of business enterprise from the small workshop (Adam Smith's pin factory) to the Marshallian family firm represented only the first step in the development of business organization. As total capital accumulated, the size of the individual concentrations composing it increased continuously, and the vertical division of labor grew accordingly.

It is best to study the evolution of the corporate firm in the U.S. environment, where it has reached its highest stage.[7] In the 1870s, the U.S. industrial structure consisted largely of Marshallian type, single-function firms, scattered over the country. Business firms were typically tightly controlled by a single entrepreneur or small family group who, as it were, saw everything, knew everything and decided everything. By the early twentieth century, the rapid growth of the economy and the great merger movement had consolidated many small enterprises into large national corporations engaged in many functions over many regions. To meet this new strategy of continent-wide, vertically integrated production and marketing, a new administrative structure evolved. The family firm, tightly controlled by a few men in close touch with all its aspects, gave way to the administrative pyramid of the corporation. Capital acquired new powers and new horizons. The domain of conscious coordination widened and that of market-directed division of labor contracted.

According to A. D. Chandler, the railroad, which played so important a role in creating the national market, also offered a model for new forms of business organization. The need to administer geographically dispersed operations led railway companies to create an administrative structure which distinguished field offices from head offices. The field offices managed local operations; the head office supervised the field offices. According to Chandler and Redlich, this distinction is important because "it implies that the executive responsible for a firm's affairs had for the first time, to supervise the work of other executives."[8]

This first step toward increased vertical division of labor within the management function was quickly copied by the recently formed national corporations which faced the same problems of coordinating widely scattered plants. Business developed an organ system of administration, and the modern corporation was born. The functions of business administration were subdivided into *departments* (organs)—finance, personnel, purchasing, engineering, and sales—to deal with capital, labor, purchasing, manufacturing, etc. This horizontal division of labor opened up new possibilities for rationalizing production and for incorporating the advances of physical and social sciences into economic activity on a systematic basis. At the same time a "brain and nervous" system, i.e., a vertical system of control, had to be devised to connect and coordinate departments. This was a major advance in decision-making capabilities. It meant that a special group, the head office, was created whose particular function was to coordinate, appraise, and plan for the survival and growth of the organism as a whole. The organization became conscious of itself as organization and gained a certain measure of control over its own evolution and development.

The corporation soon underwent further evolution. To understand this next step we must briefly discuss the development of the United States market. At the risk of great oversimplification, we might say that by the first decade of the twentieth century, the problem of production had essentially been solved. By the end of the nineteenth century, scientists and engineers had developed most of the inventions needed for mass producing at a low cost nearly all the main items of basic consumption. In the language of systems analysis, the problem became one of putting together the available components in an organized fashion. The national corporation provided *one* organizational solution, and by the 1920s it had demonstrated its great power to increase material production.

The question was which direction growth would take. One possibility was to expand mass production systems very widely and to make basic consumer goods available on a broad basis throughout the world. The other possibility was to concentrate on continuous innovation for a small number of people and on the introduction of new consumption goods even before the old ones had been fully spread. The latter course was in fact chosen, and we now have the paradox that 500 million people can receive a live TV broadcast from the moon while there is still a shortage of telephones in many advanced countries, to say nothing of the fact that so many people suffer from inadequate food and lack of simple medical help.

This path was associated with a choice of capital-deepening instead of capital-widening in the productive sector of the economy. As capital accumulated, business had to choose the degree to which it would expand labor proportionately to the growth of capital or, conversely, the degree to which they would substitute capital for labor. At one extreme, business could have kept the capital-labor ratio constant and accumulated labor at the same rate they accumulated capital. This horizontal accumulation would soon have exhausted the labor force of any particular country and then either capital would have had to migrate to foreign countries or labor would have had to move into the industrial centers. Under this system, earnings per employed worker would have remained steady and the composition of output would have tended to remain constant as similar basic goods were produced on a wider and wider basis.

However, this path was not chosen, and instead capital per worker was raised, the rate of expansion of the industrial labor force was slowed down, and a dualism was created between a small, high-wage, high-productivity sector in advanced countries, and a large, low-wage, low-productivity sector in the less advanced.[9]

The uneven growth of per capita income implied unbalanced growth and the need on the part of business to adapt to a constantly changing composition of output. Firms in the producers' goods sectors had continuously to innovate labor-saving machinery because the capital-output ratio was increasing steadily. In the consumption goods sector, firms had continuously to introduce new products since, according to Engel's Law, people do not generally consume proportionately more of the same things as they get richer, but rather reallocate their consumption away from old goods and toward new goods. This nonproportional growth of demand implied that goods would tend to go through a life-cycle, growing rapidly when they were first introduced and more slowly later. If a particular firm were tied to only one product, its growth rate would follow this same life-cycle pattern and would eventually slow down and perhaps even come to a halt. If the corporation was to grow steadily at a rapid rate, it had continuously to introduce new products.

Thus, product development and marketing replaced production as a dominant problem of business enterprise. To meet the challenge of a constantly changing market, business enterprise evolved the multidivisional structure. The new form was originated by General Motors and DuPont shortly after World War I, followed by a few others during the 1920s and 1930s, and was widely adopted by most of the giant U.S. corporations in the great boom following World War II. As with the previous stages, evolution involved a process of both differentiation and integration. Corporations were decentralized into several *divisions*, each concerned with one product line and organized with its own head office. At a higher level, a general *office* was created to coordinate the division and to plan for the enterprise as a whole.

The new corporate form has great flexibility. Because of its decentralized structure, a multidivisional corporation can enter a new market by adding a new division, while leaving the old divisions undisturbed. (And to a lesser extent it can leave the market by dropping a division without disturbing the rest of its structure.) It can also create competing product-lines in the same industry, thus increasing its market share while maintaining the illusion of competition. Most important of all, because it has a cortex specializing in strategy, it can plan on a much wider scale than before and allocate capital with more precision.

The modern corporation is a far cry from the small workshop or even from the Marshallian firm. The Marshallian capitalist ruled his factory from an office on the second floor. At the turn of the century, the president of a large national corporation was lodged in a higher building, perhaps on the seventh floor, with greater perspective and power. In today's giant corporation, managers rule from the top of skyscrapers; on a clear day, they can almost see the world.

U.S. corporations began to move to foreign countries almost as soon as they had completed their continent-wide integration. For one thing, their new administrative structure and great financial strength gave them the power to go abroad. In becoming national firms, U.S. corporations learned how to become international. Also, their large size and oligopolistic position gave them an incentive. Direct investment became a new weapon in their arsenal of oligopolistic rivalry. Instead of joining a cartel (prohibited under U.S. law), they invested in foreign customers, suppliers, and competitors. For example, some firms found they were oligopolistic buyers of raw materials produced in foreign countries and feared a monopolization of the sources of supply. By investing directly in foreign producing enterprises, they could gain the security implicit in control over their raw material requirements. Other firms invested abroad to control marketing outlets and thus maximize quasirents on their technological discoveries and differentiated products. Some went abroad simply to forestall competition.[10]

The first wave of U.S. direct foreign capital investment occurred around the turn of the century followed by a second wave during the 1920s. The outward migration slowed down during the Depression but resumed after World War II and soon accelerated rapidly. Between 1950 and 1969, direct foreign investment by U.S. firms expanded at a rate of about 10 percent per annum. At this rate it would double in less than ten years, and even at a much slower rate of growth, foreign operations will reach enormous proportions over the next thirty years.[11]

Several important factors account for this rush of foreign investment in the 1950s and the 1960s. First, the large size of the U.S. corporations and their new multidivisional structure gave them wider horizons and a global outlook. Secondly, technological developments in communications created a new awareness of the global challenge and threatened established institutions by opening up new sources of competition. For reasons noted above, business enterprises were among the first to recognize the potentialities and dangers of the new environment and to take active steps to cope with it.

A third factor in the outward migration of U.S. capital was the rapid growth of Europe and Japan. This, combined with the slow growth of the United States economy in the 1950s, altered world market shares as firms confined to the U.S. market found themselves falling behind in the competitive race and losing ground to European and Japanese firms, which were growing rapidly because of the expansion of their markets. Thus, in the late 1950s, United States corporations faced a serious "non-American" challenge. Their answer was an outward thrust to establish sales production and bases in foreign territories. This strategy was possible in Europe, since government there provided an open door for United States investment, but was blocked in Japan, where the government adopted a highly restrictive policy. To a large extent, United States business was thus able to redress the imbalances caused by the Common Market, but Japan remained a source of tension to oligopoly equilibrium.

What about the future? The present trend indicates further multinationalization of all giant firms, European as well as American. In the first place, European firms, partly as a reaction to the United States penetration of their markets, and partly as a natural result of their own growth, have begun to invest abroad on an expanded scale and will probably continue to do so in the future, and even enter into the United States market. This process is already well under way and may be expected to accelerate as time goes on. The reaction of United States business will most likely be to meet foreign investment at home with more foreign investment abroad. They, too, will scramble for market positions in underdeveloped countries and attempt to get an even larger share of the European market, as a reaction to European investment in the United States. Since they are large and powerful, they will on balance succeed in maintaining their relative standing in the world as a whole—as their losses in some markets are offset by gains in others.

A period of rivalry will prevail until a new equilibrium between giant U.S. firms and giant European and Japanese firms is reached, based on a strategy of multinational operations and cross-penetration. We turn now to the implications of this pattern of industrial organization for international trade and the law of uneven development.

Uneven Development

Suppose giant multinational corporations (say 300 from the United States and 200 from Europe and Japan) succeed in establishing themselves as the dominant form of international enterprise and come to control a significant share of industry (especially modern industry) in each country. The world economy will resemble more and more the United States economy, where each of the large corporations tends to spread over the entire continent, and to penetrate almost every nook and cranny. What would be the effect of a world industrial organization of this type on international specialization, exchange, and income distribution? The purpose of this section is to analyze the spatial dimension of the corporate hierarchy.

A useful starting point is Chandler and Redlich's scheme for analyzing the evolution of corporate structure. They distinguish "three levels of business administration, three horizons, three levels of task, and three levels of decision making...and three levels of policies." Level III, the lowest level, is concerned with managing the day-to-day operations of the enterprise, that is, with keeping it going within the established framework. Level II, which first made its appearance with the separation of head office from field office, is responsible for coordinating the managers at Level III. The functions of Level I—top management—are goal-determination and planning. This level sets the framework in which the lower levels operate. In the Marshallian firm, all three levels are embodied in the single enterpreneur or undertaker. In the national corporation, a partial differentiation is made in which the top two levels are separated from the bottom one. In the multidivisional corporation, the differentiation is far more complete. Level I is completely split off from Level II and concentrated in a general office whose specific function is to plan strategy rather than tactics.

The development of business enterprise can therefore be viewed as a process of centralizing and perfecting the process of capital accumulation. The Marshallian entrepreneur was a jack-of-all-trades. In the modern multidivisional corporation, a powerful general office consciously plans and organizes the growth of corporate capital. It is here that the key men who actually allocate the corporation's available resources (rather than act within the means allocated to them, as is true for the managers at lower levels) are located. Their power comes from their ultimate control over *men* and *money* and although one should not overestimate the ability to control a far-flung empire, neither should one underestimate it.

> The senior men could take action because they controlled the selection of executive personnel and because, through budgeting, they allocated the funds to the operating divisions. In the way they allocated their resources—capital and personnel—and in the promotion, transferral and retirement of operating executives, they determined the framework in which the operating units worked and thus put into effect their concept of the long term goals and objectives of the enterprise. . . . Ultimate authority in business enterprise, as we see it, rests with those who hold the purse strings, and in modern large-scale enterprises, those persons hold the purse strings who perform the functions of goal setting and planning.[12]

What is the relationship between the structure of the microcosm and the structure of the macrocosm? The application of location theory to the Chandler-Redlich scheme suggests a *correspondence principle* relating centralization of control within the corporation to centralization of control within the international economy.

Location theory suggests that Level III activities would spread themselves over the globe according to the pull of labor-power, markets, and raw materials. The multinational corporation, because of its power to command capital and technology and its ability to rationalize their use on a global scale, will probably spread production more evenly over the world's surface than is now the case. Thus, in the first instance, it may well be a force for diffusing industrialization to the less-developed countries and creating new centers of production. (We postpone for a moment a discussion of the fact that location depends upon transportation, which in turn depends upon the government, which in turn is influenced by the structure of business enterprise.)

Level II activities, because of their need for white-collar workers, communications systems, and information, tend to concentrate in large cities. Since their demands are similar, corporations from different industries tend to place their coordinating offices in the same city, and Level II activities are consequently far more geographically concentrated than Level III activities.

Level I activities, the general offices, tend to be even more concentrated than Level II activities, for they must be located close to the capital market, the media, and the government. Nearly every major corporation in the United States, for example, must have its general office (or a large proportion of its high-level personnel) in or near the city of New York, because of the need for face-to-face contact at higher levels of decision making.

Applying this scheme to the world-economy, one would expect to find the highest offices of the multinational corporations concentrated in the world's major cities—New York, London, Paris, Bonn, Tokyo. These, along with Moscow and perhaps Peking, will be the major centers of high-level strategic planning. Lesser cities throughout the world will deal with the day-to-day operations of specific local problems. These in turn will be arranged in a hierarchical fashion: the larger and more important ones will contain regional corporate headquarters, while the smaller ones will be confined to lower level activities. Since business is usually the core of the city, geographical specialization will come to reflect the hierarchy of corporate decision making, and the occupational distribution of labor in a city or region will depend upon its function in the international economic system. The "best" and most highly paid administrators, doctors, lawyers, scientists, educators, government officials, actors, servants, and hairdressers will tend to concentrate in or near the major centers.

The structure of income and consumption will tend to parallel the structure of status and authority. The citizens of capital cities will have the best jobs—allocating people and money at the highest level and planning growth and development—and will receive the highest rates of remuneration. (Executives' salaries tend to be a function of the wage bill of people under them. The larger the empire of the multinational corporation, the greater the earnings of top executives, to a large extent independent of their performance.[13] Thus, growth in the hinterland subsidiaries implies growth in the income of capital cities, but not vice versa.)

The citizens of capital cities will also be the first to innovate new products in the cycle which is known in the marketing literature as trickle-down or two-stage marketing. A new product is usually first introduced to a select group of people who have "discretionary" income and are willing to experiment in their consumption patterns.[14] Once it is accepted by this group, it spreads, or trickles down to other groups via the demonstration effect. In this process, the rich and the powerful get more votes than everyone else; first because they have more money to spend, second, because they have more ability to experiment, and third, because they have high status and are likely to be copied. This special group may have something approaching a choice in consumption patterns; the rest have only the choice between conforming or being isolated.

The trickle-down system also has the advantage—from the center's point of view—of reinforcing patterns of authority and control. According to Fallers,[15] it helps keep workers on the treadmill by creating an illusion of upward mobility even though relative status remains unchanged. In each period subordinates achieve (in part) the consumption standards of their superiors in a previous period and are thus torn in two directions: if they look backward and compare their standards of living through time, things seem to be getting better; if they look upward they see that their relative position has not changed. They receive a consolation prize, as it were, which may serve to keep them going by softening the reality that in a competitive system, few succeed and many fail. It is little wonder, then, that those at the top stress growth rather than equality as the welfare criterion for human relations.

In the international economy trickle-down marketing takes the form of an international demonstration effect spreading outward from the metropolis to the hinterland.[16] Multinational corporations help speed up this process, often the key motive for direct investment, through their control of marketing channels and communications media.

The development of a new product is a fixed cost; once the expenditure needed for invention or innovation has been made, it is forever a bygone. The actual cost of production is thus typically well below selling price and the limit on output is not rising costs but falling demand due to saturated markets. The marginal profit on new foreign markets is thus high, and corporations have a strong interest in maintaining a system which spreads their products widely. Thus, the interest of multinational corporations in underdeveloped countries is larger than the size of the market would suggest.

It must be stressed that the dependency relationship between major and minor cities should not be attributed to technology. The new technology, because it increases interaction, implies greater interdependence but not necessarily a hierarchical structure. Communications linkages could be arranged in the form of a grid in which each point was directly connected to many other points, permitting lateral as well as vertical communication. This system would be polycentric since messages from one point to another would go directly rather than through the center; each point would become a center on its own; and the distinction between center and periphery would disappear.

Such a grid is made *more* feasible by aeronautical and electronic revolutions which greatly reduce costs of communications. It is not technology which creates inequality; rather, it is *organization* that imposes a ritual judicial asymmetry on the use of intrinsically symmetrical means of communications and arbitrarily creates unequal capacities to initiate and terminate exchange, to store and retrieve information, and to determine the extent of the exchange and terms of the discussion. Just as colonial powers in the past linked each point in the hinterland to the metropolis and inhibited lateral communications, preventing the growth of independent centers of decision making and creativity, multinational corporations (backed by state powers) centralize control by imposing a hierarchical system.

This suggests the possibility of an alternative system of organization in the form of national planning. Multinational corporations are private institutions which organize one or a few industries across many countries. Their polar opposite (the antimultinational corporation, perhaps) is a public institution which organizes many industries across one region. This would permit the centralization of capital, i.e., the coordination of many enterprises by one decision-making center, but would substitute regionalization for internationalization. The span of control would be confined to the boundaries of a single polity and society and not spread over many countries. The advantage of national planning is its ability to remove the wastes of oligopolistic anarchy, i.e., meaningless product differentiation and an imbalance between different industries within a geographical area. It concentrates *all* levels of decision making in one locale and thus provides each region with a full complement of skills and occupations. This opens up new horizons for local development by making possible the social and political control of economic decision making. Multinational corporations, in contrast, weaken political control because they span many countries and can escape national regulation.

A few examples might help to illustrate how multinational corporations reduce options for development. Consider an underdeveloped country wishing to invest heavily in education in order to increase its stock of human capital and raise standards of living. In a market system it would be able to find gainful employment for its citizens within its *national boundaries* by specializing in education-intensive activities and selling its surplus production to foreigners. In the multinational corporate system, however, the demand for high-level education in low-ranking areas is limited, and a country does not become a world center simply by having a better educational system. An outward shift in the supply of educated people in a country, therefore, will not create its own demand but will create an excess supply and lead to emigration. Even then, the employment opportunities for citizens of low-ranking countries are restricted by discriminatory practices in the center. It is well known that ethnic homogeneity increases as one goes up the corporate hierarchy; the lower levels contain a wide variety of nationalities, the higher levels become successively purer and purer. In part this stems from the skill differences of different nationalities, but more important is the fact that the higher up one goes in the decision-making process, the more important mutual understanding and ease of communication become; a common background becomes all-important.

A similar type of specialization by nationality can be expected within the multinational corporation hierarchy. Multinational corporations are torn in two directions. On the one hand, they must adapt to local circumstances in each country. This calls for decentralized decision making. On the other hand, they must coordinate their activities in various parts of the world and stimulate the flow of ideas from one part of their empire to another. This calls for centralized control. They must, therefore, develop an organizational structure to balance the need for coordination with the need for adaptation to a patchwork quilt of languages, laws, and customs. One solution to this problem is a division of labor based on nationality. Day-to-day management in each country is left to the nationals of that country who, because they are intimately familiar with local conditions and practices, are able to deal with local problems and local government. These nationals remain rooted in one spot, while above them is a layer of people who move around from country to country, as bees among flowers, transmitting information from one subsidiary to another and from the lower levels to the general office at the apex of the corporate structure. In the nature of things, these people (reticulators) for the most part will be citizens of the country of the parent corporation (and will be drawn from a small, culturally homogeneous group within the advanced world), since they will need to have the confidence of their superiors and be able to move easily in the higher management circles. Latin Americans, Asians, and Africans will at best be able to aspire to a management position in the intermediate coordinating centers at the continental level. Very few will be able to get much higher than this, for the closer one gets to the top, the more important is "a common cultural heritage."

Another way in which the multinational corporations inhibit economic development in the hinterland is through their effect on tax capacity. An important government instrument for promoting growth is expenditure on infrastructure and support services. By providing transportation and communications, education and health, a government can create a productive labor force and increase the growth potential of its economy. The extent to which it can afford to finance these intermediate outlays depends upon its tax revenue.

However, a government's ability to tax multinational corporations is limited by the ability of these corporations to manipulate transfer prices and to move their productive facilities to another country. This means that they will only be attracted to countries where superior infrastructure offsets higher taxes. The government of an underdeveloped country will find it difficult to extract a surplus (revenue from the multinational corporations, less cost of services provided to them) from multinational corporations to use for long-run development programs and for stimulating growth in other industries. In contrast, governments of the advanced countries, where the home office and financial center of the multinational corporation are located, can tax the profits of the corporation as a whole as well as the high incomes of its management. Government in the metropolis can, therefore, capture some of the surplus generated by the multinational corporations and use it to further improve their infrastructure and growth.

In other words, the relationship between multinational corporations and underdeveloped countries will be somewhat like the relationship between the national corporations in the United States and state and municipal governments. These lower level governments tend always to be short of funds compared to the federal government, which can tax a corporation as a whole. Their competition to attract corporate investment eats up their surplus, and they find it difficult to finance extensive investments in human and physical capital even where such investment would be productive. This has a crucial effect on the pattern of government expenditure. For example, suppose taxes were first paid to state governments and then passed on to the federal government. What chance is there that these lower level legislatures would approve the phenomenal expenditures on space research that now go on? A similar discrepancy can be expected in the international economy with overspending and waste by metropolitan governments and a shortage of public funds in the less advanced countries.

The tendency of the multinational corporations to erode the power of the nation state works in a variety of ways, in addition to its effect on taxation powers. In general, most governmental policy instruments (monetary policy, fiscal policy, wage policy, etc.) diminish in effectiveness the more open the economy and the greater the extent of foreign investments. This tendency applies to political instruments as well as economic, for the multinational corporation is a medium by which laws, politics, foreign policy, and culture of one country intrude into another. This acts to reduce the sovereignty of all nation states, but again the relationship is asymmetrical, for the flow tends to be from the parent to the subsidiary, not vice versa. The United States can apply its antitrust laws to foreign subsidiaries or stop them from "trading with the enemy" even though such trade is not against the laws of the country in which the branch plant is located. However, it would be illegal for an underdeveloped country which disagreed with American foreign policy to hold a U.S. firm hostage for acts of the parent. This is because legal rights are defined in terms of property-ownership, and the various subsidiaries of a multinational corporation are not "partners in a multinational endeavor" but the property of the general office.

In conclusion, it seems that a regime of multinational corporations would offer underdeveloped countries neither national independence nor equality. It would tend instead to inhibit the attainment of these goals. It would turn the underdeveloped countries into branch-plant countries, not only with reference to their economic functions but throughout the whole gamut of social, political, and cultural roles. The subsidiaries of multinational corporations are typically amongst the largest corporations in the country of operations, and their top executives play an influential role in the political, social, and cultural life of the host country. Yet these people, whatever their title, occupy at best a medium position in the corporate structure and are restricted in authority and horizons to a lower level of decision making. The governments with whom they deal tend to take on the same middle-management outlook, since this is the only range of information and ideas to which they are exposed.[17] In this sense, one can hardly expect such a country to bring forth the creative imagination needed to apply science and technology to the problems of degrading poverty. Even so great a champion of liberalism as Marshall recognized the crucial relationship between occupation and development.

> For the business by which a person earns his livelihood generally fills his thoughts during the far greater part of those hours in which his mind is at its best; during them his character is being formed by the way in which he uses his facilities in his work, by the thoughts and feelings which it suggests, and by his relationship to his associates in work, his employers to his employees.[18]

The Political Economy of the Multinational Corporation

The viability of the multinational corporate system depends upon the degree to which people will tolerate the unevenness it creates. It is well to remember that the "New Imperialism," which began after 1870 in a spirit of Capitalism Triumphant, soon became seriously troubled and after 1914 was characterized by war, depression, breakdown of the international economic system, and war again, rather than Free Trade, Pax Britannica, and Material Improvement.

A major, if not the major, reason was Great Britain's inability to cope with the by-products of its own rapid accumulation of capital; i.e., a class-conscious labor force at home, a middle class in the hinterland, and rival centers of capital on the Continent and in America. Britain's policy tended to be atavistic and defensive rather than progressive, more concerned with warding off new threats than creating new areas of expansion. Ironically, Edwardian England revived the paraphernalia of the landed aristocracy it had just destroyed. Instead of embarking on a "big push" to develop the vast hinterland of the Empire, colonial administrators often adopted policies to slow down rates of growth and arrest the development of either a native capitalist class or a native proletariat which could overthrow them.

As time went on, the center had to devote an increasing share of government activity to military and other unproductive expenditures; they had to rely on alliances with an inefficient class of landlords, officials, and soldiers in the hinterland to maintain stability at the cost of development. A great part of the surplus extracted from the population was thus wasted locally.

The new mercantilism (as the multinational corporate system of special alliances and privileges, aid, and tariff concessions is sometimes called) faces similar problems of internal and external division. The center is troubled: excluded groups revolt and even some of the affluent are dissatisfied with the roles. [. . .]. Nationalistic rivalry between major capitalist countries (especially the challenge of Japan and Germany) remains an important divisive factor, while the economic challenge from the socialist bloc may prove to be of the utmost significance in the next thirty years. Russia has its own form of large-scale economic organizations, also in command of modern technology, and its own conception of how the world should develop. So does China to an increasing degree.[19] Finally, there is the threat presented by the middle classes and the excluded groups of the underdeveloped countries.

The national middle classes in the underdeveloped countries came to power when the center weakened but could not, through their policy of import-substitution manufacturing, establish a viable basis for sustained growth. They now face a foreign exchange crisis and an unemployment (or population) crisis—the first indicating their inability to function in the international economy, and the second indicating their alienation from the people they are supposed to lead. In the immediate future, these national middle classes will gain a new lease on life as they take advantage of the spaces created by the rivalry between American and non-American oligopolists striving to establish global market positions. The native capitalists will again become the champions of national independence as they bargain with multinational corporations. But the conflict at this level is more apparent than real, for in the end the fervent nationalism of the middle class asks only for promotion within the corporate structure and not for a break with that structure. In the last analysis their power derives from the metropolis and they cannot easily afford to challenge the international system. They do not command the loyalty of their own population and cannot really compete with the large, powerful, aggregate capitals from the center. They are prisoners of the taste patterns and consumption standards set at the center, and depend on outsiders for technical advice, capital, and when necessary, for military support of their position.

The main threat comes from the excluded groups. It is not unusual in underdeveloped countries for the top 5 percent to obtain between 30 and 40 percent of the total national income, and for the top one-third to obtain anywhere from 60 to 70 percent.[20] At most, one-third of the population can be said to benefit in some sense from the dualistic growth that characterizes development in the hinterland. The remaining two-thirds, who together get only one-third of the income, are outsiders, not because they do not contribute to the economy, but because they do not share in the benefits. They provide a source of cheap labor which helps keep exports to the developed world at a low price and which has financed the urban-biased growth of recent years. Because their wages are low, they spend a moderate amount of time in menial services and are sometimes referred to as underemployed—as if to imply they were not needed. In fact, it is difficult to see how the system in most underdeveloped countries could survive without cheap labor since removing it (e.g., diverting it to public works projects as is done in socialist countries) would raise consumption costs to capitalists and professional elites. Economic development under the multinational corporation does not offer much promise for this large segment of society and their antagonism continuously threatens the system.

The survival of the multinational corporate system depends on how fast it can grow and how much trickles down. Plans now being formulated in government offices, corporate headquarters, and international organizations sometimes suggest that a growth rate of about 6 percent per year in national income (3 percent per capita) is needed. (Such a target is, of course, far below what would be possible if a serious effort were made to solve basic problems of health, education, and clothing.) To what extent is it possible?

The multinational corporation must solve four critical problems for the underdeveloped countries, if it is to foster the continued growth and survival of a "modern" sector. First, it must break the foreign-exchange constraint and provide the underdeveloped countries with imported goods for capital formation and modernization. Second, it must finance an expanded program of government expenditure to train labor and provide support services for urbanization and industrialization. Third, it must solve the urban food problem created by growth. Finally, it must keep the excluded two-thirds of the population under control.

The solution now being suggested for the first is to restructure the world-economy allowing the periphery to export certain manufactured goods to the center. Part of this program involves regional common markets to rationalize the existing structure of industry. These plans typically do not involve the rationalization and restructuring of the entire economy of the underdeveloped countries but mainly serve the small manufacturing sector which caters to higher income groups and which, therefore, faces a very limited market in any particular country. The solution suggested for the second problem is an expanded aid program and a reformed government bureaucracy (perhaps along the lines of the Alliance for Progress). The solution for the third is agribusiness and the green revolution, a program with only limited benefits to the rural poor. Finally, the solution offered for the fourth problem is population control, either through family planning or counterinsurgency.

It is doubtful whether the center has sufficient political stability to finance and organize the program outlined above. It is not clear, for example, that the West has the technology to rationalize manufacturing abroad or modernize agriculture, or the willingness to open up marketing channels for the underdeveloped world. Nor is it evident that the center has the political power to embark on a large aid program or to readjust its own structure of production and allow for the importation of manufactured goods from the periphery. It is difficult to imagine labor accepting such a reallocation (a new repeal of the Corn Laws as it were[21]), and it is equally hard to see how the advanced countries could create a system of planning to make these extra hardships unnecessary.

The present crisis may well be more profound than most of us imagine, and the West may find it impossible to restructure the international economy on a workable basis. One could easily argue that the age of the multinational corporation is at its end rather than at its beginning. For all we know, books on the global partnership may be the epitaph of the American attempt to take over the old international economy, and not the herald of a new era of international cooperation.

Conclusion

The multinational corporation, because of its great power to plan economic activity, represents an important step forward over previous methods of organizing international exchange. It demonstrates the social nature of production on a global scale. As it eliminates the anarchy of international markets and brings about a more extensive and productive international division of labor, it releases great sources of latent energy.

However, as it crosses international boundaries, it pulls and tears at the social and political fabric and erodes the cohesiveness of national states.[22] Whether one likes this or not, it is probably a tendency that cannot be stopped.

Through its propensity to nestle everywhere, settle everywhere, and establish connections everywhere, the multinational corporation destroys the possibility of national seclusion and self-sufficiency and creates a universal interdependence. But the multinational corporation is still a private institution with a partial outlook and represents only an imperfect solution to the problem of international cooperation. It creates hierarchy rather than equality, and it spreads its benefits unequally.

In proportion to its success, it creates tensions and difficulties. It will lead other institutions, particularly labor organizations and government, to take an international outlook and thus unwittingly create an environment less favorable to its own survival. It will demonstrate the possibilities of material progress at a faster rate than it can realize them, and will create a worldwide demand for change that it cannot satisfy.

The next round may be marked by great crises due to the conflict between national planning by governments and international planning by corporations. For example, if each country loses its power over fiscal and monetary policy due to the growth of multinational corporations (as some observers believe Canada has), how will aggregate demand be stabilized? Will it be possible to construct superstates? Or does multinationalism do away with Keynesian problems? Similarly, will it be possible to fulfill a host of other government functions at the supranational level in the near future? During the past twenty-five years many political problems were put aside as the West recovered from the depression and the war. By the late sixties the bloom of this long upswing had begun to fade. In the seventies, power conflicts are likely to come to the fore.

Whether underdeveloped countries will use the opportunities arising from this crisis to build viable local decision-making institutions is difficult to predict. The national middle class failed when it had the opportunity and instead merely reproduced internally the economic dualism of the international economy as it squeezed agriculture to finance urban industry. What is needed is a complete change of direction. The starting point must be the needs of the bottom two-thirds, and not the demands of the top third. The primary goal of such a strategy would be to provide minimum standards of health, education, food, and clothing to the entire population, removing the more obvious forms of human suffering. This requires a system which can mobilize the entire population and which can search the local environment for information, resources, and needs. It must be able to absorb modern technology, but it cannot be mesmerized by the form it takes in the advanced countries; it must go to the roots. This is not the path the upper one-third chooses when it has control.

The wealth of a nation, wrote Adam Smith two hundred years ago, is determined by "first, the skill, dexterity and judgement with which labour is generally applied; and, secondly by the proportion between the number of those who are employed in useful labour, and that of those who are not so employed."[23] Capitalist enterprise has come a long way from this day, but it has never been able to bring more than a small fraction of the world's population into useful or highly productive employment. The latest stage reveals once more the power of social cooperation and division of labor which so fascinated Adam Smith in his description of pin manufacturing. It also shows the shortcomings of concentrating this power in private hands.

Notes

1. Karl Marx, "On the General Law of Capitalist Accumulation," chap. 25; "Cooperation," chap. 12; and "Division of Labour in Manufactur-

ing and Division of Labour in Society," chap. 14, part 4, in *Capital*, vol.
I (1867; Moscow: Foreign Languages Publishing House, 1961); and
Karl Marx, chap. 23, *Capital*, vol. III (1894; Moscow: Foreign Languages Publishing House, 1966).

2. Phrase used in A. M. Salomon, *International Aspects of Antitrust, Part I:
Hearings before the Sub-Committee on Antitrust and Monopoly of the Senate
Committee on the Judiciary* (Washington, D.C.: Government Printing Office, April 1966), p. 49.

3. The trends as discussed in S. Hymer and R. Rowthorn, "Multinational
Corporations and International Oligopoly: The Non-American Challenge," in C. P. Kindleberger, ed., *The International Corporation* (Cambridge, Mass.: MIT Press, 1970).

4. Substituting the words *multinational corporation* for *bourgeois* in *The Communist Manifesto* provides a more dynamic picture of the multinational
corporation than any of its present-day supporters have dared to put
forth.[. . .].

5. See R. H. Coase, "The Nature of the Firm," in G. J. Stigler and K. E.
Boulding, eds., *Readings in Price Theory* (Chicago: Richard D. Irwin,
1952). [. . .].

6. The following analysis by E. S. Mason, "The Apologetics of Managerialism," *Journal of Business of the University of Chicago* 31, no. 1 (January
1958), an attempt to justify hierarchy and inequality by emphasizing
the skill and knowledge of managers and the technostructure, is interesting and of great significance in this connection:

> As everyone now recognizes, classical economics provided not
> only a system of analysis, or analytical "model," intended to be
> useful to the explanation of economic behavior but also a defense—
> and a carefully reasoned defense—of the proposition that the
> economic behavior promoted and constrained by the institutions
> of a free-enterprise system is, in the main, in the public interest.
> It cannot be too strongly emphasized that the growth of
> nineteenth-century capitalism depended largely on the general
> acceptance of a reasoned justification of the system on moral as
> well as on political and economic grounds.
> It seems doubtful whether, to date, the managerial literature
> has provided an equally satisfying apologetic for big business.[. . .].

7. This analysis of the modern corporation is almost entirely based on the
work of A. D. Chandler, *Strategy and Structure* (New York: Doubleday,
1961); and C. Barnard, The Functions of Executives (Cambridge, Mass.:
Harvard University Press, 1938).

8. A. D. Chandler and F. Redlich, "Recent Developments in American
Business Administration and Their Conceptualization," *Business History
Review* (Spring 1961): 103-28.

9. Neoclassical models suggest that this choice was due to the exogenously
determined nature of technological change. A Marxist economic model
would argue that it was due in part to the increased tensions in the
labor market accompanying the accumulation of capital and the growth

of large firms. This is discussed further in S. Hymer and S. Resnick, "International Trade and Uneven Development," in J. N. Bhagwati et al., eds., *Kindleberger Festschrift* (Cambridge, Mass.: MIT Press, 1970).

10. The reasons for foreign investment discussed here are examined in more detail in S. Hymer, "La grande corporation multinationale," *Revue Economique* 19, no. 6 (November 1968): 949-73, and in Hymer and Rowthorn, "Multinational Corporations."

11. At present, U.S. corporations have about $60 billion invested in foreign branch plants and subsidiaries. The total assets of these foreign operations are much larger than the capital invested and probably equal $100 billion at book value. (American corporations, on the average, were able to borrow 40 percent of their subsidiaries' capital requirements locally in the country of operation.) The total assets of the 200 largest non-U.S. firms are slightly less than $200 billion. See U.S. Department of Commerce, *Survey of Current Business, 1969*, and the *Fortune* list of the 500 largest U.S. and 200 largest non-U.S. corporations.

12. Chandler and Redlich, "Developments in Business Administration," p. 120.

13. See H. A. Simon, "The Compensation of Executives," *Sociometry* (March 1957).

14. S. Gervasi, "Publicité et croissance économique," *Économie et Humanisme* (November-December 1964).

15. L. A. Fallers, "A Note on the Trickle Effect," in P. Bliss, ed., *Marketing and the Behavioral Sciences* (Boston: Allyn & Bacon, 1963), pp. 208-16.

16. See R. Vernon, "International Investment and International Trade in the Product Cycle," *Quarterly Journal of Economics* 80 (May 1966).

17. An interesting illustration of the asymmetry in horizons and prospectives of the big company and the small country is found in these quotations from *Fortune*. Which countries of the world are making a comparable analysis of the multinational corporation?

> A Ford economist regularly scans the international financial statistics to determine which countries have the highest rates of inflation; these are obviously prime candidates for devaluation. He then examines patterns of trade. If a country is running more of an inflation than its chief trading partners and competitors and its reserves are limited it is more than a candidate; it is a shoo-in. His most difficult problem is to determine exactly when the devaluation will take place. Economics determines whether and how much, but politicians control the timing. So the analyst maintains a complete library of information on leading national officials. He tries to get "into the skin of the man" who is going to make the decision. The economist's forecasts have been correct in sixty-nine of the last seventy-five crisis situations. [. . .]. [S. Rose, "The Rewarding Strategies of Multinationalism," *Fortune*, September 15, 1968, p. 105.]

18. This quote is taken from the first page of Marshall's *Principles of Economics*. In the rest of the book, he attempted to show that the economic

system of laissez-faire capitalism had an overall positive effect in forming character. As we noted above, his argument rested upon the existence of competitive markets (and the absence of coercion). Because multinational corporations substitute for the international market they call into question the liberal ideology which rationalized it.

19. A. A. Berle, Jr., in Foreword to E. S. Mason, ed., *The Corporation in Modern Society* (New York: Atheneum, 1967), p. ix, has put the problem most succinctly:

> The Industrial Revolution, as it spread over twentieth-century life, required collective organization of men and things.... As the twentieth century moves into the afternoon, two systems—and (thus far) two only—have emerged as vehicles of modern industrial economics. One is the socialist commissariat, its highest organization at present in the Soviet Union; the other is the modern corporation, most highly developed in the United States.

20. S. Kuznets, *Modern Economic Growth* (New Haven: Yale University Press, 1966), pp. 423-24.
21. See K. Polanyi, *The Great Transformation* (New York: Farrar & Rhinehart, 1944), on the consequences after 1870 of the repeal of the Corn Laws in England.
22. See K. Levitt, *Silent Surrender: The Multinational Corporation in Canada* (Toronto: The Macmillan Company of Canada, 1970); and N. Girvan and O. Jefferson, "Corporate vs. Caribbean Integration," *New World Quarterly* 4, no. 2 (1968).
23. See Adam Smith, *The Wealth of Nations* (New York: The Modern Library, 1937 edition), p. 1.

[12]
Developing Societies as Part of an International Political Economy

Michael Barratt Brown

The New Enclaves of Development

On May 9, 1980, the London *Financial Times* carried a large advertisement for the Greater Colombo Free Trade Zone under the heading "A Boon for Labour-Intensive Industries: Sri Lanka's Free Trade Zone Offers 600,000 Low-Cost, High- Productivity Workers." The advert is worth quoting *in extenso*:

> As any manufacturer knows, intelligent labour is a boon, expecially in labour-intensive industries. Sri Lanka's Free Trade Zone offers manufacturers one of the world's most educated, highly trainable labour reserves.
>
> 600,000 men and women who are young and eager to work. Sri Lanka's most valuable natural resource is its educated, intelligent, mostly English-speaking labour.
>
> Because Sri Lankans *need* jobs, the government has launched a full-scale programme to attract foreign investment in the country's Free Trade Zone.
>
> An unbeatable combination of tax incentives and business-like assistance is being offered.
>
> For instance, all manufacturers in the Free Trade Zone are automatically exempt from all taxes—for up to 10 years. This includes taxes on corporate and personal income, royalties, dividends, followed by a further concessionary tax period for a maximum of fifteen years.
>
> *Plus, there is no limit on the equity holdings of foreign investors.*
>
> Sri Lanka offers many other advantages:
>
> 1. Political stability. With a government committed to democratic parliamentary rule.
>
> 2. A booming economy. In 1978, Sri Lanka achieved a growth rate of 8.20 percent in real terms, in all sections of the economy. A figure *twice* the average growth rate during the last decade.
>
> 3. Lowest labour rates. Sri Lanka has the most competitive labour rates in Asia. The average monthly wage in manufacturing industries is only US $35. Compare your wage bill with this!
>
> 4. All the assistance you need. The Greater Colombo Economic Commission (GCEC) is the Authority for the Free Trade Zone. It's the only agency you need deal with, to set up operation in Sri Lanka.

The GCEC will leave no stone unturned to help you get started. It will help you choose the best possible location for your factory. Help you with feasibility studies, project evaluation, joint venture negotiation and business registration. Even screen job applicants for you—and then train them!

If your business is electronics, light engineering, rubber-based products, cosmetics, pharmaceuticals, electrical appliances, precision tools, vehicle assembly, or any labour-intensive industry, Sri Lanka's Free Trade Zone is well worth a good, hard look.

Sri Lanka, formerly Ceylon, is located along major air and sea routes.

It is not the picture that we have come to have in our minds of Ceylon—more a country of tea estates, coffee groves, and coconut palms, of cinnamon, pineapples, and other tropical products supplied to Europe in exchange for our manufactures. Of course there are not 600,000 Sri Lankans at work in manufacturing today, not more than a sixth of that number. But the offer is a genuine one and could be met. Nor is Sri Lanka alone in offering cheap labor for foreign manufacturing industries in free trade zones. It can be equaled in many other countries and territories—in Singapore, in Manila (the Philippines), in Taiwan, in Djakarta (Indonesia), in Mauritius, Colombia, and Bolivia, above all in Hong Kong, South Korea, and Mexico. In each of the last three there are over a million workers in manufacturing industry. There are at least another million altogether in the smaller territories. Four million out of a world total of employment in manufacturing of about 70 million is still little more than 5 percent of the total. Add to this a similar number again in the larger countries like India, Pakistan, Brazil, Argentina, and it can be seen that the developing countries enjoy about 10 percent of world manufacturing employment, rather less of world manufacturing output.

The point of the *Financial Times* advertisement, however, was to attract foreign firms into Sri Lanka, and the other free trade zones which we listed had the same aims. This reflects a recent switch of interest in foreign investment into such areas.

Thus, the proportion of their employees that the transnationals—the manufacturing companies operating in many countries—now have in developing countries is much more than 10 percent; it is more nearly 20 percent and this proportion is growing. The exports of the non-oil-producing developing countries have continued at around 12 percent of total world exports for the whole decade of the 1970s, having declined from almost twice that share in the 1950s.[1] But after the 1950s, the share of their exports accounted for by manufactured goods rose from 10 percent to 40 percent. Two-thirds of this went to developed countries; and intrafirm trade, i.e., goods moving *inside* the transnationals, makes up a third of all the trade.[2]

The developing countries' exports of manufactured goods are concentrated in a limited number of industries. One-third of the exports going to developed countries consists of textiles (14.5 percent) and clothing (21 percent); a sixth of electronics and electrical machinery, another sixth of chemicals, iron and steel, and transport equipment and other machinery, and a final third of miscellaneous manufactures. It is only in the case of transport equipment and other machinery that the bulk of developing countries' exports goes to other developing countries and not to the developed countries, and that is a point we must take up later. In the case of clothing and electronics, etc., over 80 percent of exports are to developed countries. Looked at from the other side, anything from a third to a half of imports into the United States of such items are from developing countries. What is more, the rate of increase in the 1970s of imports of manufactures into the United States, and into the European Economic Community (EEC) and Japan likewise, was of the order of 25 percent to 35 percent per year.[3]

We have been referring to the "*non*-oil-producing developing countries," and we began this essay by identifying new areas of development in them, but of course the oil-producing countries have assumed even greater importance with the rise in oil prices. In the decade of the 1970s their share of world trade rose from 6 percent to 13 percent.[4] Other mineral-exporting countries benefited from a rise in prices in the 1970s but none to the extent of the oil producers. The fear of declining reserves may be as great or greater with other minerals, but the capacity which the Organization of Petroleum Exporting Countries (OPEC) has shown to make a cartel effective is not shared by other mineral cartels. These have to deal with substitutes and scrap, as well as political differences—in a way that the oil producers do not. There is no doubt, however, that there is a huge expansion of investment by transnational companies in mineral extraction from the developing countries and that the developing countries are claiming a larger share in the value produced from their own resources. It seems that much of the remaining reserves of many minerals are to be found in the developing countries, the developed countries having already in most cases used up what resources they were endowed with.

What is developed today by transnational companies in each of the developing countries is one mineral or primary product or one or two types of manufactured goods to fit into their synergy, as they call their mix of inputs and outputs. They look for oil or some other mineral in one area, forest and plantation crops in another, cheap labor for manufacturing in a third, and everywhere the world over they look for markets. But this leads to a peculiar kind of development in developing countries in which only one part of the economy is developed—the oil wells, the ore mines, the plantations, or the free trade ports. We need to describe this as "enclave" development, because outside of the enclave little or no development takes place. Labor may move into the enclave, transport and communications will be developed to the ports. But what development there is takes place wholly at the discretion of the transnational companies from the developed countries. There is little or no spread effect outside the enclave and the profits from the operation flow back largely to the developed countries.

It is not, however, a new phenomenon for the developed economies to limit development to such enclaves in developing countries. The most striking example is provided by the emirates of the Arabian peninsula—Kuwait, Oman, Abu Dhabi, Aden—nibbles of the mainland providing oil supplies or port facilities for the developed countries. But the plantations of Malaya, Indonesia, Mauritius, or the West Indies, the mines of the Congo, Chile, Zambia, or Peru, provide similar examples of such enclave development, and the city-states of Hong Kong and Singapore give today the best indication of the nature of an enclave cut off completely from the hinterland it depends on.

Types of Developing Societies in the World Political Economy

It is a common practice to distinguish developing societies according to their income per head, and therefore their eligibility for development assistance—high-income, upper-middle, lower-middle, and low-income societies, as in Table 1.

It is more useful here to distinguish developing societies according to their type of development in the world-economy, because so much more depends on income distribution or who gets the high incomes in each society than on whether the average is high or low. Even more significant are the structural differences in the economies of these societies, the organization of the agrarian economy, the balance between agriculture and industry, and, within the industrial sector itself, the balance between industries—those engaged in labor-intensive, intermediate processing, serving metropolitan industrial production, or light industry for production of goods for domestic consumption and export or, in a few cases, heavy industry

Table 1
Definitions of Developing Countries*

High income (over $2,500 per capita in 1976)

South Europe:	Greece, Spain, Rumania
OPEC:	Saudi Arabia, United Arab Emirates, Kuwait, Libya, Venezuela
Special cases:	Israel, Singapore, Bahamas, Gabon

Upper middle ($1,000-$2,500)

South Europe:	Portugal, Cyprus, Turkey, Yugoslavia, Malta
Latin America:	Chile, Mexico, Brazil, Argentina, Uruguay, Panama
OPEC:	Iran, Iraq
West Indies:	Barbados, Jamaica, Trinidad, Surinam
Special cases:	Hong Kong, Taiwan

Lower middle ($400-$1,000)

Middle East:	Syria, Jordan
Africa:	Ghana, Ivory Coast
Latin America:	Peru
Southeast Asia:	Korea, Malaysia, Thailand, Philippines

Low income (under $400)

52 countries including:	China, India, Pakistan, Bangladesh, Sri Lanka, Nigeria, Egypt, Burma, Vietnam, Kampuchea, rest of Africa

---

*Those receiving development assistance.

that provides a basis for a more advanced, though still dependent, capitalist development. Perhaps the most striking example of this last category of countries is India, which appears in Table 1 in the lowest category of low-income countries, a classification which, therefore, is wholly misleading because it has perhaps the most advanced capitalist industrial sector of all developing societies.

The new development of enclaves in developing societies which we have just reviewed suggests at least three different types of development, to which we shall have to add a fourth to complete the picture. We may consider them in the order of influence they may have on the rest of the capitalist world economy. First, there are the oil-producing countries. Since OPEC effectively established its power in 1973, oil prices have been raised thirtyfold and the financial reserves of the oil states have increased in line. The question that has to be asked, however, is whether the result is to establish the oil-producing countries as developed rather than underdeveloped or developing economies. The answer is that no self-generating economic development has taken place in any oil-producing economy. Oil finances have tended to be invested by rich Arabs in production facilities or other forms of property mainly in the *developed* economies, and only to a limited extent in the oil states themselves.

Given the immense resources involved, it is remarkable that so little economic development has spread locally from the oil revenues. The answer must lie in the dependence of oil production and refinery processing on the giant transnational companies' expertise and capital accumulation, on the one hand, and, on the other, on the equal absence of entrepreneurial skills in local development of a broad range of manufacturing industry based upon oil wealth. One of the reasons for this is precisely the enclave development of oil production which we have already referred to in the Arabian peninsula; the other is the integration of the larger oil states like Venezuela or Iran into the industrial division of labor of the capitalist world within which the developed economies provide the dynamic for the production equally of capital plant and consumer goods. It would be necessary for new entrants to establish their own capital accumulation for self-generating economic development to take place. The nearest approach to such a development in the oil states has occurred in Mexico, in Nigeria, in Iran, and in Venezuela, but the results to date have been very limited.

If the oil states have failed to establish their own self-generating economic growth, how much less should we expect our second type of developing society—the other mineral and plantation enclaves— to succeed? They have suffered even more from both of the limitations of the oil-producing countries. First, the process of extraction is carried out by a foreign company which has the capital resources and the know-how for the job; and second, the foreign company has total control over the outlets for the product. It is an important aspect of enclave development that the financial terms governing the right to exploit a mineral resource or tropical plant like sugar, bananas, tea or coffee, or palm products, are not by any means the most important matters at issue. High levels of taxation and concessionary grants may be won by the developing countries but may simply be paid to a local elite that invests the funds in one of the developed countries. Even more important questions need to be asked about the exploitation of developing countries' resources and the nature of this exploitation. Is there any long-term advantage to the developing country in the roads and railway lines built to open up the mine or plantations, the port facilities constructed, the hydroelectricity generation plants established, the new towns, schools, and hospitals built to supply the mines or plantations? If not, the developing company may simply leave behind it a hole in the ground, a diseased tea or coffee estate, with no accumulation of funds and no infrastructure of any value to the host country.

What then of the third, and newest, type of enclave development? Are the new manufacturing enclaves of any greater value to the developing societies than the old primary product enclaves? The answer would have to depend again on the extent of the profit that stuck to the developing country and the extent of the spin-off of the manufacturing enterprises. It is worth considering for a moment the offer of concessions and facilities that was being made in the advertisement which we started this chapter with for the Greater Colombo Free Trade Zone. We may list them in the order in which they were offered to the reader of the advertisement: (1) plenty of cheap labor—cheaper than elsewhere in Asia—for labor-intensive industry; (2) educated, intelligent, English-speaking, high-productivity labor; (3) tax exemptions and concessions for ten to twenty-five years; (4) political stability under parliamentary rule; (5) booming local markets; (6) a free trade zone with assistance for its establishment; (7) a geographic location along major air and sea routes.

At the end of this list the question has to be asked: what advantages will accrue to Sri Lanka? Some of the 600,000 unemployed will be employed but by no means all and those who do find work may find it for a limited period only while their eyesight lasts in the precision work on microchip assembly to which they will be assigned without the protection of any form of trade-union organization.[5] Some limited development of ports and infrastructure must rub off. Government officials may benefit from the contracts, but the concessions on taxes and on free trade must inevitably imply that the profits flow *out* and capital accumulation takes place in the developed and not in the developing countries.

This leaves us finally with a forth type of underdeveloped economy. It has already been made clear that the great majority of developing societies have neither oil, nor other minerals, nor plantations, nor free trade zones, or, if they have, these are quite marginal to their overall economies. If we think of the largest developing societies—India, Pakistan, Brazil, Indonesia, Argentina, Nigeria, Egypt, and for the moment exclude China—we are thinking of a third of the world's population. What has happened to them in the process of world development? The answer must be that they have been developed as enclaves or as sources of cheap labor at an earlier period and have been left behind. Yet they remain integrated into the world capitalist system with a twofold role—first as continuing sources of food and raw materials, second as limited but dependent markets. This means generally that the companies based on the developed countries first established agencies for distributing the products of their advanced manufacturing technology and in time found local firms to produce under license.

Transport costs, local marketing, customs duties, and other forms of protective import control all increasingly require of companies from developed economies that they locate their plants at least for purpose of assembly in the developing countries if they are to expand their markets.[6] British capital in the nineteenth century spread its influence throughout the Empire—first in Europe, then in the United States, Canada, Australia, New Zealand, South Africa, and Latin America—in just this way through local agents who developed varying degrees of independence. U.S. capital, and later German and Japanese capital, to a large extent ousted British capital. But the giant transnational companies, mainly from the United States and the United Kingdom, still dominate the world capitalist market.

Trade and Aid in Economic Development and the Role of the Transnational Companies Today

Once established by force and conquest, settlement, plantation and colonial power, the artificial division of labor between industrial and primary production was maintained chiefly by free trade in a world market. Underdeveloped nations could escape only by state-enforced isolation, by state finance and enterprise, and by state protection of infant industries. The power of the first developed states was used largely to prevent the underdeveloped escaping from the system. Japan was too far away to control; and the USSR and later Eastern Europe, China, North Korea, Vietnam, Cuba, and the Portuguese African colonies found new national leaders capable of creating new forms of social organization and new forms of social appeal to unite their peoples behind forced measures of self-denial, autarky, and industrial self-generation. The role of the state in the developed countries had always been to protect their national capitalists' activities in trade and foreign investment. States like Japan and Russia that aspired to become developed were able to encourage state or private enterprise to adopt, and where possible to adapt, the technology of the advanced capitalist firms in industry, commerce, and finance, until they could themselves compete on the world market.

It was already becoming clear ten years ago that the transnational company was the most important economic agency in the capitalist world economy. This development was clearly foreseen in Stephen Hymer's essay reproduced in this volume.[7] The emergence of the giant transnational company has produced a major change, as it has taken inside itself many of the functions of the market. While still operating inside the world capitalist system and in competition with other giant companies, the transnationals, as we have noted earlier, move goods and finance to an increasing extent between their own related plants and enterprises in many different countries. This internal, international trade may make up as much as a third of world trade exchanges, and in the high technology industries a much larger proportion.[8]

Hymer analyzed the effects of the emergence of the giant transnationals in terms of their hierarchy of levels of activity—decision-making top jobs in the capital cities of the most advanced industrial countries; management coordination of finance and distribution at regional centers; and, third, at the bottom, the actual day-to-day production processes. He concluded from this that the power of these companies would tend to freeze the world economy into unequal development. At the same time, the hierarchy of development would be reproduced *inside* the developing societies themselves. A small ruling elite consuming the products of the most advanced industry, a middle class of lesser officials, skilled workers, and richer farmers moving up slowly into the consumer market leaving the great majority at the level of mere subsistence—underemployed or seasonally employed, divided between rural and urban life. The question that Hymer leaves open is whether the dynamics of the increasingly collusive, giant transnational companies' planning can be challenged by the developing societies. For this they would need to find new national middle-class groupings capable of using state power to generate their own economic development inside new forms of international cooperation in the world market. Ten years later, the changes wrought by the giant transnational companies on the international economy seem more permanent and the chance of challenging them that much weaker.

We can spell out the meaning of such major change in four ways: First: there is the much remarked upon fact that the wealth and power of these giant corporations is greater than that of most states apart from the superstates. The great oil companies and other mining, refining, and plantation companies like Unilever, Imperial and British American Tobacco, Anglo-American Consolidated, Goodyear, Firestone, Swift, or United Fruit, always had enormous power over the countries in which they operated and always exercised it to manage the market. This meant controlling the underdeveloped countries, to keep out competition, both from rival producers in "their" territories and from rival sellers in "their" markets. This they achieved through cartels and similar agreements to divide up the world between themselves, but they remained still nationally based firms seeking support from their nation states. A few joint Anglo-Dutch and British-American ventures showed the way to the transnational company that was to come. For, the modern transnational is much more truly *multi*national than the imperial companies of the past.

The second meaning of the change we are considering lies just in this separation of these giant companies from their original national base. It is not only that they operate in many more different countries and on a larger scale, but they are increasingly opportunistic about where they hold their funds and where they invest them. The earlier practice of repatriating profits to the home country—that is, maintaining a flow from the underdeveloped countries to one or other of the developed countries—and then reinvesting a part in new ventures overseas is not at all what happens today. This practice derived from the role of the merchant banks of London, New York, and Paris providing risk capital which even the largest companies depended upon. Today the transnational company accumulates its own reserves and banks these where interest rates are high and exchange rates advantageous, until such time as new investment opportunities occur. The dividends returning to the country of origin are but a small part of the total profits, and it is not any more likely that the funds will be invested in that country than anywhere else in the world. Ironically, it is generally from the original home country that the aid will be supplied that in effect covers the debt charges incurred by the transnational company with its underdeveloped partners.[9]

It is this opportunistic attitude of transnational companies to the nation states from which they operate, together with the huge resources they deploy, that has led to the conclusion that nation states have had their day.[10] In this exaggerated form the conclusion must be questioned and has been properly challenged.[11] But the argument is somewhat misplaced. It is undoubtedly true that a small national state is almost powerless to resist the demands of a giant transnational company *if* it wishes to get involved or is already involved with one of these companies in the economic activities within its territory. At the same time giant transnationals will look to the superstates—the United States or Japan—or to larger groupings of states like the EEC—for protection rather than to smaller states like Holland or Belgium. It is particularly true that transnationals, even those originally based in the United States or Britain, will show no national "loyalty" in their movements of funds or in their investment decisions. But none of this is to say that nation states, even small ones, have lost all their power to resist the advance of the giant companies. It is very much a matter of political will. Governments of national liberation will still find great difficulties in obtaining certain kinds of technological know-how if they do resist and they will find many markets and facilities closed to them. We shall look at this more closely in a moment.

Much of the literature has been concerned with the British problem where for historical reasons a large number of transnational companies orginated, which today increasingly place their funds and their investments outside Britain. The problem for the developing countries lies in the continuing integration of state and company in the developed countries. The downfall of Allende's government and the role of the CIA and International Telephone and Telegraph in that downfall bear witness to that. Nor is it only where the superstates are involved. The power of the South African state or the Australian state is not at all negligible when brought to bear on small neighbors like Zambia or Papua-New Guinea when the interests of giant mining companies are at stake.

Nor should it be supposed that regional integration of states offers the opportunity for more effective popular control over the activities of the transnationals. The enthusiastic support given by the giant British-based transnationals to Britain's entry to the European Economic Community indicates their appreciation of where their interests lie. Capital and goods can be freely moved throughout the Community and pressure can be brought to bear upon the communities' commissioners' policymaking in ways that national parliaments and national trade unions find it hard to rival, and a European Parliament has, as yet, neither political interest nor power to challenge. Regional groupings of developing countries have proved still less effective as countervailing force against the transnationals' power. Evidence has been most convincingly drawn from the experience of the Central American Common Market to show a great increase in dependence on the developed countries and on the transnational companies as a result of the integration of this market. On the other hand, the same study indicates that transnationals which are already well established in larger developing countries with close ties to their governments, as is the case with the Andean Pact countries, did not favor, and did everything to block, their economic integration.[12]

The third meaning of the change in the world economy which the giant transnational companies have brought about arises from the fact that their activities are more concerned today with manufacturing, where before the great imperial companies were engaged mainly in mining and primary production. In the last two decades new foreign investment, particularly by U.S.-based companies, has mainly been in manufacturing and in other developed countries. One of the reasons suggested for the failing competitiveness of the British economy is that so much British capital and so many of the British-based transnational companies are engaged in mining and primary production, whereas the giant companies based in the United States, Germany, and Japan are in manufacturing.[13] More than this, these foreign transnationals have concentrated their investment on the most advanced technology so as to establish and retain monopolistic positions in the world's markets. The implication of this for the underdeveloped countries is that, if they want modern technology for industrial development, they will have to go to the giant transnational companies for the know-how.

This then is the meaning of the free trade zones with which we started this essay. The terms offered in that advertisement for greater Colombo may be the only way in which Sri Lanka could achieve any industrial development. Where a developing country wished instead to establish its own enterprises and industries, and had the trained labor force, it might be possible to obtain licenses and patents. The royalties to be paid and the restrictive clauses attached to such arrangements have been much researched. In a study of the Andean countries made in 1969, the following facts were revealed: royalty payments were greater than remitted profits in some of their countries' balance of foreign payments; nearly all licenses had clauses restricting the export of products made with the imported technology and had clauses requiring machinery and other intermediate inputs to be obtained from the licensing company; while generally the prices charged for these inputs were far above world market prices.[14]

The fourth meaning of the concentration of trade and investment in manufactures in the hands of giant transnational companies is that the technology they have on offer is increasingly capital-intensive. This has two implications for developing countries: it may be quite unsuited to their economies, if, as is likely, they have surplus labor and are short of capital; it may also fix for them a certain division of labor that is inappropriate for their preferred social development. The first point has been given much attention by the advocates of "intermediate technology."[15] No country has probably gone further than China in setting its surplus labor to work on labor-intensive machines, to provide the foundations for an industrial revolution. But Mao always argued for "walking on two feet," and capital-intensive fertilizer factories and refineries could be seen growing up side by side with intermediate technology in the Chinese communes in the 1970s. What is more, the whole trend of the modernization program that China's leaders have embarked on since Mao's death has emphasized the need to draw upon the advanced technology of the United States, Europe, and Japan. China has the power, resources, and offshore base in Hong Kong to filter Western technology and adapt it to its own needs, but smaller and weaker countries will find the lines of their social development predetermined. For technology is not neutral; that is the second problem for developing countries in importing advanced technology. It is based upon a division of labor that separates manual and nonmanual labor, and it assumes a certain distribution of income that involves widening inequalities between the mass of the people and a small advanced sector linked to the technology, and dependent as producers and consumers on its controllers.[16] But this leads us to our last section, in which we have to explore further the links between the ruling groups in the developing societies and the world capitalist system.

The Concept of a New International Economic Order and the Role of Classes in the Developing Societies and the World Capitalist System

Under the influence of Andre Gunder Frank it became fashionable to speak of the imperial relationship in terms of center and periphery.[17] The existence of more than one center (in Europe, then in the United States, and later in Japan) led to a change of metaphor, in Wallerstein's writings, to "core" and "periphery."[18] The obvious historical fact of challenges from newcomers to "core" status encouraged Wallerstein to add a category of "semiperipheral" countries. Behind the words there are real differences of historical experience. Europe and particularly Britain established the first integration of a capitalist world market. The United States, Germany, and Japan have successively challenged Britain's leadership and sought to dominate this world market. Canada, Australia, South Africa, and other European countries also established powerful positions. Russia and some other countries in Eastern Europe and in Latin America have been the last to enter as major actors and indeed in competition in this world market, although the nature of the motivation must be somewhat different in the actions of leaders of a country with predominantly private ownership and a country with predominantly state ownership.

To emphasize with Wallerstein the totality of the world system having a single division of labor may lead us to forget the infinite diversity of the parts, and labeling them "core," "periphery," and "semiperiphery" draws distinctions in what may be much more nearly a continuum than what Wallerstein calls a "tri-modal system," or three-tiered structure.[19] What does seem clear is that there is *still* only one world system, but within it there are winners and losers—winning countries and losing countries, changing over time— but above all winning classes and losing classes. What, moreover, any analysis of class and country soon tells us is that winning classes can be distinguished by their use of the state to secure and sustain their victory. What concessions they make to those they have vanquished will depend on the nature and source of their economic strength in the world system. To study countries, above all perhaps to study developing societies, in a world system without studying the classes that are dominant and dominated in them is to fall into error. This is typified by talk of one *country* exploiting another, as if nations were homogeneous and state policies were pursued in the interests of the whole population. What the world system holds together, then, is not countries or even states but economic activities and more specifically economic classes. The crucial question for us is whether these nations and classes have real possibilities of economic development.

It is just these possibilities that politicians in both developed and developing societies have seized upon in putting forward the concept of a "New International Economic Order," which might reconcile the interests of both societies. Such a new order has been most persuasively argued in the much publicized Report of an Independent Commission on International Development Issues, prepared by men and women of great influence, under the chairmanship of Willy Brandt, and entitled *North-South—A Programme for Survival*. This report follows ten years after the Pearson report on "Partners in Development." The emphasis has moved from an earlier, more optimistic, prospect of partnership to a much more desperate response from the rich countries to the revolt and disorder that another decade of famine and frustration in the underdeveloped world has generated. It reveals, moreover, a much less confident voice from the developed world, which by 1980 is plagued with unemployment, inflation, and internecine competition. The developing countries appear as new markets for surplus manufactured products, and particularly for those where sales are slumping in the developed countries—cigarettes, milk and baby foods, pharmaceuticals (analgesics, sulfonamides, antibiotics), agricultural and industrial machinery. Combined with the threat of rising prices of oil and raw materials for the developing countries, the developed countries' need for markets becomes a splendid neoclassical example of economic mutuality.

The report is based upon three assumptions: (1) that the combined threats of famine and unemployment, exhaustion of mineral resources, and nuclear war create a crisis that is so serious as to make possible a united human effort to start bridging the ever widening gap in wealth between the developed "North"-and the underdeveloped "South"; (2) that rich and poor nations alike have a common interest in cooperating to help the poor to develop, and can overcome the conflicts between them over the division of the world's wealth; and (3) that a massive transfer of funds from the rich nations to the poor nations would enable the poor to develop their industry and agriculture and meet basic needs that are not met today. This proposal for worldwide Keynesian solutions to worldwide recession is ironically presented just when the governments of the major countries in the "North," at least, have abandoned Keynesian policies at home for earlier and more primitive nostrums of economic retrenchment and protection. But this could be precisely because there were no Keynesian policies being simultaneously pursued in the world economy. The writers of the report were, it must be said, in the main critics of their countries' governments' desertion of Keynesian policies.

The essence of Keynesian policy has always been that there are at any time great underused resources of goods and labor and capital—and this was certainly never more obvious than today with millions of unemployed in the developed countries and their factories working at well below their productive capacity—and that to evoke their use it is necessary to generate increased demand for the frustrated supply to come forward.[20] This can best be initiated, the Keynesians argue, by taxing the savings of the rich to increase the purchasing power of the poor. The rich will have a smaller share of the cake, but as the cake will be larger their slice will at least be no smaller. Unfortunately, the rich can't always believe this, and especially if they are not sure that the taxes in an international scheme will fall equally on all the rich, and, therefore, on their competitiors in capital accumulation in other nations. Ultimately, the Marxist critique of Keynesian solutions resides in just this uncertainty. The difficulty in achieving such international economic expansion has indeed always been that international agreements are made not between the peoples of each nation but between leaders representing classes whose interests may well be at stake in making any change in the status quo.

The appeal of the authors of *North-South* for the "vested interests" in the South, whose "economic power and wealth are concentrated in the hands of a small minority," "to redistribute incomes and assets to expand employment opportunities,"[21] is not, however, applied equally to the vested interests in the "North." The problem is that the system is a world system of capitalist accumulation, and it is not nations but classes that are integrated into it.

Let us take the case of the British colonies that were settled by British and other Europeans and became independent nation states in the nineteenth century, whether linked as "dominions" to the British Empire and later British Commonwealth (Canada, Australia, New Zealand, South Africa), or not (United States). We may contrast their experience of development with the underdevelopment of India under British rule in the nineteenth century. The reason for the success of the former must be found in the combination of rich but empty lands—emptied largely by the Europeans' own depredations—and in a ruling class of settler capitalists. These people were mainly small capital owners in commerce and trade closely linked to the center of capital accumulation in Britain, but gained the power in time to establish their independence from kith and kin at home. They were thus able to hold on to an increasing proportion of the profit of the investment by British capital in primary production in their lands and to generate their own industrialization and independent capital accumulation. They did this by diversifying production from the original exploitation of the mineral and agricultural wealth of their lands of settlement into a wider and wider range of manufacturing industry. This gave them cumulatively more freedom from dependence on the capital and technology of the home country. The early British history of these countries is of continual struggle between a landed and farming interest and commercial class tied closely to the British home market and a local manufacturing interest.

Once again it is the class diversity of different developing societies that must be emphasized. Andre Gunder Frank has argued that there is no national bourgeoisie in Latin America but only the local agents and accomplices of U.S. imperialism.[22] First of all, this is not a universal truth: there are certainly national bourgeoisies in Canada, South Africa, and Australia. However close their links may be with United States, United Kingdom, or Japanese capital, they have some elements of independence in their capital accumulation. Secondly, the hierarchy of nations that Frank and Wallerstein emphasize leaves no room for understanding a bourgeoisie embedded in the industrialization process of developing societies, however much this is integrated into and dependent on the world capitalist system. This is not to argue against what we saw in an earlier section on the rise of the transnational company: that it is increasingly difficult for any new major center of independent capital accumulation to become established. It can now be added that the independence of Canadian, South African, and Australian capital has probably been much reduced in recent years by the growth of the transnationals.

By contrast with the developments we have just been considering, the extent and independence of the economic development of India can only be regarded as quite specifically different. The reasons for its limitations are evident from the absence of all the predisposing factors we saw in the settler colonies: richly endowed land, but densely occupied beyond the powers of even Europeans to depopulate; not settled by the British but ruled by them indirectly through landlords, agents, princes, and a native army; first plundered and then developed in enclaves of primary production—mainly on plantations of cotton, jute, tea, copra, timber, rubber; existing local handcraft industries supplanted by imports of British manufactures; ports and railways constructed to supply the overseas trade; finally, some modern industry—mainly textiles and food processing—established through agencies of British firms to supply an elite of ruling classes—landed, commercial, or in the state service. A small national bourgeoisie, however, did emerge during the years when British manufactures were cut off and British troops needed supplies in two world wars. From this tiny bourgeoisie and from the radicalization of a section of the educated elite, the Congress Party emerged. The connection is revealing. The wars provided the chance to benefit from the world system and a section of the Indian ruling classes seized its chance. They had just enough local power thereafter, with continuing support from the transnational companies, to make something of the chance.

Can we then list the necessary and even sufficient conditions for successful economic development today within a world capitalist system? The list might still be so overwhelming as to lead to the conclusion that nothing but the establishment of a rival world socialist system could guarantee economic development for most of the developing societies in the world. The brave assumptions of proponents of a New International Economic Order may well be shown to be quite unrealistic.[23] Such a transfer of power over the earth's resources from dominant to dominated groups and classes, via aid schemes and positive discrimination in trade, could not be made in more than a very few especially well-placed countries. To generalize such a transfer would imply nothing short of a worldwide revolution. The aim of such programs prepared by leading politicians in developed countries is precisely to head off revolution by buying off certain leading groups in revolutionary movements.

What then can we conclude are the conditions for economic development within a world capitalist system? The first and most necessary condition must be access to resources for which there is a strong and growing demand on the world market and not too many rival suppliers. The resources might be mineral or agricultural or human or simply a special geographical location like Singapore or Hong Kong. But this is not a sufficient condition. The world is littered with the sites of deserted mines and forests and great populations which capitalism has exploited and abandoned. The second condition is the existence of a class or classes related to the ownership and control of these resources and capable of developing them independently of the developed centers, so as to begin their sustained capital accumulation. Once more this condition is not sufficient for successful development. History is full of stories of the rise of classes or merchants and traders and financiers, even of producers of goods and services in great demand, who have risen to power and challenged the market to concentrate accumulation in their hands and have then fallen back defeated or been incorporated into the dominant power system.

The third condition for development is the establishment of a powerful state—with both a military force and an efficient and well-organized bureaucracy working not merely as servants of the dominant class but as an integrated part of it. But herein lies a contradiction: there is a final condition. The state of a dominant class can be the organ of forced growth only to the extent that it is legitimated either by real or synthetic popular support, i.e., by the ideology that sustains it. Real popular support rather than false ideology may be easier to achieve in a small nation state than in a large one; but for economic development the bigger the state—both in numbers of citizens and in the stretch and power of its organs—the better. With the growth of transnational companies big has to mean very big.

It is, as we expected, a formidable set of conditions. There are not likely to be many candidates and there would seem likely to be a premium on those that established centrally planned economies, whether the ideological underpinnings are socialist or corporatist. Short of the establishment of a rival socialist world market, there will be little chance for the smaller nation states to develop and no chance even that the larger nation states, where socialist revolutionaries have taken power, will develop into societies bearing any resemblance, except in their ideology, to the ideal which they seek.

Notes

1. See United Nations, various *Statistical Yearbooks*.
2. W. Brandt et al., *North-South—A Programme for Survival* (London: Pan, 1980), pp. 174, 188.
3. United Nations, various *Statistical Yearbooks* and UNCTAD.
4. United Nations, various *Statistical Yearbooks*.
5. See Diana Rouse, "Cheaper than Machines," *New Internationalist* (April 1980).
6. Robin Murray, "Underdevelopment, International Firms and the International Division of Labor," in *Towards a New World Economy* (Rotterdam: 1972).
7. Stephen Hymer, "The Multinational Corporation and the Law of Uneven Development," abridged in this collection.
8. M. Panic and P.L. Joyce, "UK Manufacturing Industry: International Integration and Trade Performance," Bank of England, *Quarterly Bulletin* (March 1980).
9. M. Barratt Brown, *Economics of Imperialism* (Harmondsworth: Penguin, 1974), pp. 226-27.
10. R. Vernon, *Sovereignty at Bay* (Harmondsworth: Penguin, 1971).
11. B.Warren, "How International Is Capital," *New Left Review* 68 (July-August 1971).
12. C. Vaitsos, "The Attitudes and Role of Transnational Enterprises in Economic Integration Processes among the L.D.C.s," *Millenium* 6, no. 3 (Winter 1977-78).
13. Panic and Joyce, "UK Manufacturing Industry."
14. C. Vaitsos, "The Process of Commercialisation of Technology in the Andean Pact," in H. Radice, ed., *International Firms and Modern Imperialism* (Harmondsworth: Penguin, 1975).
15. See for a summary Frances Stewart, *Technology and Underdevelopment* (New York: Macmillan, 1977).
16. See M. Barratt Brown, "Ideology and Economic Development," *Millenium* 6, no. 3 (Winter 1977-78).
17. Andre Gunder Frank, *Capitalism and Underdevelopment in Latin America*, (New York: Monthly Review Press, 1967).
18. Immanuel Wallerstein, *The Capitalist World-Economy* (New York and Cambridge: Cambridge University Press, 1979), pp. 20-22, 98-102.
19. Ibid. pp. 68-69, 123, and 223-24.
20. M. Barratt Brown, *Economics of Imperialism* (Harmondsworth: Penguin, 1974), pp. 312-15.
21. Brandt et al., *North-South*.
22. Frank, *Capitalism and Underdevelopment*.
23. The analysis of Brandt et al., *North-South* makes no allowance for the growth of COMECON, the Eastern trading bloc.

[13]
The Structure of Peripheral Capitalism

Hamza Alavi

The Problem

There was a pervasive belief in classical Marxism that despite the destructive and exploitative nature of colonial capitalism, it would nevertheless, historically, fulfill a regenerative role for colonized societies. It would break down the old precapitalist social order and generate new social forces, setting in motion the dynamics (and contradictions) of capital accumulation and development in the colony. Among Marxists such a view still survives as a minority view.[1] Taken onesidedly, the optimistic aspect of that complex vision was, on the other hand, the prognosis and self-justification of colonialist ideology, a notion that continues to inform the theory and practice of "modernization" and developmentalism. The actual experience of peripheral capitalist societies belies such expectations.

Two influential lines of thought have emerged from attempts to explain this perverse fact. One of these is "underdevelopment theory," pioneered by Andre Gunder Frank and built on by Immanuel Wallerstein, who has articulated a concept of the "modern world system" which sees the whole world (including socialist—or postcapitalist—societies) embraced by a network of international trade and therefore by global capitalism, but on the basis of a hierarchy of states and regions within it so that "core" states exploit those of the periphery, which explains the underdevelopment of the latter. The other line of thought recognizes and emphasizes the effects of colonial capitalism on the internal structures of colonized societies and the consequences of such effects for development, which are obscured in underdevelopment theory and the conceptual scheme of the "modern world system" theory. This second view proposes instead a conception of "articulation" of the colonial capitalist mode of production and what are still regarded as indigenous precapitalist modes which, it is argued, are not dissolved by the development of colonial capitalism, as envisaged by the classical Marxist theory. Rather, it is suggested that colonial capital brings about instead a *conservation* and *dissolution* (both at once?) of the precapitalist modes of production in colonized social formations;

172

that it *subordinates* them in order to serve its own purposes. Each of these currently influential lines of thought poses major problems in terms of historical materialism. In the light of a consideration of these problems, an alternative view is presented here (given space considerations, only briefly) which attempts to grasp the structural specificity of colonial capitalism and the dynamics and contradictions of its development and to examine the manner in which precapitalist structures, although apparently surviving, are in fact profoundly transformed by the impact of colonial capital and the development of indigenous capital.

The concept of "mode of production" provides a basic point of departure for our analysis. The term designates coherent structures within social formations (i.e., societies conceived of as systematically structured entities). It designates social relations of production and identifies fundamental classes that are embedded in them, i.e., for each mode of production, a class of exploited producers and a corresponding class of exploiting nonproducers. Other "auxiliary classes" in social formations derive their significance from their relationship with either the pre-existing fundamental classes or new ascendant classes in a social formation in which a new mode of production develops.

It is a process that necessarily entails the dissolution of the old, over a period of time, through class struggle between the classes located in the respective modes of production. It is by an analysis of the modes of production and their contradictions that we can understand the patterns of class formation and class alignment, and the class struggles that ensue as a consequence. The notion of irreconcilability between the rising capitalist modes of production and precapitalist modes in a social formation is a pivotal conception in historical materialism.

Modes of production and social relations of production structured by them, rather than relations of exchange, define capitalism in a Marxist conception. Trade links do not by themselves unify societal entities structurally into a single economic system. Referring to trading nations that promoted trade between commercially and economically underdeveloped societies, Marx spoke of "merchants' capital in its pure form" that merely mediates between their respective spheres of production but does not thereby constitute them as a single structured entity. This is not to rule out possible effects of such trade, "a more or less dissolving influence [of commerce] everywhere on the producing organisation." He wrote: "Both money and commodities are elementary preconditions of capital, but they develop into capital only under certain circumstances. . . . The production and circulation of commodities do not at all imply the existence of the capitalist mode of production. . . . They may be found even in pre-bourgeois modes of production. They constitute the *historical premise* of the capitalist mode of production. . . . Once the commodity has become the *general form of the production*. . . [only then is it] on the foundations of capitalist production."[2] Marx points out that the growth of the capitalist mode of production in Western Europe "tends to extend the world market continually, so that it is not commerce in this case which revolutionises industry, but industry which constantly revolutionises commerce."[3] It is in classical political economy and Weber, rather than in Marx, that we find conceptions of capitalism founded on exchange and trade rather than social relations of production.

Underdevelopment theory and Wallerstein's conception of the modern world system are grounded on a conception of capitalism in terms of trade and exchange rather than social relations of production.[4] The incorporation of a society within the network of world trade is a sufficient condition for its designation as capitalist. This unifies the "modern world system" under a single division of labor. The relative positions of different regions in the "modern world system" are said to derive from the strength or weakness of their respective states: "By a series of accidents. . . North-West Europe emerged as the core area of this world economy" and developed "strong state mechanisms." Peripheral states, by contrast, were "weak" so that the former imposed on them "unequal exchange" on the basis of which they extracted a "surplus" from them. Wallerstein insists that capitalism was from the beginning an affair of the "world economy" and not of nation states. However, it is states, not classes, that are the essential units of his analysis, despite his disclaimers to the contrary. The argument tells us little about the origins and the *structural* and *class character* and consequences of capitalism and, specifically, peripheral capitalism.

The alternative line of thought that we have referred to focuses on the internal structures of precapitalist social formations in colonized societies that are incorporated within the domain of colonial capital, and the apparently *symbiotic* relationship between the two, as against antagonistic contradictions between them. In considering this line of thought, it might be said at the outset that every society builds on inherited societal, institutional, and cultural products of the past. Capitalism does not erase them totally and substitute new social institutions brought out of nowhere. It takes the legacies from the past as the raw materials for building its society of the future, combining them with new societal and cultural realities that it also creates. This often results in an illusion of continuity, where profound changes have occurred, when social phenomena are looked at in an empiricist way, disregarding underlying structural discontinuities and new significance and meanings that are infused into old forms thereby. This, one would argue, has happened in the case of those who see precapitalist forms *conserved* by capital rather than transformed by virtue of their subsumption under capital.

In this school of thought colonial capital is sometimes regarded as an *external* entity rather than as a new element in the social and economic structure of the colonized society itself and as a force that is internal to it. Thus Charles Bettelheim writes: "Inside social formations in which capitalist mode of production is not directly predominant, that is social formations that are capitalist social formations *because* they are subordinated to the capitalist mode of production through the world market (but in which other modes of production *predominate*), the main tendency is not to dissolution of the noncapitalist mode of production but to their *conservation-dissolution.* The predominance of this tendency is doubtless connected with a group of determining factors produced by the 'external' domination of capitalism. . . ."[5] The relationship that is expressed here by Bettelheim is that which Marx visualizes in the case of the global expansion of precolonial merchants' capital. It is quite indefensible in the case of capitalist penetration and domination of colonized economies and the introduction into them, consequently, both of new social relations of production, in the form of colonial enterprises in plantations, mining, and colonial manufactures, and also the subsumption of peasant production under colonial capital. The formula of *conservation-dissolution* has passed into common currency especially among those who are mainly concerned with predominantly peasant societies, whose subsumption under capital presents a new and unresolved problem for Marxist theory (for which capitalist relations of production are premised on the separation of the producer from the means of production). Claude Meillassoux represents such a view when, referring to labor migration between what he characterizes as the "capitalist sector" of the colonized society and the "rural one," he writes: "Because of this process of absorption [of migrant labor] within the capitalist economy, the agricultural communities maintained as reserves of cheap labour, are being *both undermined and perpetuated at the same time*" (emphasis added).[6] This formula obscures the underlying theoretical problem that I have referred to, rather than helping toward its clarification.

The debate takes a somewhat different course in discussions of the effects of colonial capitalism on highly stratified "feudal" societies of the periphery. In this case, the main tradition of Marxist thought is grounded in Lenin's influential writings on the development of capitalism in Russia. In the Russian case, Lenin recognized an irreconcilable contradiction between the dominant feudal mode of production and the rising forces of capitalism, in agriculture as well as in industry. That contradiction defined for him the stage of bourgeois-democratic revolution in Russia that would in turn inaugurate the stage of proletarian revolution. This idea was also extended to colonized "countries of the East." But the fact remains that Russia was not a colonized society and any attempt to extrapolate the argument grounded on analysis of the Russian case must first take account of the nature and specificity of the colonial experience.

In the application of Lenin's analysis, of noncolonized Russia, to colonized societies, the argument underwent an untheorized transformation. As against his original argument of an irreconcilable structural contradiction between the dominant classes located in the feudal mode of production and the capitalist mode, respectively, in the debates on "The National and the Colonial Questions" at the Second Congress of the Comintern in 1920, he recognized instead an alliance between landowning magnates in the colonial societies, designated "feudal," and metropolitan capital. This militates against his own (and a basic Marxist) notion of irreconcilability between the fundamental classes located in the two respective modes of production. On the other hand, it was also accepted that there was a conflict of interest between the rising indigenous bourgeoisies in colonized societies and the other two classes just mentioned, although both are located in the same, capitalist, mode of production. In the light of the debate that ensued, Lenin recognized that this conflict of interest did not have the character of an irreconcilable structural contradiction; that there also existed the possibility of class collaboration between the two. That was the basis of reformist "nationalist" movements. This was an accurate assessment of the political situation and movements of the time in those countries referred to in the debate, such as India. But the theoretical issues that underlie that reassessment have remained unclarified. Our present object, therefore, is to examine the structural specificity of peripheral capitalism in the light of these questions.

Basic Concepts: Modes of Production

Much of the debate in this area has been vitiated by misunderstandings and disagreements over some basic concepts. The difficulty stems, in no small measure, from the fact that Marx does not provide us with a concise and precise definition of the basic concept of "mode of production," as a concept of social structure, which he alludes to, for instance, in the "Preface to the Critique of Political Economy," designating "the Asiatic, the ancient, the feudal and the modern bourgeois...economic formation(s) of society." Contemporary Marxists who have turned to the task have done so largely under the influence of a structuralist-functionalist translation of Marxism by Louis Althusser and others, who offer a conception of the social world inhabited by reified structures. In our own attempt to clarify that basic concept we must begin with the recognition that even if Marx did not offer a definition of the concept as such, the whole of his monumental work, *Capital*, is devoted precisely to a systematic and rigorous analysis of the capitalist mode of production. We can therefore derive the concept from a careful study of that work. But first we might consider some contemporary discussions of this question in order to locate the analysis that is presented.

We have already referred to the conceptualization of capitalism by Frank, Wallerstein, and others, in terms of a global network of trade—a conception grounded on relations of exchange rather than social relations of production. This issue is taken up by Laclau in his well-known critique of Frank.[7] In redefining the concept, Laclau writes: "We therefore designate as a mode of production the logically and mutually coordinated articulation of: (1) a determinate type of ownership of means of production; (2) a determinate form of appropriation of the economic surplus; (3) a determinate degree of development of the division of labour; (4) a determinate level of development of productive forces."[8] In specifying the feudal and capitalist modes of production, Laclau limits himself to the first two of these four conditions:

> The feudal mode of production is one in which the productive process operates according to the following pattern: (1) the economic surplus is produced by a labour force subject to extra-economic compulsion; (2) the economic surplus is privately appropriated by someone other than the direct producer; (3) property in the means of production remains in the hands of the direct producer. In the capitalist mode of production the economic surplus is also subject to private appropriation but, as distinct from feudalism, ownership of the means of production is severed from ownership of labour power; it is that [which] permits the translation of labour power into a commodity, and with this the birth of the wage relation.[9]

We shall see in the light of a definition that we can derive from Marx's treatment of the capitalist mode of production in *Capital* that Laclau's definition, while specifying some levels of determination of the respective modes of production, is incomplete, and that it can lend itself to an empiricist interpretation of the notion of "relations of production" as a relationship between two individuals, obscuring the structural matrix in which individuals are located. To proceed further, it may be best to outline the structural conditions of the feudal and capitalist modes of production (FMP and CMP respectively). The concepts as they emerge from an analysis of the argument in *Capital* can be set out as follows—I have further indicated the points at which the structure of peripheral capitalism can be distinguished from that of metropolitan capitalism.

The structural conditions identified above constitute a complex unity; they are interdependent. In conceptualizing economic, or political, etc., "instances" or "subsystems" in society, they are all too often thought of either as empirically separable entities or, in a structuralist conception, each a separate "structure" constituting an entity in itself and having determinate relationships with the other "structures," namely, "economic," "political," and "ideological." This can be quite misleading. The economic "instance," for example, cannot be thought of without its basis in particular forms of property and the latter in turn entails particular structures of power and ideologies that sustain them. There is therefore a simultaneous determination of the whole societal structure, and none of the component instances that we identify analytically actually exist prior to, or independently of, the others.

To avoid some possible sources of confusion, it is equally essential to recognize that the concepts of "social formation" and "mode of production" are each concepts of a quite different order. A mode of production defines the *structure* of social relations of production; it is an analytical concept. The concept of "social formation," on the other hand, is a descriptive term. It denotes an actual and specific societal entity, with all its particularities, products of past developments, and structuration and restructuration, results of accident and design, and all historical legacies of the past and potentialities for the future. As such it refers to a particular, geographically bounded and historically given, societal entity with given resources and given forms of economic and political organization and cultural features. Social and economic relations exist not merely *within* social formations but also *between* them, such as the relationships established by colonial capital. As a concept of structure of relationships, the concept of "mode of production" does not—and in the case of peripheral social formations cannot—exclude such relationships.

We can now consider what is missing from Laclau's definition of modes of production. It covers only the first two of the structural conditions that we have derived from a reading of *Capital*, namely

Feudal mode of production (FMP)	Capitalist mode of production (CMP)	Peripheral capitalism
1. Unfree labor; direct producer in possession of means of production (land, etc.).	"Free" labor: (1) free of feudal obligations (2) dispossessed— separation of the producer from means of production.	As in CMP.
2. Extraeconomic compulsion for extraction of surplus.	Economic "coercion" of the dispossessed producer.	As in CMP.
3. Localized structure of power; the fusion of economic and political power at the point of production—a necessary condition of coercive extraction of the surplus.	Separation of economic (class) power from political (state) power; creation of bourgeois state and bourgeois law.	Specific colonial structure.
4. Self-sufficient localized economy supplemented by simple circulation of commodities.	Generalized commodity production (production primarily for sale; labor power itself a commodity).	Specific colonial structure.
5. Simple reproduction where surplus is largely consumed.	Extended reproduction of capital and rise in organic composition of capital.	Specific colonial structure.

(1) in the feudal mode, unfree labor and extra-economic compulsion in the extraction of surplus from direct producers who possess the means of production, and (2) in the capitalist mode, free labor and separation of the producer from the means of production. It could be argued that condition number 3, which is made explicit in our formulation, namely, the localization of the structure of power in the FMP as against the separation of economic and political power, and the creation of a bourgeois state, bourgeois law, and juridical equality in the CMP, on which capitalist property is based, is *implied* in the Laclau formulation. But that still leaves us with the crucial conditions of generalized commodity production and extended reproduction of capital that distinguish the CMP from the FMP, which are not to be found either in Laclau's formulation or in others that are current. These conditions are central to Marx's analysis of the two modes of production and the difference in the respective dynamics of their development. It is also precisely in these two respects that we find that the structure of peripheral capitalism is different from that of metropolitan capitalism.

It is a common misconception to think of "modes of production" as if the concept denotes societal elements within social formations. This confusion is understandable, for the concept has been used in analyses of noncolonized social formations (such as that of Russia) in their transition from feudalism to capitalism, where both have been regarded as structures that are internal to the social formation. But the concept of *structure* is not a bounded entity. It may include, and in the case of peripheral capitalism it must include, relationships that extend beyond the confines of the particular social formation. In the case of colonized societies the external nexus is not at the level of trade alone (and the trade of a peripheral social formation expresses a relationship of subordination to imperialism that shapes its pattern). Rather, the crucial link is through the domination of the economies of the peripheral social formations by metropolitan capital that has a "structural presence" in them. Their structures cannot be understood without taking into account their link with imperialism. Their structures transcend their societal boundaries.

The main structural difference between capitalism in colonial societies and in noncolonized societies is to be found in the last two conditions listed above: (1) generalized commodity production, and (2) extended reproduction of capital. In the first case, the major impact of colonial capital on precapitalist societies, in the course of their transformation into peripheral capitalist societies, was to break down their local self-sufficiency and to generate in them commodity production intended for sale, both locally and in international markets. By the same token, it drew these societies into the ambit of colonial trade, as markets for metropolitan production. This is generalized commodity production, but generalized commodity production with specific characteristics that distinguishes it from that in metropolitan societies. This difference constitutes one of the elements of the structural specificity of peripheral capitalism. In noncolonized, metropolitan, countries generalized commodity production was an "integrated" process of development, in industry as well as in agriculture and—especially in the case of the former—the production of capital goods as well as consumers' goods. That was not the case in peripheral capitalism, which brought about a disarticulated form of generalized commodity production, as contrasted with the *integrated* form in metropolitan capitalism. It must be emphasized that by this distinction we do not mean autarkic development. The point is about the character of production in different branches of metropolitan economies and those of peripheral capitalist societies, which make the latter dependent on its links with the metropolitan economies. The circuit of generalized commodity production in peripheral capitalist societies is not internally complete, as in the case of metropolitan capitalism. For then that circuit is completed only by virtue of their links with the metropolitan economy, by production for export, and as markets for colonial imports. The structural condition of generalized commodity production in peripheral capitalism is satisfied only by virtue of the link with the metropolis.

The same can be said about the process of "extended reproduction of capital," a concept in Marxist theory of capitalist development that refers to the fact that not only is the capital used up in production replaced from the proceeds, but also that the "surplus value" that is extracted from the worker contributes to the accumulation of capital and thereby to a constant enlargement of the capacity to produce.[10] In the case of peripheral capitalist societies, insofar as the surplus value generated in them is appropriated by metropolitan capitalism, this leads to a growth of productive powers not in the peripheral capitalist society but in the metropolis. The condition of capitalist development is thus satisfied but in a manner that is specific to peripheral capitalism. While both cases fulfill the conditions of CMP, as I have shown, the structure of peripheral capitalism and the dynamics of its development are, by virtue of these differences, quite distinct from those of metropolitan capitalism.

Finally, we might consider the consequences of leaving out the two structural conditions that we have identified, which are usually ignored in conceptualizing modes of production, on the basis of which we have been able to make a distinction between the structure of peripheral capitalism and that of metropolitan capitalism. One of these I have referred to above, namely the danger of an empiricist reading of the concept of "social relations of production," as relations between two sets of individuals or classes, independently of the overall matrix in which they are located. This can happen when using categories such as ownership or nonownership of property, free or coerced labor, or simple categories such as wage labor as contrasted with sharecropping or labor services. Another consequence of no small importance is that without the specification of these two conditions we arrive at a static conception of structure, whereas the project of historical materialism aims at illuminating underlying processes and dynamics of change. In the one-sided polemic against Andre Gunder Frank, his critics lose sight of the fact that it is only with capitalism that the production of commodities becomes the direct and immediate objective of all production and that generalized commodity production (which concept includes the transformation of labor power into a commodity) is a necessary condition and consequence of capitalist development. Likewise, the condition of "simple reproduction" under precapitalist modes of production, and "extended reproduction of capital" in CMP, differentiate the latter's capacity for the growth of the forces of production as compared with the relative stagnation of precapitalist societies.

Transition to Peripheral Capitalism

When capitalism begins to emerge in a social formation or, as in the case of societies that were subordinated to colonial capital, penetrates it from outside, there is a period during which the two modes of production exist side by side, in mutual contradiction, which is resolved by the ultimate triumph of the capitalist mode of production, by virtue of the transformation of the precapitalist modes and the subsumption of the processes of production (and reproduction) that existed in that sphere, under capital. That is a historical process whose course and duration is determined by the particular characteristics and conditions of existence of the precapitalist mode and the manner of the impact of capital. It is not, however, a process that unfolds purely at the economic level. In the class struggle that accompanies that process of transformation, force plays a part and, especially in the case of the subordination of peripheral social formations, the colonial state plays a crucial role. Here we are concerned not with the variety of ways in which that process has unfolded in different parts of the world, but with the common characteristics of the structure of peripheral capitalism that eventually takes shape as a result.

In the schema of the structural characteristics of the feudal and capitalist modes of production, and those of peripheral capitalism, that I have sketched out above I have indicated the specific features of the latter that result at the end of that process of transformation. In looking at the process of change itself, we can identify broadly two kinds of processes, each of which raises particular theoretical issues that we must try to clarify. One is the case where the precapitalist society in question is a highly stratified "feudal" society such as that of medieval India or latifundia in Latin America, with large landowning magnates. I will state my arguments here with brief illustrative references to the Indian case, which I have examined more fully elsewhere.[11] But the analysis can be extended to other such cases. The other type of case is that of subsumption under capital of precapitalist societies of small peasants such as those that predominate in many African countries but are not by any means absent in India or Latin America.

Evidence about the form of village organization in medieval India is conflicting and no doubt there were considerable regional differences. In northern India a hierarchy of *zamindars*, lords of the land, within the framework of the "absolutist state" of the Moghuls, lived off the surplus extracted from unfree peasants. The term *zamindar* refers to lords of varying rank and power. Historian Nurul Hasan offers a simplified classification of *zamindars* in the Moghul empire into three broad categories: (1) autonomous chieftans, (2) "intermediary" *zamindars*, and (3) "primary" *zamindars*, the last being the village *zamindar*.[12] It is this last category that is of crucial interest for us.

The *zamindar* at the village level was the kingpin of the whole system. It was he who, in the first instance, directly controlled the peasants and their labor and forcibly extracted the surplus from them. "The *zamindars* enjoyed the right to restrain the tenants from leaving their lands and to compel them to cultivate all arable land held by them."[13] As Irfan Habib points out, the *zamindars* had the right to bring fugitive peasants back by force. These are all characteristics of the feudal mode of production. Here was a localized structure of power, exercised directly over the peasant, the foundation of the elaborate hierarchy of power of the Moghul empire. This was a pattern not dissimilar to that of the absolutist state in Europe. Likewise, production was localized, for the village society was self-sufficient, with its own internal division of labor. Land

revenue was paid in cash and for that purpose the peasant cultivated cash crops that sustained a flourishing, and parasitical, urban
society. But this was by no means a case of "generalized commodity
production." The surplus drawn off in the form of land revenue
was largely consumed—a case of "simple reproduction" rather than
"extended reproduction of capital."

Colonial conquest not only displaced the crumbling power of the
Moghul empire and set up the colonial state. It also transformed
the structure of power at the local level, concomitantly with the
creation of "bourgeois landed property" whereby land became the
property of the *zamindar, dispossessing* the cultivator. Whereas before the change the peasant sharecroppers were unfree and the
surplus was extracted from them by the *zamindar* by virtue of the
jurisdiction and coercive force that he directly exercised over them,
now it was to be on a new basis. The "petty sovereignties" of the
zamindars were abolished under the new colonial dispensation that
separated political power, now vested in the colonial state, from the
economic power of the *zamindars*. The latter, who were land*lords*,
were now land*owners*. On the surface, their relationships with their
sharecroppers do not appear to be very different from what they
were before. An empiricist reading of history could easily lead one
to suppose that this was unchanged. But the *basis* of that relationship was fundamentally altered. Peasants were now legally free to
leave their *zamindar*. But being dispossessed, they could have no
access to the means of his livelihood without turning to the landowner for whom they now worked out of economic compulsion,
"freely." The peasants were thus trapped, as sellers of labor power,
by their dispossession. From now on their demand was to be for
security of tenure rather than for freedom to leave the lord.

We can therefore conclude that as a consequence of a series of
changes, implemented by the colonial state, in the decades after the
conquest of India, social relations of production in Indian agriculture were transformed. The precolonial feudal structure was dissolved, the peasants were separated from their means of production
and livelihood, land, which now became bourgeois landed property
in the hands of landowners who ceased to be landlords, their localized structures of power having been dissolved and incorporated
into the structure of the colonial state. Economic compulsion was
substituted for direct political compulsion to draw a surplus, from
"free" labor. The first three of the five structural conditions of the
capitalist mode of production were realized by that restructuring of
the social relations of production.

The process of development of a peripheral capitalist economy
was a longer one.[14] Indian cotton and silk textile industries (based

on domestic production) as well as other industries were destroyed. With the development of railways and a general improvement in the means of transport and communication, Indian agriculture was progressively turned toward the production of crops for the metropolitan market, especially cotton, jute, and indigo. Some crops, such as tea, were produced on colonial plantations; elsewhere, peasants produced food crops as cash crops, not only to feed the towns that were bases for colonial trade but also to feed peasants in other areas who had turned to the production of export crops. Thus the old pattern of localized production was broken and production of commodities for an international market as well as an expanding domestic market was taken in hand. Likewise, with the progressive destruction of local manufacturing production, a market was established for imports from the metropolis. There was therefore a movement to generalized commodity production. But, as was said earlier, this was a form of generalized commodity production that was specific to peripheral capitalism, the circuit of commodity circulation being completed via the link with the metropolis, through exports and imports. The surplus extracted by colonial capital likewise created a form of extended reproduction of capital which was generated in the colony but accumulated in the metropolis. Thus all five conditions that we have stated were realized, but in a form that is specific to the structure of peripheral capitalism.

In recent debates about the development of capitalism in Indian agriculture,[15] the various protagonists have regarded sharecropping for landowners, on the basis of largely unchanged techniques, to be "feudal." Capitalism in agriculture is identified in that view with large-scale investment in farm mechanization in recent decades. This is misconceived insofar as the change in social relations of production, discussed above, has been ignored. Nevertheless, there *is* a difference between the two situations that needs to be clarified theoretically. The difference is best understood in the light of a distinction Marx made between "formal subsumption of labour under capital" and "real subsumption of labour under capital."[16] He writes that formal subsumption of labor under capital "is the general form of every capitalist process of production," for it refers essentially to the restructuration of social relations of production under capital. The formal subsumption of labor under capital "does not, by itself imply a fundamental modification in the real source of the labour process, the actual process of production. On the contrary, capital subsumes the labour process as it finds it, that is to say, it takes over an existing labour process." By contrast, with the "real subsumption of labour under capital" the labor process is (continually) transformed, concomitantly with the rise in the or-

ganic composition of capital, the consequence of extended reproduction of capital. The formal subsumption of labor under capital
(the change in social relations of production) is "the premise and
precondition of its real subsumption.... And real subsumption begins only when capital sums of a certain magnitude have directly
taken over control of production."[17]

This pair of concepts enables us to distinguish between the first
stage of capitalist development in England, with the bourgeois revolution in the seventeenth century, and that which followed after
the Industrial Revolution of the late eighteenth century. If the logic
of the Indian argument were to be adopted, it would be the latter
that would have to be regarded as the moment of the bourgeois
revolution in England. Likewise in India, we can recognize two
phases of transformation of the rural society, the first a formal
subsumption of labor under capital and more recently a marked
movement toward real subsumption. While the argument has been
presented here with reference to India, a case of direct colonial
rule, it can be extended to other peripheral capitalist societies where
parallel, developments can be delineated. In Latin America, for
example, where initially a precapitalist colonial empire was established by the Iberian powers, a movement toward formal subsumption of labor under capital can be recognized following independence
in the nineteenth century, at the same time as these countries came
increasingly under the (indirect, economic) domination of British
imperialism. The newly independent states, under indirect colonial
domination, soon began to undertake measures that dissolved
precapitalist social relations and established institutional structures
necessary for peripheral capitalism. New classes emerged. The pace
and the manner of peripheral capitalist transformation has varied
in accordance with local specificities and conditions, but the end
result, structurally, has been the same, both for countries that have
experienced direct colonial rule and those that have experienced
indirect colonialism.

The second major problem concerning the restructuration of
precapitalist societies in the course of their transition to peripheral
capitalism is that of the subsumption of peasant production under
capital. This is a problem that has not been confronted explicitly by
classical Marxism, which has visualized the dissolution of petty commodity production as a consequence of the centralizing tendency
of capitalist production (although even in the urban and manufacturing economies of advanced capitalism such forms of production
continue, subsumed under capital). With regard to the peasantry,
the issue is of far greater significance. Lenin reiterated the classical
view when, writing at the turn of the century about the disintegra-

tion of the Russian peasantry, he wrote: "The old peasantry is not only 'differentiating'; it is being completely dissolved, it is ceasing to exist, it is being ousted by absolutely new types of rural inhabitants—the types that are the basis of a society in which commodity economy and capitalist production will prevail. These types are the rural bourgeoisie (chiefly petty bourgeoisie) and the rural proletariat."[18] Much later he was to speak instead of "the more complicated problem [which] has come to the fore—*our attitude towards the middle peasant*" (emphasis in the original).[19] But Lenin did not elaborate on the theoretical issues that underlay his fresh perspective on the peasant question.

In his earlier analysis of the manner in which the rise of capitalism was causing "disintegration of the peasantry," Lenin did identify two aspects of the process, which provide leads into the problem and also illuminate contemporary processes in peripheral capitalist societies. He recognized, firstly, the effects of the impact of capitalism in breaking down the self-sufficiency of the peasant economy and drawing it increasingly into the circuit of generalized commodity production generated by the capitalist economy and, secondly, on the increasing migration of peasants who, as a consequence of the disintegration of the peasant economy, have to look for outside employment to supplement the bankrupt farm economy and subsidize the livelihood of those who depended on it.

Among contemporary writers, Henry Bernstein has fruitfully explored theoretical issues concerning the impact of capital on the peasantry, entailing "The Destruction of Natural Economy" and the "Process of 'Commoditisation.' "[20] He underlines two problems, namely (1) that of "investigating the relations of simple commodity producers (the peasantry) with various forms of capital in varying concrete conditions," and (2) "the internal differentiation of simple commodity producers (toward capitalist farmers and wage workers)." Bernstein adds: "We have been at pains to emphasize that the latter "classic model" is a special case of the first set of relations *and not its sole or necessary form of development*" (emphasis added). One would agree with his conclusion that "peasants have to be located in their relations with capital and the state, in other words, within *capitalist relations of production* mediated through forms of household production which are a site of a struggle for effective possession and control between the producers and capital/state" (emphasis added). Empirically, the processes of the subsumption of the peasantry under capital are examined with clarity by Lionel Cliffe,[21] although he operates within the analytical framework of the "articulation" of modes of production, the "precapitalist" with the (colonial) capitalist mode. One might argue that his data and analysis point strongly, nevertheless, in the direction of the argument that, in the aftermath of the impact of colonial capital and the transformation that follows, the peasant economies have ceased to be "precapitalist." While some old *forms* may persist, their underlying structural basis is transformed.

The concept of a mode of production includes not only structural conditions of production specific to it but also conditions of its *reproduction*. In the analysis of the capitalist mode of production the conditions of "necessary labor time," which determine limits to the degree of exploitation of labor in order to ensure the reproduction of labor power, and, likewise, the concepts of "constant capital" and "extended reproduction of capital," which relate to conditions that ensure reproduction of capital, are conditions of reproduction of the capitalist mode of production. These include also the existence and functioning of the capitalist state and ancillary institutions of the capitalist social order. The existence (and conception) of such conditions of *reproduction* of a mode of production does not by any means imply that in specifying them we are suggesting that they implicate a notion of *perpetuation* of that mode of production. The same must be said of precapitalist modes of production which, as such, can exist only so long as the conditions of their reproduction are realized.

The decisive feature of the transformation of precapitalist peasant societies, as a consequence of their subsumption under colonial capital, is that whereas previously they were able to realize the conditions of their reproduction, they were no longer able to do so after their transformation by colonial capital, except on the basis of the new structural conditions of the colonial capitalist economy—as sellers of labor power, or of commodities in which their labor power is embodied, and also as markets for colonial production. Their new modes of functioning are fundamentally different from their previous, precapitalist, modes. They can no longer reproduce themselves except within the integument of capital, under which they are subsumed. The Bantustans in South Africa, for example, are an integral part of the South African capitalist economy, structurally involved in the process of capitalist production, as reproducers of labor power. They are new creations and not simply survivals of a precapitalist past that are "conserved" as such, to subserve capitalism. Rather, it is precisely by virtue of the dissolution of their precapitalist basis that they fulfill such a role, having little alternative but to serve as reservoirs of cheap labor power for the enterprises that draw on them for that purpose. That is a mark of the specific structure of peripheral capitalism, and the location in them of peasant economies.

The destruction of conditions of reproduction of precapitalist societies is achieved by peripheral capitalism in a variety of ways, including, especially, state action designed specifically for that purpose. One of these is the imposition of taxes, for which peasants are forced to realize a cash income and therefore to engage, in one form or another, in activities that relate to the working of peripheral capitalism. A critical factor consists of state-imposed changes in conditions of access to land. Precapitalist societies have procedures that regulate access to land and productive resources so that new families are set up as viable economic units as well as social ones. Under peripheral capitalism and the authority of its state, such procedures are modified and abolished so that the previous procedures of reproduction of the peasant community no longer obtain. Land that can be designated as "unappropriated" is brought under state control depriving local communities of traditionally established access to such lands. There is also, concomitantly, a destruction of peasant manufacturing—a phenomenon known to rural sociology as the "agriculturalization" of the peasant. Commenting on similar processes in Europe, Kautsky, in his celebrated work *The Agrarian Question*, pointed out that: "In this way the peasant was finally forced to become what today we understand by peasant—a pure agriculturist."[22] The combined effects of state action in putting an end to traditional forms of access to land (making land "bourgeois landed property," a term that Marx used in the context of Britain), the imposition of fiscal burdens by the state and the destruction of peasant manufacturing—both creating a new need for the peasant to earn cash—were decisive in putting an end to the ability of the precapitalist modes of production to reproduce themselves. The peasant was now firmly located in the structure of peripheral capitalism; the peasant economy and society were no longer precapitalist. To describe them as such, albeit as "conserved-dissolved," obscures questions about the manner of transformation of these societies and their future dynamics of development.

If the peasantry continues to exist (though in its radically restructured form under peripheral capitalism), unlike the urban petty commodity producer who tends to disappear more rapidly (though not entirely), the reasons are to be found in the nature of the peasant economy itself rather than in a voluntarist conception of the intentions and purposes of capitalism. This is too large a subject to discuss in the present context,[23] but one or two points need to be made. Firstly, the crucial factor that distinguishes the two cases concerns the difference in the way in which each category secures a basic minimum of subsistence. In the case of the urban petty commodity producer, commodities must be sold on the market before commodities needed for subsistence can be bought. In the case of the peasant, food and shelter are secured up to a point without having to valorize production through the market; except for taxes, rents and such dues, the peasant can postpone cash requirements by putting off consumption of commodities dependent upon outside sources. Therefore the peasant has a much greater degree of resilience. Secondly, insofar as the pauperization of the peasantry under peripheral capitalism forces the peasant's kinsfolk to migrate for outside jobs, the money so earned helps the bankrupt farm economy to survive the ravages of capitalism for a longer time. Thirdly, in agriculture itself, the rise of large-scale farming depends upon a prior dispossession of the peasant, whose lands may be taken over by agribusiness. Given the ability of the poor peasant to survive on his bit of land, supplemented possibly by outside employment, it is necessarily a slow and difficult process for capital to take over from the peasant. Moreover, large-scale agriculture must have a contiguous block of land. That again imposes special conditions that are not easy to fulfill. This can be seen in the marked contrast with the tendency toward a rapid concentration of industrial production. The rise of large-scale industry is not predicated on the prior destruction of urban petty commodity producers. On the contrary, it rises independently of them, and, having done so, turns on them the powerful thrust of its competitive power, putting them out of business, onto the labor market. Peasants by contrast are able to survive a little longer because of the logic of their own economic situation. But this is not because capital "wills" it so. On the contrary, the forces of capitalism tend toward the peasant's pauperization. Peasants may not disappear overnight. But the conditions of their existence are being progressively undermined. That is an aspect of the dynamics of peripheral capitalist development.

Large questions about class formation and class alignments, as well as the dynamics of development of peripheral capitalist societies, follow from this analysis. One broad conclusion is that the "bourgeois revolution" in these societies was accomplished by metropolitan capitalism, and that these societies are already on the road of capitalist development. But it is capitalist development of a specific character that distinguishes it from that in metropolitan societies—one that does not allow the forces of production in these societies to grow rapidly as in classical capitalism. Furthermore, in cases that are analogous to the Indian case, where we find three "fundamental" classes, they are all located in the same mode of production and they do not stand in irreconcilable contradiction vis-à-vis each other. Their common ground provides them with a basis of mutual class alliances. With regard to peasant societies which predominate in some countries, but are by no means absent from the others, our analysis suggests a shift of perspective, locating them within the structure of peripheral capitalism, in terms of which the dynamics of their development may, more profitably, be viewed.

Notes

1. See, for example, Karl Marx, "The Future Results of British Rule in India," reprinted in K. Marx and F. Engels, *On Colonialism* (Moscow: 1960). For a contemporary argument on those lines see Bill Warren, *Imperialism: Pioneer of Capitalism* (London: New Left Books, 1980).
2. Karl Marx, *Capital*, vol. 1 (London: Lawrence and Wishart, 1976), p. 949. See also *Capital*, vol. III (Moscow: 1971), pp. 321-37.
3. Karl Marx, *Capital*, vol. III, p. 333.
4. Immanuel Wallerstein's key ideas are summed up in his article, "The Rise and Future Demise of the World Capitalist System: Concepts for Comparative Analysis," *Comparative Studies in Society and History* 16 (January 1974); a slightly abridged version is reprinted in this volume.
5. Charles Bettelheim, "Theoretical Comments" in appendix I to Arghiri Emmanuel, *Unequal Exchange* (New York: Monthly Review Press, 1972), pp. 297-98.
6. Claude Meillassoux, "From Reproduction to Production," *Economy and Society* 1, no. 1 (February 1972): 103.
7. Ernesto Laclau, "Feudalism and Capitalism in Latin America," *New Left Review* 67 (May-June 1971).
8. Ibid., p. 33.
9. Ibid.
10. For a lucid exposition of the theory see Paul Sweezy, *The Theory of Capitalist Development* (New York: Monthly Review Press, 1964).
11. See Hamza Alavi, "India: Transition from Feudalism to Colonial Capitalism," *Journal of Contemporary Asia* 10, no. 4 (1980).
12. Irfan Habib, *The Agrarian System of Moghul India* (London: 1963); and Nurul Hasan, "The Position of Zamindars in the Moghul Empire," *Indian Economic and Social History Review* 1, no. 4 (1964).
13. Hasan, "Position of Zamindars."
14. For an account see Alavi, "India: Transition from Feudalism."
15. A list of references to contributions in the debate is given in Hamza Alavi, "India and the Colonial Mode of Production," in R. Miliband and J. Saville, eds., *Socialist Register 1975* (London: Merlin Press, 1975), n. 1.
16. Karl Marx, *Capital*, vol. I, pp. 1019ff.; also see chap. 16, "Relative and Absolute Surplus Value."
17. All quotations from Marx, *Capital*, vol. I, pp. 1019-38.
18. V. I. Lenin, *Development of Capitalism in Russia* (Moscow: 1956), p. 174.

19. V. I. Lenin, "Report on Work in the Countryside" for the Eighth Congress of the Russian Communist Party (Bolshevik), March 1919.
20. Henry Bernstein, "Notes on Capital and Peasantry," *Review of African Political Economy* 10 (September-December 1977).
21. Lionel Cliffe, "Rural Class Formation in East Africa," *Journal of Peasant Studies* 4, no. 2 (January 1977); see chap. 21 of this volume.
22. Karl Kautsky, *Die Agrarfrage*, "Summary of Selected Parts," trans. by J. Banajee, *Economy and Society* 5, no. 1 (February 1976): 4.
23. See Teodor Shanin, "Defining Peasants: Conceptualizations and Deconceptualizations—Old and New in a Marxist Debate," *Peasant Studies* 8, no. 4 (Fall 1979); Eric Wolf, *Peasants* (Englewood Cliffs, N.J.: Prentice Hall, 1966); Boguslaw Galeski, *Basic Concepts in Rural Sociology* (Manchester: Manchester University Press, 1972).

Part III

Political Economy

This part is devoted to the characteristics of the political economy of "developing societies" and the dynamics of their development. It opens with an extract from Paul Baran's seminal work, which marked a new stage in the analysis of peripheral capitalism and the critique of modernization theories in the 1950s and 1960s. Two short extracts from Sweezy and Amin focus on important aspects of the problem, namely the relationship between agriculture and industry, levels of exploitation, and what Amin characterizes as the internal disarticulation of the economies of "developing societies" under the impact of metropolitan capital. Bernstein's paper reviews and builds on a major debate between Warren and Emmanuel about the possibilities and limits of industrialization in "developing societies." Griffin and Khan look at the most striking result of three decades of "development strategies," namely mass poverty and its structural roots. Demographic explanations of that condition are taken up in Bondestam's critique. Contributions by Cliffe and Cohen examine the two major classes of exploited producers in "developing societies," the peasantry and the working class. Cliffe's paper also expounds one contemporary view of the impact of colonial capitalism on precapitalist societies whereby the latter are subordinated and articulated into the former; a different view was taken by Alavi in the preceding section.

Divisions into "external" and "internal" aspects of political economy are necessarily relative—issues discussed in Part II bear very closely on those in Part III. We have not been able to incorporate in this part substantial discussions of all of the major social classes and groups in "developing societies"—the papers by Cohen and Cliffe, as well as those by Shanin and Alavi to follow refer to some additional aspects of class formation. Other contributions particularly relevant to the issues taken up in this section are those of Emmanuel concerning foreign capital and of Roberts concerning the dual axis of industrialization and urbanization.

[14]
A Morphology of Backwardness

Paul A. Baran

[. . .]. The forces that have molded the fate of the backward
world still exercise a powerful impact on the conditions prevailing
at the present time. Their forms have changed, their intensities are
different today; their origin and direction have remained unaltered.
They control now as they have controlled in the past the destinies
of the underdeveloped capitalist countries, and it is the speed with
which and the processes by which they will be overcome that will
determine these countries' future economic and social development.

The way in which capitalism broke into the historical development of the now underdeveloped countries precluded the materi-
alization of what we have termed the "classical" conditions for
growth.[. . .]. As the term "underdeveloped" suggests, output in
underdeveloped countries has been low and their human and material resources have been greatly underutilized, or altogether unemployed. Far from serving as an engine of economic expansion,
of technological progress, and of social change, the capitalist order
in these countries has represented a framework for economic stagnation, for archaic technology, and for social backwardness. Thus
to the extent to which it depends on the volume of aggregate output and income, the economic surplus in backward capitalist countries has necessarily been small. Not that it has constituted a small
proportion of total income. On the contrary, [. . .] the consumption
of the productive population has been depressed to the lowest
possible level, with "lowest possible" corresponding in this case closely
to a subsistence minimum or to what in many underdeveloped
countries falls notably below that benchmark. The economic surplus therefore, while by comparison with the advanced countries
small in *absolute* terms, has accounted for a large *share* of total output
—as large as, if not larger than, in advanced capitalist countries.

So this is not where "the dog is buried," where one may find the
principal discrepancy between the situation that prevails in underdeveloped countries and what was envisaged in the classical model
of economic growth. The discrepancy is most profound, indeed
decisive, when it comes to [. . .] conditions relating to the *mode of
utilization* of the economic surplus. [. . .].

It is a typical feature of economic backwardness, if not always synonymous with it, that the majority of the population is dependent on agriculture, and that agriculture accounts for a large share of the backward countries' total output. While this ratio differs from country to country, almost everywhere a considerable proportion of agricultural output is produced by subsistence peasants who in turn constitute the bulk of the agricultural population. Their holdings are as a rule small, and their productivity (per person and per acre of land) is extremely low [. . .].

The subsistence peasant's obligations on account of rent, taxes, and interest in all underdeveloped countries are very high. They frequently absorb more than half of his meager net product. An additional drain on his disposable income results from the highly unfavorable terms of trade under which he is usually forced to operate. Exploited by middlemen of all kinds, he receives low prices for what little he has to sell, and pays high prices for the few industrial commodities that he is in a position to buy. Thus the economic surplus that is squeezed out of the peasant sector of agriculture is appropriated by the landowners, the moneylenders, and the merchants, and, to a smaller extent, by the state.[. . .].

As a German writer once remarked, whether there will be meat in the kitchen is never decided in the kitchen. Nor is the fate of agriculture under capitalism ever decided in agriculture. Economic, social, and political processes unfolding outside of agriculture, and in particular the accumulation of capital and the evolution of the capitalist class, while themselves originally largely determined by the processes that have taken place in agriculture, become with the onset of capitalism the prime movers of the historical development. In the underdeveloped capitalist countries—predominantly agrarian—this may be less obvious than in the advanced ones; it is, however, no less true.

Even in the backward capitalist country the nonagricultural sector appropriates a large share of the nation's aggregate economic surplus. It accrues there to [. . .] distinct, if closely interrelated, types of recipients. There are in the first place the merchants, moneylenders, and intermediaries of all kinds, some of them living in rural areas, but by the nature of their activities not belonging to the agricultural population. The most striking single feature of this socioeconomic stratum is its *size*. No one who has ever set foot in China of old, in Southeast Asia, in the Near East, or in prewar Eastern Europe can have failed to notice the staggering multitude of merchants, dealers, peddlers, trading-stand operators, and people with nondescript occupations crowding the streets, squares, and coffee-houses of their cities. To some extent their activities are those customary in all capitalist countries—if more conspicuous in underdeveloped countries than where the same type of "work" is carried on by correspondence or over the telephone; for the most part, however, the nature of their transactions is peculiar to the conditions prevailing in the early phases of capitalist development. [. . .].

Important as it is that the *"lumpenbourgeois"* element of the mercantile class eats up a large share of the economic surplus accruing to the class as a whole, even more portentous is the fact that such capital as is accumulated by its wealthier members is typically not turned into the *second* bracket of the nonagricultural economy: industrial production. Existing for the most part in small morsels, it can find profitable application only in the sphere of circulation where relatively small amounts of money go a long way, where the returns on individual transactions are large, and where the turnover of the funds involved is rapid. And merchants in possession of larger resources find even better opportunities for gain in buying up land yielding rent revenue, in various undertakings auxiliary to the operation of Western business, in importing, exporting, moneylending, and speculation. Thus to the extent that a transfer of capital and business energies from mercantile to industrial pursuits is at all possible, the transfer price becomes inordinately high.

To be sure, the now underdeveloped countries have this in common with the early phase of capitalist development in Western Europe or in Japan where powerful forces also tended to prevent the *exit* of capital from the sphere of circulation, where nevertheless the transition from mercantile to industrial employment of capital was accomplished in the course of time. However, what distinguishes their situation sharply from the historical past of the advanced capitalist countries is the existence of formidable obstacles barring the *entry* of such mercantile accumulations as they have into the sphere of industrial production.

Industrial expansion under capitalism depends largely on its gathering its own momentum. "Capital rapidly creates for itself an internal market by destroying all rural handicrafts, that is by spinning, weaving, making clothes, etc., for all, in fine by transforming into exchange values commodities that were theretofore produced as direct use values—a process that results spontaneously from the severance of the worker (albeit a serf) from land and ownership of his means of production."[1] Not that this dissolution of the precapitalist economy, the disintegration of its natural self-sufficiency, has not taken place in most of the now underdeveloped countries. On the contrary, as was mentioned earlier, in all areas of Western penetration, commercial agriculture to a considerable extent displaced traditional subsistence farming, and manufactured commodities invaded the market of the indigenous craftsman and artisan. Yet although, as Allyn Young put it, "division of labor depends in large part upon the division of labor,"[2] in the now backward areas this sequence did not unfold "according to plan." It took a different course: such division of labor as was bred by the initial division of labor resembled the apportionment of functions between a rider and his horse. Whatever market for manufactured goods emerged in the colonial and dependent countries did not become the "internal market" of these countries. Thrown wide open by colonization and by unequal treaties, it became an appendage of the "internal market" of Western capitalism.

While significantly stimulating industrial growth in the West, this turn of events extinguished the igniting spark without which there could be no industrial expansion in the now underdeveloped countries. At a historical juncture when protection of infant industry might have been prescribed even by the sternest protagonist of free trade, the countries most in need of such protection were forced to go through a regime of what might be called industrial infanticide which influenced all of their subsequent development.[. . .].

The amount of capital required to break into the monopoly's privileged sanctuary, the risks attendant upon the inevitable struggle, the leverages that the established concern could use to harass and to exclude an intruder—all tended to decimate the inducement for merchant capital to shift to industrial pursuits. The narrow market became monopolistically controlled, and the monopolistic control became an additional factor preventing the widening of the market.

This is not to say that such industrial development as has taken place in the backward countries did not represent a tremendous advance from the situation in which their industrial markets were entirely controlled by supplies from abroad. These had ruined native handicrafts, and smothered what little industrial development there was in the affected countries without offering the displaced artisans and craftsmen any alternative employment in industry. The corresponding industrial expansion took place in the West. To this the newly founded industrial enterprises represented, as it were, an antidote. They repatriated at least some of the manufacturing part of the original division of labor, undertook at least some industrial investment at home, provided at least some employment and income to native labor. Yet this antidote was inadequate. It not only did not suffice to offset the damage that had been done earlier; the way in which it was administered was such as to give rise to a cancerous growth no less powerful and no less harmful than the evil which in the beginning it partially cured.[. . .]. Thus in most underdeveloped countries capitalism had a peculiarly twisted career. Having lived through all the pains and frustrations of childhood, it never experienced the vigor and exuberance of youth, and began displaying at an early age all the grievous features of senility and decadence. To the dead weight of stagnation characteristic of preindustrial society was added the entire restrictive impact of monopoly capitalism. The economic surplus appropriated in lavish amounts by monopolistic concerns in backward countries is not employed for productive purposes. It is neither plowed back into their own enterprises, nor does it serve to develop others. To the extent that it is not taken abroad by their foreign stockholders, it is used in a manner very much resembling that of the landed aristocracy. It supports luxurious living by its recipients, is spent on construction of urban and rural residences, on servants, excess consumption, and the like. The remainder is invested in the acquisition of rent-bearing land, in financing mercantile activities of all kinds, in usury and speculation. Last but not least, significant sums are removed abroad where they are held as hedges against the depreciation of the domestic currency or as nest eggs assuring their owners of suitable retreats in the case of social and political upheavals at home.

This brings us to the [next] branch of the nonagricultural part of the underdeveloped country's economic system: foreign enterprise.[. . .]. The worst of it is that it is very hard to say what has been the greater evil as far as the economic development of underdeveloped countries is concerned: the removal of their economic surplus by foreign capital or its reinvestment by foreign enterprise. That such has been actually the somber dilemma stems not merely from the pronounced paucity of the direct benefits derived by the underdeveloped countries from foreign investment; it is even more clearly realized if the overall impact of foreign enterprise on the development of underdeveloped countries is given some consideration.

This is not the way in which matters are viewed in more or less official Western writing on the subject. Thus the authors of an article in the U.S. Commerce Department's *Survey of Current Business* roundly assert that "the great expansion of foreign productive facilities represented by [United States corporate] investment has been of great importance in the improvement of economic conditions abroad."[3] Although apparently less confident, Professor Mason holds that "the expansion of mineral production is, in general, not only compatible with the economic growth of underdeveloped areas but may greatly facilitate industrialization in these areas."[4] And Professor Nurkse, also all but certain, concludes that "the trouble about foreign investment of the 'traditional' sort is not that it is bad, or that it does not tend to promote development generally; it does, although unevenly and indirectly. The trouble is rather that it simply does not happen on any substantial scale."[5]

This position is based essentially on the following considerations. One is that the transfer abroad of returns on foreign investment is not to be regarded as an encroachment upon the underdeveloped country's economic surplus, for whatever is being transferred would simply not exist in the absence of foreign investment. Thus since in the absence of these transfers there would be no foreign investment, the transfers themselves imply no real cost to the paying country and cannot therefore be considered as adversely influencing its economic development.[6] Secondly, it is argued, the operations of foreign enterprise, by passing a part of its output to the native population in reward for services rendered, increase to *some* extent its aggregate income. Thirdly, it is pointed out that foreign enterprise, whatever may be its *direct* contribution to the welfare of the peoples inhabiting the underdeveloped countires, renders them a major service *indirectly* by stimulating the construction of roads, railways, power stations, and the like, as well as conveying to their capitalists and workers the business know-how and the technical skills of the advanced countries. Finally, stress is laid on the fact that Western enterprise, by remitting taxes and royalties to the governments of the source countries, places in their hands important funds for financing the development of their national economies.

As is the case with most bourgeois economic reasoning based on "practical intelligence," this is judicious and plausible on the surface. Yet encompassing merely one segment of reality, and dealing with it not historically but by the now very fashionable method that might be called "animated statics," it conveys a conception that is both biased and misleading. Let us take up these arguments in turn.

It is undoubtedly correct that if the natural resources of the underdeveloped countries were not exploited, there would be no output to provide for the transfers of profits abroad. This is, however, where the firm ground under the first of the above propositions ends. For it is by no means to be taken for granted that the now underdeveloped countries, given an independent development, would not at some point have initiated the utilization of their natural resources on their own and on terms more advantageous than those received from foreign investors. This could be dismissed if foreign investment and the course taken by the development of the underdeveloped countries were independent of each other. However,[. . .] as the case of Japan convincingly demonstrates,[. . .] such independence cannot possibly be assumed. In fact, to assume it amounts to begging the entire issue and prejudging it from the very outset. But there is still another aspect to the problem. With regard to some agricultural products, it might be thought that since they consist of recurring crops, and since an outlet for them can be found only in exports, their production and shipment abroad constitute no sacrifice whatever to the source countries. This is a grievous, albeit commonly accepted, fallacy. Quite apart from the fact that export-oriented corporations have traditionally engaged in the most predatory exploitation of the plantation land under their control, the establishment and expansion of these plantations have brought about the systematic pauperization, indeed in many instances the physical annihilation, of large parts of the native population. The cases are legion, and citing a few will have to suffice: "The one-crop culture of cane sugar in the Brazilian northeast is a good example. The area once had one of the few really fertile tropical soils. It had a climate favorable to agriculture, and it was originally covered with a forest growth extremely rich in fruit trees. Today, the all-absorbing, self-destructive sugar industry has stripped all the available land and covered it completely with sugar cane; as a result this is one of the starvation areas of the continent. The failure to grow fruits, greens and vegetables, or to raise cattle in the region, has created an extremely difficult food problem in an area where diversified farming could produce an infinite variety of foods."[7] In most of Latin America, what "helped in definitively ruining the native populations was the one-track exploitation to which almost every region was dedicated: some were given over to mining, others to coffee planting, some to tobacco and others to cacao. This specialization brought on the deformed economy which is still found in such countries as El Salvador, which produces practically nothing but coffee, and Honduras, which exports nothing but bananas." In Egypt "a large part of the irrigated land was reserved to produce cash export crops. . .particularly cotton and sugar—which further aggravated the nutritional poverty of the fellah." In Africa "the first European innovation which worked to upset native food customs was the large-scale production of cash crops for exports, such as cacao, coffee, sugar and peanuts. We already know how the plantation system works. . .a good example is that of the British colony of Gambia in West Africa, where the culture of food crops for local consumption has been completely abandoned in order to concentrate on the production of peanuts. As a result of this monoculture. . .the nutritional situation of the colony could hardly be worse." In what has represented for a long time the internal colony of American capitalism—the southern states—very similar effects were produced by sugar, and in particular by cotton. "In the United States, the cotton-growing states make up the nation's lowest income group. The statistical correlation between cotton growing and poverty is startling. Cotton culture has two harmful effects on the soil: (1) depletion of soil fertility...(2) the damage done by erosion.... All this is realized clearly now, but it was not understood and appreciated in the nineteenth century—the century that measured success in dollars and cents at the expense of lasting assets."[8]

To avoid misunderstanding, the above is not to be taken as arguing against division of labor, intranational and international specialization, and the resulting increase of productivity. What it clearly demonstrates, however, is that an intranational and international specialization that is so organized that one participant of the team specializes in starvation while the other assumes the white man's burden of collecting the profits can hardly be considered a satisfactory arrangement for attainment of the greatest happiness for the greatest number.[...].

[...] The principal impact of foreign enterprise on the development of the underdeveloped countries lies in hardening and strengthening the sway of merchant capitalism, in slowing down and indeed preventing its transformation into industrial capitalism.[...]. This is the really important "indirect influence" of foreign enterprise on the evolution of the underdeveloped countries. It flows through a multitude of channels, permeates all of their economic, social, political, and cultural life, and decisively determines its entire course. There is first of all the emergence of a group of merchants expanding and thriving within the orbit of foreign capital. Whether they act as wholesalers—assembling, sorting, and standardizing commodities that they purchase from small producers and sell to representatives of foreign concerns—or as suppliers of local materials to foreign enterprises, or as caterers to various other needs of foreign firms and their staffs, many of them manage to assemble vast fortunes and to move up to the very top of the underdeveloped countries' capitalist class. Deriving their profits from the operations of foreign business, vitally interested in its expansion and prosperity, this comprador element of the native bourgeoisie uses its considerable influence to fortify and to perpetuate the status quo.

There are secondly the native industrial monopolists, in most cases interlocked and interwoven with domestic merchant capital and with foreign enterprise, who entirely depend on the maintenance of the existing economic structure, and whose monopolistic status would be swept away by the rise of industrial capitalism. Concerned with preventing the emergence of competitors in their markets, they look with favor upon absorption of capital in the sphere of circulation, and have nothing to fear from foreign export-oriented enterprise. They too are stalwart defenders of the established order.

The interests of these two groups run entirely parallel with those of the feudal landowners powerfully entrenched in the societies of the backward areas. Indeed, these have no reason for complaints about the activities of foreign enterprise in their countries. In fact, these activities yield them considerable profits. Frequently they provide outlets for the produce of landed estates, in many places they raise the value of land, often they offer lucrative employment opportunities to members of the landed gentry.

What results is a political and social coalition of wealthy compradors, powerful monopolists, and large landowners dedicated to the defense of the existing feudal-mercantile order. Ruling the realm by no matter what political means—as a monarchy, as a military-fascist dictatorship, or as a republic of the Kuomintang variety—this coalition has nothing to hope for from the rise of industrial capitalism which would dislodge it from its positions of privilege and power. Blocking all economic and social progress in its country, this regime has no real political basis in city or village, lives in continual fear of the starving and restive popular masses, and relies for its stability on Praetorian guards of relatively well kept mercenaries.

In most underdeveloped countries social and political developments of the last few decades would have toppled regimes of that sort. That they have been able to stay in business—for business is, indeed, their sole concern—in most of Latin America and in the Near East, in several "free" countries of Southeast Asia and in some similarly "free" countries of Europe, is due mainly if not exclusively to the aid and support that was given to them "freely" by Western capital and by Western governments acting on its behalf. For the maintenance of these regimes and the operations of foreign enterprise in the underdeveloped countries have become mutually interdependent. It is the economic strangulation of the colonial and dependent countries by the imperialist powers that stymied the development of indigenous industrial capitalism, thus preventing the overthrow of the feudal-mercantile order and assuring the rule of the comprador administrations. It is the preservation of these subservient governments, stifling economic and social development and suppressing all popular movements for social and national liberation, that makes possible at the present time the continued foreign exploitation of underdeveloped countries and their domination by the imperialist powers.

Notes

1. Karl Marx, *Grundrisse: Der Kritik der Politischen Ökonomie* (Berlin: Rohentwurf, 1953), p. 411.
2. "Increasing Returns and Economic Progress," *Economic Journal* (December 1928): 533.
3. S. Pizer and F. Cutler, "International Investments and Earnings," *Survey of Current Business* (August 1955): 10.
4. "Raw Materials, Rearmament, and Economic Development," *Quarterly Journal of Economics* (August 1952): 336.
5. Ragnar Nurkse, *Problems of Capital Formation in Underdeveloped Countries* (Oxford: 1953), p. 29.
6. Cf. S. Herbert Frankel, *The Economic Impact on Under-Developed Societies* (Oxford: 1953), p. 104.
7. Josué de Castro, *The Geography of Hunger* (Boston: Little Brown, 1952), p. 97. The following passages quoted in the text are from pages 105, 215, and 221 of this outstanding work. Professor de Castro notes, incidentally, that while soil erosion and exhaustion are a plague of the entire colonial world, experts "go so far as to assert that, for all practical purposes, there is no such thing as erosion in Japan" (p. 192).
8. E. W. Zimmerman, *World Resources and Industries* (rev. ed.; New York: 1951), p. 326. Needless to say, the author discriminates unfairly against the nineteenth century. In the capitalist world of the twentieth, success is still measured by the same yardstick, the difference being only that large-scale enterprise thinks more about its longer run returns.

[15]
The Disarticulation of Economy Within "Developing Societies"

Samir Amin

Accumulation on a World Scale

The process of development of peripheral capitalism goes forward within a framework of competition (in the broadest sense of the word) from the center, which is responsible for the distinctive structure assumed by the periphery, as something complementary and dominated. It is this competition that determines three types of distortion in the development of peripheral capitalism as compared with capitalism at the center: (1) a crucial distortion toward export activities, which absorb the major part of the capital arriving from the center; (2) a distortion toward tertiary activities, which arises from both the special contradictions of peripheral capitalism and the original structures of the peripheral formations; and (3) a distortion in the choice of branches of industry, toward light branches, and also, to a lesser degree, toward light techniques.

This threefold distortion reflects the asymmetrical way in which the periphery is integrated in the world market. It means, in economistic terms, the transfer from the periphery to the center of the multiplier mechanisms, which cause accumulation at the center to be a cumulative process. From this transfer results the conspicuous disarticulation of the underdeveloped economy, the dualism of this economy, etc.—in the end, the blocking of the economy's growth.[. . .].

The developed economy is an integrated whole, a feature of which is a very dense flow of internal exchanges, the flow of external exchanges of the atoms that make up this entity being on the whole marginal as compared with that of internal exchanges. In contrast to this, the underdeveloped economy is made up of atoms which are relatively juxtaposed and not integrated, the density of the flow of external exchanges of these atoms being relatively greater and that of the flow of internal exchanges very much less. It is said that this economy is "disarticulated," "astructural," or else that the developed economy is "autocentric" whereas that of the underdeveloped countries is "extraverted."[. . .].

Now, the consequences that follow from this disarticulation are crucial. In a structured *autocentric* economy, any progress that begins in any center of the economic organism is spread throughout the entire body by many convergent mechanisms. Contemporary analysis has stressed the "leading effects" of an increase in primary demand: leading effects that are both direct—downstream (on the industries that directly consume the product), and upstream (on the industries that directly supply the branch whose demand has increased) —and indirect (on the industries that are consumers and suppliers of the foregoing); and also "secondary" leading effects (through the incomes distributed), which are likewise both direct and indirect. Formerly, analysis emphasized other channels of diffusion: the reduction in prices resulting from progress, and so along with this the change in the structure of relative prices, of demand and of real income, the possible increase in profits and change in the distribution of investments. If the economy is *extraverted*, all these effects are limited, being largely transferred abroad. Any progress realized in the oil industry will, for example, be without the slightest effect on the economy of Kuwait, since nomad stockbreeding sells nothing to and buys nothing from the oil sector, but this progress will be diffused in the West, in all the industries that consume oil.

In this sense one ought not speak of "underdeveloped national economies," but to reserve the adjective "national" for the autocentric developed economies which alone constitute a true, structured, national economic space, within which progress is diffused from industries that deserve to be regarded as poles of development. The underdeveloped economy is made up of sectors, of firms, which are juxtaposed and not highly integrated among themselves, but which are, each on its own, strongly integrated in entities whose centers of gravity lie in the centers of the capitalist world. What we have here is not a nation, in the economic sense of the word, with an integrated internal market. Depending on its geographical size and the variety of its exports, the underdeveloped economy may appear as being made up of several "atoms" of this type, independent of each other (as with Brazil or India), or of a single "atom" (Senegal, which is entirely organized around the groundnut economy, etc.).

The consequence of this is that the false, nonstructured economic spaces of the underdeveloped world can be broken up, "exploded" into microspaces, without serious danger, something that cannot be done without almost intolerable retrogression with the integrated spaces of the advanced countries. The weakness of national cohesion in the Third World is often a reflection of this fact, which is also the source of "micronationalism": the area interested in the export economy has no "need" of the rest of the country, which may indeed seem a burden upon it, and so it may contemplate establishing a "microindependence," as has been seen to happen in both Latin America and Africa.

The effects of this disarticulation are plainly to be seen in the historical geography of the Third World. The areas interested in an export product that is comparatively important for the development of capitalism at the center experience "brilliant" periods of very rapid growth and prosperity. But because no autocentric integrated entity is formed around this production, as soon as the product concerned is deprived of the interest, even the relative interest, that the center had for it, the region falls into decline: its economy stagnates and even retrogresses. Thus, Northeastern Brazil was in the seventeenth century an area of "prosperity," the scene of a real "economic miracle." It was a miracle that led nowhere: the moment the sugar-growing economy lost the relative importance it had enjoyed, the region fell into lethargy, to become later the famine area that it is nowadays. Even in Senegal, the river region was a "prosperous" one in the days of the gum trade. When natural gum was replaced by synthetic products, the region became an exporter of cheap labor, the only livelihood available to its population.[. . .].

The disarticulation of the underdeveloped economy is expressed, finally, in certain characteristic disharmonies: in the distribution of the occupied population and of the product among the sectors (especially inside the secondary sector), and in the distribution of investments.

Let us compare the distribution of secondary production, as shown in Table 1.

Table 1
Secondary Production
(percents)

	Senegal (1960)	Maghreb (1955)	Present developed countries*
Mines	5	17	5-10
Crafts, small-scale industry	7	19	5-10
Large-scale industry			
Light industry	55	30	30-40
Basic industry	0	4	30-40
Electricity, power	5	6	2-4
Building, public works	28	24	12-15

*Western and Eastern Europe, North America, Japan.

While the place held by mining varies a great deal from one underdeveloped country to another, we note: (1) the fundamental absence of basic industries throughout the periphery; (2) the relatively greater importance of building (connected with the structure of investments); (3) the different nature of the production of electricity—in the underdeveloped countries, 50 percent is provided at low tensions (80 percent in value terms), as against 20 percent in the developed countries (50 percent in value terms).

It is the same with the distribution of investments, as shown in Table 2.

Table 2
Investment
(percents)

	Maghreb (1955)	West Africa (1965)	Developed countries*
Agriculture	17	7	7
Mines, power, oil	10	7	7
Industry	11	7	35
Transport, trade, services	12	14	21
Housing	20	25	15
Infrastructure	30	40	15
Total	100	100	100

The predominance of not directly productive investment will be observed, together with the parallel smallness of the share of industrial investment in the periphery.

The term "domination" of the periphery by the center has also become one of the commonplaces of present-day writing. This domination is expressed on all planes, economic and other (especially political and ideological). On the economic plane it is expressed in the structures of the commercial exchanges and in those of the financing of growth.

As regards commercial exchanges, domination by the center is not at all a result of the fact that the exports of the periphery are made up of primary products, as current writings on the subject allege. Some countries have been exporters of primary products (Canada, Australia, etc.), and still are to a large extent, without ever having been underdeveloped; and indeed, these primary products occupy an important position in the exports of many developed countries (wheat, timber, coal, etc.). Domination results from the fact that the peripheral economies are *merely* producers of primary products—in other words, that this production is, in their case, not integrated into an autocentric industrial structure. The consequence is that, taken as a whole, the periphery does most of its trade with the center, whereas the central economies carry out most of their exchanges among themselves. It is this difference in structure that implies an essentially unequal relation of strength which is expressed in a different evolution in the rewards of labor—which the structure of the peripheral formations and the development of the monopolies at the center made possible—and in the worsening of the terms of trade. [...].

The development of capitalism at the center has increased the relative intensity of the internal flows, but in the periphery it has increased only that of the external flows. The "development of underdevelopment" analyzed above, the intensification of the structural characteristics of underdevelopment in the periphery—this is what explains the domination by the center, this and not the nature of the products exchanged. For these products have themselves evolved.

[16]
Center, Periphery, and the Crisis of the System

Paul M. Sweezy

It is a commonplace these days that capitalism is in crisis: one hears it from friends as well as foes of the system. I believe that this is a defensible thesis, provided the meaning of the term "crisis" is appropriately clarified.

First of all, it is necessary to be clear that we are talking about the overall capitalist system and not about a particular country or region. From the earliest period of its continuous existence capitalism has always transcended individual countries and regions, and by now it is a truly global system.

By speaking of the earliest period of capitalism's continuous existence, I mean roughly the fifteenth and sixteenth centuries in Western Europe. I do not mean to imply that there was no capitalism before then, or that capitalism could not have begun a continuous existence elsewhere. It will be useful, I think, to consider these two points somewhat further.

The earliest examples of what I would consider to be true capitalism emerged in a number of Italian city-states during the Middle Ages. Of these, Venice was the earliest and a prototype for the others that came later. Venice's geographical position—offshore as far as the Italian mainland was concerned and strategically located for trade and conquest between the western and eastern halves of the Mediterranean—gave it a unique opportunity, of which it took full advantage, to develop an essentially bourgeois and antifeudal society that endured for many centuries. Trade, piracy, and tribute were of course the bases of Venice's great wealth; but its capitalism was not of a purely mercantile kind. Its shipbuilding and armaments industries, absolutely crucial to the society's very existence, were capitalistically organized and employed large numbers of wage laborers, and its political and cultural superstructure foreshadowed the bourgeois epoch to come, rather than reflecting the feudal context of its own time. A number of other essentially bourgeois city-states flourished in other parts of Italy in the later Middle Ages; and in some, of which Florence was the leading example, a highly developed capitalist textile industry emerged with all the usual accompaniments of industrial strife and political class struggle. In the long run, these early sprouts of capitalism were too divided and weak to survive in a hostile feudal environment. But they did not succumb without leaving a rich legacy of economic practices (e.g., double-entry bookkeeping), political institutions, and cultural achievements which could be taken over and adapted to the needs of the Atlantic capitalist societies that emerged in the wake of the geographical discoveries of the fifteenth and sixteenth centuries and that finally established capitalism as the dominant world order for the next four centuries.

As for the possibility that a viable capitalism might have emerged in some part of the world other than Western Europe, it is obvious that this cannot be proved or disproved in any scientific sense. Yet it seems highly plausible to me: there were several regions with developed trading relations and money economies, necessary prerequisites to the emergence of a full-fledged capitalist order, and I see no reason to doubt that, given time, one or more of them would have achieved a breakthrough comparable to that which actually occurred in Europe. The point is that they were not given time. For a number of reasons, including the absence of a dominant centralized state, the situation in Western Europe was propitious, and the region got something of a head start, two aspects of which were the development of superior technologies in navigation and firepower. These, in turn, enabled the Europeans to embark on a career of pillage and conquest that transferred vast amounts of wealth to their homelands and, at the same time, stunted or actually destroyed the development potential of possible rival areas. These rival areas, instead of undergoing an independent process of capitalist development, found themselves incorporated into the emerging Europe-centered capitalist system as colonies, dependencies, or clients of one sort or another. It was in this way that capitalism as we know it today started in its very earliest infancy as a dialectical unity of self-directed center and dependent periphery.

The fact that capitalism has from the beginning had these two poles—which can be variously described by such terms as independent and dependent, dominant and subordinate, developed and underdeveloped, center and periphery—has at every stage been crucial for its evolution in all its parts. The driving force has always been the accumulation process in the center, with the peripheral societies being molded by a combination of coercion and market forces to conform to the requirements and serve the needs of the center.

Owing to the overwhelming predominance of maritime transport and naval power, the early outward thrust originating in Western Europe affected mostly coastal areas of the other continents and nearby islands. This mode of expansion continued in later times but was supplemented, at first gradually and after the introduction of railroads on a much larger scale, by the penetration and conquest of huge inland areas and populations. What followed these successive waves of expansion was not everywhere the same. We can distinguish several more or less clearly defined patterns of action and reaction.

(1) Where precapitalist societies were weak and sparsely populated, the conquerors followed one of two possible courses. (a) They established new forms of production (plantations, mining compounds) using forced labor, both native and imported from other conquered territories. The products of these enterprises (gold and silver, tropical crops) were exported to the center and sold at enormous profits. The return flow of imports was made up of subsistence goods for workers, which could not be produced locally, plus luxury goods for resident Europeans. The exchange was of course vastly unequal and may be considered the prototype of all subsequent forms of unequal exchange between center and periphery. This was the pattern that prevailed in South and Central America, parts of South and Southeast Asia, and parts of Africa. (b) The conquerors wiped out or otherwise effectively eliminated the indigenous population and established settler societies more or less closely modeled on their homelands. North America and later Australia and New Zealand were the leading examples. Where conditions were favorable, as in the United States, this type of settler colony soon developed ambitions for independent status and in time did in fact achieve independence and joined the nations at the center of the system as a rival and partner in exploiting the periphery.

(2) Where precapitalist societies were stronger and more highly developed, the Europeans sought to achieve their goals not by breaking up the existing order but by penetrating its power structure, playing off some chiefs and potentates against others, establishing effective overall colonial rule, and imposing on the local population both direct economic and indirect political forms of exploitation. India under British rule was the classic example of this pattern, but it was also widely practiced not only by the British but also by the Dutch and the French elsewhere in Asia, in parts of Africa, and in the Middle East.

(3) We come now to the final chapter in the story of European expansion, the encounter with Japan. Owing to a long history of relative isolation from outside contacts and to a geographical location that placed the country at the end of the road in which Western expansionism had embarked in Asia, Japan was a late target of the Europeans, who by that time had been joined by the North

Americans in the race for empire. When the Westerners finally did reach Japan in the middle decades of the nineteenth century, they were slow to exploit their initial advantage, largely because of mutual rivalry and preoccupation elsewhere. This enabled the Japanese rulers, forewarned by the fate of other victims of Western expansion, to devise a successful strategy of maneuvering to preserve the country's independence while at the same time taking over from the West and imposing on Japan the social relations and institutions necessary to transform the country into a full-fledged capitalist power.

Within a remarkably short time (by historical standards), Japan passed from outside the periphery of the world capitalist system directly to the center. The route chosen—or, as some might argue, forced on Japan—was both historically unique and the only one that offered a chance of success. If Japan had allowed itself to be integrated into the periphery, it would have been trapped there, as literally scores of other countries have been. This would not necessarily have precluded rapid economic development, as the history of Brazil convincingly demonstrates. But development would have been dependent, not independent, and it never would have allowed Japan to reach the top echelon of the world capitalist pyramid.

This brings us to a crucially important question: What is the difference between independent development at the center and dependent development in the periphery? There are obviously many aspects to the question, but here I shall touch on only two of the most essential.

The first relates to the relationship between agriculture and industry. The heart of the matter was put in its briefest possible form by Samir Amin, a leading figure among Third World Marxists of the post-World War II period: "Unlike the countries of the center, where the 'agricultural revolution' preceded the 'industrial revolution,' the countries of the periphery have imported the latter without having started the former stage."[1] Capitalism could never have put down roots in the center without a sustained increase in the productivity of agriculture and hence also in the agricultural surplus. This was the basis for the release of workers from the countryside; the flourishing of rural-urban trade; the emergence directly and through intermediate forms, like the putting-out system, of manufactures based on wage labor and embodying an increasingly elaborate division of labor; and only finally the introduction of machinery (the "industrial revolution") as the last step in full-fledged capitalism.

This is the only sequence that could have led to the development of independent self-sustaining capitalist societies. It is an illusion, perhaps widespread but reflecting ignorance of economic history, that industrialization somehow lies at the heart of the process of economic development. On the contrary, it is the final act and the crowning achievement of economic development; and there is no direct route to its successful realization, though of course countries like Germany and Japan, which were relatively late in embarking on the development process, could learn (as well as borrow) from their predecessors and in this way avoid mistakes and shorten the time required. But those countries that, to use Samir Amin's phrase, "imported" the industrial revolution without laying the necessary agricultural foundation have succeeded only in creating new forms of dependence.[2]

The second aspect of the difference between independent development in the center and dependent development in the periphery to which I want to call attention is simply this: the rate of exploitation is and always has been vastly higher in the periphery than in the center. In the center, the rate of exploitation is for all practical purposes the same as the rate of surplus value. This is not so of the periphery, where only a small part of the workforce is employed as wage laborers in capitalist industry, with a much larger proportion being exploited directly and indirectly by landlords, traders, and usurers, primarily in the countryside but also in the cities and towns. Here all or most of the surplus extorted from the workers not employed in capitalist industry is commercialized and becomes indistinguishably mingled with capitalistically produced surplus value. In these circumstances we can speak of a social rate of exploitation but should not confuse the concept with a rate of surplus value in the usual sense.

The high rate of exploitation in the periphery enables local ruling classes and allied elites to live on a level comparable to that of the bourgeoisies of the center, while at the same time making possible a massive flow of monetized surplus product (in the form of profits, interest, rents, royalties, etc.) from periphery to center.

The other side of the coin is a miserable, often bare subsistence or below, standard of living for workers, peasants, and the marginalized poor of countryside and urban slums. Well-meaning critics often deplore what they consider to be a drain of surplus out of the periphery that might have been invested in productive facilities catering to the impoverished masses, but this is to put the cart before the horse. The root of the problem is the high rate of exploitation, which both perpetuates poverty and at the same time prevents the growth of a mass market for consumer goods that would attract and justify investment in a local version of Marx's Department II. And, of course, the high rate of exploitation is built into the very structure of the system and protected by a formidable array of domestic and international institutional arrangements. The counterpart of the very high (and frequently rising) rate of exploitation in the periphery is a lower (and over time relatively stable) rate of surplus value in the center. There are two basic and interrelated reasons for this. On the one hand, the working class of the center is more highly developed and is in a better position to organize and struggle for its own interests. On the other hand, the bourgeoisies of the center learned through historical experience that a situation that allows the standard of living of the proletariat to rise over time (a stable rate of surplus value combined with rising productivity) is not only functional but even indispensable for the operation of the system as a whole. Without it, the growth of Department II (producing consumption goods) is stunted, the demand for the products of Department I (producing means of production) is held down, and vitally important conditions for the operation of the capital accumulation process are absent. What this means is that a high and rising rate of surplus value, however desirable it may appear to be from the point of view of the individual capitalist, would be a disaster from the point of view of the capitalist societies of the center as a whole.

Nor is this all. In the early stages of the Industrial Revolution—up to the middle of the nineteenth century—the European bourgeoisies attempted, through the anticombination laws and the like, to block the organization of the working class and in this way to boost the rate of surplus value. The result was the development of strong revolutionary currents in the newly emergent proletariat: not by chance was this the period during which Marxism, the world view of proletarian revolution, was born and began the inexorable spread that has continued ever since. Alarmed by the revolutions of 1848, the ruling classes of the advanced capitalist countries began to reconsider their strategy, responding to the struggles of the workers more flexibly and discovering in the process that the new course paid both political and economic dividends. It was during the next half century that the modern labor movement, in its trade-union and reformist political wings, took shape—against opposition that increasingly focused not on destroying the movement but on containing it within limits safe and even beneficial for capitalism. Soon after, as we shall have occasion to notice in due course, revolutionary Marxism began a "long march" from its birthplace in the center of the world capitalist system to the periphery, where conditions were—and are—more favorable to its development.

Corresponding to the contrast between the levels of exploitation in center and periphery is an equally striking contrast between the political systems in the two parts of world capitalism. In the center, by various routes and over a long period of time, bourgeois democracy became the norm and proved to be the political arangement most conducive to the maintenance of a stable rate of surplus value and class relations reasonably compatible with the functioning of the accumulation process. In the periphery, on the other hand, efforts to copy the bourgeois democratic institutions of the center (very widespread, for example, in Latin America after the Spanish colonies achieved their formal independence and sought to model their constitutions on that of the United States) either produced empty faces or were discarded by dominant classes whose way of life depended on the maintenance of extremely high rates of exploitation and who saw in any concessions to the underlying population a dangerous threat to their continued rule. From the beginning, therefore, and now as much as at any time in the past, the norm in the periphery has been military-police states of one kind or another. They are, in fact, as closely related to high rates of exploitation as two sides of the same coin.

The implications of this analysis for the countries and peoples of the periphery are far-reaching. The extremely high rates of exploitation of which they are the victims are not, as conventional bourgeois wisdom would have it, a heritage of their precapitalist past to be overcome by the kind of policies prescribed in economics textbooks and touted by governments and international agencies like the World Bank—foreign aid and investment, transfer of technology, and so on. All such activities are carried out within the framework of the existing structure and normally have both the intention and the effect of strengthening rather than changing it.

Take, for example, the investment by multinational corporations in the periphery, which has occurred on a large scale in the period since World War II and has spurred the growth of modern industry beyond anything known in previous times. The multinationals, based in the advanced countries of the center, go to countries like Brazil—which is rightly considered a prototype of this kind of development—to supply and profit from markets that already exist and can be expected to grow with the general expansion of global capitalism. Some of these are domestic Brazilian markets fueled by the spending of perhaps 20 percent of the population in the highest income brackets. Others are international markets for agricultural products, raw materials, and certain kinds of manufactures, the costs of which can be kept low through the employment of cheap labor. But there is one market, potentially by far the largest, that does not exist and that the multinationals have no ambition to create, the market that would be generated by a rising real standard of living for the Brazilian masses. The reason for what at first sight might seem a paradox is simple: for capitalists, both Brazilian and foreign, the masses are looked upon as costs, not as consumers: the lower their real incomes, the higher the profits from selling to the local upper class and the international market. The dynamic at work here has produced a most startling result: in the fifteen years since the military coup of 1964, a period frequently referred to as that of the Brazilian "economic miracle," when the Gross National Product rose at annual rates as high as 10 percent, the level of real wages *declined* by a third or more. No wonder the president of Brazil on a visit to Washington several years ago was quoted in the press as saying, "In my country the economy is doing fine, but the people aren't."

The conclusion to which both theoretical analysis and historical experience lead is, thus, that for the vast majority of the peoples of the periphery, dependent development yields not a better life and a brighter future but intensified exploitation and a greater misery. The way forward for them is therefore through a revolutionary break with the entire capitalist system, a road that is already being traveled by a growing number of countries in the periphery. [. . .].

Notes

1. Samir Amin, "The New International Economic Order," *Monthly Review* (July-August 1979): 16.
2. To avoid misunderstanding, it should be added that attributing to the countries of the periphery a failure to lay the necessary agricultural foundations for industrialization is not to deny that they have experienced certain kinds of agricultural development. The trouble is that these have centered on the cultivation of at most a few specialized crops for export, and in the process have tended to withdraw the best lands and other rural resources from vitally needed domestic production. The consequence is the paradox, almost universally observable in the periphery, of countries with predominantly agricultural economies unable to feed themselves and forced to import a large and increasing proportion of their requirements for grains and other staples from the countries of the center. This is why the first rule of a strategy for independent development in the periphery must be a determined move toward agricultural self-sufficiency, including food production. And this in turn means that industrialization must first and foremost be geared to the needs of agriculture.

[17]
Industrialization, Development, and Dependence

Henry Bernstein

The words that provide the title of this essay have acquired a new centrality and urgency in that dimension of contemporary history characterized by the emergence of the postcolonial "Third World." At the same time the meanings attached to them, and the controversies surrounding them, cannot be pursued and understood unless they are placed in the context of three further terms of unique significance in the history of the modern world: capitalism, socialism, and nationalism.

The international situation following the end of the World War II in 1945 assigned the development of the "poor" or "underdeveloped" or "backward" countries (which came to be known collectively as the Third World) a central place on the agenda of contemporary concerns. The factors that combined with each other to form a new global context include the following: the now unrivaled dominance of the United States, formally a noncolonial power, in world capitalism; the increasingly shaky grip of the European imperial powers on their colonies; the initiation of the postwar capitalist "long boom" through the reconstruction of the economies of Western Europe and Japan; the strengthening of the socialist bloc through postwar reconstruction of the Soviet economy and the addition of Eastern Europe and China; the anti-imperialist movements in Asia and Africa commanding mass popular support for the demand of national independence; the struggle of West and East for strategic advantage in a period of rapid decolonization and international "instability."

In sum, there was a major restructuring of international relations economically, politically, and ideologically. Wartime industrial production and postwar reconstruction contributed a new generation of technological innovation and experience with new forms of state economic management to the accumulation process in the industrialized capitalist countries. The expansion of the world economy arising from the postwar cycle of capital accumulation has been characterized by an immense growth of international corporations, and by their entry into the sphere of manufacturing industry (as distinct from the more traditional imperial activities of trade, finance, transport, and resource-based industries such as mining, petroleum, and export agriculture). At the political level the United Nations was established (with a commitment to decolonization, and subsequently to the development of poorer countries), and progressively enlarged as the former colonies of Asia and Africa, and the remaining smaller colonies of Latin America, gained national independence.

"Underdevelopment" or "backwardness" was identified with the heritage of imperialist rule by the independence movements of Asia and Africa, which saw the achievement of national sovereignty not only as an end in itself but as a condition necessary for "national development." The notion of "national development" (and the assessment of its prospects) encompasses the following: (1) the accumulation of capital under national control, promoting the development of the productive forces and the capacity for self-sustained growth; (2) the expansion of productive employment and the achievement of higher levels of income and social welfare—of health and nutrition, of education and participation in the political life of the nation; (3) the prospects of achieving national development are influenced to a greater or lesser extent by the position Third World countries occupy in the international economy.

This conception of "national development" in itself is neutral as far as capitalism or socialism is concerned. Indeed, the very notion of the Third World has often been taken to be suggestive of the possibility of a "third way" of development, avoiding the pitfalls of both Western capitalism (rooted in class exploitation and inequality) and Soviet-type socialism (achieved through the "totalitarian" control of society by the state in the name of proletarian ideology). At the level of international politics it is expressed in the vocabulary of "nonalignment" with regard to the rivalries of West and East; at the level of national ideology it has acquired a range of expressions, including that of various national "socialisms" that identify an indigenous historical and cultural basis for cooperation in "nation-building" and development, and reject the Marxist understanding of socialist construction as a process of class struggle.

In the conceptions of development that emerged in the context outlined above, industrialization is usually accorded a privileged status. The reason for this is straightforward. The pervasive image of the world economy created in the period of colonial imperialism is that of an international division of labor between industrial countries and nonindustrial countries (colonies in a functional if not always formal sense). Exchange between the two consists of the export of industrial manufactures by the former and the export of raw materials by the latter. Moreover, the production of raw materials for export is usually a highly specialized activity carried out through plantation agriculture and mining enterprises directly linked to the industrial economies which consume their products, and with few linkages or "spread effects" (Myrdal) in the countries where they are physically located (except negatively—for example, peasantries subordinated in various ways to the demands of export production for which they constitute a reserve army of "cheap" labor-power).

Thus "the wealth of some nations," to use Malcolm Caldwell's paraphrase of Adam Smith, is identified with their industrial power, and the poverty of others with their lack of manufacturing industry and their position in the world market as exporters of agricultural and mineral raw materials. Capital exported from the former to the latter is typically concentrated in the "enclave" sectors of production and in the financial, transport, and mercantile infrastructure they require.

Industrialization and Dependence

In the late 1940s some leading economists of the Economic Commission for Latin America (ECLA) began to analyze the implications of the international division of labor for development strategies in the nonindustrial, hence "underdeveloped" or "backward" countries. The intrinsic limitations imposed on Latin American development by the relations of the world market were exacerbated, in their view, by the deteriorating terms of trade for raw materials, so that an increasing quantity of exported raw materials was needed to acquire the same quantity of manufactured goods. Their solution was to advocate a strategy of "inner-directed" development through import-substituting industrialization, as opposed to the "outer-directed" strategy of further specializing in the export production of raw materials in which Third World countries enjoy an ostensible "comparative advantage," according to orthodox international trade theory.[1]

The nature of the Latin American experience and the interpretations it has provoked are of particular interest for several reasons: many areas of Latin America were involved in export production for a world market from the sixteenth century, the major countries of Latin America achieved political independence in the course of the nineteenth century (before most of Africa was colonized); by most conventional indicators, including those relating to industrialization, Latin America is the most developed part of the Third

World; and finally there is a long established, often radically nationalist, intelligentsia.

The ECLA strategy of "inner-directed" development (which had its analogue in the Mahalanobis conception in India, also in the 1950s) aimed to build up a national industrial base with well-developed linkages between capital goods, intermediate goods, and mass-consumption goods industries, in order to supply the internal market (and to stimulate its levels of demand) and to obviate the dependence on imports of manufactured goods. The ECLA economists believed that the strategy could be accomplished through the investment of private capital, albeit with state assistance, in contrast to the Mahalanobis strategy in India which was inspired by the example of the Soviet five-year plans and assigned a central role to state planning and investment (especially in capital goods industries) and a subordinate and strictly regulated role to private industrial capital.

The high, if uneven and unevenly distributed, rates of industrial growth in Latin America in recent decades coincided with a massive expansion of the activities of multinational corporations, in particular their diversification into manufacturing industry and the establishment of subsidiaries in major branches of industry in many Third World countries. The kinds of industrial growth experienced and their effects (as well as the effects of a new phase of the capitalization of agriculture in most Latin American countries in this period) confounded the hopes that many had invested in "inner-directed" development. The aspiration of the latter was essentially nationalist (though not anticapitalist); now it is argued that the course of Latin American industrialization has been largely determined by international capital (in line with its own needs and interests), resulting in many instances in a "denationalization" of major sectors of industry and finance (the latter through the operations of international banks, analogous to and often closely associated with those of multinational corporations). The pattern of industrialization has produced new forms, or exacerbated existing forms, of "dependence," notably (1) technological dependence, given the monopolistic control of multinational companies over advanced technologies and the leverage it gives them in supplying industrial processes, machinery, patents, blueprints, spare parts, etc., and (2) financial dependence manifested in the high rates of inflation, balance-of-payments problems, and growing external debt that have accompanied import-substituting industrialization. During its early stages the latter inevitably demands an accelerated volume of imports, and a shift in their composition toward capital goods, machinery, transport equipment, and so on. Technological and financial dependence are seen as related parts of a larger and definitive system of "dependence," complemented by a range of techniques employed in the interests of the advanced capitalist countries—the supply of vast amounts of military equipment, economic "aid," and technical assistance, the role of institutions like the International Monetary Fund and the World Bank, and the infiltration of trade unions and political parties all providing well-documented examples.

The conceptions of the ECLA economists and their apparent frustration by the forms of industrialization that Latin America has experienced provide persistent currents to topical debates about underdevelopment and development. First, the original concern with the terms of trade in the world market, and what determines them, has gained prominence again in recent years in the controversial theory of unequal exchange proposed by Arghiri Emmanuel and others (as well as politically in the topical demands for a "New International Economic Order"). Second, the experience of Latin America with its longer history of political independence (and of a nationalist intelligentsia) is now more readily assimilated to that of Asia and Africa in general conceptions of the Third World, and of "neocolonialism."[2] The notion of neocolonialism denies any major significance to the fact of political independence, suggesting that it has not altered the fundamental economic relationships constituted in the earlier (colonial) period of imperialism. Finally, and central to our present concerns, the Latin American experience has put the vocabulary of "dependence" at the center of current debates.

Earlier theories of underdevelopment as a condition of social and economic stagnation imposed on Third World countries by their position in the international division of labor have become increasingly implausible in the face of high rates of economic growth, including those of industry, and widespread social change in the last thirty years or so. The replacement of stagnationist theories by so-called dependency theory registers precisely the disillusionment with the postwar Latin American experience, which for all its dynamic character failed to satisfy a conception of development understood as truly "national" and "independent." Moreover, insofar as the latter is identified with the historical mission of a national bourgeoisie (based above all in industrial capital), then it is usually argued that no such class can exist in the conditions of contemporary imperialism, or that it is crippled as an effective agent of national development by the domination exerted by international capital. The ruling classes of the Third World (whether identified as big landowners, merchants, financiers, industrial capitalists, or as rooted in state power and property) are thus considered "junior" or "dependent" partners of international capital—the strategic political component of the notion of neocolonialism.

On other counts too the rapid rates of industrial growth have failed to "deliver the goods" expected of national development. That is to say, in many cases industrialization in recent decades has been accomplished in conditions of control exercised by authoritarian and repressive regimes (e.g., the "Brazilian miracle"); the technologies employed are capital intensive so that rates of growth of the industrial labor force are much slower than rates of growth of industry measured in terms of capital investment and growth of output; the high degree of vertical integration of multinational corporations and the accounting practices this makes possible enable them to evade regulation, and to conceal and repatriate the profits accruing from their manufacturing subsidiaries in the Third World; the limited employment effects of this kind of industrialization, and the political conditions under which it has taken place, means that it has contributed little to the welfare of the majority who remain very poor, dispossessed of the means of political expression, and subject to mass unemployment and underemployment—which in turn inhibits "the process of the formation of a home market for large-scale industry" (the subtitle of Lenin's classic work, *The Development of Capitalism in Russia*).

In sum, current theories of "dependency" retain the main tenets of underdevelopment theory while abandoning earlier stagnationist associations (if reluctantly). It is conceded that there has been some development (or simply economic growth?), but of a "dependent" kind, necessarily limited by the interests of international capital and the powerful means it uses to pursue them. The kinds of industrialization that have taken place through the direct penetration of international capital or under the umbrella of its general dominance are incapable of achieving a genuine "national" or "independent" development, expressed as the accumulation of capital under national control, the capacity for self-sustained growth, the expansion of productive employment, and higher levels of income, consumption, and social welfare.

"Independent" Capitalist Industrialization?

"Dependency theory" has now acquired the status of a contemporary radical orthodoxy concerning the frustration or "blocking" (Samir Amin) of development in the Third World due to the functioning of the capitalist world system, whether this is expressed in neo-Marxist terms (dependency as the contemporary form of imperialism), or as a nationalist response to the unanticipated effects and frustrations of "inner-directed" development strategies. It was against this new orthodoxy that the late Bill Warren directed his polemic on "Imperialism and Capitalist Industrialisation," which in turn provoked critical responses of different kinds.

Warren set out to demonstrate the following propositions:

> that the prospects for successful capitalist economic development (implying industrialisation) of a significant number of major underdeveloped countries are quite good; that substantial progress in capitalist industrialisation has already been achieved; that the period since the end of the the Second World War has been marked by a major upsurge in capitalist social relations and productive forces (especially industrialisation) in the Third World; that insofar as there are obstacles to this development, they originate not in current imperialist-Third World relationships, but almost entirely from the internal contradictions of the Third World itself; that the imperialist countries' policies and their overall impact on the Third World actually favour its industrialisation; and that the ties of dependence binding the Third World to the imperialist countries have been, and are being, markedly loosened, with the consequence that the distribution of power within the capitalist world is becoming less "uneven."[3]

At the same time Warren makes it clear what he is not dealing with, namely the ability or inability of capitalist development to satisfy the basic needs of the masses (the welfare dimension of development, noted above), and the backwardness of agriculture in Third World countries, which he admits is the "most immediate problem" they face today. He adds an important qualification that "we do not claim universality of sustained industrialisation (nor even that long-period sustained industrialisation is inconsistent with intermittent periods of stagnation, deceleration or decline)."[4] The qualification is important, not so much as a defensive gesture on behalf of the empirical evidence employed, as *theoretically* in that the statement in parenthesis applies to the Marxist investigation of the development of industrial capitalism in *any* country.

Our concern here is not to examine the statistics and empirical generalizations that Warren presents to substantiate his argument, which have been subjected to some telling criticisms.[5] For present purposes we are more concerned with conceptual and methodological questions arising from Warren's intervention in the debates about industrialization, development, and dependence. The first major point of Warren's argument concerns periodization—in effect he identifies imperialism above all (though not consistently so) with the colonial epoch and therefore rejects the position of continuity in the form of "neocolonialism." Decolonization is important for three reasons—(1) as a permissive condition for industrialization in that the monopoly of colonial power is broken and independent regimes in the Third World can exploit the room for maneuver presented by interimperialist and East-West rivalries,[6] (2) as a direct cause of industrialization through pressure for higher standards of living, particularly by urban petty-bourgeois strata,[7] and (3) because it coincided with the need for expansion of industrial capital in the postwar period. Nationalist regimes (of whatever political complexion) thus have an internal base of support for the pursuit of industrialization, are able to exploit international competition between countries and between corporations, and in this way to form alliances with foreign capitals and states to establish the conditions of indigenous industrialization.

In assessing the postwar record of industrial growth Warren employs four criteria suggested by Bob Sutcliffe[8] as the "conditions of independent industrialisation": (1) the development of a domestic market for the products of national industry; (2) a diversified industrial structure with numerous linkages, "including economically strategic capital goods industries"; (3) "national" control over the investment of capital and the accumulation process; (4) an indigenous capacity for the development of technologies appropriate to a given country's industrialization strategy.

The first two of Sutcliffe's conditions resonate the aspirations of the ECLA "inner-directed" strategy discussed in the previous section; alleged frustration of the last two conditions through the modes of operation of international capital provide the central thrust of theories of "dependency," as we have also seen. Taking each of these conditions in turn, Warren argues that "empirical observation" confirms the strong trend he asserts toward lessening dependence/development of national (industrial) capitalisms in the postcolonial Third World, devoting the most attention to the consideration of capital investment and accumulation.[9] This is not surprising since the export of capital from the advanced capitalist countries, and the nature and effects of international capital flows, have occupied a central place in Marxist thinking about world economy since the time of Lenin's *Imperialism* (1916); and for the contemporary school of "Third Worldist" political economy the penetration and generalized dominance of foreign capital is the primary agency in the reproduction of underdevelopment and dependence.

Concerning foreign capital investment, Warren concludes that quantitatively it plays only a small part in capital formation, and that qualitatively it is increasingly subject to conditions of control by nationalist regimes in the Third World that enable them to appropriate a significant share of its profits: through "rents" on international companies in extractive sectors (notably but not exclusively in the case of petroleum), through joint ventures between international companies and indigenous private or state capital, and sometimes through the outright nationalization of the subsidiaries of foreign companies and banks. Similarly, he argues that imports of advanced technology (now a more strategic role of multinational corporations than direct capital investment) represent a net gain for Third World countries, are increasingly assimilated in the industrializaton process, and thereby contribute to the development of indigenous technical culture and capacity.[10]

These findings, together with some passing remarks about the development of capitalist relations of production in agriculture, lead to the strategic conclusion of Warren's essay that "imperialism declines as capitalism grows" (imperialism having been vaguely defined as "a system of inequality, domination, and exploitation" and in effect identified with the epoch of colonial rule, as we have noted).[11] To reiterate, the essential condition of this process is the conjunction of political independence with a new stage of the global expansion of capital in the postwar period, *compelling* the industrialization of the Third World. This occurs even in the absence of a national bourgeoisie of the "classic" type (represented by the historical experience of Western Europe, the United States, and Japan), which "partly explains the importance of the state in most underdeveloped countries, where it often assumes the role of a bourgeois ruling class prior to the substantial development of that class."[12]

The "serious problems" that capitalist industrialization in the Third World still faces "are now rooted in the internal contradictions of underdeveloped countries, centered around agricultural stagnation, excessive urbanisation, growing unemployment, and the 'premature' spread of socialism prior to the development of industrial capitalism."[13] While these internal contradictions may represent the legacy of an earlier imperialism, current imperialist-periphery contradictions are "basically nonantagonistic," representing the ("normal") rivalry of (increasingly equal) national capitalisms which share a global interest in the exploitation of producing classes, and in opposition to socialist states and social forces.

The attack on the "Warren thesis" by McMichael, Petras, and Rhodes[14] derives from the very "dependency" school that Warren had attacked. While some of their specific criticisms of Warren's use of aggregated statistics are well founded, the central thrust of their article is simply to reiterate the position of dependency theory: "Capitalist development in the Third World today means dependent growth in a small proportion of countries, for the benefit of a small proportion of the population."[15] This conclusion embodies a conceptual delusion at the core of dependency theory, which is that an understanding of "genuine" or "national" development as a process which delivers the goods of increased social welfare, more egalitarian income distribution, full employment, and so on (to the benefit of the majority), virtually *excludes capitalist development by definition.* The latter refers to the development of capitalist relations of production and productive forces, manifested in the accumulation and expanded reproduction of capital (which Warren attempted to document), the fundamental mechanism of which can be nothing else than *exploitation* through the appropriation of surplus value, and creating the conditions of such exploitation.

The methodology of historical materialism suggests that there can be no universal "model" of capitalist development, disregarding the specific historical conditions, forms, and mechanisms through which it occurs (or fails to occur). Yet this is the fallacy that pervades radical views of underdevelopment and dependence: that capitalist development in the Third World is held either to be impossible (stagnationist theories), or "deficient" or "distorted" or "dependent" by reference to an implicit "model" of "normal" capitalist development realized (in very different historical conditions) by the now advanced countries of the West and Japan.[16] The result is that what may be the very conditions and effects of capitalist development—immiseration, mass unemployment, new forms of class oppression—are assimilated to an established "symptomology of underdevelopment" (J. Freyssinet's term, and exemplified by McMichael et al.), rather than being investigated as aspects of processes of contemporary change, of the development of new contradictions, and the types of struggle they give rise to. While Warren's purpose was to open up these areas to analysis and debate, the response of dependency theory is typically to close them off.

In sum, for dependency theory "capitalism" is effectively encompassed by the circuits of *international* capital which are inimical to the notion of national development it proposes. By default therefore national development can only be realized through "socialism," which thus appears as an adjunct of nationalist aspiration—and rescues the "progressive" character of the latter from any association with the historic failure of the "neocolonial" ruling class.[17] The conception of socialism arrived at by this route is no less utopian than the earlier notion of development through the agency of national capital that it replaced, as Colin Leys has pointed out.[18] Insofar as the conditions for socialist politics are generated by the contradictions of capitalist development, then an incapacity to analyze those contradictions and their concrete forms leaves "socialism" as a utopian vision, rather than the object of struggles which require appropriate analysis, programs, and organization.[19] That is the case also with those whose ideological blinkers cause them to assimilate all change in the Third World under the residual of "dependent growth."

The critique of Warren by Emmanuel,[20] best known as the theorist of unequal exchange, is of considerably more interest. Emmanuel's earlier work had led him to reject what he terms "the myth of investment imperialism," deriving originally from the work of Lenin, and manifested rather differently in the various versions of current dependency theory.[21] Accordingly, he agrees with several major points of Warren's polemic: that imported technology, licenses, and patents for industrial processes are obtained "cheaply" by the Third World as they are the products of an enormous research and development industry in the West which is subsidized by state funds; that the external debt of Third World countries (in any case not unique to them), rather than constituting an additional "drain of surplus" through interest and capital repayments, represents the effect of an in-flow of capital which can be utilized for accumulation. In one way Emmanuel goes much further than Warren in arguing that a major cause of the reproduction of "underdevelopment" is not that Third World countries have been invaded by foreign capital (the dependency position) but that they have been *starved* of it. The essential issue is the scale and rate of accumulation, not the "nationality" of the capitals involved, for example, large-scale industrial capital is much more "national" in India than in Canada.[22]

This is not the place to go into Emmanuel's theory of unequal exchange and how it bears on underdevelopment and development. It is sufficient to note that in Emmanuel's view the critical problem of capitalist development is that the growth of accumulation and production is determined by the size of markets (in turn dependent on aggregate income and the demand it generates). Accordingly international capital flows much more between the advanced capitalist countries which "are nowadays too rich not to be able to absorb themselves, without difficulty, all the new capital that is formed in them, and the underdeveloped countries are too poor to offer attractive investment prospects to this same capital, apart from their few import-substitution industries."[23] At the same time international income differences are the basis for the "drain of surplus" through unequal exchange in the world market, reducing the prospects of indigenous capital accumulation in Third World countries.[24]

Emmanuel's assessment that "Warren has attempted to prove too much"[25] is undoubtedly a fair one, and his critique of Warren's use of statistics on industrialization reveals that they aggregate capitalist enterprises, relations of production, and productive forces with "precapitalist" forms (e.g., craft production, petty commodity production), and that capitalist industrialization cannot be adequately considered in isolation from the development of capitalism in agriculture. Emmanuel is further correct in pointing out that "it is not enough to juxtapose phenomena in statistical terms; we have to organise them in a system of precise determinations."[26] Warren's argument was conducted without any (explicit) theorization (or "system of precise determinations") of the nature of international and national capitalist economy in the present period. On the other hand, dependency theories have demonstrated their incapacity for such a task, providing a description (and condemnation) of the symptoms and effects of capitalist development, rather than being able to explain them in the terms of the intrinsically contradictory nature of the process itself (something which Lenin had pointed out with respect to the Russian Narodniks of the late nineteenth century).

Futhermore, Warren's essay contains a tension between documenting the actuality of capitalist development in the Third World, and, more ambitiously, arguing that it is increasingly taking the form of national and independent industrialization. With respect to Sutcliffe's criteria, Warren notes that they have not always been necessary or sufficient conditions of independent capitalist industrialization, and he concludes that "the very notion of 'independent industrialisation,' even if clarified by specifying whether it is capitalist or socialist, is highly ambiguous. The increase in economic interdependence within the capitalist world and the collaboration of ruling, exploitative, classes throughout the world against socialism and the masses, both mean that the issue would be more accurately posed in terms of equality between previously unequal 'partners' in an increasingly interdependent relationship."[27]

While the notion of "equality" seems no less ambiguous, it can be suggested that Warren's contribution was hampered by the polemical desire to counterpose "independent" industrialization against the new orthodoxy of dependency theory. This is a very common effect—a "mirror image" effect, one could say—of ideological debate. Warren remains at least partly trapped on the conceptual terrain of his opponents by attempting to establish his conclusions in the terms they employ (the "problematic" of dependent/ independent development). To this extent he provides a different answer to that of the dependency theorists, but to a question formulated within their problematic (one in which, we have argued, issues of capitalist or socialist development are always mediated through an underlying and pervasive nationalism).

Warren correctly rejects any necessary evaluation of national development in terms of increasing welfare (which excludes capitalist development by definition), but remains engaged with his opponents' insistence on a process of accumulation under "national" control (by a national bourgeoisie or its surrogate, the postcolonial state), which leads him to underestimate the importance of the role played by international capital in Third World industrialization. He also assimilates the dependency theorists' conception of "external" and "internal" determinations: while they see the reproduction of the internal structure of underdevelopment and dependence as (almost entirely) determined by external forces (namely international capital), Warren locates the obstacles to capitalist industrialization in the internal structures of Third World countries and not as attributable to the interests of imperialism. In this way he again asserts a different position to dependency theory but within the problematic of the latter, which he failed to transcend by providing a different theoretical basis for his conclusions.[28]

Conclusion

The space opened up by Warren's intervention in the debate about industrialization has yet to be supported by an alternative theoretical framework needed to carry the debate forward—a "system of precise determinations" concerning the nature of contemporary world economy (imperialism) and the conditions of the capitalist development (or "underdevelopment") of national economies. While there are a number of contenders for this role, both "classic" theories (Luxemburg, Bukharin, Lenin) and contemporary ones (Frank, Amin, Emmanuel, Wallerstein, Kay, Mandel, among others), a number of persistent problems remain which can be drawn out from the critical discussion pursued in this essay.

(1) Perhaps the outstanding problem for contemporary political economy is the status and content of the categories "national economy" and "world economy," which cannot be taken simply as "given" entities—the former by economic activity within the political boundaries of national states, the latter by the evidence of international trade and capital flows. Which conditions and aspects of the process of value formation and of the reproduction of capital are constituted within "national economies," which are constituted within the circuits of world economy, and how do they bear on each other? This is the kind of question that dependency theory has been unable to pose, given its conception of world economy as a system of

relations between two groups of countries—the advanced capitalist countries with their "self-evident" qualities of economic independence and self-sustained growth, the absence of which no less self-evidently defines the countries of the Third World. These are the assumptions that pervade dependency theory and, as we have argued, express a conceptual terrain on which Warren remains despite his radically different conclusion (the development of increasingly equal "national capitalisms").

The point is that only by posing questions about the contemporary conditions, mechanisms, and contradictions of the reproduction of capital can we avoid a priori or "given" assumptions about "national" or "world" economy—determinate concepts appropriate to these categories can only emerge as a *result* of investigation. Furthermore, it is clear that these questions apply no less to the economies of the advanced capitalist countries than to those of the Third World. Discussions of the former can be no less bogged down by assumptions about the "nationality" of capital than discussions of the latter.[29]

(2) Sensitivity to the historically diverse mechanisms and forms of capitalist development, and of the "articulation" of noncapitalist economic, social, and ideological forms with the development of capitalist relations, should help avoid the all too familiar inability to see transitional processes occurring because they fail to conform to a predetermined and abstracted "model" of what capitalist development "should look like."

(3) Recent world history is not a tabula rasa on which modern capital can simply impose the "logic" of its own needs. Imperialism cannot rewrite its own history, and many of the contradictions facing the extension of capitalist relations of production (through the capitalization of industry and agriculture in the Third World) are the inheritance of earlier modes of operation of capital, something which Warren grudgingly recognized but the significance of which he evaded.[30] In the course of its "world-historical" career (Marx) the development of capitalism becomes ever more uneven, so that we should expect to encounter in the contemporary period an accumulation of forms of production, exploitation, and appropriation of surplus labor, representative of virtually all the historical "stages" of capitalist development, from the most "backward" and incomplete (e.g., "feudal" mechanisms of the subordination of the peasantry in the expansion of agricultural commodity production) to the most advanced forms of capitalist industry employing a growing and stable industrial proletariat.

(4) The above points contribute to an awareness of the need to transcend the more or less static dichotomy of "internal" and "ex-

ternal" factors shared by Warren and the dependency theorists despite their different conclusions. Within the framework of a theory of world economy the need to analyze *any* social formation in its specificity—as a complex ensemble of class relations and contradictions, of the economic, political, and ideological conditions and forms of class struggle—is a political task of prime importance, making even greater demands on a "system of precise determinations." This applies perhaps a fortiori to the countries of the Third World, which otherwise are aggregated and characterized by negative and residual criteria: Brazil and Senegal, India and Guatemala, Indonesia and Kenya, are lumped together by what they ultimately have in common, the inablility to achieve "national development." Warren breached this conceptual vicious circle by trying to chart the actuality of capitalist development in the Third World; the limitations in which his important contribution was trapped have to be overcome to carry our understanding further.[31]

Notes

1. Useful critical discussions of the international trade theory of "comparative costs" are to be found in F. Clairmonte, *Economic Liberalism and Underdevelopment* (New Delhi: 1960); T. Szentes, *The Political Economy of Underdevelopment* (Budapest: 1971); and A. Emmanuel, *Unequal Exchange* (New York: Monthly Review Press, 1972).
2. In contrast to the 1950s, when the notion of an "Afro-Asian" bloc was more prevalent. On the character of dependency theory as a response to the crisis of "inner-directed" development in Latin America, see T. Dos Santos, "The Crisis of Development Theory and the Problem of Dependency in Latin America," in H. Bernstein, ed., *Underdevelopment and Development* (Harmondsworth: Penguin Books, 1973); D. Booth, "Andre Gunder Frank: An Introduction and Appreciation," in I. Oxaal, A. Barnett, and D. Booth, eds., *Beyond the Sociology of Development* (London: Routledge & Kegan Paul, 1975); and P. O'Brien, "A Critique of Latin American Theories of Dependency," in ibid.
3. B. Warren, "Imperialism and Capitalist Industrialisation," *New Left Review* 81 (1973): 3-4.
4. Ibid., p. 6, n. 6.
5. A. Emmanuel, "Myths of Development Versus Myths of Underdevelopment," *New Left Review* 85 (1974); P. McMichael, J. Petras, and R. Rhodes, "Imperialism and the Contradictions of Development," *New Left Review* 85 (1974).
6. Warren, "Imperialism and Industrialisation," pp. 11-16.
7. Ibid., pp. 11, 43.

8. B. Sutcliffe, "Imperialism and Industrialisation in the Third World," in Roger Owen and Bob Sutcliffe, eds., *Studies in the Theory of Imperialism* (London: Longman, 1972), pp. 174-76.
9. Ibid., pp. 19-30.
10. The discussion of technology has acquired a new prominence associated with the focus on multinational corporations. For Samir Amin, "technological domination" is increasingly adequate for the appropriating of monopolistic superprofits, without direct investment—see Samir Amin, *Unequal Development* (New York: Monthly Review Press, 1976), p. 189; for Hamza Alavi, the "colonial" mode of production is characterized by "external dependence...in the field of capital goods and research-intensive technology"—see Hamza Alavi, "India and the Colonial Mode of Production," in R. Miliband and J. Saville, eds., *Socialist Register 1975* (London: Merlin Press, 1975), p. 192; see also Hamza Alavi, "Imperialism Old and New," in Miliband and Saville, eds., *Socialist Register 1964* (London: Merlin Press, 1964), one of the first presentations of the argument. The suggestion that "enclaves" of advanced industrial technology introduce a new form of economic and social dualism (as well as dependence) in Third World countries has been made by both liberal development economists (e.g., H.W. Singer and J. Ansari, *Rich Countries and Poor Countries* [Baltimore: Johns Hopkins University Press, 1977]), and by neo-Marxists (e.g., F.H. Cardoso, "Dependency and Development in Latin America," *New Left Review* 74 [1972], and abridged in this volume). Warren's retort that "technology is the last resort of the dependence theoreticians (as indeed it is of many fetishists)" (p. 34) is too dismissive. Technologies embody the social relations through which they are produced and employed—a strategic discussion premised on this understanding is to be found in G. Kay, *Development and Underdevelopment* (New York: St. Martin's Press, 1975), especially chap. 6, in the context of an analysis of the reproduction cycle of modern industrial capital.
11. Warren, "Imperialism and Industrialisation," pp. 41, 4.
12. Ibid., p. 43.
13. Ibid., p. 42.
14. McMichael et al., "Imperialism and Contradictions."
15. Ibid., p. 104.
16. Which are deemed to have "delivered the goods," as manifested in the "affluent society" of the postwar Western world; a view that was not only celebrated in the apologetics of bourgeois social science, but incorporated in the "New Left" political economy of Baran and Sweezy, and social philosophy of Herbert Marcuse. The argument that the Western countries have achieved ways of regulating both the basic economic contradictions of capitalism (through demand management, and massive nonproductive state expenditure preventing the "over-accumulation" of capital) and its social contradictions (through the "social contract" between capital and labor) concludes that the Western working class is no longer a revolutionary force. Imperialism "exports" the principal contradictions of capitalism to the Third World

(exploitation of which "subsidizes" the incorporation of the Western working class into bourgeois society), which is therefore the center of revolutionary socialist hopes in the present epoch. The "political economy of underdevelopment" and Third Worldist ideology thus go hand in hand, a notable example of which is the politics of unequal exchange theory as formulated by Arghiri Emmanuel (*Unequal Exchange* [New York: Monthly Review Press, 1972]), and taken up by Samir Amin in *Unequal Development* and Immanuel Wallerstein in *The Capitalist World-Economy* (New York: Cambridge University Press, 1979). See also the interesting article by A. Phillips, "The Concept of Development," *Review of African Political Economy* 8 (1977), which locates this "turn" to the Third World in the *crise de conscience* of the Western New Left of the 1950s and 1960s.

17. It is often stated, with some justification, that Marxist political theory and practice have proved inadequate in dealing with nationalism as an ideological and social force in the modern world. Socialists have to come to terms with nationalism as a contemporary reality, and should neither dismiss it nor identify with it according to a set of all-purpose prescriptions about the "national question," ostensibly derived from Lenin, Stalin, Mao, or any other source of " authority." The "progressive" or "reactionary" nature of particular nationalist politics can only be determined according to their specific conjunctures, and from the viewpoint of the struggle for socialism. This is quite different from *internalizing* nationalist perspectives in a theoretical position, which we argue is the case with the dependency theorists.

18. Colin Leys, "Underdevelopment and Dependency: Critical Notes," *Journal of Contemporary Asia* 7, no. 1 (1977).

19. These comments summarize the conclusions of an attempt at a systematic critique of theories of underdevelopment and dependence in my "Sociology of Development vs. Sociology of Underdevelopment?" in D. Lehman, ed., *Development Theory: Four Critical Essays* (London: Frank Cass, 1979), which contains a wide range of references to the recent literature; see also Leys, "Underdevelopment," and Phillips, "Concept of Development."

20. Emmanuel, "Myths of Development."

21. A. Emmanuel, "White-Settler Colonialism and the Myth of Investment Imperialism," *New Left Review* 73 (1972), and abridged in this volume.

22. Emmanuel, "Myths of Development," p. 75.

23. Ibid., p. 77.

24. There are critiques of unequal exchange theory by Charles Bettelheim (appendices to Emmanuel, *Unequal Exchange*), G. Pilling, "Imperialism, Trade, and 'Unequal Exchange': The Work of Arghiri Emmanuel," *Economy and Society* 2, no. 2 (1973); and Kay, *Development*, pp. 107-19. Emmanuel's own argument, with its skepticism about the "nationality" of capital and its insistence on imperialist "exploitation" through trade relations rather than capital exports, goes against the grain of much dependency theory, which does not prevent its assimilation by Amin in *Unequal Development*, an eclectic compendium of virtually every propo-

sition put forward by Third Worldist political economy. No less striking is the reliance of Wallerstein's "world-system" theory on the *conclusions* of Emmanuel's economics, the theoretical structure of which Wallerstein gives no evidence of comprehending (just as he never refers to the controversy surrounding unequal exchange theory). The most powerful criticism of Emmanuel derives from the work of Wolfgang Schoeller, which denies the existence of an international process of value formation, or mediation of values through the formation of an international rate of profit (one of Emmanuel's critical assumptions); see note 29 below. Ernest Mandel in his *Late Capitalism* (London: New Left Books, 1975), chap. 11, follows the same logic as Schoeller in criticizing Emmanuel, then stops and abandons the argument pursued up to that point.

25. Emmanuel, "Myths of Development," p. 63.
26. Ibid., p. 74.
27. Warren, "Imperialism and Industrialisation," p. 35.
28. "The question here arises whether the problem does not already pronounce its own nonsensicality, and whether the impossibility of the solution is not already contained in the premises of the question.... Frequently the only possible answer is a critique of the question and the only solution is to negate the question"—Karl Marx, *Grundrisse* (Harmondsworth: Penguin Books, 1973), pp. 126-27. Marx's comment is an apt one with respect to the way dependency theory has formulated the problem of "national" development; unfortunately, Warren sought to provide a different answer rather than negating the question.
29. See, for example, the discussion of the nature and effects of U.S. capital investment in Western Europe by Nicos Poulantzas, "Internalisation of Capitalist Relations and the Nation State," *Economy and Society* 3, no. 2 (1974), and the pertinent criticisms by J. Friedman, "Crisis in Theory and Transformations of the World Economy," *Review* 2, no. 2 (1978). The most developed attempts to establish *theoretically* the concepts which make it possible to use the category of national economy have been made by German economists; little of their work is available in English, but see W. Olle and W. Schoeller, *World Market, State, and Average National Conditions of Labour* (Dar es Salaam: Economic Research Bureau, University of Dar es Salaam, 1977).
30. The same point occupies a central place in the theoretical schema of Geoffrey Kay, although again it is mentioned briefly and without any elaboration; see H. Bernstein, "Underdevelopment and the Law of Value—A Critique of Kay," *Review of African Political Economy* 6 (1976).
31. This paper was written before the posthumous publication of Bill Warren's important book *Imperialism: Pioneer of Capitalism* (London: New Left Books, 1980), which develops the argument of his 1973 article and at the same time represents some significant changes of emphasis.

[18]
Poverty in the Third World:
Ugly Facts and Fancy Models

Keith Griffin and Azizur Rahman Khan

Development of the type experienced by the majority of Third World countries in the last quarter century has meant, for very large numbers of people, increased impoverishment. This is the conclusion which has emerged from a series of empirical studies of trends in levels of living in the rural areas of Asia.[1] In most of the countries we have studied, the incomes of the very poor have been falling absolutely or the proportion of the rural population living below a designated "poverty line" has been increasing, or both. Similar things almost certainly have been happening elsewhere, in Africa and parts of Latin America, for the mechanisms which generate poverty in Asia are present in greater or lesser degree in much of the rest of the underdeveloped world. Certainly there is no evidence that growth as such has succeeded in reducing the incidence of poverty.

Principal Findings

Ten empirical studies were undertaken in an attempt to determine the trends in the absolute and relative incomes of the rural poor in seven Asian countries. These seven countries were Bangladesh, India, Indonesia, Malaysia, Pakistan, the Philippines, and Sri Lanka. In the case of India it was thought that it would be meaningless to attempt to generalize about the entire country; instead, separate studies were made of conditions in four major states, viz., the Punjab, Uttar Pradesh, Bihar, and Tamil Nadu.

The seven countries included in our sample account for approximately 70 percent of the rural population of the nonsocialist underdeveloped world. Since the average income of these seven countries is below that of the rest of the underdeveloped market economy countries, it is likely that their share of the poor of the nonsocialist underdeveloped world is even greater.

In each of the seven, the scope and method of analysis had to be adapted to the available statistical information. Considerable dif-

236

ferences in the quantity and quality of evidence were therefore inevitable. Yet some broad generalizations about trends are possible.

In general an attempt was made to cover as long a time period as possible and to bring the story forward as close to the present as possible. Attempts were made to overcome distortions due to weather cycles and to incorporate the most up-to-date information. But here too it was not possible to ensure uniformity. The period covered varies from a decade to a quarter century. The most outstanding facts to be noted are the worsening distribution of income and the declining real income of the rural poor. Those studies which contain the relevant data show that the shares of the lower decile groups in aggregate income and consumption have been declining even during periods of relatively rapid agricultural growth. There are significant differences from country to country as regards the proportion of its population that has been adversely affected, but in each country for which we have data, a substantial proportion of the lowest income groups appears to have experienced a decline in their share of real income over time.

Indeed, the evidence from the case studies points to an even stronger conclusion. In almost every case a significant proportion of low-income households experienced an absolute decline in their real income, particularly since the early 1960s.

This fact emerged from two separate types of measurements that were attempted in the case studies. First, a level of real income was defined below which all households were classified as poor. In most studies such a "poverty line" was derived from an estimate of the level of income necessary to ensure a minimum diet, although the case studies differ widely as to what should be the contents of a minimum diet. In each case, however, it is found that the proportion of the population below the "poverty line" either has remained constant or has tended in recent years to increase. The data are summarized in Table 1.

In six of the eight cases in which "poverty lines" were constructed the proportion of the rural population in poverty seems to have increased, although in the Philippines the increase was modest. In Pakistan and Tamil Nadu, in contrast, the proportion of people in poverty has remained roughly constant.

One of the unsatisfactory things about "poverty lines" is that it is impossible to tell from them what has happened to the distribution of income among those below the line. This problem can be overcome in part, however, by constructing more than one line, corresponding to alternative definitions of poverty. This was done in three of the studies. In the case of Pakistan there appears to be no systematic tendency for the proportional incidence of rural poverty

Table 1
Percentage of the Rural Population Below the Poverty Line

Country or state	Year	Rural population in poverty		
		A	B	C
Pakistan	1963-64	72	54	45
	1966-67	64	52	44
	1968-69	64	53	46
	1969-70	68	46	36
	1970-71	71	47	38
	1971-72	74	55	43
Punjab, India	1960-61	18		
	1970-71	23		
Uttar Pradesh, India	1960-61	42		
	1970-71	64		
Bihar, India	1960-61	41		
	1963-64	54		
	1964-65	53		
	1970-71	59		
Tamil Nadu, India	1957-58	74	53	
	1959-60	79	54	
	1960-61	70	48	
	1961-62	66	36	
	1963-64	64	39	
	1964-65	72	46	
	1969-70	74	49	
Bangladesh	1963-64	40	5	
	1968-69	76	25	
	1973-74	79	42	
	1975	62	41	
Malaysia	1957	40		
	1970	47		
Philippines	1956-57	10		
	1961	12		
	1965	13		
	1970-71	12		

Source: The data were obtained from various chapters in Keith Griffin and Azizur Rahman Khan, eds., *Poverty and Landlessness in Rural Asia* (Geneva: ILO, 1976), mimeo, or, in the case of Malaysia and the Philippines, were derived from interpolations of data contained in that volume.

Table 1 (*continued*).

Notes: (1) The data refer to the proportion of the rual population in poverty, except in the case of Malaysia and the Philippines, where the data refer to households.
(2) The poverty lines are defined as follows: *Pakistan*: Income sufficient to yield food consumption satisfying 95 percent of the estimated caloric requirements (estimate A), or 92 percent (estimate B) or 90 percent (estimate C); *Punjab*: Rs. 16.36 per capita per month in 1960-61 prices; *Uttar Pradesh*: Rs. 14.50 per capita per month in 1960-61 prices; *Bihar*: Rs. 15.83 per capita per month in 1960-61 prices; *Tamil Nadu*: Rs. 21 per capita per month in 1960-61 prices (estimate A) or Rs. 15 per capita per month (estimate B); *Bangladesh*: Tk. 23.61 per capita per month in 1963-64 prices, corresponding to a level of income sufficient to yield food consumption satisfying 90 percent of the estimated caloric requirements (estimate A) or Tk. 17.02, corresponding to an income satisfying 80 percent of caloric requirements; *Malaysia*: 97.4 Malaysian dollars per household per month at 1965 prices; *Philippines*: 434 pesos per family per year at 1965 prices. The reader is warned that these interpolations are tentative.

to change regardless of which of three definitions of poverty is used. The implication of this is that the distribution of income within the poverty group has remained essentially unaltered. In Tamil Nadu there has been no tendency for poverty to decline when the "poverty line" is drawn at Rs. 21 per capita per month in 1960-1961 prices (estimate A), but when the line is lowered to Rs. 15 (estimate B) the proportion in poverty clearly has declined. This implies that the distribution of income among those with Rs. 21 per capita per month or less improved over the period studied. In Bangladesh, on the other hand, the proportion of the rural population with an income below the "poverty line" of Tk. 23.6 per capita per month in 1963-1964 prices rose significantly (estimate A), but the proportion below Tk. 17.02 (estimate B) rose even more dramatically, thereby indicating that inequality even among the poor became worse between 1963 and 1975.

A second type of measurement was a calculation of the real incomes of decile or quintile groups at different points of time. Here it was found that the real incomes of the lowest decile or quintile groups have been declining over time. Once again, the range over which this has occurred differs from one country to another. In the Philippines, for example, the bottom 20 percent experienced a decline in real income whereas in Bangladesh over 80 percent of the population experienced such a decline.

The other major empirical finding concerns the trend in real wages of agricultural laborers. In most of the countries for which measurements could be obtained either real wages remained constant or there was a significant downward trend. In a few cases the trend was ambiguous, although even in these cases there was always clear additional evidence that the living standards of agricultural workers had not improved. In the Indian state of Punjab, for example, a few measurements suggest that there was some increase in real wages of agricultural laborers, but the results are very sensitive to the wage series selected, the nature of the cost of living index used to convert nominal wages into real wages, and the choice of the base year. At the same time, it has been shown in our study that the proportion of agricultural laborers below the poverty line increased precisely during the period when real wages are claimed to have risen. If one is to believe both pieces of evidence, then there must have been a change in the occupational distribution of the wage-earners included in the average wage index. In fact, the compositon of agricultural laborers does seem to have changed significantly as a result of the widespread adoption of capital-intensive farming techniques, especially by the labor-hiring, large farmers. The importance of skilled labor and of operators of mechanical equipment has increased considerably. The rise in demand for workers of this type, given the initial shortage of skills, undoubtedly led to a relatively rapid increase in their wages. On the other hand, the balance between the supply and demand for more traditional types of labor became increasingly unfavorable over time, and consequently their wages failed to rise.

All the countries included in our sample are characterized by a highly unequal distribution of landownership. Statistical information usually relates to the distribution of farm size, i.e., to the area farmed and not the area owned. It is generally known that the ownership distribution is less equal than the distribution of farm size. Of the seven countries studied, the degree of inequality is perhaps the least in Bangladesh, but even there the bottom 20 percent of the holdings account for only 3 percent of the land while the top 10 percent account for over 35 percent. The Gini concentration ratio is 0.5. In the other six countries the distribution is less equal. For example, the Gini concentration ratios of the distribution of landholding for Pakistan, India, and the Philippines have been estimated to be around 0.6.[2]

None of these countries made any significant progress toward redistribution of land during the periods considered. For those countries for which information is available no significant trend toward reducing inequality can be found. Pakistan, the Philippines, and Sri Lanka initiated some land reform measures in the early 1970s. Although our studies were not able to take their effects fully into account, it is reasonably clear by now that the redistributive ·consequences of these measures are likely to be marginal.

The continuation of the highly unequal ownership of land during a period of rapid demographic growth has resulted in increased landlessness and near-landlessness. Due to a curious lack of enthusiasm on the part of the statistical authorities in these countries it is very difficult to obtain a time series on the number of landless workers. In those cases where information is available, e.g., in Bangladesh and parts of India, a marked trend toward increased landlessness can be discerned.

Causal Mechanisms

A salient characteristic of the countries we have studied is that many of the resources needed for development are at hand, unutilized or poorly utilized. Foremost among these is the intelligence, ingenuity, and effort of the labor force itself. It has long been known that part, usually a small part, of the rural work force often is openly unemployed, particularly during the slack season in regions where multiple cropping is not practiced. In addition, a larger part of the work force may be underemployed in the sense that it is engaged in tasks with a very low level of productivity. More important, perhaps, than unemployment and underemployment is the low productivity and occasionally low intensity of work arising from the poor motivation, poor health, and injustice that is found in most rural areas. The exploitation and inequality to which the majority of the rural population is subjected is demoralizing, engenders resentment, and stifles initiative and creativity. The effect is not only to lower current output below its potential but to reduce the capacity and willingness of the population to innovate. Where inequality is so severe that infants of the poor suffer from protein malnutrition, intelligence is permanently impaired and their creative talent is destroyed. In societies where material deprivation is less acute, effects on initiative and innovation may be similar because of the psychological consequences of a warped incentive system and the sociological consequences of a social structure which ensures that most of the economic surplus is captured by a small minority.

Labor is not the only resource that is poorly utilized; in many countries land and other natural resources are not efficiently exploited. Especially on the larger farms, the length of the fallow period is excessively long, the degree of cropping intensity is too low, and the amount of land in natural pastures is high. At the same time, many of the smallest farmers are forced to overexploit their land, with the result that useful land is destroyed through erosion and the exhaustion of soil fertility. Just as the economic system in the countries we have studied results in poor use (and even destruction) of part of its human resources, so too it results in poor use (and even destruction) of part of its natural resources.

Underutilization of labor and land often is accompanied by underutilization of capital. Large irrigation facilities are not used to capacity; irrigation canals and drainage ditches are allowed to fall into disrepair; fish ponds are permitted to become overgrown with weeds; mechanical equipment becomes inoperative because of a lack of spare parts. Furthermore, much of the savings potential of the peasantry remains untapped, and hence the rate of accumulation of capital remains lower than necessary.

Latent within these inefficiencies and inequities are possibilities for higher output, faster growth, and greater equality. This potential for rural development, however, has lain dormant. Instead of growing prosperity for those most in need there has been impoverishment. The crucial question is why.

It certainly is not the case that the increasing poverty of the poor is due to general stagnation in Asia, or, worse, economic decline. On the contrary, all but one of the seven countries surveyed has enjoyed a rise in average incomes in recent years, and in some instances the rise has been quite rapid; only in Bangladesh have average incomes fallen. Excluding Bangladesh, between 1960 and 1973, GNP per head increased between 1.3 percent a year (in India) and 3.9 percent (in Malaysia). Thus it is the pattern of growth in Asia that has been most unsatisfactory rather than the rate of growth. The pattern has been such that despite a fairly rapid increase in average income per head, poverty in rural areas has tended to rise. It is tempting to argue that one reason for this is that the growth has been of a type consistent with slow growth of agriculture. The basic point that is being made, however, is that in a period of increasing prosperity, poverty in rural areas has not diminished and probably has increased.

The claim that the growing poverty of Asia is due to a world food shortage or to a failure of food production in Asia to keep up with the expanding population is untenable. If one examines our seven countries individually, it transpires that in only one of them did population expand faster than domestic food production. This was in Bangladesh where, as we have seen, even GNP per capita has been falling. In India population and food production have grown at the same rate, while cereal production has expanded faster than the population;[3] in Pakistan food production may have grown fractionally faster than the population and cereal production significantly faster. In all the other countries studied food production clearly has increased faster than the population, and in some countries, notably Sri Lanka and Malaysia, the difference in growth rates has been very large.

The answer to why poverty has increased has more to do with the structure of the economy than its rate of growth. One structural feature common to all the countries studied is a high degree of inequality. Data from the six countries on which information is available suggest that in the economy as a whole the richest 20 percent of households typically receive about half the income, whereas the poorest 40 percent receive between 12 percent and 18 percent of total income. The bottom 20 percent fare even worse, of course, receiving about 7 percent of the income in the least inegalitarian country (Bangladesh) and merely 3.8 percent in one of the most inegalitarian countries (Philippines).

The degree of income inequality in rural areas is somewhat less than in the urban areas and, hence, less unequal than the average for the economy. Nonetheless, the degree of inequality is considerable. According to the available data, rural India is the least inegalitarian while rural Malaysia and the Philippines are the most. Little emphasis should be placed on these differences, however, as the data are not very precise and in the case of India in particular it is widely believed that the data understate the extent of inequality.

The counterpart to the compression of the income of the poor is the concentration of the economic surplus in a very few hands. The disposal of this surplus, in turn, largely determines the pace and composition of economic growth. The preferences of the upper income groups as between present consumption and savings will affect the rate of accumulation. The pattern of demand, itself strongly influenced by the distribution of income, will determine in large part the sectors into which investment flows. And the set of relative factor prices which confront those who invest the surplus will have an effect on the methods of production that are used, the amount of employment that is generated, the productivity of that employment, and the distribution of income.

The structure of factor markets is such that the unequal distribution of income arising from an unequal distribution of productive assets is reinforced by the operations of the price mechanism. Those who have access to the organized capital market are able to obtain finance capital for investment on very favorable terms.[4] Indeed, when nominal rates of interest are adjusted for inflation, the real rate of interest paid by large investors is often negative. This introduces a strong bias in favor of investment in the more capital-intensive sectors and in the more capital-intensive methods of production. As a result, the demand for labor is lower than it otherwise would have been. Paradoxically, the relatively high productivity of labor associated with the more mechanized processes may lead to higher wages for those who secure employment in the sector, thereby further reducing the demand for labor.[5]

This pattern of investment is accentuated in countries where a system of protection is combined with a foreign exchange rate that is overvalued and import permits for foreign equipment consequently must be allocated through a rationing device of some sort.[6] The contrived cheapening of imported goods relative to domestic labor introduces an additional bias in favor of (foreign) capital-intensity, and tends to raise the share of profits in national income while reducing the demand for labor.

The capital markets operate in such a way that a small minority of the labor force is equipped with excessively capital-intensive techniques, given the relative availabilities of investable resources and labor. At the same time, the majority of the labor force (in urban as well as in rural areas) is forced to work with techniques which are insufficiently capital-intensive. As a result, the productivity and incomes of the majority are exceptionally low compared to those employed in the so-called modern, capital-intensive sector. Crude "guesstimates" from Indonesia, for example, suggest that in the modern sector it costs about $5,000 to equip each additional worker. Expansion of employment in this sector provides for about 12 percent of the new entrants into the labor force and absorbs over 70 percent of the surplus allocated to investment. As a result, the investable surplus available for those who enter the informal urban sector and rural occupations is less than $300 per worker.

Price-cum-rationing mechanisms also are present in other parts of the economy. In fact most markets for intermediate goods and services operate in a fashion parallel to that of the capital market. For instance, electric power typically is distributed highly unevenly, many rural areas being excluded from the national network. Efficient transportation services are available to only a relatively few producers, again many rural areas being isolated from the main currents of commerce. Within the rural areas, technical assistance is concentrated on the large farmers and research programs are often oriented toward their needs. Finally, even the labor market operates to the disadvantage of the poor, monopsonistic elements being present in many localities, often associated with a high degree of concentration of land ownership.[7]

The initially high degree of inequality of income and wealth, the concentration of the economic surplus in a few enterprises and households, and the fragmented allocative mechanisms constitute a socioeconomic context in which powerful dynamic forces tend to perpetuate and even accentuate low standards of living of a significant proportion of the rural population. Four such forces, or processes occurring through time, should be mentioned.

First, there is the accumulation of capital in the private sector. The volume of private investment is a relatively low proportion of the economic surplus appropriated by those who control the national wealth. Although some capital formation occurs in rural areas, much of it is channeled into the urban areas, notwithstanding the fact that in the countries studied the urban population accounts for as little as 10 percent of the total in Bangladesh and about 30 percent in the most urbanized country, Malaysia. This "urban bias"[8] in the pattern of investment often takes the form, as we have seen, of highly capital-intensive projects in which the share of wages in value added is relatively low. As a result, the rate of growth of employment in the capital-intensive sector is slow, sometimes not even as fast as the rate of growth of the labor force. In the Philippines, for example, the proportion of the labor force engaged in manufacturing fell from 13 percent in 1957 to less than 10 percent a decade and a half later.[9]

Those unable to find a job in the capital-intensive activities must seek a livelihood either in the urban informal sector or in rural areas, or become openly unemployed. If the labor force entering these categories grows faster than the rate of capital formation in the informal sector and rural areas combined, there is likely to be a tendency toward decline in the real incomes of the most vulnerable workers in the most vulnerable sectors.

Next, these pressures are likely to be exacerbated by investment trends in the public sector. The reason for this is that in the mixed economies of Asia public capital formation essentially supports private sector activities, particularly the large and capital-intensive enterprises. This, in turn, arises from the fact that the groups on which the government relies for support are the same groups which possess most of the wealth of the country, supply the majority of technicians and administrators, and provide the leadership of the army and the dominant political alignments. Economic and political influence are closely interwoven: those who possess purchasing power also possess political power.

Then, the process of technical change may tend to have a labor-saving bias in the activities in which most capital accumulation occurs. Part of the explanation for this is that the pattern of technical innovation is certain to be influenced by the set of relative factor prices which large investors confront. It has already been shown that these factor prices encourage the adoption of relatively capital-intensive methods which economize on labor. A second reason is that most of the Asian economies under study are dependent for much of their innovation on imported foreign technology. This technology was developed in economies where labor is scarce and capital is abundant, and hence their importation into economies where the opposite conditions prevail is likely to diminish still further the number of jobs created for each $10,000 of investment.

Consequently in the sectors and activities where most of the capital accumulation occurs—in manufacturing, on the large mechanized farms, in port, airport, and highway development—there is a danger that technical change will exhibit a pattern that is increasingly labor displacing. In the remainder of the economy, however, where the majority of the labor force is employed, the investible surplus is small and producers are forced by circumstances to seek land and capital-saving technologies. At times this process may be carried to such an extent that the ratio of land and capital to labor begins to fall and a period of increasing poverty, declining labor productivity and "agricultural involution" begins.[10]

Whether or not this happens, and to what extent, depends of course upon our final dynamic process: the rate of growth of the population and associated demographic phenomena. Given the structure of the economy as it has been described and the resulting nature of the processes of capital formation and innovation, the faster the pace of expansion of the population and labor force, the stronger will be the tendency for the standard of living of some groups or classes to fall. Alas, the available estimates indicate, without exception, that the present rates of population growth in the seven Asian countries are high. The slowest estimated rate of demographic expansion is 2 percent a year (in Indonesia), while the fastest is about 3 percent (in Pakistan and the Philippines).

It is important to underline, however, that the cause of increasing poverty in Asia is not an alleged population explosion. Rapid population growth is merely a contributing factor. The basic causes are the unequal ownership of land and other productive assets, allocative mechanisms which discriminate in favor of the owners of wealth, and a pattern of capital accumulation and technical innovation which is biased against labor.

Because of the rate and pattern of investment and technical change, the number of workers that can be readily absorbed in urban areas and in nonfarm rural activities is relatively small—far smaller than the increase in the work force. Agricultural production is characterized by diminishing returns to labor, which of course in principle could be offset by high rates of accumulation and innovation. Unfortunately, however, investment in agriculture has been relatively low, especially on the small farms, yet the sector has been forced to retain a large proportion of the yearly increase in the labor force.

In consequence, the tendency toward diminishing returns and falling output per worker has not always been compensated by rising investment. As population densities and the man-land ratio have increased, the level and share of rents have risen while the wage share, wage rates, and the number of days employed per person have tended to decline. That is, at the going terms of agricultural remuneration, the demand for labor has increased less rapidly than the supply and hence the standard of living of those who depend on work as a source of income has fallen. This has affected some plantation workers, unskilled landless agricultural laborers, pure tenants, and some small landowners who have to supplement their income by engaging in paid labor.

Thus it is that in a world that is far from being perfectly competitive, a rise in national income per head and in food production per head is quite compatible not only with greater relative inequality, but with greater hunger and falling incomes for the poorest members of society. The study of Asian economic development indicates that the initial distribution of wealth and income has a decisive influence over the pattern of growth and hence over the rate of amelioration or deterioration in the standard of living of the lowest income groups. Furthermore, given the initial conditions, it is difficult to change the distribution of income by manipulating standard policy instruments—tax, subsidy, and expenditure levels, exchange rates and trade controls, monetary variables, etc. It follows from this that a "grow now, redistribute later" strategy is not a valid option in most countries; it is necessary first to "get the structure right."

Deficiencies of Formal Models

The foregoing suggests that the economic processes that produce poverty are too complex to be described adequately by a formal model consisting of a system of a large number of equations. The structure of a realistic model would be extremely complicated. Even if such a model could be set out in mathematical terms its numerical application would be virtually impossible in view of the immense difficulty of measuring all the parameters.

This, however, is not to suggest that formal models have no role to play in promoting an understanding of poverty and in planning for its eradication. What clearly is not feasible is to develop a comprehensive model of poverty that would explain all the causative factors and enable one to trace the results of all possible policies. On the other hand, some specific aspects of the process can be illuminated in important ways by the explicit specification of the major interrelationships in quantitative terms. Especially in planning for the reduction of poverty, relatively simple formal models may be able to shed light on the interaction between particular actions and the final outcomes in terms of changes in the magnitude and composition of poverty.

To achieve these goals of providing a partial explanation of poverty and indicating the impact of policy measures on the eradication of poverty, the formal models must incorporate the crucially important variables and relationships. Here we can only highlight a few of these that are often omitted from such models.

It seems reasonable to ask to what extent economists have been able to explain the ugly facts we have described above by their theorizing, including theorizing done while constructing formal models. Despite the time, energy, and ingenuity that have been lavished on theories of economic development and on the design of formal models intended either to describe or help governments plan the development process, it appears that not as much light as one would hope has been shed so far on why poor people remain poor. Perhaps one reason for this is that the building blocks of most theories and models are faulty.

Our empirical work has demonstrated that poverty is associated with particular classes or groups in the community, e.g., landless agricultural laborers, village artisans, plantation workers, etc. Yet most theories and models are couched in terms of atomistic households in a classless society. This neoclassical assumption is closely associated with an assumption of universal harmony of interests.

We do not believe it is possible to get very far in understanding the problems of the Third World until it is more widely accepted that there are classes in society and that the interests of the various classes often are in conflict. Posing the issue in this way forces one to examine the distribution of wealth (a variable neglected in most models) and then to view the distribution of income as closely related to the underlying distribution of assets. A chain of association is thereby established between class structure, the ownership of wealth, and the distribution of income.[11]

Such a framework has several advantages. First, it encourages investigators interested in problems of income distribution to abandon models framed in terms of decile rankings and the like, and to substitute instead classes or groups of persons. If it is true that certain types of growth processes reduce incomes absolutely, then this must operate through identifiable groups, classes, or persons in comparable situations, not through deciles except as a byproduct; that is, changes in the share of a particular decile reflect possibly offsetting movements in the fate of heterogeneous groups who happen to be represented in that decile.

Second, the proposed framework would encourage the investigator to confront the awkward question of the function of the state in a class society. Implicit in most models is the assumption that the state is a neutral and benevolent arbiter attempting to maximize a social welfare function. One cannot avoid concluding from the evidence of our empirical studies, however, either that the arbiter is woefully ignorant or that economists have a rather naive theory of the state. Again, if analytical methods are to help us understand what is going on, we shall have to revise our thinking on the behavior of the state.

If the state were seen as an endogenous element in the economy, an institution which reflects the underlying social forces and structure of production, and not an external agent enjoying free will, the investigator would be encouraged to examine other phenomena in a new light. For example, prices are commonly regarded as a product of a market-clearing process in a competitive environment. True, monopolistic features and other "distortions" are acknowledged, but these are treated as anomalies to be corrected by the state. In the framework we have proposed, in contrast, the possibility exists for a rational state to intervene actively in the process of price formation, not to eliminate "distortions" but to create them.

In several models, notably that of Adelman and Robinson, the extent and location of poverty are strongly influenced by changes in the agricultural terms of trade.[12] In other work, including some done by one of us,[13] emphasis is placed on differences in ease of access to resources by different groups or classes, and in particular on variations in the set of relative factor prices which different groups confront. These differences in relative prices are used to account for the techniques of production that are adopted, the pattern of innovation and the resulting changes in the distribution of income among classes. What we are now suggesting is (1) that prices should be incorporated into formal models concerned with poverty, (2) that provision should be made for the possibility that different groups will face different sets of prices, and (3) that the state should be treated as a "price maker" with a class bias which determines who faces what prices.

Such an approach to the problem of development is likely to lead us to alter our conception of the nature of poverty. Many economists work with an absolute income concept and this leads them naturally to think in terms of minimum income requirements, poverty lines, basic needs, and all that. Others view poverty in terms of relative low income and hence focus on the degree of inequality, shares in income of the bottom deciles of the population, Gini coefficients and the like. Perhaps it would be better, however, to work with a structural definition of poverty, in which poverty is regarded as a product of a social system and reflects differences in access of various groups to sources of economic and political power.

This view of the nature of poverty would sever the link once and for all between, on the one hand, the extent of poverty (and its direction of change) and, on the other, the level of average income (and its rate of growth). A preoccupation with questions of income inequality would remain, but these issues would be examined within an analytical framework in which the distribution of productive wealth, the resulting class hierarchy of society, and the behavior of the state play leading roles. Dynamic processes—the appropriation and disposal of the investible surplus, the pattern of private and state investment, the speed and nature of technical innovation—could then be explained, at least in part, in terms of the fundamental characteristics of the economy.

Above all, a structural definition of poverty focuses attention on where one should look for remedies. The provision of welfare services and income transfers are ruled out because they do not remove the underlying causes of poverty. Efforts devoted to expanding the output of allegedly key commodities, e.g., food, are exposed as being inadequate because of the lack of connection between changes in production and changes in purchasing power in the hands of the poor. Thus our conceptualization of poverty makes it clearer why both micro and macroeconomic tinkering are almost certain to fail. The remedy lies in structural change, in changing the distribution of productive wealth (and consequently the distribution of economic power) and in increasing the participation of the poor in decision making (and consequently enabling them to exercise political power).

Notes

1. See Keith Griffin and Azizur Rahman Khan, eds., *Poverty and Landlessness in Rural Asia* (Geneva: ILO, 1976), mimeo. Much of this paper consists of extensive quotation from chap. 1 of the book and an attempt to summarize the main empirical findings of the other chapters.
2. These estimates, for 1960, are reported in IBRD, *Land Reform*, World Bank Paper, Rural Development Series (July 1974).

3. In the period 1956-1957 to 1973-1974 agricultural output per head increased 1.3 percent a year in Bihar, 3.2 percent in the Punjab, 1.0 percent in Tamil Nadu and 1.4 percent in Uttar Pradesh. That is, per capita agricultural output increased significantly in all of the states studied, yet the data in Table 1 above indicate that only in Tamil Nadu did the incidence of rural poverty fail to increase. Thus it is unlikely that the major explanation for the persistence and even increase in poverty is slow agricultural growth.

4. See, for example, Ronald I. McKinnon, *Money and Capital in Economic Development* (Washington, D.C.: Brookings Institution, 1973).

5. Thus the sequence is (1) "cheap" finance capital leads to (2) adoption of "excessively" mechanized techniques which, in turn, results in (3) high productivity of labor. This both provokes a demand for and facilitates the payment of (4) higher wages which then leads to (5) a second round reduction in the quantity of labor demanded.

6. See I.M.D. Little, T. Scitovsky and M. Scott, *Industry and Trade in Some Developing Countries* (New York: Oxford University Press, 1970).

7. See Keith Griffin, *Land Concentration and Rural Poverty* (New York: Macmillan, 1976).

8. See Michael Lipton, *Why Poor People Stay Poor: Urban Bias in World Development* (London: Temple Smith, 1977).

9. ILO, *Sharing in Development: A Programme of Employment, Equity and Growth for the Philippines* (1974), Tables 77 and 78, pp. 433 and 434.

10. Clifford Geertz, *Agricultural Involution: The Process of Ecological Change in Indonesia* (Berkeley: University of California Press, 1968).

11. One of the virtues of the accounting system advocated by Graham Pyatt and Erik Thorbecke is that it does focus on particular groups of households and the associated asset and income distributions. See their *Planning Techniques for a Better Future* (Geneva: ILO, 1976).

12. I. Adelman and S. Robinson, *Income Distribution Policies in Developing Countries: A Case Study of Korea* (New York: Oxford University Press, 1977).

13. Keith Griffin, *The Political Economy of Agrarian Change* (New York: Macmillan, 1974).

[19]
The Political Ideology of Population Control

Lars Bondestam

The ideological motives for population growth control can be summarized as follows:

—The nonrenewable resources of the world are limited. So are the possibilities of a further increase in the production of renewable goods, particularly food. Thus, the high standard of living in the center is threatened by the increasing demands in the periphery, which are due to its growth of population.

—Population grows faster than job opportunities, causing increasing unemployment. This leads to social unrest not only among the growing body of unemployed but also among the active laborers, whose wages are forced down because of oversupply of labor-power. This unrest may easily pass into an open and violent opposition against the established capitalist order of society. There are imminent risks of socialist ideas gaining terrain.

—The poorest and the least intelligent people reproduce faster than the others. When the unintelligent and incapacitated increase and the intelligent constitute a correspondingly smaller and smaller share of the population, society will degenerate.

These three motives coincide to some extent. In all of them, social problems are seen as caused by that part of the population which grows the fastest. But this same part of the population consumes least, totally as well as per capita, and seen both from a national and from an international perspective. Officially, only the problem of limited resources is looked upon as an international concern. But in reality, drastic political changes in favor of the poor masses in the periphery are a headache not only for those in power in the respective countries but for corresponding groups in the center as well. Thus, the division into three motives, which we made with the purpose of exposing the neo-Malthusian ideology, is blurred when the ideology is put into practice.

With the rapid development of the productive forces during the last century, much of the original Malthusian model of explanation had to be abandoned. The vacuum has been filled with a big dosage of dogmatics and mishandled statistics, despite the better knowl-

252

edge of demography and of the political and economic role of population that we have today. [...].

In neoclassical development models a large amount of population data are combined with economic data, on top of which hypotheses are placed on the relations between level of consumption, distribution between investments and consumption, economic growth, productivity, school enrollment, susceptibility of the population to family planning programs, etc. All these data and hypotheses are then computerized and the result shows the degree of development, globally or of the respective country, at a certain point of time, e.g., the year 2000. Output depends on input, i.e., on "facts" and subjective hypotheses concerning functional relations between them. A certain combination of input data corresponds to the best result (highest welfare, measured in Western terms). Thanks to the biased assumptions, the models show what they are supposed to show: the earlier the world or the respective country introduces population growth control and the more money that is allocated toward this sector, the more developed the world or the country will be in the year 2000. Notwithstanding the fact that these models cost millions of dollars and are printed on glossy paper, their reliability is not enhanced. For several reasons they are useless:

—They are usually strictly mathematical and are supposed to be valid in a stereotyped way for all regions of the world or of the periphery without exception. Consequently, they do not, and cannot, take into consideration the political structure and the traditional values of the various countries or the political and economic heterogeneity of the world.

—They do not take into consideration possible political decisions which may lead to dramatic consequences for development (e.g., land reform).

—They do not take into consideration changes in the world market (e.g., higher oil prices, lower cocoa prices, higher demand of copper).

—They do not, and obviously cannot, take into consideration sudden and unpredictably altered conditions of survival and of economic growth and development. (What happens if the capital city is destroyed by an earthquake, if the grain yield is spoiled by drought or flood, if the peasants revolt?)

—They take for granted that all citizens of the respective countries take part in the money economy on equal conditions and that the distribution of consumption within countries or continents is absolutely fair, which is never the case. [...].

The all-pervading characteristic of this type of model is the blind acceptance of the prevailing market mechanisms, with the subsequent emphasis on the growth of GNP per capita. When the growth of production is lagging behind the growth of population, everything goes to consumption and nothing is left over for investments. Likewise, a high fertility results in a very broad-based age pyramid, i.e., the number of people of working age is small relative to those of dependent age (up to, say, fifteen years). Thus, too many consumers in relation to producers weakens the economic capacity of the population. But if population growth is reduced, GNP per capita will increase faster, the percentage of economically active people in the total population will rise, and more can be spent on consumption as well as on investments in higher production, more housing, etc. This is a tempting argument, but a false one.

First, contrary to what is stressed in the neo-Malthusian models, we generally find a positive correlation between population growth and production growth, i.e., the more people the bigger the total labor force and the market and the more is produced. (Kenya, for instance, is "more developed" than Ethiopia but produces less, simply because the population of Kenya is smaller than that of Ethiopia.) Thus, a higher population growth in fact encourages a faster increase in total production. A comparison of sixty-seven underdeveloped countries (each with more than 1 million inhabitants) shows that, contrary to what the neo-Malthusians claim, during the period 1960-1970 there was no connection between population growth and growth in GNP per capita (according to the 1972 *Atlas*). Actually, the coefficient of correlation was slightly positive, which is in agreement with a statement by Colin Clark, who has insisted that countries with a higher population growth also show a faster growth in GNP per capita. Although it casts doubt upon the Malthusian argument, it is not definitely refuted by such ambiguous statistics. With the very heterogeneous economic structures of the underdeveloped countries, cross-national statistical analysis is notoriously deceptive, but it can at least be used to demask simplistic reasoning.

Second, from the asserted general connection between a fast increase in population and a decrease in per capita consumption (a "natural law"), it would, according to the neo-Malthusian models, automatically follow that a smaller size of population results in a higher standard of living. This inconsistently implies that starvation in one area after a while would benefit the whole country (compare the discussion above, concerning the "desirability" to limit the growth of the poor in order to secure the living standard of the rich). This Malthusian paradox was already pointed out by Marx in his study of Ireland: despite the potato famine of the mid-1840s taking almost 800,000 lives and despite the ensuing mass emigration to

America, the Irish economy stagnated, unemployment increased, and average per capita consumption decreased.

Third, there is no guarantee that a higher average production per capita will automatically change the distribution between consumption and investment in favor of the latter, neither in poor communities where the struggle for immediate survival gets priority, nor among the landed bourgeoisie who often prefer the foreign banks and imported luxury goods to economic growth in the national interest. Moreover, the argument that a higher percentage of people in economically active ages to total population will strengthen the economy and increase the savings is unrealistic so long as a higher production is primarily accomplished through higher labor productivity, and unemployment in the periphery often amounts to 20-30 percent.

Fourth, the rapid decreases in the birth rates, which the modelers predict birth control programs will lead to, are unrealistic. [. . .]. Such programs in the periphery have so far succeeded in decreasing the birth rate by at most two per mil units. Despite these bitter and costly experiences the unrealistic political targets are translated into mathematical assumptions: an artifical decrease in the birth rate by half in twenty to thirty years is a common prophecy in these projections. Such playing with figures can, no doubt, only be politically motivated.

Although qualitatively different from the technocratic and mechanistic projections of various optimistic neoclassical economists, another neo-Malthusian approach is the prophecies of future crises, which increased in popularity as a reaction to the political movement of spring 1968. In these pessimistic visions there is no way out of the economic and social degeneration caused by the population growth. One can still scent the ghost of Malthus: humans are put in a corner with mouths and stomachs but with no hands, as passive spectators of their own inevitable decay. As a member of the periphery, survival is made dependent upon the goodwill of the center— the "New World Poor Law." The inherent contradictions of capitalism are not recognized, but the uneven growth of production is steered by undefined and elusive forces. Yearly fluctuations in food supply are made the irony of fate. Hunger and famine become inevitable allies.[. . .].

When Marx analyzed relative overpopulation he referred to the victims of capital accumulation in Europe during the early phase of the Industrial Revolution. However, in order to better understand the economic conditions of the broad masses of the periphery the concept demands a widened definition. The majority of the population is small subsistence peasants who are too weak to withstand external economic pressures. Because of the very biased ownership and control over land in many countries, most of the farming population has to depend on small plots of land which hardly sustain a minimum of subsistence. Simultaneously, a minority of big farmers enjoy extensive areas of fertile land. In these countries the relative overpopulation is striking, not measured in the average population density but in the small peasants' access to land. The rural economic structure in Central America of the mid-1960s may serve as an illustration. Here the landownership was concentrated to a small group: whereas 90 percent of the holdings constituted less than 20 percent of the land, 1.4 percent of the holdings grasped 52 percent of the total areas. This means that over half of the total cultivated area was in farms which were, on average, 170 times as large as the plots of the poor peasants. While a few powerful landowners and foreign companies produce a surplus for export, lack of land and food is a reality for a major part of the peasant population. The latter belong to the relative overpopulation of the rural areas.

During the early industrialization in Europe people were to some extent "pulled" from the countryside to the towns. A growing industry swallowed some of the labor that was released from the agriculture through rationalizations and the introduction of more potent techniques of farming. In the periphery of today the situation is somewhat different: people are evicted from agriculture and "pushed" to towns, often against their own will and usually without finding new jobs. Land was expropriated by the colonial powers or concentrated on big estates, and large areas were transferred from food to cash crops. These are processes which were started in the eighteenth and nineteenth centuries. They were the foundation of the biased agricultural structure which has developed in several countries during this century. The last decades have been characterized by rural economic growth and more poverty, side by side.

The so-called green revolution gave new hope for the 1960s. In several countries wheat and paddy production increased, thanks to the application of high-yielding-varieties (HYV) and of fertilizers. But technical backlashes turned optimism into another era of pessimism in the early 1970s. Moreover, those who could take the main advantage of the higher production were the middle peasants and above, i.e., those who were creditable and who could afford the high costs of modern inputs. Poor peasants, who could not get access to the new technology, not even on credit, fell out of the picture in this "revolutionary process." In several countries this led to a further concentration of land ownership and a strengthening .of the capitalist mode of production.

Mexico was the first victim of the "green revolution," introduced by the Rockefeller Foundation and Norman Borlaug (which later rendered him a Nobel Prize in Peace). The wheat yield reached unprecedented levels but not for the benefit of the active farming population. In 1960 over half of the agricultural laborers were landless. In the countryside 28 million people lead a life as wretched as before the Mexican revolution. Twenty percent of all arable land and 60 percent of all irrigated land are still in the hands of a few big landowners, who produce 90 percent of all marketed foods. A few own much land, many own little, and more still own nothing. Consequently, Mexico City grew from 1.5 to 10 million inhabitants between 1940 and 1970 and is now the second biggest city in the Third World. [. . .]. Mexico cannot any longer accommodate its own people, and seven million Mexicans are permanent or seasonal laborers in United States, working for wages close to the minimum of subsistence. Mexico not only exports its surplus population but also its surplus food: every day vegetables and truckloads of live cattle find their way to the rich market in the north. That is how the average American is able to gobble up some two kilos of meat every week, while the southern neighbors go hungry.[. . .].

Capital-intensive investments in industry usually tie a certain portion of the domestic capital (joint ventures between foreign and domestic public capital are an effective means for the transnational companies to eliminate competition and to avoid labor disputes, in both cases with assistance from the host state); this leaves less capital for local investments in the labor-intensive sectors, which further accelerates the rate of unemployment. Since they are too poor, a majority of the population is locked out from the consumption of locally manufactured goods above their basic needs. Only a minority of the employees have incomes sufficiently high to allow for the purchase of goods beyond these needs. With the exception of light industries, like breweries, food, and textiles, we can without exaggeration assert that when the needs of the upper and middle classes are satisfied, the market is more or less exhausted. New investments become less and less profitable, unless directed toward the export market (cf. U.S. investments in Latin America, and Japan's in Southeast Asia), and the growth of those industries which produce for the local market is hampered. Capitalism places a pitfall in the way of development, unemployment persists, and the circle is closed.

Ethiopia can illustrate this argument. Prior to 1975 the exploitation of the peasantry and the poverty in towns meant that the circulation of money was mainly limited to the small upper and middle classes. With almost nonexistent purchasing power in the rural areas and the low purchasing power in the towns, the market for manufactured goods was limited. This was the main bottleneck to an expanding industry in Ethiopia. Industry production increased by 15 percent yearly during the second half of the 1960s—a fast relative growth but slow in absolute terms, due to the low starting point. These 15 percent can be broken down into an increase in labor productivity of 11.3 percent and a growth of employment of 3.3 percent yearly. That is, the increase in production was three-fourths due to imported new machinery in a progressively more capital-intensive industry, mainly controlled by foreign interests. In 1970 only some 100,000 people worked in the industrial sector (industries with more than five employees), corresponding to much less than 10 percent of the potentially economically active urban population (all able-bodied nonstudents aged 15-60). The employment growth rate of 3.3 percent should be compared with the population growth of the bigger industry areas which was 7-8 percent. Accordingly, unemployment rose in the bigger towns, in absolute as well as in relative figures. Those with a job often had a working-day of ten hours or more. The labor exchange offices of the three biggest towns—Addis Ababa, Asmara, and Dire Dawa—were able to find jobs for 22 percent of those who were in search of work in 1968 but only for 9 percent three years later. The profit motive, not the necessity of more employment, governed the model of economic growth. A too high degree of capital-intensity in production and long working-days preserved a high rate of unemployment and a ruthless competition for work, whereby wages could be forced down to levels even below the poverty line. Those in Ethiopia who could not find productive work or employment in the state sector either had to live as parasites on relatives or to join the already overpopulated private service sector as domestic servants, street vendors, shoe-shiners, bar girls, etc. (the situation has not really changed today, half a decade after the overthrow of the old feudal system).[. . .].

It is too often stressed that the reproduction of population in the Third World is the result of unplanned and irrational behavior and, therefore, a purely biological concern. This biological phenomenon is portrayed as the main obstacle to socioeconomic development, and it is suggested that an artificial reduction of fertility would contribute to the eradication of the most serious manifestations of underdevelopment. This is the view held by many "scientists" who have not attempted a definition of "underdevelopment" or an investigation of trends in births and deaths and their interrelations with the economic causes of misery, hunger, and famine. These "scientists" deny that the causal connection is the reverse, namely that high birth and death rates and rapid population growth subsist as consequences of the socioeconomic conditions. A reduction in fertility and in the rate of population growth can therefore only be achieved through means which concentrate on the very causes of this high growth rate, i.e., the unfavorable socioeconomic conditions of the masses. In the light of the present situation in most parts of the periphery, there is therefore no rationale for a policy which aims at decreasing the growth of its main asset in the development process— its people.

To tackle population without recognizing its political and economic environment ultimately leads to results unaimed at or even to failures. The individual's economic situation, which is partly decisive of one's social behavior and general welfare, is a reflection of the economic system of the society to which the individual belongs. But as the Third World looks today, this system depends to a large extent on external economic relations which prevent self-reliance. These relations are well known: the connection between the Sahel famine and European colonialism and neocolonialism, between the starvation wages of the Chilean laborer and the CIA and ITT of the United States, between the underdeveloped agriculture of Colombia or Pakistan and the American Public Law 480 (dealing with U.S. grain "aid"), between the undernourished child in Brazil or South Asia and Rockefeller Center in New York.

To control the reproduction of the poor people is a piece of cynicism unless they have themselves asked for it and unless they are allowed to take active part in the planning of such a program. To facilitate for people to plan their families according to their own wishes is a matter of course. If a woman finds it essential to limit her number of children, she should be given the opportunity to do so, but she should also be given the right to education, a productive job, a stable economy, a meaningful social standard, and other fruits of a well-planned development. Population control means that people are controlled by others, family planning means that people control themselves. The two concepts are irreconcilable.

[20]
The Dimension of Environment

Malcolm Caldwell

[. . .] During the centuries-long period of Western expansion and establishment of global political and economic dominance, the handful of countries successful as predators were able to break out of the constraints which had, throughout the span of human history, necessarily limited the extent to which labor could be freed from subsistence agriculture to devote its energies and dexterity to providing for needs other than those of the stomach and of the barest subsistence. Labor devoted to manufacturing industry, to commercial enterprise, and to administration, much though it may contribute to enriching society, has to rely upon others to grow the food it consumes. Historically, the surplus of food devoted to supporting the nonagricultural population of industrial countries has come from two sources: first, from improved productivity in domestic agriculture, enabling a shrinking working population engaged in the fields to reap a growing harvest; and, second, from purchases of food made abroad from the proceeds of sales of manufactured goods (and of certain services, such as shipping, insurance, and the like).

We may analyze the economic history of the last few centuries, centuries which have seen the emergence of drastic disparities in wealth between one group of countries (the overdeveloped) and another (the underdeveloped), in two ways: one way is to apply the tools developed by Marx and his successors to account for the development of capitalism (and its concomitant and reciprocal colonialism/neocolonialism/imperialism); the other is to shift our focus to the physical exchanges involved and to account for the outcome in "real" terms (in terms, that is, of the flows of raw material resources and of the increasing utilization, geographically uneven in impact, of finite, nonrenewable, mineral reserves, among which the fossil fuels are of particular importance and significance)[. . .].

It is worth saying here that, in my view, the phenomena of underdevelopment and overdevelopment [. . .] cannot be understood without an insight into the role of the fossil fuels in determining their very different, though causally related, fates. Nor can the significance of the possibilities for what I have called "transcending" under- and overdevelopment [...] be fully appreciated until the objective natural limits to our manipulation of our environment, viewed in the context of the crisis of world capitalism and imperialism, have themselves been adequately grasped [...].

[21]
Class Formation as an "Articulation" Process: East African Cases

Lionel Cliffe

The article from which these extracts are taken seeks to isolate a method by which African social structures, and especially their rural dimensions, can be analyzed. It rejects those approaches which see Africa as a special case: views which see African rural dwellers not as "peasants" but as "cultivators,"[1] "husbandmen";[2] or which sees African rural society in idyllic terms as essentially classless and egalitarian; or as corresponding to some social type whose distinctness is characterized as "tribal" society.[3] Whether any of these views once had any validity, as conceptualizations of present realities they suffer from a myopic disregard of the vast changes that have occurred. But not only are African rural societies in motion; they are subject to a particular impulse: their incorporation into, and transformation in a direction dictated by, capitalism. However, in two basic regards the process of capitalist transformation differs from that in the advanced capitalist countries, which progressed "under their own steam," as it were, from feudalism to capitalism. Africa, and this history it shares with the rest of the so-called Third World, was never "feudal"; and moreover its capitalist path was one imposed from outside. Such a perspective points the way to an approach which does not lose sight of the specifics of the African experience but situates them within a more global process. Thus a method is put forward for exploring the resulting process of class formation in terms that owe much to French Marxist anthropologists (notably Rey[4]): as an *articulation* of modes of production that existed in different parts of Africa with the capitalist mode.[5]

This kind of class analysis thus sees the actual patterns of class formation as shaped by two sets of forces: as a "resultant" of the interaction between the trends set in play by the incorporation into the capitalist system, and by the structure of the pre-existing social formation. We shall look at each of these in turn. However, this is a more complex task than developing a single model of the interaction of some generalized "African mode of production" with the capitalist mode. Nor can one arrive at a picture of the contemporary social formation of one of the existing African countries by looking at the interplay of *its* precapitalist mode with capitalism.

262

Apart from the fact that the unevenness of capitalist development has led to marked regional differences within as well as between countries, the indigenous social formations were many and varied and did not follow the present national boundaries. National class structures cannot be documented only in terms of the interplay between bourgeoisie and proletariat, petty bourgeoisie and other classes which have a national character, on the one hand, and different regional peasantries on the other.[6] A class analysis of contemporary states has to start from what were in the past distinct social formations, even if they have come more recently to interact with each other and through their incorporation into a state and national economy have led to the emergence of some national classes.

Precapitalist Modes of Production in Africa

An examination of the process of articulation must start from some first approximation of the precapitalist modes of production found in Africa. I shall in fact suggest, on the basis of differences in property relations and in the size and form of distribution of any surplus, that certain distinct modes of production were found in East Africa. First, there were societies that produced almost no surplus. Often based on shifting cultivation, with a sparse population and segmented sociopolitical structures, they consisted of small, nonhierarchical communities of subsistence-producing families. This may be what people have in mind when they talk about a "tribal" society. However, a more thorough specification of the actual relationships of production is essential, which would determine the formation's own internal dynamic. This is a point emphasized by Sahlins,[7] who came to the interesting conclusion about these presurplus, pre-exchange economies, characterized by what he terms a "domestic mode of production": that the absence of surplus was not due to the lack of potential inherent in the environment or technology. There was a potential abundance, which social relations and not the limitations of "nature" or the productive forces prevented from being realized. It is further necessary to be aware even of the nonantagonistic productive relations associated perhaps with a certain division of labor or various arrangements of reciprocity,[8] for often these would be transposed into antagonisms with the articulation with capitalism. At a certain point, the voluntary and mutual help on the farm from neighbors, relatives, or beer parties is subtly transposed into the hiring of casual labor. But, most important, it is necessary to examine the relationships of production in such social formations to realize that often there were crucial and qualitative inequalities in the access to the means of production. One such approach highlights the control by elders of the labor of women, the main producers, which is a feature of some societies, and so sees many African societies as characterized by a "lineage mode of production."[9]

At the other end of the scale were found societies in which feudal relationships of production were discernible (e.g., in the "Inter-Lacustrine Kingdoms"), in that not only were the masses of the society subject to the rule of individual lords, but these latter also claimed rights over a proportion of the land and the peasants who dwelt on it and thereby extracted surplus in the form of surplus product or *corvée* labor from the peasants. These feudal patterns were never as widespread in East Africa as, say, in Ethiopia. They were found in a few social formations where state systems had evolved, existing and coexisting with other modes of production such as the slave mode, whose presence in the immediate precolonial centuries was more widespread than was once realized. A third category consisted of less centralized and hierarchical "chiefly" societies where the state was only in the process of emergence. These certainly produced a surplus, which in turn supported a division of labor more complex than that based on age groups and sex. But the appropriation of part of the surplus by political authorities or even via their privileged access to land or to livestock was typically through a straight levy not based on certain property rights. This corresponds to what Samir Amin and others have referred to as the *tributary* mode of production,[10] thus generalizing the Asiatic mode to Africa.

The differences between these modes were liable to offer different options when subject to capitalist penetration, whether in the form of extraction of surplus by colonial capital external to the particular rural society, or in internal relations of production and distribution within the society with the onset of commodity production, or as differing types of alliances between external and internal class forces—as we shall see in examining some case studies.

Whatever the relations of production associated with these three basic types, or the particular mix of them within the social formation, many parts of Africa had in common the dependence on family-based, small-scale agriculture. They probably also shared the common guarantee that no family was denied access to land, the means of livelihood. But the fact that land was not everywhere a "property," that rights to it were vested in the extended family and not the individual, and that generally no propertyless class existed, should not blur the essential characteristic that production was small scale and individual, at least in the sense of the family or wife, even though occasionally supplemented by exchange. This realization is crucial in assessing the likely impact when capitalist social relationships impinge on this small production unit. As Marx rightly warned with respect to Russian agriculture, the communal ties of reciprocity in labor use and free access to land were unlikely to be effective proof against more individualistic property and labor relationships with the growth of commodity production.[11]

A fourth, "pastoral," mode of production, not based on crop husbandry, should be recognized as dominant or at least present in several areas which were wholly or largely dependent on livestock. The difference in production relations lies not merely in the fact that they revolve around cattle (or goats or camels) rather than land as the basic means of production. The notion of ownership, even though hedged about with complex kin and other relationships that provided for redistribution, existed, as was not usually the case with land. Moreover, unlike land, a larger herd of cattle, camels, or goats did not require a proportionate increase in available labor. Not only was the ownership of livestock often markedly unequal, and confined to men, but often some adult males with families owned none or less than would guarantee subsistence. Even though most analysts have stressed the benevolent social obligations which protected such people, their relationships to the larger herders would nevertheless involve some form of dependence and thus subservience, either as part crop cultivators, or as herders of someone's animals (either as "tenant-keepers" or as junior family members). Again, this kind of social formation was so shaped that different groups were differently affected, and relationships were transposed by the contact with the capitalist market economy when it finally caught up with the pastoral and semipastoral areas of East Africa.

The Penetration of the Capitalist Mode of Production

The other set of variables shaping the social formation that emerges from the articulation process arises from the different role that different rural societies were expected to perform in the capitalist economy that was instigated. During the colonial phase, African territories tended to have a particular economic role forced upon them as part of a division of labor within a metropolitan-dominated economic system. Different African colonies were looked upon as either sources of minerals, plantation crops, areas for European settlement, or suppliers of peasant-produced cash crops, surplus value from African labor being extracted in each case through very different means. In the first three cases, a capitalist mode of production was introduced de novo, but in order to obtain the necessary labor force economic and political pressures were exerted on the indigenous agricultural modes of production. The result of this kind of articulation was not the complete destruction of the subsistence production of the family farm or of rural artisans—although it did imply considerable modification both in attaching the economy through labor migration to a cash nexus and in promoting "underdevelopment" through the absence of a labor force, and often the blocking of cash-crop production or any other channel for earning a cash income. The ensuing patterns of change in the relationships of production were very different from those in a colony where the emphasis was on promoting the production of cash crops within the existing peasant agriculture. Here again, however, the initial effect was not to replace or destroy the subsistence production or self-provision of basic housing and other necessities, but to incorporate these activities within a system of commodity production. There was what Charles Bettelheim has referred to as a partial conservation and a partial dissolution of the indigenous modes of production.[12]

There were important regional differences within countries—depending on the potential for local export-crop production, the proximity to settler-occupied areas and to towns, and the penetrability of the local political system and the peasant economy—within the division of labor that evolved with the colonial economy. Thus we can identify the following different emphases that were forced on different local societies either by deliberate colonial policy or by circumstances: (1) labor-supply areas, (2) cash-crop-producing areas, (3) quiescent areas, and (4) frontier areas.

The latter two require some further explanation. There were "quiescent" areas which were not regarded as suitable for cash cropping and whose labor force was not required, and where the indigenous mode of production was consequently disturbed to a more limited extent; indeed, the main aim of colonial policy was to maintain social control until there was a need for their labor-power or their land. The history of most of the pastoral areas follows this pattern. The "frontier" areas resulted from the fact that, with increasing population and the extension of communication, population expanded, and just as European farmers initiated capitalist modes of production in areas of settlement, so too there were "frontiers" opened up by the spread of the African population. This process did not involve the grafting onto existing relationships of new ones that were symptomatic of capitalism. Rather, wholly new patterns were created, which usually smacked more completely of capitalist relationships—although some carry-over of property or "working" relations from either the area of settlement or of emigration would often occur.

One final observation of a general nature needs to be made about the different forms of attachment to the capitalist system. There is a tendency to imagine that, because farming is still almost universally carried on by simple hand techniques on a small, family scale, the mode of production has not effectively changed from precolonial days—that it remains at a pre-peasant stage. This is particularly so of our categories (1) and (3), the labor supply and quiescent areas, which are referred to as "subsistence" or even "backward" areas. Anthropologists describe farming systems or land tenure in the present tense, not clarifying whether they are describing remembered traditions or whether they are mistaking current realities for those traditions. Planners in the 1960s could offer as one of their main goals, as they did in all the East African countries, the expansion of the market into the many areas which were still in the "subsistence economy." It will in fact be our contention later, following Rey, that although during much of the first (colonial and even contemporary) stages of articulation capitalist pressures had left the basic patterns of production of food and other basic needs (tools, housing, etc.) undisturbed, still characterized by simple techniques of production and not involving market exchange, it would be entirely mistaken to consider that the rural areas of East Africa, even those which are clearly not producing for the international market and which seem to be so remote and "backward" technologically, are free of involvement in the broader capitalist network and unmarked by those relationships characteristic of capitalism. The truth is that for three or four generations East African peasants have been, perhaps only partially but nevertheless inextricably, involved in cash transactions: they have had to pay a tax in the form of cash, and a limited range of purchased products has become a necessity. For these purposes people in all areas have not only been involved in relationships of exchange but in turn have had to involve themselves in new relationships of production: they have had to sell their labor-power or their produce.

The Process of Articulation

This process of the involvement in exchange and in commodity production did not occur overnight and it is important to study the mechanisms through which it has occurred. The work of Rey is

instructive here in that he extracts from Marx's work two stages
through which the articulation goes before reaching a point where
the capitalist relations are dominant. But he first reminds us that
while these stages have their parallels in transitions from all
precapitalist modes of production, they are not necessarily the same
as in the historical case of European transition from feudalism to
capitalism. In the first phase, there is a separation of agriculture
from manufacture, leaving peasant subsistence production of food
in existence, while promoting an expansion of agricultural production and thus of the market for manufactures on the one hand and
at the same time releasing labor to be absorbed in capitalist production in industry. But this set of processes occurred in a different
manner in Europe, even Russia, from the comparable pattern in
Africa. The European articulation was one where the expulsion of
free labor and the expansion of a marketed surplus from agriculture—
preconditions for capitalist production—were created by the internal dynamic of the reproduction of feudalism itself: through the
mechanism of landed proprietors and their appropriation of land
for their own use and by conversion of rent payments in kind or
labor to money. Economically, once this process had begun, there
was an "open" system into which a capitalist mode of production
could penetrate; politically in this stage of articulation there was an
alliance between the feudal class of landed proprietors and the
bourgeoisie. But in the colonial situation capital was an exterior
force facing a closed system of rural handicrafts and peasant subsistence production and thus, in Rey's analysis, the first stage of the
articulation of nonfeudal and capitalist modes is faced with "the
impossibility of destroying the closed circle of agriculture and rural
handicrafts without recourse to noneconomic means."[13] And thus
the solution Marx noted in India where the English "rulers and
rentiers . . . simultaneously deploy their political and economic power
to shatter the small economic communities" is generalized.[14] Our
East African evidence shows that in the early stages it was necessary
to use force, combined with judicious alliances with indigenous
strata, to achieve the two initial objectives: the extraction of a labor
force for capitalist production in plantations, settler farms, commerce, administration, and some modicum of industry, and to generate peasant production of export crops. In the first generation of
colonial rule, various patterns of what amounted to forced labor
had to be used to extract labor power from the Kikuyu and other
East African societies. And administrative direction using the authority of the local rulers was the mechanism used for introducing
the first cash crop, cotton, both by the British in Buganda and by
the Germans in eastern Tanzania.[15]

A second stage in the articulation is one where coercive noneconomic intervention is no longer essential, which Rey sees as corresponding "to the actual situation in most of the ex-colonial countries."[16] Characterizing it a little differently from Rey, some industry has grown up on the basis of those displaced from the land; rural handicrafts have been destroyed and capitalism now supplies the simple means of production and a few manufactured consumer goods to the peasantry as well as for the "surplus" consumption of locally privileged classes, but subsistence food production has still not been displaced and indeed is necessary to provide for the reproduction of labor, much of which is unstable and only partially and temporarily urbanized and proletarianized and consequently heavily exploited. At the same time economic mechanisms, the circulation of money and commodities, are now sufficient to draw out surplus value in the form of labor or of produce from the agricultural mode of production, which in turn has become more geared to capitalist relations of production as well as exchange.

Before going on to examine concrete instances of transition through these stages, some general points about the nature of this last element in the second stage of articulation, the emergence of capitalist relations or production in the agricultural mode of production, must be noted. First, it must be stressed that in no sense, at this stage, is the sum of relationships of production "capitalist." Property rights may well retain precapitalist traits, the alienation of the worker from the product of his or her labor is far from complete, subsistence production and "peasant" production (by the family on the family farm) for the market may still be widespread and certainly there will be no complete polarization of classes into farmer and laborer. Indeed, these categories may not have finally emerged at all. Second, the extent of capitalist elements in the relations will clearly vary, not only as a result of the general unevenness of development but depending (in roughly descending order) on their role as pioneer, cash-crop producing, labor supplying, or quiescent areas. But, as was spelled out earlier, the resulting "articulated" mode of production and the exact structure of classes to which it gives rise will not only be a function of the extent and form of capitalist penetration, but of the pre-existing mode of production. Our earlier discussion of the concept of "articulation" allows a further refinement of this formulation, however. The process may not involve simply more or less rapid "dissolution" but conflicting tendencies: what Balandier has termed trends of "destructuration" and "restructuration" (where the same institutional forms may take on different functions with the articulation with external capitalist relations and, in the process, a new lease on life).[17]

Finally, in this connection it is time to be a little more explicit about the different dimensions of the "relationships of production," so that we can observe more closely the components of this complex and varied process of the emergence of capitalist elements in the actual process of agricultural *production.* Three aspects of the relations can be picked out, those between (a) people and means of production (especially land)—*property* relations; (b) people and their labor-power—*labor* relations, and (c) people and the product of their labor—basically the question of "surplus." In a mode of production that is capitalist, the characteristic pattern of these relationships would be private ownership of land (and unequal distribution), labor-power a "commodity," the product of labor alienated, and labor thereby exploited through the extraction of surplus value. Feudalism also has its characteristic relations of land ownership and concentration, labor attached to the land and surplus extracted in the form of rent. Equally, the different precapitalist patterns in East Africa had distinctive property relations where land might be communally controlled or allocated if not "owned," or virtually "free"; labor was that of the family (variously supplemented), which retained (with a few exceptions) complete rights to the produce; if there was surplus it was usually extracted by exchange or as tribute. But in analyzing the articulation of capitalist relations with the pre-existing production relations in agriculture, it is more useful to see the relationships associated with capitalism as tendencies. Thus the actual process would be marked by trends toward individualization of land and its concentration, a modification of labor-use, both family labor and "exchange" labor, involving cash transactions and alienation from produce; an expansion of surplus production and the appropriation of surplus value. It must also be noted that any such changes observable in the base are going to generate, and to be visible through, changes in all social relationships. Shifts in land tenurial arrangements lead to subtle changes in inheritance and thus in family patterns. Kinship is also reshaped by changes in the organization and division of labor, and in the appropriation of the products of labor. Two characteristics of these patterns need to be stressed. First, the changed patterns are *"resultants,"* shaped by both parents, reflecting characteristics of both the capitalist and the indigenous. So that in many land-scarce areas, such as that of the Kikuyu, land is now "alienable" and a saleable commodity, but this "capitalist" pattern is qualified by restrictions requiring clan or lineage consent to sale to outsiders. Under similar pressures, the Nyakyusa people in southwest Tanzania retained taboos on the sale of land but changed inheritance from being through brothers to through the father.[18] In Kenya, land rights and then in turn inheritance and marriage have been transformed into bourgeois forms of legislation, but in the actual use of land and in family patterns old (now illegal) patterns persist.[19] A second noteworthy feature of these changes is that although often subtle, undramatic, and seemingly insignificant, they do represent qualitative transformations. Thus labor has become a *commodity* and antagonistic relationships have emerged not when the hiring of laborers is general or even when a few rich peasants start paying casual harvesters, but when the extended family or neighborhood helpers are no longer welcomed with a meal or beer but have their school fees or a debt for medicine paid.

An approach to analyzing the process of class formation in the rural areas has been suggested which starts from an awareness that different regions within what are now national societies will have different patterns of class formation, as they represented different precolonial social formations and have been incorporated on different terms into the international capitalist system. The range of patterns can be illustrated by the following matrix:

Mode of production dominant or present in precolonial formation	*Mode of incorporation into capitalist economy*			
	Labor supply	Commodity-producing	Frontier	Quiescent
Feudal	—	—	—	—
Tributary	—	—	—	—
Lineage	—	—	—	—
Slave	—	—	—	—
Pastoral	—	—	—	—

Having isolated the two components whose interaction determines the dynamic of a society, it then becomes possible to identify the actual classes that are distilled out in such a local society and also their contribution to the broader class cleavages which evolve across these regions with the growth of the larger national society during and after colonialism. The following thumbnail sketches will try to capture the process at work in the articulation of two different precolonial social formations found in particular ecological areas, cultural groups, or political units within East Africa with the capitalist mode of production.

Labor Extraction and Land Deprivation in a Kenyan Society

The Kikuyu peoples, now numbering some 2 million, are spread around the foothills of Mt. Kenya and the Aberdares, to the north of what is now Nairobi. They had colonized this area as a result of the lineage founders clearing land to establish an estate (*githaka*). The growing numbers of families within the lineage (*mbari*) would be allocated land which is controlled (but not "owned") by a leader chosen to succeed the founder. As the mbari grew to become more of a subclan—through successive generations and through other men marrying into it (*muthoni*) or asking for the use of land (*ahoi*) —the *githaka* could not meet their needs, and some of those with less priority to land (younger sons, *ahoi*) would be pushed out to found new *mbari*. The rich soils and altitude made possible a form of smallholder farming, growing bananas, millet, and several other crops plus the herding of goats and a limited number of cattle, on a more or less permanent basis. Even so, this did not lead to individual permanent claims to land nor did the potential surplus give rise to any hierarchal superstructure other than a loose network of age-grades and councils which cut across the *mbari* kinship network.

At the turn of the century European settlers began to seize land to the west and south of the Kikuyu, who found themselves affected in very dramatic and immediate ways. The actual loss of land was not as significant as two other factors: the settlers' demands for labor (sought primarily from their nearest, settled neighbors) and their sealing off of any possibilities for further Kikuyu expansion. In the first phase of colonial rule, a labor force was extracted by characteristically brutal measures by the colonial state. The actual imposition of colonial rule was a bloody process of putting down persistent, widespread, but never centralized, resistance. Appointed chiefs were created under a very "direct" form of administration, which recruited forced labor, enforced a head tax and then in turn pushed people into jobs to pay it.

A second stage of articulation fairly quickly set in, which meant that economic pressures alone would be sufficient to provide a constant labor supply without the use of political power (at least in a direct way). The spread of the market and manufactured goods to replace simple handicrafts intensified the demand for cash beyond the raising of tax. At the same time, the power of the colonial state (clearly dominated by settler interests) led to virtual prohibition, as in almost all labor-supply areas of East Africa, of the growing of export cash crops like coffee. Thus selling labor-power was the only available form of involvement in the cash nexus for most Kikuyu. At the same time, there was a rapid "destructuration" of indigenous institutions: the age councils were swept aside as a political body by the chiefly administration; and the *mbari* and the relationships within it were subject to intense internal pressures which could no longer be resolved through expansion. With increasing land shortage and the emergence of land as a "commodity" under the pressure of shortage, and the primitive accumulation that had been fostered by wage labor and the cash economy generally, plus a strong state and missionary presence, the colonial servants and the heads of *mbari* began to acquire more land. The property relations within the *mbari* system were eroded. General insecurity of tenure resulted. The *ahoi* and others with less claim to land were forced off the land—and into wage employment in the towns or in the "white highlands" as farm laborers, or as "squatters," where they entered into a capitalist mode of production but through a feudal relationship, supplying corvée labor in return for the use of the land. By the 1940s the possibilities for absorption in the urban/settler capitalist sector were insufficient to absorb the growing number of landless; the mass of small peasants were becoming increasingly impoverished as a result of the denial of cash-crop opportunities and the dwindling size of many plots; and the acquisition of land by the salaried and the officials, often through concessions from the colonial authorities or missions, or through their own control of the courts hearing land cases, had created what has been described as a "landed gentry."[20] The explosive situation surrounding this three-tiered class structure—large farmers, small peasants, and landless laborers—was ignited when some spontaneous unrest by squatters, farm laborers, and radical groups of workers in Nairobi was greeted by the forced repatriation of those virtually landless elements among the Kikuyu back to the overcrowded reserves. It was these elements, with at least "passive support" from the sea of small peasants, who were thus forced into armed struggle. These various strata among the peasants were not only engaged in a class struggle against the colonial state and the settler-capitalist, but also saw the privileged class of Kikuyu landed officials as their chief target of attack, and the latter were in fact the basis for the formation of a "loyalist" faction by the colonial government.

The revolt was contained militarily but the colonialists realized that a political solution would depend on some major change in socioeconomic structure. Some administrators urged an "English" two-tier class structure through some kind of "enclosure," thus creating a class of yeoman farmers "too busy on their land to worry about political agitation."[21] The final formula was to preserve and confirm the three-tier structure in a modified form by allowing the small-time, independent "middle" peasants to keep land rather than allowing them to be bought out in a completely free market in land—and also give them and the already large farmers not only security in the form of a freehold individual title to holdings but also new economic opportunities through the consolidation of the several tiny fragments into a single more substantial holding and through lifting the embargo on coffee and other cash crops. Thus in the Kikuyu areas, a third stage of articulation was launched by an intervention which instituted capitalist property relations in land, promoting further capitalist relations of *distribution* and further polarization of the landed toward capitalist production. It confirmed and in a relative sense worsened the situation of the landless, the *mutarukiire* ("ragged ones") as they are called, but also isolated them politically from the majority of middle peasants, who showed themselves supportive of the status quo as a result of the effective counter-revolutionary economic and land reforms. Thus in 1966 when an embryo challenge to the neocolonial development strategy was mounted by a radical party, it was only able to win support from the minority of landless in the Kikuyu areas. The contradiction that was politically relevant was no longer between capitalist farmers and poor and middle peasants, but between all classes of landholders and the landless.

Commercialization of "Feudalism"—Buganda

Buganda was only the largest of several "kingdoms" in western Uganda and northwestern and other parts of Tanzania, and always the one with the most elaborated hierarchy. A productive pattern of settled agriculture based on bananas yielded a considerable surplus to support the court and its centrally appointed bureaucracy. The relations of distribution through which this political class extracted its requirements were transformed into relations of production of a clearly feudal type in the early stages of colonial rule. The British adopted a totally different economic strategy here from that in Kenya. Instead of promoting a basically settler economy, they sought to induce the settled and seemingly organized peasants they first found in Uganda to embark on the production of export cash crops. In particular they were attracted by the potential for a market and for raw materials that seemed inherent in Buganda's relatively prosperous, fertile area with its centralized system. They in fact made a "deal" with the chiefs, strengthening their political power vis-à-vis the Kabaka (king), and institutionalizing a more completely feudal pattern of property and social relations. Some 3000 square miles were designated *mailo* estates, large tracts of land, and the peasants cultivating them were assigned to the aristocracy. The intention was that the landlord-chiefs would then use their access to land and their potential control of the population to establish cotton plantations.

In fact, this piece of social engineering was not as successful as they had expected nor as effective as their slightly different strategy of allowing individual peasant cotton producers that was followed in less hierarchal societies. The landowners found it easier merely to extract a money-rent. The emphasis was thus shifted after World War I; what have often been seen in the history textbooks as mere changes in the administrative structure of Buganda giving the Kabaka more power (and incidentally some of the clan leaders, *bataka*, more freedom) vis-à-vis the *mailo* chiefs, was in fact a new economic policy of backing the emerging commercial peasant farmer. Producers who were tenants were given security of tenure. And with new marketing and other support a class of farmers emerged from the richer peasants, both tenant and freehold land users, and some of the inheritors of *mailo* land who went in for commercial production. But although not European settlers, nor even operating on the same scale (farming tens rather than thousands of acres), they too had a labor problem. And so, as in Kenya, other areas of the country were held back; cash crops could not be grown in the less fertile, nonfeudal northern districts, in order to generate a supply of migrant labor. Later, when Buganda switched to coffee, some of the embargoes in the north were lifted, and the main labor supply came from nearby and overcrowded Rwanda and Burundi and even some parts of northwestern Tanzania. Many of the Rwandans settled, becoming "proletarians," not just "migrants"; and in fact various estimates in recent times have suggested that perhaps as much as a third of the kingdom's population were immigrants, and although it was possible for some to acquire land and settle, many were landless (dependent) laborers.

A complex class structure has as a consequence evolved from the original division into *bakopi* (peasants) and *bakungu* (the members of the hierarchy or chiefs). Moreover, some consciousness of the several classes exists. Mafeje suggests that the following distinctions are made: *basajja banene* (literally "big men" or "men of affairs" —used to described landowners who are still substantial); *basajja bagagga* (literally "rich men" or "men of profit"—those who have emerged from the peasantry to become capitalist farmers); among the peasant strata, *balimi balunga* (literally "good cultivators"; peasants oriented to commodity production, perhaps equivalent to kulaks).[22] Thus a class of capitalist farmers exists, but they are not simply the lineal descendants of the feudal class of *mailo* estate owners. Much of that land has been fragmented—already a generation ago there were 50,000 owners of such land, of whom 15,000 held more than ten acres and only 2,500 of those had more than five tenants.[23] Some *mailo* descendants are no more than middle peasants today—although with the advantage over farmers with similar acreages of having free land. A few have progressed from landlords to capitalist farmers, while a number of commoners have gone beyond the kulak stage to reach equivalent economic status. But Mafeje argues that despite their privileged access to credit, mechanized equipment, and markets, the influence of feudal relationships and values and getting rent without recourse to the demeaning prospect of work has made this emerging class poor vehicles for agrarian capitalism.[24]

The remaining classes have not been in a position to challenge the underdevelopment that is being reproduced nor the reproduction of the class structure. The peasantry proper is stratified between rich, middle, and poor peasant strata, but is divided into free landholders and tenants (some of the latter not impoverished sharecroppers but farmers seeking larger commercial holdings). The prospect of any common political action is made less likely by the different consciousness of Ganda and immigrants, perhaps half of whom have now settled on land that they farm themselves. The peasants of course distance themselves from that half of the immigrant population that remains as laborers, although in this transitional situation the latter are as much retainers as an agricultural proletariat. Moreover, the relative abundance of land still means that those pressures which brought cleavages to a head in parts of Kenya are not operative.

Concluding Remarks

It should be made clear at this point that Kenya and Uganda experienced typically uneven development. The Kikuyu and Buganda patterns should not be regarded as "typical." In Kenya, most of the other populous areas were not such significant areas of labor supply nor so highly commercialized. Their limited cash cropping tended to produce a group of rich peasants rather than commerical farmers, and a petty bourgeoisie of traders and officials related to them, and there has not been a corresponding emergence of a landless class even though some poor peasants may hire themselves out. A few areas, mainly pastoral, have certainly been involved in relationships of exchange (and exploitation) with the outside economy but their mode of production was until recently little changed. In Uganda, a smaller scale version of the Buganda experience did occur in most of the areas that had state systems. The other main category of area was in most cases not producing much of a surplus in precolonial times, was held back from commerical agriculture during the early part of the colonial period, but later experienced some cash-crop production and as a result at least some differentiation of different strata among the peasantry.

The assemblage of a picture of the class structure of the society as a whole also requires the identification of the nonrural classes: the petty bourgeoisie of trader and businesspeople and the educated, bureaucratic element that grew out of, in a more or less concentrated form, the different rural situations. Indeed, the rural relationships of production themselves can only be understood in relation to these other elements.[25] Major contradictions between the whole peasantry and the state bureaucracy, or the marketing system, or the plantation owner may be more critical than those between kulak and poor peasant. In particular, the contradiction with the international bourgeoisie through an array of exchange relationships may well represent the major contradiction.

Conversely, there will be shifting alliances between certain of the local agricultural classes or strata and the dominating national and international classes. Indeed, the "typical" pattern has been for a colonial "indirect rule" alliance to give way to a kulak-bureaucratic bourgeoisie-international capital pattern as the basis for the neocolonial state in Africa.

Notes

1. L.A. Fallers, "Are African Cultivators to Be Called 'Peasants'?" *Current Anthropology* 2, no. 2 (1961).
2. W. Allan, *The African Husbandman* (Edinburgh: Oliver and Boyd, 1965).
3. Some examples of the use of "tribal" as a societal type are I. Schapera, *Migrant Labour and Tribal Life* (London: 1947); J. van Velsen, "Labour Migration as a Positive Factor in the Continuity of Tonga Tribal Society," in A. Southall, ed., *Social Change in Modern Africa* (London: 1961); and even a Marxist writer in an otherwise instructive treatment of African peasants, R. Stavenhagen, *Social Classes and Agrarian Societies* (New York: Doubleday, 1975), talks about "tribal tenure of land." For a critique see A. Mafeje, "The Ideology of Tribalism," *Journal of Modern African Studies* 9, no. 2 (1971).
4. P-P. Rey, *Les Alliances des Classes* (Paris: 1973).
5. Lionel Cliffe, "The Agrarian Question and the 'Mode of Production' Debate in Africa," in H. Alavi, A. G. Frank, and K. J. Harriss, eds., *Relations of Production in Indian Agriculture* (forthcoming).
6. J.S. Saul and R. Woods, "African Peasantries," in T. Shanin, ed., *Peasants and Peasant Society* (Harmondsworth: Penguin, 1971), develop this notion of different regional "peasantries." See also K. Post, "'Peasant-

278 *Lionel Cliffe*

isation' and Rural Political Movements in Western Africa," *European Journal of Sociology* (1973).
7. M. Sahlins, *Stone Age Economics* (Chicago: Aldine, 1972).
8. "Reciprocity" as a mechanism of exchange is a concept developed by Karl Polanyi and used by George Dalton and other anthropologists.
9. E. Terray, *Marxism and "Primitive" Society—Two Studies* (New York: Monthly Review Press, 1972), following Meillassoux, uses this concept.
10. S. Amin, *Accumulation on a World Scale* (New York: Monthly Review Press, 1973).
11. Marx to Zasulich, March 8, 1881.
12. A. Emmanuel, *Unequal Exchange* (New York: Monthly Review Press, 1972), appendix I.
13. Rey, *Les Alliances des Classes*, p. 65 (my translation).
14. K. Marx, *Capital*, vol. II.
15. C.C. Wrigley, *Crops and Wealth in Uganda*, East African Studies, no. 12 (Kampala: East African Institute for Social Research, 1959); J. Iliffe, *Agricultural Change in Modern Tanganyika* (Dar es Salaam: Historical Association of Tanzania, 1971).
16. Rey, *Les Alliances des Classes*, p. 68.
17. G. Balandier, *Sociologie actuelle de l'Afrique Noire* (Paris: P.U.F., 1963).
18. P. Gulliver, *Land Tenure and Social Change Among the Nyakyusa* (Kampala: East African Institute of Social Research, 1959).
19. Kenya Government, *Report of a Mission on Land Consolidaton and Registration* (Nairobi: Lawrence Commission, 1965).
20. M.P.K. Sorrensen, "Counter-revolution to Mau Mau: Land Consolidation in Kikuyuland, 1952-60," East African Institute of Social Research Conference, 1963; and *Land Reform in the Kikuyu Country* (Oxford: Oxford University Press, 1967).
21. Ibid.
22. A. Mafeje, "The Farmers—Economic and Social Differentiation," in A.I. Richards, F. Sturrock, and J.M. Fortt, eds., *Subsistence to Commercial Farming in Present-Day Buganda* (Cambridge: Cambridge University Press, 1973).
23. L.A. Fallers, ed., *The King's Men* (London: Oxford University Press, 1964).
24. Mafeje, "The Farmers"; "Buganda Land Reform," in C. Leys, ed., *Dualism and Rural Development in East Africa* (Copenhagen: 1973).
25. One example which attempts this is C. Leys, "Politics in Kenya: The Development of Peasant Society," *British Journal of Political Science* 1 (1970).

[22]
Workers in Developing Societies

Robin Cohen

To talk about a "working class" in the developing societies of Africa, Asia, Latin America, the Caribbean, and the Middle East might initially appear premature, both in a numerical and sociological sense. It has become embedded in the popular consciousness of metropolitan societies that developing nations are "peasant" societies, locked in a rural universe and producing goods won from the soil in the "traditional" manner of generations of tillers. Few contemporary scholars of peripheral societies would now be insensitive to the massive changes in rural lifestyles wrought by the expansion of the capitalist world system since the sixteenth century. Communal systems of land tenure have been all but totally undermined. In many countries land holdings have become consolidated, crops are produced for reasons of commerce rather than subsistence, while the processes of urbanization, migration, and industrialization are everywhere visible and accelerating rapidly. Despite these observed processes, however, there remains a curious reluctance to accept that a new working class of considerable dimensions and with a potentially great political significance has already been created in the fields, factories, and backyard slums characteristic of peripheral cities.

The scholars' reserve is, in a sense, understandable—for the intitial problems of definition of what constitutes a "working class" in such an environment are indeed formidable. If we accept only a minimalist view, e.g., "those working in full-time wage employment in establishments employing over ten persons" (a definition often favored in labor legislation and by planners and international agencies), the number of "workers" in peripheral societies is indeed low. However, such a restrictive definition ignores the fact that the land is often deserted in favor of contract, seasonal, or temporary wage labor. There is, in short, a large group of the population which is simultaneously and ambiguously "semiproletariat" and "semipeasant" whose situation is described below. Equally, within the *favelas* and shantytowns, large numbers of individuals who are sometimes designated as "unemployed" or as a "sub-" or "lumpenproletariat" are in fact intermittently employed performing services or in small workshops employing a handful of workers and apprentices. In the case of this group, the ambiguity arises from the fact that it comprises people who can at the same time be considered self-employed or employees.

As long as the definitional parameters of the working class in the periphery remain restricted by the model derived from contemporary central societies, so the importance of workers will be minimized. But the denigration of the working class also arises from persistent misconceptions at the political and ideological levels. The first misconception is that the working class is not only small in numbers but is also "privileged," especially in relation to the unemployed, petty traders, and rural dwellers. This view is often simply held as self-evident; at the level of the peripheral state it is frequently invoked to hold down wage demands in the interests of "development." But it is also given theoretical status by a number of authors, Frantz Fanon being a notable example of a polemicist who holds that the working class can be seen as "bourgeois."[1] A similar notion of privilege in relation to other segments of the population is seen in the use of the concept of a "labor aristocracy," initially used to distinguish craft from manual workers, then by Lenin to typify metropolitan workers fattened by imperialism, and now to characterize a section of—or indeed the total—wage labor force in the periphery (see the review by Waterman, n. 17). From the notion of privilege stems a second ideological misconception, this time found in the writings (or more often the commentaries on the writings) of practicing revolutionaries on three continents—including Mao Zedong, Che Guevara, and (again) Fanon. The common conception is that revolutions in the peripheral countries are "peasant revolutions"; the role of workers is therefore seen as marginal or irrelevant. The study of peasants as revolutionaries has acquired formidable academic support,[2] but by overreacting to the Marxist view of the exclusive authenticity of proletarian struggle, there is a danger of underestimating the real level of worker participation in revolutionary change.

Other serious reservations about the prevailing orthodoxies can be indicated. Take, for example, the initial conventional wisdom that capitalist social relations have not seriously penetrated the countryside. In terms of our present concern, the major index to refute this claim would be evidence of the extent of wage employment in the countryside. One interesting, if still controversial, viewpoint is that there existed a proletariat of a kind (in respect of the typical labor process, with a "hidden" wage and work practices) in the plantations of the New World—in Brazil, Central America, the U.S. South, and the Caribbean—at roughly the same time as the European proletariat emerged.[3] While the delineation of a "plantation proletariat" in the New World can perhaps be considered rather esoteric, there seems little doubt that the intensification of commerical agriculture, combined with population pressure, has led in recent decades to the emergence of millions of new agricultural laborers compelled to work for wages. The process is dramatically evident in India—surely the "peasant" country par excellence. There, even allowing for problems in the definition and collection of the statistical evidence, R. Sau's conclusions from his comparisons of the 1961 and 1971 decennial censuses seem inescapable. Of the three categories ("cultivators," "agricultural laborers," and "other workers") comprising the rural work force, the number of cultivators and other workers has stabilized, while 28 million more agricultural laborers have appeared over the ten-year period—exactly the same increase in the rural work force as a whole.[4] Thus, in the case of India alone, assuming the trend has continued through the 1970s, roughly as many rural laborers (who have virtually escaped any sociological attention) have been created as comprise the total population of France. Finally, with respect to the development of a rural working class, it is necessary to note how the enormous expansion of agribusiness in the post-1945 period has created a modern plantation system and numerous agriculturally related jobs. The case of Del Monte, the California-based transnational, is instructive. By 1967, the company owned canneries and plantations in twenty countries—including Kenya, the Philippines, Guatemala, and Mexico. In the Bajio Valley of Mexico alone, 5250 workers are employed in Del Monte's field-factory.[5]

If the existence of a working class in the countryside can now be roughly documented, it is clear that it has not been adequately theorized, either politically or sociologically. Lenin, for example, tended to assimilate the "rural proletariat" into the urban one, and drew no firm distinction between the forms of struggle characteristically found in urban and rural areas. The initial form of resistance by a rural community is indeed to try to cling to its own means of production (land, tools, and labor-power) and thereby prevent the full process of proletarianization from unfolding. It is for this reason that most colonial governments resorted extensively to forced labor, rather than the "lure" of wages. In another sense, it was not in the interests of colonial capital (in particular) to detach workers too violently or completely from the land: their low-wage policies could then be justified by reference to the idea that workers had a supplementary income from their agricultural produce. The contradiction between a necessary supply of labor-power to the towns and plantations and the benefits that a viable peasant economy conferred by subsidizing the cost of the reproduction of labor was partially resolved by the development of migrant labor systems. The individuals enmeshed in these systems became, as it were, "peasant-workers," or, if one prefers an even more adventurous term, the "peasantariat." In the countryside, peasant-workers resisted recruitment by communal flight, evasion of the taxes designed to draw them into the wage economy, and desertion from the labor gangs. At the point of production, they evolved an ingenious set of strategies, graphically described in the case of Southern Rhodesia by C. van Onselen, involving symbolic and cultural protests, theft, sabotage, and the reduction of tasks, labor time, and productivity.[6] Protests against the migrant system were normally constrained by the inconsistent relationship the peasantariat had to the means of production—a relationship that led to sporadic, localized, and individualistic forms of class consciousness. The importance of an attachment to the land, albeit increasingly only an emotional one, has led Teodor Shanin to argue that even in the case of postwar migrants to Europe, "in their social and political characteristics, labor migrants carry aspects of peasanthood not only in the traces of the past in the present, but also in terms of actual relations and contacts, both real and imaginary."[7] While the "traces of the past" typically act to mediate the development of a full proletarian consciousness, an important limiting case is one where the retention of an independent means of production causes workers to take *more*, not less, risks and to adopt more militant postures than those of their coworkers with fully urban backgrounds.[8] This case was repeated recently in Iran, where construction workers, with a base in the villages to which they could retreat, openly challenged the postrevolutionary regime with respect to its economic and employment policies.

As well as creating a dependence on wages in the countryside and a class of peasant-workers, the spread of capitalist social relations into peripheral societies has propelled the growth of more conventionally described urban and industrial workers. The pattern of industrialization exhibits large regional variations, but P. Ranis provides a useful generalization in the case of Latin America. He identifies three phases: First, the 1880-1930 period, when a small light industrial sector, concentrating on clothing, textiles, handicrafts, and furniture, developed. Second, from the Depression of 1930 to the early 1940s, when the strategy of import substitution was predominant and household and consumer goods were produced locally. Third, from the late 1950s to the 1960s, when infrastructural and heavy industrial plant was laid down while employment in the service sector showed explosive growth.[9] The Latin American pattern can be contrasted with the subsequent expansion of export-oriented manufacturing in peripheral capitalist countries (a trend pioneered in Hong Kong, Taiwan, and South Korea). Other notable export-geared manufacturing bases have been established in northern Mexico, Singapore, Malaysia, the Philippines, and elsewhere. As the editors of a recent collection on workers and peasants note, "there is no doubt we are in the midst of a substantial relocation of industries on a worldwide scale, a trend being orchestrated and led by transnational companies."[10] The recent Brandt Commission has now popularized the term "newly industrializing countries" to cover such structural shifts in global manufacturing.[11] The working class in peripheral countries is thus set for an enormous quantitative expansion, especially if the number of workers in the small open-air sweat shops (the so-called informal sector) is considered. The informal sector is, in addition, likely to experience greater growth as rural populations are further displaced and as planners expect to assist the informal sector through easier access to credit, training to upgrade skills, technical advice on product improvement, and the provision of better tools and infrastructural facilities.[12]

An expanded notion of the working class must also include those from peripheral zones who have been sucked into the central economies—the advanced capitalist societies—as migrants or immigrants. The migrants are normally escaping a reproduction sector that does not even permit the replacement of labor-power at existing levels of nutrition and they are destined for jobs that are dirty, unskilled, and dangerous, with low status and poor pay, at least by metropolitan standards. The numbers involved are considerable. By 1975, workers from peripheral zones constituted 10 percent of the labor force in Western Europe as a whole. In France, they represented 11 percent of the total labor force, while in Switzerland the proportion surpassed 25 percent. Since the mid-1960s, the United States has also experienced a huge influx of workers from the Caribbean (including Puerto Rico) and Mexico. Illegal migrants alone are estimated at anything from 2 to 7 million.[13] These migrations are also paralleled by migration to industrially active zones within the periphery—thus there are enormous inflows of labor from Asia to the Gulf states, from Colombia to Caracas in Venezuela, and from neighboring countries to South Africa, particularly to the Rand area.

Given the limited political and civic rights and low levels of organization characteristic of a work force that can easily be expelled from production, there is frequently a low level of political organization and consciousness among migrant workers. One author has gone so far as to argue that the use of migrants has become a structural requirement for monopoly capitalism both in the sense that they help to iron out the stops and starts of the economy and in that they help to fracture the class composition of indigenous workers.[14] Migrants have, however, begun to organize defensively within their communities and at their places of work around such issues as residential and legal rights, and the need to join or organize trade unions. These modes of organization are slowly cutting into the capacity of the advanced capitalist states to use migrants as a flexible "reserve army."

But what levels of consciousness, and forms of organization and action, can be anticipated from workers within developing countries themselves? It is first necessary to discount the argument that they constitute en masse a privileged group. Such a characterizaton may be applied, with reservations, to a narrow band of salaried workers and to exceptional cases like that of the white working class in South Africa. But the bulk of unskilled and semiskilled workers have been wrongly compared to the peasantry in terms of the income of the employed head of an urban household, ignoring the fact that this relative advantage is offset by the higher cost of living in the towns, the practice of transferring income from urban to rural households, and the larger size of the dependent urban household.[15] This last point is particularly important in understanding the political and social role of workers in peripheral capitalist societies. There is little evidence to suggest that the urban poor, the small-scale traders, or the peasantry have accepted the image of selfish unionized urban workers held by planners, officials, and politicians. On the contrary, there appears to be a wide acceptance of workers and their principal class organs, the trade unions, as articulators of a wider set of grievances and ideologies than those that can simply be reduced to a wage demand. In Latin America, workers have been deeply influenced by anarchist, syndicalist, and socialist views, and strikes and other manifestations of dissent often spread far beyond the confines of the dues-paying membership. In the Buenos Aires General Strike of 1907, for example, a socialist newspaper estimated a participation of 93,000 workers in sixteen trades. Of these, some 31,000 had participated actively in union activities while only 10,000 regularly paid dues.[16] In Africa and Asia, workers' organizations were usually in the forefront of anticolonial and nationalist struggles, even though a good deal of disillusionment with the leadership of the postcolonial states soon set in. On the other hand, workers in peripheral capitalist societies have rarely succeeded in establishing viable workers' parties or in influencing the character or policies of socialist parties (though some exceptions to this statement can be recorded in Argentina, Mexico, and Chile).

Workers have tended instead to participate in politics on the basis of immediate issues and grievances, including rent strikes, marches, demonstrations, and strikes. Workers in larger establishments in particular have shown a capacity to participate in class action and to achieve a political impact quite disproportionate to their relatively small numbers. The strategic concentration of workers in the big towns and cities close to the centers of power has allowed workers to severely damage the credibility of postcolonial governments, especially those of recent provenance. Worker-led protests have culminated in a change of government in a significant number of countries. In the last few years alone, a strike movement in Egypt, starting in January 1977, escalated into an uprising of the urban and rural poor. One year later, the national trade-union center of Tunisia, previously known for its moderate character, enraged the government sufficiently for its protests to be treated as tantamount to an insurrection.[17] The revolutionary movement in Iran, it is now easy to forget in the turmoil of events, was also triggered by strikes by petroleum workers. In the late summer of 1978, guerrilla action in Nicaragua was followed by a general strike that led ultimately to a civil war and a rupture with the United States. The contagion has now spread, mainly through the agency of workers and students, to other Central American countries. Strikes in what Western newspapers have called "Africa's most stable country," Liberia, led to the collapse of the legitimacy of the True Whig Party, and the assassination of its president in a coup d'état in April 1980.

Finally, it remains only to make some brief remarks about the role of workers in peripheral socialist societies. It has already been argued that the participation of workers has been downgraded by those who have interpreted revolutionary political action as stemming largely from the peasantry. Detailed studies of the Algerian, Cuban, and Chinese cases confirm the errors of this view.[18] But it is important to emphasize (as does Petras),[19] that there is an interaction between potentially revolutionary classes and fractions of classes. While the impetus, organization, ideology, and leadership of a revolutionary struggle might begin in the urban areas, the success of revolution in the periphery seems to depend on its linking with the bulk of social forces located in the countryside.

Notes

1. F. Fanon, *The Wretched of the Earth* (Harmondsworth: Penguin Books, 1967).

2. See B. Moore, *Social Origins of Dictatorship and Democracy* (Boston: Beacon, 1966); E. Wolf, *Peasant Wars of the Twentieth Century* (New York: Harper & Row, 1969); T. Shanin, "The Peasantry as a Political Factor," in T. Shanin, ed., *Peasants and Peasant Societies* (Harmondsworth: Penguin Books, 1971); and H. Alavi, "Peasants and Revolution," *Socialist Register 1965* (London: Merlin Press, 1965).

3. S. Mintz, *Caribbean Transformations* (Chicago: Aldine, 1974).

4. R. Sau, "Rural Workforce in India: Proletarianisation or Immiserisation of the Peasantry?" *Labour, Capital, and Society* 12, no. 1 (April 1979).

5. North American Congress on Latin America (NACLA), "Del Monte: Bitter Fruits," *Latin America and Empire Report* 10, no. 7 (September 1976).

6. C. van Onselen, *Chibaro: African Mine Labour in Southern Rhodesia, 1900-1933* (London: Pluto Press, 1976).

7. T. Shanin, "The Peasants Are Coming: Migrants Who Labour, Peasants Who Travel, and Marxists Who Write," *Race and Class* 19, no. 3 (Winter 1978).

8. R. Sandbrook and R. Cohen, eds., *The Development of an African Working Class: Studies in Class Formation and Action* (London: Longman, 1975), p. 312.

9. P. Ranis, "The Workers and the State in Latin America: Patterns of Dominance and Subordination," *Civilisations* 29, nos. 1-2 (1979).

10. R. Cohen, P.C.W. Gutkind and P. Brazier, eds., *Peasants and Proletarians: The Struggles of Third World Workers* (New York: Monthly Review Press, 1979), p. 12.

11. Brandt Commission, *North-South—A Programme for Survival* (London: Pan Books, 1980), p. 12.

12. Ibid., p. 130.

13. M.J. Piore, *Birds of Passage: Migrant Labour and Industrial Societies* (Cambridge: Cambridge University Press, 1979), p. 1.

14. M. Castells, "Immigrant Workers and Class Struggles in Advanced Capitalism," in Cohen et al., eds., *Peasants and Proletarians.*

15. Sandbrook and Cohen, eds., *Development of African Working Class*, p. 3.

16. H. Spalding, *Organized Labor in Latin America: Historical Case Studies of Urban Workers in Dependent Societies* (New York: Harper & Row, 1977), p. 24.

17. P. Waterman, "The 'Labour Aristocracy' in Africa: Introduction to a Controversy," *Development and Change* 6, no. 3 (1975): 177.

18. See I. Clegg, *Workers' Self-Management in Algeria* (New York: Monthly Review Press, 1971); M. Zeitlin, *Revolutionary Politics and the Cuban Working Class* (Princeton: Princeton University Press, 1967); and J. Chesneaux, *The Chinese Labor Movement, 1919-1927* (Stanford: Stanford University Press, 1968).

19. J. Petras, "New Perspectives on Imperialism and Social Class in the Periphery," *Journal of Contemporary Asia* 5, no. 3 (1975).

Part IV

State and Revolution

Part IV is devoted to issues of power, domination, and resistance in "developing societies." It begins with a paper by Hamza Alavi devoted to the conceptualizaton of the state and its social bases. Teodor Shanin considers different aspects of the debate concerning revolution and its agencies, relating it to the issues of state and class. The last two items are essentially related. Colin Leys considers the guiding principles of U.S. strategies concerning *political change* and *political order* in "developing societies," with reference to the work of one of its major theorists, who personifies a shift in emphasis from the former to the latter. Gabriel García Márquez, the great Latin American novelist, documents in the closing item the poignant reality that those strategies meant in the tragedy that overtook Chile.

Contributions in other parts of the volume that are of particular relevance to issues that are taken up in this part are those by Harry Magdoff, Arghiri Emmanuel, Paul Baran, Paul Sweezy, Robin Cohen, and Basil Davidson. The editors have been unable to incorporate, as originally planned, discussions of the organization of power at the local level and of political movements in "developing societies." The reading list at the end of the volume should help to fill that gap.

[23]
State and Class Under Peripheral Capitalism

Hamza Alavi

Given the central role that is accorded to the state and public policy in "modernization" theory, it is rather striking to see how little thought is given to an examination of the nature of the state itself, its location within the matrix of a class-divided society, and its relationship with contending social forces. The state is, rather, thought of as an entity that stands outside and above society, an autonomous agency that is invested (potentially) with an independent source of rationality (enriched by "technical assistance" from metropolitan countries), and the capability to initiate and pursue programs of development for the benefit of the whole of society. There is an implicit disjunction between the state and society, slurring over questions about the social foundations of political power and the making of public policy. The problematic of the state is then narrowed down to that of the efficacy of its public institutions and organs to achieve objectives and programs of "modernization," focusing especially on the respective roles of "ruling elites," political parties, the bureaucracy, and the military.

Theories of "modernization" are, however, explicitly or implicitly theories of capitalist development, inasmuch as they are premised on the creation and maintenance of the basic structures and institutions of a capitalist society, which may be contrasted with the notion of revolutionary change that would aim to make a decisive break with the internal structures and the encompassing international framework of global capitalism. Both kinds of change involve the dissolution and transformation of precapitalist social and economic structures, but each in a different way. In "modernizing" societies, the direction of such change is toward their subsumption under peripheral capitalism, an aspect of the problem that is discussed in my article "The Structure of Peripheral Capitalism" (see above).

Some general notions about the state and society do, of course, underlie discussions of its role in "modernization" theory. Functionalist theory, in particular, has been extremely influential in shaping ideas in political sociology and the sociology of development, providing their master concepts.[1] To grasp the full implications of the functionalist position one must bear in mind its key organizing conception: essentially society is constituted on the basis of the complementarity and reciprocity of roles in the social division of labor. This contrasts with notions of exploitation and oppression, domination and subordination, and antagonism of class interests. Structures, such as those of the political system and the state, thus exist to carry out necessary functions, which can but be for the good of the whole society. An alternative view, one that does not reify society as a whole (as functionalist theory does), but proceeds instead from the idea of the social process being constituted by interactions of free acting individuals—the "market model" —nevertheless arrives at very similar conclusions to those of functionalist theory on issues of relevance here. Analogous to the economic market is a political market (and political entrepreneurs aiming to maximize votes), to which individuals in a society bring their demands and supports; these are converted by the political system into outputs in the form of legislation, the application of laws, and authoritative allocations of value. Given "free competition," the system produces a "fair" result, just as in the economic market. No questions are raised about the preconditions of a particular division of labor in society, or the consequences of class divisions that determine the capacities of members of different classes in the political and the economic markets, or their different relationship to the state, in the context of their mutual opposition. Instead of a conception of a society systematically divided into antagonistic classes, in accordance with the social relations of production, we have here a picture of an indefinite heterogeneity of interests vying with each other, with the state playing a neutral role, maintaining the rules of the game, aggregating the variety of contending interests into coherent policies, and holding society together for the good of all its members rather than the interests of its dominating, exploiting classes.

Both functionalist theory and the "market model" yield pluralist conclusions about the way in which political systems work, as against recognition of structured class interests in conflict. In the literature on "modernization" theory, considerations about the state and society are all too often adduced eclectically from different and essentially conflicting theoretical traditions—not only the two referred to above but also a third which in fact militates against pluralist conceptions. These are ideas derived from "elite theory," which visualizes necessarily privileged individuals and groups in society and the state, occupying positions of power and authority. But their dominant position is associated not with their class positions and economic power, or their class associations, but with their personal attributes and social values. Modernization theory thus attaches a crucial importance to the so-called "Westernizing elites," the bearers of Western technology and rationality who must take over from "traditional elites." The self-acknowledged role of the modernizing elites is to change "traditional society," a conception that detaches them, in a sense, from their own society and roots them externally. The conception of the state that underlies this conception, in contrast to the functionalist view and the market model, is that of the state as an autonomous agency operating on society, rather than its product. The emphasis is not on consensus or free play of the political market, but on the capabilities and efficacy of the modernizing elites and their instrument, the state, which are the bearers of forces of progress. This is the self-image of bureaucracies, of ambitious military leaders, of monarchs who discover that they have a mission for their country. Such a voluntaristic conception of modernizing elites, however, begs questions about their social roots and commitments in a class-divided society, as well as about the "structural imperatives" (see below) and constraints within which they operate.

To grasp issues about the state and development, therefore, it is essential to examine underlying questions about the state and classes under peripheral capitalism. For that we can identify four different levels at which relevant questions may be posed. The first concerns the nature and role of the state in society at its most general level, namely, its central role in the creation and reproduction of the social order that constitutes the necessary precondition for the functioning of a (peripheral) capitalist economy. A second set of questions concerns the "instrumental" nature of the state for and on behalf of particular groups and classes that seek control over it. These two aspects of the state have figured prominently in contemporary Marxist debate, which we do not have space enough to go into fully here. We will note, very briefly, the main issues in order to expound our key concept of the "structural imperative," and we will then proceed to identify and analyze special issues that arise in the context of peripheral capitalist societies. A third set of questions is about the nature and character of those who occupy positions of authority and power within the state apparatus, the "servants of the state." Are they in fact masters rather than servants? If they enjoy a degree of autonomy, how far does (or can) it extend? Do they have interests of their own, independent of those of the dominant classes? Finally, we might examine a view of the state not as an "actor," operating on behalf of dominating classes, but as an arena of class struggle—the state not as a homogeneous and monolithic entity but as a differentiated one, within which we may discover more than one locus of power. We may consider possibilities of class struggle *within* the framework of the state itself, as against confrontations by subordinate classes *against* the state of the dominant classes. In this case, once again, questions arise about the limits of gains that might be possible within the framework of the state as an arena of class struggle, short of a revolutionary seizure of power by subordinate classes. There are questions here also about the depth of penetration of civil society by institutions of the state—a question that is of particular importance in the context of precapitalist societies being subsumed under (peripheral) capitalism.

To take up the first question, the fundamental and overriding function of the state is to realize and maintain the organizational prerequisites of the capitalist social order. Capitalist production and exchange presupposes, simultaneously, a kind of equality in society and a basic inequality. In contrast with differential rights and statuses among different categories of individuals in precapitalist societies, capitalist production and exchange are founded on juridical equality between individuals: there is a free, contractual, basis of exchange in capitalist society in which labor-power itself is a commodity to be bought and sold freely. But this latter condition presupposes a fundamental inequality in the disposition of resources in society with the creation of a class of owners of the means of production and a class of dispossessed workers on the basis of capitalist property, and concomitant laws and institutions on which capitalist production and exchange depend. The idea that the role of the state is to maintain the foundations of the social order is shared by Marxist theory and sociological theories; where they differ is in their idea of the social order that is maintained. But in structural-functionalist sociology and the functionalist version of Marxist theory, the role of the state is limited to this most general level,[2] for in both these conceptions individuals and groups (and classes) are but agents and bearers of reified structures and it is the latter which operate in accordance with their inexorable logic, which unfolds in manifestations of social processes. They are not brought about by willed actions of individuals and classes. Both structural-functionalist sociology and functionalist Marxism would rule out, therefore, the other questions outlined above, namely, the "instrumental" character of the state under the control of "ruling classes" and, even more emphatically, the possibility of the independent interests of those who are in control of the state apparatus—or our last question, namely, the state itself being an arena of class struggle—for in this light the state is an entity with its own designated functions.

We will not attempt to summarize here arguments deployed in the famous debate between Ralph Miliband and Nicos Poulantzas in which some of the main issues were taken up, but the reader should, nevertheless, keep these in mind in the course of our present discussion.[3] We must recognize that a one-sided interpretation of either position would be an oversimplified interpretation of Marx's ideas on the subject. This was shown by Miliband in a seminal essay in which he pointed out, possibly for the first time, two alternative conceptions of the state in Marx's work, to be combined as elements of a single complex theory.[4] Miliband expounded the "Bonapartist" conception of the state, which Poulantzas later fastened on to, to the exclusion of the other, instrumentalist, conception. Miliband, it must be pointed out, though not a functionalist Marxist, rejects crude "instrumentalist" conceptions of the state. If such a view, he points out, is taken "to mean...that the state acts *on behalf* of the dominant or 'ruling' class,...[that] is one thing; but [to say] that it acts *at the behest* of that class...is an altogether different assertion, and, as I would argue, a vulgar deformation of the thought of Marx and Engels."[5]

Both the functionalist Marxist and the crude "instrumentalist" view of the state can be seen to be reductionist, inasmuch as in both the state acts exclusively in pursuance of the "common affairs of the whole bourgeoisie," even though in the former version this is qualified by the concept of "relative autonomy" of the state vis-à-vis particular fractions or sections of the bourgeoisie—precisely so that the state may act on behalf of capital as a whole, untrammeled by particularist demands. Both these views thus rule out the capacity of contending *classes*, other than the "whole" bourgeoisie, to press their demands (with varying degrees of success) on the state. As we shall see, this problem is of particular importance in peripheral capitalist societies where we may have more than one dominant class, e.g., not only the indigenous bourgeoisie, but also the metropolitan bourgeoisie and landowning classes. Furthermore, we can consider whether there does exist the possibility of successful class struggle by subordinate classes in winning at least some limited gains—a question that is ruled out in both these versions of the Marxist theory of the state. Both, moreover, offer a one-dimensional view of the making and implementation of state policies, as if at all times the state unerringly follows the interests of a dominant class. If the last possibility is admitted, we must consider in particular the conditions and limits of such deviations. The working of the state under peripheral capitalism in fact opens up a much larger range of questions than those that have been confronted by the Marxist theory of the state in the context of advanced capitalist countries.

At this point it may be useful to expound our concept of the "structural imperative," mentioned earlier, which is not as "deterministic" as it sounds. Quite the contrary: it enables us to understand the degrees of freedom, and deviations from the requirements and demands of capital, in the working of the state under (peripheral) capitalism. The "structural imperative" refers to the basis of economic calculation in a capitalist society and the conditions that govern their outcome, both at the level of the individual enterprise and at the level of the state. It defines the conditions of profitable economic behavior and the allocation of resources, delineates "efficient" from "inefficient" allocation with reference to performance on the market, and draws a line between solvency and insolvency. It refers also to the dynamics of capitalist development and its contradictions, which are analyzed in Marxist political economy.[6] But the notion of the "structural imperative" does not mean that it determines in advance actions of individual capitalists or those of the capitalist state, as if they were perfectly programed—as implied in the conception of the capitalist state in functionalist Marxism. Neither individual capitalists nor the guardians of the capitalist state possess perfect knowledge and foresight, and their calculations are always fraught with uncertainty. Firms, after all, do go bankrupt.

At the level of the state, not only these but also other, ideological, factors intervene which account, conjuncturally, for deviations in the actions of the state from the interests of the "ruling classes." Ideology is not a simple one-dimensional problem of the propagation of the ideology of the ruling class, as proposed by functionalist Marxism; it is a somewhat more complex process which is more adequately captured in the works of Antonio Gramsci and those who have elaborated his seminal ideas. At the level of the state, therefore, these factors intervene, making for deviations from the perfect pursuit of capitalist rationality. Does this then mean that the actions of the state are capricious and do not follow any logical course—that they are autonomous? No. If that were the case, we would not speak of a "structural *imperative*." It is the imperative of capitalism, however, not by virtue of the fact that it predetermines *actions* of individual capitalists and the capitalist state. Rather, its imperative character lies in the fact that it determines the *consequences* of all such actions; it makes the new situations, successively, the basis on which fresh calculations are made and "corrective" action contemplated.

Thus at particular moments, conjuncturally, actions of capitalist enterprises and those of the capitalist state can be out of line with the logic of the capitalist economy and its "objective" needs—contrary to the functionalist Marxist view. But such deviations cannot continue without negative consequences for the capitalists and the capitalist state, thus setting in motion fresh evaluations—and, indeed demands—from the bourgeoisie for a change in the course of policy to bring it into line with their objective requirements, even if this is still done imperfectly. It is in this way, through a continuous process of re-evaluating and correcting policies and programs, that the logic of the capitalist economy, the "structural imperative," imposes itself in the long run upon state policy. That is one sense in which one might meaningfully speak of "economic determination in the last instance." It is thus not a mechanistic, deterministic, concept. There is another sense in which this is true too: with the progress of capitalist development, its underlying contradictions unfold and give rise to conditions and forces that operate and have effects quite independent of the will and actions of the ruling class.

In that light, given the relative autonomy of state action within the limits and constraints of the "structural imperative," we can recognize cases where state action helps and accelerates capitalist development and cases, often against the background of a populist rhetoric, where it obstructs and slows it down without undermining the institutional and structural bases of the capitalist economy (and thus proceeding to a revolutionary transformation of the society). Capitalism itself is not transcended as long as the state guarantees the continuity of capitalist social relations of production and its class structure by virtue of capitalist property that separates the producer from the means of production by interposing between them an exploiting class. This applies also to "public sector" enterprises, which operate within the framework of peripheral capitalism and are subject to its imperatives. State-sponsored or state-owned enterprises are in such cases no more than "bearers of capital," one more form of the organization of capital, which takes many forms by way of individual or corporate ownership. Following this line of thought, some Marxists speak of a "bureaucratic bourgeoisie that is in command of such enterprises."[7] But if this line of thought is to be pursued, an analytical distinction must be made between state enterprises and the officials who run them, whose decisions are subject to the rules of capitalist solvency (even if this is not actually achieved in practice—nor is that always so in the private sector without public help) on the one hand, and, on the other hand, those in charge of the state apparatus, the state bureaucrats who are not in the same way governed by the calculations of profitability.

The concept of the "structural imperative" understood in this way allows us to distance ourselves from the essentially deterministic logic of functionalist Marxism, as well as from the cruder versions of the instrumental conception of the state, without throwing overboard the notion of instrumentality altogether. It alerts us to the fact that the state bureaucracy itself calculates its policy to accord with the dictates of capitalism without having to receive orders from the capitalist class. But, at the same time, given a degree of indeterminacy in the making of public policy, it is also of the utmost importance for all the dominant classes in peripheral capitalist societies (as will be discussed below) to be represented in the state apparatus and to press their demands, for which purpose they establish viable modes of class representation in the state. These take a variety of forms: political parties, independent class organizations, formal representation within the state apparatus on committees, etc., as well as factions within the state apparatus established by virtue of the class origins and/or class affiliation and commitments of members of the bureaucracy and the military.

We will consider presently the problem of rival interests between the dominant classes within peripheral capitalist societies. The concept of the "structural imperative" understood in this way allows us to recognize the possibility of disjunction, within limits and at particular moments, between the making of public policy and the contending interests of the dominant classes, the indigenous bourgeoisies, the metropolitan bourgeoisies, and landowning classes, as well as the fact that such deviations not only have limits but cannot persist over a long period of time, for they are soon overtaken by the consequences of such policies, which bring into play forces for an alteration of the course, so that state policies are brought into line with the requirements and demands of peripheral capitalism. This view of the "economic determination in the last instance" allows us to account for the stupidity and miscalculations of the guardians of the state, and for the degree of freedom that they possess in possibly pursuing their own interests by virtue of being in charge of the state apparatus, a question that we shall consider below. But first we must return to the question of the plurality of dominant classes in peripheral capitalist societies, which is unlike that in advanced capitalist countries where we have only one dominant class to contend with—a fact which has shaped Marxist debates on the theory of the state in a particular mold, one that does not easily fit the case of the peripheral capitalist societies.

The problem of identifying the ruling classes and class alignments in peripheral capitalist societies is more complex than in advanced capitalist countries. To comprehend this problem, we must recall that for each mode of production, such as the feudal mode or the capitalist mode, Marxist theory recognizes pairs of "fundamental classes," the class of exploited producers and the exploiting class, whose social relations of production are constitutive of that mode. Where capitalism has triumphed and dissolved precapitalist modes, as in the advanced capitalist countries, the bourgeoisie and the proletariat are the fundamental classes. Where, as in noncolonized prerevolutionary Russia, which Lenin analyzed, we have a social formation in which the feudal mode was still dominant but the capitalist mode was rising and challenging that earlier mode, we have fundamental classes located in the respective modes in antagonistic contradiction. The development of the one necessarily entailed the dissolution of the other. The interests of the two "fundamental classes" in two modes of production in the same social formation are irreconcilable; the contradiction between the two is resolved only by structural change. Besides the "fundamental classes," Marxism also recognizes the existence of "auxiliary classes," such as petty producers and traders, professional classes, and so on, whose structural significance is derived from their location vis-à-vis the dominant mode of production and their relationship to the fundamental classes, which are the rival contenders to be the ruling classes.

In peripheral capitalist societies, however, we are presented with a pattern of class formation and class alignment that is different both from that of the advanced capitalist countries and that of Lenin's picture of noncolonized Russia awaiting its bourgeois revolution. The actual process of class formation and restructuration in Africa, Asia, and Latin America is a consequence of the impact of colonial capitalism (in the case of Latin America, also of the precapitalist Iberian colonial conquest) and is quite varied, in accordance with differences in their respective precapitalist social formations, and differences in their encounters with colonialism and the manner of their subsumption under peripheral capitalism. For our present purposes, at the risk of some oversimplification, we may distinguish two basic types of situations. One is that of societies where we find well-established landowning classes, no longer "feudal," as I have argued, but owners of capitalist landed property exploiting the labor of dispossessed peasants. With the establishment of the peripheral capitalist state, and the institutions of a capitalist economy, we also find the growth of indigenous bourgeoisies, at varying levels of development, including not only a comprador bourgeoisie that is ancillary to foreign capital, but also an industrial bourgeoisie whose relationship with foreign capital is ambivalent. Foreign capital opposes the development of this local rival but at the same time, insofar as it does develop, certain sections of foreign capital (especially those engaged in high technology industries) will seek collaborative relationships with it. In addition, foreign capital—the metropolitan bourgeoisie on its own—has a structural presence in postcolonial societies and their state apparatus—its hand is not removed with independence any more than it is absent in those countries that have not been subjected to direct colonial rule. In fact, the metropolitan bourgeoisie is represented in peripheral capitalist societies and the state doubly. It is represented in the first instance through its own local presence, organization, and resources. But this direct presence is greatly reinforced through the mediation on its behalf of the respective metropolitan states in their dealings with states in peripheral capitalist societies. It cannot be therefore regarded as external to these societies.[8]

We find that in peripheral capitalist societies that have a plurality of "fundamental classes" we cannot designate any one of them, unambiguously, as the "ruling class"; both the "instrumentalist" version of the Marxist theory of the state and the functionalist version, as they are at present formulated, are unable to offer a suitable theoretical framework in terms of which this problem can be resolved. Furthermore, unlike, for example, Lenin's model of prerevolutionary Russia, these three classes are not located in antagonistic modes of production (as I have tried to demonstrate in my article, "The Structure of Peripheral Capitalism," above), which would predicate an antagonistic contradiction between them so that a rising class must triumph, bringing about the dissolution of the other two in a restructured society. I have argued that the three classes are located in the single structure of peripheral capitalism, which admits their competing interests without a structural contradiction between them.

It may be argued that these are not three separate classes but only "fractions" of a single class, analogous to the division of the bourgeoisie in advanced capitalist countries into different "fractions," such as industrial capital, finance capital, and commercial capital. But there is a fundamental difference between the two cases. In the advanced capitalist countries (and on those lines in peripheral capitalism too), such "fractions" are essentially *complementary* in their functions, so that it is only by their coming together that "capital as a whole" is constituted in the overall organization of capitalist production and exchange. It is that essential underlying complementarity that constitutes them, together, into a single class. But that is by no means the case with respect to the indigenous bourgeoisie, the metropolitan bourgeoisie, and the landowning classes in peripheral capitalist societies. Each of these constitutes a whole class in that sense; their roles are mutually exclusive rather than complementary. We cannot therefore think of them, together, as constituting a single (ruling) class. Given that fact, neither the instrumentalist conception of the bourgeois state, as thought of in the Marxist theory of the state in the context of advanced capitalist countries, nor even less the functionalist Marxist theory, can provide a satisfactory explanation of the basis of state power in peripheral capitalist societies with a plurality of "fundamental classes." We can therefore recognize the problematic of state and class under peripheral capitalism as a distinct one.

A second, alternative, class configuration is found in some countries of Africa where the indigenous population has consisted mainly of peasant communities ("tribal" societies) without large landowning classes such as those that we encounter in Asia, Latin America, or other parts of Africa. In the wake of the colonial economic domination and transformation, expatriate bourgeoisies were implanted in these societies—not only representatives of the metropolitan bourgeoisie itself, but a comprador bourgeoisie recruited mainly from Asian countries to underpin the colonial economy. After decolonization, with the summary expulsion (or more subtle squeezing out) of the Asians, a class vacuum was created. Inasmuch as theorists have failed to recognize the structural presence in these societies of the metropolitan bourgeoisie, they have been confronted with an apparently paradoxical picture of having only subordinate "fundamental classes," i.e., working classes, but not a superordinate one that might be designated as the "ruling class." In their search for a ruling class, in that context, some Marxist theoreticians have turned to the "new petty bourgeoisie," the salaried middle class drawn from the indigenous population that operates the state apparatus (an "auxiliary class") as the "ruling class."[9] Misconceived analysis grounded in such a view would disappear if we were to bring into the picture the role and structural presence of the metropolitan bourgeoisie in peripheral capitalist societies as a "fundamental class."

The political role of the educated salaried middle classes in peripheral capitalist societies is, however, of very considerable importance and should not be dismissed too easily, by designating them as an "auxiliary class." Especially in countries that have experienced direct colonial rule, that class has acquired special characteristics that distinguish it socially and culturally from other indigenous groups. Their appropriation of an alien language and culture, English or French, distances them from those in their society who lack the kind of education that they have had. They are subject to a far greater extent than any other class in peripheral capitalist societies to influences and ideas that emanate from the metropolitan countries. By virtue of the fact that they also hold the upper echelons of the bureaucracy and the military, they hold a place of strategic importance, particularly for the metropolitan powers.

Members of the educated middle class play an active and vigorous role in the politics of peripheral capitalist societies and much of the thrust of their political demands is directed toward positions of power in the state apparatus as such. The state is their biggest and the most remunerative employer—and, given corruption and nepotism, for their kin. We find a tendency for this class perpetually to fracture on the basis of ethnic, regional, linguistic, or sectarian loyalties, which on the surface may appear to contradict the traditions of the liberal, secular, "Western" ideologies that they have imbibed. In fact, they inhabit more than one cultural domain. Their lifestyle remains "Westernized," especially as expressed in material objects that fetishize Western culture. Their ideas, more importantly, are impregnated with the logic of capitalist rationality, even if, as in the case of "modernist" translations of their traditional culture and religion, they express such ideas in the idiom of tradition. A partial return to the indigenous culture can be an enriching but exotic experience for them. But their training in statecraft has a decidedly "Western" stamp. They have internalized the calculus of capital. They have a distinctive presence in peripheral capitalist societies and states, one that is qualitatively different from that of their counterparts in the advanced capitalist societies.

A consideration of the classes from which the state apparatus is mainly recruited leads us to the third of the main questions we began with, namely, the nature and character of the bureaucracy and the military, of those who occupy positions of power and authority in the state. In a simple instrumentalist conception, their function is a purely derivative one, as the term implies. Equally so in the functionalist Marxist view, such as that propounded by Poulantzas, for whom the specificity of the bureaucracy is dissolved within a conception of the functions of the bourgeois state. The issue is pursued there with reference to the *class origins* of the bureaucracy, which are considered to be of no significance. But I would not dismiss the significance of class origins as readily: members of the higher echelons of the bureaucracy and the military are very often recruited from landowning or rich farmer families or the bourgeoisie (who can afford to give them the required higher education). It is not surprising, therefore, that despite commitments, in some cases at the highest levels, to programs such as land reform, these have failed to be implemented effectively, for the class that is affected is directly represented within the state apparatus by virtue of the class origins of its officials, and is able thereby to undermine the implementation of measures directed against itself. Likewise we encounter cases of *class affiliation*, irrespective of the class origins, of officials who acquire close links with either the metropolitan bourgeoisie or the local bourgeoisie, whose interests they pursue vigorously and usually effectively.

These are both aspects of the mode of class representation in the state.

The problem of the nature and character of the state bureaucracy that we need to consider further relates not to the modes of class representation but to whether the state as such establishes interests in society quite independent of the respective classes; and if so, what such interests can be and what are the limits within which they may be pursued, subject to the structural imperatives of peripheral capitalism that I have referred to. We can begin by recognizing that there is an almost universal tendency on the part of regimes in peripheral capitalist societies to acquire an authoritarian character and proliferate military dictatorships. This phenomenon is too often explained away by suggesting that it is a response to class struggles waged by workers and peasants. But such an explanation, while possibly true in some cases (most notoriously, of course, in the case of Chile), is by no means true of the majority of such cases where movements among, and the organization of, subordinate classes are in fact quite weak, and actual resistance, if there is any, is sporadic and localized. One would not wish to minimize the repressive character of the state in peripheral capitalist societies in relation to the subordinate classes and the effective intervention of the state, through legislation and administrative means as well as through the institutionalized violence of police and military action, to suppress attempts on the part of subordinate classes to organize themselves and to act in their own behalf. And the ideological apparatus of the state, as well as that deployed by the dominant classes, is also preoccupied with the task of containing the thrust from below. But this explanation appears to be insufficient when confronting the realities of many countries where highly centralized and undemocratic regimes have appeared.

At a totally different level, however, we find that it is not the subordinate classes alone that confront the state as an alien force. The fundamental classes also have to do the same—and here it is mainly the administrative arm of the state that is deployed against them, even while upholding their fundamental interests. Unlike in the advanced capitalist countries where the state has developed in the wake of a single dominant class, and state institutions and power have developed largely in keeping with the requirements of that class and are therefore "subordinate" to it, we find that in peripheral capitalist countries there is instead a very considerable accretion of powers of control and regulation over the "dominant" fundamental classes in the hands of a powerful and centralized state; here the fundamental classes do not have any *direct* control over the state. On a previous occasion I referred to this syndrome

as the "overdeveloped" state, in the sense that the excessive enlargement of powers of control and regulation that the state has
accumulated and elaborated extend far beyond the logic of what
may be necessary for the orderly functioning of the social institutions of the society over which the state presides.[10] Referring to a
society where there is more than one "fundamental class," I explained this relatively autonomous development of the state and its
extensive power by virtue of the fact that precisely because of the
plurality of the dominant classes, whose rival interests are mediated
by the state, which therefore sits in judgment over their respective
demands, the state must enjoy a degree of freedom vis-à-vis each
of them individually.

In opting for the interests of one class, the state by definition acts
against the rival claim. It is therefore not an "instrument" of any
one of them. Nor can we in this case meaningfully take recourse to
the functionalist Marxist formula of the state as the reproducer of
the social order that upholds the ruling class *as a whole*. The plurality of classes that we are concerned with in the present context does
not constitute a single class, and the functionalist formula too therefore makes little sense in that context. It would not be difficult to
document instances where the state in peripheral capitalist societies
has failed to pursue consistently the interests of any single one of
the three dominant classes—including the metropolitan bourgeoisie, the most powerful of three, for even metropolitan capital (and
the metropolitan state on its behalf) must now *negotiate* with the
state. It cannot impose policies on these states—although it must be
added that the degree of autonomy varies greatly. But crude statements of "dependency" are generally misleading and obscure the
fact that metropolitan capital (of which there are several, competing) often has to accept disappointments or compromises. Its relationship with the postcolonial state is no longer like that of the period
of colonial rule, whether the direct or the indirect variety. This
occurs even in societies where metropolitan capital is not confronted
with competing indigenous fundamental classes. There are many
factors that underlie this new equation of interstate relationships
and the relatively greater degree of freedom of peripheral capitalist states following decolonization—issues that we cannot pursue
here. On the other hand, we must recognize the very considerable
economic dependence of peripheral capitalist societies on metropolitan capital.

The question that we must return to is that of the purposes for
which this relative autonomy of the state, and those at the head of
it, is deployed. Their relative autonomy places unprecedented opportunities for profit at their disposal. These arise in two ways:

First, states under peripheral capitalism deploy, in the name of "development," vast economic resources, often considerably exceeding the amount of private investment. Such resources are drawn in part from a proportion of the surplus value currently generated within the economy, but this is multiplied by resources drawn by borrowing from abroad. This scale of public expenditure establishes an independent economic base and a vested interest for those in command of the state, so that state expenditures and programs cannot always be rationalized and justified by reference to the needs and requirements of the economy and the dominant "fundamental classes."

Demands for state expenditure and the manner of their disbursement are influenced not only by the private benefits those who are in charge of the program derive from them. In part they are influenced also by the collective demands of sections of the state apparatus, most notoriously the military, which has a vested interest in channeling public funds into projects that serve its interests—often to the detriment of the economy as a whole and therefore of the "fundamental classes," which are thereby deprived of resources. Associated with this direct appropriation and use of economic resources, we find the deployment of state power itself vis-à-vis the "fundamental classes" by way of a proliferation of state controls that create a series of hurdles that potential investors must overcome— and that they do by bribing state officials at all levels. This opens up another channel by which those in command of the state apparatus siphon off a part of the surplus for their own private gain.

But both these ways of deploying state power and its command over economic resources can operate only within the continued and unimpaired framework of peripheral capitalism itself. It is within this framework that private gains can be enjoyed. Even more, the enrichment of public officials, politicians, bureaucrats, and the military officers bears its best fruit when they can invest their ill-gotten gains, and for that they must again operate within the framework of peripheral capitalism. Insofar as this guarantees the commitment of the guardians of the state to maintaining the structure of peripheral capitalism, the loss of a proportion of the surplus is a price that the "fundamental classes" pay for the ultimate preservation of their own collective interests. Finally, it must be pointed out that the management of the state and the economy as a whole is itself subject to the "structural imperative." In the final analysis, therefore, state policies must remain within the framework and logic of peripheral capitalism; otherwise those in command of the state would find themselves in the grip of crises that they cannot resolve.

In order to maintain this relative autonomy vis-à-vis the dominant classes (not to speak of the subordinate classes), state authorities in peripheral capitalist societies try to prevent the creation and functioning of effective representative political institutions through which these classes can mobilize to bring pressure to bear upon the state authorities. Even where they nominally exist, parliamentary institutions and political parties atrophy and effective power gravitates into the hands of those who are at the head of the state apparatus—and the bureaucracy and the military rather than the political parties are their primary source of power. India is often cited as the exception, a genuine parliamentary democracy in a peripheral capitalist society. But a close examination of the Indian political system shows that the control of the bureaucracy by those at the head of government has played a far greater role as the basis of state power, including the management of factions within the "ruling party" itself, than is generally (and superficially) acknowledged.[11] Elsewhere the power of the bureaucracy and military is far more blatant.

Military rule is all too often believed to be merely an instance of intensified repression—there are, of course, many instances where the military is brought into power precisely for that purpose (notoriously, Chile). But such a view of the role of the military in peripheral capitalist states obscures three of its crucial aspects: First, civilian and parliamentary regimes by no means preclude a full deployment of the military against struggles and movements of subordinate classes. We may again cite the Indian example, where despite an elected parliamentary government, extreme repression has been used and the military fully deployed for that purpose.[12] In fact, the simple equation of military rule with the unleashing of repression obscures its other, equally important, aspects. One is its *juridical* significance. It is not just that military rule makes possible the use of a greater amount of physical violence against the people, but that martial law supersedes all constitutional and legal constraints. It makes possible arbitrary rule not only with regard to repressive actions but also with regard to "administrative" ones. The military puts itself forward as a law unto itself, needing no other source of "authority." Another aspect is ideological. Here—and there are several historical cases where this has been of central importance—the military genuinely enjoys a degree of "legitimacy" among the common people and puts itself forward as the guardian of the integrity of the state. Until 1971 this was the case in Pakistan, where the military stepped into the political arena at times of political crisis, claiming to rescue the state from "self-seeking politicians." Until its total loss of credibility, the military possessed sufficient "charisma" to enable it to do this. Similarly, we may cite the example of Turkey, where the military has also laid claim, with some effect, to the legacy of the nationalist struggle under the leadership of Kemal Attaturk and by virtue of that claim has been able to step into the political arena with some force of political legitimacy—as an ideological force, therefore, and not merely by virtue of its repressive powers. Such resources of legitimacy are expendable, however, and are quickly dissipated when people see the real face of the military in power. Recognizing this, the more sophisticated among military leaders often prefer to keep a civilian government nominally in office, as long as they themselves hold effective power in the background. But ambitious military commanders do not always allow such considerations to stand in their way, and civilian political regimes all too often prove fragile.

The question of legitimacy in fact is a crucial aspect of any state, for in the long run a state is not viable if it must resort to constant violence against the people. An ideological force is needed. Although the bureaucracy in most peripheral capitalist societies is at the core of state power, inasmuch as it shapes its day-to-day actions (and in the final analysis this is what counts), it is generally unable to legitimize itself and rule in its own name. The role of political parties and variously elected parliamentary assemblies is to provide such legitimacy. But elections open the way for forces from civil society to impinge themselves upon the state to some degree. Where this has led to a crisis, military solutions have been sought. Government by political parties does not, however, necessitate genuine elections or mass mobilization. It is often the case (especially in one-party systems) that the "ruling party" is an empty shell, buttressed by the bureaucracy, which not only sees no need to mobilize mass support but fears it.

Our fourth major question was whether we must view the state only as an entity, one that exists and acts in a variety of ways as discussed above for and on behalf of ruling classes; or whether we can combine that view with a view of the state as a set of institutions that constitute an arena of class struggle. We suggest that both these aspects of the state are necessary to arrive at an adequate conception of the state. In much of the preceding discussion we have in fact referred to the struggle among three contending "fundamental classes," which seek various forms of representation in the state and vie with each other to direct the formulation and implementation of public policy along lines that serve their particular class interests. By that token we have looked upon the state as an arena of class struggle among rival fundamental classes. Likewise, within much narrower limits subordinate classes may also find it possible to establish positions within the political system and the state and achieve a degree of class representation in order to achieve some limited gains—such policies can exist in conditions of electoral politics, where rival parties need to rally some degree of mass support. But the possibilities of such gains by subordinate classes is necessarily limited by the structural imperatives of peripheral capitalism.

We may distinguish certain primary conditions, which follow from the structural imperative and concern the very foundations of the social order of peripheral capitalism. On those there can be no compromise and the state will not yield. On the other hand, it is also possible to conceive of other areas in which there is scope for compromise, and where concessions can be made in the face of mass struggles, concessions which will blunt the thrust of mass movements and, for the fundamental classes, hopefully aid in the orderly incorporation of the subordinate classes into the framework of state power of peripheral capitalism. But that power itself— and its social base—is not transcended; that can only happen if there is a revolutionary rupture and a dissolution of the peripheral capitalist state, along with peripheral capitalism itself.

Notes

1. The U.S. Social Science Research Council Committee on Comparative Politics, under the chairmanship of Gabriel Almond, played a most influential role during the 1960s in extending the application of functionalist theory to the analysis of "developing societies." The central ideas of this approach were spelled out by Almond in his "Introduction: A Functional Approach to Comparative Politics," in G.A. Almond and J.S. Coleman, eds., *The Politics of the Developing Areas* (Princeton: Princeton University Press, 1960).
2. Nicos Poulantzas remains the most outstanding and influential exponent of the political theory of functionalist Marxism. Cf. N. Poulantzas, *Political Power and Social Classes* (London: New Left Books, 1973). For a critique, see Simon Clarke, "Marxism, Sociology, and Poulantzas' Theory of the State" in *Capital and Class*, no. 2 (1977).
3. Nicos Poulantzas, "The Problem of the Capitalist State" in *New Left Review* 58 (1969)—a review of Ralph Miliband, *The State in Capitalist Society* (London: 1969); Ralph Miliband, "The Capitalist State—Reply to Nicos Poulantzas," *New Left Review* 59 (1970); Ralph Miliband, "Poulantzas and the Capitalist State," *New Left Review* 82 (1973).
4. R. Miliband, "Marx and the State," in R. Miliband and J. Saville, eds., *Socialist Register 1965* (London: Merlin Press, 1965).
5. R. Miliband, "Poulantzas and the Capitalist State," p. 85n.

6. Paul M. Sweezy, *The Theory of Capitalist Development* (New York: Monthly Review Press, 1964). Originally published in 1942, this work remains unsurpassed as a clear exposition of Marxist political economy.
7. I.G. Shivjee, *The Class Struggles in Tanzania* (New York: Monthly Review Press, 1976).
8. Michaela Von Freyhold, "The Post-Colonial State and Its Tanzanian Version," *Review of African Political Economy* 8 (1977).
9. Examples of this approach are: John Saul, "The State in Post-Colonial Societies: Tanzania," *Socialist Register 1974* (London: Merlin Press, 1974); Wolfgang Hein and Konrad Steinzel, "The Capitalist State and Underdevelopment in Latin America: The Case of Venezuela," *Kapitalistate* 2 (1973)—both these articles are reprinted in Harry Goulbourne, ed., *Politics and the State in the Third World* (London: 1979), a book that offers a useful collection of articles. It will be clear that Saul's "Nizers" refers to the same class category as Hein and Steinzel's "Patriziat," but they arrive at diametrically opposed conclusions.
10. Hamza Alavi, "The State in Post-Colonial Societies," *New Left Review* 74 (1972), reprinted in Goulbourne, ed., *Politics and the State*.
11. C.P. Bhambri, *Bureaucracy and Politics in India* (Delhi: 1971); Myron Weiner, "India's New Political Institutions," *Asian Survey* 16, no. 9 (1976).
12. Ranajit Guha, "Indian Democracy: Long Dead, Now Buried," *Journal of Contemporary Asia* 6, no. 4 (1976).

[24]
Class, State, and Revolution:
Substitutes and Realities[1]

Teodor Shanin

The radical upsurge of 1968 and its aftermath were linked to and followed by a renewed debate between the socialists about the nature of revolutions and the tactics of revolutionary struggle. A search for the agencies of revolutionary change and an analysis of its impediments formed the crux of a threefold debate. The prospects of social revolution and the search for the revolutionary class of our time have provided the first focus. Those sneeringly referred to by their adversaries as "Third Worldists" opposed "Proletarianists" —to coin an equally ugly term. A second argument cross-cut the first, concentrating on revolutionary organizations and their relation to the classes or "masses"; the issue of a "vanguard" revolutionary party, of a guerrilla "foco," etc.[2] The third problem, the last to be confronted but not the least in importance, has been that of state and revolution, or more specifically of the nature of the state in societies where revolutions have been contained, of the states which revolutionaries challenge, and of the state within which a revolution becomes institutionalized.

The political context that triggered off and fed the debate is not far to seek: 1968 Vietnam, France, United States, China, and Czechoslovakia; the death of both Che Guevara and Allende in the Latin American backyard of the United States; the many "stabilizations" that followed; and the increasing malaise of those craving rapid change yet faced with the strength and violence of the world's many "Establishments." No less significant for the argument were the dramatic lessons in the inadequacies of theoretical thought, "left" and "right" alike: the 1968 wave of radicalism; the split between China and the USSR; the depth of the economic crisis in "the West"; China's Cultural Revolution; the impact of the Organization of Petroleum Exporting Countries (OPEC), Cambodia, Khomeini, or the Ogaden—none of which had been predicted, or even adequately explained *ex post factum*. New events within an increasingly global scene have challenged, exploded, and transformed the structures of our understanding and the boundaries of intuitive plausibility. The exceptional significance of evidence drawn from the so-called developing societies for the reconsideration and redefinition of contemporary social science is consequent on it: tensions between reality and social theory have been most explicit, and the challenge to deduction more illuminating and profound, precisely in those societies.

The Empirical Peasantry and the Hypothetical Proletariat

The reconsideration of established concepts in the light of new, often non-European, developments lies at the core of the post-1968 debate. The discussion of the early 1970s about revolutionary classes and perspectives was both an example of it and an important case in itself. The argument unfolded within the basic framework of the Marxist tradition. This implied a common commitment to change aimed at abolishing the social base of exploitation and domination of human by human. It accepted a sociological perspective whose major components are the determining impact of political economy and of class conflict within social structure. It accepted revolutionary violence as the probable and indeed usual—though not obligatory— way of bringing about the necessary social changes. At this point, however, paths began to diverge.

One group of analysts looked to the "Third World" as the area where revolutionary conditions are ripe and where revolutions, which might develop into socialist ones, are in the cards. The industrial working class of the advanced capitalist societies, on the other hand, was increasingly diversified in numbers and sunk in a complacency, derived in part from the benefits of the imperial spoils. The main weight of global capitalist exploitation fell most heavily upon the "developing societies," in particular on the peasants and the urban poor of peasant background, who together form the major oppressed class(es) there. The established industrial working class in these countries has been privileged in relation to the peasant majority, the poorest urbanites, and the unemployed. It is also relatively small in numbers and will remain so until the imperialist controls that result in "underdevelopment" are broken. Therefore, "the masses in the exploited dependencies," i.e., the underprivileged classes— the peasants, the urban poor, *and* the workers, plus, perhaps, the "intelligentsia"—"constitute a force in the global capitalist system which is revolutionary in the sense Marx considered the proletariat of the early period of modern industrializtion to be revolutionary."[3]

Against this, others stuck to the more orthodox Marxist guns. The most advanced technology, the centers of power and knowledge, lie in the industrial societies, and it is therefore from there that socialism has to be estabished around the globe. It is the social character of the industrial working class—its unity on the shop floor, its skills acquired in dealing with advanced technology, its size, its propertylessness, and its explicit relations of conflict with the capitalists—which make it into the most revolutionary—indeed the only—revolutionary and socialist class of our times.[4]

A closer look indicates that some of the very premises of that comparison were spurious. The peasants of the "Proletarianists' " argument often seem realistic enough, their images backed by political experience and study. It is the image of the proletariat that has remarkably little to do with the actual life of the contemporary working class in industrialized capitalist societies. Indeed, the more one tries to match the real working class with its hypothetical model, the more the model looks either prehistoric, i.e., irrelevant to our times, or ahistoric, i.e., utopian. It is this hypothetical proletariat that outstrips real peasants in its revolutionary and socialist potential.

Let us try to turn this comparison of incomparables into comparative analysis of real social classes in a real world. An article by N. Harris published as part of the third-worldist/ proletarianist debate provides a list of characteristics of the peasantry, or rather, of its political shortcomings—as compared to the proletariat of an industrial metropolis.[5] Let us go through that list, comparing the political characteristics of empirical peasants with those of empirical industrial workers, rather than attempting to deduce them from a "historico-philosophical theory whose supreme virtue," in Marx's words, "consists of being supra-historical."[6]

Peasants in their political struggles tend to fight for land rather than for broader political aims, to be preoccupied with local day-to-day concerns rather than with general long-term aims and complex ideologies. That, no doubt, is true. But so do industrial workers: wages, pensions, and holidays simply take the place of land, rent, and taxes (the name for this limitation of horizons in the revolutionary lexicon is "bread and butter issues," "unionism," or "economism"). Only at long intervals and under conditions of extraordinary crisis have the workers directly attacked the system of property relations by seizing the means of production, whatever the explanation and immediate impulse—in Russia in 1917-1918, in northern Italy in 1919, in Shanghai in 1927. So did Mexican peasants under Zapata, Russian peasants in 1905-1906, and again in 1917-1919, and Chinese peasants in 1926. Both peasants and proletarians in these confrontations dominated the political scene for a short while, were eventually "calmed down" by reforms and/or brutal suppression, and finally lost impetus and impact while different social forces took over.

The workers develop nationwide class consciousness and class organiza-tion, becoming consequently "a class for itself," while the peasants remain disunited and politically naive. (Harris uses the example of the Rus-sian peasants who, while fighting landlords, worshipped the tsar.) The claim that there are important differences between workers and peasants holds true for the reasons indicated, i.e., that working in large industrial structures facilitates organization and self-organization. Not surprisingly therefore, workers have often shown superiority over peasants in organizing nationwide associations and adopting nationwide symbols. But the relationship is anything but one-to-none. The political and revolutionary potential of the workers is by no means constant. We will return to this point shortly. On the other hand, the "green movements" of the peasantry in Eastern Europe between World Wars I and II provide ample proof that peasants have the capacity to consolidate as a class and to create their own organizations through which to fight for political power. Poland, to give a specific instance, has seen powerful peasant parties (the S.L., Piast, etc.), a real peasant prime minister (Witos, who to the horror of his staff was said "not to use handkerchiefs,"), and even, in the 1930s, a nationwide and reasonably successful peasant "general strike." The differences are therefore mainly ones of de-gree and context. Incidentally, the bulk of Russian workers wor-shipped the tsar in 1904 as much as did peasants, as "Bloody Sunday" in January 1905 clearly proved. Only by 1917 had the bulk of the Russian working class finally shed this faith—but by that time so had a crucial part of the peasants.

The peasants do not control their leaders; they are the object and tool, rather than the subject, of political action. That has been true, once again, for peasants and workers alike. The article pointed to the fact that the Communist Party of China was not an agent of the Chinese peasant class, and that its leadership was drawn mainly from the urban intelligentsia; one could add that it was mainly of rural origin and that it directed and utilized the rank and file, at times against the immediate interest of peasants. No doubt this was substantially so. The same seems to apply to the relations between the Bolsheviks and the Russian workers. Lenin's writings (from *What Is To Be Done?* onward), and in particular the type of organi-zation he built, made this clear and legitimized it within the socialist movement as one of the necessities of revolutionary action.

Time has not made that debate obsolete. The essentials of the "proletarianist" view have been repeated with few modifications. Some of the recent writings deconceptualized peasants altogether, labeling them the "rural detachment of the petit bourgeoisie."[7] What is at issue is not simply the social and political characteristics of peasants within different areas and conditions. (Indeed, a similar conceptual denigration could be documented for other social classes and groups in contemporary societies.) The image of the peasant is clearly used as an "antimodel"—an abstraction and a punching bag— in order to elevate the hypothetical proletariat and to justify its monopoly over the revolutionary imagination.

There are reasons why this type of reification—which depends on false comparisons—has persisted within Marxist orthodoxy. Wishful thinking is, as always, one reason—a wish to see change in the world we ourselves live in, since it is industrial workers who form the massive "lower class" in the societies to which Western intellectuals belong. Taken to extremes this turns into the fallacy of dismissing deductively and automatically as "unscientific" any evidence or analysis not reducible to the simple "proletarians are revolutionary" proposition. Secondly, some of these images of peasants result from faithfully following Marx's views of over a century ago. Marx lived in a world in which peasants had formed the majority for millennia, while the industrial working class was only in its diapers, something new, promising, and exciting. During the following century, there was a particularly rapid transformation of urban-industrial society in the centers of world capitalism. Hence, whereas the majority of students of "developing societies" can still recognize contemporary peasants from the picture drawn by Marx in the *Eighteenth Brumaire*, and his comments there seem still remarkably "fresh" and useful,[8] a contemporary industrial worker in Detroit or Coventry is nearly unrecognizable in terms of nineteenth-century descriptions of workers, whether they be by Marx, Booth, Zola, or Dickens. Marx was, after all, a better scholar than a prophet—an epitaph which would no doubt please him greatly. Finally, peasants (and intellectuals) do not fit well into global theoretical structures of elegant simplicity. Those who prefer pure deduction to social investigation do not like them.

The manifest disparity between "proletarianist" images and actual reality does not mean that "peasantism" is the "correct" alternative. Quite the contrary. Recent history has brought into question any belief in a single, natural, and sole revolutionary class. Revolutions have happened. They will no doubt happen again, and provide abundant evidence of class-determined political action. But the same evidence also demonstrates that different classes can be revolutionary, and that the revolutionary potential of the "same" class may vary greatly in different social and historical contexts. That is why one cannot simply deduce revolutionary potential from a general definition. The central question is what are the general conditions under which successful revolutions "from below" occur.[9]

In other words, what must we concentrate on in making such an analysis, what are the component elements, and what are the relationships and contradictions between these components in a general "model" of revolution in which class analysis in a narrow sense constitutes a major and necessary input, but is insufficient on its own.

Model and Context

During the 1968 wave of revolutionary optimism, the discussion of revolution tended naturally to focus on the "revolutionary army," i.e., on those who are, or may become, revolutionaries. It usually underestimated the intrinsic power of the systems of social domination to mobilize resources, to manipulate, and to readjust. Those capacities are not only immense, but still growing, and a more realistic way of putting the questions is, "How do revolutions take place and succeed at all?" rather than, "Why do revolutions not take place more frequently?"

Lenin, a man well versed in the practice, theory, and art of revolution, reminded us that there are two sides to the equation in his remark that revolutions occur when neither the ruled nor the rulers are able to go on living in the old way. That is true, but it needs further specification. If we define successful revolution as a leap (quanta-transformation), involving massive popular intervention, in social structure, property relations, systems of domination, class divisions, as well as in typical forms of cognition, the transformation of the state, and the removal of its rulers, then the processes that preceded and led to revolution have in the twentieth century universally displayed four major characteristics.[10] (1) A major crisis causing severe dislocation of society and its day-to-day functioning; (2) a major crisis of the governing elite, affecting its ability to govern; (3) a crystallization of classes and subclasses expressed in a sharp increase in self-identification, organization, and militancy along class lines; and (4) an effective revolutionary organization providing leadership in the political struggle. A heuristic model would have to recognize that while each of these elements is partly determined by the other three, each must also be analyzed on its own terms, i.e., its own specific characteristics and dynamics.

Revolutions, moreover, are always embedded in an *inter*national context, relevant and often decisive for their outcome. In the most politically direct and analytically trivial sense, foreign intervention can preclude revolution or defeat it; it can also promote it and

)

accelerate it. More significant, if contradictory, is the long-term impact of the world economy and polity, reflected in the fact that all of the internally generated and successful revolutions of our century have occurred in the type of societies we call "developing," i.e., societies at the underprivileged pole in a world capitalist system of inequalities, with consequences for important features of their internal structures. It indicates a particular kind of state, a particular kind of class system, and a particular kind of revolution.

The Epiphenomenal State and the Substitute Bourgeoisie

To return to the four-prong model, the build-up to a revolutionary situation entails a societal crisis that stops or impedes the functioning of structures of domination as well as day-to-day social life, a situation in which, in Mandel's expression, society "fails to deliver the goods." A major economic collapse or a military defeat are the principal obvious cases. The importance of functional breakdown on this scale lies in the impossibility of resolving it by resorting to the coercive and manipulative responses that are effective in a social system that operates "as usual." Only circumstances of the most extreme kind will induce masses of people to engage in a head-on clash with the powers that be, and to endangering safety, livelihood, and lives.

Second, revolutionary situations and prospects reflect the nature and dynamics of the rulers, and in particular the conditions under which the governing elite loses its grip. This deterioration of the ability to govern does not come about simply as a result of an increase in the pressure of revolutionary forces and/or a general social crisis, but has its own partly autonomous logic. The weakness or decline of the dominant class and/or of its direct links with the governing elite are contributory, but, once again, a crisis of governing cannot be reduced to a crisis of class hegemony.

The issue of "state and revolution" relates the two major conceptual clusters referred to above. The contemporary state is the principal machinery of social domination and ordering which links territorially delimited and hierarchically organized social structures with the social group(s) which govern them. Laymen and scholars share the assumption of the state's exceptional significance as the major unit of institutionalized and monopolized power, day-to-day administrative and enforcement procedures, economic action, identification, political mobilization, legitimation, and social reproduction in its broadest sense. A revolution is necessarily a war against the state: "The basic question of every revolution is that of state power."[11] A successful revolution is first of all a victory over the state, and its transformation.

At the core of Marxist tradition lies a challenge to the liberal belief in the parliamentary state as a simple tool for managing society, serving "everybody's" interest evenly within the framework of a "social contract" between rational equals and/or as a neutral computer-like mediator of class interests. The principal alternative view, offered by Marx and Engels, was to approach the state as a tool of class domination, an executive committee of the ruling class. In their work and that of their successors (notably Kautsky and Lenin), the very existence of the state was seen as the product of the irreconcilable nature of conflict in class society, and was therefore limited to class societies. Cases in which those who made policy and managed society did not directly express the will of the dominant class or even challenge it—e.g., under absolutism or Bonapartism—were explained by the transitional balance of class forces that made for the relative autonomy of the state administration, enabling it to play a "balancing" role. This autonomy was always restricted, in the long run, by the interests of the dominant classes. An attempt by Bucharin to ask what the new phenomenon of an increasingly interventionist state might mean for the Marxist theory of the state was rapidly forgotten. Only recently have new conceptualizations of the state, emphasizing its "relative autonomy," been developed in the work of Marxist analysts; these come increasingly to stress the "institutional materiality" of the state, its role in organizing the power bloc of class forces, and its economic functions.[12]

To the Marxist tradition, the postcolonial state has offered therefore a significant analytical challenge. These states seemed to have been "parachuted" by colonial rule and then taken over, lock, stock, and barrel, i.e., in their territorial claims, administration, and legal structures, by "independence movements." A dominant class in the classical capitalist sense of control over the means of production (clearly distinct from the management of the state) often did not seem to exist to any significant extent, e.g., in Tanzania. The first serious Marxist conceptualization of the special characteristics of such states was offered by the term "overdeveloped state": overdeveloped, that is, with respect to its imported characteristics, and as against the relative underdevelopment of its indigenous class structures. In that view, while a state's origins might be colonial, its actual power base and its "relative autonomy" rested on a new class balance between the metropolitan bourgeoisie, which retained its influence, the local bourgeoisie, and the local landlords, who together constituted the dominant class coalition.[13] A much cruder "one-dimensional" version was also offered, in which the power base of such a state was seen simply to be the reflected power and interest of neocolonialism— the state within "developing societies" was merely the local executor of the multinationals and of metropolitan rule—a foreign policeforce speaking the native tongue.

There is no doubt of the major importance of the insights of Marxist analysis, classical and new, referred to above: the functioning of the state as a repressive power in the service of the propertied classes; its role in "developing societies" as a local partner of the multinationals; and the way confrontations and balances of class forces structure and underlie the organization of state power. However, this is an incomplete model, and the experience of "developing societies" offers a significant reason why this should be so. In most Marxist analyses, the state is treated as epiphenomenal, a reflection of underlying class forces, local and foreign, or the setting for their interplay—a conceptual equivalent of the class-neutral state of pluralist theories of society, which acts as a management computer; alternatively, the state is seen as an expression of the structural needs of capital accumulation only. The determinative capacity of the state to shape and reshape society is dismissed or passed over in silence via the conceptual reduction of the state to its assumed class dimensions and/or the functional needs of capital and/ or the impact of imperialism and/or the inertia of the past class and colonial rule. (Within the pluralist paradigm, a similar reduction of the state to a vector of influences, factors, "needs," and rational arguments takes place.) Even the very possibility of considering the opposition between state and dominant classes is at times removed altogether by an image of a state fully tailored to class needs.

There are three fundamental deficiencies in such a line of thought. First, while states can be shown to be shaped, produced, and determined by class interests and action, they have also produced class structures, transformed them, or made them disappear, as when a bourgeoisie or a peasantry has been created by deliberate state policy, as in Kenya, Pakistan, Tanzania, or Brazil. Nor has this happened only in states of the capitalist era. In the China of Chin Shih (third century B.C.), to cite one example, a state-initiated agrarian reform effectively abolished the rural proletariat-cum-serf classes that the polarization and debt-enslavement of the peasantry had created, returning China to "square one," i.e., to a gigantic system of small-holder agriculture serving the imperial interest—a revolution from above in clear contradiction to the immediate interests of the dominant class of the large landowners. Both of the possible routes of determination must thus be considered.

Second, the state is treated as if it operated outside the context of political economy—a laissez-faire utopia that still colors economics as a discipline. A mode of analysis that focuses on political economy and defines it as social production and reproduction, making use of human labor through the control of the means of production to produce surplus value, applies also to the contemporary state. The state operates within the economy in two ways. It works indirectly through taxation, monopolies, monetary policies, the national debt, employment, patterns of spending, and welfare services—a point increasingly incorporated in the theoretical fold. In all those ways the policymaking process structures economic life and redistributes surpluses, which service social functioning, the reproduction of social relations, and social control as well as passing on costs to "the taxpayers," without which the whole contemporary process of capitalist profitmaking would not work.[14] But the state does not just offer "infrastructure" to support or simply reproduce the necessary conditions for capitalism to flourish. It simultaneously operates as a major capitalist enterprise or "holding company" in the direct sense of creating surplus value, cooperating and at times competing with national and multinational capital, aiming at the control of labor, the maximization of profits, and the securing of their privileged use for its personal, i.e., for a specific social group—a "state bourgeoisie" according to some, a "technocracy" to others, an "entrepreneurial bureaucracy" to yet others. Whatever term is used, the contents indicate a social category with specific corporate interests, a position within the process of production, control of surpluses, and strategies of its own. The state and its managers are a politicoeconomic force in terms of resources, production, power, surpluses, and personnel, quite apart from the *extra*economic power which they wield. In "developing societies," the scope of state economy broadens so that typical examples of it would include not only state-owned factories and mines but also state monopolies, e.g., the state boards controlling main export crops, such as coffee in Ghana or cotton in the Sudan, which are bought/extracted cheaply from their producers to be sold dearly on international markets, with the remainder siphoned off for the maintenance of the privileged "state apparatus." Such monopolies add an important exploitative dimension—a gigantic dispersed "manufacture" in Marx's sense, the socioeconomic equivalent of an early bourgeoisie exploiting a smallholder economy.[15] The ways in which any "actually existing" capitalism in a "developing society" is run depend upon the class struggle of exploited and exploiters, on the "structural imperatives" of capitalist profitmaking, and also on the confrontation and compromise within a "triple alliance" of local property owners, multinational companies, *and* those who control the state economy in its indirect *and* direct sense.[16]

Third, "state" and "state apparatus" are at times treated as two separate phenomena, an analytical distinction elevated into an assumed social reality, i.e., "state" is depicted as an abstraction of "us all," served by "civil servants," while "state apparatus" simply serves its extrastate masters, who are the only determinant of the political scene. The direct manifestation of the "state" is the "state apparatus," and, analytical divisions apart, the one without the other belongs where disembodied spirits do. Marx's description, adopted by Lenin, of the "organs" of the state provides a good initial list of the bureaucratic core organizations but also reflects that description's historicity and initial limitations. It included "standing army, police, bureaucracy, clergy and judiciary."[17] The necessary additions today would include the administrators of the economy, welfare, education, the mass media, and possibly the ruling party. The last four are, arguably, exchangeable for the "clergy" of Marx's designation; the first is notably absent in his list. The sum total of the "organs" is a system of controls, legitimation, and privileges, but also of human beings organized, selected, and reproduced according to partly autonomous rules. To a great extent the social reality and "materiality" of the state lie here. Furthermore, the bureaucratic system of hierarchical supervision and promotion means the concentration of power in the hands of a relatively small group, with its specific characteristics, internal life, the potential for interchange between its different sectors, ideological patterns, and consciously established strategies—a governing elite in direct control of the "state apparatus." The term "elite" has often been challenged, especially by Marxists, and is often treated as an eclectic admixture that threatens verbal orthodoxies. It has some considerable limitations which must be kept in mind, but it is still the only term for which no substitute as yet exists, one which denotes a real enough social phenomenon, i.e., the characteristics of a small, internal, linked group at the top of major bureaucratic structures, and wielding power through them.[18]

Attempts to analyze developing societies have produced another image, one as unrealistic as the notion of the state as "epiphenomenal." It is the image of the state's total independence of, and supremacy over, the rest of the social matrix—the faith in the manipulative omnipotence of the state typical of many modernizers of the 1950s and 1960s. International experience has since eroded much of the confidence that easy and quick solutions will result once the correct plan or advice has been adopted (and its "twin" belief that the failure of a strategy is simply the result of mistakes or treason).

A revolution begins with an attack on the state/state apparatus. The very "revolutionary situation" is a consequence of the state's failure to contain revolutionaries: to manipulate or suppress opposition, to "run" its administration and economy. With few exceptions, it also means the collapse of unified strategy, and often of nerve "at the top." What also seems to be necessary is the establishment of alternative political focuses of authority to those of the state. That is why a centerpiece of a revolutionary situation is the fragmentation of the governing process, which challenges the state's monopoly of it in what Trotsky called "dual power" and Charles Tilly refers to as a "situation of multiple sovereignty"—a political and ideological "base" outside the spheres of domination and control by the "organs" of the state.[19] We shall return to this presently.

The nature of so-called developing societies has accentuated some of the general aspects of state organization: the significance of the state economy and of the state bureaucracy are made more obvious by the weakness of the native bourgeoisie and/or the low "classness" of the other social classes. The state is often the main employer and the main source of economic enterprise in what is at times referred to as "state capitalism"—a capitalist economy run by noncapitalists. It may mean a process of eventual transformation of state bureaucrats into "capitalists." It is never only that. The oppressive nature of state intervention through "revolutions from above" is particularly salient in "developing societies." So are the exceptionally high levels of exploitation and social polarization. The special political characteristics—the military regimes' brutality of oppression and instability—are not an aberration but reflect the specific nature of the state in "developing societies." The less secure its control, the more visible the oppressive nature of the state.

The social structure of "developing societies," their characteristically "uneven" development, the "disarticulation" between aspects of social and economic structures, the relatively weak domination of the ruled by the rulers (with the ruled excluded from political life rather than politically incorporated), and the immense concentration of control at the "top" lead to rapid and erratic changes within the political elite—plots, coups d'état, assassinations. The relative weakness of the state's grip offers opportunities when a revolutionary organization, weak as it may be, faces a political elite, a state, and a dominant class that prove even weaker. The politics of global dependency, the class nature of "developing societies," and the character of the state in these societies explain why every successful self-generated revolution for over a century has taken place in a "developing society."

Class and Classness

Within the main European tradition of class analysis, social classes are treated as the major subgroups of contemporary society, defined by their common basic interests and their position in the system of political economy, expressed in a distinctive consciousness and shaped by conflict relations with other classes.[20] The most illuminating aspect of this analysis lies in its insights concerning the relation between the objective and the subjective in political action. Group interest and group consciousness are mediated by social conflict, which leads to the crystallization of a class as a recognizable and self-recognized entity, i.e., a "class for itself." It means also that the revolutionary character of a social class is historical, i.e., relative and changing. Insofar as a "class" in its full meaning is defined as a self-conscious social category rooted in the ways political economy works, we must assume and consider different and changing levels of its coherence and powers of determination. The problem is not only one of class, but also of the extent of "classness."

The attempt to pinpoint the revolutionary class of our time has often rested on an analogy that runs as follows: just as the bourgeoisie overthrew feudalism, with the advance of the new and more plentiful forces of production, so will the proletariat, in due time, overthrow capitalism and build a new world in its own image, i.e., a classless society. Both the metaphor and the extrapolation are wrong. Feudalism was *not* overthrown by its main class of exploited producers, i.e., the peasantry, but by classes representing new social characteristics and located in the relatively independent towns. (That was of course also true in the past—it took Stalin's brazen illiteracy to claim that a slave revolt overthrew Rome.) If an antifeudal revolution is to be used as a model, we would not look to the "blue collars" of today as the class that is to make a revolution. But analogies, right or wrong, do not validate theories. Their validation, such as it is, lies with analysis of reality. Let us look at the industrial workers of today in those terms.

Paul Sweezy provided an analysis of the development and contemporary position of the working class that has been largely ignored. It deviates from the unidirectional interpretation of the Marxian "class in itself"/"class for itself" duality,[21] suggesting instead a typical three-stage pattern of development. In a simplified form it runs as follows. In the first stage, a conservative technology of a handicraft system—"the manufacture"—was linked to an essentially conservative working class of assembled craftsmen. In the second stage (which Marx observed in England and France), revolutionary breakthrough in technology and the new social relations introduced by industrialization gave rise to a massive and fairly homogeneous proletariat and the possibility that a powerful revolutionary push by them might result in revolution, e.g., England in the 1840s, France in 1848 and 1871, Russia in 1905 and 1917. However, when and if revolutions fail to mature, a new situation begins to develop. The tremendous rise in productivity means for the working class of contemporary industrial societies,

> a sharp reduction in their relative importance in the labor force,...the proliferation of new job categories, and...a gradually rising standard of living for employed workers. In short, the first effects of the introduction of machinery—expansion and homogenization of the labor force and reduction in the costs of production (value) of labor power (i.e., its standards of living secured through organization)—have been largely reversed.

All this, together with increased social mobility, means that "once again, as in the period of manufacture, the proletariat is highly differentiated; and once again occupational and status consciousness has tended to submerge class consciousness."[22] The significance of that historiography for the understanding of revolution is obvious. It makes sense of the influential socialist metaphor of the turn of the century about revolution "moving east"—from England to France, then to Germany, then possibly to Russia, China, and "the Orient." By that token, workers in the "developing societies," especially those in the industrialization upsurge (as well as their opposite numbers within the socialist "developing societies" of today), would have the highest potential for revolutionary action. The scenario sounds realistic.

What is the historical experience of relevance for contemporary peasants? The Taiping revolt in nineteenth-century China was a forerunner of a new lease of revolutionary life for the peasantry, which truly begins in the countryside of Russia in 1905-1907 and in Mexico in 1910. This new revolutionary spirit spread through many peasant lands with the crisis of "modernization" and the pressure of the market, of the state, and of hegemonic cultures transferred from elsewhere. Eric Wolf has pointed to the fact that in all of the six main political upheavals of our century—Mexico, Russia, China, Vietnam, Algeria, and Cuba[23]—peasant revolt was central. He explains this by a triple crisis: a demographic crisis, an ecological crisis, and a crisis of authority, leading to, and making effective, a new peasant militancy, despite the handicaps of segmentation, dispersal, and technological backwardness. It was the "middle" (economically) and the "tactically mobile" peasants of the geographical fringes, i.e., those who preserved more of the specific peasant characteristics, who formed the core of such rebellions, at least initially. The revolutionary potential of peasant hostility toward landowners, town dwellers, and the state has proved extraordinarily powerful in our times, even if its results have been anything but a peasant utopia on earth. The specific characteristics of peasant political action are too complex to be discussed en passant, and such an analysis has been attempted elsewhere.[24] Its important political assets are size, spread, localized "roots," and food production—all facilitating guerrilla struggle. As against those assets stand the social limitations already mentioned. Once again, the historical nature of analysis must be remembered. The changes within the peasantry under the impact of capitalism also means at some stage its destructuration, i.e., its disappearance as a class.

The revolutionary potential of workers and peasants has often been debated. It may be useful to broaden that list. When considering classes in terms of their historical promise for revolutionary action, one should remember first a variety of other classlike entities referred to, if noticed at all, as strata, groups, or subclasses.[25] These may be the remnants of classes that are disappearing or the first nuclei of new class formations. National and racial minorities in some circumstances display patterns of political action that resemble the model of classes-in-themselves developing within systematic conflict into classes-for-themselves, especially when these are ethnoclasses, i.e., groupings in which ethnic and class specificity are linked. Finally, a particularly important revolutionary role has been played by a number of transient social groups that show classlike characteristics, i.e., common interests, way of life, patterns of cognition, and related self-consciousness that provide a basis for unity of political action. The very rise of such groups often reflects social crisis. Russian soldiers in the 1917-1918 period, students on university campuses in some countries and periods, the "city poor" of Algeria's casbah in the 1940s, the "educated young men" in Ghana when Nkrumah rose to power, and the Iranian peasant-workers in construction projects in 1979 provide a variety of examples. It was the ability of revolutionary elites to build coalitions of classes and of such groups that was crucial in the revolutionary struggle. These groups are "unstable," i.e., in constant flux, but then so are revolutionary situations.

This brings us to the issue of "intellectuals," who can be identified in terms of formal education, the role they play in the social division of labor and the specialization of "mental" as against "manual" aspects of social production and reproduction. One trouble with this group is that it does not fit well into Marxist class analysis and yet keeps popping up as a major component of every revolutionary situation with which Marxists are deeply concerned. The basic yardstick of "relation to means of production" fails to identify intellectuals at all, and in the USSR of the 1930s they were officially declared a service substratum of any ruling class.[26] That was quite in line with later conceptualizations, such as that which categorizes them as owners of "cultural capital," and as such barely distinguishable from the bourgeoisie. Gramsci, in his search for a more realistic theory of revolution and political action, suggested that every social class "creates within itself, organically, one or more groups of intellectuals who give it homogeneity and consciousness of its functions," but he also recognized sociocultural continuity as the work of the "traditional" type of intellectuals "who carry over the symbolic systems and cultural framework established in the past." Importantly, while defining intellectuals in terms of their specialized social functions, Gramsci opposed "looking for distinguishing criteria within the sphere of intellectual activity rather than of the whole general complex of social relations within which their activities...are to be found."[27] Those cryptic prison notes have barely been improved on theoretically.

One must distinguish once again between intellectuals in industrial societies and those in "developing societies." In the first, their function and position link them to a continuum of "free professions," "white collar" office workers, technicians, etc. The boundaries of such a group are vague, its internal cohesion doubtful, and its diversity increased by the essential individualism of the type of work specific to them. Some of them perform the functions of legitimation for those who rule and operate a variety of cultural forms of social control, e.g., the official "media," performing the task of Gramsci's "egemonia" as against domination by direct coercion. Yet on the other hand, the functional and formal commitment of intellectuals to "rationalism" and/or "creative freedom" necessarily leads to conflict between some of them and the organized irresponsibility of the contemporary state. These conflicts are basically unresolvable within existing social systems, making intellectuals more responsive to demands for a full-scale overhaul of society. Also, things have changed considerably since the nineteenth-century image of a few intellectuals who, by virtue of sheer numerical insignificance, cannot do much more than influence others. The number of students in France of 1968 was greater than the number of workers in General Motors, then the world's largest capitalist industrial enterprise. In some situations intellectuals have been known to move as a group into direct, massive, and effective political confrontation, as the U.S. anti-Vietnam war and antisegregation organizations have shown.

The position of intellectuals in "developing societies" has been often cited as the very epitome of the conflict situation and of marginality. Though they are the direct result of the "diffusion of knowledge" from industrial societies, these intellectuals cannot be treated simply as an "educational phenomenon." They go through ten to twenty years of systematic training along "Western" lines, which makes for a sharp division from the majority of their own people, yet they are alienated from the metropoles as well. As "organic intellectuals" they are a class-creation transplanted into places where the very classes they represent have often failed to materialize. In these conditions especially, they may form a relatively autonomous social entity with a classlike character. (Looking at the "English-speaking class" of contemporary India or Singapore, one is even tempted to call them an "ethnoclass.") They are very aware of the world outside the "developing societies" and of the social "backwardness" at home, yet are unable to bring about the changes believed necessary. In the permanent atmosphere of political crisis within "developing societies," access to and the art of literacy (and at times poetry), to the technology of publications, and to forums of speech give them a particularly powerful social resonance. Some of the "educated" are absorbed into the ruling group, while others resolve their personal frustrations by emigrating. However, such personal solutions often prove impossible, and not only for material reasons. Subject to powerful and overlapping conflicts, their social marginality, their consciousness of crisis, and their feelings of shame (Marx once called shame "a revolutionary sentiment") produce the commitment to social change and the readiness to sacrifice necessary in revolutionary action. It is not accidental that it is the Russian word "intelligentsia" that is usually used to define a politically conscious and committed intellectual stratum in a revolutionary situation; the category of "young intellectuals" introduced by C. Wright Mills may also be useful here.[28]

Students (already referred to as a transient classlike group) display the basic qualities of an "intelligentsia," which puts them at odds with the "existing system" but adds some sociopolitical qualities that often turn them into a spearhead of revolutionary struggle. Physically and intellectually, the campus provides a unifying base that helps to overcome the social atomization of the intellectuals. At earlier stages of socialization, the crass stupidity and brutal cynicism of social arrangements (not least within the very structure of the university) impress more strongly, while temporary and partial detachment from control by family, bureaucratic networks, and career requirements may increase militancy. The impact of university "degrees" on their future careers and the temporary character of the student phase place limits on this process. However, such limitations are never fully effective, and while student numbers rapidly outrun any predictions, continuing conditions and traditions introduce every generation anew to radical ideas and/or political struggle.

No list of components (of social classes, in our case) is sufficient to understand a totality and how it "works"; but analysis of basic components is necessary and each of them cannot be reduced to the logical deduction from a totality, i.e., "a society," a mode of production, etc.[29] In our case, the nature of the totality discussed is assumed, if partly submerged, due for discussion in another text. For lack of a better word, it is global capitalism in its specific "developing societies" representation, the "peripheral capitalism" of most recent terminology.

Permanent Vanguard and Revolutionary Class

The belief in the necessity of a revolutionary vanguard, supreme to and apart from the "class" in cohesion, consciousness, and organization, yet related to it, of "Jacobins indissolubly joined to the organization of the proletariat which has become conscious of its class interest," forms the essence of Lenin's tactical heritage and more importantly of his success as a revolutionary.[30] It developed further Kautsky's idea of the necessary injection of scientific thought and its proponents into the working class to help it to establish its socialist "self." It also absorbed the preoccupation of the German Social-Democrats, from the time of Engels onward, with efficiency, science, and large-scale organization which become synonymous with socialism of the future. The very idea of a "vanguard" constituted a basic revision of classical Marxism as expressed in the last section of the *Communist Manifesto*. Developed within the social context of Russia—the first "developing society" of the day and under a highly oppressive regime—it grew out of a specific revolutionary experience. Gramsci's *Modern Prince* attempted to update this analysis for the more "advanced," more complex, more democratic, and "more capitalist" societies, an issue still very much under debate— indeed, increasingly so.

The class/vanguard interdependence, i.e., the two last factors in the "model" of successful revolution suggested in the second section above, has been the centerpiece of the post-Marx new revolutionary experience, its successes and failures. Yet attempts to distill that experience have been remarkably limited, especially insofar as the comparative analysis of relevant evidence is concerned. A recent article by M. Waltzer reveals a refreshing disrespect of traditional icons, and takes up a debate begun by Rosa Luxemburg seventy years ago but often forgotten since.[31] The author compares the revolutionary vanguards of different revolutions, beginning with the Puritans in seventeenth-century England, and singles out their common qualities: conceptual cohesion supported by systematic schooling, zealous activism, a discipline rooted in self-imposed control (both individual and collective), and a deeply egalitarian ethos. He then considers the diverse impact of the vanguard's special characteristics on these revolutions, e.g., the length of the Puritans' prerevolutionary activity and organization as against the relative newness of the Jacobins in eighteenth-century France. Next he turns to the key question of the power relations and possible conflicts between the "class" and the "vanguard." He shows that it is the underdevelopment of classes which underlies vanguard dictatorships. Moreover, in his view a vanguard often consciously aims at preventing the independent development of a class, e.g., substituting new emergency goals once the revolution is won.

Waltzer's main conclusion is that the "Period of Terror" of the French Revolution was the dictatorship of the Jacobin vanguard, while the "Thermidor" was the passing of power to the dominant class of the revolution. The author states, therefore, his case for Thermidor as a victory of the revolutionary class over its vanguard, replacing that vanguard and creating a new society after its own image. Thermidor is seen as the fulfillment of the Marxist vision of a revolutionary class free to shape its revolutionary regime without tutelage—a challenge, if there ever was one, to Lenin's and Trotsky's usage of the word "Thermidor" as the symbol of counterrevolution in Russia.

Waltzer's argument seems overgeneralized by far, his "revolution" embracing Puritans in 1640 and the Vietcong in the 1960s. Without specifying the types of society in question, his conclusions claim too much (and possibly too little). Further, the study is unrelated to the earlier debate between Rosa Luxemburg and others and is thereby impoverished. Yet the issue of the specific dynamics of a revolutionary elite and the problem of its interdependence and interaction with its "class" or "masses" is central to the revolutionary process. The low "classness" characteristic of "developing societies" makes this interaction particularly important there. Also, a realistic study of that field challenges a major source of radical mystification— the verbal and analytical substitution of a revolutionary elite for class(es), especially for those class(es) that do not quite come up to the revolutionary mark or fail to materialize at all.

What often follows is the substitution of a committee of a few men for the vanguard, crowned by the leader's substitution for the committee. We are only at the beginning of an understanding of the phenomenon of the "party of cadres" organization, its internal dynamic, and the ways it is interdependent with its following of supporters. What is already clear is that one must distinguish different types of class political participation in accordance with the role played by the "vanguard" parties. Spontaneous, amorphous, and massive class action, without national leadership or organization, has at times proven effective, e.g., the resistance of the peasants in Russia in 1905-1906 and 1919. Another category of class action is that in which an oppressed social class produces "from within" its own leaders and organizations to lead it into revolutionary action, e.g., Zapata in Mexico. More important is the fact that there has never been a case in which a twentieth-century revolution was ultimately victorious in those ways. Revolutions may also be won through a third category of class action—a "guided class action" in which a class was led and controlled by a revolutionary elite of relative outsiders, with their own conceptions of reality, organization, and corporate interest. No simplistic answer or dismay will suffice here. The revolutionary martyrology explains that well enough. Lenin insisted on the necessity of an elite of professional revolutionaries to lead the working class into socialism and became the first head of a socialist regime. Rosa Luxemburg made clear the intrinsic dangers to socialism of such an organizational framework and died in prison. Political success determines (at times misleadingly) the ways we treat leaders, theories, and theorists.

Substitutes and Realities

The turn of the century has seen a new type of revolution, which commenced in Russia in 1905 and has since spread rapidly. Its social context has come to be described as that of "developing societies." It is new in its global setting, with characteristic class structures, forms of state organization, and types of social crisis. It has been conceptualized, by revolutionaries and counterrevolutionaries alike, in theoretical terms drawn from the past, mainly from Western and Central Europe in the nineteenth century, and especially from the Parisian experience of 1848 and 1871. All of the successful revolutionary leaders of the twentieth century have fundamentally revised their views in the course of their political practice, but the theory of revolution on the part of practitioners and of social scientists alike has lagged behind. The main product of this lag has been conceptual blindness, in which social realism is systematically sacrificed to terms that mislead and run counter to the evidence, but fit grand theories and presupposed schemes. That is the type of analysis in which illusionism is dressed up and comes to inhabit make-believe worlds, where a hypothetical proletariat, a nonexistent peasantry, and an intangible intelligentsia, in lieu of a revolutionary class, face an epiphenomenal state ruled by classes one cannot find or by a military dictatorship treated as "bourgeoisie" —an unending chain of mystifications. At the roots of the contemporary debate among socialists about classes, states, and revolutions lies this tendency toward reification and verbal substitution posing as radical theory. To confront it not only clears the air for realistic analysis, but serves socialism as well.

But what about a *socialist* revolution? A proper answer to that cannot be attempted here, but we can offer a few notes as a step toward further debate. To begin, the initial success of any socialist revolution would carry the characteristics of the revolutions discussed above, whatever its additional qualities might be. Next, at the risk of sounding tautological, the only irreplaceable and absolutely necessary element in socialist revolution, in the light of past experience, are the socialists who execute it: their commitment, their ability to see reality, and their capacity to build up powerful mass alliances, using every crack in the social system of domination and exploitation. Furthermore, the class nature of the revolutionary agencies of change necessarily differs between the initial stage of the struggle (against the prerevolutionary state) and the periods that follow. The most severe of all the problems of socialist revolution has proven to be not how to make it, but how to keep it socialist in the sense that word carries in the socialist classics. We seem to have to learn that daily, invariably taken by surprise. In real terms, we still know very little about the social mechanisms operating within revolutionary states and/or societies ruled by socialists, yet that is the crux of the matter insofar as socialist revolution is concerned. Moreover, realistic analysis of postrevolutionary societies is necessary if we are to understand and demystify issues like state, class, party, planning, or social transformation in the nonsocialist "developing societies" too.

To conclude, for socialists the suggested analysis calls not for conceptual evacuation of the social battlefields by the working class (and/or consequent despair), but rather the recognition that the industrial working class was never innately and eternally placed there. Class militancy is relative, and this goes for every class in historical reality. Simple solutions do not work: a proletarian revolution does not necessarily produce socialism, nor does socialism equal proletarian rule. The "laws of motion" and the unfolding crisis of capitalism on a world scale are central to any analysis of the possibility of socialism, and explain the constant challenge of revolutionary forces, but that does not mean that these will result in an inevitable grand finale with an optimistic and rational outcome.

Socialism is not some imminent "promise" or law of nature, but a possibility, something to be fought for. The first view might be anxiety reducing, but the second is more realistic. It means that socialists will not have socialism delivered to them by "laws of history" or natural revolutionary classes or their substitutes, but will have to rely heavily on themselves, their own militancy, their readiness to make sacrifices, and not least their capacity to understand the world they live in and to offer alternatives that will work both as revolutions and as socialist societies. That is precisely what makes realistic analysis more politically relevant than the histrionics of propaganda, even for the best of causes. It means that in the struggles for social justice, the specific social context of the "developing societies" will be particularly important. It means, finally, that the struggle for socialism is going to be more complex, more difficult, and more bitter than our predecessors expected, and that defeat is possible. Let us face that fact and get on with the job.

Notes

1. This paper is based on an earlier polemical paper published as "Class and Revolution: The Empirical Peasantry, the Hypothetical Proletariat, and the Evasive Intelligentsia" in the *Journal of Contemporary Asia* 1, no. 1 (1972). The first, second, and fourth sections follow it closely. Elsewhere considerable changes have been introduced or, in places, a completely new text and analysis offered.
2. Dramatized by Régis Debray, *Revolution in the Revolution* (New York: Monthly Review Press, 1967).
3. Paul M. Sweezy, "The Proletariat in Today's World," *Tricontinental* 9 (1968): 33.
4. For example, Ernest Mandel, "The Laws of Uneven Development," *New Left Review* 59 (1970).
5. N. Harris, "The Revolutionary Role of the Peasants," *International Socialism* (December/January 1969). See also a reply by Malcolm Caldwell, "The Revolutionary Role of the Peasants," in the same issue.
6. For the full text, see the beginning of the second section of this essay.
7. For example, an article by James Petras, "Revolutions and the Working Class," *New Left Review* 111 (1978), in which the specificity of the

"developing societies" was essentially disregarded, the revolutionary capacity of the proletariat assumed to be innate, and any public way to prove or disprove it dismissed as self-evidently unnecessary, indeed slanderous of the subject matter. The quotation is taken from J. Ennew, P. Hirst, and K. Tribe, "Peasants as an Economic Category," *Journal of Peasant Studies* 4, no. 4 (1977). For a different view, see Teodor Shanin, "Defining Peasants: Conceptualizations and De-Conceptualizatons," *Peasant Studies* 14, no. 4 (1980).

8. Karl Marx and Frederick Engels, *Selected Works* (Moscow: 1973), vol. 1, especially pp. 478-83.

9. "Revolution from below" in the sense attached to the phrase in Isaac Duetscher, *The Great Contest* (London: 1960), i.e., when popular mass intervention plays a major role.

10. We shall not go into the debate over definitions of what revolutions are. For a recent summary of a large range of different theories and definitions of revolution, see A.S. Cohen, *Theories of Revolution* (London: 1975).

11. V. Lenin, "Dual Power," *Collected Works*, vol. 24 (Moscow: 1963-1968), p. 38.

12. See, for discussion, Ralph Miliband, "Marx and the State," *Socialist Register 1965* (London: Merlin Press, 1965). The paper anticipated the further development of the concept of relative autonomy by Nicos Poulantzas, *Political Power and Social Classes* (London: New Left Books, 1973 [first published in 1968]).

13. See Hamza Alavi, "The State in Post-Colonial Societies," *New Left Review* 74 (1972). Also John Saul, *State and Revolution in East Africa* (New York: Monthly Review Press, 1979).

14. For an illuminating discussion, see James O'Connor, *The Corporations and the State* (New York: 1974), who has also advanced the very useful analysis of the capitalist state, distinguishing its accumulation/legitimation and conflict-regulation, but has little to say about what we have called "state economy" in its "direct sense." For work along similar lines, see C. Offe, "Political Authority and Class Structure," in P. Connerton, ed., *Critical Sociology* (Harmondsworth: Penguin Books,1976).

15. The discussion follows an analysis presented in V. P. Danilov, L. V. Danilova, and G. V. Rastyanikov in *Agrarnye Struktury Stran Vostoka* (Moscow: 1977).

16. For discussion of the idea of "structural imperatives" see the preceding paper by Alavi. For the actual mechanism of economic interdependence, see Peter Evans, *Dependent Development: The Alliance of State, Multinationals, and Local Capital in Brazil* (Princeton: Princeton University Press, 1979).

17. From Karl Marx, "The Civil War in France," *Selected Works*, vol. 2, p. 217, adopted verbatim in V. Lenin, *State and Revolution, Collected Works*, vol. 25, p. 418.

18. Consider C. Wright Mills, *The Power Elite* (New York: 1956) and its possible extension to societies with different social structures.

19. See, for discussion, Rod Aya, "Theories of Revolution Reconsidered," *Theory and Society* 8, no. 1 (1979).
20. For an exemplary discussion, see S. Ossowski, *Class Structure and Class Consciousness* (London: 1963).
21. Karl Marx, *The Poverty of Philosophy* (Moscow: 1958), p. 166.
22. Sweezy, "The Proletariat in Today's World," p. 30.
23. Eric Wolf, *Peasant Wars of the Twentieth Century* (New York: Harper & Row, 1969). A somewhat different approach to the issue of the revolutionary potential of different peasant substrata is taken by Alavi in "Peasants and Revolution," *Socialist Register 1965*.
24. Teodor Shanin, "Peasantry as a Political Factor," *Sociological Review* 14, no. 1 (1966); reprinted in Teodor Shanin, ed., *Peasants and Peasant Societies* (Harmondsworth: Penguin Books, 1971). The concept of "classness" and the taxonomy of class actions discussed below were introduced there for the first time.
25. For example, the "lumpen-proletariat" as discussed by Bruce Franklin in *Monthly Review* 21, no. 8 (1970), and Peter Worsley, "Frantz Fanon and the Lumpenproletariant," *Socialist Register 1972*.
26. Stalin's speech on the constitution of the USSR in *Problems of Leninism* (Moscow: 1945).
27. Antonio Gramsci, *The Modern Prince* (New York: 1968), pp. 129, 119-20, and 120-21.
28. C. Wright Mills, "The New Left," in *Power Politics and People* (New York: 1963). For a good discussion of the Russian intelligentsia, see I. Berlin, *The Listener* (May 2, 1968). For recent discussion of major relevance, see Eric Hobsbawm, "Intellectuals and the Labour Movement," *Marxism Today* (July 1979). For another view see an old yet by no means outdated collection of J. Kautsky, *Political Change in Under-developed Countries* (New York: 1967), especially the papers by Shils, Benda, Matossian, and Watnick.
29. One cannot improve on the formulation by Marc Bloch: "The knowledge of fragments, studied by turns, each for its own sake, will never produce the knowledge of the whole; it will not even produce that of the fragments themselves. But the work of reintegration can come only after analysis. Better still, it is only the continuation of analysis...." *The Historian's Craft* (Manchester: 1954). p. 155. For a discussion of the epistemology involved see Shanin, "Defining Peasants." For a different approach or stress, see the paper by Leys which follows.
30. For discussion see V. Lenin, "One Step Forward, Two Steps Backwards," *Collected Works*, vol. 7, and Rosa Luxemburg, "The Role of Organization in Revolutionary Activity," *Selected Political Writings* (New York: Monthly Review Press, 1971).
31. M. Waltzer, "A Theory of Revolution," *Marxist Perspectives* (1979). The earlier paper referred to is Luxemburg, "The Role of Organization."

[25]
Samuel Huntington and the End of Classical Modernization Theory

Colin Leys

In the conceptual fragmentation and conflict that has overtaken development studies, the leading place often seems to be held by the "dependency" or "underdevelopment" theorists. This school first became widely known in the West toward the end of the 1960s, particularly through the polemical attack led by Andre Gunder Frank on U.S.-dominated "modernization" theory. Since then the *dependentistas* have been severely criticized in their turn by Marxists, but there would appear to have been no serious reply from the orthodox right.

This appearance is deceptive, however, especially in the United States, and perhaps above all among political scientists in the U.S. sphere of influence—which is still a considerable one. It is true that the ideologists of developmentalism had no answers to the devastating critique of Andre Gunder Frank, Susanne Bodenheimer, and others.[1] However, their "paradigm-enforcing" powers were immense. For a long time the *dependentistas'* attack was simply ignored.[2] Instead of a scientific debate, there was a retreat from confrontation with anti-imperialist theory, while efforts were made to consolidate a major transformation in imperialist development theory that was already under way when the onslaught by Frank and others occurred. This was a shift to a concern with the maintenance of *order*. The revolution in Cuba, followed by the accumulating humiliation of U.S. policy in Vietnam and the revolutionary instability and increasing reaction in Latin America and South Asia, undermined the original optimistic assumption of orthodox development theory: that the process of development involved drawing the populations of the Third World out of their traditional isolation into a modern social system that would be participative, pluralistic, and democratic. A growing number of U.S. social scientists began to recognize that this was not in fact the destiny of Third World countries developing in the framework of U.S. imperialism ("leadership"). Increasingly, their thinking turned from a concern with the processes of "modernization" (the processes of transformation into advanced, capitalist, and hence pluralist and democratic societies) to a concern with the maintenance of social *control*.[3]

Yet a complete break with the theoretical apparatus inherited from the optimistic phase of development ideology was neither practicable nor desirable. The need was to transform that apparatus—whose central animating concept was *modernization*—in such a way as to incorporate the new concern with maintaining order and, wherever possible, at the same time "co-opt" the more persuasive themes of dependency theory and even Marxism itself. How this task has been carried out, in various branches of theory, lies beyond the scope of this essay. What is attempted here is to bring out the general nature of the ideological reconstruction involved by examining the work of one political scientist who, more than any other, led the way in initiating it.

"Modernization"

In order to explain Samuel Huntington's contribution, it is first necessary to sketch the main elements of "modernization" theory itself.

The distinction between "traditional" and "modern" societies was derived from Max Weber via Talcott Parsons. A society was called "traditional" in which most relationships were "particularistic," rather than "universalistic" (e.g., based on ties to particular people, such as kin, rather than on general criteria designating whole classes of persons); in which birth ("ascription") rather than "achievement" was the general ground for holding a job or an office; in which feelings rather than objectivity governed relationships of all sorts (the distinction between "affectivity" and "neutrality"); and in which roles were not clearly separated: for instance the royal household was also the state apparatus ("role diffuseness" vs. "role specificity"). A society in which the opposite of all these was true was "modern."[4] Other features generally seen as characteristic of traditional societies included things like a low level of division of labor, dependence on agriculture, low rates of growth of production, largely local networks of exchange, and restricted administrative competence. Again, modern societies displayed the opposite features.

"Modernization," then, referred to the process of transition from traditional to modern principles of social organization, and this process was what was currently occurring in Asia, Africa, and Latin America.

From today's vantage point it is easy to see that the traditional/modern distinction was at bottom simply a pair of very arbitrary abstractions from the contemporary situations of the periphery and the center (respectively) of the world capitalist system; and that the concept of modernization was no more than a proposal to consider the former as a once-universal original state and the latter as a universal end state, with the so-called modernization process serving as a (quite fictitious) surrogate for the historical processes that have actually taken place, or are taking place, at both the periphery and the center. However, those political scientists who were unaware of the ideological nature of these formulations saw in them the basis for an attempt to conceptualize "*political development*" as "one element of the modernization syndrome," i.e., the modernization process itself at the level of politics.[5] This gave rise to a multiplicity of proposals: "political development," it was suggested, involved democratization, political "mobilization," the "building" of nation states, administrative and legal development, secularization, equality, "subsystem autonomy," etc., etc.

According to Huntington himself, the starting-point for his own theorizing was a rejection of the concept of "political development" because it indeed had no clear meaning.[6] In its place he proposed to discuss merely political *change*. If this had been true, it would have implied at least an attempt to break with "modernization" theory. But it was not true. In his main book, *Political Order in Changing Societies*, published in 1968, a central place is occupied by the concept of "political decay," a condition signalized by unrest, violence, corruption, and coups, and one which retains all the normative and teleological content of the concept of "political development," only expressed as its *opposite*.[7] And this continuity, this preservation of the essential concepts of modernization theory but in forms adapted to the new concern with order, is, as we shall see, a fundamentally significant aspect of Huntington's thought. However, in three respects Huntington did make a major break.

First, he really did switch attention to a kind of political change— *revolution*—which was the central issue of contemporary Third World politics. Previous writers had, remarkably, largely failed to do this. The concepts with which they proposed to analyze Third World politics were thinly disguised abstractions from the pluralist interpretation of U.S. politics, according to which politics consists of incremental adjustments to the evolving balance between competing interests, mediated by competing electoral machines which "aggregate" the interests of "groups" drawn from all "strata" of society. In Huntington's conception of politics, by contrast, the central place was given to potentially revolutionary struggles for state power by radically discontented social forces—workers, students, urban "middle classes," peasants, etc. Huntington's view of Third World politics seemed above all *realistic*.

Second, Huntington's work seemed genuinely theoretical. It was very difficult to extract from the previous literature on "political development" anything that really proposed explanations of large-scale, important political phenomena. There were more or less elaborate classificatory systems or typologies, but very little usable theory. Huntington, by contrast, offered to explain, among other things, why pressures for change assumed a reformist or revolutionary character, why reforms or revolutions succeeded or failed, and why, in the absence of either reform or revolution, Third World countries tended to pass under personal, arbitrary, and authoritarian rule ("praetorianism").

These two changes have a lot to do with the academic and practical influence of Huntington's work. Attention has been diverted from them, however, by the third departure that Huntington made from previous orthodoxy: his open and abrasive commitment to the maintenance of order as the supreme political value. As Donal O'Brien has shown, Huntington's views on this issue were not very different from those of numerous other leading U.S. political scientists of the later 1960s, but they were more "stringently and unambiguously expressed."[8] Throughout his work there runs a strong current of dislike for the confusing, disturbing, and contradictory aspirations of the masses, and an admiration for any "elite," bureaucracy, or "leadership" capable of containing, channeling, and if necessary suppressing them. We shall return below to the significance of the particular form taken by Huntington's obsession with authority. For the moment, however, the important point is that it was in *spite* of this, as much as because of it, that Huntington's work achieved the influence it did. Refreshing as it might be to many members of the beleaguered U.S. professoriate in 1968, the open fear of, and distaste for, the masses that Huntington expressed was hardly a viable posture for most of them.[9]

Huntington's Argument

Conventional wisdom among both social scientists and policymakers in the United States, Huntington noted, held that the poorer people are, the more prone they will be to use violence to remedy their situation (the more "unstable" politics will be). Accordingly, U.S. policies toward the Third World had, at least in theory, been directed toward securing economic growth in the belief that this, coupled with reforms made possible by growing output, would lead toward political "stability." But according to Huntington, the statistical evidence shows that there is more stability in countries with the lowest per capita incomes than in countries somewhat less poor. Huntington's interpretation of this is that as "modernization" (defined as "social mobilization plus economic development") occurs, more and more people become politically active, or become active in ways that impinge more and more on the central government ("political participation"), because increased social mobility leads to raised expectations which at an early stage of economic growth cannot be met. Economic growth also leads at first to heightened inequality, which also prompts greater "political participation." Unless political institutions are capable of handling this expanded "participation," it will assume destabilizing forms (demonstrations, strikes, riots, or even armed struggle) and/or lead to corruption (equally liable to give rise to instability in the long run).

What determines whether the increased "level of participation" produces these destabilizing consequences or not is the degree of "institutionalization" of the "polity." Strongly institutionalized polities socialize (i.e., formally and informally induct) the newly participant citizens into the channels and norms of political action that are prescribed by the existing structures. This leads to "civic" politics. "Civic" politics may or may not take a democratic form: "constitutional democracies and communist dictatorships are both participant polities."[10] Participation, in other words, need not (and Huntington thinks should not) mean popular control of government, but rather governmental control of the people through their "involvement" in the organs of the "polity" that make this possible. Weakly institutionalized polities, on the other hand, are easily overwhelmed by new "groups," which enter politics ("participate") on their own terms, giving rise to "praetorianism," in which "the wealthy bribe, students riot, workers strike, mobs demonstrate, and the military coup" [sic].[11]

Praetorianism—of which military rule is the usual *form*—may easily degenerate into chaos. In such a situation, revolution may become the only possible form of *lasting* political change—because only a social movement capable of making a revolution will be capable of establishing a new, durable political order. Revolution, then, is for Huntington a form of political change that results from a severe discrepancy between the scale of the forces newly participating in politics and the capacity of political institutions to assimilate or contain them.

Revolutions are not, according to Huntington, primarily about economic issues: "A revolution is a rapid, fundamental and violent domestic change in the dominant values and myths of a society, in its political institutions, social structure, leadership and government activity and policies."[12] "Ascending or aspiring groups and rigid or inflexible institutions are the stuff of which revolutions are made."[13] The conditions leading to revolution are the simultaneous "alienation" from the existing political order of the urban middle class and the peasantry, and their ability to collaborate, usually on a nationalist program. These conditions are rarely adequately met, however, because of the tendency of the urban middle class to become more conservative as it grows larger, and because of the basic divergence of aims between it and the peasantry. The endpoint of revolution is "the creation and institutionalization of a new political order"; "the measure of how successful a revolution is is the authority and stability of the institutions to which it gives birth."[14] In this respect the communists have proved the most successful revolutionaries, because Leninism equipped them with an effective theory of political organization and so made possible a new political order in which mass participation is combined with "a government really able to govern."[15]

The important question about any *reform*, for Huntington, is not its merits per se but simply whether it averts revolution or acts as a catalyst for it. The Alliance for Progress in Latin America was based on the idea that reforms would avert revolution. Huntington, however, thinks that in some circumstances reforms may have the opposite effect. In particular, reforms that respond to the demands of the urban intelligentsia make revolution *more* likely because the intelligentsia are revolutionary from "psychological insecurity, personal alienation and guilt, and an overriding need for a secure sense of identity":[16]

> Programs catering to the demands of the radical middle class only increase the strength and radicalism of that class. They are unlikely to reduce its revolutionary proclivities. For the government interested in the maintenance of political stability, the appropriate response to middle-class radicalism is repression, not reform.[17]

By contrast, reforms catering to peasant demands can avert revolution, because

> no social group is more conservative than a landowning peasantry, and none is more revolutionary than a peasantry which owns too little land or pays too high a rental. The stability of government in modernizing countries is thus, in some measure, dependent upon its ability to promote reform in the countryside.[18]

Such, in the barest outline, is Huntington's central argument. Let us now examine it more closely.

A Critique

To grasp the significance of Huntington's work we have to analyze it on two levels: first, from the standpoint of bourgeois social science, and second, from that of historical materialism.

Huntington's Work as Social Science

(1) *As social science theory.* One commentator, reviewing Huntington's argument six or seven years later, called it "an elegant, simple, lucid and promising theory."[19] In fact, on closer inspection it proved to be vague, tautologous, circular, and confused. Its two central concepts, "participation" and "institutionalization," were nowhere adequately defined. "Participation" included, apparently, any kind of conscious relationship whatever with the polity, no matter how ritualistic or empty, since, as we have seen, Huntington declared that today's Russians have "a high degree of popular participation in public affairs."[20] Conversely, "institutionalization" was defined as "the process by which organizations and procedures acquire value and stability," but this process was nowhere specified either. Instead, Huntington put forward four "measures," or tests, of the "level of institutionalization of any political system": the adaptability, complexity, autonomy, and coherence of its organizations and procedures. Adaptability, Huntington suggested, could be measured by the *age* of an organization or procedure: "The probability that an organization which is one hundred years old will survive one additional year...is perhaps one hundred times greater than the probability that an organization one year old will survive one additional year."[21] A moment's thought shows that this is absurd. Presumably recognizing this, Huntington added that another measure is the ability of an organization or procedure to survive challenges to its existence. Thus tsardom, passing the age test with flying colors, failed the "challenge" test in 1917. But the challenge test, in this case, was a revolution—i.e., an "explosion of participation."[22] So the theory seems to state that revolutions occur when the institutionalization of the "polity" is insufficient to handle the scale of participation, and the evidence that it is insufficient is that revolutions occur—i.e., it is circular. Huntington, however, suggests yet a third measure of adaptability, the ability of an institution (organization or procedure) to abandon challenged functions and replace them with others and so survive. But this reasoning too is circular. The evidence that an institution is adaptable is that it changes functions and survives; the evidence that it is not that it fails to change

functions and comes to an end. Tsardom and the French monarchy failed, Huntington says, while the British monarchy succeeded, in finding something else to do but practice absolutism.[23] The evidence of failure is once again the success of revolution, with the same circular consequences.

The other measures of institutionalization (complexity, autonomy, and coherence) suffer from exactly the same difficulty. Thus the measure of "autonomy" is whether social forces "outside" the political system succeed in forcing themselves "into" it or not; the measure of coherence is whether the institutions of the polity rest on a consensus sufficiently strong to preserve them; and so on.

In short, the thesis that political change is a product of the relation between participation and institutionalization turns out to be spurious because "institutionalization" is defined in terms of the response of institutions *to* "participation" (whatever *that* means). It is not possible to catalogue here the multiple other shortcomings of Huntington's argument considered as theory, nor is it really necessary: they have been carefully pointed out by others, though in muted, not to say somewhat deferential, terms.[24]

(2) *Evidence*. Part of the reason for the failure to push home the criticism of Huntington's work as unscientific may well have been the massive quantity of facts deployed in it. "Dazzlingly comprehensive"... "his empirical knowledge seems encyclopedic"—most readers, like these reviewers, are intimidated by a great show of scholarship, and Huntington spared no effort to achieve one. The range of cases referred to, and the number of sources cited, were indeed impressive, even for a writer amply endowed with research assistance.

But it is obviously not the quantity but the quality of the factual evidence, and the use made of it, that matters. The reader with some knowledge of any part of the Third World soon finds, for example, that the use made of materials relating to that area leaves a great deal to be desired. Thus when seeking to illustrate the rule that "the longer a nationalist party fought for independence, the longer it was able to enjoy the power that came with independence," Huntington says that "TANU and its predecessor had a 32-year history when Tanganyika became independent."[25] But TANU's predecessor (the Tanganyika African Association) could hardly be said to have "fought for independence" before it was transformed into TANU. Or, to take a very different example from the same text, when it is a question of illustrating the functional adaptability of political institutions the British monarchy is cited, but when it is a question of distinguishing form from content, "Britain preserved the form of the old monarchy, but America preserved the substance. Today America still has a king, Britain only a crown."[26] The careful reader soon realizes that the great flood of information with which he or she is being presented cannot be taken on trust. The central thesis—that stability is due to a high ratio of institutionalization to political participation—is supported by citing evidence from a study that compared "26 countries with a low ratio of want formation to want satisfaction and hence low 'systemic frustration' and 36 countries with a high ratio and hence high 'systemic frustration.' "[27] Remarkably enough, one of the twenty-six "satisfied countries" was the Union of South Africa. The thought eventually occurs that the quality of the data used may be inversely related to the quantity supplied. Formidable as it is, the volume of data too often serves precisely to dazzle, not to illuminate. Furthermore, the observant reader also notices, sooner or later, that the usual relation between the evidence presented and the hypotheses put forward is that of illustration. The effect is to make the hypotheses appear plausible, not to test them. It is difficult to find any point on which the author tries to identify cases that would constitute potentially "disconfirming" instances for the hypothesis in question, as the textbooks on methodology prescribe.

A few attempts have been made to test the empirical validity of Huntington's argument using the kind of cross-national statistical comparisons favored by the behavioral school to which the modernization theorists in general belong. One found a strong correlation between the ratio of social mobilization to institutionalization and political instability and violence, another found no correlation between them, and a third "unhappily reported the difficulties of selecting the correct indicators, partly due to 'the thoughtful but ambiguous formulation of key theoretic concepts' by Huntington."[28]

(3) *Scientism.* Of course, many other well-regarded works on politics may be faulted for poor evidential support. What makes this criticism more than usually pertinent is that Huntington's use of evidence so often takes a *scientistic* form. This is particularly true of the sections of *Political Order* in which the main steps of the argument are put forward. The main form of scientism is pseudo-quantification. The text abounds with propositions about "the levels of middle class participation," "the rate of increase of social frustration," "the degree of corruption," and so on. This way of writing encourages acceptance of an argument by suggesting that appropriate quantitative data have been collected that verify the general statements made.

When relevant data are cited, this sometimes appears to serve to disguise a serious circularity in the argument. For instance, the statement that "the faster the enlightenment of the population, the more frequent the overthrow of the government" is based on an alleged positive correlation between the rate of change of primary school enrollments and "instability."[29] The fact that there was almost certainly a similar correlation between the rate of growth of police forces and instability in the countries studied reminds us that the evidence cited only serves to support the conclusion drawn if one already accepts—on other grounds—a theory that indicates a causal connection between the rate of increase in school enrollments and revolution. Yet it is to support the plausibility of such a theory that the correlation is adduced ("the relation between social mobility and political instability seems reasonably direct").

At other times data are cited that in no way justify the lawlike conclusion drawn. For example:

> Burma and Ethiopia had equally low per capita incomes in the 1950s: the relative stability of the latter in comparison to the former perhaps reflected the fact that fewer than 5 per cent of Ethiopians were literate but 45 per cent of the Burmese were. Similarly, Cuba had the fourth highest literacy rate in Latin America when it went communist, and the only Indian state to elect a communist government, Kerala, also has the highest literacy rate in India. *Clearly*, the appeals of communism *are usually* to literates rather than illiterates.[30]

In these examples, the quantitative form of the statement does refer to quantitative data. In other cases, however, there are no such data to refer to: the alleged relation is pure invention. For instance: "In general, the higher the level of education of the unemployed, alienated, or otherwise dissatisfied person, the more extreme the destabilizing behavior which results."[31]

To what kind of audience is reasoning of this sort addressed? The answer is painfully clear: it could only be addressed to the U.S. graduate school victims of a behavioralist *déformation professionelle* —people who have been taught to regard a statistical correlation as the epitome of proof, and not to be too concerned about the real meaning of the statistics in question, or too clear about the logic connecting any such correlation to an argument.[32]

Taken as a whole, Huntington's method is less that of inquiry than of propaganda, and when the context is borne in mind, it strongly recalls Marx's distinction between the scientific inquiries of the classical economists and their mid-nineteenth-century successors:

> In France and England, the bourgeoisie had conquered political power. From that time on, the class struggle took on more and more explicit and threatening forms, both in practice and in theory. It sounded the knell of scientific bourgeois economics. It was thenceforth no longer a

question of whether this or that theorem was true, but whether it was useful to capital or harmful, expedient or inexpedient, in accordance with police regulations or contrary to them.[33]

Huntington's Work as Ideology

The problem that remains to be considered is why Huntington's work, with so many serious, not to say fatal, deficiencies of logic, methodology, and factual support, should have become as influential as it did.[34] The essence of the matter is this: Huntington revitalized the ideology of modernization—i.e., that *partially* adequate, but systematically mystified, view of the ex-colonial world that formed the basis for imperialist strategic action—in a highly significant way.

First, as already mentioned, he broke the connection that "modernization" had previously had with U.S. pluralism. Second, he appropriated some of the central terms of Marxism, while simultaneously appearing to invert Marxism's tenets.

The break with pluralism was more than the mere abandonment of the democratic ideal implicit in earlier modernization writing. For Huntington, Third World societies do not consist of groups competing, in fluctuating and shifting combinations, for influence over the "outputs" of government; nor do "modern" systems differ from "premodern" or "modernizing" systems in this respect. In all political systems, the key is domination, or as Huntington says, "power": "Power is something which has to be mobilized, developed, and organized. It must be created."[35] Huntington therefore wastes no time looking for the functional equivalents in the Third World of "interest articulation" and "interest aggregation," for example, as earlier modernization theorists did. For him, the central reality everywhere is the building of regimes capable of imposing their will on society. The basic problem of most Third World countries is that they lack such regimes. Even those who hesitated to endorse this latter view (especially since Huntington thought this was the United States' problem too) could see that his conception of politics was much better adapted than the pluralist model to the conflictual realities of the Third World, from General Geisel's Brazil to Indira Gandhi's India—or, indeed, Castro's Cuba.

This brings us to the relation between Huntington and Marxism. In considering this, it must be borne in mind from the outset that Huntington's theory was not coincidentally, but directly and intimately, connected with the war in Vietnam. From 1966 to 1969 he was chairman of the Council on Vietnamese Studies of the U.S. Agency for International Development's South-East Asia Advisory

Group, and in 1967 he visited Saigon on behalf of the State Department "to investigate ways in which political power could be developed in Vietman."[36] The following year—the year in which *Political Order* was published—he wrote an article in which he explicitly interpreted the Vietcong's success as due not to its ideals but to its ability to impose authority in rural areas where authority was lacking:

> There is little evidence to suggest that the appeal of the Viet Cong derives from material poverty or that it can be countered by material benefits.... The appeal of revolutionaries depends not on economic deprivation but on political deprivation, that is, on the absence of an effective structure of authority.[37]

According to Huntington, the authority of the Vietcong in the rural areas was unlikely to be overthrown, but on the other hand, the U.S. entry into the war in 1965 had led in the following three years to about 3 million people fleeing the countryside for the cities, where they came under the authority of Saigon. Huntington considered that as a result, the possibility of successful revolution in South Vietnam was being undercut because "the good Maoist expectation that by winning the support of the rural population, it [the Vietcong] could eventually isolate and overwhelm the cities" was being invalidated by "the American-sponsored urban revolution."[38] The answer to wars of national liberation was, therefore, "forced-draft urbanization and modernization which rapidly brings the country in question out of the phase in which a rural revolutionary movement can hope to generate sufficient strength to come to power."[39]

If this article revealed starkly the political thrust of the 1968 book, it is equally important to stress that defeating the *revolution* in Vietnam did not, for Huntington, necessarily entail defeating the *Vietcong*. On the contrary, he accepted that the Vietcong's power in the rural areas could not in practice be destroyed, and he proposed that a negotiated peace settlement be based on this fact, and that the Vietcong-National Liberation Front should be encouraged to "enter the political process" through participation in electoral politics, at first locally and eventually on a national level: "If as a result of this process the VC-NLF secured control of the Central Government, the United States would obviously regret the outcome but could also accept it and feel little compulsion to re-intervene."[40]

In other words, Huntington carried his antirevolutionary outlook to its logical conclusion by separating it from anticommunism. For him, it was the ideal of a fundamental reconstruction of society that was pernicious, because utopian and destructive of order.[41] He did not see the Vietcong as a revolutionary force in this sense, but as a force potentially capable of imposing order. The lesson that Third World countries such as Vietnam needed to learn—how to build and impose authority—could, he said, be learned in Moscow and Peking and not in Washington.[42] Indeed, far from being anticommunist, Huntington expressed almost unqualified admiration for the political regimes of Stalin and Mao, criticizing Stalin only for weakening the party from 1936 onward, and Mao for launching the Cultural Revolution.

This practical insight—that *it was not communism, not even as embodied in the Vietcong, that was the real enemy, but revolution, to which the bureaucratized Communist parties were equally opposed*—was what Huntington's book developed ideologically, by a double process. First, Marxism—the theory and practice of the emancipation of labor—was treated dismissively, as a *partial* theory ("Marx focussed on only one minor aspect of a much more general phenomenon...") and as politically naive ("Lenin was not a disciple of Marx, rather Marx was a precursor of Lenin.... Marx was a political primitive...").[43] In place of Marx, Huntington elevated Lenin and "Leninism"—which, however, turned out to be Stalinism: "Marxism, as a theory of social evolution, was proved wrong by events; Leninism, as a theory of political action, was proved right.... Lenin laid down the prerequisites for political order.... In Leninism the party is not just institutionalized; it is deified."[44] Very few of Huntington's U.S. readers would know the difference; one cannot be sure that Huntington knew it himself. The important point was, in any case, that "Marxism" was wrong.

Second, in "accepting" Leninism (read: Stalinism) simply as an up-to-date and efficient doctrine of authority, Huntington was able to accept (or rather to appear to accept) what most previous modernization theorists had been at pains to ignore—social classes and revolutionary movements—as central phenomena of Third World politics. In effect, Huntington seemed to be taking over the well-known Marxist concepts for dealing with Third World realities while dispensing with—or even inverting—the revolutionary theory in which they were normally contained. Moreover, Huntington demonstrated how this could be done without making any significant change in the essential structure of the ideology of modernization. What this implies is that what he appropriated from Marxism was not its concepts but only a selection of the connotations of the terms denoting these concepts—connotations which he then attached to *different* concepts, compatible with the rest of the ideology.

The essence of this process can be illustrated from virtually any part of *Political Order*. Take social classes. For Marx, social classes were the prime movers of history, formed through struggles within and over specific relations of production inherited from the past. The analysis of the formation, organization, alliances, defeats, and victories of revolutionary classes and their antagonists, and of the gradually developing consciousness of their interests and historical tasks, constituted for Marx a tightly bounded and intricate theoretical and empirical task, with all-important implications. By contrast, Huntington's concept of class entails no such consequences. The classes or groups he writes about (he more often uses the latter term) are not considered as the products (let alone the makers) of determinate historical relations of production. They appear as empirically "given" universal categories (though a somewhat mixed bag—lumpen-proletariat, industrial workers, middle-class intelligentsia, landowners, peasants), which are assumed to exist more or less everywhere. They are no more than occupational or socioeconomic aggregates, mere reservoirs of potentially "participant" *individuals*, who may or may not be "mobilized" by "elites." Huntington's Third World may thus seem to contain social classes, but they are conceived in such a wholly ahistorical, unanchored, empiricist way that virtually anything may be said about them without excessive fear of contradiction.[45]

This enables Huntington to appear to accept Marxist concepts while simultaneously "disproving" Marxism. An obvious example is his discussion of the "lumpen-proletariat," a term taken directly from Marx, but referring in Huntington merely to the newly immigrant urban "poor"—a concept as distant from Marx's as it is vague. Huntington's main point about this "lumpen-proletariat" is that is is "on the surface, the most promising source of urban revolt," but that in fact, in the 1960s it did not prove to be so.[46] Probably most of Huntington's readers would have been surprised to know that (1) Marx's concept of the lumpen-proletariat had very little to do with the urban "poor"; and (2) Marx considered the lumpen-proletariat to be the natural ally of reaction, and Engels made noncooperation with the lumpen-proletariat a point of political principle for the working class.[47] In other words, Huntington, by appropriating Marx's term but attaching it to an altogether different concept, was able to give the appearance of sophistication and realism, and to seem to be "disproving" Marxism, while in reality attacking a not very plausible straw man. Huntington's treatment of "industrial workers" (the proletariat?), the "middle classes" (petty bourgeoisie?), and "peasantry" proceeds in the same fashion. The reduction of the Marxian concept of "classes" to the concept of mere "economic groups" permits discussion to be divorced from any consideration of the actual historical conditions in which they have been and are developing, the actual course of their struggles, the role of imperialism in those struggles, etc.

In effect, Huntington introduces "classes" into the ideology of modernization simply as forms in which the *masses* threaten the maintenance of *order*; and their capacity to do so, in his formulation, is already given by the "institutionalization" of the "polity," i.e., in practice, by the capacity of the "regime" (which never has a class character) to co-opt, deflect, or repress this threat. As Henry Bernstein aptly remarks:

> The determining model of modernity, from which everything else follows, is itself non-problematic as it is already "given" by the historical development of the West. This mode of conceptualization can only produce answers that are already determined by the way in which questions are posed.[48]

Similarly with "revolution." Marx's concept is historical, and carries a very specific socioeconomic content: for him, a revolution is always a specific process of transition through which a particular country or region passes, from an epoch dominated by one mode of production (such as feudalism or capitalism) to a new epoch dominated by a new mode of production. For Huntington, however, "revolution" refers (as we have seen) simply to any "rapid, fundamental, and violent change." For historical materialism, the question of whether a revolution can or will occur in a given society at a given moment, and what its significance or historical "content" may be, is always a problem of analyzing the development of the *contradictions* to which the existing mode of production gives rise, and their expression in class struggles; whereas for Huntington, revolutions are merely pathological modes of restoring order. Thus instead of Marx's concept, embedded in a theory for assessing the prospects for particular class alliances to make particular transformations of particular societies, Huntington's concept makes revolutions mere aberrations in the global march toward the mass consumption society, to which the whole of modern history is ultimately reduced by modernization theory.

In Conclusion

Huntington thus revitalized the ideology of modernization in several ways at once. He offered a crude but substantive phenomenology of classes-groups, power struggles, revolutions, corruption, militarism, and the like, important parts of which seemed to be taken over from a simultaneously discredited Marxism, and all of which could be—in the form given by Huntington—integrated into the ahistorical and protean schema of tradition-modernity. As scientific theory it was false. As propaganda it was crude, though not necessarily ineffective, especially within the closely patrolled intellectual confines of most U.S. political science departments. But as a model of ideological reconstruction it was pathbreaking, a dramatic example of the "ideological flexibility of which bourgeois thought is capable," and one which was to have a profound influence on bourgeois thinking about development in the 1970s.[49]

Notes

1. Andre Gunder Frank, "The Sociology of Underdevelopment and the Underdevelopment of Sociology," *Catalyst* (Summer 1967), also in Frank, *Latin America: Underdevelopment or Revolution?* (New York: Monthly Review Press, 1969), pp. 21-94; Susanne J. Bodenheimer, "The Ideology of Developmentalism: American Political Science's Paradigm-Surrogate for Latin American Studies," *Berkeley Journal of Sociology* 15 (1970): 95-137; Gail Omvedt, "Modernisation Theories," in A. R. Desai, ed., *Essays on Modernisation of Underdeveloped Countries*, vol. 1 (Bombay: 1971) Henry Bernstein, "Modernization Theory and the Sociological Study of Development." *Journal of Development Studies* 7 (1971): 141-60.
2. As far as I can tell no review of Frank's first three books (all published in the United States) has ever appeared in the *American Political Science Review*, *Journal of Politics*, *World Politics*, *Comparative Politics*, or *Economic Development and Cultural Change*—the last of these being the journal whose school of thought Frank explicitly attacked in his celebrated 1967 critique of the modernization perspective.
3. For this context see the excellent early commentary by D.C. O'Brien, "Modernization, Order, and the Erosion of a Democratic Ideal," *Journal of Development Studies* 7 (1971): 141-60; also M. Kesselman, "Order or Movement? The Literature of Political Development as Ideology," *World Politics* 26 (1973): 139-54.
4. Parsons, *The Social System* (New York: 1951), pp. 58-67; also Frank, "Sociology of Underdevelopment," pp. 24-25.
5. "The Change to Change: Modernization, Development, and Politics," *Comparative Politics* 3 (1971): 283-322.
6. Ibid., p. 301.
7. An earlier statement of the central argument of the book was entitled "Political Development and Political Decay," *World Politics* 17 (1965): 386-430. The continued presence of the concept of "political development" in the 1968 book is also marked by the fact that the term itself often recurs too: e.g., pp. 7, 192, 398, etc. Huntington's later claim to have dropped it was quite spurious.

8. O'Brien, "Modernization, Order," p. 368.

9. The open advocacy of counterrevolutionary positions by U.S. academics following Huntington's example in the early 1970s tended to seem ridiculous in the context of the successive defeats for U.S. power in the Third World; see, e.g., Nelson Kasfir, "Departicipation and Political Development in Black African Politics," *Studies in Comparative International Development* 9 (1974): 3-25, and Norman H. Keen, "Building Authority: A Return to Fundamentals," *World Politics* 26 (1973-74): 331-52. Henry A. Landsberger and Tim McDaniel ("Hypermobilization in Chile, 1970-1973," *World Politics* 28 [1975-76]: 502-41) concluded that: "Historically, mobilization seems to have been more of a hindrance, i.e., a 'bad thing,' than a help to radical governments, at least after the old centers of power have been weakened with its help. The real problem is then whether 'the masses' can be controlled. If the government has enough coercive power to do that . . .it may not need to mobilize the masses in the first place."

10. Huntington, *Political Order in Changing Societies* (New Haven: Yale University Press, 1968) p. 89.

11. Ibid., p. 196.

12. Ibid., p. 264.

13. Ibid., p. 275.

14. Ibid., p. 266.

15. Ibid., p. 342.

16. Ibid., p. 371.

17. Ibid., p. 373. Those interested in the principle of value-freedom in social science should note that Huntington is careful only to draw this conclusion for governments interested in the maintenance of political stability. By implication, those interested in their own overthrow could disregard it.

18. Ibid., p. 375.

19. Gabriel Ben-Dor, "Institutionalization and Political Development: A Conceptual and Theoretical Analysis," *Comparative Studies in Society and History* 17 (1975): 310.

20. Huntington, *Political Order*, p. 1.

21. Ibid., pp. 13-14.

22. Ibid., p. 266.

23. Ibid., pp. 15-17.

24. See Ben-Dor, "Institutionalization and Political Development"; Dean C. Tipps, "Modernization Theory and the Comparative Study of Societies: A Critical Perspective," *Comparative Studies in Society and History* 15 (1973): 199-226; Kesselman, "Order or Movement"; and Dexter W. Lehtinen, "Modernization, Political Development, and Stability," *Stanford Journal of International Studies* 9 (1974): 219-45.

25. Huntington, *Political Order*, p. 425.

26. Ibid., p. 115.

27. Ibid., p. 55.

28. Michael C. Hudson, "Conditions of Political Violence and Instability: A Preliminary Test of Three Hypotheses," *Sage Professional Papers in*

Comparative Politics 1, no. 5 (1920): 252-53; cited in Ben-Dor, "Institutionalization and Political Development," p. 316, where he also refers to R. and A.L. Schneider, "Social Mobilization, Political Institutions, and Political Violence: A Cross-National Analysis, *Comparative Political Studies* 4 (1971): 69-90. The study that found no correlation is Lethinen, "Modernization, Political Development, and Stability."

29. Huntington, *Political Order*, p. 47.
30. Ibid., p. 49. My emphasis.
31. Ibid., p. 48.
32. As is well known, the highest form of statement in the behavioralist canon is a probability statement. Huntington's use of the term "probability" on p. 42 of *Political Order* is instructive.
33. Postface to the second ed. of *Capital*, vol. I (Harmondsworth: Penguin Books, 1976), p. 97.
34. A survey of U.S. professors in 1974 found that *Political Order* was the book most often cited as among the "most important in the field"; see H.C. and M.C. Kenski, *Teaching Political Development and Modernization at American Universities: A Survey* (Tucson: University of Arizona Press, 1974), pp. 9-10.
35. Huntington, *Political Order*, p. 144.
36. John Gretton, "The Double-Barrelled Character of Professor Huntington," *Times Educational Supplement* 29 (June 1973), p. 10.
37. "The Bases of Accommodation," *Foreign Affairs* 46 (1968): 644.
38. Ibid., p. 650.
39. Ibid., p. 652. Perhaps these events are already sufficiently remote for it to be necessary to remind the reader that the "American-sponsored urban revolution" and "forced-draft urbanization and modernization" refer to the saturation-bombing and scorched-earth techniques by which the United States and the Saigon regime attempted to deny the countryside to the Vietcong, at an estimated cost of 2 million killed or wounded and 8 million refugees—out of a total South Vietnamese population of some 16 million.
40. Ibid., pp. 655-56.
41. Huntington, *Political Order*, p. 371.
42. Ibid., pp. 137-38.
43. Ibid., pp. 37 and 336.
44. Ibid., pp. 337-39.
45. Huntington's use of "class" is evidently closer to Weber's than to Marx's, but is not rigorously based on Weber's usage either.
46. Ibid., pp. 278-83.
47. Engels, "Prefatory Note to *The Peasant War in Germany*," Marx-Engels, *Selected Works*, vol. I, p. 646.
48. Henry Bernstein, "Sociology of Development vs. Sociology of Underdevelopment?," in D. Lehmann, ed., *Development Theory: Four Critical Essays* (London: Frank Cass, 1979).
49. Ibid., "Conclusion": Bernstein's penetrating essay should be read by everyone interested in the process of construction and reconstruction of bourgeois social science.

[26]
The Death of Salvador Allende

Gabriel García Márquez

It was toward the end of 1969 that three generals from the Pentagon dined with five Chilean military officers in a house in the suburbs of Washington. The host was then-Lt. Col. Gerardo Lopez Angulo, assistant air attaché of the Chilean Military Mission to the United States, and the Chilean guests were his colleagues from the other branches of service. The dinner was in honor of the new director of the Chilean Air Force Academy, Gen. Carlos Toro Mazote, who had arrived the day before on a study mission. The eight officers dined on fruit salad, roast veal, and peas, and drank the warmhearted wines of their distant homeland to the south where birds glittered on the beaches while Washington wallowed in snow, and they talked mostly in English about the only thing that seemed to interest Chileans in those days: the approaching presidential elections of the following September. Over dessert, one of the Pentagon generals asked what the Chilean army would do if the candidate of the left, someone like Salvador Allende, were elected. Gen. Toro Mazote replied: "We'll take Moneda Palace in half an hour, even if we have to burn it down."

One of the guests was Gen. Ernesto Baeza, now director of national security in Chile, the one who led the attack on the presidential palace during the coup last September and gave the order to burn it. Two of his subordinates in those earlier days were to become famous in the same operation: Gen. Augusto Pinochet, president of the military junta, and Gen. Javier Palacios. Also at the table was Air Force Brig. Gen. Sergio Figueroa Gutiérrez, now minister of public works and the intimate friend of another member of the military junta, Air Force Gen. Gustavo Leigh, who ordered the rocket bombing of the presidential palace. The last guest was Adm. Arturo Troncoso, now naval governor of Valparaíso, who carried out the bloody purge of progressive naval officers and was one of those who launched the military uprising of September 11.

That dinner proved to be a historic meeting between the Pentagon and high officers of the Chilean military services. On other successive meetings, in Washington and Santiago, a contingency

350

plan was agreed upon, according to which those Chilean military men who were bound most closely, heart and soul, to U.S. interests would seize power in the event of Allende's Popular Unity party victory in the elections.

The plan was conceived cold-bloodedly, as a simple military operation, and was not a consequence of pressure brought to bear by International Telephone and Telegraph. It was spawned by much deeper reasons of world politics. On the North American side, the organization set in motion was the Defense Intelligence Agency of the Pentagon, but the one in actual charge was the Naval Intelligence Agency, under the higher political direction of the CIA, and the National Security Council. It was quite the normal thing to put the navy and not the army in charge of the project, for the Chilean coup was to coincide with Operation Unitas, which was the name given to the joint maneuvers of American and Chilean naval units in the Pacific. Those maneuvers were held at the end of each September, the same month as the elections, and the appearance on land and in the skies of Chile of all manner of war equipment and men well trained in the arts and sciences of death was natural.

During that period Henry Kissinger had said in private to a group of Chileans: "I am not interested in, nor do I know anything about, the southern portion of the world from the Pyrenees on down." By that time the contingency plan had been completed to its smallest details, and it is impossible to suppose that Kissinger or President Nixon himself was not aware of it.

Chile is a narrow country, some 2660 miles long and an average of 119 wide, and with 10 million exuberant inhabitants, almost 3 million of whom live in the metropolitan area of Santiago, the capital. The country's greatness is not derived from the number of virtues it possesses, but, rather, from its many singularities. The only thing it produces with any absolute seriousness is copper ore, but that ore is the best in the world, and its volume of production is surpassed only by that of the United States and the Soviet Union. It also produces wine as good as the European varieties, but not much of it is exported. Its per capita income of 650 dollars ranks among the highest in Latin America, but, traditionally, almost half the gross national product has been accounted for by fewer than 300,000 people. In 1932 Chile became the first socialist republic in the Americas and, with the enthusiastic support of the workers, the government attempted the nationalization of copper and coal. The experiment lasted only thirteen days. Chile has an earth tremor on the average of once every two days and a devastating earthquake every presidential term. The least apocalyptic of geologists think of Chile not as a country of the mainland, but as a cornice of the Andes in a misty sea, and believe that the whole of its national territory is condemned to disappear in some future cataclysm.

Chileans are very much like their country in a certain way. They are the most pleasant people on the continent, they like being alive, and they know how to live in the best way possible and even a little more: but they have a dangerous tendency toward skepticism and intellectual speculation. A Chilean once told me on a Monday that "no Chilean believes tomorrow is Tuesday," and he didn't believe it either. Still, even with that deep-seated incredulity, or thanks to it, perhaps, the Chileans have attained a degree of natural civilization, a political maturity, and a level of culture that sets them apart from the rest of the region. Of the three Nobel Prizes in literature that Latin America has won, two have gone to Chileans, one of whom, Pablo Neruda, was the greatest poet of this century.

Henry Kissinger may have known this when he said that he knew nothing about the southern part of the world. In any case, United States intelligence agencies knew a great deal more. In 1965, without Chile's permission, the nation became the staging center and a recruiting locale for a fantastic social and political espionage operation: Project Camelot. This was to have been a secret investigation which would have precise questionnaires put to people of all social levels, all professions and trades, even in the farthest reaches of a number of Latin American nations, in order to establish in a scientific way the degree of political development and the social tendencies of various social groups. The question-naire destined for the military contained the same question that the Chilean officers would hear again at the dinner in Washington: what will their position be if Communism comes to power? It was a wily query.

Chile had long been a favored area for research by North American social scientists. The age and strength of its popular movement, the tenacity and intelligence of its leaders, and the economic and social conditions themselves afforded a glimpse of the country's destiny. One didn't require the findings of a Project Camelot to venture the belief that Chile was a prime candidate to be the second socialist republic in Latin America after Cuba. The aim of the United States, therefore, was not simply to prevent the government of Salvador Allende from coming to power in order to protect American investments. The larger aim was to repeat the most fruitful operation that imperialism has ever helped bring off in Latin America: Brazil.

The Coup Is Postponed

On September 4, 1970, as had been foreseen, the socialist and Freemason physician Salvador Allende was elected president of the republic. The contingency plan was not put into effect, however. The most widespread explanation is also the most ludicrous: someone made a mistake in the Pentagon and requested 200 visas for a purported Navy chorus, which, in reality, was to be made up of specialists in government overthrow; however, there were several admirals among them who couldn't sing a single note. That gaffe, it is to be supposed, determined the postponement of the adventure. The truth is that the project had been evaluated in depth: other American agencies, particularly the CIA, and the American ambassador to Chile felt that the contingency plan was too strictly a military operation and did not take current political and social conditions in Chile into account.

Indeed, the Popular Unity victory did not bring on the social panic U.S. intelligence had expected. On the contrary, the new government's independence in international affairs and its decisiveness in economic matters immediately created an atmosphere of social celebration. During the first year, forty-seven industrial firms were nationalized along with most of the banking system. Agrarian reform saw the expropriation and incorporation into communal property of six million acres of land formerly held by the large landowners. The inflationary process was slowed, full employment was attained, and wages received a cash rise of 30 percent.

The previous government, headed by the Christian Democrat Eduardo Frei, had begun steps toward nationalizing copper, though he called it Chileanization. All the plan did was to buy up 51 percent of U.S.-held mining properties, and for the mine of El Teniente alone it paid a sum greater than the total book value of that facility. Popular Unity, with a single legal act supported in Congress by all of the nation's political parties, recovered for the nation all copper deposits worked by the subsidiaries of American companies Anaconda and Kennecott. Without indemnification: the government having calculated that the two companies during a period of fifteen years had made a profit in excess of $800 million.

The petty bourgeoisie and the middle class, the two great social forces which might have supported a military coup at that moment, were beginning to enjoy unforeseen advantages, and not at the expense of the proletariat, as had always been the case, but, rather, at the expense of the financial oligarchy and foreign capital. The armed forces, as a social group, have the same origins and ambitions as the middle class, so they had no motive, not even an alibi, to back the tiny group of coup-minded officers. Aware of that reality, the Christian Democrats not only did not support the barracks plot at that time, but resolutely opposed it, for they knew it was unpopular among their own rank and file.

Their objective was something else again: to use any means possible to impair the good health of the government so as to win two-thirds of the seats in Congress in the March 1973 elections. With such a majority they could vote the constitutional removal of the president of the republic.

The Christian Democrats make up a huge organization cutting across class lines, with an authentic popular base among the modern industrial proletariat, the small and middle rural landowners, and the petty bourgeoisie and middle class of the cities. Popular Unity, while also interclass in its makeup, was the expression of workers of the less-favored proletariat, the agricultural proletariat, and the lower middle class of the cities.

The Christian Democrats, allied with the exteme right-wing National Party, controlled the Congress and the courts; Popular Unity controlled the executive. The polarization of these two parties was to be, in fact, the polarization of the country. Curiously, the Catholic Eduardo Frei, who doesn't believe in Marxism, was the one who took best advantage of the class struggle, the one who stimulated it and brought it to a head, with an aim to unhinge the government and plunge the country into the abyss of demoralization and economic disaster.

The economic blockade by the United States, because of expropriation without indemnification, did the rest. All kinds of goods are manufactured in Chile, from automobiles to toothpaste, but this industrial base has a false identity: in the 160 most important firms, 60 percent of the capital was foreign and 80 percent of the basic materials came from abroad. In addition, the country needed $300 million a year in order to import consumer goods and another $150 million to pay the interest on its foreign debt. Credits advanced by the socialist countries could not remedy the fundamental lack of replacement parts, for much of Chilean industry, agriculture, and transportation is based on American equipment. The Soviet Union had to buy wheat in Australia to send to Chile because it had none of its own, and through the Commercial Bank of Northern Europe in Paris it made several substantial loans in cash and in dollars. But Chile's urgent needs were extraordinary and went much deeper. The merry ladies of the bourgeoisie, under the pretext of protesting rationing, galloping inflation, and the demands made by the poor, took to the streets beating their empty pots and pans. It wasn't by chance, quite the contrary: it was very significant that that street spectacle of silver foxes and flowered hats took place on the same afternoon that Fidel Castro was ending a thirty-day visit, a visit that had brought an earthquake of social mobilization of government supporters.

President Allende understood then, and he said so, that the people held the government but they did not hold the power. The phrase was more bitter than it seemed, and also more alarming, for inside himself Allende carried a legalist germ that held the seed of his own destruction: a man who fought to the death in defense of legality, he would have been capable of walking out of Moneda Palace with his head held high if the Congress had removed him from office within the bounds of the constitution.

The Italian journalist and politician Rossana Rossanda, who visited Allende during that period, found him aged, tense, and full of gloomy premonitions as he talked to her from the yellow cretonne couch where, seven months later, his bullet-riddled body was to lie, the face crushed in by a rifle butt. Then, on the eve of the March 1973 elections, in which his destiny was at stake, he would have been content with 36 percent of the vote for Popular Unity. And yet, in spite of runaway inflation, stern rationing, and the pot-and-pan concert of the merry wives of the upper-class districts, he received 44 percent. It was such a spectacular and decisive victory that when Allende was alone in his office with his friend and confidant, the journalist Augusto Olivares, he closed the door and danced a *cueca* all by himself.

For the Christian Democrats it was proof that the process of social justice set in motion by the Popular Unity party could not be turned back by legal means, but they lacked the vision to measure the consequences of the actions they then undertook. For the United States the election was a much more serious warning and went beyond the simple interests of expropriated firms. It was an inadmissible precedent for peaceful progress and social change for the peoples of the world, particularly those of France and Italy, where present conditions make an attempt of an experiment along the lines of Chile possible. All forces of internal and external reaction came together to form a compact bloc.

On the other side, the parties making up Popular Unity, with internal rifts much deeper than has been admitted, were unable to reach an agreement in their analysis of the March vote. The government found itself facing demands from one extreme to take advantage of the evident radicalization of the masses which the election had revealed and make a decisive leap forward in the area of social change, while from the more moderate wing, which feared the specter of civil war, there was pressure to have faith in a regressive agreement with the Christian Democrats. It is quite obvious now that those feelers on the part of the opposition were simply a distraction in order to win more time.

The truck owners' strike was the final blow. Because of the wild geography of the country, the Chilean economy is at the mercy of its transport. To paralyze trucking is to paralyze the country. It was easy for the opposition to coordinate the strike, for the truckers' guild was one of the groups most affected by the scarcity of replacement parts and, in addition, it found itself threatened by the government's small pilot program for providing adequate state trucking services in the extreme south of the nation. The stoppage lasted until the very end without a single moment of relief because it was financed with cash from outside. "The CIA flooded the country with dollars to support the strike by the bosses, and that foreign capital found its way down into the formation of a black market," Pablo Neruda wrote a friend in Europe. One week before the coup, oil, milk, and bread had run out.

During the last days of Popular Unity, with the economy unhinged and the country on the verge of civil war, the maneuvering of the government and the opposition centered on the hope of changing the balance of power in the armed forces in favor of one or the other. The final move was hallucinatory in its perfection: forty-eight hours before the coup, the opposition managed to disqualify all high officers supporting Salvador Allende and to promote in their places, one by one, in a series of inconceivable gambits, all of the officers who had been present at the dinner in Washington.

At that moment, however, the political chess game had got out of the control of its players. Dragged along by an irreversible dialectic, they themselves ended up as pawns in a much larger game of chess, one much more complex and politically more important than any mere scheme hatched in conjunction by imperialism and the reaction against the government of the people. It was a terrifying class confrontation that was slipping out of the hands of the very people who had provoked it, a cruel and fierce scramble by counterposed interests, and the final outcome had to be a social cataclysm without precedent in the history of the Americas.

A Basis for Brutality

A military coup under those conditions could not be bloodless. Allende knew it. "You don't play with fire," he had told Rossana

Rossanda. "If anyone thinks that a military coup in Chile will be like those in other countries of America, with a simple changing of the guard at Moneda Palace, he is flatly mistaken. If the army strays from the bounds of legality here, there will be a bloodbath. It will be another Indonesia." That certainly had a historical basis.

The Chilean armed forces, contrary to what we have been led to believe, have intervened in politics every time that their class interests have seemed threatened, and they have done so with an inordinately repressive ferocity. The two constitutions which the country has had in the past hundred years were imposed by force of arms, and the recent military coup has been the sixth uprising in a period of fifty years.

The blood lust of the Chilean army is part of its birthright, coming from that terrible school of hand-to-hand combat against the Auracanian Indians, a struggle which lasted 300 years. One of its forerunners boasted in 1620 of having killed more than 2000 people with his own hand in a single action. Joaquin Edwards Bello relates in his chronicles that during an epidemic of exanthematic typhus the army dragged sick people out of their houses and killed them in a poison bath in order to put an end to the plague. During a seven-month civil war in 1891, 10,000 died in a series of gory encounters. The Peruvians assert that during the occupation of Lima in the War of the Pacific, Chilean soldiers sacked the library of Don Ricardo Palma, taking the books not for reading, but for wiping their backsides.

Popular movements have been suppressed with the same brutality. After the Valparaiso earthquake of 1906, naval forces wiped out the longshoremen's organization of 8000 workers. In Iquique, at the beginning of the century, demonstrating strikers tried to take refuge from the troops and were machine-gunned: within ten minutes there were 2000 dead. On April 2, 1957, the army broke up a civil disturbance in the commercial center of Santiago and the number of victims was never established because the government sneaked the bodies away. During a strike at the El Salvador mine during the government of Eduardo Frei, a military patrol opened fire on a demonstration to break it up and killed six people, among them some children and a pregnant woman. The post commander was an obscure fifty-two-year-old general, the father of five children, a geography teacher, and the author of several books on military subjects: Augusto Pinochet.

The myth of the legalism and the gentleness of that brutal army was invented by the Chilean bourgeoisie in their own interest. Popular Unity kept it alive with the hope of changing the class makeup of the higher cadres in its favor. But Salvador Allende felt more secure among the *carabineros*, an armed force that was popular and peasant in its origins and that was under the direct command of the president of the republic. Indeed, the junta had to go six places down the seniority list of the force before it found a senior officer who would support the coup. The younger officers dug themselves in at the junior officers' school in Santiago and held out for four days until they were wiped out in an aerial bombardment.

That was the best-known battle of the secret war that broke out inside military posts on the eve of the coup. Officers who refused to support the coup and those who failed to carry out the orders for repression were murdered without pity by the instigators. Entire regiments mutinied, both in Santiago and in the provinces, and they were suppressed without mercy, with their leaders massacred as a lesson for the troops. The commandant of the armored units in Viña del Mar, Colonel Cantuarias, was machine-gunned by his subordinates. A long time will pass before the number of victims of that internal butchery will ever be known, for the bodies were removed from military posts in garbage trucks and buried secretly. All in all, only some fifty senior officers could be trusted to head troops that had been purged beforehand.

The story of the intrigue has to be pasted together from many sources, some reliable, some not. Any number of foreign agents seem to have taken part in the coup. Clandestine sources in Chile tell us that the bombing of Moneda Palace—the technical precision of which startled the experts—was actually carried out by a team of American aerial acrobats who had entered the country under the screen of Operation Unitas to perform in a flying circus on the coming September 18, National Independence Day. There is also evidence that numerous members of secret police forces, from neighboring countries were infiltrated across the Bolivian border and remained in hiding until the day of the coup, when they unleashed their bloody persecution of political refugees from other countries of Latin America.

Brazil, the homeland of the head gorillas, had taken charge of those services. Two years earlier it had brought off the reactionary coup in Bolivia which meant the loss of substantial support for Chile and facilitated the infiltration of all manner and means of subversion. Part of the loans made to Brazil by the United States was secretly transferred to Bolivia to finance subversion in Chile. In 1972 a U.S. military advisory group made a trip to La Paz, the aim of which has not been revealed. Perhaps it was only coincidental, however, that a short time after that visit, movements of troops and equipment took place on the frontier with Chile, giving the Chilean military yet another opportunity to bolster their internal position and carry out transfer of personnel and promotions in the chain of command that were favorable to the imminent coup. Finally, on September 11, while Operation Unitas was going forward, the original plan drawn up at the dinner in Washington was carried out, three years behind schedule but precisely as it had been conceived: not as a conventional barracks coup, but as a devastating operation of war.

It had to be that way, for it was not simply a matter of overthrowing a regime, but one of implanting the hell-dark seeds brought from Brazil, with all of the machines of terror, torture, and death, until in Chile there would be no trace of the political and social structures which had made Popular Unity possible. The harshest phase, unfortunately, had only just begun.

In that final battle, with the country at the mercy of uncontrolled and unforeseen forces of subversion, Salvador Allende was still bound by legality. The most dramatic contradiction of his life was being at the same time the congenital foe of violence and a passionate revolutionary. He believed that he had resolved the contradiction with the hypothesis that conditions in Chile would permit a peaceful evolution toward socialism under bourgeois legality. Experience taught him too late that a system cannot be changed by a government without power.

That belated disillusionment must have been the force that impelled him to resist to the death, defending the flaming ruins of a house that was not his own, a somber mansion that an Italian architect had built to be a mint and which ended up as a refuge for presidents without power. He resisted for six hours with a submachine gun that Fidel Castro had given him and was the first weapon that Salvador Allende had ever fired. Around four o'clock in the afternoon, Maj. Gen. Javier Palacios managed to reach the second floor with his adjutant, Captain Gallardo, and a group of officers. There, in the midst of the fake Louis XV chairs, the Chinese dragon vases, and the Rugendas paintings in the red parlor, Salvador Allende was waiting for them. He was in shirtsleeves, wearing a miner's helmet and no tie, his clothing stained with blood. He was holding the submachine gun, but he had run low on ammunition.

Allende knew General Palacios well. A few days before he had told Augusto Olivares that this was a dangerous man with close connections to the American Embassy. As soon as he saw him appear on the stairs, Allende shouted at him: "Traitor!" and shot him in the hand.

According to the story of a witness who asked me not to give his name, the president died in an exchange of shots with that gang. Then all the other officers, in a caste-bound ritual, fired on the body. Finally, a noncommissioned officer smashed in his face with the butt of his rifle. A photograph exists: Juan Enrique Lira, a photographer for the newspaper *El Mercurio*, took it. He was the only one allowed to photograph the body. It was so disfigured that when they showed the body in its coffin to Señora Hortensia Allende, his wife, they would not let her uncover the face.

He would have been sixty-four years old last July and he was a perfect Leo: tenacious, firm in his decisions, and unpredictable. "What Allende thinks, only Allende knows," one of his cabinet ministers had told me. He loved life, he loved flowers, he loved dogs, and he was a gallant with a touch of the old school about him, perfumed notes and furtive rendezvous. His greatest virtue was following through, but fate could grant him only that rare and tragic greatness of dying in armed defense of the anachronistic booby of bourgeois law, defending a Supreme Court of Justice which had repudiated him but would legitimize his murderers, defending a miserable Congress which had declared him illegitimate but which was to bend complacently before the will of the usurpers, defending the freedom of opposition parties which had sold their souls to fascism, defending the whole moth-eaten paraphernalia of a shitty system which he had proposed abolishing, but without a shot being fired. The drama took place in Chile, to the greater woe of the Chileans, but it will pass into history as something that has happened to us all, children of this age, and it will remain in our lives forever.

(Translated by Gregory Rabassa)

Part V

Community, Culture, and Ideology

Part V is devoted to questions about individuals in communities and about patterns of cognition specific to "developing societies." It begins with a short extract from Raymond Williams concerning the impact of urbanization and the new world metropoli on changes in consciousness. Bryan Roberts' paper then discusses the linked issues of urban life and patterns of industry specific to "developing societies." The article by Frances Pine looks at the family and the position of women, relating patterns of division of labor to gender and age. The short quotation from Octavio Paz introduces the issue of cultural confrontation as seen by creative artists in "developing societies." Roger Dale examines the complex and sometimes contradictory aspects of education, which is all too often thought of as a panacea for a "developing society's" problems. Anthony Smith discusses the important issue of the role of the press and the struggle over the control of information. The extract from a paper by Tom Nairn discusses nationalism—a major state ideology of the "developing societies." Basil Davidson concludes this section, and the volume, with a piece discussing the different ways in which people in centers of metropolitan power and those living in "developing societies" perceive each other and, in that light, themselves, within a process that is necessarily one.

Contributions of relevance to the dual focus of Part V are to be found in other parts of the book, in particular in the items by Arghiri Emmanuel, Paul Sweezy, Hamza Alavi, Teodor Shanin, Colin Leys, and Gabriel García Márquez.

[27]
The New Metropolis

Raymond Williams

In current descriptions of the world, the major industrial societies are often described as "metropolitan." At first glance this can be
taken as a simple description of their internal development, in
which the metropolitan cities have become dominant. But when we
look at it more closely, in its real historical development, we find
that what is meant is an extension to the whole world of that division of functions which in the nineteenth century was a division of
functions within a single state. The "metropolitan" societies of Western Europe and North America are the "advanced," "developed,"
industrialized states; centers of economic, political, and cultural
power. In sharp contrast with them, though there are many intermediate stages, are other societies which are seen as "underdeveloped": still mainly agricultural or "underindustrialized." The
"metropolitan" states, through a system of trade, but also through a
complex of economic and political controls, draw food and, more
critically, raw materials from these areas of supply, this effective
hinterland, that is also the greater part of the earth's surface and
that contains the great majority of its peoples. Thus a model of city
and country, in economic and political relationships, has gone beyond
the boundaries of the nation state, and is seen but also challenged
as a model of the world.

It is very significant that in its modern forms this began in England. Much of the real history of city and country, within England
itself, is from an early date a history of the extension of a dominant
model of capitalist development to include other regions of the
world. And this was not, as it is now sometimes seen, a case of
"development" here, "failure to develop" elsewhere. What was happening in the "city," the "metropolitan" economy, determined and
was determined by what was made to happen in the "country"; first
the local hinterland and then the vast regions beyond it, in other
people's lands. What happened in England has since been happening ever more widely, in new dependent relationships between all
the industrialized nations and all the other "undeveloped" but economically important lands. Thus one of the last models of "city and
country" is the system we now know as imperialism.[. . .].

[. . .]The effects of colonialism on the English imagination have gone deeper than can easily be traced. All the time, within it, there was the interaction at home, between country and city, that we have seen in so many examples. But from at least the mid-nineteenth century, and with important instances earlier, there was this larger context within which every idea and every image was consciously and unconsciously affected. We can see in the industrial novels of the mid-nineteenth century how the idea of emigration to the colonies was seized as a solution to the poverty and overcrowding of the cities. [. . .]. The lands of the Empire were an idyllic retreat, an escape from debt or shame, or an opportunity for making a fortune. An expanding middle class found its regular careers abroad, as war and administration in the distant lands became more organized. New rural societies entered the English imagination, under the shadow of political and economic control: the plantation worlds of Kipling and Maugham and early Orwell; the trading worlds of Conrad and Joyce Cary. [. . .].

Most novels are in some sense knowable communities. It is part of a traditional method—an underlying stance and approach—that the novelist offers to show people and their relationships in essentially knowable and communicable ways. The full extent of Dickens's genius can then only be realized when we see that for him, in the experience of the city, so much that was important, and even decisive, could not be simply known or simply communicated, but had, as I have said, to be revealed, to be forced into consciousness. And it would then be possible to set up a contrast between the fiction of the city and the fiction of the country. In the city kind, experience and community would be essentially opaque; in the country kind, essentially transparent. As a first way of thinking, there is some use in this contrast. There can be no doubt, for example, that identity and community become more problematic, as a matter of perception and as a matter of valuation, as the scale and complexity of the characteristic social organization increased. Up to that point, the transition from country to city—from a predominantly rural to a predominantly urban society—is transforming and significant. The growth of towns and especially of cities and a metropolis; the increasing division and complexity of labor; the altered and critical relations between and within social classes: in changes like these any assumption of a knowable community—a whole community, wholly knowable—became harder and harder to sustain. But this is not the whole story, and once again, in realizing the new fact of the city, we must be careful not to idealize the old and new facts of the country. For what is knowable is not only a function of objects—of what is there to be known. It is also a function of subjects, of observers—of what is desired and what needs to be known. And what we have then to see, as throughout, in the country writing, is not only the reality of the rural community; it is the observer's position in and toward it; a position which is part of the community being known.

Thus it is still often said, under the pressure of urban and metropolitan experience, and as a direct and even conventional contrast, that a country community, most typically a village, is an epitome of direct relationships: of face-to-face contacts within which we can find and value the real substance of personal relationships. Certainly this immediate aspect of its difference from the city or the suburb is important; it is smaller in scale; people are more easily identified and connected within it; the structure of the community is in many ways more visible. But a knowable community, within country life as anywhere else, is still a matter of consciousness, and of continuing as well as day-to-day experience. In the village as in the city there is division of labor, there is the contrast of social position, and then necessarily there are alternative points of view. [...].

[28]
Cities in Developing Societies

Bryan Roberts

The discussion of urban life in developing societies is often conducted in terms of the contrast between rural and urban ways of life and of the special problems that such differences pose for societies that are in the middle of a rapid transition from being rural to being urban. The consequence is a focus on the assimilation of rural migrants into towns or cities and on the coping behavior of illiterate populations in the face of the anonymity and complex organization of the modern city. In contrast, I shall argue from a perspective that sees underdevelopment as a condition of the whole society; uneven and combined development is as characteristic of urban economies as it is of rural ones. Indeed, a city's social and spatial organization embodies, in concentrated form, the global economic and political forces that produce uneven development, and the different degree to which and the different stages at which developing societies were incorporated into the world economy has had lasting effects on their pattern of urbanization.

In the contemporary period, industrialization has become an increasingly dominant force in most developing societies. Cities are not only the main location of industry, but they potentially provide a social and political context that fosters the type of labor supply and patterns of consumption required by modern industry. Industrialization, however, has been limited and uneven in its impact on the urban economy. Some enterprises are highly productive, capital-intensive, and technologically sophisticated, producing, for example, pharmaceutical or petrochemical products and requiring relatively little labor to do so. Others produce modern consumer goods and use labor-intensive processes, assembling with the use of "cheap" local labor the products of a technology based primarily in the developed world. Such enterprises are often closely integrated with production processes elsewhere, developing few economic linkages to the local urban economy and thus limiting the amount of employment that is generated. Neither type of modern industrialization fosters the rapid growth of employment in the skilled, technical, or white-collar grades. Moreover, industrial concentration destroys the basis for craft-type industry in small towns and in rural areas, displacing population.

Most urban employment is concentrated in the service sector and in informal economic activities, including begging, petty trade, and a multitude of ill-equipped artisan workshops. Recorded urban unemployment in developing societies is usually low, but under-employment, defined in terms of jobs of very low productivity and remuneration, is very high, encompassing half or more of the economically active population of some of the largest cities. A recent International Labour Organization survey of urban employment in eight Latin American countries, for example, suggests that the informal employment sector, defined mainly as the self-employed, is increasing more rapidly than the formal employment sector.[1] The formally employed are becoming a decreasing proportion of the urban working class. Proletarianization is thus as slow and problematic a process in the cities of developing societies as it is in the rural areas.

Urbanization in the Developing World

Developing societies, almost without exception, are increasingly concentrating their populations in urban places. In 1920, 4.8 percent of the population of Africa, 5.7 percent of that of South Asia, 7.2 percent of that of East Asia, and 14.4 percent of that of Latin America lived in places of 20,000 or more inhabitants; by 1975, the respective percentages were 18.1, 17.4, 23.7, and 40.5.[2] Two traits of this urbanization deserve attention. First, there is considerable variation between countries and, significantly, between continents of the developing world in both the rate and extent of urbanization. Second, the increase in urbanization begins consistently from the mid-nineteenth century onward, but accelerates, in most countries, in the period following World War II.

The most convincing explanation for these variations in urbanization lies in differences in the character of the local economies and the manner of their incorporation into an integrated world economy in the course of colonial expansion, especially following the Industrial Revolution. That incorporation took place in two phases, consequent on the political and technological changes that became accentuated from the late 1940s onward. The first phase essentially consisted in a restructuring of economies and societies in the developing world to produce export goods. These goods ranged from minerals to a wide variety of agricultural products, but, to different degrees, their production depended on the mobilization of labor, the payment of wages, and the development of communications, including urban centers to handle the administrative, police, and commercial functions that ensured production and shipped it onward. Urban places arose either as intermediate service points on the export routes or, as in the case of the mining townships, around production points. The expansion of wage labor opportunities in place of rural self-subsistence also increased the commercialization of local economies, providing the purchasing base for the return flow of manufactured goods that came from the industrializing nations. Labor was freed from semifeudal or communal ties by means of taxation and laws weakening traditional institutions.

Elements of this restructuring predate the nineteenth century. The Latin American economies had been transformed from the Spanish conquest onward to meet the demand of the European economies for precious metals and some agricultural products. But most other parts of the developing world were less radically affected before the end of the nineteenth century. India, for example, was an important source of capital accumulation for Britain well before the nineteenth century through tax revenue and commerce. This integration into the British economy was achieved, however, through the intensification of existing forms of production through extracting a greater part of the surplus of the peasantry.[3] Indeed, there are signs of *de*urbanization in this first period of colonial rule in India as the existing industrial base was destroyed to make way for British imports. Only in a few places in India did there occur the extensive resettlement of population and the disarticulation of existing forms of production in the rural areas that followed Latin America's conquest.

These variations are the basis for differences in the pattern of urbanization in the developing world. Those areas, such as Latin America, which were earliest integrated into the world economy and most extensively restructured to that end are the areas which urbanize most rapidly and most extensively. The more that a country becomes organized around and dependent on export production, entailing a restructuring of the agrarian sector and the development of urban service centers, the more urbanized it becomes from the nineteenth century onward. W.P. McGreevey establishes a close correlation between the per capita value of exports in the Latin American countries at the end of the nineteenth century and the extent to which their populations are concentrated in large cities.[4]

The impact of the expanding world economy was uneven, depending on where the major sources of export production were located and on the nature of local labor and material resources. One effect of this was a regionalizing one. Peasant small-holdings coexisted to various degrees with different forms of organization of export production in mining and different forms of plantation agriculture, and with large landholdings producing goods for the internal market. In this situation there arose particular regional identities and class structures formed by the struggles of elites, workers, and peasants to profit from or defend themselves against the exploitation inherent in new economic opportunities.

Integration into the capitalist world economy, especially from the nineteenth century onward, was the main trigger for the capitalist development of the developing world. Compared to the changes wrought in the European countries, those in the developing world required a more sudden and drastic reordering of the pre-existing society. Labor, for example, had usually to be coerced to work for wages in the new enterprises either directly or indirectly, through taxation or the destruction of the relatively self-sufficient village economies. In many places such devices failed, and labor was massively imported in the form of slaves or indentured labor from Africa and Asia and migrants from Europe. Italians were brought to power the coffee plantations of Brazil by the state government of São Paulo and Chinese and Indian labor by the British colonial authority to power the rubber plantations and tin mines of Malaya.

Consequently, the form that capitalist development took varied in legal and political structure and in the combinations of production relations on which capital accumulation was based. These were enduring legacies affecting, for example, the nature of class struggle and resulting in different patterns of urbanization. In some places, plantation agriculture discouraged the development of small and intermediate sized towns, leading to a situation in which one dominant provincial or national center existed alongside a relatively undifferentiated rural economy of poor sharecroppers and laborers. In other places, small-holding agriculture producing for export or for the domestic market gave rise to flourishing centers of commerce and local industry. Such differences continue to affect contemporary urbanization. In Malaya, the continuance of a thriving export economy since independence, based on small-holder production of rubber, makes the rural areas a continuing attraction, resulting in a relatively low contemporary rate of urbanization.

Certain traits of the large urban centers that arose on the basis of export-led growth are general enough to require attention. Robert Redfield and Milton Singer distinguished two basic cultural roles that cities or rather their elites can play in societal change.[5] One role, the orthogenetic, is that of adapting local traditions so that these become fertile means of organizing and mastering new conditions. The other role, the heterogenetic, is that of introducing new ideas and styles of life into traditional society, which become places of dissent and heresy. It is the heterogenetic role of cities that becomes increasingly marked from the nineteenth century onward in developing societies. The elements of disequilibrium in economic exchange or in styles of life between cities and their hinterlands become more pronounced since the city is no longer the center of things for local societies, but one point more in a chain of relationships that leads outward. Indeed, the city becomes the milieu in which foreign tastes and foreign products first develop a market among elites and other urban groups. It is in the city that philosophies generated in the dominant countries find an audience, that styles of life prevalent there are adopted by urban elites, and that foreign religions find their cult. The city in developing societies becomes the place of residence of immigrant entrepreneurs, colonies of which establish themselves in distinct urban areas. Native urban elites imitate foreign customs.

The countryside by contrast often comes to be seen as the true repository of national values and national culture. Peasant or tribal economies appear to retain their customary form. They provide a subsistence base that can be supplemented by wage labor in mines or plantations; temporary labor for harvests or for longer periods can easily be obtained by the owners of mines and plantations because wives and children can remain at home to cultivate the small plots that are insufficient to maintain the family for the whole year. The labor so acquired has minimal needs for housing or welfare services; some of its food is brought from home. At the same time, village or tribal institutions exist as frameworks of security or residence, both for the migrant and for his or her family at home. Tribal groupings in the Copperbelt of Central Africa, village associations in the mines and plantations of Peru—these are examples of the presence of rural institutions in urban situations created by increasing integration into a world economy. In the villages, on the other hand, fiestas, religious observances, and kinship groupings have often acquired a new vitality and social significance, and their practices and symbolism have become ever more complex as they are adapted to take account of the distinct but interlocking spheres of activity of the village and the urban work center.

The first phase of integration into the world economy was based on rural production systems. Consequently, urbanization was a slow process. In some areas, there may even have been periods in which urbanization was reversed as population moved to colonize regions in which new types of agricultural production were being developed. Also, the improvements in transport, especially the railroad, centralized communications and commerce, concentrating growth in the largest cities at the expense of smaller urban places. The primate city phenomenon in which the largest city was several times larger than the next in size became general in developing countries, especially in Latin America and in those parts of Africa and Southeast Asia whose economies were extensively organized around export production.

These various processes had a common significance for the second, industrial, phase of urbanization. To different degrees, the economies of countries in Latin America, Asia, and Africa became commercialized, from at least the end of the nineteenth century onward, with wage labor an increasingly common form of providing for, or supplementing, family subsistence and with the purchase of manufactures becoming generalized even at the village level. Population growth reinforced these trends. This growth was itself in part a product of increasing integration into the world economy as improvements in health care and disease control followed the penetration of commerce and new production systems. Increasing population meant, however, more pressure on land resources, which in most areas were curtailed by an inequitable distribution that became more concentrated as elites seized the opportunities offered by large-scale production for urban or export markets. A common response of peasant households to this situation was to diversify, supplementing agriculture with wage labor, crafts, and trade that made use, often at different times and different places, of the labor of men, women, and children. Diversification and population mobility created an internal market for labor, and for industrial and agricultural commodities.

These variables must be examined in each specific case if the differences in the patterns of twentieth-century industrialization in developing countries are to be understood. Other equally important variables are the presence of political institutions capable of implementing industrialization in terms of labor and low tariff legislation or in terms of a powerful class able to commit itself to industrialization. Consequently, developing countries have varied in the extent of industrialization. Some, such as Argentina, began to industrialize late in the nineteenth century on the basis of a population that was already completely dependent on market relations, and on a relatively homogeneous dominant class that controlled a powerfully organized state and was to derive substantial advantages from financing industry. In other countries, industrialization came later and more slowly, depending on the extent to which the population remained in subsistence or near-subsistence agriculture, whether as peasants, small-holders, sharecroppers, or impoverished farmworkers. Likewise, as F. Cardoso and E. Faletto stress, where foreign enterprises or colonial governments controlled most local production, the relative weakness of national bourgeoisies reduced the likelihood of a strong nationally based industrialization.[6] The pattern of industrialization in developing societies is thus shaped by the particular pattern of class conflict. The strength of the local industrial bourgeoisie, of labor unions, and of the state are variables influencing decisions by both private enterprise and government to invest in industry. The balance of class forces will determine the form of control over industry.

Poverty and Urban Social Organization

The evident and extreme poverty found in the cities of developing countries is a useful point of departure for analyzing the detailed workings of urban political and social life because it raises, in acute form, the question of who benefits from the prevailing pattern of industrial development. Cities vary in the extent of the poverty of their inhabitants. According to World Bank estimates made in 1976, roughly half the urban households in Southeast Asian cities for which data were available fell below the "absolute poverty line," which was defined in terms of an income insufficient to meet minimum daily dietary requirements plus a small amount for necessary nonfood expenditures.[7] The approximate estimates for African cities showed that between 20 and 40 percent of their inhabitants fell below this line. In Latin America there were estimated to be fewer "poor" in terms of this definition.

The most graphic description of urban poverty is that of Oscar Lewis in his various accounts of families living within what he called the "culture of poverty."[8] For Lewis, this was the context that explained the traits he observed among the urban poor in Mexico and Puerto Rico. Some of these traits were attitudinal, such as feelings of helplessness, hopelessness, and a cynical indifference to politics. Others were behavioral, such as marital instability, alcoholism, or the inability to organize politically or economically. Lewis stressed that not all the urban poor lived within the culture of poverty. Thus, workers in large-scale enterprises who were able to form labor unions were excluded. So too were members of solidary, ethnic, or religious groups, who were viewed by Lewis as retaining a strong sense of corporate identity to offset the disorganizing impact of urban life. Lewis emphasized that it was the uneven development of the economies of developing countries under capitalism that gave rise to the conditions of the culture of poverty, destabilizing rural areas without adequate employment opportunities in the towns. The significance of the culture of poverty was that it encapsulated the poor so that the associated behavior traits became normal means of adapting to life. Children brought up in this culture learned the pattern of behavior, internalized it, and were thus incapable of escaping their poverty.

Lewis's accounts of the life of the urban poor are, however, partial ones that, as we shall see, overemphasized the passivity and fatalism of the urban poor. His research made clear, however, that poverty was not, as some previous commentators suggested, a pathological condition sustained by the inability of rural inhabitants to adjust to modern urban life. The pattern of behavior that Lewis describes represents a rational adaptation to material deprivation, income insecurity, and residential instability. Moreover, Lewis stressed the high degree of social organization among the poor based on personal relationships, recreation, and such institutions as religion. To counteract the notion that urban life in developing countries was anonymous and disorganizing, he entitled one early article "Urbanization Without Breakdown."[9]

Contrary to the suppositions of sociologists such as Louis Wirth[10] or Georg Simmel,[11] the metropoli of developing countries are not places in which secondary relationships become more significant for coping with urban life than primary relationships, or in which frequent encounters with strangers lead to increasing impersonalization and an individualization of mental life. Research in different parts of the world suggests instead that in the large cities kinship and friendship ties, ethnicity, and religion organize and give meaning to the lives of the mass of the inhabitants. Surveys from Asia, Africa, and Latin America show that migrants to the cities obtain their first jobs and housing through the help of kin or fellow-villagers.[12] I found that such relationships and those with friends continued to organize the lives of long-term residents in two very poor neighborhoods of Guatemala City. Even when people moved away from a neighborhood, my informants would keep contact with them, dropping in to see them if they happened to be in that part of the city.[13]

Caste and tribe are also reported to be salient bases of association in cities in Asia and Africa: residence, work, and urban political allegiance continue to be partly determined by caste position as, for example, among the "untouchable" caste of Jatavs in Agra.[14] Likewise in African cities, tribal categories remain important in organizing social interaction even after independence from colonial rule.[15]

The stress of such studies is on the uses to which ethnicity is put, both by members and nonmembers of an ethnic group. Ethnicity at times serves to strengthen political organization among low-income populations, enabling coresidents or coworkers to mobilize effectively against employers or government officials belonging to economically privileged ethnic groups. At other times, ethnicity weakens class-based political organization, as when political bosses use ethnicity as a basis for patronage and rivalry. Similar contradictions are found in the economic sphere. Members of an ethnic group help each other find work, but ethnic entrepreneurs also exploit their fellows by obtaining low-cost labor and a monopoly of markets.

The religion that thrives in the cities of the developing world is an institution shaped by the economic and social insecurity of urban life. In Latin America, urban religion has a strong popular cast. It is based on intensive participation in such mass activities as pilgrimages or folk religious festivals rather than on the formal sacraments of the church. Sects such as Pentecostals, Seventh Day Adventists, and Mormons organized in closely interacting communities flourish in the slums of most Latin American cities. In Brazil, Umbanda, a spirit cult, has become a major religious movement for the urban poor.[16]

Urban life in cities of developing societies is rich in social relationships, but economically highly insecure. The poor seek relationships and frames of meaning that enable them to cope with intense economic competition, scarce and unstable job opportunities, and the lack of adequate social infrastructure in the shape of welfare provision, adequate housing, and health care. The activity of the poor contributes to what outside observers often view as the "color" and vitality of life in these cities. Streets bustle with a range of activities as people ply their trade, seek out and greet friends, or participate in religious celebrations. Petty traders circulate around the city, "protect" cars, or line up for football tickets to resell at a premium. Entrepreneurship is common among the poor, as well as among the not-so-poor, as might be expected in urban situations in which often a third or more of the economically active population is self-employed.

Housing

Symptomatic of this pattern of urban life are the squatter settlements that proliferate in almost all cities of the developing world. Called by various names (*favela, villas miserias, bidonvilles, "katchi abadi"*), they represent attempts by the poor to provide their own shelter in face of the overcrowding and high rents of existing housing. Estimates for Asian cities show that in almost all of these at least 30 percent of housing is provided by slum/squatter settlements.[17] Similar estimates have been made for Latin America. In most cases, squatter settlements appear on the outskirts of the city and on government-owned land that has relatively little utility for commercial or industrial purposes. Striking but common examples are locations on land used for rubbish-dumps, on swampy ground, or over lagoons. Often the squatter settlement is the product of a relatively organized invasion of prospective sites by poor urban residents. In some cases, reported from Latin America, books were drawn up of subscribers prior to the invasion of the land, trucks were hired to transport the invaders and their property, and the mass media was contacted to ensure coverage of the invasion—timed to coincide with a national holiday.[18]

From the first days, the squatter settlements show considerable amounts of internal organization.[19] Committees are established to defend the settlement, to "plan" the streets, and to number the houses. Over time, such committees often organize residents to install sewage systems, a water supply, to pave roads, and to obtain electricity. In short, the settlers urbanize their neighborhood with little or no help from government.[20] Though these committees often degenerate with time as charges of corruption and political bias are raised against them by other residents, their achievements appear to have been substantial. In one squatter settlement, I documented the following public facilities provided almost entirely by the contributions and labor of the residents: a church, a public meeting hall used also for literacy classes, a consumer's cooperative, a sewage system, piped water, some paved streets, and electric lighting.[21]

Squatters build their housing, often beginning with materials such as matting, cardboard, or planking and, when they accumulate sufficient resources, rebuild with brick or concrete. As a consequence of these investments of time and money, squatter settlements upgrade themselves into areas which often have the appearance of regular urban neighborhoods. Some of the Brazilian *favelas*, for example, now show substantial housing improvements, with some of the housing stock similar to that of middle-class neighborhoods. Self-construction enables families to suit their housing to the changing needs of the family cycle and of income opportunities. Extra rooms or floors can be added when resources permit and the family expands. Some part of the space can be made over to a shop or workshop. Pigs, chickens, and some crops are often reared in the compound. These features of squatter settlements have led some commentators to view them as part "solutions" to the problems of housing in the Third World, arguing that they encourage community organization and make best use of the initiative and small-scale resources of the urban poor. To some extent this is true enough, but, as we shall see, community organization and self-help among the urban poor are also part of a pattern of exploitation by which the poor sustain an economic development that mainly benefits the upper-income groups in their societies.

Squatter settlements are closely integrated into the urban economy. Their populations work mainly outside the settlements and in the industrial or city center zones. One study calculated that even large squatter settlements only generated between 5 and 16 percent of their population's employment.[22] Those who live in the squatter settlements are heterogeneous in occupation and in experience of urban living. Surveys have reported squatters to include white-collar workers, policemen, factory workers, and construction workers, as well as the self-employed and the unemployed. The low wages paid to skilled and white-collar workers make squatting an attractive alternative to the overcrowding of the cheap city tenements and to the expense of other types of housing.

Squatting is, then, the response of urban residents to inadequate housing conditions, not an indication of desperate action by homeless recent migrants. Many residents have lived in the city for a number of years before moving to the squatter settlement or were born in the city.[23] In the phase when a city is rapidly growing through migration, the first place of residence for a migrant is often the cheap rental area of the city center. As a city enters subsequent phases of expansion and its squatter settlements become consolidated, so too migrants begin to move directly to join kin or fellow-villagers in these settlements.

In many cities, government sponsors the building of "low-cost" housing; in some countries strong labor unions have succeeded in pressuring government to build housing for their members. However, such low-cost or sponsored housing rarely gives shelter to anything but a very small proportion of the urban population. Government-subsidized housing has proved too expensive, in most countries, for any but the best-paid industrial workers or white-collar workers. Housing built for specific groups of workers covers only a fraction of the employed working class. Consequently, encircling and interspersing affluent middle-class neighborhoods and the housing estates of a small minority of skilled and white-collar workers is a heterogeneous mix of decaying urban tenements, of housing compounds with rooms arranged around small courtyards, and of a variety of self-constructed housing ranging from shacks to well-built detached houses of brick or concrete.

There is a certain logic to the disorder of cities in developing societies. Certain parts of the city will be planned in similar ways to the cities of the advanced capitalist world: suburban areas of high-cost housing, often with their own shopping malls; city center commercial and office districts built with the latest technology and materials; and all these areas connected by superhighways. These are the locations that provide profitable opportunities for the large-scale construction industry, for real estate, and for commercial investment. These areas are, however, in a constant state of seige from informal land and business uses. The pressures to reduce the costs to government and formal enterprise of maintaining large urban populations are reflected in the inadequate (and unequal) provision of public services, in the toleration of violations of zoning and health regulations, and in the failure to keep up existing infrastructue. The appearance of these cities is simultaneously one of constant decay and ultramodern renovation.

Since both housing and jobs have been left to the play of market forces in highly unstable economies, there is little match between where people live and where they work. The journey to work in cities such as Mexico and São Paulo is often as much as two hours each way, imposing costs of time and money on an already impoverished population. It is not surprising, then, that there have been significant movements of urban protest in many cities of developing countries. Squatting and the conflicts over squatting are examples. Others include the burning of buses and trains, and demonstrations for the improvement of urban amenities. The surprising fact is that protest has not escalated further than it has, resulting in significant changes in the political system of developing societies. To explore this issue, we need now to look more carefully at the workings of the urban economy and its implications for class organization.

Urban Economic Organization

Some insight is provided by emphasizing the structural dualism of the urban economy in developing countries. Two sectors of the economy can be identified, one of which is the modern sector made up of technologically sophisticated large-scale enterprises and of associated services such as banking and government, the other of which is small scale, often based on self-employment and on unpaid family labor and is informally organized in terms of work routines, labor recruitment and regulation, marketing, and price-setting. This second sector, often called the informal sector, is informal not only because of the unsystematic nature of its working procedures, but in terms of its relationship to state regulation.[24] The informal sector obviously falls outside state regulation where it consists of illegal activity but does so mainly because it is too small scale and ad hoc to be easily subject to government social security and health and safety regulations. In contrast, the formal sector is more likely to be subject to such regulations, though this sector derives compensation from market monopolies, subventions for imports of capital goods and tax concessions, which far outweigh the costs of observing the existing and often minimal government requirements.

This apparent separation of the two sectors of the urban economy, insulating one from another, in fact contributes thereby to the overall stability of the urban system. The poverty of workers in the informal sector becomes an issue for that sector and is not seen to be the responsibility of those who command the formal sector. T.G. McGee indicates some of the factors in the social organization of the informal sector in the city that contribute to its relative self-containment.[25] He shows the extent to which the informal sector consists in peasant-type economic activities within the city. The rationale of economic activity in the informal sector is different from that in the formal sector, being, for example, directed to satisfying the consumption needs of households and to providing employment for household members. Activities will be undertaken that are not necessarily the most profitable in terms of returns for labor invested, but will enable the head of household to use all the labor that he or she is committed to maintain to exploit every possible economic opportunity.

The labor of the poor has a low opportunity cost in situations where there is no generalized system of unemployment relief, making viable activities that would otherwise be "uneconomic." Survival becomes under these conditions a question of social relations. Kin, friends, or neighbors provide job opportunities and exchange skills, labor, or materials. Such relations, and their relative availability, underpin the viability of the informal economy and of an individual's chances of success within it. They also limit the possibilities of capital accumulation, which depends on profit-maximizing strategies in which unwanted labor is shed or replaced by machines. Time invested in maintaining and extending social ties can inhibit accumulation. This point is made by Clifford Geertz in his contrast of the logic of the bazaar with that of the formal economy.[26] In the bazaar, a multitude of ad hoc transactions is as much a cultural expression, cementing alliances and understandings, as it is an economic activity. Social security is provided at the expense of profit maximization. Bazaar-type enterprises are unlikely to expand into large modern firms; on the other hand, the lack of capital concentration means that a plethora of small enterprises survive and maintain many in employment.

Part of the reason for industrial investment in the developing world is the relative cheapness of labor there in comparison to the advanced capitalist world. The urban environment is not, however, conducive to cheap labor. Costs of housing, of transport, of utilities, and of the total reliance on the market for food and clothing push up the costs of subsistence and thus the minimum wage that workers need to survive. The cheapness of urban labor in developing societies thus depends, as Portes has pointed out,[27] on the availability of products and services that are produced with a minimum cash outlay, outside the formal capitalist system, on the basis of largely unpaid personal labor. Squatter settlements are a form of mutual aid in which people obtain land at minimal cost and build housing themselves, often from materials begged or scavenged. Squatting and self-construction is thus an integral part of a pattern of capitalist development based on wages whose levels are so low that they are insufficient to pay the costs of regular housing. Analyzing the failure of government policy aimed at eradicating squatter settlements in Rio de Janeiro, Portes provides data to show how even the small amount of government-financed housing provided to resettle squatters proved too expensive, leading to massive defaults in rental payments.

The exchange of services between kinsmen, friends, and neighbors likewise reduces the cost of urban subsistence and makes it possible for workers to offer their labor cheaply. Cheap transport is often offered by small enterprises run by family workers. The multinational corporations, the state, and national capital benefit from the downward pressure on wages exercised by the informal economy.

This focus on urban dualism needs to be substantially modified in two ways to capture properly the dynamics of urban organization. First, the relationships between formal and informal sectors are more extensive and the economic dependence of the informal sector more complete than appears in dualistic analyses. Second, there is a considerable differentiation within the informal sector, creating a continuum with the formal sector that includes medium-sized capitalist enterprises employing fifty or so workers, small workshops, artisans who work from their homes, street vendors, and shoeshiners.

Caroline Moser establishes these points in a review of studies of the informal sector in Africa, India, and Latin America.[28] These studies describe the close linkages that develop between small-scale enterprise and the formal sector. For example, the encouragement of petty-commodity production by merchant houses is used as a strategy for developing local markets and increasing the penetration of local economies by Western-style goods. Most small-scale economic activity is in fact located in enterprises that are dependent on modern capitalist production for their raw materials or equipment and that either service the goods of the formal sector or provide inputs for that sector. The small-scale activities of cities of developing countries are thus creations of modern capitalism rather than residues of traditional economic practices. They persist because they represent a superexploitation of local labor that directly or indirectly cheapens production costs in the formal sector.

Car and truck repair workshops are among the most common enterprises of the small-scale sector of the urban economy; so too are shops repairing electrical goods. These repair services are offered cheaply, encouraging the expansion of the market for consumer durables through an active second- and third-hand market for cars or domestic appliances. The small repair shops provide,an extensive market for the products of the spare parts industries. The linkages between formal and informal sector are often directly exploitative. The hoards of apparently independent street traders are often employed by large-scale merchants.[29] A major part of the shoe industry in Mexico is organized in a similar way, with merchant houses putting out leather to small, specialized workshops and taking back the finished product for sale in formal retail outlets or in the street markets of the towns and cities. Alison Scott provides similar examples of large-scale enterprises in Lima, putting-out assembly operations of shoes and domestic appliances to small enterprises located in squatter settlements.[30]

The range of economic strategies available to urban businesspeople results in an immense variety of enterprises, differing in scale and structure. One consequence is that labor markets are to some extent segmented, leading to what R. Edwards, M. Reich, and D. Gordon describe as primary (i.e., formal sector) and secondary (informal sector) labor markets.[31] The conditions of work and the salaries are in general better in large-scale enterprises. In many developing countries, it is only in the large-scale sector that workers have social security protection against illness and retirement. Equally important is the regularity of work in the large-scale sector: hours are controlled by labor legislation, and in many countries workers are protected against summary dismissal. To some extent, large-scale enterprises operate an internal labor market, creating the means to encourage commitment to the enterprise and to differentiate the labor force.

The difference between the large- and small-scale sector is not, however, as sharp as appears at first sight. The large-scale sector is mainly staffed by unskilled and semiskilled workers. A large proportion of these are temporary workers who are taken on and laid off depending on the work cycles of the enterprise. Wages for the unskilled or semiskilled sector, especially the temporary category, are low and usually below what can be earned in the small-scale sector as the owner of a repair shop or small store. One of the most important categories of employment in developing cities is the construction sector, in which jobs have characteristics of both the primary and secondary sectors. Construction firms pay their skilled workers and technicians relatively well and may even include most of the work force in a social security scheme. Employment for most of the workers is, however, insecure and cyclical, with foremen recruiting gangs through personal networks for specific jobs.

The routine nature of much employment, even in the large-scale, technologically sophisticated enterprises, means that skill levels as measured by education and formal training are not highly significant in differentiating access to employment. Though credentials, such as completion of primary education, are important for obtaining work in large-scale enterprises, such a level of education is within reach of increasing numbers of the urban-born population. Indeed, studies in many developing cities indicate that the most significant variable affecting access to formal employment is the social network. Workers recruit their kin or fellow villagers with the agreement of foremen or managers who see such recruitment practices as ensuring a loyal and reliable work force. In Mexico, where labor unions control recruitment to many large-scale enterprises, union members pass on their place to kin at retirement or nominate them to vacancies. The result is that households and neighborhoods are heterogeneous in terms of the employment of their members. Thus a 1970 survey in Mexico City identified a considerable number of households that contained workers in both the formal and informal sectors. The survey also identified, however, the beginnings of a working-class tradition in the large numbers of industrial workers who came from homes where a parent had been an industrial worker.

Class Relations and the State

Two features of the class relations in the cities of developing countries can be drawn from the above account. First, there is a certain ambiguity in the class location of much of the working population. Some will be employers, in that they pay others to work in their small enterprise, but they are also likely to be dependent on working for large-scale enterprises who put out work to them or supply them with credits in cash or materials. Many shift back and forth between being owners of small business that employ others and being wage workers in large-scale enterprises when the opportunity arises or cash is needed.

Second, class relations are overlaid by other social relations because of the saliency of kinship, common village origin, or ethnicity for urban life. These relations are made salient through the workings of the urban economy which, as we have seen, generates job instability and ad hoc practices in labor recruitment. The relative absence of a state-provided system of social security also reinforces relationships such as those of kinship or ethnicity, which provide a system of mutual aid. Nonclass sources of identity, such as ethnicity or kinship, do not necessarily entail intraclass divisions. Yet the fact that many of the urban population of developing countries spend their lives within a set of relationships and cultural understandings that separates them from others in a similar class position inevitably weakens and fragments class consciousness.

The final factor to take into account in analyzing urban organization is the state and the conflicts that arise over its control. The state modifies the relations between formal and informal sectors, but in ways that depend upon the balance of class forces in each country. Where the state is controlled by the industrial bourgeoisie, repressive action is often used to weaken labor organization and lessen worker benefits. Under these conditions, medium-sized capitalist enterprises competing for a share of the market make their profits through cheap labor and through massive violation of the environment. In this situation, the apparent dualism of the urban economy is less evident. Instead there is likely to be a continuum of large to small enterprises, differentiated by the degree of their access to capital. In other situations, the absence of a powerfully organized capitalist class results in a state in which class interests are more evenly balanced. Thus, organized labor may receive concessions in return for political support. These concessions may raise wages in the formal sector and provide workers with social security benefits.

The state also directly affects the urban economies of developing societies through the employment and income opportunities it creates. A recent Mexican estimate puts at 4 million the number of federal or state employees, a large part or the majority of whom are likely to live in Mexico City. State-owned industries, which are numerous in Mexico (as in other developing countries), would add many more to these figures. State employment is also important in provincial cities where, in the absence of large-scale private industry, the state may be the largest single source of jobs. In towns in the peripheral regions of Brazil, the revenues received by residents from state pension and social security payments are at times almost as large as the incomes generated by local employment.

The development of state organization becomes a significant factor in obscuring class interest and class opposition and in hindering the political organization of the working class. The state exercises considerable influence and control over the urban population through repression, patronage, and the social services. Since the state has replaced the industrial capitalist as the major employer of the urban population, grievances over conditions of work, or over wages, are directed at the same target as are those over housing and urban services. The state rather than the private employer thus becomes the major target for working-class hostility, as well as the most evident source of benefits. Repairing the corruption and inefficiency of the state often becomes, in this situation, the major focus for political organization. The aim of politics becomes that of replacing "bad" officials with "good" ones or with an "incorruptible" military. The class basis of urban inequality tends, in this context, to pass unnoticed by the mass of political participants.

The significance of these suggestions depends on the particular context of urban development. States in developing countries vary in their class basis and in the strength of their organization. Cities differ in their degree and type of industrialization and in their rates of growth. Such variations and the uneven development of the urban economy make it foolhardy to give any definitive account of class organization in the cities of developing societies. The conclusion must, then, be tentative, stressing the contradictory nature of the trends that are emerging. There is little evidence of any inherent split between a working class employed in large-scale enterprises, that employed in small-scale enterprises, and the self-employed. All these groups face basic deprivation in cities in which wages are generally low and housing and other urban services are inadequate. Different categories of workers organize together in neighborhood action groups as well as in the workplace. Their protests have often been effective and, in the more complex industrial economies, such as Brazil, the combination of urban and industrial protest has been sufficiently powerful to bring concessions from strongly entrenched authoritarian regimes. Other processes work to fragment working-class organization and consciousness. The urban working class is a highly mobile one, both geographically and socially. Social mobility is a consequence of the recent formation of the industrial working class and of substantial rural-urban migration. Moreover, changes of job are common in an unstable economy, including movements back and forth between city and provinces. Social security among the working class is, in this situation, based on particular relations such as those of kinship, ethnicity, and religion.

Conclusion

In their present form, cities in developing societies have little future. Already overcrowded and still expanding fast, many will be larger than any cities in the advanced capitalist world by the end of the century. The problems of employment and housing reviewed above will be severely aggravated in such a future. Population dispersal and economic decentralization are possible alternatives to the path of increasing urban concentration. Some observers, such as John Friedmann and Clyde Weaver,[32] see the alternative as the development of relatively self-contained areas based on a dispersed population, the communalization of productive wealth, and the diversification of the territorial economy—the "agropolitan" approach. They argue that this is the only way to avoid the income concentration and grossly inequal access to basic resources that characterize contemporary urban concentrations in developing societies. To opt for such an alternative requires, however, immense political will; it involves fundamentally changing the present pattern of economic development and industrial growth, and the balance of class power generated by it. Yet many cities in developing societies already contain the seeds of their own dissolution. Stable income opportunities are becoming relatively scarcer with the slow expansion of employment in the formal sector. Income distribution becomes more uneven and social tensions increase. As the cities grow larger the inadequacies of their infrastructure become sharper, imposing increasing burdens on the mass of the population. This situation cannot be contained by the dominant classes of these societies. Either through political will or bitter reaction to unmanageable problems, decentralization will eventually take place.

Notes

1. PREALC, *The Employment Problem in Latin America* (Santiago: International Labour Office, 1976), table 3.

2. Bryan R. Roberts, *Cities of Peasants* (London: Edward Arnold, 1978), table 1.1.
3. Hamza Alavi, "India: Transition from Feudalism to Colonial Capitalism," *Journal of Contemporary Asia* 10, no. 4 (1980).
4. W. P. McGreevey, "A Statistical Analysis of Primacy and Log Normality in the Size Distribution of Latin American Cities, 1750-1960," in R. Morse, ed., *The Urban Development of Latin America, 1750-1920* (Stanford: Stanford University Center for Latin American Studies, 1971).
5. Robert Redfield and Milton B. Singer, "The Cultural Role of Cities," *Economic Development and Social Change* 3 (1954): 53-73. Reprinted in T. Shanin, ed., *Peasants and Peasant Societies* (Harmondsworth: Penguin Books, 1971).
6. F. H. Cardoso and E. Faletto, *Dependency and Development in Latin America* (Los Angeles: University of California Press, 1979).
7. Joan M. Nelson, *Access to Power* (Princeton: Princeton University Press, 1979), pp. 17-19.
8. Oscar Lewis, *La Vida: A Puerto Rican Family in the Culture of Poverty—San Juan and New York* (New York: Vintage Books/Random House, 1968), pp. xlii-lii.
9. Oscar Lewis, "Urbanization Without Breakdown: A Case Study," *Scientific Monthly* 75, no. 1 (July 1952).
10. Louis Wirth, "Urbanism as a Way of Life," *American Journal of Sociology* 44 (July 1938).
11. Georg Simmel, "The Metropolis and Mental Life," in Paul K. Hatt and Albert J. Reiss, eds., *Cities and Society* (New York: Free Press, 1951).
12. Nelson, *Access to Power*, pp. 72-108.
13. Bryan R. Roberts, *Organizing Strangers* (Austin and London: University of Texas Press, 1973).
14. Owen M. Lynch, *The Policies of Untouchability* (New York: Columbia University Press, 1969).
15. Abner Cohen, ed., *Urban Ethnicity* (London: Methuen, 1964).
16. Peter Fry, "Two Religious Movements: Protestantism and Umbanda," in John D. Wirth and Robert L. Jones, eds., *Manchester and São Paulo: Problems of Rapid Urban Growth* (Stanford: Stanford University Press, 1978), pp. 177-202.
17. F. Lo, K. Saith, and M. Douglass, "Uneven Development, Rural-Urban Transformation, and Regional Development Alternatives in Asia," paper presented at the Seminar on Rural-Urban Transformation and Regional Development Planning, October 31-November 10, 1978, Nagoya, Japan.
18. William Mangin, "Latin American Squatter Settlements: A Problem and a Solution," *Latin American Research Review* 11, no. 33 (1967).
19. Peter C. Lloyd, *Slums of Hope? Shanty Towns of the Third World* (New York: St. Martin's Press, 1979), pp. 163-85.
20. J.F.C. Turner, *Housing by People* (London: Marion Boyers, 1976).
21. Roberts, *Organizing Strangers*.
22. Robert Alden Lewis, "Employment, Income, and the Growth of the Barriadas in Lima, Peru," unpublished Ph.D. thesis, Cornell University, 1973, p. 298.

23. Nelson, *Access to Power*, p. 100-05.
24. Keith Hart, "Informal Income Opportunities and Urban Employment in Ghana," *Journal of Modern African Studies* 11, no. 1 (1973): 61-89.
25. T.G. McGee, "Catalysts or Cancers? The Role of Cities in Asian Society," in Leo Jakobson and V. Prakashy, eds., *Urbanization and National Development* (New York: Halstead Press, 1971).
26. Clifford Geertz, *Peddlers and Princes: Social Development and Economic Change in Two Indonesian Towns* (Chicago: University of Chicago Press, 1963).
27. A. Portes, "Housing Policy, Urban Poverty and the States," *Latin American Research Review* 14, no. 2 (1979): 3-24.
28. Caroline Moser, "Informal Sector or Petty Commodity Production," *World Development* 6, no. 9/10 (1978): 1041-64.
29. Ray Bromley, ed., "The Urban Informal Sector: Critical Perspectives," special issue of *World Development* 6, nos. 9-10 (September-October 1978).
30. Alison Scott, "Who Are the Self-employed?" in Ray Bromley and Chris Gerry, eds., *Casual Work and Poverty in Third World Cities* (New York: Wiley, 1978).
31. R. C. Edwards, M. Reich, and D. M. Gordon, eds., *Labor Market Segmentation* (Lexington, Mass.: D. C. Heath, 1975).
32. John Friedmann and Clyde Weaver, *Territory and Function: The Evolution of Regional Planning* (Los Angeles: University of California Press, 1979), pp. 193-207.

Family Structure and the Division of Labor: Female Roles in Urban Ghana

Frances Pine

Most works on the roles and status of women in society empha-size family structure and a kinship-based division of labor. The reasons for this are self-evident: in the eyes of both social scientists and the social actors themselves, there is generally a strong associa-tion among women, the domestic sphere, and the organization of family and kinship activities. Age and gender serve, on either a formal or informal basis, as major organizational mechanisms in all known societies, and in preindustrial society often provide the pri-mary differentiating principles in the division of labor.[1] A signifi-cant aspect of the process of economic development is the separa-tion of certain types of economic activities from the kin- or family-based production unit, or the allocation of economic tasks on the basis of criteria other than age, gender, or kinship. Never-theless, in both "developing" economies and in "developed" socie-ties, gender remains a crucial element, in real if not in jural terms, in the division of labor. Equally, while the structure and function of the family inevitably change with economic development, and spe-cifically with the process of urbanization, its significance in social and economic organization, in socialization, and in reproduction may alter but not necessarily diminish. My aim in this article is first to provide a general discussion of the problematic—women, family structure, and the division of labor—and second, to place the dis-cussion within the context of "developing" or peripheral societies with specific reference to materials on urbanization in West Africa.

In the past decade, the growth of academic and popular femi-nism in the West has resulted in a major shift in sociological and anthropological approaches to female roles and the sexual division of labor. Modern Western feminism emerged from the general climate of politicization and reassessment that was the aftermath of the widespread unrest throughout Europe and the United States in 1968, and, like other contemporary movements, made its impact in both political and theoretical terms.[2] The search for the social ori-gins of female oppression under capitalism, and specifically within the nuclear family, led feminist theoreticians to the social sciences, and their work in turn influenced the nature of debate within the social sciences themselves. Whereas previously women had by and large been relegated to the position of a residual category by social scientists, feminist writers opened an arena for debate and began to question prevalent models of family structure and the division of labor. In an attempt to understand both its roots and its persistence under widely diverse historical and economic conditions, female subordination was examined in cross-cultural perspective, and prime importance was accorded to the significance, in theoretical terms, of social relations between men and women.[3] On the one hand, this has been an apt redressing of the balance; it is no longer easy to justify "male-centric" models in academic writing, nor to take it as an a priori assumption that men are the prime social actors, and male activities the only ones of general social significance. On the other hand, the stress on women as a focal point of social analysis has in itself presented the social sciences with various theoretical problems that have yet to be adequately resolved.

One of the most crucial, and complex, questions in the discussion of female roles and status is that of universality: to what extent can we assume a uniformity among women, either between societies or even within one specific society? The use of gender as a differenti-ating principle is physiologically founded and universal, but its articulation is socially created and culturally specific. Activities as-cribed to women in certain cultures are barred to them in others, and attributes of "maleness" in some societies are those of "female-ness" in others.[4] While gender unites all women as a category, gender boundaries are cross-cut, time and time again, by other divisive factors in the wider political economy. A woman in a shanty-town in a city in a developing country may have more in com-mon, in social, economic, and political terms, with her male counterpart than she will with either an upper-class educated woman in the same city, or a woman in a society as culturally distinct as a European peasant society or a Western state of advanced capitalism.

These points should not be seen as negating the significance of the study of women and of male and female relations; rather, they should be borne in mind as caveats against too broad or simplistic an analysis. In many preindustrial societies, age and gender are the major criteria for role differentiation; internal stratification on any other basis is minimal or nonexistent. In such cases, it is fairly easy to describe and analyze the social relations between men and women, and to correlate sex roles with economic activity and family struc-ture. However, in societies where internal stratification is greater, as, for example, in preindustrial slave-based states, in peasant soci-eties that are partially integrated into a national economy, and most of all in "developing" or "developed" nations, age and gender appear to take on at most a secondary significance, while other factors such as class or stratum membership become the major forces determining socioeconomic relations. Nevertheless, the argument that in all known societies, and within each class or stratum in more complex societies, some degree of inequality and some relation of subordination obtain between men and women as social categories should in itself be adequate cause for analyses that focus on gender roles and relationships, and attempt to reach a comprehensive view of the interrelation among gender, family structure, and economic organization.

The first social scientist to view the family not as an absolute, but as a variable structure that arose out of specific historical and economic conditions, and to relate family structure to the sexual division of labor and the position of women, was Friedrich Engels.[5] Writing in the latter half of the nineteenth century, when the work of Charles Darwin on evolution was gaining influence in the social as well as the natural sciences, Engels argued against the idea that the monogamous nuclear family was the "normal" or "correct" family structure. Drawing heavily on the works of Morgan, Bachofen, and others, he postulated a process of social evolution, beginning with a stage of promiscuity and mother right and culminating, concurrently with the emergence of private property, in the monogamous family and the control of female labor and female sexuality by males under the auspices of the patriarchal state. Private property was vested in male hands because, under each form of family, male activities were those involving the external social and economic spheres, while female activities centered around the household and child-rearing. The desire on the part of men to perpetuate their property holdings through their own sons led to the institution of monogamous marriage and the control by males of female sexuality.[6] Thus, for Engels the oppression of women arose historically from a sexual division of labor within which women operated in the household and men in the public sphere.

While much of Engels' ethnographic reconstruction must be viewed as highly doubtful at best—there is little evidence now to suggest that anything approximating a society based upon promiscuity, mother right, or primitive communism ever existed—his attempt to depict the relationship between the sexes as one arising from and changing with specific historical conditions was extremely important. The salient point here, in terms of contemporary analysis, is that Engels related family structure to economic conditions, and claimed that an increase in the division of labor, and the development of a system of unequal value that weighed heavily in favor of the products of male labor under a state political system, inevitably led to the devaluation of female "nonproductive" labor in the household, and to the subjugation of women.[7]

The assumption that the sexual division of labor is one which *naturally* places women in the household or private domain and men in the public one is integral to Engels' thinking.[8] This dichotomy between socioeconomic spheres has been elaborated upon and criticized by the majority of contemporary writers addressing themselves to the problem of female roles and the division of labor. The domestic sphere is usually taken to encompass roles and activities centering around child-rearing and the household, while the external or public sphere extends beyond the boundaries of the domestic group, and involves production for exchange, links between groups, political and often ritual activity.[9] Thus, the domestic sphere is equated with household labor, which is often undervalued and considered nonproductive because it does not produce surplus value, with socialization of children and child care, which are also often undervalued, and with consumption. The external sphere is correlated with production, with economic activity which has both social and economic value, and with authority structures which transcend the level of the family.[10] For Engels and Marx, the central problem lay not in an equation between women and the household or domestic sphere, but in the process by which the family became a unit of oppression and domestic labor lost its economic value.

Evidence from hunting and gathering societies suggests that a rigid equation of female roles with a domestic sphere and male roles with a public is not a universal fact, but rather an aspect of social organization that may often be associated with sedentary life and with a diversified economy.[11] Michelle Rosaldo, Peggy Sanday, and Karen Sacks have argued that women will have higher status in societies where there is little differentiation between the domestic and the public spheres, or where women are economically and politically active in the public sphere, than they will in societies where the domestic and external spheres are rigidly separated or where women as a category are barred from participation in public life.[12] Thus, in certain preindustrial societies with complex divisions of labor, such as the West African indigenous states, although male and female economic spheres can be best described as quite distinct, it can be argued that the relatively high status of women resulted as least partially from their monopoly over certain areas of the external economy, and their right to control their own labor and the products of their labor.

The allocation of sex roles in any society is integrally connected to indigenous ideologies of correct male and female activities and behavior.[13] Even in industrial states, which have no jural basis for a sexual division of labor, or which in fact have legislation *against* such discriminatory labor allocation, we find a sex-based division of labor in statistical terms. It is clear, therefore, that the discussion of sex roles and female status cannot rest purely on a description of economic activity or even upon a dichotomy between societies that *ascribe* roles on the basis of gender and those that accord legally "open" achievement of roles regardless of gender. Rather, the sexual division of labor in any society must be considered in conjunction with ideologies of male and female attributes on the one hand, and in conjunction with the organization of the economy, in terms of family, kin, or externally controlled production, on the other.

Perhaps the most difficult question to answer in this context is why, or indeed whether, the social classification of male and female is in itself enough to predicate relations of inequality. Felicity Edholm, Olivia Harris, and Kate Young succinctly phrase the crucial issue here: "The association of women with domestic tasks...does not explain of itself why such tasks should be consistently undervalued within the process of social production, nor why, by extension, whatever tasks assigned to women tend to be less highly valued than those undertaken by their male counterparts...it does not explain the sex *hierarchisation* of tasks."[14] These authors argue that in certain societies the sexual division of labor is based upon separate but complementary productive activities, both men and women control the products of their own labor, and gender-based economic relationships are characterized by reciprocity. On the other hand, when the unit of production is the domestic unit, as in peasant society, male and female labor is concentrated in the same productive process, and sex-role hierarchization, with differential control over labor and its products, is more likely to occur. In many tribal economies, men and women perform totally different economic tasks, and sustain a system of balanced reciprocity of necessary goods and services, both within the household and outside it. This is probably best illustrated by reference to the connection between family or kinship organization and the division of labor. In peasant societies the household works as one productive unit in one productive process. Domestic labor is usually controlled by females, on the basis of an age hierarchy, but is ideologically undervalued in relation to agricultural, or external, work. Agricultural tasks are differentiated, on the basis of age and gender, within the productive process, but that differentiation may be minimal, and women often perform as much, and at least as tedious, labor as men. The product of this combined male and female labor is usually under male control, as is female labor throughout the process of production. Female activities, although actually essential, are considered to be less important.[15] Hence we can speak of a hierarchization of economic tasks.

If we consider the interrelation between family structure and the division of labor in preindustrial societies, we can argue that when economic activity is organized primarily in terms of gender, and when the family is not united as a single unit of production but as the center for different types of productive activity—as, for example, when women gather and men hunt—women are likely to have a greater potential for autonomy and for high status than in societies where the domestic unit is the sole or primary unit of production and men and women work regularly as part of the same economic team. The type of family, and the importance of the marriage tie compared to other bonds of kinship, are of significance here.

Broadly speaking, it can be said that in preindustrial societies, social and economic relations are embedded in kinship. Kinship exists as a system of organization at most levels of social life. Personal relations are often couched in kin terms, and any kindship relationship contains within it a clearly defined set of reciprocal rights and obligations. In lineage-based societies, i.e., societies organized on the basis of groups where membership of the group is determined by descent from a common ancestor, a person's social identity is defined primarily by his or her position within the lineage and its branches, in conjunction with age and gender. Lineage membership determines whom one may or may not marry, it confers the rights to land and to labor, and it defines political and ritual activity. In matrilineal societies, there is some justification for arguing that the woman is likely to command a higher status, as her children gain their social identity from her and not from their father, and as she is usually entitled to land and property in her own right. Nevertheless, in most matrilineal cases, ultimate external authority lies not with the woman but with her brother. In many preindustrial societies, the family (if we define it as a couple and their offspring and possibly grandparents or grandchildren or other very close kin residing together)[16] may be of less importance than wider kin relationships. Marriage, like other relations of kinship and affinity, is generally defined in jural and moral terms by an established set of rights and duties; however, while a marriage can often be ended if these conditions are not met, kinship relations are permanent. It is often the wider kindred that ultimately provides the individual with support and aid, and kin as well as spouse often have the right to command the labor of an individual. In other words, the local kin group, and the family, together perform most of the functions of education, socialization, organization of labor, and so forth, which are in industrial economies often associated with the state or with outside agencies. While women may hold a social position subordinate to men in some ways, they do usually have the right to support and help from their kin.

If we consider the socioeconomic organization that usually obtains in peasant society, we find a rather different order. The household, and to a lesser extent the wider kindred, is the focus for both production and consumption. On the whole, the marriage bond takes precedence over other kin and affinal ties, and it is as a member of a household, rather than of a wider kin group, that a person is socially defined. The two- or three-generation family is the unit of both production and consumption; it is the continuation of the small-holding enterprise, rather than either the individual or the lineage or a wider kin group, which is central to socioeconomic organization. The labor, social behavior, and status of the individual is integrally connected with his or her position within the domestic unit as a whole. Authority is placed with the senior generation within the household, and may well be termed "patriarchal." The difficulty in analyzing male/female relationships in peasant economies lies in the fact that the individual peasant household is clearly subservient, as a unit, to some more powerful body such as the state or large landowner, and that within the household all individuals are firmly and inextricably linked in a continuous process of production and consumption. Nevertheless, it is clear that labor is differentiated on the basis of age and gender, and that cultural attitudes surrounding this differentiation result in the subordination of the younger to the older and the female to the male. The difference between the exploitation of the junior by the senior generation, and of females by males, lies in the fact that in time the young reach their majority and replace the parental generation, while differentiation based upon gender is unalterable. William I. Thomas and Florian Znaniecki have shown clearly the extent to which the peasant family exists on the basis of both the subordination of the individual to the enterprise, and the interdependence, albeit ranked, between the generations and the sexes.[17]

In all preindustrial societies, some form of social differentiation exists between the sexes, and between young and old. The form this differentiation takes is largely dependent upon family or kinship structure and on the organization of labor and production, and is articulated on both a practical and an ideological level. On the whole, however, it can be said that economic relations are embedded in social relations, and the use of age and gender in the allocation of power and authority, control over labor and the products of labor, is formal and legitimate. Roles are on the whole ascribed rather than achieved, and it is difficult to separate kinship, economic, social, and political roles; that is to say, roles tend to be multiplex rather than singlestranded.[18] The family or the wider kin group provides the framework for economic organization and the division of labor, and performs many of the basic functions of education, socialization, orientation, and welfare.

With the emergence of a capitalist economy and society, the relations of production change, and concurrent changes take place in role allocation and in the division of labor. The growth of wage labor divorces economic tasks from the domain of the family or kindred, and creates a situation whereby role recruitment and the division of labor is based, in legal terms, not on ascribed characteristics of age, gender, and kinship, but on achieved qualities such as training, skill, and education. The nature of the family changes as well. In developed capitalist economies, the family or kin group loses its legitimate function as the unit of production, and its function as the unit of consumption may also be curtailed. Labor changes from production for subsistence and exchange within a small and clearly defined community to work for remuneration, which is necessary to meet subsistence needs. Rather than serving as a major system of organization in all aspects of life, as in precapitalist societies, the family now takes on a primarily social and moral character. This too is the result of the diversification of roles and activities. In the urban economy, the role of the individual in the process of production alters. Rather than being involved in productive activities geared toward meeting his or her needs directly, the urban dweller takes one part in a complicated process of production and distribution; housing, food, clothing, various commodities, and various services which in indigenous economies are produced directly within the division of labor, or are exchanged for payments in kind, become things which must be paid for from money earned at other work. Equally, socialization, education, and other processes which are integrally associated with family structure in small-scale societies fall, at least partially and often wholly, under the jurisdiction of the state.

What characterizes the urban environment in peripheral or "developing" countries is that it is betwixt and between. In the densely populated cities in many parts of the developing world, elements of both the developed capitalist urban economy and precapitalist social organization can be found. This is not, however, a simple case of "developing" cities being divided into two socioeconomic sectors, one of which is advanced and capitalist, and the other of which is "backward" or "underdeveloped." Rather, these cities demonstrate distinctive patterns of their own, comparable directly to neither the highly diversified and specialized life of developed metropolises, nor the multiplex and integrally related role structure of small-scale, precapitalist systems. While it is beyond the scope of this essay to discuss urbanization and the urban economy in "developing" nations, several general points must be made: First, the "developing" countries, because of their unique and unequal relationship with the developed capitalist states, should not be seen as mimicking, belatedly, European transitions from precapitalist to capitalist economy. The form their "development" takes is causally linked to their peripheral position in relation to capitalist developed nations. Second, the "urbanization process" in most "developing" countries has been rapid and has resulted in a vast urban population that far exceeds in numbers the jobs available on a permanent or "formal" basis. Third, the process of industrialization and the penetration of a capitalist mode of production have been neither even nor widespread, and only a small proportion of urban dwellers is in fact incorporated into the capitalist sector of the economy. Finally, the nature of the government, or the state machinery, in most developing countries is such that any grassroot potential for political or economic change is severely limited; further, most of the functions of social welfare common in the West are simply not met. All of these factors influence, in various ways, the roles of women and the structure and function of the family in "developing" cities. Although the following discussion focuses on Ghana, I would argue that the patterns described are by no means specifically Ghanaian, but reflect general trends throughout the "developing" world.

Urban growth in Ghana has accelerated rapidly since independence in 1957. In 1921, 5 percent of all Ghanaians lived in cities of over 5000; by 1970 the official figure was 29 percent and was still increasing.[19] The combination of the policies of Africanization of state administration, high expenditures on education, and the creation of many low-paid jobs in the public service made the city the gathering place for both the educated and the semieducated or uneducated. As in most developing countries, the focus of development was the cities, and the rural areas lagged behind. The rapid growth of urban centers, which could not be self-sufficient, and the substantial government input into roads, transport, and communication, opened the urban areas to petty commodity traders and created a market for various small-scale services. Rural migrants flocked to the cities, on either a temporary or a permanent basis, and urban unemployment became a serious problem.[20] For a large number of urban dwellers, regular wage or salaried employment is now an impossibility; figures on official employment, however, fail to indicate the extent to which "hidden" economic activity takes place within the vast informal sector of the urban economy.

The distinguishing factor between the formal and the informal sectors is usually taken to be the regular wage. In Keith Hart's words, "The key variable is the degree of rationalisation of work—that is to say, whether or not labour is recruited on a permanent and regular basis for a fixed income."[21] The formal sector consists of regular organized occupations with steady pay, the informal of self-employment, irregular employment, and often intermittent or varying remuneration. People work within the informal sector for a variety of reasons: they may lack the qualifications necessary for access to the formal economy; they may have these, but be unable to find employment; they may have the desire, strong in Ghanaian culture, "to be your own boss"; they may straddle the two sectors, making enough in neither for self-sufficiency, but managing on a combination of the two; or they may leave the formal sector to start their own businesses. While the latter category are entrepreneurs by choice, and are behaving as capitalists, as P. Kennedy points out, "the majority of the urban poor do not usually enjoy the luxury of this kind of opportunity...the force which propels them towards self-employment is economic necessity."[22]

The effect of uneven development on the "developing" urban economy in terms of male and female activity is complex. On the one hand, differential access to and control of the means of production and of capital creates an ever widening division between social classes, to the extent that gender divisions appear to be of little consequence. In terms of the socioeconomic hierarchy, class appears to replace both age and gender in the division of labor. However, it is apparent that, despite laws granting equal opportunity to men and women, the position of each is by no means equal *within* a class or economic sector. In the formal sphere of the economy, men dominate most "modern" occupations and professions, while women are highly represented in numerical terms in the "helping professions" of nursing, teaching, and clerical work. This pattern has evolved in Ghana over the past three decades. In the period immediately after independence, work such as nursing and teaching carried high prestige and commanded, for a Ghanaian, a relatively high income. As other spheres of employment developed—in managerial work, the local bureaucracy, industry, and so forth—men left their previous positions for work higher on the economic scale, and women replaced them. Concurrently, the relative status and income of these occupations diminished. There has then been a slow but steady division of roles along the lines prevalent in Western society. As in the developed countries, the highest positions are retained by men even in those occupational categories that are predominantly female.[23]

In terms of the specificity of development, however, it is the informal sector which is more interesting. As in the formal sector, there is, in statistical terms, a gender-based division of labor. However, this division approximates more closely that prevalent in indigenous society than in the developed nations; the activities performed by each sex can be seen as reflections of certain aspects of the indigenously defined multiplex roles of "wife," "mother," "husband," and so forth, but are partially or totally removed from the context of kinship and of the encompassing precapitalist social order. Similarly, while female roles in this sector often correspond to "domestic" roles in indigenous society, and male roles to "external" ones, the lack of a comprehensive framework, in terms of household, kinship, and socioeconomic structure, makes these distinctions primarily ideologically based. Although the informal sector comprises a high proportion of the entire urban population, and a disproportionate number of women, it can be argued that, due to the peculiarly distorted process of development in urban areas, these people are marginal to the urban economy. In a study of Nima, a slum in Accra, which houses 8 percent of the city's population, Hart examined the economic activities of the under- and unemployed.[24] At the time of his study, 23 percent of the adult work force of Nima was described as "not economically active," and only 60 percent of the males, and 5 percent of the females, were engaged in wage employment. Most of the employed women were sales workers, while the men were mainly artisans and laborers. Hart argues that even those working in wage labor received such low wages that they could not cover their daily expenses. The high cost of living and the low wage structure created a web of borrowing, repaying, and borrowing again; the majority of workers attempted to supplement their meager incomes in any way possible. Hart divides informal sector activities into several categories. Primary and secondary activities include market gardening, crafts, gin distilling, and beer brewing. The latter are predominantly female, as they are throughout Africa. Tertiary enterprises are usually part-time and involve some capital—services such as renting accommodation, private transport for hire, and the like. Small-scale distribution is also an area for supplementary enterprise; the goods being bought and resold are often stolen. Both men and women work in "irregular full-time employment," providing such services as haircutting, laundering, and the like. Finally, various illegitimate activities are prevalent. For men, the most common is that of the hustler, "a jack of all trades, mostly shady. He can be found pushing Indian hemp, selling smuggled or stolen goods, touting for a prostitute, operating a street roulette wheel, getting involved in rigged horseraces. . . ."[25]

For those with some capital, hoarding, money lending, and pawnbroking are possible although unpopular. For women, by far the most common form of "illegitimate" activity is formal or semiformal prostitution.[26]

The most prevalent activity for women throughout Ghana, as in much of West Africa, is petty commodity trading. Numerically speaking, women exercise a monopoly in this field: over 80 percent of those involved in "sales" occupations are women.[27] Various reasons can be given for the plethora of women in petty trade activities. First, many activities in the informal sector are considered "unsuitable" for women; men without formal education can perform irregular manual labor, construction, driving, mechanical repairing, and maintenance work. Second, petty trading is easily accommodated to child care; it does not necessarily entail long absences from home, can often be carried out at home, and is organized in such a way that small children can accompany their mothers if necessary, and when old enough be enlisted as aides. Third, small-scale marketing of domestic surplus is a traditional occupation of many West African women. Finally, in an economy with an abundance of labor and a lack of capital, marketing activities provide a seemingly bottomless vessel for surplus labor. A problem inherent in the discussion of trade and marketing in urban Ghana is that the term covers a wide range in terms of commodities sold, type of personnel, and extent of business. Some people work full-time and some part-time; some are self-employed and work alone while others engage the services of others on a regular basis. A trader may be the head of an import-export business, may rent a kiosk in the marketplace, or may hawk his or her wares on the street. A shopkeeper may have several thousands of pounds worth of stock to the street sellers' packets of matches and single cigarettes. The "market queen," or highly successful market woman, is often taken as epitomizing West African female traders, but this is by no means an accurate portrayal. The majority of women involved in urban petty commodity trading have few alternatives; they trade because they have to, and their income is minimal and sporadic. On the one hand, the female monopoly suggests female dominance in the field; on the other hand, as in other economic spheres, there is a distinction between male and female trading activities. As Sidney Mintz has pointed out, "For reasons that are not always clear, we have little evidence that women traders in [developing urban] situations have demonstrated a continuing capacity to expand their operations, to innovate significantly in trade, or to get firmly inside the sphere of export intermediation."[28] Most Ghanaian women occupied in trade are among thousands of petty and itinerant traders. Men dominate the two most lucrative areas, those of wholesale original supply and of large-scale importing and wholesale, while local sellers, regional bulk buyers, intermediaries, and small-scale urban retailers tend to be women.[29]

A final point about the informal sector is that it is here that child labor plays an important role. In small-scale societies, age is a significant element in the division of labor. Children begin to participate in the productive process from an early age. The notion that the use of child labor is both nonproductive and inhumane, and should be barred from the wage market, is prevalent in developed societies and is usually enforced by strong legislation, but is, historically speaking, a recent phenomenon.[30] In the formal sector of the Ghanaian economy, and among the middle and upper classes, employment is predominantly adult; here too this sector parallels the developed urban economies. In the informal sector, and among the marginal poor, however, children are economically active, as housemaids, child-minders (often to the middle and upper classes), and assistants in trading and other activities. In the context of this discussion, child labor is significant for two major reasons: first, it is mobilized primarily within the areas of the economy that are dominated by women, thus creating a dynamic whereby women and children are structurally opposed to, or separated from, men in terms of economic divisions, and reinforcing a strong trend toward separation of the sexes in urban domestic arrangements; and second, child labor in the informal sector serves both as an economic and as a socializing factor, often replacing formal education and thereby creating a second dynamic, which opposes the children of the different classes— those whose parents and kin can afford to keep them in educational institutions and thus give them access in adult life to the formal sector, and those who must help their parents or kin economically, and in so doing minimize their own opportunities to move eventually into the formal sector. The existence of child labor among the lower classes thus perpetuates the major divisions of sex and class in the urban economy.

The complexities of the urban economy remove labor from the context of family or kinship organization and concurrently result in changes in the structure and function of the family and the kindred. While it is difficult to isolate an urban "norm" in terms of family pattern, we can again identify certain syndromes, and correlate them with class membership. A widely held idea in the social sciences is that with urbanization, the kin network of an individual diminishes, and the nuclear family, based upon a "companionate" relationship between spouses, becomes increasingly common.[31] However, various studies have emphasized the growth of female-headed, or "matrifocal," families among the developing countries' urban populace. These models are not necessarily mutually exclusive; rather, evidence suggests that different family patterns are likely to obtain among the middle and upper classes and the marginal poor.[32]

In certain ways, the process of economic diversification can be seen as widening the gap between the external/economic sphere and the domestic sphere, in both practical and ideological terms, and undermining the structure of interdependency between the sexes and between age groups and kin. Basically, the diversified economic structure of the city is such that indigenous patterns of extended family household, complementary labor, and interdependence of kin cannot take the same form. Housing shortages, style of housing, the breakup of the extended family through migration, and the isolation of economic roles from the social sphere all serve to negate indigenous residence and economic patterns.

Among urban Ghanaian upper and middle classes, the relationship between husband and wife is usually depicted as moving toward the ideal of Western middle-class companionate marriage, centered around the conjugal pair and their offspring. Although husband and wife may remain economically independent in terms of earnings, the nuclear family becomes the vehicle for property accumulation, and for the transfer of property from generation to generation. Often better off than their kin, members of these classes see kin as a potential threat to, or drain on, their resources rather than as a network of security. Functions indigenously covered by the domestic group and the extended kindred here become separated from each other, and take on a primarily economic character. For example, domestic labor may remain the responsibility of the woman, but she may hire another woman or a child to perform these tasks for her, and work herself in other employment. Equally, while the state does not provide an adequate welfare system, members of these classes are able to pay for medical services, for education, and so forth, and to remove these processes from the network of kinship reciprocity and obligation.

Legal marriage, under civil or customary law, is less prevalent among the urban poor although consensual unions, frequently serial, and "visiting" relationships of an enduring nature are common. The members of a low-income couple tend far more than the upper and middle class to live separately, often with kin, and to be involved in day-to-day reciprocal relationships with kin. This causes a further separation of male and female spheres as defined by a conjugally based domestic group, and the pattern reaches its extreme in the syndrome of the female household, in which kinswomen, often of different generations, live together with their children, cooperate in child care and domestic labor, and often share economic activities and responsibilities. This pattern has often been associated with urban poverty and viewed in the light of the "culture of poverty" argument: it is seen as a cultural adaptation that is somehow deviant, but self-perpetuating. Rather than viewing it in this light, it is more useful to ask why any other pattern should be expected. It may well be argued that in many complex societies with uneven economic development, the nuclear family, as an economic and domestic unit in which the members are interdependent, is a viable or at least desirable alternative primarily for the middle and upper classes. Among the marginal poor, the family has minimal viability as a unit for the holding and transfer of property. There is minimal basis for cooperation or reciprocity between males and females, as their economic and social spheres tend to be quite separate, and as neither has a capacity to command a high income. For women, especially those with children, a sporadically employed or unemployed male may be more of a liability than an asset, while female kin can offer each other mutual aid, companionship, and labor. Although the strengthening of the marital tie may be feasible and beneficial for the upper classes, it does not hold the same promise for the urban poor. If anything, the occupational diversity, the heterogeneity, the lack of moral sanctions present in a small closed community, and above all the undermining of the reciprocal rights and obligations between men and women in the urban environment further separate the male and female spheres.

In terms of family and kinship, it is more useful to look at the wider kinship relationships between the urban poor than to concentrate upon variations on, or lack of, conjugal unions. Often, it is the extended kindred, rather than either the nuclear family or the state, which fulfills the various functions of welfare, mutual aid and support, and, to a large extent, education and socialization. This pattern is most clearly seen in the context of migration. In West Africa, there is a continual flow of people backward and forward between the cities and the rural areas. Both men and women leave the rural areas in order to work in the cities, but maintain strong links with their rural kin, and eventually aim to return. Children are sent from the rural areas to urban kin for education or to help in the household, and are sent "back to the village" when conditions are hard in the cities, when rural kin need help, or when it is considered "healthier" or better for them. Equally, there is a continual flow of goods and money between rural and urban kin. The fact that many of the urban peripheral poor can be considered as "peasant-workers," whose primary allegiances and social links are centered in the rural areas, also makes analysis of family and kinship as settled or steady patterns in urban areas difficult. Considered from this point of view, the urban family can be viewed as a flexible, transitory, or ad hoc formation, which takes its structure from the adaptive strategies of its members to temporary residence in the urban world. On the one hand, migrant workers live, work, and form social networks in the cities; on the other hand, their primary social, economic, and kinship ties are focused not on urban life but on their rural places of origin.

Two distinct theoretical trends are identifiable in the literature on urbanization, the sexual division of labor, and women and development. One stresses the breakdown of ascriptive roles and the consequent "emancipation" of women from the constraints of indigenous society; the second emphasizes a maintenance or increase of sex-based differentiation in the cities. Those of the former opinion concentrate on the "choices" open to, and the strategies used by, urban women to improve their situation, while those of the latter see the constraints of the urban economy as effectively limiting the alternatives available. The first is a model based upon individual action, the second upon a determinant system. The assumption that the lag in female education in cities, their relatively low-income potential, and their overrepresentation in the informal economic sector can be changed by "improving" individual conditions, for example by birth control, which was common in development theory in the 1960s, is germane here. As Esther Boserup and others have pointed out, such arguments failed to take into account the extent to which both cultural and ideological factors influence female roles, and the extent to which such measures are in fact ineffectual, or even counterproductive, in terms of the constraints imposed upon women by the wider political economy.[33] Within a system which removes female domestic labor from its socioeconomic context, consistently undervalues a large proportion of indigenous female economic roles, and offers no security network on which to fall back, women's strategies should be seen as more related to survival than to emancipation. There can be little incentive for limiting numbers of children when child labor is widespread, and when children offer a potential for security in later life. Equally, emphasis on female kin, and on the extended kindred, above that on the conjugal relationship, can be seen in terms of mutual aid and survival. The urban environment separates out aspects of combined female roles, and either devalues them completely, as in the case of domestic labor in one's own home, or undervalues them, as in the case of domestic labor performed for others, sexual services for payment, and petty commodity trading, by removing them from the context of clearly defined reciprocal rights and obligations in the indigenous economy.

Women have been referred to as a "neglected human resource in development."[34] While this is a valid claim, it is difficult to see how the overall situation of women in developing urban centers can change without a basic reordering of the political economy. Cultural classifications of female labor and female attributes are retained in the urban economy, and are reinforced by an ideology which undervalues female labor. Aspects of indigenous domestic and external female roles are translated into the urban economy as isolated economic or maintenance activities. The gap between the domestic and the public/external sphere increases with the devaluation, on the one hand, and the underevaluation, on the other, of female domestic labor, with the replacement of the family or kin-based productive process, and with the isolation or separation of indigenously reciprocal male and female roles. The end result is a distortion of the basis of gender classification in economic terms. While women perform many of the same activities in the urban environment as in indigenous society, the context in which they do so is one of survival rather than subsistence.

Notes

1. See J.S. La Fontaine, ed., *Sex and Age as Principles of Social Differentiation* (New York: Academic Press, 1978).
2. See Juliet Mitchell, *Women's Estate* (Harmondsworth: Penguin Books, 1971), part 1.
3. See Michelle Rosaldo and Louise Lamphere, eds., *Women, Culture, and Society* (Stanford: Stanford University Press, 1974); Rayna Reiter, ed., *Toward an Anthropology of Women* (New York: Monthly Review Press, 1975); Ernestine Friedl, *Women and Men: An Anthropologist's View* (New York: Holt, Reinhart and Winston, 1976); *Critique of Anthropology (Women's Issue)* 3, nos. 9 and 10 (1977).
4. See La Fontaine, ed., *Sex and Age*; Claude Lévi-Strauss, "The Family," in Harry Shapiro, ed., *Man, Culture and Society* (New York: Oxford University Press, 1971).
5. F. Engels, *The Origins of the Family, Private Property, and the State* (London: Lawrence and Wishart, 1973).
6. "The overthrow of mother right was the *world historical defeat of the female sex.* The man took command in the home also; the woman was degraded and reduced to servitude" (Engels, *Origins of the Family*, pp. 120-21).
7. Ibid., p. 137.
8. "The first division of labour is that between men and women for the propagation of children" (Marx and Engels, quoted in ibid., p. 129).

9. Michelle Rosaldo, "Women, Culture, and Society: A Theoretical Overview," in Rosaldo and Lamphere, eds., *Women, Culture, and Society*, p. 23.

10. See Annette Kuhn, "Structures of Patriarchy and Capital in the Family"; Beechey, "Women and Production: A Critical Analysis of Some Sociological Theories of Women's Work"; McIntosh "The State and the Oppression of Women," all in Annette Kuhn and Annemarie Wolpe, eds., *Feminism and Materialism* (London: Routledge & Kegan Paul, 1978).

11. See Patricia Draper, "!Kung Women: Contrasts in Sexual Egalitarianism in Foraging and Sedentary Contexts," and Kathleen Gough, "The Origin of the Family," both in Reiter, ed., *Toward an Anthropology of Women*.

12. Draper, "!Kung Women"; Rosaldo, "Women, Culture, and Society"; Peggy Sanday, "Female Status in the Public Domain," and Karen Sacks, "Engels Revisited: Men, the Organization of Production, and Private Property," both in Rosaldo and Lamphere, eds., *Women, Culture, and Society*.

13. See Wallman, "Difference, Differentiation, Discrimination," *Journal of Community Relations Commission* (Summer 1976).

14. Edholm, Harris, Young, "Conceptualising Women," *Critique of Anthropology* 3, no. 9 (1977), p. 123.

15. See Conrad Arensberg and S.T. Kimball, "The Small Family Farm in Ireland" in Anderson, ed., *The Sociology of the Family* (Harmondsworth: Penguin Books, 1971), and W.I. Thomas and F. Znaniecki, *The Polish Peasant in Europe and America* (1918; New York: Octagon Press, 1971).

16. For discussions of family form in cross-cultural perspective, see Lévi-Strauss, "The Family"; Gough, "The Origin of the Family"; W. Goode, *World Revolution and Family Patterns* (New York: Free Press, 1963); Anderson, *Sociology of the Family*; and J. Goody, ed., *Kinship* (Harmondsworth: Penguin Books, 1971).

17. Thomas and Znaniecki, *The Polish Peasant.*

18. See J.S. La Fontaine, "The Free Women of Kinshasa," in Davis, ed., *Choice and Change* (London: London School of Economics, 1974).

19. 1970 Population Census of Ghana.

20. See S. Amin, *Neo-Colonialism in West Africa* (New York: Monthly Review Press, 1973), pp. 43-47; Keith Hart, "Urbanization, the Post-Colonial State and Petty Commodity Production in Ghana," unpublished paper presented at the Past and Present Society Annual Conference on Towns and Economic Growth, University College, London, 1975, pp. 6, 7; Gloria Marshall, "The State of Ambivalence: Right and Left Options in Ghana," *Review of African Political Economy* 5 (1976).

21. K. Hart, "Informal Income Opportunities and Urban Employment in Ghana," *Journal of Modern African Studies* (1973): 11, 68.

22. P. Kennedy, "Cultural Factors Affecting Entrepreneurship and Development in the Informal Economy of Ghana," *IDS Bulletin* 8, no. 2 (1976): 18.

23. See J. Z. Giele, "United States: A Prolonged Search for Equal Rights," and M. Sokolowska, "Poland: Women's Experience under Communism," both in J.Z. Giele and A. Smock, eds., *Women: Roles and Statutes in Eight Countries* (New York: Wiley, 1977); HMSO, "Social Commentary: Men and Women," *Social Trends* 5 (1974).
24. Hart, "Informal Income Opportunities."
25. Ibid, p. 74-75.
26. See also D.F. McCall, "Trade and the Role of Wife in a Modern West African Town," in A. Southall, ed., *Social Change in Modern Africa* (Oxford: Oxford University Press, 1961); M. Little, *African Women in Towns* (Cambridge: Cambridge University Press, 1974).
27. See Peil, "Female Roles in West African Towns," in J. Goody, ed., *Changing Social Structure in Ghana* (International African Institute, 1975).
28. S. Mintz, "Men, Women and Trade," *Comparative Studies in Sociology and History* 13 (1968): 265.
29. M. Katzin, "The Role of the Small Entrepreneur," in M. Herskovits and M. Harwitz, *Economic Transition in Africa* (Evanston, Ill: Northwestern University Press, 1974); D. Garlick, *African Traders and Economic Development in Ghana* (Oxford: Clarendon Press, 1971).
30. See C. Schildkraut, "Roles of Children in Urban Kano," in La Fontaine, ed., *Sex and Age*.
31. See Goode, *World Revolution and Family*; C. Oppong, *Marriage Among a Matrilineal Elite* (Oxford: Oxford University Press, 1974).
32. M. Tanner, "Matrifocality in Indonesia and Among Black Americans," and K. Stack, "Sex Roles and Survival Strategies," both in Rosaldo and Lamphere, *Woman, Culture, and Society*; Morris, "Women Without Men," *British Journal of Sociology* (September 1979); and R.T. Smith, "The Matrifocal Family" in J. Goody, ed., *The Character of Kinship* (Cambridge: Cambridge University Press, 1973).
33. E. Boserup, *Women's Role in Economic Development* (New York: St. Martin's Press, 1970).
34. Human Resources in Development Division, UNESCO, "Women: The Neglected Human Resource in African Development," *Canadian Journal of African Studies* 5, no. 2 (1972).

[30]
Culture of Dependency:
Arts and Political Ethos

Octavio Paz

[...] Political crises are moral crises. [...]. Those years [the 1940s] saw the beginnings of the third period of our contemporary history, a stage that the North American historian Stanley R. Ross has called the Mexican Thermidor: ideas were transformed into formulas and the formulas into masks. Although moralists are scandalized by the fortunes amassed by the old revolutionaries, they have failed to observe that this material flowering has a verbal parallel: oratory has become the favorite literary genre of the prosperous. More than a style, it is a stamp, a class distinction. And alongside oratory, with its plastic flowers, there is the barbarous syntax of our newspapers, the foolishness of North American television programs with the Spanish dubbed in by persons who know neither English nor Spanish, the daily dishonoring of the language on loudspeakers and the radio, the loathsome vulgarities of advertising—all that asphyxiating rhetoric, that sugary, nauseating rhetoric, of satisfied people whose gluttony has made them lethargic. Seated at Mexico, the new lords and their courtesans and parasites lick their lips over a gigantic platter of choice garbage. When a society decays, it is language that is first to become gangrenous. As a result, social criticism begins with grammar and the re-establishing of meanings. This is what has happened in Mexico. Criticism of the present state of affairs was begun, not by the moralists, not by the radical revolutionaries, but by the writers (a handful of the older but a majority of the younger). Their criticism has not been directly political—though they have not shied away from treating political themes in their works—but instead verbal: the exercise of criticism as an exploration of language and the exercise of language as an exploration of reality.

The new literature, poetry as well as the novel, began by being at once a reflection on language and an attempt at creating a new language: a system of transparencies, to provoke reality into making an appearance. But to realize this proposal it was indispensable to cleanse the language, to flush away the official rhetoric. Hence these writers had to deal with two tendencies inherited from the Revolution and now thoroughly corrupt: nationalism and an "art of the people." Both tendencies had been protected by the revolutionary regimes and their successors. The resemblances between the official aesthetics of Stalinism and the officious aesthetics of Mexican politicians and hierarchs are instructive. Mexican mural painting—originally a vigorous movement—was a prime example of this mutual accommodation between the regime and the "progressive" artists. The criticism directed at a showy nationalism and an art of patriotic or revolutionary slogans was more moral than aesthetic: it criticized imposture and servility.[...].

The advent of this critical and passionate art, obsessed with double images of daily marvels and banalities, of humor and passion, surprised and disturbed the new class in power. This was natural enough. That class, made up of entrepreneurs, bankers, financiers, and political bosses, is only now taking its first steps along the path which their counterparts in Europe and the United States have been walking for more than a hundred years; it takes them at precisely the moment when the nations that have been its models and the object of its admiration and envy are beginning to suffer substantial changes in both technology and economics, in both the social sphere and the spiritual, in both thought and feeling. What is sunrise in Mexico is sunset there; what is daybreak there is still nothing at all in Mexico. The modernity in which the regime's hierarchs believe is not modern any longer; hence the horror and panic with which they react to the writers and artists, who in their eyes represent those tendencies toward dissolution, criticism, and negation that are undermining the West. The long-kept truce between the intellectuals and those in power, a truce initiated by the Revolution and prolonged by the necessities (the mirage) of development, has now ended. Mexican culture has recovered its vocation as critic of society. [...].

[31]
Learning to Be...What?
Shaping Education in "Developing Societies"[1]

Roger Dale

One of the last facets of the Western impact on developing societies to be opened up to criticism or even close scrutiny and analysis has been education. It has been considered one of the few obviously valuable spinoffs of colonial and postcolonial exploitation. It is seen as self-evidently "a good thing." First, it is held to civilize the backward peoples of the world, to remove them from the chains of ignorance and superstition in which they have been confined for centuries. This attitude often has about it a strong whiff of (usually "Christian") duty: that it is our duty to the values of our civilization to propagate them far and wide, and bringing them to the poor and hungry people of the world is the least we can do to mitigate those intransigent material hardships they suffer. Of course, this is something of a caricature and its ethnocentric and patronizing assumptions are now widely acknowledged, but it would be a mistake not to recognize that such views continue to inform the moral dimension of educational aid.

Dissatisfaction with the assumptions of this "civilizing" approach to education helped produce the second major justification for education. This is that education contains the means whereby "developing" nations can become self-sufficient intellectually, and hence eventually entirely self-sufficient. Once they are educated to Western levels, "developing" countries will be able both to decide for themselves how they wish to develop and to achieve these goals. In this view, education (almost) alone is not subject to the general condemnation of Western penetration and exploitation of the developing world, and is the major means by which that penetration and exploitation can be resisted, and even turned to good effect, at both societal and personal levels.

Of course, this "liberationary" view of education is also a caricature, but it does not exaggerate excessively the hopes and expectations for it. (These are not, of course, confined to the Third World. Education has everywhere frequently been seen as a panacea for, or prophylactic against, all social ills.) This makes it particularly important to analyze the actual place and effect of education in the Third World. I propose to do this by first examining briefly the

408

assumptions about, and implications for, education of two major sociological approaches to "development," by looking at the characteristic forms education has taken in developing societies, and finally, by trying to determine the demands of, and possibilities for, education in developing societies.

The common sense views about the contribution of education to development I have just outlined do in fact have a lot in common with the way education is conceived of in modernization theory. Modernization theory was not only a theory but a prescription. It set up a target—"modernity," as represented by the contemporary West—and a pattern of progress toward that target. This "catching up" process was very largely based on achieving economic growth, to which education was seen as able to make a most significant contribution. It will be useful, therefore, to indicate very briefly those of the major tenets of modernization theory that have particular associations with education.

First, it involves conceptualizing "postcolonial backwardness" as it presents itself to the core, Western, countries, rather than as it presents itself to those experiencing it. In fact, it becomes rather more than that; certainly in the earlier phases of the postcolonial period, when the bases of most education systems in "developing" countries were being laid, it was effectively the only way of conceiving of the problem. It was often held by postcolonial leaders themselves, who typically had absorbed it both directly and indirectly during their studies in the West; and it was (and largely remains) much the dominant way of conceiving of the problem in the mass media,[2] to say nothing of its prominence in the Western textbooks so pervasive in the secondary schools and universities of developing societies. As Renato Constantino puts it, writing about the Philippines, "We never thought that we too could industrialize because in school we were taught that we were primarily an agricultural country by geographical location and by the innate potentiality of our people."[3] "Catching up" to the advanced countries by means of economic growth would have the simultaneous, and from a Western point of view equally important, effect of ensuring the continuing and yet firmer binding-in of the former colonies to a peripheral place in the world capitalist system.

During this same period, the technical-functional theory of education became very popular.[4] Technical-functional theory is concerned with demonstrating that education contributes to economic growth and how it does so. Its starting point is the correlation between economic growth (as measured by per capita GNP) and level of education (as measured for instance by literacy level); the theory was designed to explain this correlation. Its major propositions can be set out quite briefly. Its first contention is that economic growth requires technological development. Technological development creates the needs for new skills. Schools exist to equip people with these skills, and hence increases in demands for skill create the need for expanded schooling systems. So, countries with the most technologically sophisticated economies will have the highest demand for skills and hence the highest levels of education; thus may the correlation be explained. From this it is but a short step to arguing that a developed education system is at least a precondition, and maybe a cause, of economic growth—and this appears to be confirmed by the well-known argument that investment in education is more effective than any other kind of investment in securing economic growth.

It is not, however, merely at the level of providing a variously skilled labor force that education is held to contribute to modernization (though it often seems like it). For, as Peter Berger points out, "Technological and economic processes (associated with economic growth) do not occur in a vacuum, especially when they take place with the rapidity that is common today. Rather, they contribute a turbulent force that affects, increasingly, all the institutions and the entire culture of the society in question."[5] Education is, along with the military and the police, the most prominent "modern" institution in most developing countries. It is expected to display the chief characteristics required of the institutions to be built in the developing world. These are typically taken to involve a shift from the values of particularism, ascription, and diffuseness, to universalism, achievement, and specificity. Thus it is desirable that schools should be open to everyone regardless of gender, religion, caste, tribe, or whatever, should treat them all in the same way, and should display the virtues of specialized institutions over multifunctional ones like the family. They should also demonstrate the superiority of technical rationality over traditional rationality.

Schools are also expected to contribute to the making of modern individuals. This is based on similar premises to institution-building, namely, that there is a causal association between particular personal values and psychological types, and successful growth and development, and that therefore replacing particular kinds of (traditional) values and personal qualities with more "modern" ones is a key step in the march of progress. A further premise of this argument is that "traditional man" is, as Caroline Hutton and Robin Cohen put it, "at root 'obstacle man.' Man as obstacle is one standing in the way of economic advancement which would be to his own advantage."[6] Modern people, as opposed to traditional people, are prepared to act on their world rather than fatalistically accept it;

welcome rather than distrust change; see the sense of deferring gratification; are not constrained by irrational religious or cultural forms; have a cosmopolitan rather than a local orientation; and recognize the instrumental value of educational.[7] (Perhaps the best known and most fully developed work in this area is that of David McClelland on the need for achievement.)[8]

The "developing" countries are quite clearly heavily dependent on outside aid to expand their educational systems beyond very rudimentary levels, and this fact gives international aid organizations (such as the World Bank and philanthropic foundations) a great deal of influence (as Robert Arnove has pointed out),[9] since their contributions are typically not to basic minimum programs of education, but are essential to, and therefore very influential over the direction of, expansion beyond existing minimum provisions. These international organizations have been and continue to be particularly influenced by technical-functional theory, of which they may be seen as the major "carriers." Though their policies effectively strengthen and expand capitalism, these organizations do not compel defenseless poor countries to adopt in toto Western models of schooling. The point is rather that they use their undoubted power in the support of a model of economic growth and national development, and of education's place in it, whose desirable outcome is compatibility with Western capitalism. This is important because capital cannot by its own devices secure either compatibility—i.e., active rather than passive acceptance of absorption into the capitalist world economy—or effective continuity of that absorption. This is not, of course, to say that educational aid is the only, or even a major, factor in perpetuating Western hegemony. It is important to note, if only to quench incipient paranoia and nip conspiracy theories in the bud, that the World Bank does not explicitly and in detail enforce the virtues of the U.S. or any other way of life. It does not, in fact, lay down *precise* models for education systems. It has operated rather in such a way that its economic focus blinds it to any other basis for appraising or evaluating education systems.

It is important to note too that national aid to education in developing countries may have "ulterior motives," as is indicated in the title of Philip Coombs' book, where education is referred to as the fourth dimension of foreign policy.[10] The clearest example of such a use is probably found in the work of the Alliance for Progress in Latin America after Fidel Castro took power in Cuba.

The most widely canvassed alternative to modernization theory, and what is probably the currently dominant explanation of underdevelopment, is contained in the broad range of theories known as "dependency" theory. The relatively small amount of work in this broad tradition which explicitly focuses on education tends to see it as a form of cultural imperialism.[11] In these analyses education is seen as part of the process whereby peripheral countries are maintained in that position, part of the "development of underdevelopment," part of a process which promotes and safeguards the economic and commercial interests of the developed world. These analyses move beyond the exclusively economic analysis of mainstream dependency theory to continue the process by which dependency theory turns modernization theory on its head by arguing that education, far from being a key component in development, modernization, self-sufficiency, and so on, is in fact yet another instrument of enslavement, a way of tightening, rather than loosening, the dependency bond.

Such analyses do move us beyond the silence about education and its effects on any other noneconomic internal structures in developing societies. But their stance is still very largely one of economic reductionism, with the pattern of education in developing societies determined by the needs and interests of Western capitalism: internal structures, including education, remain dominated by such needs and interests and have no autonomy or space for independent development. Broadly similar is what might be called the "neocolonial" explanation of education in developing countries.[12] Proponents of this approach have devoted special attention to the role and importance of multinational companies in publishing and other media in maintaining or bringing about a "servitude of mind" among students in developing societies, through the perpetuation of Western content, structure, and forms in their education systems. They have shown how such companies have contained to dominate the publishing markets of former colonies and hence left students in those countries with little option but to follow subjects and courses developed in and for the West, regardless of their local relevance. This reinforces a psychological and academic dependence on the developed world.

Whereas in modernization theory the predicted contribution of education to development is both clear and positive, in the cultural imperialism approach it is less clear but nevertheless obviously negative (i.e., it contributes to "misgrowth"). In the neocolonialist approach it is rather clearer but scarcely less negative than in the cultural imperialist approach. The neocolonialist approach sets out to indicate much more precisely just how education contributes to the "development of underdevelopment." If the cultural imperialism model, with its stress on the direct contribution of education as just one more way of meeting the needs and interests of international capitalism, is valid, then not only is there little or no flexibility or autonomy available to developing countries in designing their education systems, but neither is there any obvious way of bringing about any but the least significant changes in those systems short of a change in the whole capitalist world system whose demands determine their shape.

Rather more flexibility is allowed by the neocolonialist approach. This represents both its strength and its weakness. It represents its strength because it demonstrates that an important aspect of the situation that developing countries find themselves in can be changed in significant ways; some kind of educational import substitution is possible. But if we examine the likely outcome of such policies we find that they are unlikely to be effective largely because the effect of the developed countries' influence and impact on the education systems of developing countries is not confined to whatever "servitude of the mind" results from the use of Western textbooks and materials. It is quite possible to imagine that all textbooks could be written in local languages and serve locally developed curricula without any significant change taking place in the overall effect of the education system. This is because the relationship between developed and developing countries, which lays down the broad parameters within which education systems can operate, is not altered by changing the education of the developing country's elite. And this shows both the strength and weakness of theories of cultural imperialism. Its strength is that it recognizes the supreme importance of the world economic context which shapes everything all countries do; its weakness is in not recognizing that that does not mean that everything that happens in developing countries is closely determined as a result.

The interplay of external controls and internal possibilities becomes clear if we look at some important alternative ways of conceiving of and organizing education systems in developing countries. The first and probably the best known is the Paolo Freire solution,[13] which seeks to raise people's consciousness of their situation through education and thus to produce liberated individuals in sufficient numbers to bring about a peaceful erosion of capitalism. However, attempts to implement this on a large scale demonstrate (with Freire's own exile from Brazil as the outstanding example) that though there may be "space" for independent individual action, it cannot be assumed that it will achieve a societal dimension and thus become effective as a social force acting against internal and external constraints. The second form of alternative is to use what internal space is available to proceed toward a more "authentic" national development. However, we should be clear that it can by no means necessarily be assumed that such "independent" initiatives will loosen the bonds of dependency or, indeed, radically alter the internal structure of the developing society. Such initiatives are much more likely to strengthen the domination of existing elites, which in turn entails not challenging the country's place within the world system. The outstanding example of an apparently sincere attempt to use the education system to weaken rather than reinforce the bonds of dependency and to open up the possibility of independent development is Tanzania.[14] However, the attempt has not so far been conspicuously successful due to internal and external pressures to maintain an education system more directly reflective of the needs and interests of capitalism, and to internal pressures to deviate from the capitalist path in different ways. The third alternative is a kind of desperate educational atavism which, despairing of the possibility of escaping from the dependency relationship, seeks as far as possible to ignore it, or at least to minimize its effects, through summoning up a chimerical golden age which existed before capitalist penetration.

The major problem, however, is that the reality of education systems in developing countries is rather different from the predictions and assumptions of both modernization and cultural imperialist theories (though to a rather lesser extent neocolonialist theories). They certainly do not take the form one would expect if their chief (or even only) function was to provide a technically sophisticated labor force for international capitalism. There is, for instance, typically a huge overproduction of graduates from every level of the education system. University and secondary school graduates are as likely to be qualified in the humanities or social sciences (especially law) as they are in technology or physical science. Notoriously, even where there are large numbers of scientifically and technologically qualified personnel, it is extremely unlikely that there will be sufficient jobs available that demand their level of knowledge and expertise. Two reasons underlie the failure to explain such education systems in developing countries. First, both modernization and dependency theories grant too little autonomy and importance to the intranational context in which education systems are located and operate. Both regard the developing education systems' chief function to be contributing to the strengthening of the country's economic ties with the rest of the world. Neither sees as important their internal context and contribution to noneconomic development. Second, just as education is assumed to play the same role everywhere, so it is assumed to be received everywhere in the same way, that it is to say, in the same way as it was intended to be received by those who planned it. This is very far from the case even within advanced countries; when what is being talked about (in cultural imperialist or neocolonialist approaches) is an externally imposed education system, the possibilities for deliberate or accidental modification of meaning are obviously much greater.

In spite of its apparent nonfunctionality, education remains extremely popular in developing countries. At a societal level, it is a demonstration of the declared intention of implementing the commitment to egalitarianism and progress of so many developing societies, though the availability and effectiveness of education are far from universal and tend to follow and reinforce existing status and regional inequalities. It is, more realistically, the most important route to the achievement, or confirmation, of wealth and social status, as well as the only route to prestigious and relatively extremely well-paid modern sector jobs, a very significant proportion of which are in state employment. Thus in terms of personal strategy, the more education, the better; any form of educated employment provides an opportunity structure. It is clear, too, as Ronald Dore points out, that it is well worth a graduate waiting for a modern sector job, even if it means being supported by one's family, when, "in the late sixties the Ugandan graduate just entering the civil service could expect his income to be fifty times the average income per head in Uganda. Even in India, after a much longer period of independence under governments with a much more explicitly egalitarian philosophy, the ratio was twelve to one."[15]

One major and neglected consequence of the education policies adopted by or imposed on developing societies is the "brain drain" they generate. Thus one important aspect of higher education as a personal strategy for self-advancement is its consequent contribution to the advantage of developed rather than developing countries. This is by virtue of the fact that it opens up a route for educated individuals to take up lucrative careers in advanced societies. Richard Devon notes this as a consequence of the tremendous emphasis which providers of education aid have placed on aid to tertiary education. As he puts it, "Countries like India which sorely need paramedics and technicians are exporting doctors and engineers from the medical schools and institutes of technology which development assistance has been instrumental in building."[16] He quotes UNCTAD figures to show that over the period 1961-1972, the imported capital value of skilled immigration from the less developed countries to Britain, the United States, and Canada was estimated at $51 billion; over the same period the total cumulative net flow of development assistance from these countries to less developed countries was $46 billion. A personal strategy aimed at becoming a surgeon in Britain or an engineer in Canada is far from unrealistic, then, even in countries with little indigenous demand for, or ability to absorb, such skills.

The problem is that though in terms of what it provides developing societies, education may seem to be a very poor investment, it goes on growing at a tremendous rate (between 1950 and 1970 estimated total enrollment in developing societies grew by over 300 percent at the primary level, by nearly 600 percent at the secondary level, and by over 600 percent at the tertiary level)[17]—and the evidence suggests that demand is nowhere near being met.

How is this explained? It is clear that technical-functional theory cannot explain it; the empirical evidence does little to support the theory. There is little evidence to suggest that beyond a certain point there is a continuously rising demand for occupational skills and knowledge. Rather, it appears that the provision of qualified graduates of educational institutions greatly outstrips the need for them. Similarly, it is not clear that work-related skills are learned in school (beyond basic literacy and numeracy, which are by no means universal preconditions of effective job performance), and it cannot be assumed that the curriculum is heavily vocationally biased in any case. Again, there is little evidence to suggest that the best educated workers, or those with the best qualifications, are the most effective or productive.

What schools provide is not qualifications but credentials. Credentials, as Randall Collins argues,[18] have become the key cultural currency, the possession of which provides their holders with the entries to variously prestigious levels of employment. The chase for educational credentials is endlessly inequitable, for beyond a certain point, fairly rapidly reached in most developing societies, expanding equality of educational opportunity merely leads to credential inflation. Possession of educational credentials may be used to confirm the social status of an elite job holder, rather than his or her ability to perform it.

Education is the major path in many developing countries to positions of social privilege and power; elsewhere it reinforces the status and power of already dominant groups. Education is thus clearly tied up with the production and reproduction of elites, while appearing to offer an equitable basis for the allocation of desirable occupational and social positions to those developing countries which explicitly, if frequently rhetorically, embrace an egalitarian socialist ethic. Formal equality of access to schools does not guarantee equality of outcome from them and in any case, provision of education is hugely inequitable. Even where there is a good level of educational provision, the likelihood is that the existing

elites will be able to exploit it better, or buy extra education resources to improve their credentials. Joel and Rachel Samoff, for
instance, describe how the existing elite in the Kilimanjaro district
of Tanzania was able to adapt to the fact of schooling as the legitimate route to power and wealth through its ability to manipulate
the level and nature of schooling provision in the area. As they
conclude, "Access to wealth leads to access to schools which in turn
provides access to power."[19]

It is not, however, that the education systems that have grown up
in developing societies are merely irrelevant: in a number of ways
the forms they take and the results they produce are positively
harmful. The very much greater rate of growth of nominal credentials, empty of content, and unrelated to social needs, which are
geared merely to formal qualifications for chronically scarce modern sector jobs, produces a truly enormous rate of educated unemployed. One example, that of Sri Lanka, may demonstrate the extent
of the problem. Ronald Dore writes of the situation there:

> At the beginning of the seventies the schools were producing annually
> about 70,000 children with eight years education, nearly 100,000 with
> the first "Ordinary Level" certificate, and another 12,000 with higher
> level certificates. At the same time, the total number of wage and
> salary jobs coming available was altogether probably no more than
> 70,000—*and* there were all the disappointed aspirants of previous
> years joining them in the competition.[20]

The rapid growth of educated unemployment is an eloquent
comment on the failure of such societies to break out of the stran-
glehold of underdevelopment. It is important in emphasizing the
pervasiveness of credentialism not to assume that it alone explains
why education systems in developing countries are as they are.
What is required is an analysis of the situations in developing societies which have created the problems to which particular forms of
education are a response. To do this we need to understand in
much more complex ways than those set out in dependency theory
the nature and effects of capitalist penetration of Third World
social formations. We may take John Taylor's work on the impact
of colonial capital on those societies as a useful point of departure
to examine the problem further.[21]

Very briefly, Taylor sees a "restricted and uneven capitalist development specific to Third World formations which is structured
both by the reproductive requirements of the industrial capitalist
mode of production *and* by the possibilities for the continuing
reproduction of the non-capitalist mode or its elements, embodied
in particular divisions of labour." He recognizes that the reproduc-

tion of noncapitalist modes can be a barrier to capitalist penetration; such reproduction will, in particular circumstances, take the form of resistance to capitalist penetration. The barriers to capitalist penetration which derive from the continuing strength and prominence of noncapitalist classes have a major ideological dimension. It is here that education has a major role to play. Taylor goes on to suggest:

> Unless imperialism can establish the political dominance of a class or alliance of classes which can gain ideological support amongst sectors of the population of the capitalist mode, the reproduction of capitalist social relations necessary for the enlarged reproduction of the capitalist mode cannot be guaranteed...its continuing reproduction...requires both an ideological and a political foundation, a commitment to its adequacy as a superior form of production in the ideologies that structure daily life, and a permanent access to political power to guarantee its population.[22]

Most of the latter part of that quotation reads like a program for education aid and, indeed, Taylor identifies the introduction of educational ideologies as one of the ways through which "the new ideologies required for the reproduction of the indigenous capitalist mode emerge."[23] However, he notes that the dominant capitalist ideologies (of such institutions as schools) are nevertheless necessarily penetrated by elements of noncapitalist ideologies. This has been important, for example, in the educational apparatus where, particularly during the colonial period, the contradictions between the theoretical ideologies promoted by the state and the matrix of ideologies originating in the apparatus of the previously dominant mode generated political ideologies that played a crucial role in independence movements.

Capitalism, then, does not penetrate noncapitalist formations smoothly and without resistance, either economically, politically, or ideologically. Education plays a key role in all this, though not exactly that attributed to it in both liberal and radical ideology—of smoothing the transition from underdeveloped to modern society through the provision of a radical, suprapolitical consensus about national goals and how to achieve them. It is very important to note, however, that because education does not do all the things it promises (or threatens), it cannot thereby be inferred either that it has no effect or that all its effects are negative. For while it is clear that education does not achieve all that liberal ideology claims for it, it is equally clear that development cannot take place without some sort of education system. Any solution to the problem of education in developing societies will have to start from the idea of transforming rather than of eliminating it. This is particularly important when so many criticisms of the effects of education in developing societies come very close to throwing out the baby with the bath water.

Rather than begging the question of what education does in developing societies by asserting a priori that it is involved with modernization, or increasing dependence, we should concentrate on the problems it solves and creates in and for the state. The forms taken by the problems it is to help solve obviously differ according to the world economic and political locations of the state and its own history, but the basic problems will center on directly assisting and providing a favorable context for the expansion of capitalism, and for the legitimation of that expansion and of the state's own role in it.[24] The problems that the (necessary) use of education creates *for* the state, however, take on a rather similar pattern, as has been suggested above. This is because (1) its effects cannot be entirely predicted or controlled, and (2) it becomes a weapon in the very struggle it is intended to thwart.

The demand for education, once created, cannot be turned off like a tap. As long as education is quite clearly the major, if not the only, route to wealth and power in a society, that demand is likely to continue to rise. This is especially so when the creation of a viable alternative route would depend on a total uncoupling of educational achievement from occupational position, which is impossible for the very reason that while in the majority of cases the process and outcome of educational credentialism are vocationally irrelevant, in a quite significant minority they are of the greatest importance. Developing societies are then stuck in the position of being unable to do without education, and also unable to control the demand for it—attempts to either limit its availability or deflect the demand into more "relevant" and less potentially threatening channels have so far been almost equally politically unpopular and ineffective.

This inability to control demand for education is the quantitative aspect of the way that education as a solution in fact also contributes to the problems of those whom it serves. The qualitative aspect is at least equally important. This is because it is impossible to educate people to the level where they are able to run a country or a branch plant without exposing them to ideas which would undermine the very basis of that country or company. Revolutionary as well as conservative ideologies are transmitted through education; it creates (especially in association with high levels of educated unemployment) an oppositional intelligentsia as well as providing the techniques to run the system smoothly. It was thus an ironic but inevitable consequence of colonial education that it produced articulate and sophisticated socialist leaders of postcolonial countries. Yet it is from that fact, and from these leaders' inability to transform their countries as they would wish, that we can infer most clearly both the potential of education and its limitations in the developing societies. It can do much to develop, extend, and exploit—but much less to bring about—the conditions of self-directed development.

Notes

1. The title, of course, refers to the famous Faure Report, *Learning to Be*, which represents the quintessence of the "education as a human right" approach to education in developing societies.
2. See Anthony Smith, "Reflections and Refractions on the Flow of Information," *Times Higher Education Supplement* (London), March 28, 1980; reprinted in this volume.
3. Quoted in Keith Buchanan, *Reflections on Education in the Third World* (Nottingham: Spokesman Books, 1975), p. 34.
4. Randall Collins has done as much as anyone to identify technical-functional theory as an application of a more general functionalist theory of stratification and to expose its shortcomings. See Randall Collins, "Functional and Conflict Theories of Educational Stratification," *American Sociological Review* 36 (1975): 1002-19.
5. Peter L. Berger, *Pyramids of Sacrifice* (London: Allen Lane, 1977), p. 51.
6. Caroline Hutton and Robin Cohen, "African Peasants and Resistance to Change: A Reconsideration of Sociological Approaches," in Ivor Oxaal, Tony Barnett, and David Booth, eds., *Beyond the Sociology of Development* (London: Routledge & Kegan Paul, 1975), p. 115.
7. This list is distilled from Alex Inkeles and David H. Smith, *Becoming Modern* (London: Heinemann, 1975); and Everett Rogers, *Modernization Among Peasants* (New York: Holt, Rinehart and Winston, 1969).
8. David C. McClelland, *The Achieving Society* (Princeton: Van Nostrand, 1961).
9. See Robert F. Arnove, "Comparative Education and World Systems Analysis," *Comparative Education Review* 24 (February 1, 1980): 48-62. On the effect of international organizations on national educational policies, see Roger Dale and Ann Wickham, "International Organizations and National Education," unpublished paper presented to the International Sociological Association Education Research Committee, Paris, August 1980.
10. Philip Coombs, *The Fourth Dimension of Foreign Policy: Educational and Cultural Affairs* (New York: Harper & Row, 1964).

11. See, for example, Martin Carnoy, *Education as Cultural Imperialism* (New York: McKay, 1974).
12. See, for example, Philip Altbach and Gail Kelly, *Education and Colonialism* (London: Longmans, 1974).
13. Most notably laid out in Paolo Freire, *Pedagogy of the Oppressed* (Harmondsworth: Penguin Books, 1972).
14. See Bill Williamson, *Education, Social Structure, and Development* (London: Macmillan, 1979), chap. 5.
15. Ronald Dore, *The Diploma Disease* (London: Allen and Unwin, 1976), p. 30.
16. See Richard Devon, "Education and the Development of Underdevelopment," *Comparative and International Education Society Newsletter* 47 (April 6-7, 1978).
17. UNESCO, *Statistical Yearbook 1972* (Paris: Unesco, 1972).
18. Randall Collins, *The Credential Society* (New York: Academic Press, 1979).
19. Joel Samoff and Rachel Samoff, "The Local Politics of Underdevelopment," *Politics and Society* 6, no. 4 (1976): 417.
20. Dore, *Diploma Disease*, p. 4.
21. John Taylor, *From Modernization to Modes of Production* (London: Macmillan, 1979).
22. Ibid., pp. 236-37.
23. Ibid., p. 267.
24. For an expansion of this assertion, see Roger Dale, "Education and the Capitalist State: Contributions and Contradictions," in Michael W. Apple, ed., *Economic and Social Reproduction in Education* (London: Routledge & Kegan Paul, 1982).

[32]
Reflections and Refractions
on the Flow of Information

Anthony Smith

The influence of Western media over the consciousness and culture of developing societies has become an important new issue in the years of East-West detente. So long as the world appeared to be divided into two quite separate and opposed ideologies, "North-South" questions lay submerged by "East-West" Cold War issues and their aftermath. With the arrival of a number of Third World countries at a position of economic power in the 1970s, and with the partial blurring of the great intellectual rifts of the Cold War, there has grown up an important geopolitical controversy over information, that is to say, over how the flow of information created by and required by modern industries is controlled, as it passes between the relatively prosperous "northern" societies and the formerly colonized "southern" societies.

Over the last five years or so a series of international conferences has been held at which many Third World spokespeople have argued that Western journalism plus Western control of the international corporations dealing in information (i.e., news agencies, international telecommunications networks, computer industries, publishing companies, etc.) have become a kind of intellectual occupation, leading to a systematic undermining of the political gains achieved by the national independence movements of the 1960s and 1970s. The geopolitics of information is something more than an echo of the "North-South" dialogue in the economic sphere. The developing nations have found in the information industries some positive leverage on world power in general.

In the course of the half-decade the debate has taken a number of fresh turns and is no longer directed primarily against the four major Western news agencies (Reuters, Agence France Presse, Associated Press, United Press International) which were originally made to take the brunt of the shrill accusation that the West operated a systematic machinery of disinformation, against the interests of the Third World. Today, with the imminent publication of the MacBride Report,[1] prepared at the request of the secretary-general of the United Nations Educational, Scientific, and Cultural Organization (UNESCO) who wanted a survey of the entire field of world information problems, the information debate reaches into broader and far more difficult terrain. The questions addressed by MacBride are inseparable from the questions addressed by the now-published Brandt Report,[2] which urges a major rethinking of North-South relations. MacBride's document is clearly cumulative, and contains a compendium of the arguments and allegations that have been made during the course of the years, as well as the counterarguments and counterallegations; in aggregating them it becomes evident that the performance of Western journalism, which remains at the heart of the controversy, is but one of a number of historic processes that cannot be dealt with by lecturing a few journalists or denouncing their employers. What the participants in the debate now acknowledge is that the information industries are responsible in large measure for the shaping of the relationship and mutual image of world sectors, but they are so only within the constraints of certain realities of power; it is these which give rise to the sense of plausibility, the perception of relevance, the newsworthiness, which are the core of journalistic judgment.

Those whose profession it is to report the world play a unique role in creating its realities but are so locked into their own routines of fact collection, into their national "mind-sets," and into the sense of the needs and the comprehension of their audiences, that they are not really free agents in the sense that their accusers have imagined. So long as the audiences of the Western nations remain the major paying audiences for the whole machine of international information and entertainment, then the assumptions of those audiences will remain intellectually dominant.

One may cite the reporting of Iran since the cracking of the shah's regime; the ayatollah, so long as he remained in Paris, was treated, together with his followers, as an eccentric turbanned zealot, later turning into an inexplicable tyrant; the Iranian insurrection was reported in terms of its impact upon oil prices, jobs, the balance of world power, almost anything except its attractiveness for Iranians themselves who had endured some decades of a regime which they increasingly disliked.

Reporters from Western Europe and the United States were so firmly convinced that the shah's occasional harshness was a necessary aspect of the process of "modernization" that they completely neglected—with a handful of exceptions—to look at the failure of "modernization" to reach down through the population or to deliver anything of tangible value (still less of cultural value) to the Iranian people. The disappearance of the shah was a terrible shock to the Western media, which had reported Iran's affairs through the prism of a Western model of what was happening and what "modernization" meant.

What the Third World has been arguing during the years of the great information debate is basically that this systematic failure on the part of the Western information apparatus to comprehend the dynamic of postcolonial history has led to appalling distortions which are (or were) shared by Western diplomacy as well as the Western press. In other words, the West comes to believe its own lies and recirculate them.

The international issue which arises from these lies is the fact that the Western apparatus of information is also the dominant apparatus for informing the whole of the world. The Soviet, Chinese, and Third World news agencies are frail, poorly equipped, undertrained affairs and tend to be so subject to the ideological control of their respective governments as to be impotent as systems of information. It is the relative freedom of the Western press which contributes to its power and expertise and therefore to its influence over the population of the very countries which it most damagingly misrepresents.

From the point of view of an observer in the West, however, the problem is more complicated than that—the faults of the press are as evident when they report their home societies as when they report other cultures, but that cuts little ice in Asia, Africa, and the Middle East where the specialist reporters and agency journalists of the four major companies exercise a disproportionately large influence.

There is a general crisis of concept and purpose in Western journalism and the North-South debate points up one classic symptom of it. For the whole of the present century the foreign reporter has used two main protections against the accusation of irresponsibility: the first is his adherence to a policy of "objectivity" which has meant in practice the belief that the journalist is fundamentally a collector of facts, and the second is the belief that there can reside in an individual observer of another culture a kind of expertise which guarantees the validity of his judgments, or at least supports his or her right to make them.

In the case of ethnographers, anthropologists, novelists, filmmakers, historians, and many other intellectuals, a much livelier realization has dawned that dominant societies bring a major built-in bias to the task of observing nondominant cultures. All these areas of disquisition have come to treat their own methods with a healthy skepticism, especially when it comes to attempts at intercultural interpretation. Not so journalism, which continues to pin its own justification to a set of intellectual methods which are seldom examined critically by those who employ them.

Watergate has brought about a great revival of faith in the efficacy and reliability of journalistic methods, although there exists today a small body of journalists from North and South who specialize in reporting Third World concerns from different professional and deliberately "Third World" standpoints. A school of journalism which calls itself "developmental" has grown up which argues that the Western bias is built into the construct of the news story, as this is imparted in Western schools of journalism: it argues that the mere collection of unassimilated "stories" is a method by which Western newsgatherers structure an image of the world around Western beliefs and superstitions about the Third World and thus serve to "reproduce" prevailing realities.

The readers of the North are treated to a flow of imagery about the Third World which emphasizes instability, violence, starvation, and insurrection because these phenomena fall easily into the categories of Western popular journalism. In their place the "developmental journalists" substitute the notion of processes, trends, and analyses of society's needs. Reporting ceases to be a form of entertainment and becomes instead a structured form of education. Not appropriate for the columns of the Western press, but practical, cynics wryly observe, in societies in which governments in any case dominate the press. It is possible to describe the problems of a country in terms which automatically exonerate its rulers, if the reporter concentrates on processes and problems and ignores hard spot news, real and spectacular events.

The idea that there can in reality be widely practiced a new form and doctrine of journalism has become current within UNESCO, which has been the powerhouse of the whole information debate. There are, of course, a number of genuine "developmental journalists" around the world, but a wide variety of despicable governmental practices can also be justified in the name of the new doctrine. Since the debate on international information flow started up, the treatment of Western journalists in a number of Third World countries has noticeably deteriorated. UNESCO has opened a Pandora's box which has resulted in a strengthening of many rulers who have nothing but contempt for the processes of a free press, whether "developmental" or not.

One senior official of the United Nations Development Program, Narinder Aggarwala, who has long been an advocate of a new form of Third World journalism, points out that some of the most basic facts about India, for example, are never alluded to by the reporters who cover India's disasters, electoral conflicts, problems of public and social life. India has doubled its food production in the last twenty years and is now the eighth largest industrial country in the world with the third largest technically trained labor force. That suggests a different picture from the one normally depicted in the radio, television, and print journalism of the agencies and special correspondents. Journalists who come from the Third World, however, are no more willing in general to write about national and economic development than their colleagues in the West. Indeed, the failure of a "new journalism" to take hold within the Third World is itself a reflection of the way in which norms and standards of journalism are basically Western ones which travel throughout the globe through the sheer dominance of Western institutions.

The paradoxes of this domination are widespread. Within the countries of Asia and Africa, for example, elite populations have sprung up around the capital and regional centers that have passed through the stage of "modernization" and have become committed to the culture of the West. The mass culture of the West has in effect become the elite culture of much of the Third World, and Western culture thus continues the task of alienating these social groups from a direct involvement with their own societies, presenting them and their children with appalling cultural dilemmas, decommitting them from their ethnic cultures but giving them only a peripheral role within the culture whose centers are in New York, London, Paris, Berlin, Rome.

Yet the Third World is not complaining about an excess of Western information overall. Rather the reverse is the case. There are legal, institutional, and financial blockages in the flow of international information which are further contributing to the information gulf that yawns alongside the North-South economic gulf. Developing countries have a need to protect their own indigenous authors and artists and require a system of copyright which will lead the wealth earned by their intellectuals to flow back into the originating society; at the same time, they require access to the information store of the West—through translation, reproduction, importation— despite the copyright controls which are imposed in the originating countries.

There is great international pressure being exerted at present through the relevant international bodies for a general reconstruction of the copyright system to favor the needs of developing societies which are trying to benefit from the greater flow of scientific and technical knowledge. The processes of state and private subsidy, foundation and state patronage, which help the creation of technical knowledge are of course much more highly developed in the North than in the South; technicians and writers in the North have a much wider range of sources of income than those in the South and the laws of copyright have been designed over the decades to protect the blocs of publishing and media capital of Western societies. It is likely that in the wake of the MacBride Report, UN agencies will make much greater efforts to loosen the controls and permit a broader flow of information in both directions.

In the field of electronics lies the greatest of all obstacles to the equitable flow of information around the world. The more widespread the use of modern computer-based technologies for circulating information, the more difficult it becomes for Third World societies to participate in the intellectual life of the late twentieth century. In the United States a great war is breaking out between the giant corporations, instigated by Congress itself which is forcing a higher level of competition upon the multinationals as a way of regulating them.

The result is that an equipment war fought between U.S., Japanese, and German multinationals is taking place across the globe. New electronic information services are being offered which have the effect of removing indigenous information for processing in the United States or by U.S. companies. True, transborder data flow, as it is commonly called, helps to render the participating countries mutually dependent, but the overall effect of the satellite-borne message systems which are to be used in the 1980s by the multinationals is that of a giant pipette sucking information out of the weaker societies.

For example, remote sensing by satellite enables the nation which controls the technology to have access to knowledge about mineral resources, military movements, the state of harvests in developing societies which themselves lack the expertise to process the information, thus leaving them vulnerable to foreign corporations who wish to exploit their resources. Then there is the Satellite Business System (SBS) which will soon begin to send intracorporate mail, electronically, from place to place, eventually broadening into an international carrier of letters and telephone messages; SBS is the means by which IBM will compete for the message market against AT&T. The results will, no doubt, be of great benefit to the consumer, but SBS will mean the decline of physical postage services, and the evaporation of local control over industrial and governmental information from societies which are technically weak. (Britain could also be one of the losers.) SBS will have concomitant benefits and the disadvantages lie precisely in those areas on which national sovereignty and independence rely—the indigenous control of local information.[3]

The information issue spins itself out into area after area of national policy. Take, for example, the position of the newspaper industry in those Asian countries whose capital city today sports a

Western-owned English-language daily paper. Vernacular newspapers in Asian countries are expensive to print and very expensive to distribute outside the city of publication. They have waited several decades for the chance of milking the new elites of their advertising power, which could now begin to bring in revenue sufficient to transform the vernacular press and, in so doing, help to render it less reliant on political and governmental patronage.

However, in these Asian cities, the elites turn unsurprisingly to the new English-language dailies, mainly owned abroad, which are mopping up the advertising potential generated by the prosperous urban elites. It is a cultural tragedy in its way but also a political one in that the phenomenon is helping to defer the development of a healthy independent journalism of the kind which the Third World is constantly preached at for failing to develop.

What the information issue consists of, at heart, is the fear that Western professional practices and information technology are robbing the Third World of its chance of sovereignty. This group of societies has, on the whole, been coping badly with the task of building political democracy and equally badly with the task of building media freedoms. However, it might be argued that the more insecure a nation's grasp on its own sovereignty, the less likely it is that political democracy or press freedom can be established. The current discussion about North-South information inequality is dogged by the failure or unwillingness of Western journalism and the Western information industry to comprehend the fear that lies behind the autocracy and press harassment of many Third World governments. It has already taken one or two generations to create successful independence movements and commence the process of building separate notions of national consciousness. It takes a mental and educational, as well as a political, revolution for Ashantis to see themselves as a Ghanaians; yet a century ago it seemed just as difficult for Piedmontese to begin to see themselves as Italians or Hanoverians as Germans. The threat of sheer cultural swamping by Western information is perhaps a greater threat to sovereignty than was colonialism itself— greater but less tangible, because the pressure for it lies in institutions that no one in the West seems fully to understand, still less to control.

Notes

1. *Many Voices—One World* (*The MacBride Report*), report by the International Commission for the Study of Communication Problems (Paris: UNESCO, 1980).

2. W. Brandt et al., *North-South—A Programme for Survival* (London: Pan, 1980).
3. See Robert E. Jackson, "Satellite Business Systems and the Concept of the Dispersed Enterprise: An End to Sovereignty," *Media, Culture and Society* 3 (July 1979); also Herbert I. Schiller, "Computer Systems: Power for Whom and for What?" *Journal of Communication* 28, no. 4 (Autumn 1978).

[33]
Nationalism and "Development"

Tom Nairn

[. . .]If someone were producing an updated version of Gustave Flaubert's *Dictionnaire des idées réçues* for the use of politics and social science students, I think the entry "nationalism" might read as follows:

> *Nationalism*: infrequently used before the later nineteenth century, the term can nonetheless be traced back in approximately its contemporary meaning to the 1790s (Abbé Baruel, 1798). It denotes the new and heightened significance accorded to factors of nationality, ethnic inheritance, customs, and speech from the early nineteenth century onward. The concept of nationalism as a generally necessary stage of development for all societies is common to both materialist and idealist philosophies. These later theoretical formulations agree that society must pass through this phase (see, e.g., texts of F. Engels, L. von Ranke, V. I. Lenin, F. Meinecke). These theories also agree in attributing the causes of this phase to specific forces or impulses resident within the social formations concerned. Nationalism is therefore an internally determined necessity, associated by Marxists with, for example, the creation of a national market economy and a viable national bourgeois class; by Idealists with the indwelling spirit of the community, a common personality which must find expression in historical development. Both views concur that this stage of societal evolution is the necessary precondition of a subsequent, more satisfactory state of affairs, known as "internationalism" ("proletarian" or "socialist" internationalism in one case, the higher harmony of the World Spirit in the other). This condition is only attainable for societies and individuals who have developed a healthy nationalism previously. While moderate, reasonable nationalism is in this sense praised, an immoderate or excessive nationalism exceeding these historical limits is viewed as unhealthy and dangerous (see entry "Chauvinism," above).

The gist of this piece of global folklore (which unfortunately embraces much of what passes for "theory" on nationalism) is that nationalism is an inwardly determined social necessity, a "growth-stage," located somewhere in between traditional or "feudal" societies and a future where the factors of nationality will become less prominent (or anyway less troublesome in human history). Regrettably, it is a growth-stage which can sometimes go wrong and run amok. This is mysterious. How can adolescence become a deadly disease? Whatever the doctors say about this, they agree on the double inwardness attaching to nationalism. It corresponds to certain internal needs of the society in question, *and* to certain individual, psychological needs as well. It supplies peoples and persons with an important commodity, "identity." There is a distinctive, easily recognizable subjectivity linked to all this. Whenever we talk about nationalism, we normally find ourselves talking before too long about "feelings," "instincts," supposed desires, hankerings to "belong," and so on. This psychology is obviously an important fact about nationalism.

The universal folklore of nationalism is not entirely wrong. If it were, it would be unable to function as myth. On the other hand, it would be equally unable to function in this way if it were true—that is, true in the sense that concerns us in this place. It is ideology. This means it is the generally acceptable "false consciousness" of a social world still in the grip of "nationalism." It is a mechanism of adjustment and compensation, a way of living with the reality of those forms of historical development we label "nationalism." As such, it is perhaps best regarded as a set of important clues toward whatever these forms are really about.

The principal such clue is the powerful connection that common sense suggests between nationalism and the concept of development or social and economic "growth." It is true that the distinctively modern fact of national*ism* (as opposed to nationality, national states, and other precursors) is somehow related to this. For it is only within the context of the general acceleration of change since about 1800, only in the context of "development" in this new sense, that nationhood acquired this systemic and abstract meaning.

However, it is not true that the systemic connotation derives *from the fact of development as such*. This is the sensitive juncture at which truth evaporates into useful ideology. It is simply not the case (although humanity has always had plenty of reasons for wishing it were the case) that national-ism, the compulsive necessity for a certain sociopolitical form, arises naturally from these new developmental conditions. It is not nature. The point of the folklore is of course to suggest this: to award it a natural status, and hence a "health" label, as if it were indeed a sort of adolescence of all societies, the road we have to trudge along between rural idiocy and "modernity," industrialization (or whatever).

A second significant clue is that pointing toward social and personal subjectivity. It is true that nationalism is connected with typical internal movements, personnel, and persons. These behave in similar ways and entertain quite similar feelings. So it is tempting to say, e.g., that the Italian nationalism of the 1850s or the Kurdish or Eritrean nationalism of the 1970s rests upon and is generated by these specific internal mechanisms. They express the native peculiarities of their peoples, in a broadly similar way—presumably because the people's soul (or at least its bourgeoisie) needs to.

However, it is not true that nationalism of any kind is really the product *of these internal motions as such*. This is the core of the empirical country-by-country fallacy which the ideology of nationalism itself wishes upon us. Welsh *nationalism*, of course, has much to do with the specifics of the Welsh people, their history, their particular forms of oppression, and all the rest of it. But Welsh nationalism —that generic, universal necessity recorded in the very term we are interested in—has nothing to do with Wales. It is not a Welsh fact, but a fact of general developmental history, that at a specific time the Welsh land and people are forced into the historical process in this fashion. The "ism" they are then compelled to follow is in reality imposed upon them from without; although of course to make this adaptation, it is necessary that the usual kinds of national cadres, myths, sentiments, etc., well up from within. All nationalisms work through a characteristic repertoire of social and personal mechanisms, many of them highly subjective. But the causation of the drama is not within the bosom of the *volk*: this way lie the myths of blood and *geist*. The subjectivity of nationalism is an important objective fact about it; but it is a fact which, in itself, merely reposes the question of origins.

The real origins are elsewhere. They are located not in the folk, nor in the individual's repressed passion for some sort of wholeness or identity, but in the machinery of world political economy. Not, however, in the process of that economy's development as such— not simply as an inevitable concomitant of industrialization and urbanization. They are associated with more specific features of that process. The best way of categorizing these traits is to say they represent the *uneven development* of history since the eighteenth century. This unevenness is a material fact; one could argue that it is the most grossly material fact about modern history. This statement allows us to reach a satisfying and near-paradoxical conclusion: the most notoriously subjective and ideal of historical phenomena is in fact a by-product of the most brutally and hopelessly material side of the history of the last two centuries. [. . .].

Unable to literally "copy" the advanced lands (which would have entailed repeating the stages of slow growth that had led to the breakthrough), the backward regions were forced to take what they wanted and cobble it on to their own native inheritance of social forms. In the annals of this kind of theorizing the procedure is called "uneven and combined development." To defend themselves, the peripheral countries were compelled to try and advance "in their own way," to "do it for themselves." Their rulers—or at least the newly awakened elites who now came to power—had to mobilize their societies for this historical shortcut. This meant the conscious formation of a militant, interclass community rendered strongly (if mythically) aware of its own separate identity vis-à-vis the outside forces of domination. There was no other way of doing it. Mobilization had to be in terms of what was there; and the whole point of the dilemma was that there was nothing there—none of the economic and political institutions of modernity now so needed.

All that there *was* was the people and peculiarities of the region: its inherited *ethos*, speech, folklore, skin-color, and so on. Nationalism works through *differentiae* like those because it has to. It is not necessarily democratic in outlook, but it *is* invariably populist. People are what it has to go on: in the archetypal situation of the really poor or "under-developed" territory, it may be more or less all that nationalists have going for them. For kindred reasons, it had to function through highly rhetorical forms, through a sentimental culture sufficiently accessible to the lower strata now being called to battle. This is why a romantic culture quite remote from Enlightenment rationalism always went hand-in-hand with the spread of nationalism. The new middle-class intelligentsia of nationalism had to invite the masses into history; and the invitation card had to be written in a language they understood.[...].

It is only too easy to deduce from this picture a certain theory of nationalism. I will call this the anti-imperialist theory. It lays primary emphasis upon the successive waves of peripheric struggle, from the early nineteenth century up to the generalized Third World rebellion of the present-day. And, of course, it views the phenomenon in a highly positive moral light. There may have been aberrations and excesses, but nationalism is mainly with the angels of progress. This point of view is given its most cogent expression at the end of Ernest Gellner's celebrated essay on nationalism. "By and large this does seem a beneficent arrangement," he argues, because if the nationalist response to development had not occurred then imperialism would have simply intensified, and "this politically united world might well come to resemble the present condition of South Africa...."[1]

The anti-imperialist theory is better than stories about demonic urges and irrepressible atavism. It does relate nationalism to the wider arc of historical development (in the way we say was necessary), and it does encompass some of the mechanisms of that process. It combines a degree of theoretical consciousness with its strong practical and political impulse, the impulse of solidarity with the underdevelopment struggles which are still proceeding over most of the globe. Yet it is really incorrect. In effect, it is a sort of compromise between historical materialism and common sense: between the much more ambiguous truth of nationalism and those mythologies I mentioned previously. As such, it renounces the difficult task of gripping both horns of the dilemma and—for the most sympathetic of motives—clings aggressively to one of them. In many cases (though not in Gellner's), it comes down to little more than a more sophisticated justification of romantic nationalism, now transformed into "Third Worldism."

The truth is less palatable. Anti-imperialist theory lets go of the real logic (or illogic) of uneven development, because it lets go of the totality of the process.

Note

1. Ernest Gellner, *Thought and Change* (London: 1964), pp. 177-78.

Ideology and Identity:
An Approach from History

Basil Davidson

The problem of "otherness" in cultural history is as old as Adam and Eve, and is not really my subject here. Yet something may usefully be said about it at the close of a volume concerned with the realities of a "Third World" whose very name derives only from a relationship with other "worlds," above all with the "world" of industrialized states and their economic structures, and which otherwise has no such identity or corresponding awareness of itself. This exercise may possibly be more than useful: it may even be necessary to any further unfolding of "our" understanding of "them" —coming from whichever "side" you may prefer—and therefore to the fruitfulness of work projected by studies such as these. For if the pursuit of health, wealth, and happiness—and to the old formula should we not now add liberty?—makes all men brothers (assuming sisters, naturally, while the collective noun seems lacking), then where along the resulting relationship-continuum, as between one "world" and another, stands person A or person B? Or again, where along that continuum from the merely mystifying to the validly heuristic is the place for objectivity to take its stand: for science, that is, and synthesis? Is there any such place for objectivity, and, if not, what is that subjectivity which can be useful instrumentally, not only to "them" as well as to "us" but also to a collective "them/us"? We can answer this question for "us" and apply the answer that we find to "them," and this is what we are doing all the time even when we prefer not to say so: but how can we know, in truth, that we are prescribing for more than ourselves?

Dogmatists have naturally had no difficulty here. For religious missionaries of whatever faith or denomination, it has been good objective truth that sauce for the goose must be sauce for the gander. The more dogmatic of the missionaries, especially after about 1880 with the onset of new forms of "First World" imperialism (or do I mean "Second World"? I can never be sure), were content to extend that formula to the "civilizing mission" of colonial enclosure, forced labor, mining profits, and the rest. The less dogmatic went much less far, as it is pleasant to remember. "What do we mean," asked the awkward Bishop Tozer in 1870, "when we say that England and France are civilised countries and that the greater part of Africa is uncivilised?" "Surely," he went on, very teasingly for a bishop, "the mere enjoyment of such things as railways and telegraphs and the like do not necessarily prove their possessors to be in the first rank of civilised nations.... Nothing can be so false as to suppose that the outward circumstances of a people is the measure of its barbarism or its civilisation."[1]

They were words lost on the wind for the most part, since this was just what the vast majority of Bishop Tozer's colleagues and their like supposed and intended to continue to suppose. Attachment to a community equipped not only with a Christian God but also with telegraphs and railways, and above all cash, was to be the ground on which all people must stand if they wished to be civilized. Latterday dogmatists have said the same, if in different terms. There is, for instance, the dogmatism deriving from the concept of capitalist hegemony. Many have defined it with a ponderous certainty but none, in recent years, so clearly as Walt W. Rostow in his famous "five stages" from a "traditional society" (whatever that may be) to one of high mass-consumption (unemployed not counted): a progression which, seemingly, assumes that all societies everywhere follow the same track, no matter what their history, and terminate—must indeed terminate unless disaster overtakes them on the way— somewhere in the Texas of the 1960s.[2] This way of understanding the world might be called the Church of Fifth Stage Adventism: or, more vulgarly, the school of whatever-is-good-for-General-Motors-is-good-for-everyone-else. Then, of course, we have the reverse dogmatism which has declared that this or that prescription for anticapitalist revolution, and so this or that attachment to this or that—precisely defined—series of instrumental attitudes and/or interpretations of supposed reality (as distinct from researched reality, but I will come back to this point) must be the only rightful, because the only effective, ground of universality.

Yet for nondogmatists, or anyone striving to be such, the problem is far from simple; and it is rendered continually more complex by awareness of the fact that history is not a neatly linear progression nicely adjusted to all peoples and cultures, but rather a process fractured and confused by an open-ended quantity of different "stages" and consequences. Consider, in this respect, only the apparently simple but really very tortuous matter of nationalism. In the industrialized countries, by 1945 if not before, the concept of nationalism no longer seemed, at least in any automatic way, to offer a desirable future. Two frightful wars across the world had taught the contrary, for in each of them the driving initiative, the crucial aggression, had come from nation states whose internal logic—whose nationalist logic—called for expansion by any means to hand. You could label this imperialism if you wished, but it still remained obvious that imperialism without nationalism was unthinkable. Any further development of society must therefore depend upon "getting beyond nationalism": under the banners of socialism, for some, or for others of a different kidney, under those of a transnational capitalism. Yet in Africa—and here I confine myself to the African part of the "Third World"—this was precisely the moment, in 1945 and after, when the banners of nationalism not only seemed, but really were, the only ones that could promise an exit from colonial subjection. The goose might have tired of the sauce, but not the gander. And with good reason.

Of course it was possible for progressives, whose ponderings on the subject may be taken seriously (as against the "community" propaganda of corporations eager for the untrammeled movement of their assets, including labor) to get round this contradiction that nationalism had become "bad" for one world while remaining "good" for another. But the getting round it could not be elegant. They could (and often did) argue that African nationalism presumed the growth of middle classes and a corresponding development of working classes, and therefore, in time, the same "outlet to socialism" as in the industrialized countries. All national roads, in short, would lead to the same end—and the end would be desirable. This might pass for acceptable logic so long as it was based on little information: but with information, as the post-1945 years have shown, the logic could be very hard to see. Yet in any case and with whatever reservations, progressives during the 1950s were bound to approve of those very processes of nationalism which they had come, and very understandably, to deplore at home in the industrialized "world." Few of them made the reservation entered by Thomas Hodgkin: that "even if we were guilty of the sin of historicism"—though if it came to that, he added, he should still prefer Marx to Popper— "the end of the historical process to which we looked, and still look, forward—a new beginning in fact as much as an end—was not the bourgeois territorial state but the world socialist commonwealth and the withering away of the state."[3]

Most non-Marxist or non-*marxisant* progressives, on the other hand, appeared to believe that the coming of the "bourgeois nation state" (and I put in the quotation marks merely to indicate a terminological shorthand) could offer precisely the liberating processes and guarantees in Africa that it had singularly failed to provide elsewhere. As for the nonprogressives, insofar as they gave sign of thinking about the matter at all, it was to welcome the rise of the "bourgeois nation state" in colonial territories, now ex-colonial, as one more proof that Europe knew best. So much could repeatedly be seen in the assumption that the parliamentary model à la Westminster or Palais Bourbon could and would provide all that was required for everything afterward to go swimmingly ahead. Nothing could be more illustrative of an intellectual provincialism than the British imperial custom, as late as the 1960s, of continuing to speed copies of Erskine May with suitable wigs and maces to the new parliaments of the ex-colonial states; nor, in its amused irony, than the careful acceptance by African dignitaries of their manifest obligation to conform. The French set their own example, but it was really just the same. "There is Marianne," a brand-new chairperson of a brand-new assembly in French-speaking Africa once said to me, while pointing with a cautious smile to the plaster-pale figure of the state symbol on the wall above his chair, "and here are we. She so white, and we so black. . . ."

An anecdote, no doubt; and yet the relationship-continuum is nothing if not anecdotal, at least in the sense that Marc Bloch was meaning when he affirmed that historical facts are psychological facts.[4] Given the dimension in which this is undoubtedly true, the facts of any history being the facts that have been psychologically selected, an approach from history may still yield some firm ground, in this elusive field, for a consideration of the relationship-continuum of our own time and in which all of us, whether as actors or spectators (or supposing ourselves spectators) are of necessity involved.

2

It was a common ground of colonial or imperial ideology, for many years, to consider the populations of Africa as being deviant in their nature from the developmental potentialities of a "normal rationality." The "natives" might begin as children like other children, but they failed to become adults like other adults. They remained "grown-up children." They failed to "develop." One may argue that such attitudes, which would be called racist now, were part of the scaffolding necessary to allow otherwise honest or well-meaning people to subjugate and expropriate other people in ways they would have found disgraceful if practiced at home. The fact remains that such attitudes become easily rooted into dominant cultures, and were accepted as patently rational. Among many sensible people who held them there was, for example, the chief social administrator of the Belgian Congo (Katanga:Shaba) copper mines of the Union Minière. Writing in a scientific spirit in 1946 Dr.

Léopold Mottoulle could affirm with a perfect confidence of being enlightened as well as right, that

> the coloniser must never lose sight of the fact that the Negroes have the minds of children, minds which are shaped by the methods of the educator: they look and listen, feel and imitate. The European must in all circumstances show himself a calm and thoughtful chief, good without weakness, benevolent without familiarity, active by method and above all just in the repression of faults as in the reward of goodwill.[5]

How otherwise should one deal with children save by a sage paternalism?

The study of alienation at this point is clearly into the psychopathology of colonial rule and its own rationale. I cannot follow it here, but its course would show, I think—and as S. Ramon has argued in discussing the whole question of "deviancy" and its conception—that "each action against any sort of deviancy strengthens the conformists in their conformity,"[6] and tends to reinforce those very influences which may deprive the supposed "deviant" of his or her innate sense of "normality." Behind the good Dr. Mottoulle's formulations lay a long paternity; and inferiority begets its own children. The colonial years were laden with their experience.

Was it so in earlier times? Is it in any case the fact that humanity has always diminished and twisted with distance—distance geographical or social: rather like those neighbors of the Lugbara who became ever more peculiar and inverted (for the Lugbara) as the kilometers clocked up between?[7] There may be something in this. Writing in the fifth century B.C., Herodotus had evidently to cope with rather few problems of racist mythology, of built-in assumptions (or neuroses) about sin and virtue, either as to himself or to the Greeks for whom he wrote, and whether in respect of the peoples of the Nile and North Africa or even of those "blameless Ethiopians" who lived beyond the reach of his travels and who were, or so he told the Greeks, said to be the best-looking people anywhere. Doubts began in Asia rather than Africa, for beyond the Asian Issedones were the one-eyed Arimaspians, clearly not quite satisfactorily human, and beyond them again the griffins who guarded the gold, obviously still less so. But who had ever seen them? On the other hand, the Greeks were close to their neighbors over the water; and anyone who cares to look at the busts and portraits of Africans made in those times, and right on through the Hellenist centuries, will find the relationship to have been one of interested acceptance of a "different but equal" humanity.[8] And was it the same the other way round? At least from what Herodotus says and implies, it seems to have been so.

This "different but equal" relationship persists. If Malfante is telling an Italian audience in 1447 that the black peoples who live in "innumerable and great territories" south of the Sahara desert "are in carnal acts like the beasts," with their women "bearing up to five at a birth," and so on, he is only retelling the travelers' tales of the caravans of the long-distance trade. Such tales about the "black peoples" were akin to those of the Thousand and One Nights, of Sinbad and Aladdin, made up for stay-at-homes in Baghdad who "longed to travel for profit and adventure" but all the same preferred that others should travel for them; and nobody is taking them seriously. So little, indeed, that after a Scots privateer lands a black lady at the port of Leith in 1508 (or possibly 1509), fourteen knights from the nearby royal court at Edinburgh are found jousting for the honors of her friendship, and it is King James IV himself who, literally enough, carries off the prize. There is, in short, a harvest of amusing stories; but when it comes down to business Othello is no "grown-up child" but the captain of Venetian armies, and greatly prized as such.

Africans might come into that Europe in the status of captives, and therefore of slaves, but they were tested for their qualities and used according to their merits; and it was the same elsewhere. At least one of the great Ottoman generals of the early sixteenth century, sweeping his Turkish host across North Africa, was an ex-captive slave from the Balkans (apparently a Croat), and in this respect he offered a precedent for a long Ottoman future. "Yes, and some widows of good family who brought some of these female slaves" captured in Africa, records the Portuguese chronicler Azurara, only nineteen years after mariners from Portugal have sailed south beyond Cape Bojador, "either adopted them or left them a portion of their estate by will, so that in the future they married right well, treating them as altogether free." It has been argued that Azurara was improving on the truth, but I fail to see why he should have wished to do so. The antislavery agitations were immensely far ahead in 1453.

The interested acceptance of a different but equal humanity gives way to new attitudes in the seventeenth century, at least on the European side; and this shift along the continuum, this cultural response to new forms of exploitation, is hard to interpret without placing the changed nature of the conditions of enslavement in the center of the picture. A changed nature: one has to insist on that. Medieval and early postmedieval slavery was, for the most part, only another form of servitude within precapitalist modes of production and their corresponding cultures: "It was a personal service in the widest sense of the word, which, when the master served was of high rank and wealthy, carried with it great advantages, as well as social prestige."[9] A slave within that context was generally better off than the majority of rural producers, if only because slaves were expensive and hard to replace, while serfs were not. But the plantation and mining slavery which derived from the maritime slave trade, above all in the Americas, was something else. Within that, slaves became chattels whose cost of replacement grew progressively smaller as the years went by: smaller, that is, in relation to the market value of their product and sometimes to the ease of their replacement. Much turned on that. A crude but not misleading display of the shift in attitude may be had from comparing, for example, the narratives of early European voyages to the West African coast (the Portuguese arriving there in the 1440s, with their competitors beginning to offer a serious rivalry some fifty years later), with those of the eighteenth century when the trans-Atlantic trade was at its height. The attitude of different but equal has almost entirely disappeared. In its place is the attitude that takes the different as being deviant, as being necessarily inferior: humanly, that is, and inherently. The travelers' tales are taken seriously now.

Installed within the history of capitalism, the relationship-continuum reflects its steering forms of exploitation. There are, of course, exceptions. These derive, though for a long time rarely, from attitudes of scientific interest rather than philanthropic enlightenment, the latter being always liable to slide into a mere paternalism. Characteristic of this scientific interest is the work of Thomas Winterbottom, a physician whose two-volume account of the population of Sierra Leone, published in 1803, formed perhaps the first attempt at what would afterwards become the discipline of social anthropology.[10] Later again there were men such as the nineteenth century Thomas Hodgkin who put themselves against the rising flood of travelers' tales which were now set forth, at any rate after about 1850, as scientific truth. These exceptions belong to an interesting tradition of its own. It points ahead, but is very much a minority tradition within dominant attitudes of public contempt that found their most influential exponent in the writings of the British traveler Richard Burton during high Victorian times. Africans, by now, have become those "retarded children" who are incapable of growing up, and knowing, as Samuel Baker affirmed in his confident diary of 1863, "neither gratitude, pity, love, nor self-denial." Having "no idea of duty; no religion; but covetousness, ingratitude, selfishness, and cruelty"—how the "deviancy" piles up! —"all are thieves, idle, envious and ready to plunder and enslave their weaker neighbors."[11] Baker inclined to the view that the

climate was the real culprit. Only the temperate latitudes, somewhere around those of southern England, could apparently enable
humankind to produce its "highest development."

And on "the other side"? The records are unhappily few, but
those we have suggest that peoples first confronted with the spectacle of white-skinned visitors were struck with astonishment, and
applied to their oracles for explanations which varied from down-
right disbelief to divine dispensation. Robin Horton has given us a
possibly typical example. He recalls a story of the Kalabari of the
Niger Delta about the coming of the Europeans, and, as it was felt
by the Kalabari, the deplorable threat that this must hold for the
natural order:

> The first white man, it is said, was seen by a fisherman who had gone
> down to the mouth of the estuary in his canoe. Panic-stricken, he
> raced home and told his people what he had seen: whereupon he and
> the rest of the town set out to purify themselves—that is, rid them-
> selves of the influence of the strange and monstrous thing that had
> intruded into their world.[12]

Here the relationship was between two "worlds" that knew nothing
of each other: in this respect, if no other, Burton and the Kalabari
fisherman make a pair.

Where Africans became accustomed to Europeans and to European reasons for being in Africa, there followed an acceptance
which naturally varied from the gullible to the shrewd. Among the
gullible, there was a sixteenth-century king of Kongo (what is now
northern Angola) who persuaded himself that his "royal brother"
of Portugal would really send him useful technicians, including
artisans capable of building a ship in which he could conduct his
own trade with Europe outside the Portuguese royal monopoly.
Such gullibility frayed with the years: "I hear your countryman
done spoil West Indies," a Niger Delta ruler was remarking to some
British visitors in 1841; "I think he want come spoil we country
too."[13] Or else, along the same lines, there is the conclusion of the
Ethiopian emperor Tewodros II, who explained in the early 1860s
that: "I know their game. First traders and missionaries, then am-
bassadors, then the cannon. It's better to get straight to the cannon."[14] It wasn't, in his case, but one can see his point.

Much could be done to build a picture of the continuum as
seen from the African side, but the materials will evidently remain
slight. They generally indicate that the culture of the capitalist enclosure had rather little influence on African interpretations and responses until at least the close of the nineteenth century, and even,
for many populations, until later times. Does this yield any useful

conclusions? Here I will only note that the Africans of the colonial period, transformed into the objects of other peoples' history, took up attitudes of resistance to this transformation that varied, in time and place and circumstance, from warlike enterprise to efforts at accommodation. Yet their ability to succeed in either, especially in accommodation, was necessarily limited by their lack of access to reliable information. They did not, and usually could not, know where the springs of European motivation lay. As late as the 1890s a puzzled king of Asante (modern Ghana) thought that he might well be able to stave off British invasion by offering the British all that they could conceivably wish for, so far as he could see, in terms of commercial privilege. Let them accept his proposal that they form a chartered British royal company with very extensive rights for "opening up" his kingdom, and surely there would be no need for them to possess the country. But he soon learned better, for the British were determined to possess the country. How could he possibly understand why? Even the schools of British historiography are still divided on the answer.

And later? What men like Tewodros had urged was understandably forgotten. The period of high imperialism placed most of the relevant European cultures in so marked a position of technological and organizational superiority over colonized peoples as to make it feasible to assert an all-round and, as it were, predestined superiority; and the assertion was widely accepted. For the few who could achieve higher education, the Gold Coaster Attoh Ahuma's call of 1911 seemed irresistibly well grounded: Africans "must find a way out of Darkest Africa...must emerge from the savage backwoods and come into the open where nations are made." One must accept, in other words, the "model" of one's own metropolitan nation state, Britain or France or whatever, for in that alone could salvation from "Darkest Africa" be found.

A split personality consequently developed among such persons (very few till 1945, many more thereafter): they became what another Gold Coaster, Kobina Sekyi, called "hybrids...born into one race and brought up to live like members of another race." And as a postcolonial future began to loom ahead, and even arrive, the prestige of the "European models" (and, of course, the North American "model") grew still more, and most of all in universities. No wonder: for, as Sir Eric Ashby remarked in a famous report on British colonial universities but applicable elsewhere, students and staffs in these universities had become "isolated from the life of the common people in a way which has no parallel in England since the Middle Ages." It is going to take some time to end that isolation, and many tears. Recent developments, at last, have made a start.

3

I should like to persevere a little further along this line of thought. It may be helpful.

The dominant tradition of the English about themselves and their empire—and others have shared it—has been that a new industrial civilization carried them into an increasingly egalitarian democracy. Not, that is, into a democracy *sui generis*: no, but into the only form of democracy deserving of respect as being both effective and desirable. For a long time other peoples, through some inherent defect of human nature, had failed to make the grade; while the "colonial peoples" could only continue, some more woefully and others less, in the stagnation of one or other "savage despotism" corresponding to their deprived and naturally inferior humanity. One may admire or regret this dispensation. The fact remains that attitudes deriving from it (or, rather, from belief in its veracity) have gone so deeply into the heuristic structures that have shaped and often still shape the teaching of history in schools and universities as to have become, impressively often, the common coin of political and other assumptions about the "Third World": most obviously, no doubt, in the news media. In England—and is it so different in France, in the United States, in other industrialized polities?—this dominant tradition has correspondingly weighed with large effect on the relationship-continuum, reaching across the broad spectrum of society and exerting such power as to have achieved, as well, a reflection in the large acceptance of the same tradition by a majority of Africans educated in England during this century. However banal, the tradition is thus an aspect of our "problem of otherness."

On the first part of the proposition, that the condition of the English people became steadily "more equal" during and after the Industrial Revolution (broadly, after about 1780), rather than "less equal," the place for discussing it is clearly not here. But as to the second part, that (as an Oxford professor, Reginald Coupland, affirmed some fifty years ago) "the heart of Africa was scarcely beating" before the colonizing Europeans came upon the scene, and was not going to beat any faster till the Europeans got down to work, something more may be offered. One point is that it developed in no small measure from the experience of the Atlantic slave trade, as well as from the polemics on either side of that commerce. But as a piece of common coin whose value was—still is?—mainly unquestioned, it developed much more from the new imperialism of the 1880s and later.

Nothing being known of Africa's history, or that which had been known having been forgotten or ignored, the new imperialists conveniently assumed that there was none to know. Even when social anthropology grew into a discipline seriously concerned with the study of Africa's cultures, it continued to assume a correspondingly ahistorical approach. Reflecting Hegel's unforgotten dicta of the 1830s, this anthropology considered the "today" of these cultures as though they had known no "yesterday" and would be just the same "tomorrow" if they were left to themselves. This is not to say that it failed to make great strides, notably in English with Bronislaw Malinowski and the "functionalists," beyond the armchair speculation of earlier times. These cultures were often very usefully examined, whether in their structure or their rationality; but they were still examined in an "ethnographic present" which supposed them to be static, and, as such, not in the least "different but equal" but "entirely other." Unlike "our" cultures, "theirs" called for no historical explanation; and it remained for E. E. Evans-Pritchard in his well-known Marett lecture of 1950 (and in another of 1961) to argue within his own discipline for a contrary view.[15]

To say that an ahistorical approach to Africa's cultures mirrored the needs and interests of the colonial administrations in whose service or with whose approval these social anthropologists necessarily had to work is at best a partial truth. The deeper truth is that it mirrored the dominant tradition of imperialist culture. "The modern version of a naturalistic study of society," Evans-Pritchard pointed out, contesting its validity, "claims that for an understanding of the functioning of a society there is no need for a student of it to know anything about its history, any more than there is need for a physiologist to know the history of an organism to understand it. Both are natural systems and can be described in terms of natural law without recourse to history."[16] So indeed it was generally held and practiced; and there may be few neater demonstrations of the nature and effect of imperialist alienation.

This truncated view of African life-without-history marked in any case an intellectual decay: another component, one could argue, of the imperialist condition. Even briefly before the onset of the new imperialism, attitudes had been different. Those English who were concerned with reaching operative conclusions in that somewhat earlier period had still grappled with the "different but equal" proposition, even if the long influence of the Atlantic slave trade had greatly confused it for them. They thought themselves superior (and I am offering the English case only as one example: readers who are not English may offer their own); but they did not think they were superior by an inherent virtue, and they were often

quite unresponsive to travelers' tales. The notable English states-
man William Ewart Gladstone is a case in point. Much against the
English current, by the time of his old age, he thought it perfectly
legitimate for the Sudanese of the Mahdia to embark on war to rid
themselves of foreign rulers, a view which altogether failed to make
the grade in any subsequent text for use in English schools almost
down to our own time, where, for the most part, the Sudanese of
the Mahdia have appeared as "savage fanatics" bent on purposes
totally perverse. But let me offer, as an example in point, the case
of a Colonial Office blue paper of 1874 concerned with the Gold
Coast (modern Ghana). The date is interesting because this was the
very moment when the British government began to turn away
from the doctrine of mere "presence"—that is, of ensuring a commercial monopoly vis-à-vis other European powers—and, reluctantly enough, to embrace the doctrine of imperial enclosure. The
subject matter is interesting, too, for it was largely concerned with
discussing the "legal character and limitations of British power
upon the Gold Coast," and hence with a description of Gold Coast
social institutions, and especially the nature and extent of slavery
there.[17]

The paper was much in the "different but equal" tradition that
generally, by now, had ended. One has to admit, of course, that it
was scarcely a document from orthodox English sources: at that
time, almost entirely Oxbridge sources. Not only was its author an
Edinburgh lawyer, Sir David Chalmers, but the materials that he
used were those provided by a Scots magistrate who had served for
eighteen years on the Gold Coast in the days when the doctrine of
mere presence had not only held sway, but had seemed the only
sensible approach. The magistrate in question, Brodie Cruickshank,
had published his conclusions about Gold Coast forms of government in 1853, and they were notably different in tone and appreciation from what would come later: that is, they assumed possible
and valid comparisons between "their" history and "ours."
Cruickshank took such note as he could of the history of the principle polity of the country, that of Asante, and its coastal overlord-
ship or claims thereto; and he found that its political system was an
intriguing variant of what the Scots themselves had known, being
"not a despotism, nor a constitutional monarchy, nor an oligarchy,
nor a republic, but [partaking] something of the qualities of each of
these different forms."[18] He also discussed the nature and extent of
"domestic slavery," an issue of especial interest to the Colonial Office in 1874, twenty years later. The blue paper rehearsed Chalmers's conclusions, and roundly declared that "the great majority
of the people of the Gold Coast are in actual slavery." But it went

on, again drawing on Cruickshank's descriptions, to explain that this slavery "differs *toto caelo* from that species of slavery which it was deemed necessary to abolish in the West Indies, namely the praedial slavery of the great mass of an inferior race"—and here we see the dominant tradition beginning to insert assumptions not made by Cruickshank, a child of the 1800s—"to a handful of civilised men working for fortune and ruling by terror."

Now the point that bothered the British Colonial Office of the 1870s was that Britain could not possibly be seen to approve of slavery. "Domestic" or otherwise, slavery might continue to exist beyond reach of Britannia's saving arm. But what would happen if Britannia's arm should now enclose the Asante state? The question possessed its urgency. Sir Garnet Wolseley had in fact already sailed for that distant land of which so little was known, together with an armory of warlike stores which included thirty foghorns and a hundred railway-guard whistles, no doubt for use in the mysterious jungles. And Wolseley was going to invade Asante; diplomatic varnish aside, that was what he was going there for. So the "grave question" remained for the British government, continued the blue paper, whether if it "were for certain reasons to desire to take the Gold Coast...more fully under British dominion, the toleration of domestic slavery would not be generally regarded as a violent departure from those principles which this country has in modern times persistently practised?" If the Gold Coast were "taken," must not slavery be brought to an end there? Yet how could this be done? Those who knew the country might reply that Gold Coast slavery was a bird of a quite different feather, and not slavery at all in any familiar sense, not wage labor, nor clientage, nor vassalage, nor serfdom but partaking "something of the qualities of each of these different forms." Never mind all that: for what member of parliament or prying opposition newspaper was going to bother with such fine distinctions?

By this time, in fact, the relationship-continuum was settling into its familiar groove. After the 1870s it became the general assumption, no matter what information might have come back from Africa in earlier times, that any useful development of African society must necessarily derive from European (or, at least, white) precedent, example, and convenience. This idea took a little time to get itself established against clearly subversive Tozerisms which continued to hold, though muttering now pretty much in the background, that there was more to civilization than railways and telegraphs (or, as it turned out more and more frequently, mining concessions). But established it became; and by 1900, with colonial enclosure almost complete and "pacification" getting under way, the assumptions of Fifth Stage Adventism can be said to have carried all before them, even if appropriate Tablets of the Law had still to be inscribed.

Enshrined as an immanent truth applicable to all situations, this attitude of *necessary* "white" precedence justified the culture of the new imperialism. It marshaled poets, prophets, and grave philosophers, often even scientists, and was continuously sustained and enlarged by the instrumentality of its racism. In due course it opened the way for latter-day mythologies of "development," supposing as these generally have (and still do) that Africans, having no history of their own, can have had no development of their own. Here we reach the characteristics of the relationship-continuum in our own time. The earlier mythologies of race had justified the Atlantic slave trade and trans-Atlantic slavery. Those of the new imperialism justified the colonial enclosure. Now it is the "development" of the industrialized world—more specifically, of Western Europe and North America—that must be transferred to Africa if the Africans are to be saved. With this, imperialist alienation from the reality of "them" appears complete.

Now this matrix of assumptions, laid down long ago but thickened and compacted by the culture of successive generations of technologically superior "whites," is what has generally governed the relationship-continuum in this our period of decolonization and "Third World emergence." None of its unyielding toughness, we may note, has discouraged whole regiments of planners and political scientists from bouncing on this matrix as though it were a trampoline. We see them going up and down, often with an impressive energy; but they stay in the same place. On one side we see all those (in Africa as well as outside Africa, let us remember) who project development in Africa in the remainder of this century, or beyond, as depending on a proper application of the lessons of *external* cultures and economies which sprang from specific circumstances at a specific time in history; who therefore "test" the credentials of this or that regime, policy, party, or whatever by its capacity to deliver "democracy"—that is, the parliamentary democracy of the bourgeois nation state or some native attempt to reproduce it—as though this were some kind of consumer good like cars or cash in Switzerland (the best of all consumer goods, no doubt, as guaranteeing all others); and who, quite logically, then translate a public demonstration of the failure of these "lessons in democracy" as a license to pursue their own careers and leave the devil to take the hindmost.

On the other side, scarcely less depressing, we have those (fewer in Africa, as yet, but appearing there as well) who fall into the

vulgar structuralism of an armchair "Marxism" and believe, apparently, that what must be "right" for the "Third World" (but here I
am sticking to Africa) is somehow immanent within a "revolutionary recipe"—drawn up, of course, without taint of filthy factual
evidence— rather as though (and characteristically for such ideal-
ists) the truth about "what should be done" is only to be found
among a gallery of abstract images. And then between the two sides
we have of course a range of variables, some leaning this way and
others that, whose upshot goes toward the production of a "literature of development" which, often if not always, is little or nothing
more than another bout on the trampoline. Often if not always? No
doubt that emphasis is an exaggeration unjust to those among us
who are not content to bounce upon the trampoline, but who, lately
with very interesting results, now begin to move forward into reality along paths of their own making and discovery.[19] Yet these are
still exceptions to the rule. And the rule, or so it seems to me, leads
us to one clear conclusion. This is that a prime need now is to
return to study of the evidence.

4

This may appear at first sight a fruitless conclusion; otiose, too,
for preceding essays have emphasized it. And then, at what other
time in history has the evidence been so much studied? When has
the evidence been more abundant? When were there ever so many
workers in the field, so many others prepared to join them? Even at
the level of the television there is now a supply of documentary film
whose productions are not always, by any means, a mere "glimpse
of the exotic." And if our newspaper media generally continue to
treat Africa (for example) as a cross between a menagerie and a
madhouse, their alienating influence is probably smaller than it
ever was before. Why then insist once more on study of the evidence?
  Let me restrict myself to a single line of thought, for otherwise
this writing will get still further out of hand. It refers to that point
along the relationship-continuum where the notion of solidarity
occurs. I do not know what status the notion of solidarity may be
awarded by Althusserians and their kind—does it enjoy, perhaps,
its own "relative autonomy"?—and perhaps it does not greatly matter. Still less need it matter that other antagonists on the orthodox
side of idealism should draw aside their academic skirts in horror at
the proposal that the notion of solidarity not only can be, but in fact
always should be, a morally integral aspect of scholarship. Along

the relationship-continuum, in any case, the notion of solidarity has its crucial place. The place is crucial because it marks the moral acceptance of the fact and obligation of human unity that has geared and driven the wheels of all effective liberating action—I should like to say revolutionary action, but perhaps the word is too much loaded with its own inheritance—since recorded history began. Without this motivating insight, we have chronology or propaganda. With it, we have history.

So far as England is concerned within the context of a mature capitalism—and others, again, may supply their own examples—this notion of solidarity with the "Third World" may be said to have received its first explicit formulations with the thought of William Morris and his co-workers during the 1880s. These people saw the new imperialism then taking shape as an extension of the domestic alienations they knew so well, and they analyzed it in terms which laid the groundwork for later thinkers in what became the same tradition: broadly, the tradition of Marx and Engels. But they lacked access to the evidence, and they had to work from small and uncertain materials. As everybody knows, Marx had met the same problem. All the same, they saw that imperialism was not something done only to one's own people. Given that "a people which enslaves another forges its own chains," imperialism was bad for the English, or at any rate for most of the English. But leaving Marx-on-India aside as a mere proof that Marx was capable of error and therefore reassuringly human, imperialism was also bad for those it was "done to" overseas. They saw imperialism, in other words, as a two-way guarantee of misfortune. The same theme became familiar to the Second International, no matter if its parties failed to practice what they preached—whenever, that is, they happened on a chance to practice. And the same notion of solidarity stood at the center of the origins and early life of the Third International, a fact in no way removed by the later evolution (or petrification if you prefer) of that enterprise.

All these and many other aspects of the notion of solidarity, made manifest in the period between the world wars in spite of aberrations, distortions, contradictions, and plain betrayals, led to one large consequence in 1945 and after. It helped to open the way for that process of decolonization which derived, immediately, from the nature and development of the anti-Nazi war: from the development, that is, which flowed out of the need to win a "necessary and historic confrontation"[20] between what its contenders, on our side, felt increasingly as a fight between the forces of the past and those that could liberate the future. Of course it was also true that decolonization served other ends than those of liberating the future; but that is too obvious a point for any comment here. So far as the notion of solidarity was concerned, the years in the wake of World War II proved fruitful of a great reinforcement: scholarship, to go no further, began to be able to stand once more on the old ground of "different but equal."

More directly to our theme, those years likewise saw the beginnings of a systematic scholarly research into a subject hitherto not thought to exist: that is, into Africa's history and, more widely as the years proceeded, into the processual development of the cultures of the Africans. Over against such reinforcement, however, there was a loss to be faced; and this loss was not a small one. For the years in the wake of World War II were themselves followed by the onset and persistence of a political ice age known as the "Cold War" when, in Edward Thompson's lapidary words, whatever happened or could happen in terms of analysis or interpretation "seemed to congeal in an instant into two monstrous antagonistic structures, each of which allowed only the smallest latitude or movement within its operative realm."[21]

Out of this, along into the 1960s and beyond, there came a mutual reduction. The "antileft" (*sensu largo*) applied its "development strategies," concerned increasingly with the mechanics of making "free enterprise" work, under the assumption that Africa (for example) could be "rescued" only in the measure that Africans meekly followed father, no matter what the actual evidence might show. The "left" (same sense) meanwhile rediscovered the Marxist tradition but in a mode that seemed to turn, reductively, toward a simple "purification" of the sacred texts within a post-Stalinist, or at any rate anti-Stalinist, world. Much of this remained interesting, even new; but much of it, again, was neither. Somewhere between the two, in any case, reality tended to become the victim. The tests applied by one orthodoxy—is this state friendly, is this structure capitalist, is this country "safe for the West"?—were reflected all too often in opposite tests applied by another orthodoxy: is this party Marxist, is this program revolutionary, is this situation progressive? Either way, as you see, the alienation remained considerable.

I am not saying that no good work was done. On the contrary, the years since the 1960s have seen a number of useful theoretical formulations and debates, as for example in relation to concepts of "center" and "periphery." Yet the tendency to armchair or aprioristic judgments remained on stage. Another anecdote: the leader of a successful liberation movement in Africa, Amilcar Cabral, came to London in 1971. He spoke to various audiences, one of which was a group of excellent intellectuals of the left who had neither studied his country (Guinea-Bissau) nor his movement (PAIGC), nor even, as it seemed, read his available texts, yet were emphatically concerned to measure his Marxist and revolutionary credentials. He replied with a plea for study of the reality in which his movement had taken shape and of what it was actually doing, since, as he explained, the reality of what *is* happening cannot be separated from the conceptualization of what *should* happen, or be made to happen. Practice and theory march together, in other words: but practice comes first, theory after.

Yet might it not be said of some of these intellectuals, if not of all, and if perhaps a little harshly, what Marx advanced against Proudhon in his well-known letter to Annenkov of 1846? "So it is the men of learning, the men who know how to get God's secret thoughts out of him, who make history. The common people have only to apply their revelations. . . . The solution of present problems does not lie for [Proudhon] in public action but in the dialectical rotations of his own mind."[22] For Cabral, *per contra*, "nobody could create the theory of the struggle for liberation without participation in the struggle."[23] Here indeed are two opposed approaches. The one has relied on the alchemy which holds that if the gold of social progress will not come out of the crucible of theory, then there is something wrong with the elements being used;[24] the other has applied to the facts of reality.

In this sense the living experience of these recent years seems to have been a notably rich one. Among others, though perhaps none so clearly, the leader of the successful Mozambique liberation movement, Samora Moisés Machel, has echoed Cabral's insistence that "ideas derive from practice," even if, as he too insists, an effective derivation of such ideas, or at least their codification and subsequent application, must come from a Marxist approach: "Ideas come from praxis. Now we want the people to synthesize this praxis, to have the capability to synthesize their experience." The peasants of Mozambique had learned the essence of the—in this case colonial—exploitation of person by person from their own experience of it:

> No Marxist went there to say: "Look, this is exploitation, this is this and that is that." They didn't read it in any books, but they felt it. . . . It was these peasants who struggled and brought about the victory. . . . They struggled and made *poder popular* [the assembly-delegate system of participation promoted by FRELIMO], class power, triumph over feudal and bourgeois power. . . . They didn't know where the door of the university was. They didn't even know the way there.

And in a passage which would surely have warmed the young Marx's heart, Machel continued: "In the process of the struggle we synthesize our experiences and heighten our theoretical knowledge. It's different from first studying the theory of how to wage a war and then going out to do it. We did it, and now we synthesize; we resolve [our synthesis] day by day."[25]

It is time to conclude. Given all this, together with all that much more which could be adduced in support, there is now a considerably pressing need to get the cart of theory back behind the horse of practice: I mean the practice of rigorous inquiry such as also becomes, in the measure that it can become effective, a form of participation, a form of that "public action" which alone can solve "present problems." And the need for this appears all the larger because, in our time, the "Third World" has marched itself out of its old intellectual tailism, sometimes toward destinations which have proved dead ends, even tragic ones, but at other times (the times that make history) toward destinations which are qualitatively new, original, and capable of solving problems. Now this is not to indulge a new mythology of "Third World" primacy, arguing that whatever may be done there is to be accepted as being inherently right to be done there. The ending of one tailism is no argument for the beginning of another. But it is to propose that the notion of solidarity has acquired a new force and potential along the relationship-continuum: or, as I suggested a little earlier, that scholarship can stand once more on the ground of "different but equal"—only this time in circumstances of an almost infinitely smaller ignorance of "the other" than was possible in the sixteenth century.

An outrageous comparison in time? Not really so, I think. The relationship of assumed inferiority of the "Third World" can be traced back at any rate to around 1650 (which is not to argue, please, that the period before that was any kind of golden age): to the foreshadowings, in other words, of capitalist enclosure and the evolving domination of industrialized economies and their cultures over all others. There is rather little difficulty in showing that dominant attitudes to Africa now, as between Africa and "the West" (but is "the East" really different from "the West" in this respect?), derive from the new imperialism of the late nineteenth century; and that the attitudes of colonial times derived in their turn from the relations of exchange developed in precolonial times (however reinforced by colonial relations of exchange); and that the most characteristic and influential form of the attitudes then developed took their force from the Atlantic slave trade and its ancillary connections, going back at any rate to circa 1650. That is a long chain of cause and effect which retains no little of its binding strength today, as the present operations of almost any transnational corporation may quickly confirm. All the same, we are living now in a period when the chain begins to be broken. As in other regions of the "Third World," it is even possible to mark a point in history when the "tide of influence" from Europe to Africa was not only checked, but even reversed for the first time in half a millennium, and when the "periphery" proved that it need not depend for its destiny upon the decisions of the "center." This was shown by the influence on Portugal and on all the allies of Portugal of the liberation movements in the Portuguese colonies: the influence, centrally with other influences, which overturned in 1974 a European dictatorship (and all its supportive assumptions) such as fifty years of European protest had failed to shift by as much as an inch. Where else has any such development been seen since medieval times?[26]

We live, in short, at the probable ending of one long epoch in this whole relationship, and at the conceivable beginning of a very different one: conceivable if far from guaranteed, for people make their own history, and there is no saying beforehand what they will be up to. Conceivable all the same, and if the impressive papers preceding in this volume have a message, which perhaps they do, it is surely this: that we live in a time of new and wider possibilities, not least in the study and perception of other societies. Their reality and ours—from whichever "side" you take it, on whichever "side" you stand—begin to converge: not in the phenomena of these realities, remaining as these will as richly various as human nature, but in their ever more evident requirement of conjoint acceptance. "They" are beginning to be "there" as much as "we" are—either way you take it, from whatever way you come—in forms and intensity never before possible in consciousness. And as they take shape there, and as we see them in their solidity and in all the lineaments of their condition, and as the same perception occurs in reverse, so in the same measure can we and they approach and stand on common ground, and, in doing that, find the synthesis which can realize conjoint potentials. The moral acceptance of solidarity, the recognition of our shared nature, plight, and possibilities beyond all the barriers of cultural and ethnic history, is no longer, if it ever was, an eccentric addition to scholarship, a sentimental icing on the academic cake. It becomes in this realm, if not in others too, the manifest essence of purposive study.

Notes

1. Bishop William George Tozer, *Pastoral Letters* (Zanzibar: U.M.C.A., 1904), pp. 189-91. H.A.C. Cairns, *Prelude to Imperialism* (London: Routledge & Kegan Paul, 1965), p. 218, remarks that Tozer "was one

of the few Britons who deliberately repudiated any inherent connection between Christianity and the late-nineteenth century Western culture in which it was embedded."

2. W.W. Rostow, *The Stages of Economic Growth* (Cambridge: Cambridge University Press, 1960).

3. Thomas Hodgkin, "Where the Paths Began," in C. Fyfe, ed., *African Studies Since 1945* (London: Longman, 1976), p. 15.

4. Marc Bloch, *Apologie pour l'histoire* (Paris: Armand Colin, 1967), p. 101.

5. L. Mottoulle, *Politique sociale de l'Union Minière du Haut-Katanga pour sa main-d'oeuvre indigène* (Brussels: Inst. Royal Coloniale Belge, 1946), pp. 5-6.

6. S. Ramon, "Man and His Shadow: Models of Normality and Non-Normality," in T. Shanin, ed., *The Rules of the Game: Models in Scholarly Thought* (London: 1972), p. 110.

7. John Middleton, *Lugbara Religion* (Oxford: Oxford University Press, 1960).

8. See the photographs assembled in F.M. Snowden, Jr., *Blacks in Antiquity* (Cambridge, Mass.: Belknap Press of Harvard University Press, 1970), and those in J. Vercouter et al., *The Image of the Black in Western Art* (Lausanne: Menil Foundation, 1976), vol. I, *From the Pharoahs to the Roman Empire*.

9. S.D. Goitein, *A Mediterranean Society*, vol. 1: *Economic Foundations* (Berkeley: University of California Press, 1967), p. 130.

10. Thomas Winterbottom, *An Account of the Native Africans in the Neighbourhood of Sierra Leone* (London: 1803).

11. Sir Samuel Baker, *The Albert N'yanza* (London: Macmillan, 1898), p. 153.

12. Robin Horton, "African Traditional Thought and Western Science," *Africa* 37, no. 2. (1967).

13. In J.B. King, in *Journal of Royal Geographical Society*, quoted in E. Isichei, *The Ibo People and the Europeans* (London: Faber, 1973), p. 81.

14. In R. Battaglia, *La Prima Guerra d'Africa* (Turin: Einaudi, 1958), p. 124.

15. E.E. Evans-Pritchard, *Essays in Social Anthropology* (London: Faber, 1962).

16. Ibid., p. 19 (Marett lecture of 1950).

17. Colonial Office, Gold Coast No. 47 (1874).

18. Brodie Cruickshank, *Eighteen Years on the Gold Coast*, 2 vols. (London: 1853), vol. 1, p. 232.

19. For two differently angled but corresponding examples, see Adrian Adams, *Le Long Voyage des gens du Fleuve* (Paris: Maspero, 1977), and Lionel Cliffe, "Rural Class Formation in East Africa," *Journal of Peasant Studies* 6 (January 1977): 2—not to mention the essays in this book.

20. E.P. Thompson, *The Poverty of Theory* (London: Merlin, 1978), p. 264.

21. Ibid., p. 265.

22. Quoted here from *Karl Marx: Selected Works*, 2 vols. (London: Lawrence and Wishart, 1945), vol. 1, p. 376.

23. In Amilcar Cabral, *Our People Are Our Mountains* (London: Mozambique Angola Guiné Information Centre, 1971), pp. 20-23.

24. See Brecht's sarcastic lines "after the [Berlin] uprising of 17 June"
    when "the people had forfeited the confidence of the [East German]
    government":

> Would it not be easier
> In that case for the government
> To dissolve the people
> And elect another?

    (*Bertolt Brecht Poems*, trans. J. Willett [London: Eyre Methuen, 1970],
    p. 440.)

25. Interview with I. Christie and A. Isaacman in *Southern Africa* 12 (July/
    August 1979): 6.

26. See, for example, the unanimous declaration of the assembly of the
    Portuguese Armed Forces Movement in Guinea-Bissau, *Boletim Informativo*
    1 (June 1974): 1: "The colonized peoples and the people of Portugal
    are allies. The struggle for national liberation has contributed power-
    fully to the overthrow of fascism and, in large degree, has lain at the
    base of the Armed Forces Movement [which overturned the Portugese
    dictatorship in the coup of April 1974] whose officers have learned in
    Africa the horrors of a war without prospect, and have therefore un-
    derstood the roots of the evils which afflict the society of Portugal."

Part VI

Appendix

Further Reading
on the Sociology of Developing Societies

Compiled by Chris Allen

This list, compiled with the help of contributors to this and other volumes in the series, includes both general studies on developing societies and selected area or country case studies, notably those of broad theoretical interest. It is designed for use by those teaching or following relevant courses and thus concentrates on material readily available in English, although this has meant the omission of many excellent works. In general, only the original publishers are listed; many of the books will be available in U.S. or British editions as well. Shortage of space has forced difficult decisions between competing studies—especially case studies—and the representation of many authors by only a fraction of their output. Further material can be found in the bibliographies in the works listed below and in the "further reading" sections of the various companion volumes in this series. The arrangement of the list roughly follows the schema of this volume, while within each section the arrangement is neither alphabetic nor in order of merit, but reflects grouping of items by content, by continent, or in their order of publication.

1. Statistical Sources (Annual)

1.1 WORLD BANK. *World Development Report*. New York: Oxford University Press. (Includes commentary on developmental issues and area analyses.)
1.2 UNITED NATIONS. *Statistical Yearbook*. New York: United Nations. (Mainly economic.)
1.3 UNESCO. *Statistical Yearbook*. Paris: UNESCO.
1.4 FOOD & AGRICULTURE ORGANIZATION. *The State of Food and Agriculture*. Rome: FAO.
1.5 FOOD & AGRICULTURAL ORGANIZATION. *Production Yearbook*. Rome: FAO.
1.6 UNITED NATIONS CONFERENCE ON TRADE AND DEVELOPMENT. *Handbook of International Trade and Development Statistics*. New York: United Nations.
1.7 GENERAL AGREEMENT ON TARIFFS AND TRADE. *International Trade*. Geneva: GATT.

2. General Readers

2.1 RHODES, R., ed. *Imperialism and Underdevelopment*. New York: Monthly Review Press, 1970.
2.2 BERNSTEIN, H., ed. *Undervelopment and Development*. Harmondsworth: Penguin Books, 1973.
2.3 DE KADT, I. and WILLIAMS, G.P., eds. *Sociology and Development*. London: Tavistock, 1974.
2.4 OXAAL, I., BARNETT, T., and BOOTH, D., eds. *Beyond the Sociology of Development*. London: Routledge & Kegan Paul, 1975.
2.5 MACK, A., PLANT, D., and DOYLE, U., eds. *Imperialism, Intervention, and Development*. London: Croom Helm, 1979.

For an earlier generation of analysis, see:
2.6 WALLERSTEIN, I., ed. *Social Change: The Colonial Situation*. New York: Wiley, 1966.
2.7 FINKLE, J.R. and GABLE, R.W., eds. *Political Development and Social Change*. New York: Wiley, 1966.

3. The Making of the Third World
(see also 7.42; 7.49)

(a) General interpretations of the history of the Third World and its relations with Europe and America

3.1 BARRATT BROWN, M. *After Imperialism*. London: Heinemann, 1963. (Covers 1800-1962.)
3.2 HOBSBAWM, E.J. *Industry and Empire*. Harmondsworth: Penguin Books, 1969.
3.3 BAIROCH, P. *The Economic Development of the Third World Since 1900*. London: Methuen, 1975.
3.4 WALLERSTEIN, I. *The Modern World-System*. 2 vols.; New York: Academic Press, 1974, 1980. (Covers up to 1750.)
3.5 FRANK, A.G. *World Accumulation, 1492-1789*. New York: Monthly Review Press, 1978. (See also item 3.22.)
3.6 CALDWELL, M. *The Wealth of Some Nations*. London: Zed, 1977.
3.7 KIERNAN, V. *America: The New Imperialism*. London: Zed, 1978.
3.8 WORSLEY, P. *The Third World*. London: Weidenfeld & Nicolson, 1964.
3.9 FIELDHOUSE, D.K. *The Colonial Empires: A Comparative Survey from the Eighteenth Century*. London: Weidenfield & Nicolson, 1966.

(b) Area studies: Asia, Latin America, Middle East, Africa (see also 7.47)

3.10 SCHURMANN, H.F. and SCHELL, O., eds. *China Readings*. 3 vols.; Harmondsworth: Penguin Books, 1967-68.
3.11 CHESNEAUX, J. et al. *China from the Opium Wars to the 1911 Revolution*. Hassocks: Harvester, 1977.
3.12 CHESNEAUX, J. et al. *China from the 1911 Revolution to Liberation*. Hassocks: Harvester, 1977.
3.13 WERTHEIM, W.F. *Indonesian Society in Transition*. Rev. ed.; The Hague: Van Hoeve, 1964.
3.14 GEERTZ, C. *Agricultural Involution: The Process of Ecological Change in Indonesia*. Berkeley: University of California Press, 1963.
3.15 GOUGH, K. and SHARMA, H.P., eds. *Imperialism and Revolution in South Asia*. New York: Monthly Review Press, 1973.
3.16 NEHRU, J. *The Discovery of India*. London: Meridian, 1946.
3.17 FRANKEL, F.R. *India's Political Economy, 1947-1977*. Princeton: Princeton University Press, 1978.
3.18 TRUONG, BUU LAM. *Patterns of Vietnamese Response to Foreign Intervention*. New Haven: Yale University Press, 1967.
3.19 HODGKIN, T.L. *Vietnam: The Revolutionary Path*. London: Macmillan, 1981.
3.20 NGO VINH LONG. *Before the Revolution: The Vietnamese Peasants under the French*. Cambridge, Mass.: MIT Press, 1973.
3.21 PARRY, J.H. *The Spanish Seaborne Empire*. London: Hutchinson, 1966.
3.22 FRANK, A. G. *Capitalism and Underdevelopment in Latin America: Historical Studies of Chile and Brazil*. Rev. ed.; New York: Monthly Review Press, 1969.
3.23 GALEANO, E. *Open Veins of Latin America: Five Centuries of the Pillage of a Continent*. New York: Monthly Review Press, 1973.
3.24 STEIN, S. and STEIN, B. *The Colonial Heritage of Latin America*. New York: Oxford University Press, 1970.
3.25 WOLF. E.R. *Sons of the Shaking Earth*. Chicago: University of Chicago Press, 1959. (Mexico.)
3.26 FURTADO, C.P.S. *Economic Development in Latin America: From Colonial Times to the Cuban Revolution*. Cambridge: Cambridge University Press, 1970.
3.27 CARDOSO, F. H. and PALETTO, E. *Dependency and Development in Latin America*. Berkeley: University of California Press, 1979.
3.28 AMIN, S. *The Maghreb in the Modern World*. Harmondsworth: Penguin, 1970.
3.29 HALLIDAY, F. *Arabia Without Sultans*. Harmondsworth: Penguin, 1974.
3.30 HALLIDAY, F. *Iran: Dictatorship and Development*. Harmondsworth: Penguin, 1979.
3.31 DAVIDSON, B. *Africa in Modern History*. London: Allen Lane, 1978.
3.32 RODNEY, W. *How Europe Underdeveloped Africa*. London: Bogle-L'Ouverture, 1972.
3.33 BRETT, E.A. *Colonialism and Underdevelopment in East Africa*. London: Heinemann, 1973.
3.34 BENDER. G. *Angola under the Portuguese*. London: Heinemann, 1978.

4. The Global Context

(a) Dualist and modernization theories: classic presentations (see also 2.7)

4.1　BOEKE, J.H. *Economics and Economic Polity of Dual Societies as Exemplified by Indonesia.* New York: Institute of Pacific Relations, 1953.
4.2　ROSTOW, W.W. *The Stages of Economic Growth: A Non-Communist Manifesto.* Cambridge: Cambridge University Press, 1960.
4.3　EISENSTADT, S.N. *Tradition, Change, and Modernity.* New York: Wiley, 1973.

For non-Marxist critiques see:

4.4　MYRDAL, G. *Economic Theory and Underdeveloped Regions.* London: Duckworth, 1967. (See also 5.2.)
4.5　CLAIRMONTE, F.F. *Economic Liberalism and Underdevelopment: Studies in the Disintegration of an Idea.* Bombay: Asia Publishing House, 1960.

(b) Theories of imperialism (see also 3.1-3; 3.6; 3.7; 4.30; 4.34)

4.6　KEMP, T. *Theories of Imperialism.* London: Dobson, 1967.
4.7　MAGDOFF, H. *The Age of Imperialism: The Economics of U.S. Foreign Policy.* New York: Monthly Review Press, 1969.
4.8　MAGDOFF, H. *Imperialism: From the Colonial Age to the Present.* New York: Monthly Review Press, 1978.
4.9　JALÉE, P. *The Pillage of the Third World.* New York: Monthly Review Press, 1968.
4.10　ARRIGHI, G. *The Geometry of Imperialism.* London: New Left Books, 1978.
4.11　WILLIAMS. G. "Imperialism and Development," *World Development* 6 (1978): 925-36. (Extensive bibliography.)
4.12　COHEN, B.J. *The Question of Imperialism.* London: Macmillan, 1974. (Skeptical non-Marxist discussion.)

(c) Theories of underdevelopment (see also 5.16; 5.24)

4.13　BARAN, P. *The Political Economy of Growth.* New York: Monthly Review Press, 1957.
4.14　BARAN, P. and SWEEZY, P. *Monopoly Capital.* New York: Monthly Review Press, 1966.
4.15　FRANK, A.G. *Latin America: Underdevelopment and Revolution.* New York: Monthly Review Press, 1969.
4.16　FRANK, A.G. *Dependent Accumulation and Underdevelopment.* New York: Monthly Review Press, 1978.
4.17　EMMANUEL, A. *Unequal Exchange: A Study of the Imperialism of Trade.* New York: Monthly Review Press, 1972.

4.18 AMIN, S. *Accumulation on a World Scale.* New York: Monthly Review Press, 1974.

4.19 AMIN, S. *Unequal Development.* New York: Monthly Review Press, 1977.

4.20 BECKFORD, G.L. *Persistent Poverty: Underdevelopment in Plantation Economies.* New York: Oxford University Press, 1972.

4.21 THOMAS, C. *Dependency and Transformation.* New York: Monthly Review Press, 1974.

4.22 KAY, G. *Development and Underdevelopment.* London: Macmillan, 1975.

4.23 WALLERSTEIN, I. *The Capitalist World Economy.* Cambridge: Cambridge University Press, 1979.

4.24 MURRAY, R. "Underdevelopment, the International Firm and the International Division of Labour," in *Towards a New World Economy* (Rotterdam: Rotterdam University Press, 1972), pp. 159-248.

4.25 WARREN, W. *Imperialism: Pioneer of Capitalism.* London: New Left Books, 1980. (Critical of most of the above; see Bernstein in this volume.)

4.26 ROXBOROUGH, I. *Theories of Underdevelopment.* London: Macmillan, 1979.

(d) Theories of underdevelopment: commentary and critique
(see also 2.1; 2.4; 2.5; 5.17; 6.50)

4.27 PALMA, G. "Dependency: A Formal Theory of Underdevelopment or a Methodology for the Analysis of Concrete Situations," *World Development* 6 (1978): 881-924. (Useful bibliography.)

4.28 LEHMANN, D., ed. *Development Theory: Four Critical Essays.* London: Frank Cass, 1979.

4.29 LEYS, C. "Underdevelopment and Dependency: Critical Notes," *Journal of Contemporary Asia* 7, no. 1 (1977):92-107.

4.30 BREWER, A. *Marxist Theories of Imperialism.* London: Routledge & Kegan Paul, 1980.

4.31 TAYLOR, J.G. *From Modernisation to Modes of Production.* London: Macmillan, 1979. (See review by Mouzelis in *Journal of Peasant Studies* 7, no. 3 [1979]:353-74.)

(e) Soviet theories of development

4.32 SZENTES, T. *The Political Economy of Underdevelopment.* Budapest: Akedemia Kiado, 1973.

4.33 CLARKSON, S. *The Soviet Theory of Development.* London: Macmillan, 1978. (See, for recent Soviet thought, J.K. Valkenic, *World Politics* 32 [1980]:485-508.)

*(f) The global economics of underdevelopment
(see also 4.7; 4.9; 5.1; 5.2; 5.7; 5.9; 5.13; 5.14)*

4.34 BARRATT BROWN, M. *The Economics of Imperialism.* Harmondsworth: Penguin Books, 1974.

4.35 HYMER, S. *The Multinational Corporation: A Radical Approach.* Cambridge: Cambridge University Press, 1979.

4.36 RADICE, H., ed. *International Firms and Modern Imperialism.* Harmondsworth: Penguin Books, 1975.

4.37 UNITED NATIONS. *Transnational Corporations in World Development: A Reexamination.* New York: United Nations, 1978.

4.38 MEDAWAR, C. *Insult or Injury? An Enquiry into the Marketing of British Food and Drug Products in the Third World.* London: Social Audit, 1979.

4.39 STEWART, F. *Technology and Underdevelopment.* London: Macmillan, 1978.

4.40 FROBEL, F., HEINRICH, J., and KREYE, O. *The New International Division of Labour.* Cambridge: Cambridge University Press, 1980.

4.41 BATCHELOR, R.D., MAJOR, K.L., and MORGAN, A.D. *Industrialisation and the Basis for Trade.* Cambridge: Cambridge University Press, 1980.

4.42 NORE, P. and TURNER, T., eds. *Oil and Class Struggle.* London: Zed, 1980.

4.43 PAYER, C. *The Debt Trap.* Harmondsworth: Penguin, 1974. (IMF and World Bank.)

4.44 COLLINS, J., LAPPÉ, F.M., and KINLEY, D. *Aid as Obstacle.* Washington: Institute for Food and Development Policy, 1980.

4.45 TANZER, M. *The Race for Resources: Continuing Struggles over Minerals and Fuel.* New York: Monthly Review Press, 1980.

4.46 MURRAY, R. *Multinationals Beyond the Market.* Hassocks: Harvester, 1981.

4.47 MURRAY, R., ed. *Socialist Transformation and Development in the Third World.* Hassocks: Harvester, forthcoming.

5. Political Economy

*(a) The morpohology of backwardness
(see also 3.14; 4.43; 5.43; 6.11; 7.7-10)*

5.1 BRANDT, W., et al. *North-South: A Programme for Survival.* London: Pan, 1980.

5.2 MYRDAL, G. *Asian Drama: An Enquiry into the Poverty of Nations.* 3 vols.; Harmondsworth: Penguin Books, 1969.

5.3 CASTRO, J. de. *The Geography of Hunger.* London: Gollancz, 1952. (See also A. Sen, *Poverty and Famines* [Oxford: Clarendon, 1981].)

5.4 KJEKSHUS, H. *Ecology, Control and Economic Development in East African History.* London: Heinemann, 1977.

5.5 GEORGE, S. *How the Other Half Dies.* Harmondsworth: Penguin Books, 1976.

5.6 LIPTON, M. *Why Poor People Stay Poor: Urban Bias in World Development.* Cambridge, Mass.: Harvard University Press, 1977. (See review by T.J. Byres in *Journal of Peasant Studies* 6 [1979]:210-44.)

5.7 LAPPÉ, F.M. and COLLINS, J. *Food First: Beyond the Myth of Scarcity.* New York: Ballantine, 1979.

5.8 BONDESTAM, L. and BERGSTROM, S., eds. *Poverty and Population Control.* New York: Academic Press, 1980.

5.9 BYRES, T. and NOLAN, P. *Inequality: India and China Compared, 1950-70.* Milton Keynes: Open University, 1976.

5.10 CASSEN, R.H. *India: Population, Economy, Society.* London: Macmillan, 1978.

5.11 MAMDANI, M. *The Myth of Population Control: Family, Caste, and Class in an Indian Village.* New York: Monthly Review Press, 1972.

5.12 HILL, P. *Rural Hausa: A Village and a Setting.* Cambridge: Cambridge University Press, 1972. (Northern Nigeria.)

5.13 PEARSE, A. *Seeds of Plenty, Seeds of Want: Social and Economic Implications of the Green Revolution.* Oxford: Clarendon, 1980.

5.14 GRIFFIN, K. *The Political Economy of Agrarian Change.* London: Macmillan, 1974.

5.15 HARVEY, C. et al. *Rural Employment and Administration in the Third World.* Farnborough: Saxon House, 1978.

5.16 SUTCLIFFE, R.B. *Industry and Underdevelopment.* London: Addison-Wesley, 1971.

5.17 FRANSMAN, M., ed. *Industry and Accumulation in Africa.* London: Heinemann, 1982.

5.18 LEWIS, O. *Children of Sanchez.* New York: Random House, 1961.

5.19 LEWIS, O. *La Vida.* New York: Random House, 1966. (Urban poverty in Puerto Rico and among Puerto Ricans in New York.)

5.20 BERGER, J. and MOHR, J. *A Seventh Man.* Harmondsworth: Penguin Books, 1975. (African and Middle Eastern migrants in Europe.) (See also part 4 of 5.30.)

5.21 ILLICH, I. *Tools for Conviviality.* London: Calder & Boyars, 1973. ("End to industrial development" school.)

(b) Class and class formation (see also 4.18; 4.19; 4.26; 4.31)

5.22 WOLF, E.R. and HANSEN, E.C. *The Human Condition in Latin America.* New York: Oxford University Press, 1972.

5.23 KITCHING, G. *Class and Economic Change in Kenya.* New Haven: Yale University Press, 1980.

5.24 PETRAS, J. *Critical Perspectives on Imperialism and Social Class in the Third World.* New York: Monthly Review Press, 1978.

5.25 O'CONNOR, J. *The Origins of Socialism in Cuba.* Ithaca: Cornell University Press, 1970. (Prerevolutionary.)

5.26 EVANS, B. *Dependent Development: The Alliance of Multinational, State and Local Capital in Brazil.* Princeton: Princeton University Press, 1978.

5.27 SHILS, ED. *The Intellectuals and the Powers and Other Essays.* Chicago: University of Chicago Press, 1972.

5.28 BATATU, H. *The Old Social Classes and the Revoluionary Movements of Iraq.* Princeton: Princeton University Press, 1979.

5.29 LIPSET, S. and SOLARI, A., eds. *Elites in Latin America.* New York: Oxford University Press, 1967.

5.30 COHEN, R., GUTKIND, P., and BRAZIER, P., eds. *Peasants and Proletarians: Struggles of Third World Workers.* New York: Monthly Review Press, 1979. (Useful if unselective bibliography.)

5.31 BROMLEY, C. and GERRY, C. *Casual Work and Poverty in Third World Cities.* London: Wiley, 1977. (See also their issue of *World Development* 6, no. 9/10 [1978].)

(c) Peasantry and rural society (see also 5.6; 6.32-34; 6.38; 6.47; 7 [e])

5.32 SCOTT, J.C. *The Moral Economy of the Peasant: Rebellion and Subsistence in Southeast Asia.* New Haven: Yale University Press, 1976. (See also critiques by S.L. Popkin in *Theory and Society* 9, no. 3 [1980]:411-71 and M. Adas in *Journal of Social History* 13 [1980]:521-46.)

5.33 POPKIN, S.L. *The Rational Peasant: The Political Economy of Rural Society in Vietnam.* Berkeley: University of California Press, 1979.

5.34 SHANIN, T., ed. *Peasants and Peasant Societies.* Harmondsworth: Penguin Books, 1971.

5.35 SHANIN, T. "The Nature and Logic of Peasant Economy," *Journal of Peasant Studies* 1 and 11 (1973-74), pp. 63-80, 91-106, 186-206.

5.36 STAVENHAGEN, R. *Social Classes in Agrarian Societies.* Garden City: Anchor Books, 1975.

5.37 BERNSTEIN, H. "African Peasantries: A Theoretical Framework," *Journal of Peasant Studies* 6 (1979): 421-43.

5.38 SHANIN, T. "Defining Peasants: Conceptualisations and Deconceptualisations," *Peasant Studies* 8, no. 4 (1980).

5.39 NEWBY, H., ed. *International Perspectives in Rural Sociology.* New York: Wiley, 1978. (Useful bibliographical surveys.)

5.40 DESAI, A.R., ed. *Rural Sociology in India.* Bombay: Popular Prakashan, 1969.

5.41 GOUGH, K. *Rural Society in Southeast India.* Cambridge: Cambridge University Press, 1981.

5.42 GOODMAN, D. and REDCLIFF, M. *From Peasant to Proletarian: Capitalist Development and Agrarian Transitions.* Oxofrd: Blackwell, 1981.

(d) Modes of production (see also 4.31)

5.43 WOLPE, H., ed. *The Articulation of Modes of Production.* London: Routledge & Kegan Paul, 1980.

5.44 CLAMMER, J., ed. *The New Economic Anthropology*. London: Macmillan, 1979.
5.45 SEDDON, D., ed. *Relations of Production*. London: Cass, 1978.
5.46 FOSTER-CARTER, A. "The Modes of Production Controversy," *New Left Review* 107 (1978):47-77.
5.47 KAHN, J.S. and LLOBERA, J.R. *The Anthropology of Pre-Capitalist Societies*. London: Macmillan, 1981.

6. State and Revolution

(a) The state and state power (see also 4.26; 5.26)

6.1 SKOPCOL, T. *States and Social Revolutions: A Comparative Analysis of France, Russia, and China*. Cambridge: Cambridge University Press, 1979.
6.2 GOULBOURNE, H., ed. *Politics and State in the Third World*. London: Macmillan, 1980.
6.3 LEE, J.M. *Colonial Development and Good Government*. Oxford: Clarendon, 1967.
6.4 WRIGGINS, H. *The Ruler's Imperative: Strategies for Political Survival in Asia and Africa*. New York: Columbia University Press, 1969. (Written wholly from the ruler's standpoint.)
6.5 HUNTINGTON, S.P. *Political Order in Changing Societies*. New Haven: Yale University Press, 1968. (Classic authoritarian account; see Colin Leys' critique in this volume.)
6.6 O'DONNELL, C. "Reflections on the Patterns of Change in the Bureaucratic-Authoritarian State," *Latin American Research Review* 13, no. 1 (1978): 3-38.
6.7 O'CONNELL, J. *The Corporations and the State*. New York: Harper & Row, 1974.

(b) Development, bureaucracy, and state power (see also 5.15; 7.6; 7.8; 7.9)

6.8 SEIDMAN, R.B. *Development, Law and the State*. London: Croom Helm, 1978. (See also C. Sumner, ed., *Crime, Justice, and Underdevelopment* [London: Heinemann, 1981].)
6.9 BHAMBRI, C.P. *Bureaucracy and Politics in India*. Delhi: Vikas, 1971.
6.10 HYDEN, G. *Beyond Ujamaa in Tanzania: Underdevelopment and an Uncaptured Peasantry*. London: Heinemann, 1980.
6.11 HEYER, J., ROBERTS, P., and WILLIAMS, G., eds. *Rural Development in Tropical Africa*. London: Macmillan, 1981.
6.12 MOORE, B. *The Social Origins of Dictatorship and Democracy: Lord and Peasant in the Modern World*. Boston: Beacon Press, 1966.
6.13 BRAIBANTI, R., et al. *Asian Bureaucratic Systems*. Durham, N.C.: Duke University Press, 1966. (Elitist account of bureaucracy.)

(c) Nationalism
(see also 3.18; 3.19; 3.31)

6.14   GELLNER, E. *Thought and Change*. London: Weidenfeld & Nicolson, 1964. (Chapter 7.)
6.15   NAIRN, T. "The Modern Janus," *New Left Review* 94 (1975):3-29.
6.16   ZUBAIDA, S. "Theories of Nationalism," in G. Littlejohn et al., eds, *Power and the State* (London: Croom Helm, 1978), pp. 52-71.
6.17   AMIN, S. *The Arab Nation*. London: Zed, 1978.
6.18   HODGKIN, T.L. *Nationalism in Colonial Africa*. London: Muller, 1956.

(d) Authoritarian regimes
(see also 5.26)

6.19   COLLIER, D., ed. *The New Authoritarianism in Latin America*. Princeton: Princeton University Press, 1980.
6.20   MALLOY, J.M., ed. *Authoritarianism and Corporatism in Latin America*. Pittsburgh: University of Pittsburgh Press, 1977.
6.21   SWEEZY, P.M. and MAGDOFF, H., eds. *Revolution and Counterrevolution in Chile*. New York: Monthly Review Press, 1974.
6.22   STEPAN, A. *Authoritarian Brazil: Origins, Politics, and Future*. New Haven: Yale University Press, 1973.
6.23   STEPAN, A. *The State and Society: Peru in Comparative Perspective*. Princeton: Princeton University Press, 1978.

(e) The role of the military/The military and the state
(see also 6 [d])

6.24   VAN DOORN, J., ed. *Armed Forces and Society*. The Hague: Mouton, 1968.
6.25   VAN DOORN, J., ed. *Military Profession and Military Regime*. The Hague: Mouton, 1969.
6.26   FIRST, R. *The Barrel of a Gun: Political Power in Africa and the Coup d'État*. London: Allen Lane, 1970.
6.27   STEPAN, A. *The Military in Politics: Changing Patterns in Brazil*. Princeton: Princeton University Press, 1971.
6.28   PERLMUTTER, A., and BENNETT, V.P., eds. *The Political Influence of the Military: A Comparative Reader*. New Haven: Yale University Press, 1980.
6.29   BENOIT, E. *Defense and Economic Growth in Developing Countries*. Lexington, Mass.: Lexington Books, 1973.
6.30   LUCKHAM, R. "Militarism," *Institute of Development Studies Bulletin* 8, no. 3 (1977):38-50 and 9, no. 1 (1977): 19-32. (International capital, arms trade, military, and class struggle.)
6.31   LUCKHAM, R. *The Nigerian Military*. Cambridge: Cambridge University Press, 1971. (Sociology of military and coups.)

(f) Peasant politics
(see also Alavi in 3.15; 3.20; 5.25; 5.32; 5.34; 5.39; 6.1; 6 [h]; 7 [e])

6.32 SCHMIDT, S.W. et al., eds. *Friends, Followers, and Factions.* Berkeley: University of California Press, 1977. (Clientelism.)
6.33 ALAVI, H. "Peasant Classes and Primordial Loyalties," *Journal of Peasant Studies* 1, no. 1 (1973):23-62.
6.34 SHANIN, T. *The Awkward Class: Political Sociology of a Peasantry in a Developing Society, Russia 1910-25.* Oxford: Clarendon, 1972.
6.35 WOLF, E.R. *Peasant Wars of the Twentieth Century.* New York: Harper & Row, 1971.
6.36 MIGDAL, J.S. *Peasants, Politics, and Revolution.* Princeton: Princeton University Press, 1974.
6.37 STAVENHAGEN, R., ed. *Agrarian Problems and Peasant Movements.* New York: Doubleday, 1970.
6.38 PAIGE, J.M. *Agrarian Revolution: Social Movements and Export Agriculture in the Underdeveloped World.* New York: Free Press, 1975. (See critique by M.R. Somers and W.L. Goldfrank in *Comparative Studies in Society and History* 21 [1979]:443-58.)
6.39 MAR, D.J. *Vietnamese Anticolonialism, 1885-1925.* Berkeley: University of California Press, 1971.
6.40 BERG, L. and BERG, L. *Face to Face: Fascism and Revolution in India.* Berkeley: Ramparts, 1972.
6.41 DESAI, A.R., ed. *Peasant Struggle in India.* Bombay: Oxford University Press, 1980.
6.42 HOFHEINZ, R.M. *The Broken Wave: The Chinese Communist Peasant Movement, 1922-28.* Cambridge, Mass.: Harvard University Press, 1977.
6.43 SELDEN, M. *The Yenan Way in Revolutionary China.* Cambridge, Mass.: Harvard University Press, 1971.
6.44 JOHNSON, C.A. *Peasant Nationalism and Communist Power: The Emergence of Revolutionary China, 1937-45.* Stanford: Stanford University Press, 1962.
6.45 HORNE, A. *A Savage War of Peace: Algeria, 1954-1962.* London: Macmillan, 1977.
6.46 MARCUM, J. *The Angolan Revolution.* 2 vols.; Cambridge, Mass.: MIT Press, 1969, 1978.
6.47 FANON, F. *The Wretched of the Earth.* New York: Grove Press, 1967.

(g) Politics of the working class and urban poor (see also 5.30; 7.6)

6.48 NELSON, J.M. *Access to Power: Politics and the Urban Poor in the Developing Nations.* Princeton: Princeton University Press, 1979.
6.49 POST, K.W.J. *Arise Ye Starvelings!* The Hague: Mouton, 1978. (The 1938 revolt in Jamaica.)
6.50 LACLAU, E. *Politics and Ideology in Marxist Theory.* London: New Left Books, 1977. (See chap. 4, on populism.)

6.51 WATERMAN, P., ed. *Third World Strikes*. Zug: Interdocumentation, 1979. (On microfiche only; see also *Development & Change* 10 [1979], issue on Third World strikes.)

6.52 CHESNEAUX, J. *The Chinese Labor Movement, 1919-1927*. Stanford: Stanford University Press, 1968.

6.53 SPALDING, H.A. *Organized Labor in Latin America, 1850-1960*. New York: New York University Press, 1977.

6.54 ANGELL, A. *Politics and the Labour Movement in Chile*. Oxford: Oxford University Press, 1972.

6.55 SANDBROOK, R. and COHEN, R., eds. *The Development of an African Working Class*. London: Longman, 1975.

6.56 GUTKIND, P., COHEN, R., and COPANS, J., eds. *African Labor History*. Beverly Hills: Sage, 1979.

6.57 OUSMANE, S. *God's Bits of Wood*. London: Heinemann, 1970. (The 1947-48 rail strike in French West Africa.)

(h) *Revolution and counterrevolution (see also most of 6 [f] and 3.12; 3.15; 3.18; 3.19; 3.30; 5.23)*

6.59 CHALIAND, G. *Revolution in the Third World*. Hassocks: Harvester, 1977.

6.60 MILLER, N. and AYA, R., eds. *National Liberation: Revolution in the Third World*. London: Collier-Macmillan, 1971.

6.61 GOUGH, K. *Ten Times More Beautiful: The Rebuilding of Vietnam*. New York: Monthly Review Press, 1978.

6.62 WOMACK, J. *Zapata and the Mexican Revolution*. New York: Knopf, 1969.

6.63 CHALIAND, G. *The Palestinian Resistance*. Harmondsworth: Penguin Books, 1972.

6.64 SNOW, E. *Red Star Over China*. 1938; New York: Grove Press, 1968.

6.65 BELDEN, J. *China Shakes the World*. 1949; New York: Monthly Review Press, 1970.

6.66 CROOK, D. and CROOK, I. *Ten Mile Inn: Mass Movement in a Chinese Village*. New York: Pantheon, 1979.

6.67 HINTON, W. *Fanshen*. New York: Monthly Review Press, 1966.

6.68 SARKESIAN, S., ed. *Revolutionary Guerrilla Warfare*. Chicago: Precedent, 1975.

6.69 TABER, R. *The War of the Flea: A Study of Guerilla Warfare*. London: Paladin, 1970.

6.70 HOBSBAWM, E. "Vietnam and the Dynamics of Guerilla Warfare." *New Left Review* 33 (1965):58-69.

6.71 KITSON, F. *Low-Intensity Operations: Subversion, Insurgency and Peacekeeping*. London: Faber, 1971.

7. Community, Culture, and Ideology

(a) Urbanization and urban culture
(see also: 5.19, 5.31; and on migration 5.20, 5.30)

7.1 ABU-LUGHOD, J. and HAY, R., eds. *Third World Urbanization*. Chicago: Ma'aroufa, 1977. (Includes useful bibliography.)

7.2 SLATER, D. "Towards a Political Economy of Urbanisation in Peripheral Capitalist Societies," *International Journal of Urban and Regional Studies* 2, no. 1 (1978): 26-52.

7.3 McGEE, T. *The Urbanisation Process in the Third World*. London: Bell, 1971. (Partly updated in *Development & Change* 10 [1979]: 1-22.)

7.4 ROBERTS, B. *Cities of Peasants: The Political Economy of Industrialisation in Latin America*. London: Arnold, 1978.

7.5 LOMNITZ, L.A. *Networks and Marginality: Life in a Mexican Shanty Town*. New York: Academic Press, 1977.

7.6 ECKSTEIN, S. *The Poverty of Revolution: The State and the Urban Poor in Mexico*. Princeton: Princeton University Press, 1977.

(b) Gender, production, and the family
(see also 5.30)

7.7 BOSERUP, E. *Woman's Role in Economic Development*. London: Allen & Unwin, 1970.

7.8 ROGERS, B. *The Domestication of Women*. London: Kogan Page, 1980.

7.9 YOUNG, K., ed. "The Continuing Subordination of Women in the Development Process," *Institute of Development Studies Bulletin* 10, no. 3 (1979).

7.10 LEWENHAK, S. *Women and Work*. London: Fontana, 1980.

7.11 GOODE, W.J. *World Revolution and Family Patterns*. New York: Free Press, 1963.

(c) Women, culture, and politics
(see also 5.23)

7.12 ETIENNE, M. and LEACOCK, E., eds. *Women and Colonization*. New York: Praeger, 1980.

7.13 BECK, L. and KEDDIE, N., eds. *Women in the Muslim World*. Cambridge, Mass.: Harvard University Press, 1978.

7.14 ROHRLICH-LEVITT, R., ed. *Women Cross-Culturally: Change and Challenge*. The Hague: Mouton, 1975.

7.15 REITER, R., ed. *Towards an Anthropology of Women*. New York: Monthly Review Press, 1975.

7.16 SMITH, M. *Baba of Karo: A Woman of the Muslim Hausa*. London: Faber, 1954.

7.17   YOUNG, K. et al. *Of Marriage and the Market.* London: CSE Books, 1981.

7.18   DAVIN, D. *Woman Work: Women and the Party in Revolutionary China.* Oxford: Clarendon, 1976. (Chinese women's movement.)

7.19   CROLL, E. *Feminism and Socialism in China.* London: Routledge & Kegan Paul, 1978.

7.20   OBBO, C. *African Women: Their Struggle for Economic Independence.* London: Zed, 1980.

7.21   DE CHUNGARA, D.E. *Let Me Speak! Testimony of Domitila, A Woman of the Bolivian Mines.* New York: Monthly Review Press, 1978.

(d) Cultural formation: education, the media, etc.

7.22   CARNOY, M. *Education as Cultural Imperialism.* New York: McKay, 1974. (See also critique by E. Epstein in *Theory & Society* [1978]: 255-76.)

7.23   ILLICH, I. *Deschooling Society.* London: Calder & Boyars, 1971.

7.24   DORE, R. *The Diploma Disease: Education, Qualification and Development.* London: Allen & Unwin, 1976.

7.25   FREIRE, P. *Pedagogy of the Oppressed.* Harmondsworth: Penguin Books, 1972.

7.26   FREIRE, P. *Pedagogy in Process: The Letters to Guiné-Bissau.* New York: Seabury Press, 1978.

7.27   BUCHANAN, K. *Reflections on Education in the Third World.* Nottingham: Spokesman, 1975.

7.28   WILLIAMSON, B. *Education, Social Structure and Development.* London: Macmillan, 1979.

7.29   SILVERT, K. and REISSMAN, L., eds. *Education, Class, and Nation.* New York: Elsevier Scientific, 1976.

7.30   ALTBACH, P. and KELLY, G., eds: *Education and Colonialism.* London: Longman, 1977.

7.31   LE BRUN, O. "Education and Class Conflict,", R.C. O'Brien, ed., *Dependence in Senegal* (Beverly Hills: Sage, 1979), pp. 175-208.

7.32   BERGER, P. L., BERGER, B., and KELLNER, H. *The Homeless Mind: Modernisation and Consciousness.* Harmondsworth: Penguin Books, 1974.

7.33   SMITH, A. *The Geopolitics of Information: Western Media and the Third World.* London: Faber, 1980.

7.34   CONSTANTINO, R. *Neocolonial Identity and Counter-consciousness.* London: Merlin, 1978.

7.35   PAZ, O. *The Other Mexico: Critique of the Pyramid.* New York: Grove, 1972.

7.36   PAZ, O. *Labyrinth of Solitude: Life and Thought in Mexico.* New York: Grove, 1962.

(e) Religious consciousness and political action (see also 6.12)

7.37   ADAS, M. *Prophets of Rebellion: Millenarian Protest Movements Against the Colonial Order.* Chapel Hill: University of North Carolina Press, 1979.

7.38 SCOTT, J. C. "Protest and Profanation: Agrarian Revolt and the Little Tradition," *Theory and Society* 4 (1977): 1-38, 211-46.
7.39 JORGENSEN, J. G. *The Sun Dance: Power for the Powerless.* Chicago: University of Chicago Press, 1972.
7.40 HODGKIN, T. L. "Mahdism, Messianism and Marxism," in Gutkind, P. and Waterman, P. eds. *African Social Studies* (New York: Monthly Review Press, 1977), pp. 306-23.
7.41 HODGKIN, T. L. "The Revolutionary Tradition in Islam," *Race & Class* 21 (1980): 221-37.

(f) Race and ethnocentrism

7.42 KIERNAN, V. *The Lords of Humankind: European Attitudes Towards the Outside World in the Imperial Age.* London: Weidenfeld & Nicolson, 1969.
7.43 COX, O. *Caste, Class and Race.* New York: Monthly Review Press, 1970. (See critique by R. Miles in *Ethnic and Racial Studies* 3 [1980]: 169-87.)
7.44 FANON, F. *Black Skin, White Masks.* London: McGibbon & Kee, 1968.
7.45 ZUBAIDA, S., ed. *Race and Racialism.* London: Tavistock, 1971.
7.46 BRODY, H. *The People's Land: Eskimos and Whites in the Eastern Arctic.* Harmondsworth: Penguin, 1975.
7.47 CURTIN, P. D. *The Image of Africa: British Idea and Action 1750-1850.* Madison: University of Wisconsin Press, 1964.
7.48 STREET, B.V. *The Savage in Literature.* London: Routledge & Kegan Paul, 1975.
7.49 HERMASSI, E. *The Third World Reassessed.* Berkeley: University of California Press, 1980.
7.50 ASAD, T., ed. *Anthropology and the Colonial Encounter.* London: Ithaca, 1973.
7.51 SAID, E. *Orientalism.* London: Routledge & Kegan Paul, 1978.
7.52 SHARIATI, A. *Marxism and Other Western Fallacies.* Berkeley: Mizan Press, 1979.
7.53 USMAN, Y.B. *For the Liberation of Nigeria.* London: New Beacon, 1979.
7.54 RANGER, T. "Colonialism in Africa and the Understanding of Alien Societies," *Royal Historical Society Transactions* 26 (1976): 115-41.

8. Politics and Society: Novels by Local Authors

8.1 GARCÍA MÁRQUEZ, G. *A Hundred Years of Solitude.* London: Cape, 1970.
8.2 GARCÍA MÁRQUEZ, G. *Autumn of the Patriarch.* London: Cape, 1977.
8.3 GARCÍA MÁRQUEZ, G. *In Evil Hour.* London: Cape, 1980.

8.4   VARGAS LLOSA, M. *Conversations in the Cathedral*. New York: Harper & Row, 1975.

8.5   VARGAS LLOSA, M. *The Time of the Hero*. New York: Harper & Row, 1979.

8.6   NGUGI WA THIONGO. *Petals of Blood*. London: Heinemann, 1977.

8.7   FARRAH, N. *Sweet and Sour Milk*. London: Allison & Busby, 1979.